BARRON'S

AP®

World History: Modern

PREMIUM

WITH 5 PRACTICE TESTS

NINTH EDITION

John McCannon, Ph.D.

Department of History
Southern New Hampshire University
Manchester, New Hampshire

About the Author

John McCannon earned a Ph.D. in history from the University of Chicago in 1994. He has taught Russian, European, and world history at several universities in the United States and Canada and is a former editor of the *Canadian Journal of History*. He has worked as an Advanced Placement Reader for the College Board and is the author of *Red Arctic: Polar Exploration and the Myth of the North in the Soviet Union* (1998) and *A History of the Arctic: Nature, Exploration, and Exploitation* (2012). He is currently an associate professor of history at Southern New Hampshire University.

About the Contributor

Pamela Jordan received a Ph.D. in political science from the University of Toronto in 1997. In addition to her academic background, she has worked as a news writer for Facts on File News Services, Inc., and as executive director of a nongovernmental organization affiliated with the United Nations. Dr. Jordan is the author of *Defending Rights in Russia: Lawyers, the State and Legal Reform in the Post-Soviet Era* and *Stalin's Singing Spy: The Life and Exile of Nadezhda Plevitskaya*, and is also an assistant professor of political science at Southern New Hampshire University.

Acknowledgments

Both the author and contributor would like to thank Jennifer Giammusso, whose editorial supervision has made the preparation of this manuscript's various editions a smooth and successful process. We are also grateful to those assisting with art direction and production assistance and to the anonymous reviewers who have commented insightfully on this manuscript as it has evolved over the years.

Published by Kaplan, Inc., d/b/a Barron's Educational Series
750 Third Avenue
New York, NY 10017
www.barronseduc.com

ISBN: 978-1-5062-5339-8

10 9 8 7 6 5 4 3 2 1

Kaplan, Inc., d/b/a Barron's Educational Series print books are available at special quantity discounts to use for sales promotions, employee premiums, or educational purposes. For more information or to purchase books, please call the Simon & Schuster special sales department at 866-506-1949.

Contents

UNIT 2: 1450–1750

UNIT 3: 1750–1900

UNIT 4: 1900 TO THE PRESENT

PRACTICE TESTS

As you review the content in this book to work toward earning that **5** on your AP World History: Modern exam, here are five essential points you should focus on.

Barron's Essential

1 **Know the course themes.** As important as factual knowledge is, you can't and won't be able to know every detail about the history of the world, nor will the exam focus on fact memorization. You need to think about how the facts fit into the wider contexts addressed by the themes. Not only will the multiple-choice questions be geared in this way, the essay questions will be theme-inspired. As a reminder, the official course themes are: interaction between humans and the environment development and interaction of cultures state building, expansion, and conflict creation, expansion, and interaction of economic systems and development and transformation of social structures.

2 **Understand historiography.** Historiography, the study of how historians think and write about history, is a topic of importance. What topics do historians choose to focus on? What sources and documents do they use as evidence, and how do they evaluate the strengths, weaknesses, and biases of that evidence? How do historians determine what causes a major event or development? How do they contextualize specific events and trends more broadly? A number of multiple-choice questions will ask you to analyze images, quotations, and excerpts from historical writing. The document-based question (DBQ) is designed expressly to make you think like a historian.

3 **Remember your rubrics.** The best-written and most insightful essays in the world will score poorly if they do not follow the rules. AP readers follow the rubrics closely as they assess papers, and following directions matters. Understand where your points come from and how to earn them. Focus particularly on crafting good thesis statements and presenting evidence effectively.

4 **"How" and "why" (and "how are they alike?") are more important than "who" and "when."** Names, dates, and other such details are never unimportant in the study of history. Mastery of facts can earn you extra points on essay questions and increase your chances of answering multiple-choice questions correctly. However, the exam is far more likely to emphasize how things were done, or why they happened, rather than who did them or when. Causes and effects matter greatly as well. Also, as you study any topic, always consider how it *compares* with similar topics in other times and places.

5 **Focus on interactions.** Note the number of times the word "interaction" appears in the course themes and historical periods. This is a topic of major interest, and you should concentrate on it throughout your studies. Note that interaction can take place on several levels—local, regional, interregional, and global—and in many forms.

INTRODUCTION

How to Use This Book

TO TEACHERS AND STUDENTS

This book can be used in one of two ways. For those taking (or teaching) a course in world history, or for those who have recently taken such a course, it can serve as a helpful supplement to coursework. For readers who are not taking, or have never taken, a course in world history, this book can serve as an independent study aid.

This introductory unit offers strategies for the various question types encountered on the AP World History: Modern exam. These will include multiple-choice questions and several questions requiring written answers: short-answer questions, a document-based question (DBQ), and a long essay question.

Units 1 through 4 contain content-based review information, corresponding to the breakdown of material found in the official AP framework. Because the AP World History course now covers content only from 1200 C.E. onward, an additional unit, called Unit Zero, is included to acquaint readers with concepts and context from earlier eras that will help make sense of the core material. Each of the main units is divided into Short Cut and Scenic Route sections. The Short Cut sections should suffice for those readers who need (or only have time for!) a quick review. The Scenic Route sections allow readers to explore topics in more detail, should they so desire.

TO THE TEACHER

This book's review chapters can be used to summarize or reinforce particular classroom or homework assignments. The Short Cut sections, with their unit overviews, allow students to examine historical events from a broad perspective. They are based on the course frame-work's major themes, and they also place events and developments in the comparative con-text that the AP curriculum emphasizes.

The book's two practice tests can be used near the end of the academic year as the culmination of an AP World History: Modern course—and as practice for the actual AP exam.

This introductory unit should be covered with students at the beginning of an AP World History course and then at several points afterward. The sooner students are familiar with how AP exams work, the more comfortable they will be with the exam experience itself. This is particularly important with respect to the written portions of the exam, where familiarity with the rules and procedures is indispensable.

TO THE STUDENT

This book can be used for independent review, whether or not you are taking, or have ever taken, a course in world history. *How* you use it will depend on your circumstances.

Short Cuts vs. Scenic Routes. To serve students with different needs, this book divides each content-based unit into two sections: a Short Cut overview, suitable for quick review, and a series of in-depth chapters called the Scenic Route.

Which path should you choose? It depends.

Perhaps you are using this book in conjunction with an AP course in world history, or at least over a long period of time. If so, you can take full advantage of the Scenic Route portion of each unit, along with the Short Cuts. The more time you give yourself to study, the more thoroughly you will be able to absorb information and ideas. Even if AP questions don't tend to test factual knowledge for its own sake, the more you know, the easier you will find it to eliminate incorrect answers on the multiple-choice questions, or to come up with evidence and supporting details for your essays. The Scenic Route sections can assist you with that.

However, if you have taken a world history course and simply need a refresher, or if you have limited time to study and are cramming at the last minute, you should focus mainly on the Short Cuts, along with the practice exams *and* the "strategies" sections of this introductory unit.

No matter how much time you have to study, be sure to focus not just on *what* the exam covers but also on *how* to take the exam itself. Knowing the exam process is arguably as important as knowing the course material.

Suggested Timelines

Different students master material at different paces, and your own circumstances may leave you with more or less time to prepare. Three possible timelines for study are provided here. Adapt as necessary to your own situation and abilities.

7-DAY TIMELINE

With such limited time, it is best to concentrate on test-taking methods and big-picture issues.

<pre>
DAY 1   Read this introductory unit carefully. Take one of the model exams to get a sense
         of how ready you are.

DAY 2   Read and study Unit Zero and the Short Cut section for Until 1.

DAY 3   Read and study the Short Cut section for Unit 2.

DAY 4   Read and study the Short Cut section for Unit 3.

DAY 5   Read and study the Short Cut sections for Unit 4.

DAY 6   Read and study all the Short Cut sections.

DAY 7   Review the introductory unit. Take the second practice test.
</pre>

4-WEEK TIMELINE

Having roughly a month to prepare will allow you some time to examine topics in depth, in addition to focusing on essentials.

WEEK 1 Read this introductory unit to learn how the AP exam works. Take one of the in-book practice tests. Then study Units Zero: Foundations and 1, focusing on the Short Cut sections. If time permits, or if you have specific knowledge gaps to fill, turn to the Scenic Route chapters as needed.

WEEK 2 Study Units 2 and 3, using the same approach as above (including one of the practice tests).

WEEK 3 Study Unit 4 (and anything in Unit 3 left over from week 2), using the same approach as above (including one of the practice tests).

WEEK 4 Take the rest of the practice tests. Review the introductory unit, Unit Zero: Foundations, as well as the Short Cut sections for Units 1 through 4.

SCHOOL-YEAR (9-MONTH) TIMELINE

This is the ideal scenario. Here, you are likely using this book as a supplement to a world history course. If so, proceed at the same pace and in the same order as your teacher and classmates. Otherwise, the following will give you a good grounding.

MONTH 1 Read this introductory unit. Take one of the practice tests to get a sense of how ready you are. Study Units Zero: Foundations and 1.

MONTH 2 Study Unit 2. Use extra time to review the Short Cut section for Unit 1.

MONTH 3 Study Unit 3. Use extra time to review the Short Cut section for Unit 2.

MONTH 4 Study the first half of Unit 4. Use extra time to review the Short Cut sections for Units 2 and 3.

MONTH 5 Study the second half of Unit 4. Take one of the practice tests. Use extra time to review earlier Short Cut sections.

MONTH 6 Review all Short Cut sections. Take one of the practice tests. Assess your strengths and weaknesses.

MONTH 7 Skim Units 1 through 4, focusing on weak points. Use the Short Cut sections to help you think about themes and comparisons.

MONTH 8 Continue reviewing the Short Cut sections. Reread the introductory unit. Take one of the practice tests.

MONTH 9 Take any remaining practice tests. Review as needed. Skim Short Cut sections and the introductory unit a final time.

General Notes

Dates are given according to the standard Western calendar, with one exception. The abbreviations B.C.E. ("before common era") and C.E. ("common era") are used, rather than the traditional B.C. ("before Christ") and A.D. (*anno domini*, or "year of our Lord").

This usage shows more respect to non-Christian cultures. The Western calendar is only one of many systems used worldwide to measure time. According to the Hebrew calendar, for example, year 1 is the equivalent of 3760 B.C.E. Year 1 of the Muslim calendar, by contrast, is 622 C.E.

Dates with no designation—those that appear simply as numerals—are assumed to be C.E.

Names and terms from a variety of languages are used throughout this book. Many, such as Russian, Chinese, Arabic, Japanese, and Hebrew, use alphabets different from the Latin script used by English speakers. There is no single, consistent way to convert one alphabet to another. Consequently, when referring to people or terms transliterated from non-Latin scripts, this book will try to use versions that are both linguistically accurate and easily recognizable. Be aware that certain well-known names and terms have several variants. These include Genghis Khan versus Chinggis Khan (or Jenghiz Khan), Mao Tse-tung versus Mao Zedong, Mohammed versus Muhammad, or Sundiata versus Son-Jara. Be prepared to encounter different versions like this in different textbooks and readings.

THE AP EXAM IN WORLD HISTORY: MODERN: AN OVERVIEW

Format

Advanced Placement exams are typically administered every May. The AP World History: Modern exam lasts a total of 3 hours and 15 minutes.

Students are allowed 55 minutes to complete 55 multiple-choice questions.

The written portions of the exam last a total of 140 minutes. They include the following questions:

- **SHORT-ANSWER QUESTIONS.** Lasts 40 minutes. Students must complete three questions, each of which calls for a three-part response to quoted material or a general proposition or historical argument.
- **DOCUMENT-BASED QUESTION (DBQ).** Roughly 60 minutes, including an optional period of 15 minutes to read 7 documents.
- **LONG ESSAY QUESTION (LEQ).** Roughly 40 minutes. Students must choose one of three questions. All three will focus on the same course theme and test the same reasoning skill, but each will deal with a different time period.

The exam begins with the multiple-choice questions, followed by the short-answer questions. The next portion of the exam includes both the DBQ and the LEQ. It will begin with the optional 15-minute document-reading period mentioned above. You may use this time to read documents, make notes, and outline your essays (highly recommended), or you may start writing immediately (less advisable). You may work on the DBQ and LEQ in whichever order you like, and you must decide for yourself when to finish one essay and move on to the other.

Grading

The multiple-choice section of the exam is worth 40 percent of the overall score. The short-answer questions are worth 20 percent, the DBQ is 25 percent, and the LEQ is 15 percent.

Grades for the exam are calculated according to a complex formula that converts raw scores from the multiple-choice and written portions of the text into a final standard score ranging from 1 (the worst) to 5 (the best).

This 1-through-5 score is what students see when they receive their results. Scores can be interpreted as follows:

5: Extremely well qualified. Accepted by the majority of colleges and universities for some kind of academic credit or benefit. Earned in recent years by roughly 10 percent of students.

4: Well qualified. Accepted by many colleges and universities for some kind of academic credit or benefit. Earned by roughly 15 percent of students.

3: Qualified. Accepted by many colleges and universities for some kind of academic credit or benefit, but often of a limited nature. Earned by roughly 25 percent of students.

2: Possibly qualified. Accepted by only a few colleges and universities for academic credit or benefit, generally quite limited. Earned by roughly 25 percent of students.

1: No recommendation. Not accepted anywhere. Earned by roughly 25 percent of students.

Universities and colleges have widely varying policies regarding AP exams. You should contact the school of your choice to determine what benefit, if any, a particular score will give you.

Time Frame

As of 2019–2020, the AP World History: Modern exam will focus on human history worldwide, from 1200 C.E. to the present. The distribution of multiple-choice questions pertaining to any given time period within this eight-century span will be roughly as follows:

- Unit 1 (1200–1450): 16 to 20 percent of questions
- Unit 2 (1450–1750): 24 to 30 percent of questions
- Unit 3 (1750–1900): 24 to 30 percent of questions
- Unit 4 (1900–the present): 24 to 30 percent of questions

Themes

The AP World History: Modern exam is broad in scope and seeks to test critical and interpretive skills, not just the mastery of facts and data. The study of world history challenges students to examine questions from a big-picture point of view, as well as to draw meaningful comparisons between different societies and time periods.

Six overarching themes form the heart of the AP World History: Modern course.

- **GOVERNANCE.** What political forms do societies adopt, and who rules whom in any given time and place? What state-building and administrative techniques do governments use to maintain order and exercise power? How and why do revolutions take place, and what impact do they have? Beyond monarchies, empires, and nation-states, what regional and international bodies—such as the United Nations—have exerted influence throughout history? How have expansion, conflict, and diplomacy affected world history?

- **CULTURAL DEVELOPMENTS AND INTERACTIONS.** What do societies believe religiously, philosophically, and politically? What artistic and intellectual traditions do they develop? How and when does the interaction of peoples lead to cultural sharing—or to cultural clashes?

- **TECHNOLOGY AND INNOVATION.** How have societies responded to the human desire for greater safety, prosperity, and efficiency? What techniques and devices have they adapted or innovated over time? What scientific insights and technological innovations have they developed? How have they coped with the intended and unintended consequences—cultural, socioeconomic, and environmental—of scientific and technological advancement?
- **ECONOMIC SYSTEMS.** How do people in a society make a living? What goods and services do they produce, and what resources do they use? How do trade and commerce affect societies and the way they interact? What systems have societies used to organize labor throughout history? What impact have these systems, including industrialization, capitalism, and socialism, had on modern history?
- **SOCIAL INTERACTIONS AND ORGANIZATION.** Who has power and status within a society? What norms determine how a society's members are grouped, which social classes exist, and how those classes interact with each other? Why do some societies lean more toward hierarchy and others toward social mobility? What roles do cities play in social and economic development? How are gender relations governed? How are ethnic and racial minorities defined and treated?
- **HUMANS AND THE ENVIRONMENT.** How has the natural world shaped the development of human societies, and how have humans, seeking resources and using various tools and technologies, shaped the natural world in return? Where have human societies migrated and settled, and how and why did they do so? How have diseases and ecological changes affected humans throughout history?

No more than 20 percent of multiple-choice questions will cover topics dealing exclusively with European history. U.S. history will rarely be discussed in its own right but generally in comparative contexts or in relation to global trends.

Basic understanding of world geography is crucial for success on the AP World History: Modern exam. You must be able to identify major regions according to the terminology used by the AP World History: Modern course: not knowing the difference between "East Asia" and "Southeast Asia," or between "Central Asia" and "the Middle East," will lead to harmful errors. For more information on the geographical labels used by the AP course, see the appendix (Map of Selected World Regions) included at the end of this book.

HISTORICAL THINKING SKILLS

A key purpose of the AP World History: Modern course is to foster certain thinking skills used by professional historians and emphasized in university-level courses. Six of these, described below, are especially important. While it helps to command as much factual knowledge as possible, it is crucial to *use* facts in the following ways in order to do well on the AP exam.

- **DEVELOPMENTS AND PROCESSES.** Can you identify and explain historical developments and processes?
- **SOURCING AND SITUATION.** Can you analyze the sourcing and situation of primary and secondary sources? Can you insightfully discuss a source's purpose, point of view, intended audience, and potential limitations (including bias or limited perspective)?
- **CLAIMS AND EVIDENCE IN SOURCES.** Can you identify and analyze a source's key claims, arguments, credibility, and use of evidence? Can you compare arguments and explain how a source's argument might be supported, qualified, or rebutted?

- **CONTEXTUALIZATION.** Can you connect specific events and facts to wider settings and to broader trends? Can you identify, describe, and explain how a specific development or process is situated within a larger historical context?
- **MAKING CONNECTIONS.** Can you take advantage of historical reasoning to analyze patterns and connections between historical developments and processes? Examples of historical reasoning skills include comparison (analyzing likenesses *and* differences), causation (understanding cause and effect, assessing competing explanations for why something happens), and continuity and change (tracing a process or development over time, paying attention not just to what changes but to what stays largely the same).
- **ARGUMENTATION.** Can you put forward a defensible claim about a historical trend or development? Can you communicate this argument in the form of a clear and effective thesis statement, and can you back it up with specific pieces of historical evidence? Can you make connections within and between historical periods and different regions? Can you discuss the strengths and limitations of sources and arguments?

MULTIPLE-CHOICE QUESTION STRATEGIES

The AP exam will require you to answer 55 multiple-choice questions. Each individual question includes four answer options; you will pick the one that BEST answers the question.

Multiple-choice questions will be grouped in approximately fifteen to twenty clusters, typically of three or four questions. More detail on this is provided below.

You will have 55 minutes to complete this section of the test.

One point is awarded for each correct answer. Incorrect answers, whether blank or wrong, are not penalized. For an overall AP score of 3, you need to answer approximately 50 percent of the multiple-choice questions correctly (assuming an acceptable performance on the other portions of the exam). To receive an overall AP score of 4 or 5, you should aim to answer at least 70 percent of the questions correctly.

Tips for the Multiple-Choice Questions

Things to bear in mind for the multiple-choice section of the exam:

- **KEEP YOUR PACE BRISK.** On average, you have 60 seconds to work on each question. While you should read each question as carefully as possible, you will not have time to think deeply about any given one. A good way to keep from bogging down is to take a first run through the entire exam, skipping anything you cannot answer quickly and confidently. Return to the more difficult questions by going through the exam a second time. Even during this second reading, don't spend too much time on any single question. As described below, if something seems too hard, make the best possible guess and move on.
- **LEAVE NOTHING BLANK.** AP exams used to penalize wild guessing by deducting a quarter-point for every wrong answer. This is no longer the case, so leaving anything unanswered only hurts you. Once you've completed the questions you're sure about and guessed intelligently at the harder ones, use the last minute or so of your time to fill in every remaining blank, even if you do so randomly.

- **START BY ELIMINATING INCORRECT ANSWERS.** Every distractor, or wrong answer, is supposed to sound at least somewhat plausible. Still, a quick but careful reading generally allows you to eliminate at least one wrong answer, if not two. This is the first thing you should do. If you can quickly pick the correct answer from the two or three that remain, do so. If you can't, flag the question and come back to it during your second run through the exam.

- **MAKE EDUCATED GUESSES.** Especially during your second run through the exam, if a question proves too difficult, make an educated guess and move on. Obsessing over one stubborn question, even if you get it right, is a bad investment of your time—which would be better spent working on several medium-hard questions. (Remember: you don't need to answer *all* the multiple-choice questions to get a 4 or 5 on the exam! Instead, use your time to ensure that you get three-quarters or so of them right.)

- **TRUST YOUR INTUITION—TO A POINT.** Most experts say that the answer you choose first is generally the correct one, *if* you know the material and have read the question carefully. Unless you have a concrete reason to change your mind, go with your instinct. (But don't use this as an excuse for lazy reading or sloppy thinking!)

Sample Multiple-Choice Questions

Multiple-choice questions on the AP World History: Modern exam will test the historical reasoning skills described above, rather than raw factual knowledge.

Multiple-choice questions are organized into question sets, or clusters, each generally containing three or four questions. Expect to see about fifteen to twenty clusters. Each cluster will require you to interpret and analyze a particular type of stimulus material. Stimulus materials may include quotations (either from primary or secondary sources), maps, images, graphs, charts, and political cartoons.

Often, clues to the correct answer are contained in the question itself and can be obtained by careful and logical reading of the stimulus material. Many questions will ask that you link the stimulus material with key concepts and broad developments covered by the AP World History: Modern curriculum. Factual knowledge may not be tested directly, but the more of it you possess, the easier you will find it to eliminate incorrect distractors in favor of correct answers. Some questions will probe your knowledge of broader context, requiring you to identify what happened after, or as a result of, whatever is described by the stimulus material.

The following are examples of various multiple-choice questions sets, along with answers and explanations.

Questions 1.1 to 1.3 refer to the two following passages.

The story of my great-grandmother was typical of millions of Chinese women [before the 1911 revolution]. She came from a family of tanners. Because her family was not intellectual and did not hold any official post, and because she was a girl, she was not given a name. Being the second daughter, she was simply called "Number Two Girl." [She never met her husband] before her wedding. In fact, falling in love was considered shameful, a family disgrace. Not because it was taboo, but because young people were not supposed to be exposed to situations where such a thing could happen, partly because it was immoral for them to meet, and partly because marriage was seen above all as a duty, an arrangement between two families. With luck, one could fall in love after getting married.

from Jung Chang, *Wild Swans: Three Daughters of China* (1991)

It is a truth universally acknowledged, that a single man in possession of a good fortune must be in want of a wife. This truth is so well fixed in the minds of the surrounding families, that he is considered as the rightful property of some one or other of their daughters.

from Jane Austen, *Pride and Prejudice* (1813).

1.1. The observations made in the above quotations are best understood in the context of which of the following?

    (A) The use of religious doctrine to regulate the role of women in society
    (B) The impact of industrialization on family structures
    (C) The oppression of women due to the rise of social Darwinist ideologies
    (D) The shaping of marriage customs by prevailing social and economic norms

ANSWER: **D**

Contextualization and process of elimination help to answer this question. Neither quotation speaks directly to religion or industrialization, making A and B unlikely. While oppression is evident in the first quotation, it is not overtly so in the second, and has nothing to do with social Darwinism in any case, so C is incorrect. In both cases, but in different ways, the impact of social and economic factors on marriage is at stake, and those are what tie the questions together.

1.2. The tone of the second quotation best reflects which of the following assertions about marriage practices during the period in question?

    (A) Women in nineteenth-century Europe had little choice in whom they married.
    (B) Families in nineteenth-century Europe took economic considerations seriously when selecting marriage partners for children.
    (C) The early industrial era enormously unbalanced gender relations in nineteenth-century Europe.
    (D) Romantic attachment did not figure into marriage decisions among most nineteenth-century Europeans.

ANSWER: **B**

Interpretation and reading comprehension are important here. The quotation does not deny the lack of choice on the part of women, nor does it speak of the possibility of romantic love where the choice of marriage partners is concerned, making A and D doubtful. While C may or may not be true, it has little if any bearing on the quotation. Austen's comments touch squarely on how marriage in many societies was seen largely as an economic partnership.

1.3. The two quotations best support which of the following conclusions?

    (A) Until well into the 1900s, traditional patriarchy severely limited women's personal choices in many parts of the world.

    (B) By the 1800s, women had largely thrown off social and economic limitations on their family choices.

    (C) In many parts of the world, economic partnership was considered a crucial aspect of an acceptable marriage.

    (D) During the nineteenth century, women worldwide bitterly resented limitations placed on their marriage options.

ANSWER: **C**

Interpretation, historical knowledge, and context come into play here. Considering the gender inequalities that still persist today, it would be mistaken to assume that B was true more than a century ago; it is patently false. Both A and D describe historical truths, and both are relevant to the first quotation. However, the wry humor expressed in the second quotation does not make it suitable as evidence to support either answer. Answer C speaks to a broader reality that encompasses both quotations.

Questions 2.1 to 2.3 refer to the excerpt below.

Although humanity evolved in Africa and is self-evidently an expression of the continent's exceptional fecundity, the species appears to have been unable to exploit its full potential within the boundaries of the continent—in terms of either numbers or achievements... All the accepted markers of civilization occurred first in non-African locales—metallurgy, agriculture, written language, the founding of cities. This is not to make a qualitative judgment. Indeed, the civilized art of living peaceably in small societies without forming states that was evident in Africa prior to the arrival of external influences is a distinctively African contribution to human history.

from John Reader, *Africa: A Biography of the Continent* (1997)

2.1. The excerpt above most directly challenges which of the following propositions?

    (A) Non-European civilizations deserve closer attention from scholars in all fields.

    (B) Societies that lag behind technologically offer little to overall human development.

    (C) The Atlantic slave trade affected the continent's historical direction less than is commonly supposed.

    (D) Environmental factors played a central role in curtailing economic growth in Africa.

ANSWER: **B**

Identifying arguments and the interpretation of texts are the key to this question. Answers A and D are arguably true but are not spoken of in the passage. Answer C might form the subject of an interesting debate but is also not touched on in the passage. By contrast, the author's assertion about the importance of the peaceful mode of existence found in early African societies directly contradicts the idea communicated in B.

2.2. The existence of which of the following does the most to contradict the passage's characterization of Africa in its earliest stages of development?

    (A) The East African slave trade
    (B) High degrees of linguistic and ethnic diversity
    (C) States such as Nubia and Kush
    (D) The profusion of different deities and religious pantheons

ANSWER: **C**

Contextualization and historical knowledge are important. Many clusters will contain at least one question that depends on knowing trends or information related to the stimulus material but not contained in it or alluded to it directly. Answer A, for example, which is certainly not a peaceful or desirable trend, comes after the period spoken of in the passage. Answers B and D speak to factors that were indeed relevant before the emergence of external influences, but while the differences they describe *can* lead to conflict, they do not necessarily have to. On the other hand, one could argue that the emergence of strong states like Nubia and Kush (answer C) at such an early date undercuts the assertion made by the passage's author.

2.3. Which of the following would have contributed most to limiting the development of African societies in the way described by the author?

    (A) An extremely high degree of ethnic and linguistic diversity
    (B) The impact of disease-causing pathogens in tropical parts of Africa
    (C) A relatively small supply of metal deposits compared to Europe and Asia
    (D) The environmental obstacles posed by the aridity of the Sahara Desert

ANSWER: **A**

Many factors kept African societies from developing along the same lines as those in Europe or Asia, although the author arguably overstates the degree to which this was the case. Answer C is factually untrue. The environmental impact of the Sahara and the prevalence of tropical diseases, as described in B and D, played a significant role in shaping African societies. But since the author is mainly concerned with the comparative rarity of large social and political units in Africa prior to contact with outsiders, the barriers posed by linguistic and ethnic difference, as in answer A, should be seen as paramount.

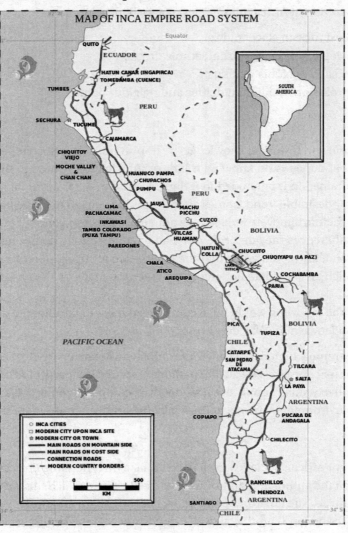

3.1. This map is best understood in light of which of the following historical trends?

(A) The expansion of infrastructure

(B) Widespread imperial conquest

(C) Missionary activity and religious conversion

(D) Competition over trade routes

ANSWER: **A**

Context-based questions are commonly included in multiple-choice clusters. They often require you to match the stimulus material with a key concept from the AP World History: Modern curriculum. All the answers refer to key concepts. While B is relevant to the growth of the Inca Empire, and while C and D are the sort of things that a map of this type might refer to, the answer that makes the most sense for a map emphasizing a road network—an important piece of infrastructure—is A.

3.2. What physical difficulty would the Incas have had to overcome in the construction of the road system depicted in the map?

    (A) The marshiness of the Amazon River basin
    (B) Desert conditions in regions such as Patagonia
    (C) The steepness of the Andes Mountains
    (D) The lack of suitable pack animals in most of South America

ANSWER: **C**

Like 2.2 above and 3.3 below, this question depends on knowing trends or information related to the stimulus material but not contained in it or alluded to directly. Answer D is false—llamas and alpacas are common to the continent—and while A and B correctly characterize the regions they describe, they are not core to the Incan homeland. Despite the rugged terrain, the Andes Mountains, featured in C, were home to many sophisticated societies in the pre-Columbian era.

3.3. Which of the following did most to disrupt political and economic relations among the populations depicted on the map?

    (A) The arrival of European colonizers
    (B) Warfare among major urban centers
    (C) Overpopulation and environmental degradation
    (D) Widespread and virulent epidemics

ANSWER: **A**

This question tests causation, and, as in 3.2, knowledge of outside material is helpful. Answers B through D refer to common causes of imperial downfall, but A speaks most directly to what brought down the Incas.

Questions 4.1 to 4.3 refer to the chart below.

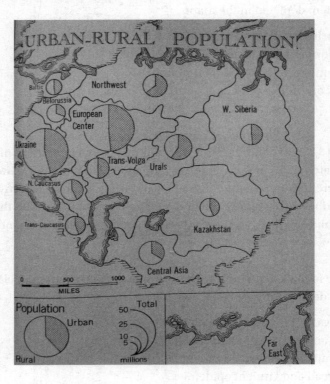

4.1. The information presented in the chart above is best interpreted in light of which of the following contexts?

    (A) Forced migration of labor in a dictatorial regime

    (B) Mobilization of a country's homefront during an armed conflict

    (C) Expansion of agriculture at the expense of heavy industry

    (D) Urbanization in a modernizing society

ANSWER: **D**

Contextualization is at the heart of this question, although geographic knowledge is useful as well. Labels like "Ukraine" and "Siberia" should indicate that the map depicts Russia and the regions surrounding it, and if they are all being treated as parts of a single modern state, the state must be the Soviet Union, or USSR. Answers A and B refer to policies or events related to the USSR, but the map gives no evidence that it is speaking of them. Most modern societies, the USSR included, move in a direction opposite from that described in C. That leaves D, which is also best suited to the map's subject, the proportion of city dwellers to rural inhabitants.

4.2. Examination of the chart would allow one to conclude most safely that

(A) more people in the nation's Northwest live in cities than in its European Center.
(B) Western Siberia has a larger agrarian population than Ukraine.
(C) Central Asia and Belorussia are, by percentage, the least urbanized of the nation's western regions.
(D) the Baltic is home to more urban dwellers than the Trans-Caucasus.

ANSWER: **C**

This question relies on careful interpretation of evidence. As with all graph-, chart-, and map-related questions, be careful to choose only those answers that can be supported by the information actually provided. One can reasonably assume that larger circles refer to larger populations, making A and B false. Answer D cannot be chosen, not only because both regions appear to have populations of roughly the same size, but because one would have to know exact numbers, not just percentages, to pronounce confidently on what it says. Answer C can be safely answered by a comparison based on proportion, rather than exact numbers.

4.3. Which of the following most likely brought about the condition depicted in the chart?

(A) The First and Second Five-Year Plans
(B) World War II
(C) The Russian Civil War
(D) Glasnost

ANSWER: **A**

This question touches on causation and requires knowledge of information not directly described by or depicted in the stimulus material but related to it. Knowing that this is the USSR should enable you to review key events like those described in the answers. Mikhail Gorbachev's glasnost policy had to do with cultural openness, making D unlikely, and both B and C refer to devastating events which depleted the Soviet population and disrupted industrial growth. The Five-Year Plans of the 1930s urbanized and industrialized the USSR, transforming what had recently been an overwhelmingly agrarian society into a more urban one—although more progress was needed before the USSR could be considered a fully urban society.

5.1. The image above is best understood as depicting which of the following trends?

(A) Imperialism

(B) Transnational migration

(C) Nonviolent decolonization

(D) Economic globalization

ANSWER: **A**

This question tests contextualization, interpretation, and general knowledge of key trends. A common motif in political cartoons of this sort is to depict the division or conquest of territory by outside powers as the ripping up of a map or the slicing up of a pie. The only answer that makes sense in this context is A, which relates to the establishment of spheres of influence in China by foreign powers during the late 1800s and early 1900s.

5.2. The imagery contained in the cartoon indicates most strongly that which of the following is true?

(A) That the artist saw China as dealing with outside powers from a position of strength

(B) That the artist approved of foreign nations' actions against China

(C) That the artist was of Western origin

(D) That the artist hoped to inspire antiforeign resistance among the Chinese

ANSWER: **C**

The distress evident on the face of the character symbolizing China—which is clearly being taken advantage of—makes A unlikely. The artist's attitude is not expressed directly, but appears to be neutral or mildly disapproving, and the target audience does not appear to be Chinese, so B and D are weak choices. The word "China" in French on the pie, the foregrounding of cartoon figures of European (and Japanese) leaders, and the very plain stereotyping of the Chinese and Japanese figures all speak to a cartoonist of Western—probably French—origin.

5.3. The development depicted in the cartoon left China's government increasingly vulnerable to which of the following events?

    (A) The First Opium War of 1839–1842
    (B) The Chinese revolution of 1911–1912
    (C) The victory of the Chinese Communist Party in 1949
    (D) The Rape of Nanking in 1937

ANSWER: **B**

Causation is being tested here as well as context and knowledge of events not alluded to by, but certainly related to, the stimulus material. Answers C and D refer to events too distant in the future to be directly related to a cartoon from the late 1800s or the earliest 1900s. The Opium War described in A definitely led to China's geopolitical decline, but clues in the cartoon indicate that the Opium War occurred before this cartoon and was therefore a cause of what the cartoon depicts and not a result. Germany (shown second from left) was not a nation until after 1871, and Japan did not begin participating in the carving-up of Chinese territory until the 1890s. The result of China's growing weakness and distintegration was the revolution of 1911–1912, as in B.

SHORT-ANSWER QUESTION STRATEGIES

This section will come immediately after the multiple-choice portion of the exam. It will ask you to use content knowledge and various historical skills to provide written responses to three short-answer questions. You must complete the first and second questions; you will then have the choice to complete the third or fourth.

You will have 40 minutes to complete this section of the test, giving you roughly 13 minutes to answer each question.

The first two short-answer questions can cover any time period between 1200 and the present. The first will require you to assess some sort of secondary source; the second will test you on primary source material. The third and fourth questions will not provide any specific stimulus material. The third question will cover the period from 1200 to 1750; the fourth will focus on the years between 1750 and the present.

Each question will ask you to do three things, each of which will be worth a point. You are not required to develop a thesis. Your main strategy here is to complete all three questions within the set amount of time and to clearly indicate that, in each case, you have satisfactorily accomplished all three goals. Lengthy answers are not necessary—one long paragraph, or perhaps two or three short paragraphs, should suffice.

Use the two passages below to answer all parts of the question that follows.

It is nowadays common for Indian history textbooks to treat the various "empires" that successively occupied the stage of Indian history as so many successive repetitions with merely different names for offices and institutions that in substance remained the same: namely, the King, the Ministers, the Provinces, the Governors, and so on. But D. D. Kosambi, in his *Introduction to the Study of Indian History*, rightly observed that this repetitive succession cannot be assumed, and that each regime, when subjected to critical study, displays distinct elements. We know most, of course, about the Mughal Empire, which displays so many striking features. In its large extent and long duration, it had only one precedent, in the Mauryan Empire, some 1,900 years earlier. Some scholars regard it as the fulfilment of the political ambitions embodied in Indian polity for three millennia. And yet there is also a temptation to see in the Mughal Empire a primitive version of the modern state. Its existence belongs to a period when the dawn of modern technology had occurred in Europe, and some of the rays of that dawn had also fallen on Asia. Can it then be said that the foundations of the Mughal Empire lay in artillery, the most brilliant and dreadful representative of modern technology, as much as did those of the modern absolute monarchies of Europe?

M. Athar Ali, "Towards an Interpretation of the Mughal Empire," 1978

The prevailing view of the Mughal Empire has been based on the mistaken assumption that this state was a kind of unfinished, unfocused prototype of the British Indian Empire of the late nineteenth and early twentieth centuries. A more fruitful approach is to treat the Mughal Empire as one example of the [older-fashioned] patrimonial-bureaucratic empire, featuring a depiction of the emperor as a divinely-aided patriarch, the household as the central element in government, members of the army as dependent on the emperor, the administration as a loosely structured group of men controlled by the imperial household. It seems clear that to accept this interpretation of the empire is to accept the necessity of re-examining the entire structure of Mughal political activity.

Stephen P. Blake, "The Patrimonial-Bureaucratic Empire of the Mughals," 1979

1. a) Provide ONE piece of historical evidence (not specifically mentioned in the passage) that would support Ali's interpretation of the Mughal Empire's fundamental nature.

    b) Provide ONE piece of historical evidence (not specifically mentioned in the passage) that would support Blake's interpretation of the Mughal Empire's fundamental nature.

    c) Explain ONE way in which the views about Mughal governance expressed in the two passages led the authors to propose different interpretations of the empire's fundamental nature.

POSSIBLE ANSWERS: The scholarly debate at stake here is whether the Mughal Empire is best seen as the product of early political modernization—and a departure from earlier regimes ruling India—or as a government that followed older patterns of rulership. Ali promotes the first argument, while Blake, using the label "patrimonial" (in which the state is considered the personal property of a monarchical ruler), takes the second position. The easiest way to answer Part A is to mention the Mughal Empire's success as a "gunpowder empire," along with Ottoman Turkey, an adoption of modern technology that buttresses Ali's thesis. One could also discuss the empire's elaborate bureaucracy, much of which was in fact kept in place by the British as they extended their colonial reach over India. In favor of Blake's argument in Part B, one could easily mention how religious policy—especially pertaining to Muslim rulership over India's Hindu majority—varied incredibly widely based on the personal preferences of any given emperor, from Akbar's remarkable tolerance to Aurangzeb's extreme Islamic rigidity.

In explaining the differences between the two views, as Part C requires, it might be tempting to point to the two authors' national differences, one being Indian, the other not. However, the debate does not seem to revolve on this question, and even though one might be able to say that patriotism inclines Ali to favor an argument depicting Mughal India as more modern than Blake appears to think, highlighting this sort of difference in this case runs the risk of stereotyping national viewpoints. (Still, be aware that national perspectives will sometimes affect debates of this type, especially when it comes to Western imperial treatment of other parts of the world, so in some instances it could be worth bringing up.) Perhaps the best way to answer this part of the question would be to point out that Ali seems mostly concerned with the Mughal Empire's place as a particular stage in India's long history, while Blake is mainly interested in the Mughal Empire as a political system typical of its era and in comparison with other regimes in Eurasia during a particular time.

Use the image below to answer all parts of the question that follows.

Hiroshige III, "Foreign Buildings along the Kaigandori Viewed from the Yokohama Wharves," 1870.

2. a) Describe ONE <u>change</u> in Meiji-era Japan that allowed the technological developments depicted in the image accompanying this question.

    b) Identify ONE way that the image accompanying this question reflects a <u>continuity</u> in Japanese social or cultural practice during the nineteenth century.

    c) Explain ONE way in which Japanese society changed as a result of Meiji-era industrialization.

POSSIBLE ANSWERS: The reasoning skill addressed by this question is continuity and change over time; the topic is modernization in Japan during the late 1800s. Part A can easily be answered by referring to the thorough industrialization of Japan carried out by Emperor Meiji after his restoration in the 1860s. Among other things, this involved the adoption of Western science, technology, and military methods on a large scale. On the other hand, hints of Japan's traditional ways can be detected in the print. These include the presence of older sailboats and people dressed in non-Western costume, which can be used for Part B.

Meiji did not settle for technological change but insisted on as thorough a Westernization of Japanese society and culture as possible, especially for elite classes. Japan incorporated Western-style education, European clothing styles, and the metric system. Samurai families lost their officially privileged status, and a new constitution created a parliamentary body (the Diet) with limited suffrage but more open than ever before. Any of these items could be mentioned to answer Part C.

Answer all parts of the question that follows.

3. a) Identify ONE similarity in how Silk Road trade affected East Asia and Europe between 1200 C.E. and 1600 C.E.

    b) Identify ONE difference in how Silk Road trade affected East Asia and Europe between 1200 C.E. and 1600 C.E.

    c) Explain ONE reason for the difference between the effects of Silk Road trade on East Asia and those on Europe.

POSSIBLE ANSWERS: Following the AP World History: Modern exam format, this question tests comparison, the skill not tested by Question 2, which focuses on continuity and change over time. Question 4 will also test comparison. Some years, the skills might be reversed, with Question 2 testing comparison and Questions 3 and 4 testing continuity and change over time.

The key similarity that could be used to answer Part A is that both regions were deeply affected by the process of cultural diffusion, with various technologies, artistic styles, and religious practices spread back and forth along the Silk Road. A major difference, in response to Part B, would be that Europe was the beneficiary of new technologies traveling westward from East Asia via the Middle East (and also that Europe was spurred to its campaign of oceanic exploration by a desire to access Asian goods more directly), while the impact on East Asia tended to involve the diffusion of religious beliefs and Chinese cultural influences. The most obvious reply to Part C is that Europe was so much less technologically and cultural advanced than East Asia that technological innovation flowed toward Europe and that it had an incentive to purchase Asian goods, whereas the reverse was definitely not true.

Answer all parts of the question that follows.

4. a) Identify ONE <u>similarity</u> in how the experience of World War I affected the Middle East and South Asia.

   b) Identify ONE <u>difference</u> in how the experience of World War I affected the Middle East and South Asia.

   c) Explain ONE reason for the difference between the effects of World War I on the Middle East and those on South Asia.

POSSIBLE ANSWERS: Like Question 3, this question tests comparison, although, time-wise, it focuses on the second half of the course.

With respect to Part A, the most obvious similarity linking these two regions after World War I is that they both remained largely under Western imperial influence. Britain retained control over India, Burma, and Singapore; the Philippines remained in American hands; and France and the Dutch continued to rule Indochina and the Dutch East Indies (Indonesia), respectively. The Ottoman Empire surrendered much of its Middle Eastern and North African possessions to the Allies. On the other hand, in answer to Part B, it can be pointed out that Western powers dominated South Asia during the interwar period much more heavily and directly than they did the Middle East. Most of South Asia remained under outright colonial rule. In the Middle East, many countries gained their freedom outright or were placed under the mandate system, in which—at least in theory—Western powers were meant to guide their mandates toward self-governance as quickly as possible.

The major reason for the difference, as called for by Part C, was that South Asia had already been colonized by Western powers, and it required more effort to change that relationship. In the Middle East, by contrast, new relationships had to be invented in the wake of World War I, thanks to the sudden collapse of Ottoman authority there, and also due to the fact that some groups under Ottoman rule, such as the principalities of the Arabian peninsula, had demanded autonomy or independence as their price for cooperating with the Allies against Turkish forces.

FREE-RESPONSE (ESSAY) QUESTIONS: GENERAL TIPS

The free-response section of the Advanced Placement exam lasts 100 minutes. During this time, you will write two essays: a **document-based question** (DBQ) and a **long essay question** (LEQ). The latter will test a particular historical reasoning skill, such as comparison, causation, or the ability to track continuity and change over time.

This section of the exam begins with a 15-minute reading period, during which you are allowed to read both questions, examine the DBQ documents, and plan your responses (taking notes and making outlines). Alternatively, you can start writing immediately. Either way, you can write the essays in whichever order you wish, and you can use the time however you please; no one will tell you when to finish one essay or start another. It is strongly suggested to use the 15-minute reading period to read the documents and outline both answers. The rest of the time should be divided more or less evenly, with perhaps 45 minutes spent on the DBQ and 40 minutes on the LEQ. Time management is crucial: students often fail to complete all three questions because they have not practiced writing essays in 40 or so minutes.

A commonly followed guideline is to write the DBQ first. The documents will be fresh in your mind, and because the DBQ operates according to the most complicated rules, it will be good to have it out of the way. Just make sure to leave enough time for the LEQ!

Using the Rubrics: Follow the Directions!

Unlike the multiple-choice questions, which are graded by machine, your essays are evaluated by human beings: high-school teachers, university professors, and other specialists who gather every June to serve as AP readers. In about a week, the average AP reader will mark literally hundreds of essays. In 2013, for example, more than 225,000 students took the AP World History exam, and approximately 1,000 readers assessed their work. AP readers are careful and well-trained. Still, they read so many essays in such a short time that special care is needed to ensure that the quality of your work stands out.

The first step toward doing this is to follow the directions! Each essay has its own set of rules, outlined in an official rubric, and AP readers are trained to judge your work according to the rubric. You will lose points if you don't observe the rules. (Actual rubrics are included in the sections below.)

How does the scoring system work? An AP reader will give your DBQ a score of zero through 7 and your LEQ a score of zero through 6. Key elements to be judged include **argument development** (including the effective use of **evidence** and the crafting of a **thesis** statement), **contextualization** and, in the case of the DBQ, **analysis of primary sources**.

THE THESIS: HALF THE BATTLE

Your essay should begin with a short and easy-to-spot **thesis**: a capsule statement of your central argument or insight. *The thesis is NOT your subject but the interesting thing you're going to say ABOUT your subject.* Both rubrics require a "historically defensible" thesis (it must be true and make sense), and the first thing an AP reader will do is to search for it. If he or she can't find it or doesn't like it, your entire essay is in trouble. If you start with a good thesis, not only will you earn points right away, you'll put your reader in the kind of receptive mood that boosts your chances of getting even more points.

So it's worth taking time to craft a good thesis. Here are some guidelines to help. (Additional suggestions are provided in the essay-specific sections that follow.)

- **PUT IT FRONT AND CENTER.** Your thesis should appear in the first paragraph. In fact, it should *be* the first paragraph. (The thesis can consist of more than one sentence, as long as the sentences are consecutive.) Technically, you're allowed to state your thesis in the conclusion, but it's a bad idea to make your reader hunt around. Put the thesis in your introduction.
- **KEEP IT SHORT.** Your thesis paragraph should contain no more than two or three sentences. Not only are you racing the clock, but for the most part, any material that contributes to the thesis statement can't be counted toward the points you're hoping to earn for argument and evidence. Extra material will be wasted—so save it for the essay's main body.
- **ADDRESS ALL ASPECTS OF THE QUESTION.** How you do this depends on which essay you're writing, but no matter what, the thesis must touch on all aspects of the question. These include the time period, the geographical area(s), and the topics presented by the question. "Address" does NOT mean simply restating the question.

■ **BE SPECIFIC AND ANALYTICAL.** Vague language weakens your thesis. As noted above, restating the question is not helpful. Neither is relying on lazy and unspecific assertions like "industrialization proved important in Europe and Japan during the 1800s" or "religious life in India changed substantially between 600 B.C.E. and 600 C.E." Analysis, which your reader will want to see, involves discussing HOW and WHY something happened and the RESULTS and EFFECTS that followed. The more concrete you can be, the better.

OTHER GENERAL REQUIREMENTS: ANALYSIS, EVIDENCE, AND CONTEXT

Although each essay is unique in its way, the rubrics for both require you to do several things beyond generating a thesis. As you build the main body of your essay (the three to five paragraphs that follow your thesis), think constantly about how you can fulfill these requirements.

Analysis

Your essay cannot just describe or narrate; it must *analyze* and *explain*. It must follow a clear and logical line of reasoning. (This is why the thesis is so important—it gets your essay off to a good start and provides it with an argumentative direction.) The details of how to argue effectively vary from question to question, but you must explicitly deal with questions of *how* and *why*, and explain the context and signficance of things, rather than simply list facts or story-tell. Also remember that your argument must address *all* parts of the question assigned to you—all (or almost all) of the documents, change *and* continuity, cause *and* effect, differences *and* similarities. Another key part of building an argument involves the evaluation of sources, whether primary or secondary. The author's intended purpose, format, point of view, strengths, and weaknesses—all of these should be discussed whenever appropriate.

Evidence

Don't just say it, prove it! Concrete details help you make your case, and this is where you can put factual knowledge to good use. Who traded which goods with whom? Who enacted which policies? What environmental or medical disasters had a bearing on your question—or which new technological innovations, artistic trends, or religious developments? Not only do specific nuggets of relevant information make your general comments more convincing, AP readers are told to look for a minimum number of them before awarding points. That number varies from question to question, but the more you include, the better you'll do. Bear in mind, however, that you cannot merely list pieces of evidence. You must explain them, contextualize them, and demonstrate an understanding of their significance and their relevance to your thesis and argument.

PROVIDING CONTEXT

Think about what trends are unfolding worldwide during the era you're writing about. Does your topic fit into a general trend? If so, how? If not, does it run against the grain of a general trend in an interesting way?

Some examples:

- growth of trade networks in Africa before 1500 (topic) > expansion of Islam (context)
- rise of the Atlantic slave trade (topic) > growing appetite for cheap labor caused by exploitation of colonies, plantation monoculture, and early industrialization (context)
- cultural and intellectual advancement in Europe during the Renaissance (topic) > flourishing of arts and culture in technologically advanced societies worldwide between 1200 and 1750 (context)
- the fall of a particular empire (topic) > does it relate to a larger migratory pattern? or a widespread environmental trend? or something else? (context)
- the rise of religious fundamentalism in the modern era (topic) > does this contradict or run counter to the general tendency for modern societies to become more secular? (context)

MISCELLANEOUS POINTS

Other things to remember as you write your essays:

- **DOING WHAT THE QUESTION ASKS.** Before answering any essay question, look at the question's action verb—what is it asking you to do? Analyze? Compare? Evaluate? Make sure you respond accordingly. OTHER THINGS to watch out for: Double-check the time period(s) you're being asked to write about. Also, if the question allows you to choose between time periods or from a list of regions, be sure you understand the terms of the choice. Is it either/or? Do you pick two items from a list of three? Are you supposed to provide examples from at least two of whatever it is the question is asking you about? Finally, make sure you understand which historical reasoning skill is being targeted by the question.
- **ACCEPTABLE LENGTH.** There is no hard-and-fast rule for how long your essay should be. Page length may vary depending on how large your handwriting is and whether you write concisely or need more words to make your point. As a rule, high-scoring LEQ responses should run 2.5 to 3.5 pages long—assuming normal-sized handwriting and no skipping of lines. Because of their complexity, DBQ essays tend to be longer, with high-scoring examples averaging 4 to 5 pages. Whatever the type, any essay shorter than 2.5 pages is unlikely to score well. (If you wish to judge by word count, rough equivalents would be 600–700 words for LEQ responses and 900–1,000 words, sometimes slightly more, for DBQs.)
- **PARAGRAPHS.** Dividing your essays into paragraphs will organize your thoughts and make your prose easier to read. Indent clearly. You should end up with four to six paragraphs, depending on how many main points you make in the body of your essay and on whether you add a formal conclusion. Your DBQ may contain more paragraphs than your LEQ.

- **CONCLUSION ... OR NOT.** Formal papers generally feature a conclusion that restates the thesis and expands upon it. If you have time to write one, it adds an elegant touch—but it's not strictly necessary, and it won't by itself add points. If you're pressed for time, you're better off strengthening your essay's main body. If you do write a conclusion, don't waste time simply repeating what's in your introduction. Use it to squeeze in more evidence or to make an extra contextual or analytical point. (Also, while it's better to state your thesis in the introduction, as suggested above, the conclusion is the one other place you can locate the thesis if for some reason you don't start with it.)
- **LEGIBILITY.** AP readers do their best to decipher sloppy handwriting. However, neatness makes it easier to appreciate your work. Write quickly, but try your best to be legible.
- **GRAMMAR, SPELLING, AND STYLE.** Substance matters more than style on the AP exam, and readers are not meant to concern themselves with misspellings or grammatical mistakes. Still, fluent prose free of errors makes a better impression, and the more sophistication you display in your writing, the better.
- **PLAN ... AND PAY ATTENTION.** It's been said several times but deserves repeating: before writing each essay, take some time—approximately 5 minutes—to plan your answer. And pay attention to the clock!

DOCUMENT-BASED QUESTION (DBQ) STRATEGIES

Although you are allowed to choose differently, the DBQ, as noted earlier, should be the first essay you write. Its elaborate rules make it the one essay you don't want to be working on if you start running short on time.

Unlike the other essays, the DBQ requires you to perform well on two fronts. Not only does the essay itself have to be solid (complete with a good thesis), but you must demonstrate skillful handling of the documents. The procedure for this is complex enough that you should familiarize yourself with it and practice it ahead of time.

Approaching the Document-Based Question

When the essay portion of the AP exam begins, you will be shown a set of 7 documents. Some will be written texts, but others will be image-based (photographs, cartoons, artwork) or consist of charts and graphs. The documents and their creators may or may not be well-known. You may (and should) use the 15-minute reading period to examine them and plan your answer.

The DBQ will focus on some time period between 1450 and the present. When taken together, the documents address a particular theme or issue, typically with a fairly narrow focus when it comes to era, geography, and topic. For example, a DBQ might ask about industrialization in nineteenth-century Asia or European imperialism in a specific part of the world. Or about a noteworthy cultural trend, technological innovation, trade network, or sociological development. A DBQ will tie your use of the documents to one of several historical reasoning skills: you may be told to compare and contrast two things, to trace continuity and change over time, or to analyze causes and consequences. You will organize the documents into **groups** (typically **three** of them). You will discuss the documents' **context** as well as their creators' **point of view** or **purpose**. Also, to test your understanding of how documents can sometimes be of limited usefulness, the DBQ will ask you to **identify additional evidence** that, if provided, would shed further light on the question.

Below is the official AP scoring guide for the DBQ.

Generic Scoring Guide for AP World History Document-Based Question
(maximum total = 7 points)

A. THESIS/CLAIM (1 point)

1 point: Responds to the prompt with a historically defensible thesis/claim that establishes a line of reasoning.

B. CONTEXTUALIZATION (1 point)

1 point: Describes a broader historical context relevant to the prompt.

C. EVIDENCE (3 points)

1 point: Uses the content of at least **three** documents to address the topic of the prompt.

1 point: Uses the content of at least **six** documents to address the topic of the prompt.

1 point: Uses at least one additional piece of specific historical evidence (beyond that found in the documents) relevant to an argument about the prompt.

D. ANALYSIS AND REASONING (2 points)

1 point: For at least **three** documents, explains the relevance of point of view, purpose, historical situation, and/or audience to an argument.

1 point: Demonstrates a complex understanding of the historical development focused on by the prompt, using evidence to confirm, modify, or qualify an argument.

How do you put all this together for a good score?

The DBQ Thesis

As noted above, this is your central argument. For the DBQ, you must first match your thesis to the task you are being asked to perform (comparison, discussion of causes and consequences, examination of changes and continuities). Second, you cannot simply develop a thesis about the historical subject(s) covered by the question. It must be something the documents can support as well.

MATCHING YOUR DBQ THESIS TO THE DOCUMENTS

If your DBQ is about East Indian diaspora communities in Africa and the documents concern the role of East Indians in African trade networks, it would be a mistake to base your thesis on the question of whether East Indians experienced racial prejudice in Africa. Interesting as that question might be, it would not allow you to use the documents properly. On the other hand, you could introduce the issue in the essay's main body as additional historical context.

Contextualization

You must explicitly relate the documents and your argument about them to a broader historical context. What major topic, theme, or larger subject—such as slavery, nationalism, industrialization, or the treatment of a minority group, to take only a few examples—seems to be at stake? What time period and part(s) of the world are the documents drawn from? This should not be difficult to figure out, but you have to demonstrate your understanding clearly and thoroughly. This point cannot be earned simply with a single phrase or sentence.

EVIDENCE: GROUPING THE DOCUMENTS (MAGIC NUMBER = 3?)

Earlier versions of the AP exam required the sorting of documents into groups. This is no longer formally required but can still be an effective way to structure your essay. Certain documents may have an important element in common or relate to your argument in a particular way and can therefore be discussed jointly. Ideally, you will end up with three groups of documents, although two could be acceptable. DBQs are generally designed in such a way as to allow more than one "correct" way to group your documents.

MAPPING DBQ GROUPS

As you outline your essay, it's worth sketching out a chart that sorts all the documents into the groups you've come up with. This will keep you from forgetting any of the documents as you write. Also, you might jot down notes about (a) point of view or purpose for as many documents as you can, and (b) where you'd like to identify the need for additional evidence (see below). As a bonus, mapping your groups will automatically give your essay the proper structure: thesis paragraph + paragraph for group 1 + paragraph for group 2 + paragraph for group 3 (if needed) + a conclusion (where you might choose to add more context or identify additional evidence).

EVIDENCE: USING DOCUMENT CONTENT (MAGIC NUMBER = ALL DOCUMENTS)

Every document should be used meaningfully to support your thesis. (The rubric permits you to use three documents for partial credit and six documents for full credit, but aim to use them all if there are seven documents.) Proper "use" does NOT mean simply listing or describing the documents, or parroting the information contained in the captions. You must demonstrate an understanding of each document's purpose and the context in which it was written or created (also see below). In addition, analysis means showing how the document relates to your central argument. Generally, you will use a document as evidence to corroborate your thesis, but sometimes a document will complicate or contradict your argument. In that case, you will want to show your ability to account for and explain ambiguities and exceptions.

CITING DOCUMENTS

How should you cite the documents? AP rules for attribution used to be more elaborate. These days, it is enough to refer to document number, title, and/or author. In other words, if the source for Document 5 is "Gloria Steinem, American feminist, 'Far from the Opposite Shore' (1978)," you can cite it any of the following ways: "Steinem," "Far from the Opposite Shore," "Document 5," or "Doc. 5."

EVIDENCE: BEYOND THE DOCUMENTS (MINIMUM NUMBER = 1, MAGIC NUMBER = 2)

To test your understanding of the strengths, weaknesses, and uses of various historical sources, the DBQ requires you to comment on what's missing from the documents you have available. Can you think of ADDITIONAL evidence to support or qualify the argument you have made about those documents? (In previous versions of the exam, the DBQ asked students to identify an extra document or two that might supplement the ones provided and, while the logic here is similar, the new rules allow for a more flexible response.) Can you think of an episode, a trend, or a fact to contextualize the documents? Or to provide a missing point of view? (Is only one gender represented? Or one social class, religion, or nationality, or one side of a controversy?) Be sure to explain WHY the extra evidence you're describing would be helpful. You can either do this while you discuss the actual documents, or you can do it in a separate paragraph—perhaps in your last paragraph.

ANALYSIS AND REASONING: POINT OF VIEW/PURPOSE/HISTORICAL SITUATION/ AUDIENCE (MINIMUM NUMBER = 3, MAGIC NUMBER = 4 ... OR MORE?)

Demonstrating your capacity for analysis is best done by discussing some or all of these factors with respect to as many documents as possible. Describe the context in which a document appeared, or what perspectives, biases, and motivations it can be said to express. Can it be considered wholly or even partly reliable? Analyzing point of view or purpose is easiest if the author/creator is famous and you can bring in "outside" factual knowledge about him or her, but this is often not the case. Typically, you will have to make judgment calls about how an author/creator's (or audience's) occupation, social-institutional status, nationality, gender, religion, or political views might shape his or her point of view. The rubric does not require you to do this for all documents, but THREE is mandatory and FOUR (or more if you can manage it without sacrificing other points) provides you with a safety margin.

ANALYSIS AND REASONING: COMPLEX UNDERSTANDING

Have you done all of the above-mentioned things thoroughly and particularly well? This last point cannot be earned simply by inserting a fact here or there or by adding a sentence or two. It is meant as a reward for students who show a comprehensive and coherent understanding of the historical development on which the question touches and who connect the documents to that topic repeatedly and in a sophisticated fashion. Awareness of course themes and broader events and processes is helpful. So is the ability to use the appropriate reasoning skill in a balanced way: Does your argument take into account continuity AND change? Similarity AND difference? Cause AND effect, as well as MULTIPLE causes and effects? While the essay as a whole will have to do well to score this point, the concluding paragraph is an excellent place to address these "big picture" issues.

Sample Question

The following question is based on the accompanying Documents 1–7. (The documents have been edited for the purpose of this exercise.)

1. Evaluate the extent to which pan-Arabism and pan-Africanism have differed in their nature and political effectiveness in the modern era.

Document 1

Source: Gamal Abdul Nasser, Arab nationalist and president of Egypt, "The Philosophy of the Revolution," 1959.

As I often sit in my study and think quietly of this subject, I ask myself: "What is our positive world in this troubled world, and where is the scene in which we can play that role?"

Can we ignore that there is a Muslim world to which we are tied by bonds which are not only forged by religious faith, but also tightened by the facts of history? … It is not in vain that our country lies to the southwest of Asia, close to the Arab world, whose life is intermingled with ours. … It is not in vain that Islamic civilization and Islamic heritage, which the Mongols ravaged in their conquest of the old Islamic capitals, retreated and found refuge in Egypt, where they found shelter and safety as a result of the counterattack with which Egypt repelled the invasion of these Tartars at Ain Jalut.

All these are fundamental facts, whose roots lie deeply in our life. Whatever we do, we cannot forget them or run away from them.

Document 2

Source: Julius Nyerere, president of Tanzania, "The Dilemma of the Pan-Africanist," 1966.

I believe there is a danger that we might now voluntarily surrender our greatest dream of all.

For it was as Africans that we dreamed of freedom; and we thought of it for Africa. Our real ambition was African freedom and African government. The fact that we fought area by area was merely a tactical necessity. We organized ourselves into the Convention People's Party, the Tanganyika African National Union, the United National Independence Party, and so on, simply because each local colonial government had to be dealt with separately.

The question we now have to answer is whether Africa shall maintain this internal separation as we defeat colonialism, or whether our earlier proud boast—"I am an African"—shall become a reality. It is not a reality now. For the truth is that there are now 36 different nationalities in free Africa, one for each of the 36 independent states—to say nothing of those still under colonial or alien domination. Each state is separate from the others: each is a sovereign entity. And this means that each state has a government which is responsible to the people of its own area—and to them only; it must work for their particular well-being or invite chaos within its territory.

Can the vision of Pan-Africanism survive these realities? I do not believe the answer is easy. Indeed I believe that a real dilemma faces the Pan-Africanist. On the one hand is the fact that Pan-Africanism demands an African consciousness and an African loyalty; on the other hand is the fact that each Pan-Africanist must also concern himself with the freedom and development of one of the nations of Africa. These things can conflict. Let us be honest and admit that they have already conflicted.

Document 3

Source: Map of the Arab world with national flags.

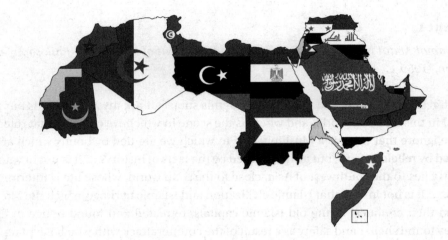

Document 4

Source: Declaration of the Rights of the Negro Peoples of the World, adopted at the Convention of the Universal Negro Improvement Association, New York City, 1920.

Be it Resolved, That the Negro people of the world, through their chosen representatives in convention assembled in Liberty Hall, in the City of New York and United States of America, from August 1 to August 31, in the year of our Lord, one thousand nine hundred and twenty, protest against the wrongs and injustices they are suffering at the hands of their white brethren, and state what they deem their fair and just rights, as well as the treatment they propose to demand of all men in the future.

We complain:

I. That nowhere in the world, with few exceptions, are black men accorded equal treatment with white men …

II. In certain parts of the United States of America our race is denied the right of public trial accorded to other races when accused of crime, but are lynched and burned by mobs, and such brutal and inhuman treatment is even practised upon our women.

III. That European nations have parcelled out among themselves and taken possession of nearly all of the continent of Africa, and the natives are compelled to surrender their lands to aliens and are treated in most instances like slaves.

VIII. In Civil Service and departmental offices we are everywhere discriminated against and made to feel that to be a black man in Europe, America and the West Indies is equivalent to being an outcast and a leper among the races of men, no matter what the character and attainments of the black man may be.

In order to encourage our race all over the world and to stimulate it to a higher and grander destiny, we demand and insist on the following Declaration of Rights:

1. Be it known to all men that whereas, all men are created equal and entitled to the rights of life, liberty and the pursuit of happiness, and because of this we, the duly elected representatives of the Negro peoples of the world, invoking the aid of the just and Almighty God do declare all men, women and children of our blood throughout the world free citizens, and do claim them as free citizens of Africa, the Motherland of all Negroes. …

37. We hereby demand that the governments of the world recognize our leader [Marcus Garvey, elected Provisional President of Africa] and his representatives chosen by the race to look after the welfare of our people under such governments. …

39. That the colors, Red, Black and Green, be the colors of the Negro race.

40. Resolved, That the anthem "Ethiopia, Thou Land of Our Fathers" shall be the anthem of the Negro race!

Document 5

Source: Pan-African mural in Tanzania, present day.

Document 6

Source: "Pan-Arabism—The Only Sensible Way Forward," Yemen Times, 2012.

The fact is that the Arab world—if, indeed, such an entity still exists—has rarely been as splintered as it is now, as evidenced by the divisions in the Arab League over Syria and Iran. There are great disparities in GDP and standards of living—and chasms between liberals and conservatives and systems of governance. The youth of the Middle East and North Africa region wave their respective country's flag and listen to patriotic songs but rarely proclaim themselves to be proud Arabs.

Arab traditions are being watered down to make way for western-imported lifestyles. In some countries, traditional dress has almost disappeared along with time-consuming dishes, cast aside because kids prefer burgers and French fries.

It bothers me to see young Arabs aspiring to become western clones when, if they only knew it, their own family-oriented culture of respect, hospitality and generosity is rich and should be preserved. Superficially, Arabs may not have a lot in common nowadays but that culture is rooted in all Arab lands along with a shared language and faith-based societal mores.

When Arab Spring states are undergoing transition and no one knows how Syria will look six months from now, the idea of a unified Arab bloc may sound ridiculous. But when the dust has settled, Arab leaders should hold a conference, to revisit pan-Arabism/Arab nationalism to decide once and for all whether closer cooperation would be beneficial for all or whether Nasser's grand plan should be filed in the dustbin of history.

Like it or not, from a geopolitical standpoint big is beautiful. It took two world wars for Europe to cotton on. The NATO alliance of countries from North America and Europe has afforded protection to all and the EU club provides even the smallest of its European members with international clout as well as a financial cushion.

Document 7

Source: Leopold Sedar Senghor, Senegalese poet, "In Memoriam," 1945.

Today is Sunday.
I fear the crowd of my fellows with such faces of stone.
From my glass tower filled with headaches and impatient Ancestors,
I contemplate the roofs and hilltops in the mist.
In the stillness—somber, naked chimneys.
Below them my dead are asleep and my dreams turn to ashes.
All my dreams, blood running freely down the streets
And mixing with blood from the butcher shops.
From this observatory like the outskirts of town
I contemplate my dreams lost along the streets,
Crouched at the foot of the hills like the guides of my race
On the rivers of the Gambia and the Saloum
And now on the Seine at the foot of these hills.
Let me remember my dead!
Yesterday was All Saints' Day, the solemn anniversary of the Sun,
And I had no dead to honor in any cemetery.
O Forefathers! You who have always refused to die,
Who knew how to resist Death from the Sine to the Seine,
And now in the fragile veins of my indomitable blood,
Guard my dreams as you did your thin-legged migrant sons!
O Ancestors! Defend the roofs of Paris in this dominical fog,
The roofs that protect my dead.
Let me leave this tower so dangerously secure
And descend to the streets, joining my brothers
Who have blue eyes and hard hands.

Sample Answer

During the global wave of decolonization that followed the end of World War II, two political ideologies seemed poised to gain permanent prominence: pan-Africanism and pan-Arabism. Both movements followed the same logic, attempting to empower previously colonized peoples by encouraging a sense of unity based on broad cultural and ethnic identities, rather than narrow national ones. A key difference, however, is that pan-Africanism defined itself mainly in terms of opposition to racial and colonial oppression, whereas pan-Arabism was in a better position to appeal to a common linguistic and religious heritage. In the end, while both achieved certain successes, both proved weaker than the lure of traditional nationalism and fell far short of their original aspirations.

[This paragraph moves steadily toward a thesis, which is given in the last sentence. The paragraph IDENTIFIES the question's major elements (the subject, time period, and task, which is comparison and involves similarities *and* differences). It spells out a similarity and a difference, then QUALIFIES them by indicating specifically what will be said about them. It contributes to ANALYSIS (and ARGUMENT DEVELOPMENT) by explaining how ideological expectations were foiled by nationalist realities in the long term. Finally, it also starts the process of CONTEXTUALIZATION and USING EVIDENCE BEYOND THE DOCUMENTS by "explaining the broader historical events, developments, or processes"—in this case, post-World War II decolonization—"immediately relevant to the question."]

REMEMBER: Vague language = weak thesis! Be as specific as possible—but without getting swamped. Don't forget that your thesis shouldn't be too long or contain too much detail.

Group	Document Nos.	Category	Point of View or Purpose or Audience
1	4, 7	roots of pan-Africanism; defining self in relation to white majority	political activism, aiming for public persuasion; poet making artistic-intellectual appeal
2	2, 5	goals of post-WWII pan-Africanism	national leader, directly promoting ideology; public art, expressing optimism
3	1, 6, 3	pan-Arabism: potential and failure	national leader, directly promoting ideology; journalist, arguing for revival of ideology; graphic image subtly indicating its failure
	evidence outside document	Biafra and Rwanda as direct indications of pan-Africanism's weaknesses? views from ordinary people whose concerns tend to be national or even local, and not transnational?	
	CONTEXT = different region or era *and/or* insights from a nonhistorical discipline	compare and contrast with transnational entities in post-WWII Asia? *and/or* note possible helpfulness of info from *economics* about the extent of trade integration among African and Arab nations?	

[The above chart shows how this essay will organize the documents. It also leaves room for notes about each document's point of view (or purpose, or audience, or context); the additional piece(s) of evidence that need to be identified and explained; and the elements needed to demonstrate context. You should create such a map when you write your own DBQ.]

Pan-Africanism had deeper roots than pan-Arabism, and much of it sprang from the discontent felt by African-descended populations who lived among abusive white majorities or under white colonial rule. These experiences are spoken of by the 1920 "Declaration of the Rights of the Negro Peoples of the World" (document 4) and the 1945 poem "In Memoriam," by Leopold Senghor (document 7). Senghor, from the French colony of Senegal, describes the alienation he feels living in Paris, surrounded by French whites—supposedly his "brothers," but completely different, and to be feared, with their "faces of stone," "blue eyes," and "hard hands." The contrast between his native landscape and holidays with the streets of Paris and the Catholic Day of

All Saints reminds him that he does not belong. As a central figure in the Negritude movement, Senghor stressed African identity as a source of strength for all those of African descent living under white rule, no matter where or under which colonial authority. The same viewpoint was expressed even more forcefully by the delegates to the 1920 Convention of the Universal Negro Improvement Association in New York City. The idea here was that all those of African descent shared a common problem—white oppression, whether in the United States, the Caribbean, Europe, or Africa itself under colonial rule—and a common heritage, and should therefore band together, regardless of language or specific tribal origin. The Convention's "Declaration" went so far as to nominate an actual president of Africa, and to designate a song about Ethiopia as its anthem.

[This paragraph accomplishes several goals. First, it DEVELOPS THE ARGUMENT introduced in the thesis paragraph. It also engages in DOCUMENT ANALYSIS by detailing the point of view—and purpose—of two documents and linking the documents to the central argument. Incidentally, all the documents will eventually be used to support the argument, the other core task involved with document analysis. Some EVIDENCE BEYOND THE DOCUMENTS is provided here by identifying the poet Senghor as a member of the NEGRITUDE school. Relevant "outside" information and factual knowledge can be helpful in this way.]

Document 2, an essay from the 1960s by Tanzanian president Julius Nyerere, carries the pan-African vision into the post-World War II era, when many African nations overthrew colonial regimes or were in the process of doing so. Along with Kwame Nkrumah, who won freedom for Ghana from British rule, Nyerere was one of this time period's most outspoken supporters of pan-Africanism. (Also like Nkrumah, Nyerere can be viewed in the larger context of "third world" political leaders such as Sukarno of Indonesia, Nehru of India, and Nasser of Egypt, all of whom sought ways to strengthen their newly liberated countries and keep them free of Western political interference and economic domination.) Nyerere identifies a key "dilemma" of pan-Africanism: the fact that African independence has to be achieved country by country, after which it is tempting for each country to focus narrowly on its own interests. He argues vehemently that Africa can prosper only if such temptations are overcome in favor of a larger, more cooperative understanding of what it means to be African. The mural pictured in document 5 is a visual representation of this utopian ideal, which seeks to unite a billion people under one inclusive label, bridging all other ethnic or linguistic differences. Neither document, however, sufficiently addresses the huge difficulties involved with uniting peoples as diverse as those in Africa actually are. While politicians like

Nyerere and Nkrumah managed to establish transnational organizations like the Organization of African Unity (now the African Union), conflict and disunity have tended to greatly outweigh pan-African unity in the decades since World War II. Differences in language, ethnic and tribal identity, and local culture and religion seem to have proven stronger than abstract ideology.

[This paragraph, like the previous one, continues to DEVELOP THE ARGUMENT and support the thesis. It provides DOCUMENT ANALYSIS by analyzing the point of view or purpose of both documents. A good deal of EVIDENCE BEYOND THE DOCUMENTS (mentioning Nyerere in conjunction with other African and Asian leaders, discussing the Organization of African Unity) is included here. Facts are not simply listed but used to explain and analyze.]

Documents 1, 6, and 3 all have to do with pan-Arabism. Gamal Nasser, who had just risen to power in Egypt as a nationalist leader, and would outrage much of the West by establishing Egyptian control over the Suez Canal, ranks with Nyerere as a major political figure in the "third world" during the 1950s and 1960s. Like the pan-Africanists, Nasser saw pan-Arabism as a means to build strength and defy the militarily stronger and more economically prosperous nations of the West. To that end, he even managed to join Egypt to Syria and Iraq in a short-lived United Arab Republic. Much more so than pan-Africanism, pan-Arabism had the potential to foster transnational unity, because most people in the so-called "Arab world" shared a common language (Arabic), a common history and cultural heritage, and, in most cases, a common religion (Islam). Document 6, a recent newspaper editorial, makes this exact point in calling for a revival of the pan-Arab ideal in order to preserve Arab identity in the face of Westernization. However, the fact that document 6 has to call for pan-Arabism in 2012 clearly indicates that, even with the advantage of a common tongue and heritage, pan-Arabism—like pan-Africanism—yielded few concrete political results. Some of the region's smallest nations may have fused together as the United Arab Emirates, but this is hardly a political powerhouse. Document 3, a graphic showing the "Arab world," with each nation linked to its individual flag, does not say anything overtly—but by its very nature speaks to the failure of pan-Arabism to overcome national differences in favor of a larger regional identity. Like Nkrumah and Nyerere, Nasser failed to cement in place a larger dream of union.

[With this final group of documents, ARGUMENT DEVELOPMENT continues, and the thesis is supported by analysis. EVIDENCE OUTSIDE THE DOCUMENTS is provided at several points. DOCUMENT ANALYSIS is demonstrated by addressing point of view or purpose in each case.]

As rich as the current selection of documents is, additional perspectives would shed more light on this comparison between pan-Africanism and pan-Arabism. While political elites are well represented, the point of view of non-state actors is not, and there is much historical evidence to show that the concerns of most ordinary people tend to be local or national, and rarely transnational. Even political leaders who theoretically supported pan-Arabism, like Gaddafi in Libya and Nasser himself, cared more for their own nations' interest in the end. With respect to Africa, numerous episodes—such as the Biafra War (in which the Igbo minority tried to secede from Nigeria in the late 1960s) and the 1994 genocide committed in Rwanda by the Hutu against their Tutsi neighbors—provide evidence of the real-life difficulties involved with realizing the dream of pan-African unity. Finally, to contextualize this topic even farther, it would be useful to compare it with trends in Asia during this period. There, too, especially in South and Southeast Asia, many nations decolonized, and a number of them tried to form transnational coalitions or alliances. While pan-Asianism was not attempted to the same degree that pan-Arabism and pan-Africanism were, organizations such as the Southeast Asian Treaty Organization (SEATO) and the Association of Southeast Asian Nations (ASEAN) emerged to accomplish at least some of the same things that pan-Africanists and pan-Arabists hoped to bring about in their own regions.

[What should you do in your last paragraph? As a reminder, this could be where you state your thesis, but it's preferable to use the introduction for this purpose (as this essay does).

If you have enough time, and if you've already earned the point for EVIDENCE BEYOND THE DOCUMENTS that comes from discussing extra evidence that would be helpful, you could wrap things up with a formal conclusion.

That's one approach. This essay illustrates another, which is to forego a formal conclusion (which by itself doesn't directly earn points) and concentrate separately on CONTEXT AND EVIDENCE BEYOND THE EVIDENCE. This provides the feel of a finishing touch, because you're reflecting on—and adding to—what you've just written. It also draws more attention to your analytical thinking about sources than if you shoehorn discussion of additional documents into other paragraphs. The major risk, of course, is that if you leave this until the end and run out of time, you won't do it at all. So if you adopt this approach, budget your time wisely!]

LONG ESSAY QUESTION (LEQ) STRATEGIES

In addition to the DBQ, you will complete a long essay question (LEQ). Although you can write this essay before the DBQ if you wish, it is recommended that you save it for last, because of the DBQ's complexity. Aim to spend roughly 40 minutes on the LEQ.

On this portion of the exam, you will be offered a choice: three possible LEQs will be presented, and you will select one. All three options will test the same historical-reasoning skill and focus on the same course theme but cover a different time period: the first will cover 1200–1750, the second will focus on 1450–1800, and the third will do the same for 1750 to the present. The reasoning skill will vary from year to year, rotating through causation, comparison, and continuity/change over time (CCOT).

Generic Scoring Guide for AP World History Long Essay Question
(maximum total = 6 points)

A. THESIS/CLAIM (1 point)
1 point: Responds to the prompt with a historically defensible thesis/claim that establishes a line of reasoning.
B. CONTEXTUALIZATION (1 point)
1 point: Describes a broader historical context relevant to the prompt.
C. EVIDENCE (2 points)
1 point: Provides specific examples of evidence relevant to the topic of the prompt.
1 point: Supports an argument in response to the prompt using specific and relevant examples of evidence.
D. ANALYSIS AND REASONING (2 points)
1 point: Uses historical reasoning (for example, comparison, causation, CCOT) to structure an argument that addresses the prompt.
1 point: Demonstrates a complex understanding of the historical development focused on by the prompt, using evidence to confirm, modify, or qualify an argument.

Approaching the Long Essay Question

The LEQ is less complicated than the DBQ, but as the rubric above makes evident, certain tasks need to be accomplished the right way to earn full credit.

THE THESIS

As with the DBQ, this is your central argument. It is generally easier to develop an LEQ thesis—the main issue is to make sure it relates directly to the question prompt and also to both aspects of the targeted thinking skill (similarities and differences for comparison, causes and effects for causation, and continuities and changes for CCOT).

CONTEXTUALIZATION

Also, as with the DBQ, you must relate the documents and your argument about them to a broader historical context. Remember to demonstrate this understanding clearly and thoroughly and not simply with a single phrase or sentence.

EVIDENCE (MINIMUM NUMBER = 2, MAGIC NUMBER = 4 OR MORE?)

As noted in the free-response general tips, concrete details help you make your case. Make factual knowledge work for you. Note, however, that simply listing pieces of information will not suffice; as the rubric indicates, you will earn only one point for this. To earn both points for evidence, you need to show a deeper understanding of them and to relate them directly to your thesis. Include as much evidence as you feasibly can. Readers are told to look for a minimum number of pieces of evidence as they tally up points. This changes from year to year, but TWO is a baseline minimum. To be safe, include THREE of FOUR pieces, depending on the question—and even more if time permits and you've taken care of the question's other elements.

RULES OF EVIDENCE: To begin with, your evidence must be APPLICABLE, or relevant, to the question's main topic. Obviously, this means avoiding errors or irrelevancy. (Talking about the elimination of foot binding—a Chinese practice—as evidence of change in the status of women in sub-Saharan Africa would do no good.) Applicability can be trickier when a question deals somehow with relationships *between* two regions or two topics. In that case, each piece of evidence must apply to both things, not just one. (For instance, if you're writing about trade between Asia and Africa between 300 C.E. and 1450 C.E., mentioning the Silk Road—a Eurasian trade route—will do you no good unless you discuss how goods traded along that route made their way *to and from Africa.* Similarly, if you're dealing with the relationship between legal systems and gender relations, alluding to India's *sati* ritual and Hindu custom will not help unless you connect it with religiously based *laws.*)

Another guideline is to BE SPECIFIC when presenting evidence. If you're describing technological innovations that facilitated the growth of maritime networks between 600 C.E. and 1450 C.E., don't settle for saying that "shipbuilding and navigational techniques improved." Mention concrete items like the lodestone compass, the lateen sail, the dhow, the junk, the ability to predict weather patterns like the monsoon season, and the adoption of the sternpost rudder. Not only is this more likely to impress your reader, you may be credited with more pieces of evidence (see the point directly below).

Make each piece of evidence look DISTINCT. You don't want your reader lumping together items that you consider to be separate bits of evidence. This can happen, though, if you present evidence lazily—as in this description of the Columbian Exchange: "Among the items that passed back and forth between the Old and New Worlds were corn, potatoes, coffee, the horse, tomatoes, bananas, and sugarcane, not to mention diseases like smallpox and measles." That's a lot of evidence, right? Maybe … but a reader might just count it as ONE piece of evidence, under the heading of "items passing back and forth," or perhaps two pieces (food items + diseases). See how a fairly easy repackaging improves things: "The global impact of the Columbian Exchange proved astounding in many ways. High-yield crops like corn and potatoes traveled from the Americas to Afro-Eurasia, where they improved diets and boosted population growth. The horse, transplanted to the New World, dramatically altered the lifestyle of many Native American peoples. Bananas, sugarcane, and coffee from the Old World grew well in the New World, giving rise to plantation agriculture and long-term dependence on slavery."

See the difference? Even if the underlined passages weren't there, breaking one long list into three distinct sentences increases the chance of earning credit for three pieces of evidence.

Finally, remember that each historical thinking skill requires a roughly EVEN SPLIT between two things: similarities *and* differences in the case of comparison, cause *and* effect in the case of causation, change *and* continuity in the case of CCOT. Make sure your body of evidence addresses both sides in a balanced fashion.

Analysis: Using the Targeted Reasoning Skill

Developing an argument to support your thesis is key to LEQ success. Be sure to use the targeted reasoning skill—comparison, causation, or continuity/change over time—to shape your central argument. Whatever skill is being tested, remember to address BOTH SIDES of it (similarities and differences for comparison, causes and effects for causation, continuities and changes for CCOT). Your argument should not neglect one in favor of the other.

Analysis and Reasoning: Complex Understanding

Have you done all of the above-mentioned things thoroughly and particularly well? As with the DBQ, this last point will go to those who demonstrate an advanced and sophisticated understanding of the prompt, using their evidence to *explain* and *evaluate*. See the corresponding heading under the DBQ advice for more detail, and remember that much can be done to earn this point in your conclusion.

Sample Questions

Below are three sets of questions, each reflecting how the AP exam, in any given year, might target a particular historical reasoning skill and course theme. Below, one sample answer—responding to one of the comparison questions—is provided.

POSSIBLE COMPARISON QUESTIONS (COURSE THEME = STATE BUILDING)

1. In the period 1200 to 1500, states in Europe and in India used various techniques of conquest and rulership to consolidate and centralize their authority.

   Develop an argument that evaluates the extent to which states in each region succeeded in their goals of political consolidation and centralization.

2. In the period 1450 to 1800, the Ottoman Empire and China employed various strategies to legitimate their political authority.

   Develop an argument that evaluates the extent to which each state succeeded in this goal.

3. In the period after 1900, both Latin America and the Middle East significantly modernized their political systems.

   Develop an argument that evaluates the extent to which this process was accomplished in each region.

POSSIBLE CAUSATION QUESTIONS (COURSE THEME = SOCIAL STRUCTURES)

1. In the period 1200 to 1500, the rise of interregional trade led to the emergence of diaspora communities in many regions.

   Develop an argument that evaluates the extent to which the rise of interregional trade in one or more regions contributed to the emergence of diaspora communities.

2. In the period 1500 to 1800, economic changes altered systems of social stratification in many states.

   Develop an argument that evaluates the extent to which economic developments in one or more states led to changes in systems of social stratification.

3. In the period 1750 to 1900, economic modernization caused various forms of coerced labor to be adopted in many regions.

   Develop an argument that evaluates the extent to which economic modernization led to the adoption of coerced labor in one or more regions.

POSSIBLE CCOT QUESTIONS (COURSE THEME = HUMANS AND THE ENVIRONMENT)

1. In the period 1200 to 1500, scientific and technological innovation allowed societies around the world to affect the environment in profound ways.

   Develop an argument that evaluates the extent to which scientific and technological innovation caused environmental change during this period.

2. In the period 1450 to 1800, epidemic diseases significantly affected human societies in various parts of the world.

   Develop an argument that evaluates the extent to which epidemic diseases shaped human societies in one or more parts of the world during this period.

3. In the period 1800 to 2000, large-scale agricultural production has had an increasingly large impact on the environment.

   Develop an argument that evaluates the extent to which large-scale agricultural production has caused environmental change during this period.

Sample Answer (based on Comparison #3 from the questions listed above)

The first half of the twentieth century brought immense changes to many parts of the globe. Among these was increased modernization in a number of non-Western regions, including Latin America and the Middle East. Both places faced similar obstacles, such as relative socioeconomic backwardness, heavy influence from outside powers, and limited success in the past with representative government. There were, however, key differences as well. Latin American states, with their generally longer history of independence, tended to be more modern already. Traditional religion was less of a barrier to change in Latin America than in the Middle East, and events like the world wars and the Great Depression affected both areas differently. On the whole, these differences outweighed the similarities, causing Latin America to make more progress toward modernization than the Middle East.

[As it builds to the THESIS in the last sentence, this paragraph briefly identifies the question's subject, time period, and task (referring to at least one similarity and one difference). It also qualifies some similarities and differences by spelling out precisely what they are. Finally, it provides analysis by making an assertion about the outcome of the trend in question—and by explaining why things turned out the way they did.]

At the beginning of this period, both Latin America and the Middle East suffered from social and economic underdevelopment. Wealthy elites, whether colonial, corporate, or royal and aristocratic, benefited from the unbalanced exploitation of a handful of commodities. In Latin America, these included foodstuffs (beef, coffee, bananas, and other fruit) and natural resources such as copper, steel, fertilizer, and, in some countries, oil. Oil was even more central to the economies of the Middle East, just as it is today. This "banana republic" overexploitation of resources discouraged the healthy diversification of economies and kept societies rigidly stratified, with small upper classes dominating large, impoverished majorities. Although some of this changed between 1900 and 1945, it limited modernization throughout the period. Another similarity is that Latin American and Middle Eastern states tended to be heavily influenced by outside powers, both before and during this half century. Prior to World War I, much of the Middle East was ruled by the Ottoman Empire or fell into European spheres of influence—and even though the Ottomans fell after WWI, European spheres of influence grew even larger when the post-WWI mandate system placed much of the Middle East, especially the Ottomans' former Arab possessions, under French and British custody. Most Latin American states had been free since the wars of independence of the early 1800s, but foreign investors (like America's United Fruit Company) wielded much power over Latin American governments, and the U.S. government regarded the region as part of its political sphere of influence. The Pan-American Union and even Franklin Roosevelt's Good Neighbor Policy were instruments of U.S. diplomatic interests throughout Latin America. Even when these outside interests did not deliberately oppose modernization (and they often did), it was rarely in their interest to actively support economic diversification, and because dealing with cooperative elite classes was easier than negotiating with elected governments representing a range of popular interests, they did not necessarily support democracy either.

[This paragraph deals with SIMILARITIES. Note that it does not attempt to give a complete narrative of either region's history during this period. Instead, it compares two points directly and in detail. It DEVELOPS THE ARGUMENT by using several pieces of concrete EVIDENCE to illustrate the comparisons, and it balances its coverage of both regions—not only is roughly equal attention devoted to each (not strictly necessary, although it's a good idea), but the pieces of evidence are evenly split between them. Pieces of evidence are not merely listed but contribute to analysis by concentrating on HOW and WHY modernization was slowed by the two factors dealt with in this paragraph.]

On the other hand, important differences moved Latin America farther down the path toward modernization. To begin with, Latin American states, while non-industrialized by the standards of Western Europe and North America, had undergone more industrialization than most parts of the Middle East. With this kind of foundation to build on, countries like Mexico and Argentina, for example, found it easier to create sizable industrial sectors after WWI. Latin American states also had a tradition of constitutional rule stretching back to the era of Simón Bolívar in the early 1800s, and while those constitutions were not always perfectly followed, they created a more favorable climate for progress when it came to gender equity, enlarging the middle classes, and reforming electoral systems. Less of this was possible in the Middle East. Another crucial difference involves the role of religion. Although Catholicism was overwhelmingly central to Latin American culture, and although it tended to exert a conservative influence over public life there, by this point in history it was not nearly as much a barrier to social and economic progress as traditional Islam still was in the Middle East. It is no coincidence that the Middle Eastern states that modernized most were the small handful where energetic Westernizing autocrats—most famously Mustafa Kemal Ataturk of Turkey and Reza Khan Pahlavi of Persia (Iran)—defied the will of Muslim clerics, secularized their states, industrialized their economies and educational systems and, in Ataturk's case, gave women the vote. By the early twentieth century, such fierce conflict with institutional religion was far less necessary for Latin America to modernize. In the Middle East, by contrast, it remains a struggle even today to balance modernization with respect for Islamic tradition.

[This paragraph moves on to DIFFERENCES, three of which are described. Coverage of the two regions is not exactly balanced 50–50, but it does not need to be. Numerous pieces of evidence are provided, and these ARE more or less divided equally between the Middle East and Latin America. As in paragraph 2, evidence is presented in such a way as to strengthen analysis and not just to story-tell or to fill the paragraph with raw information.]

Another comparison to consider is the prevalence of dictatorship in both regions during these years. Whether they were monarchs or autocratic strongmen, authoritarian leaders in both regions were often the agents of modernizing change. In the Middle East, the primary impulse for economic and social modernization was typically the will of determined authoritarians, such as the above-mentioned Ataturk and Pahlavi. Among the Latin American dictators who promoted industrialization and other modernizing changes were the Perons in Argentina and the Vargas government in Brazil. One last point that calls out for attention is the pronounced trend toward authoritarian rule worldwide during this period. A truly contextual view of this topic must take into account the rise of dictatorial or non-democratic regimes in places like Asia (Japanese militarism during the 1930s, warlords and Chiang Kai-shek in China after the collapse of Sun Yat-sen's democratic revolution) and Europe (most notably Lenin and Stalin in Russia, Mussolini in Italy, and Hitler in Germany). As with the regions discussed more directly by this question, dictatorship in these other places arose in some cases due to political and economic crises like the Depression, and in other cases due to pressures brought about by rapid modernization.

[Rather than compose a formal conclusion, this essay uses the last paragraph to provide another direct and relevant comparison. More important, it aims to provide greater context by extending the argument to other geographical regions. As with the DBQ, the conclusion could be used to state the thesis, although it's much better to do so in the introduction—as is done in this sample essay.]

UNIT ZERO

FOUNDATIONS

Unit Zero: Foundations

GENERAL REMARKS

As revised in 2019–2020, the AP World History: Modern exam now covers a much shorter time period than it used to, testing only material from 1200 C.E. to the present. This does not mean, however, that background information from earlier eras has lost all importance. Starting in medias res ("in the middle of the story") can be confusing without at least some understanding of what happened beforehand. Organized according to the AP **course themes**, this transitional Unit Zero: Foundations provides a brief survey of key concepts and essential points.

 TIP

Pay special attention to this unit's overview of world religions (under the "Cultural Developments" theme). Most of these had taken shape by around 600 C.E., if not long beforehand, but you will be expected to know their basic principles and the many ways they have affected world history since 1200 C.E.

GOVERNANCE (AND GEOGRAPHIC ORIENTATION)

The map in the Appendix at the end of this book will give you a good sense of the **geographic labels** preferred by the AP World History: Modern course. Study it closely.

Complex forms of government arose with the gradual appearance of the first cities and states between the Neolithic Revolution (ca. 10,000 years ago) and the emergence of the earliest civilizations (between 3500 and 2000 B.C.E.). Premodern governments took many forms, most often **monarchy** (rule by a central leader) or **oligarchy** (rule by a small elite). Some became **empires**, acquiring new territory by military conquest or diplomatic pressure.

Over the centuries, governments increased their effectiveness by devising a variety of **state-building techniques**, many of which remain standard today. Among these are the writing of law codes, the development of bureaucracies and systems of tax collection, a reliance on elite classes (such as aristocratic nobles or state officials) to share political and administrative responsibility, the creation of infrastructure for transport and communications, the mobilization of labor (for large-scale building projects or military service), and the use of religion and other sociocultural norms to justify the right to rule.

One way of categorizing governments is the degree to which they are **centralized** or **decentralized**. While we take centralized **nation-states** for granted today, many premodern societies were more loosely organized. Think of **feudalism**, a system in which weak monarchs delegate much of their political power to noble elites, or the division of a territory into autonomous **city-states** that coexist cooperatively at some times and compete fiercely at others. Many regions at various times in the past were bound together more by cultural and linguistic ties than by straightforward political unity. Another factor to bear in mind, both before and after 1200, is the **interaction between sedentary/urban societies and migratory/nomadic peoples**—these relationships often involved war and conflict but also played a crucial role in the transfer of ideas and technology.

Although Unit 1 will introduce you to the political world of 1200 C.E., it is worth knowing some of the key states and empires that came beforehand, some of which proved permanently foundational to the regions they governed. Several places experienced **classical periods** before 1200 C.E., characterized by socioeconomic advancement, a high degree of political cohesion, and an enduring cultural legacy. These periods are typically remembered as golden ages of unity and stability long after their societies' collapse or disintegration.

In Europe, starting in the 500s B.C.E., the city-states of ancient **Greece**, followed by the mighty state of **Rome**, created a civilizational bedrock whose intellectual, artistic, and political influence remains profound even now. After Rome's fall in the late 400s C.E., most of Europe plunged into a long medieval era continuing till the 1300s and 1400s C.E.—as detailed in Unit 1—and marked by extreme instability until after about 1000 C.E.

The Middle East, home to the world's oldest civilizations—Mesopotamia and **Egypt**, emerging in the 3000s B.C.E.—fell largely under the rule of **Persia** for many centuries, not counting intervals when Alexander the Great and, later, the Roman Empire conquered territory there. The rise of Islam in the 600s C.E. caused most of the region to come under the sway of Arab-dominated political-religious states called caliphates, the grandest and most powerful of which was the **Abbasid Caliphate** (750–1258), which ruled from Baghdad and achieved its golden age in the 800s.

The formation of large, centralized states was rarer in Africa than elsewhere, but advanced societies appeared throughout the continent. In ancient times, the region of Nubia, south of Egypt, provided a home to several advanced cultures. Later, much of North Africa, including Egypt, came under the influence of the Islamic caliphates. The eastern coast was dominated by **Swahili city-states**, cosmopolitan centers of trade and cross-cultural interchange. Also prominent in the sub-Saharan interior was the imposing city of **Great Zimbabwe**. The most complex states took shape in West Africa, most notably **Ghana**, which reached its peak between 800 and 1200 C.E., to be followed by the successor states described in Unit 1.

In East Asia, one of the world's oldest civilizations emerged in China, along the Huang He, or Yellow River. Until the twentieth century, China's political history was measured in dynasties, and while periodic breakdowns occurred, the Chinese consider themselves to have experienced an unbroken tradition of nationhood since 2000 B.C.E. Many of the core features of Chinese governance were set into place during the **Qin** dynasty of the 200s B.C.E. and the **Han** dynasty that followed from the 200s B.C.E. through the 200s C.E.. Both dynasties centralized the state and expanded it by means of imperial conquest. It was during the latter—commonly remembered, like Roman rule in Europe, as a golden age of power and achievement—that the Han Chinese became the country's dominant ethnic group. The later Tang (618–907) and **Song** (960–1279) are famous for artistic and intellectual grandeur and remarkable technological advancement, although, as described in Unit 1, the Song was vulnerable to political weakness. In Japan, the **Heian** era (795–1185), a period of immense cultural refinement, is thought of as the country's classical age before its descent into centuries of feudalism and samurai warfare.

NOTE

From humanity's earliest days, the populations of Africa and Eurasia interacted constantly, and the AP World History: Modern course frequently uses the term *Afro-Eurasian* to describe trends spanning all three continents. North and South America were originally settled by migrating peoples from Asia, who crossed a land bridge that existed only temporarily. Until the late 1400s C.E., the Americas developed in cultural and environmental isolation from the Afro-Eurasian world.

South Asia and Southeast Asia were governed by a wide diversity of states, the largest of which appeared on the Indian subcontinent. The **Mauryan** (300s–100s B.C.E.) and **Gupta** (300s–500s C.E.) empires presided over India's classical age, although neither of them fully united what is today modern India. Other notable states in the region were the **Khmer Empire** (800s–1400s C.E.), in present-day Cambodia, and the **Srivijayan Empire** (500s–1100s C.E.), based on the islands that now make up Indonesia. A complex mix of Buddhist and Hindu culture and religion deeply influenced this region, with Islamic elements making themselves felt later in certain areas.

In the Americas, the largest and most complex states were to be found in Mexico and neighboring Mesoamerica (Central America), as well as in South America's Andes Mountains. Oldest were the **Olmecs** (ca. 1400–400 B.C.E.), considered to be Mesoamerica's "mother civilization" because of how their artistic and religious practices—including the construction of pyramids—seem to have influenced later cultures, such as the **Mayans** (200s–900s C.E.), Toltecs (800–1000), and **Aztecs** (Mexica) (1200s–1500s). The high reaches of the Andes witnessed the emergence of the Chavín as early as 1000 B.C.E., as well as the Moche (200s–700s C.E.) and, by the 1300s, the **Incas**, featured in Unit 1. In North America, groups like the **Ancestral Puebloans** (once commonly known as the Anasazi) occupied the U.S. Southwest from about 400 C.E. (or perhaps earlier) to 1300, living in complex dwellings known as pueblos. To the north and east, in the Ohio and Mississippi River valleys, sophisticated societies that built cities and large earth mounds emerged. The most advanced of these cultures was the **Mississippian civilization**, which arose around 700 C.E. and survived until the arrival of Europeans, as narrated in Unit 1.

POLITICAL AND IMPERIAL OVERREACH

States collapsed for a variety of reasons and in a variety of ways. The end could come suddenly or gradually, and it could be due mainly to **internal** or **external** **factors**. Especially in the case of empires, the problem stemmed from **overreach**: the state assumed too many responsibilities or expenses, conquered too much territory, or caused itself too many social problems for the authorities to handle.

Pay attention to how major states before and after 1200 C.E. met their end. Typically, a combination of factors, not just one cause, brings about a state's downfall. Challenges commonly faced by states in decline or crisis include

- unwise or corrupt political leadership
- rebellions and social upheavals caused by overtaxation or elite injustice
- civil wars
- conquest of more territory than can be effectively governed
- economic downturns and disruptions of regional trade patterns
- neglect of infrastructure, such as roads or waterways
- war with one or more advanced states or the sudden appearance of a powerful enemy
- constant, long-term frontier harassment by raiding or migrating nomads
- external environmental factors, such as climate change, natural disasters, or the appearance of new diseases
- self-inflicted environmental problems, such as overpopulation, overuse of wood (deforestation), overuse of water (desertification), or the silting of rivers and the erosion of soil caused by large construction projects or overfarming

CULTURAL DEVELOPMENTS AND INTERACTIONS

From earliest times, humans produced art, music, and stories, both for individual enjoyment and for social purposes. They pondered abstract ideas, giving rise to philosophical and scientific insights, as well as ethical and religious systems. Such cultural traditions have been important to all peoples over time.

Many aspects of a society's culture are developed on their own, arising as a result of **independent innovation**. Others are borrowed from or imposed by other societies by means

What about science?

Earlier versions of AP World History placed culture, science, and technology under the same thematic heading, whereas now, the course splits culture and technology into separate categories. Science, confusingly enough, touches on both: it involves ideas (appropriate to the culture theme) *and* practical application (suitable for the technology theme). For the sake of convenience, this book will deal with scientific ideas and discovery under the technology theme. In test-taking terms, this distinction is unlikely to make much practical difference— although you should read any related free-response questions carefully.

of a process called **cultural diffusion**. (This also applies to technology, as described in the section that follows.)

A bedrock cultural development in most civilizations is the invention of **writing**, which allows for complex recordkeeping, the efficient storage and transfer of ideas and information, and the creation of **literary traditions**, typically built on foundational texts like the Gilgamesh epic from Sumeria, India's Rig Veda, and the Greek Homeric poems. (Some societies did not adopt systems of writing until the modern era, instead maintaining rich **oral traditions**, as among griot storytellers of West Africa, or devising alternative forms of recordkeeping, such as the quipu, or "talking knots," found in the Andes.) Certain languages, including Latin, Sanskrit, Mandarin Chinese, and Arabic, held a special status as **classical** or **liturgical** (scriptural) **languages** and achieved intellectual or religious dominance in large parts of the world over long periods of time. A **lingua franca**, such as Swahili in East Africa or the sign language used by many Native Americans, is a tongue adopted (or sometimes invented) for common use, especially for purposes of trade, in a region with many languages.

Artistic traditions appeared in all parts of the world, with regionally distinct styles of sculpture, painting, music, pottery, weaving, and other art forms. Architecture served artistic purposes as well as practical ones (providing living space and defense), and it also came to play political and religious roles in many societies: works of **monumental architecture**, which required enormous expenditures of resources and labor, impressed onlookers with their grandeur and displayed the power of the government, the ruling church, or both. Examples include **pyramids** (in both Egypt and Mesoamerica), ziggurats, and earth mounds; temples and churches; palaces and other seats of power; fortifications and defensive walls; and elaborate schemes of **urban planning**.

Several civilizations pioneered the mode of rational thought known as **philosophy**. Generations of Greek thinkers, culminating in Socrates, Plato, and Aristotle during the 400s and 300s B.C.E., created the intellectual foundation on which most Western thought rests. Asia experienced a similar phenomenon at roughly the same time—in India, thanks to the explosion of ideas caused by religious debates over Vedism, and in China during the "Hundred Schools of Thought" era that birthed Confucianism and other new belief systems.

NOTE

In many societies, the blending of old and new beliefs was common, as was the mixing of practices from more than one religion. This is called *syncretism*, and it is illustrated by the absorption of ancestor veneration into Buddhist and Confucian ritual, by the incorporation of Vedic concepts into the newer religion of Hinduism, and by the persistence of pagan beliefs among newly Christianized peoples.

Religions, developed by all societies to address questions of ethics and morality, the possibility of an afterlife, and humanity's place in the universe, grew more complex with the advent of civilization. Religious beliefs crossed borders, sometimes peacefully through trade and **missionary activity**, sometimes by **forced conversion**. Older forms of worship, like **shamanism**, persisted among hunter-foragers, and **ancestor veneration**, equally ancient, remained popular even in settled communities—for example, China and Rome. Most common in advanced societies were **polytheistic systems**, best illustrated by the Sumerian-Babylonian and Egyptian gods of the Middle East, the Olympian deities worshipped by the Greeks (and borrowed by the Romans), the Vedic gods of India, and China's "celestial bureaucracy."

Hebrew Monotheism and Judaism

Among the earliest of the major faiths that still exist today was the Hebrew monotheism that evolved into **Judaism**. According to Judaic tradition, the **Hebrews**, in the time of

Abraham, entered into a covenant as the chosen people of the god Jehovah. The resulting religion, **Judaism**, is considered the first **monotheistic** faith. It may have arisen around 2000 B.C.E., although the term "Jewish" was not commonly used until after the 900s B.C.E. To the extent one can match Hebrew scripture with historical chronology, the Hebrews migrated to Egypt around 1700 B.C.E., were enslaved there, and then escaped under **Moses** around 1300 to 1200 B.C.E.—the exodus celebrated during the **Passover** holiday. Moses led the Hebrews to the "promised land" of Canaan (present-day Israel) and is said to have handed down the **Ten Commandments** and the **Torah** ("teaching"), the first five books of the **Tanakh**, or Hebrew scriptures. The Hebrew kingdom reached its zenith in the 900s B.C.E. under **David** and his son **Solomon**, the two of whom established a capital at Jerusalem and built the **First Temple**. After Solomon's death, the Hebrew kingdom split up, then suffered conquest between the 700s and 500s B.C.E. by the Assyrians, the Neo-Babylonians, and the Persians.

During this era, Jewish doctrine took more formal shape, but the Jewish people began to scatter. In the 500s B.C.E., the Neo-Babylonians uprooted Hebrews from their land and tore down the First Temple, and although the Persians allowed them to return to Jerusalem and erect a second temple, many chose to remain in their new homes, beginning the **Jewish diaspora**. The population was scattered even further by the Romans, who responded to Jewish rebellions by destroying the second temple and dissolving what remained of the Jewish state. The main source of Roman-Jewish tension was the Jews' monotheistic refusal to worship the Roman emperor as a living god, as other subject peoples agreed to do.

In the face of conquest and exile, religious adherence helped Jews to preserve their sense of identity. During this period, especially around the 400s B.C.E., rabbis codified Jewish scripture (the **Tanakh**) and added their own commentaries (the **Talmud**, or "Instruction"). Jewish law operated on a retributive principle—an eye for an eye, a tooth for a tooth—that was common throughout the ancient Middle East. Dietary restrictions were strict, and marriage outside the Jewish community was strongly discouraged. Although women were respected in the home, Hebrew society as a whole was patriarchal, and like neighboring peoples in the eastern Mediterranean, the Hebrews practiced slavery. On the other hand, Jewish scripture insisted on treating slaves humanely and, more generally, placed a premium on charity. Jews also came to believe that a messiah ("anointed one") would someday appear as a savior to free them from foreign oppression.

Zoroastrianism

The origins of **Zoroastrianism** are difficult to uncover, with the birth date of its founder, Zoroaster, ranging from 1700 to 500 B.C.E. Most believed that Zoroaster lived around 1000 B.C.E., probably in eastern Iran. Zoroastrian scripture, the **Avesta**, was compiled over many centuries, and the religion emerged as a major faith in Persia by the 500s B.C.E., when it was adopted by Darius the Great to justify his rule as king of kings. Zoroastrianism was **monotheistic**, venerating a single god: **Ahura Mazda**, the world's creator. The good deeds of worshippers were said to assist Ahura Mazda in his cosmic struggle against Ahriman, the evil spirit of chaos. An end time of judgment was predicted, with an afterlife promised to the worthy. Kept alive today by only a few followers—the Parsi sect in parts of Iran, Pakistan, and India—Zoroastrianism influenced much of the Middle East for centuries, and many of its core elements found their way into Judaic and Christian doctrines as they evolved.

From Vedism to Hinduism

The polytheistic faith of **Vedism** is thought to have been brought to India around 1500 B.C.E. by foreign invaders; its best-known scripture is the *Rig Veda*. It set into place a rigid **caste system**—later adopted by Hinduism—and taught that all creatures possessed a soul that yearned to be reunited in spiritual perfection with the World Soul (Brahman). This was achieved by undergoing a cycle of life, death, and **reincarnation**. According to the law of deeds (**karma**), a person's actions in one life determined one's rebirth in the next. Vedism placed value on elaborate rituals to dozens of gods, obedience to the brahmin class, and accepting one's lot in life—an excellent example of a religion justifying social hierarchy.

NOTE

Because Hindu deities are considered to be reflections of the creator god Brahma, some argue that Hinduism can theoretically be categorized as monotheistic. While philosophically interesting, this is a minority viewpoint, and the AP World History course generally regards Hinduism as polytheistic.

After 700 B.C.E., growing discontent with the brahmins' authority sparked intense religious struggle. Central to these debates was a series of essays and poems called the **Upanishads**, which proposed that people could liberate themselves from the cycle of life, death, and reincarnation without relying so heavily on the priestly class. As discussed below, the new faith of Buddhism emerged as part of this new thinking, but for most people in India, Vedism was not rejected outright but absorbed into the larger set of beliefs known as **Hinduism**. This process took a long time but was essentially complete by the 300s B.C.E. Today, the vast majority of people in India are Hindu, and sizable Hindu populations live elsewhere in South and Southeast Asia.

Hinduism recognizes tens of thousands of gods and goddesses, making it the most polytheistic religion in the world. The Vedic gods had their place, but three newer deities attracted the largest followings by the 200s B.C.E. **Brahma** is the masculine personification of the World Soul. **Vishnu** the Preserver is a savior figure and a great friend to humanity. **Shiva** the Destroyer, the dancing god of creation and destruction, reflects the duality of life and death. Hinduism's great mother goddess is Shakti.

From Vedism, Hinduism inherited the concepts of **karma** and **reincarnation**. Another legacy was the **caste system**, thought to have originated after 1500 B.C.E., when Indo-European invaders from the north relegated manual labor to the darker-skinned natives. Already by the 600s B.C.E., this scheme had stratified society into four distinct classes: priests; warriors and rulers; farmers and artisans; and servants and serfs. Over time, the system grew more complex and came to include a category of "untouchables," who performed degrading tasks like the handling of human waste and burial of the dead. The **Law of Manu**, a Hindu text compiled between 200 B.C.E. and 200 C.E., justified the caste system by arguing that acceptance of one's social status was a moral duty: good behavior as a member of a lower caste would result in good karma, increasing the likelihood of rebirth into a higher caste.

Hindu society was highly patriarchal. Women were considered legal minors even as adults, with no right to divorce or to own property. It was believed that women could not achieve spiritual union with the Brahman in their lifetimes but had to wait to be reincarnated as a man. The most extreme form of female subservience was the **sati ritual**, in which widows of certain castes were required to burn themselves to death on the funeral pyres of their deceased husbands. This practice was discouraged by India's colonial masters, the British, during the nineteenth century and outlawed by the Indians themselves in the twentieth.

Buddhism

Several movements besides Hinduism arose in India during the transition from traditional Vedism. One of these was **Buddhism**, based on the teachings of **Siddhartha Gautama**, a nobleman from northern India around 500 B.C.E. Appalled by the pain and poverty endured by the common people, Gautama abandoned his aristocratic life to seek an answer to the question of human suffering. His search is said to have caused his spiritual **enlightenment**, after which he took the name Buddha, "the awakened one." Followers recorded his teachings in texts called sutras. In the 200s B.C.E., the Mauryan emperor Ashoka became a great supporter of Buddhism, spreading it throughout India and beyond its borders. It reached China before 100 C.E. and has since influenced all of Asia.

Although Buddhism originated with one person, a staggering variety of beliefs and practices now fall into the category "Buddhist." In its earliest form, Buddhism was less a religion and more a philosophy meant to correct the worst features of Vedism. Like Hinduism, Buddhism postulates that souls evolve toward spiritual perfection by means of birth, death, and **reincarnation** and according to the law of **karma**. However, Gautama rejected the caste system and argued that anyone could achieve **nirvana**, or liberation from the wheel of life, without the aid of priests or rituals. All that was needed was to realize the Four Noble Truths and to follow the Eightfold Path of good conduct. At no time did the Buddha claim to be divine.

After the Buddha's death, the tradition he founded split into many denominations, roughly divided into three major schools. The oldest is **Theravada** (also referred to as Hinayana). Prominent in South and Southeast Asia, Theravada emphasizes simplicity and meditation and remains closer to the Buddha's actual teachings. One newer school, **Mahayana**, caught on farther to the north, especially in Japan, Korea, and parts of China. Mahayana involves more ritual and symbology than the Buddha spoke of, mainly due to syncretism: upon reaching new lands, Buddhism often blended with local beliefs. In some Mahayana denominations, the idea of nirvana came to resemble a heavenly afterlife, and the Buddha came to be seen as divine. Other elements appeared as well, such as the concept of hell and complex pantheons of gods and bodhisattvas (saintlike souls who had achieved nirvana but chose to remain in the earthly realm to help living humans). Related to Mahayana doctrines is **Tibetan Buddhism**, sometimes referred to as Vajrayana or Tantric Buddhism. Especially popular among the Mongol and Turkic peoples of Central Asia, its most famous practitioner is the Dalai Lama.

Confucianism

Like Buddhism, **Confucianism** grew out of a philosophy founded by an individual who made no claim to divinity. A government official during China's unstable Spring and Autumn Period, **Confucius** (ca. 551–479 B.C.E.) lived through war and political chaos; in retirement, he pondered the proper relationship between society and the individual. His teachings, compiled by followers after his death, are contained in the *Analects*.

Confucianism took for granted the existence of the **celestial bureaucracy** of traditional Chinese gods but was more concerned with wise and ethical conduct in this world. Confucius proposed that **social harmony** could be created by a combination of benevolent rulership from above and good behavior from below. Order and **hierarchy** are paramount, and the well-being of the group comes before that of the individual. As long as the ruler performs his duties well, his people are obliged to obey him. This notion squared well with the **mandate of heaven** ideology that emerged during the Zhou period and remained central to Chinese political thought. Above all, Confucianism stressed **filial piety** and envisioned society as a perfect family, with junior members paying respect to their elders. This made it a good fit with China's long-standing tradition of **ancestor veneration**. A highly **patriarchal** system, Confucianism firmly established women as subservient. Men ruled, fought wars, and received educations. They could keep more than one wife, as well as concubines, and could divorce any woman who failed to produce an heir. Women were exclusively homemakers and mothers. They were allowed a limited education, but they were prohibited from owning property, and brides had no dowry system to provide them with financial security.

In theory, these hierarchical relationships rested on the concept of mutual respect. Central to Confucian thought was a "golden rule" similar to that found in Christianity: "Never do to others what you would not like them to do to you." (Confucius's assumption that people are inherently good contrasted with the logic behind a rival doctrine in China, **Legalism**, which viewed people as innately immoral and advocated harsh punishments as the only way to control them.) Confucianism coexisted and at times competed with Daoism and Buddhism. Starting in the 100s B.C.E., under the Han emperor Wudi, Confucianism was frequently supported by the state as an official code of conduct. By the 600s C.E., a newer variation, **Neo-Confucianism**, appeared. Even when it was not in official favor, Confucianism's influence persisted and has lasted into the modern era, even under the communist regime.

Daoism

Like Confucianism, **Daoism** (or Taoism), a more mystical strain of thought, took shape in China during and after the 500s B.C.E. Its founder is said to be **Laozi** or Lao-tse (ca. 600 B.C.E.). Its central text, the **Tao-te Ching**, is attributed to Laozi but was most likely written in the 300s or 200s B.C.E.

Daoists seek to be in harmony with the **dao** (the "way" or "path"), the invisible yet irresistible force that governs the universe. Daoism is deliberately antirational, using parables to understand the world in nonlogical ways. In one famous example, a Daoist teacher asks whether he is a man awakening from a dream in which he was a butterfly or a butterfly dreaming that it is a man.

Flexible and individualistic, Daoism was easily reconciled with **ancestor veneration** and respect for the **celestial bureaucracy** of gods. It influenced many cultural practices, including traditional medicine, martial arts, and through its embrace of alchemy and astrology, the sciences of metallurgy and astronomy. Fortune-telling was crucial to Daoism, and the **I-Ching** ("Book of Changes"), one of its key texts, teaches how to read the future. Daoism added a philosophical tone to Chinese poetry, especially during the Tang dynasty. Daoist ritual was interwoven with the architectural art of **feng shui**, or harmonious placement, which orients buildings and the items inside them in ways that ensure good fortune. Daoism's most famous symbol is the **yin-yang**, a circle whose dark and light halves are divided by a double-curved line, illustrating that nothing is absolute.

Daoism spread quickly throughout China, and elements of it were transported to the many parts of Asia where China exerted cultural influence. In all these places, it was common for people to blend Daoist, Buddhist, and Confucian practices syncretically.

Christianity

Growing out of the Judaic tradition, **Christianity** was founded by **Jesus of Nazareth** (ca. 4 B.C.E.–29 C.E.)—later known as the Christ, from the Greek translation of the Jewish term "messiah." According to the Christian Bible, Jesus was born into a Jewish family of humble background. As a teacher, he sought to reform Jewish laws and traditions. To him, charity and compassion were more important than obeying rabbis and observing customs. During his ministry, Jesus claimed to be the messiah foretold by Hebrew prophecy. Although many Jews expected the messiah to restore the Hebrew kingdom politically, Jesus spoke of a heavenly kingdom instead, calling himself the "Son of God."

Christ's teachings proved popular among the common people and the poor. On the other hand, his claims to be the messiah and his questioning of tradition angered conservatives within the Jewish religious establishment, and rumors that he had named himself "king of the Jews"—a misinterpretation of what he meant by being the messiah—aroused anxiety among the Jews' Roman overlords. When Jesus came to preach in Jerusalem during the Passover season, Jewish religious authorities demanded that the Romans arrest him. They did so, putting him to death by crucifixion.

The Bible depicts Jesus claiming that he would rise from the dead before returning to God in heaven. Afterward, his disciples preached that this had happened, and a new religion dedicated to him began to spread. Followers believed not just in the Resurrection but also a Second Coming, when all souls would be subjected to a Day of Judgment—with virtuous Christians admitted to heaven and nonbelievers damned to hell.

Roman law banned Christianity, and yet the new faith gained a large following over the next three centuries. Crucial to organizing the early church was the apostle **Paul**, who began as a persecutor of Christians but suddenly converted and, between 45 to 64 c.e., worked with Christ's chief disciple, **Peter**, to establish new centers of worship. Paul's main contribution was to widen Christianity's appeal beyond its original community of Jewish followers. By decreeing that Christians did not have to observe Jewish dietary restrictions or circumcise male believers, Paul made it easier to convert Greeks, Romans, and others within the Roman Empire.

Christianity caught on among many groups, especially those who felt powerless in Roman society: noncitizens, slaves, commoners, and women. The new religion was open to all and held out the hope of a happy afterlife to those whose present lives were drab or miserable. The early church gave women influential roles, but as it grew more hierarchical, it took a more patriarchal stance. Many of the church fathers described below used the Old Testament story of Adam, Eve, and the serpent to assign women the blame for humanity's "original sin," and Paul's writings in particular put women in a secondary position. They were to obey men and were barred from positions of leadership, including priesthood. Cultures that adopted Christianity were affected by this worldview for centuries to come.

In 313 c.e., Roman persecution ended when the emperor **Constantine** legalized Christianity with the Edict of Milan. By the end of the century, Christianity had become not just the empire's official faith but the only legally permitted one. During the 300s and 400s, the church formalized its hierarchy of priests and bishops, with the pope at the top and with men only as priests. Theologians now known as the church fathers established a body of dogma, or officially agreed-upon beliefs, with unacceptable views condemned as heresy. They also compiled the books of the **Bible**, combining texts from Jewish scripture (the Old Testament) with the four Gospels and other materials (the New Testament). Among the most famous of the church fathers are Jerome (347–420), who completed the first Latin translation of the Bible, and **Augustine** (354–430), whose *City of God* provided the intellectual basis for further Christian doctrine.

After Rome's collapse in the 400s, the Christian church drifted apart in terms of leadership and doctrine. In the west, **Roman Catholicism** remained dominant and provided much of Europe with a badly needed force for cultural unity. In the east, the church, based in cities like Constantinople, evolved into **Eastern Orthodoxy** and several other eastern churches. The split between Catholicism and Orthodoxy became final in the Great Schism of 1054.

Islam

The youngest of the world's major religions, **Islam** is linked with Judaism and Christianity in many ways. Despite their stormy, even tragic, relationships with each other, these three **monotheistic** faiths contain many similarities and possess an eventful shared history.

Islam arose in the Arabian Peninsula due to the efforts of **Mohammed** (also Muhammad, 570–632), a merchant from the town of Mecca. In 610, Mohammed, while meditating in the nearby mountains, experienced a profound vision in which the archangel Jibril, or Gabriel, is said to have delivered the word of Allah (Arabic for "God") to him. With the help of his wife and other key supporters, Mohammed preached and formed a religious community. In 622, he and his followers were forced out of Mecca by leaders of the local polytheistic faith and fled to the city of Medina. This flight—the **Hegira**—marks the beginning of the Islamic calendar. In 630, Mohammed returned to Mecca and converted the city. He died in 632, but his new religion survived and grew. The teachings of Mohammed are contained in the **Qur'an** (Koran), and the holy language of Islam is **Arabic**. **Sharia** is the codification of traditional Islamic law.

Mohammed claimed to be the final prophet in the Abrahamic tradition. While he believed his interpretation of that tradition to be the purest and truest, he respected many figures from Judaism and Christianity as important teachers and therefore instructed Muslims to acknowledge Jews and Christians as "**people of the book**." Muslims are to live by the **Five Pillars of Faith**: to confess one's faith ("there is no god but Allah"); to pray five times daily, facing in the direction of Mecca; to fast during the month of Ramadan; to give alms to the poor; and to attempt a pilgrimage (hajj) to Mecca at least once in one's lifetime. Other traditions include abstinence from alcohol and pork, avoiding the portrayal of human or animal images in art, and polygamy (Muslim men were allowed to take up to four wives so long as they could support them properly). Islam's holiest city is **Mecca**, but Medina and Jerusalem (where Mohammed is said to have ascended to heaven) are important as well.

A high degree of **patriarchalism** restricted the conduct of Muslim women, who were often secluded in women's quarters and required to veil themselves when in public. In the past, as today, the degree to which these customs were observed depended on class, region, and individual circumstances. Islam commanded men to treat women with respect, and women in much of the Islamic world enjoyed the right to inherit, have dowries, and own property—but even so, women's status remained secondary.

NOTE

Islamic theology divides the world into two states: dar al-Islam ("house of peace") and dar al-Harb ("house of war"). The former includes those lands where Islam is the dominant faith. In early times, the expansion of dar al-Islam was encouraged. Many moderate Muslims now consider dar al-Islam to be a wider community including all places where their religion can be practiced freely.

As it expanded between the 600s and 800s, early Islam made no distinction between political allegiance and religious affiliation: to be a Muslim meant also to belong to a political and social community, or **umma**, linked by religious belief. After Mohammed's death, the umma was governed by a **caliph**, or "successor," who was both a religious and political leader. The first caliph was Mohammed's father-in-law, Abu Bakr, and the history of the various caliphates is described elsewhere. Islam did not survive these early years without discord: a succession crisis in the mid-600s led to civil war and the **Sunni-Shiite split**. Sunnis, who make up more than 80 percent of all Muslims, supported the war's victors, the Umayyad caliphs. The followers of Mohammed's son-in-law Ali, who was killed during the war, formed the Shiite movement as a minority denomination. Divisions between the two remain relevant today.

TECHNOLOGY AND INNOVATION

As tool-using creatures of high intelligence, human beings from the start have used technology to perform tasks more efficiently, to make their lives safer and more comfortable, and to shape the environments in which they live. They have also sought to comprehend the world around them and to explain natural phenomena, giving rise over time to scientific understanding.

Technological innovations have played a massive role at all times and in all aspects of human history. Although they have often proved beneficial, they have just as often led to unintended, sometimes unwelcome, consequences.

Building-block technologies include **metallurgy**—the first transitions from stone tools to ones made of bronze occurred in the Middle East and China between 4000 and 3000 B.C.E., with iron tools appearing by about 1200 B.C.E.— the invention of the **wheel**, and the mastery of **pottery** and **weaving**. Bows and arrows, chariots, and other **weapons** became important, as did **farming tools**, including hoes, plows, horse collars, and yokes for oxen and cattle. Crucial for labor and transport were **wheeled vehicles** and the **stirrup**—which, in combination with improved **saddles**, increased the usefulness of domesticated animals like camels and horses.

At sea, most early societies were restricted to **coastal navigation**, lacking both the technology to sail safely across long stretches of open ocean and the know-how to keep from getting lost when familiar land was not in sight. Among the earliest to master long-distance, **open-water navigation** were the Vikings, with their famous longboats, and the Polynesians, whose outrigger canoes ventured throughout the vast Pacific. In the Indian Ocean basin and the adjoining Pacific, innovations such as the **lateen sail** and the **stern rudder** made deep-sea voyaging even more reliable for large vessels like the Arabian and Indian **dhow** and the Chinese **junk**. (Also crucial was the **magnetic compass**, mentioned below.)

Many peoples developed an excellent working knowledge of **mathematics**, **medicine**, **engineering**, and **astronomy**. Often, they did not fully understand the scientific principles behind such fields but nonetheless became gradually adept at learning **empirically**, or by means of systematic observation. (Greek philosophers between 600 and 200 B.C.E., heavily influenced by Egyptian learning, are considered to have been among the first in the ancient world to move toward forms of **scientific thinking**, even if their findings and observations were not always correct.) The measurement of time and the calculation of **calendars** became more accurate over time. At the same time, the quest to properly define a **decimal system**, complete with the **concepts of pi and zero**, was ongoing. In Afro-Eurasia, scholars from Gupta India are credited with success in this area as well as with inventing the misnamed **Arabic numerals**. Some Mesoamerican peoples, including the Maya, arrived at the concept of zero on their own.

In Eurasia, during the centuries approaching 1200 C.E., a number of key inventions appeared. Middle Eastern scholars in the 700s significantly improved the **astrolabe**, an instrument that measured the altitude of heavenly bodies and—in addition to advancing the science of astronomy—hugely aided navigation. Similarly, the **magnetic compass**, developed in China, became known in the Middle East and Europe after about 1000.

Also from China, just before 1100, the **Song water clock** was the most accurate timepiece ever made to that date and arguably the most elaborate and precisely crafted mechanical device in the world at the time. It should be no surprise to hear, then, that **gunpowder** originated in China as well, around the 800s or 900s, as did the **horse collar**, so vital to agricultural production.

Woodblock printing, which appeared in China in the 200s C.E., allowed faster reproduction and dissemination of information. This innovation spread throughout Eurasia and eventually gave rise to the more revolutionary concept of **movable-type printing**. Early versions of this practice arose in Song China during the 1000s and were known in Korea during the 1200s, but they remained expensive and limited in scope. Not until the 1400s in Europe would a cost-effective and mass-producible form of movable-type printing emerge.

ECONOMIC SYSTEMS

All societies generate economic activity in different ways and to varying degrees of complexity by producing and consuming goods and services. **Modes of economic production** help to shape forms of social organization; they are detailed below in the "Social Interactions and Organization" section. Of importance before 1200 C.E. were **hunting and foraging**, **pastoralism**, and **agriculture** as well as artisanry and craft production. Later units cover **industrial** and postindustrial production.

The exchange of goods and services, or **trade**, took place on an individual basis (such as barter) but also on local, regional, and transregional levels. Within societies, trade led to the formation of **marketplaces** and strengthened contacts among villages, cities, and rural communities. Connections created by regional and transregional trade spread ideas, religious beliefs, and technologies over great distances. Trade motivated the development of **water transport** (aided by innovations in shipbuilding technology and navigational science) and **overland transport**, including **caravans** (which benefited from increasingly efficient exploitation of pack animals and wheeled vehicles). Until the invention of railroads and modern highways, water transport tended to be faster and more cost-effective than land transport, causing trade to flourish especially along rivers, lakeshores, and coastlines.

Where trade took solid hold, the value of goods and services had to be calculated and converted systematically and reliably. A key tool for doing so was the **standardization of weights and measures**; another was the invention of **currency**. Many substances—including beads, shells, and salt (the source of the word "salary")—were used as currency, but **coins** (invented in the Middle East by the Lydians around 600–500 B.C.E.) and **paper money**, or banknotes (developed in China between the 600s and 1100s C.E.), gradually caught on as the most important. In places where communications were good and political circumstances stable, commerce was boosted by the rise of **banking** and the extension of **credit** (including loans with interest as well as promissory notes or bills of exchange that could be redeemed like cash). These practices required trust but allowed for the safer and simpler transfer of wealth, even between places far apart from each other.

Transregional trade routes operated over surprisingly long distances and eventually formed the interlocking networks that gave birth to economic globalization. As 1200 C.E. drew near, the most significant routes in Afro-Eurasia were the **Mediterranean trade network**, the system of **trans-Saharan caravan routes** that crossed large parts of Africa, the sea lanes of the

Indian Ocean basin, and the overland **Silk Road** that joined the Middle East and East Asia. All of these are discussed further in Unit 1. In the Americas, Mesoamerican peoples traded far to their north and south, and in South America, a thriving commerce arose between the Andes and the Amazon basin.

SOCIAL INTERACTIONS AND ORGANIZATION

Whether simple or complex, social structures determine how individual members of a community are categorized and grouped as well as how they interact with each other. Who exercises power and influence, and how is labor organized? What roles do different people play, based on their occupation or class, their gender, or their ethnic, religious, or linguistic identity? Is social status rigidly fixed or more fluid? How does a given society treat minority populations?

Economic modes of production did much to influence social organization. Rather than produce food themselves, the earliest societies supported themselves by **hunting and foraging** (also known as hunting and gathering), living off resources taken directly from the land. Around 10,000 years ago, thanks to the Neolithic Revolution, some groups learned how to domesticate animals and plants, giving rise to **pastoralism** (herding) and **agriculture** (the systematic cultivation of plants). Hunter-foragers and pastoral herders tended to remain **nomadic**, while agriculturalists shifted to a more **sedentary**, or settled, existence. All three lifestyles persisted long after the Stone Age ended.

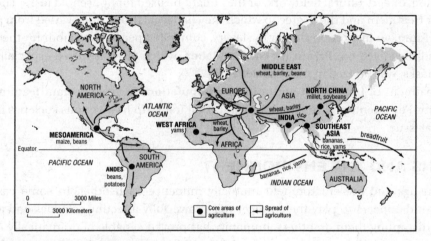

The Practice of Agriculture, ca. 8000 B.C.E.
During the transition from the Paleolithic Era to the Neolithic, communities in the Middle East and northern China began to practice agriculture systematically.

All societies exhibit some form of **class distinction**, defining members by wealth, ancestry, or occupation. Such distinctions tended to be minor in hunter-forager societies and somewhat more noticeable among pastoralists. Agriculture, by contrast, required intensive labor and cooperative effort, leading to the formation of **villages** and eventually **cities**. The concepts of **private property** and **land ownership**, along with sharper distinctions between wealthier and poorer **social classes**, came to seem more natural. **Food surpluses**, which allowed people not directly involved in food production to develop other skills, encouraged the **specialization of labor**.

The gender division of labor was felt as early as the Stone Age, with various tasks assigned by sex among hunter-foragers because of basic physical differences. These distinctions sharpened greatly among pastoralists and especially agriculturalists, giving rise in most parts of the world to a long-standing gender inequality that in many ways continues today. Regulation of women's conduct also took many forms, including veiling in public, harsher penalties for adultery, limited property rights, inequality before the law, foot binding in China, and the Hindu ritual of *sati* (the burning of a widow on her dead husband's funeral pyre).

Certain roles, such as political, military, and religious leadership, were valued more than others, causing the phenomenon of **social stratification**. A people's system of ranking social classes is known as a **hierarchy**, and each society has its own way of deciding how difficult it is for an individual to move from one class to another (the concept of **social mobility**). In earlier periods of history, status was almost always hereditary, and religion often played a role in justifying hierarchies. **Elite classes** were quite small, and social stratification tended to be rigid. (The strictest hierarchies, in which movement between classes is all but impossible, are known as **caste systems**.) Elite classes typically enjoyed legal and financial advantages, such as more lenient treatment before the law and immunity from taxation. In most parts of the world since the rise of agriculture, male-dominated **patriarchalism**— reinforced by **gender inequity** and the **gender division of labor**—has tended to be the norm. Matriarchal societies were extremely rare.

At the bottom of any hierarchy are those whose labor is coerced. **Slavery**, the most common form of forced labor, was widespread until recent times and still exists in some parts of the world. In ancient times, people fell into slavery in many ways. Some were prisoners of war or captives taken in raids. Many were owned and traded privately, others belonged to the state. **Debt slavery** and **indentured servitude** put people to work for owners who had paid money or taxes they owed. In some societies, slave status was hereditary. Slaves might perform hard labor, such as mining, construction, or agricultural fieldwork, or they might be used for household tasks. The severity of their treatment and the degree to which they had legal protections varied from place to place. **Serfdom**, an institution similar to slavery, compelled peasants to labor for the owners of the land they lived on. **Prison** (or **convict**) **labor**, which often involved especially back-breaking tasks, was utilized in many societies.

The treatment of **immigrant** and **minority populations** is an important feature of any community. Pay attention throughout the units that follow to how various societies handled this crucial issue.

HUMANS AND THE ENVIRONMENT

Human beings and the environment mutually influence each other. In some cases, the natural world appears to play the stronger role, powerfully affecting societies and at times seriously disrupting them. In others, humanity has proved capable of dramatically controlling or transforming the environment, especially with advanced technology at its disposal. Human impact on the environment can be deliberate or inadvertent—with societies sometimes remaining completely unaware of the changes they are causing—and **unintended consequences** are common in the history of humankind's interaction with nature.

One subject of concern to the AP exam is the environmental impact of human technology and economic activity. Even the simplest forms of economic production, such as hunting and foraging and pastoralism, affected the environment. The development of agriculture— typically accompanied by population growth and technological improvements—had an even heavier impact. Plant and animal species selected artificially by humans came to dominate many regions, even where they were not native. Forest clearing and systems of water management, such as **irrigation**, vastly increased humanity's ecological footprint. The same is true of **engineering projects** such as swamp dredging, dam building, canal digging, road building, and urban planning—all becoming more common as agricultural communities grew larger and more advanced. Forms of **resource extraction** strained the environment as well. These included **mining**, hunting, and fishing.

Among the stresses placed on the environment by various societies at various times were **erosion**, **deforestation**, desertification, soil depletion, **species extinction**, and the diversion of rivers and other waterways. In some cases, such damage contributed to the fall or decline of the society that caused it.

Another crucial topic related to the environment is human **migration**. The peopling of the earth by *Homo sapiens* began around 100,000 years ago as hunter-forager groups left Africa—humanity's birthplace, according to the **"Out of Africa" thesis** accepted by the overwhelming majority of scholars— for the Middle East and eventually the rest of Eurasia. Around 50,000 years ago, settlers from Southeast Asia reached Australia and other parts of Oceania. Hunting peoples from Eurasia moved into the Americas, most likely around 15,000 years ago, across the **Bering land bridge** that spanned Siberia and Alaska during periods of heavy glaciation. By 8000 B.C.E., the time of the Neolithic Revolution, humans had settled all but the most inhospitable parts of the globe.

Other noteworthy migrations to be aware of include the spread of **Indo-European** pastoralists from Central Asia to many corners of Eurasia in the 1000s B.C.E.; the disruption of classical empires like Rome, Han China, and Gupta India by **Asiatic steppe nomads** like the Huns in the early centuries C.E.; and the pressure placed on Rome and early medieval Europe by the movement of **Germanic tribes** and **Viking raiders** between 300 and 1000. Many of Africa's present-day peoples are descended from the **Bantu migrations**, which ranged throughout much of the continent between 1500 B.C.E. and 1000 C.E. A vast expanse of the Pacific was settled by the mammoth **Polynesian migrations** between 1500 B.C.E. and 1200 C.E.

Another major facet of environmental history involves the **transfer of foodstuffs** and **diseases** in response to human migration and economic activity. Trade and the diffusion of the concept of agriculture from one society to another caused various foods (and farming techniques) to travel far from their point of origin, sometimes with profound effects. Early examples include **sugar**, which may have arisen in New Guinea and was systematically extracted from cane and crystallized in India between 500 B.C.E. and 500 C.E., during which time it spread to China and the Middle East. It arrived in Europe on a large scale after 1000 C.E. as a result of the Crusades. Bananas and citrus likewise originated in Southeast Asia, reaching the Middle East, the Mediterranean, and Africa by the 600s and 700s C.E. **Cotton** was grown in India between 2000 and 1000 B.C.E., and the practice gradually spread throughout Afro-Eurasia. (The cultivation of cotton arose independently in the Americas as well.) Around the 900s C.E., important improvements in rice farming were imported from Southeast Asia to China and East Asia in the form of drought-resistant **Champa rice** from Vietnam. Champa rice grew fast enough to permit two harvests per year, substantially increasing food production. In Oceania, the **coconut palm** spread throughout the Pacific, thanks to the Polynesian migrations.

Pathogens, or disease-causing agents such as viruses and bacteria, followed wherever humans migrated or settled. In most times and places, disease is a normal part of everyday existence, and in some cases, ailments become **endemic**, or persistently native, to a particular region. (Malaria, which affects many tropical areas in this way, is a classic example.) Periodically, **epidemic** and **pandemic** outbreaks have devastating consequences over large areas, sometimes on a civilization-changing scale. (Technically, epidemics are regional or

NOTE

Episodes of climate change (including the human-caused one we are presently undergoing) have proved important throughout history. As noted earlier, the end of the Pleistocene ice age approximately 12,000 years ago gave rise to the Neolithic Revolution around 10,000 years ago. Closer to 1200 C.E., especially in the northern hemisphere, a warming trend called the medieval climatic optimum greatly affected patterns of migration and settlement—not to mention economic activities like agriculture, trade, and hunting and fishing—roughly between 800 and 1300. The general cooling that followed is referred to as the Little Ice Age and is discussed in Units 1 and 2.

transregional in scope, while pandemics are global, but the distinction between the two can be fuzzy.) Diseases known to have played important historical roles prior to 1200 C.E. include **smallpox**, **measles**, **bubonic plague**, **malaria**, yellow fever, sleeping sickness, cholera, and typhus.

A fact of towering importance in premodern environmental history is the **ecological isolation of Afro-Eurasia from the Americas**. With the vanishing of the Bering land bridge, many of the plants, animals, and diseases that became commonplace in Africa and Eurasia went unknown in the Americas, and vice versa. (One fateful repercussion: populations native to the Americas possessed no immunities to Afro-Eurasian diseases and were cut down in unimaginable numbers by them after 1500 C.E.) The environmental encounter between the so-called Old and New Worlds, the result of European exploration in the 1400s, is known as the **Columbian Exchange**; it will receive much attention in Unit 1.

UNIT 1

1200–1450

Unit 1: Short Cut

GENERAL REMARKS

The period between 1200 and 1450 was a time of growing political consolidation, technological aptitude, and socioeconomic and cultural sophistication. World population continued to rise, and regional and transregional exchanges increased in scale and frequency.

Although less advanced societies continued to be found in all parts of the globe, this era witnessed the emergence of many **centralized states and empires**, whose effective **bureaucracies** made them capable of governing large and diverse populations and mobilizing resources over great distances. **Cities** played a larger role than ever as hubs for political leadership, economic activity, and cultural and artistic dynamism. Increasingly **organized religions**, along with **shared artistic and cultural traditions**, fostered social cohesion and a stronger sense of identity.

In certain places, these developments were part of a general recovery from the weakening or collapse of **classical civilizations** that had existed beforehand but then entered into decline between the 200s C.E. and about 1000 C.E., depending on the region in question. In some areas, as in Europe after the fall of Rome, a lengthy period of backwardness and decentralization followed the end of a classical period. In others, as in China after the Han dynasty, the transition was less traumatic or lasted a shorter time. In either case, many of the cultures that arose or matured after 1200 C.E. continued to draw upon the legacy left by their classical predecessors.

One important historical question is whether the civilizations of this era are better studied as **nation-states** (countries as formally defined political entities in the modern sense of the word) or **cultural spheres** (areas defined less by political boundaries and more by ethnic similarities, shared cultural and religious traditions, or government by a larger imperial or regional power). Examples of the latter include the Islamic world, which stretched from West Africa to the Indian subcontinent and beyond; European Christendom during the medieval era; the "Sinosphere" of East and Southeast Asia, where Chinese influence held strong sway; and pre-Columbian Mesoamerica.

The other central trend of this age was the continued growth of **networks of communication and exchange**. (On a related note, **increased productive capacity** became the economic norm in most parts of the world.) Although the Americas remained isolated, vibrant **systems of interaction** arose to link the various civilizations of Africa and Eurasia. Trade, religious influence, technological transfer, and cultural diffusion all marked this era. **Diaspora communities**, **migration**, and the **movement of nomadic peoples** such as the Vikings, Bantu, and Mongols greatly affected settled societies. A key question pertaining to this period is how nomadic movement compared in importance to **cities** as a cause of historical change. Even though the world was not as joined together as it later became, it was moving swiftly and steadily toward interaction on a truly global scale.

BROAD TRENDS

Governance, 1200–1450	
Europe	Byzantium (Constantinople, 300s–1453) transition from feudalism to centralized nation-states city-state government on Italian peninsula (Venice) and elsewhere (Novgorod) papal-imperial struggle and the medieval ideal of Christendom Mongol rule over Russia (Golden Horde) fall of Constantinople and Ottoman conquest of Byzantium (1453)
Middle East	Abbasid Caliphate (Baghdad, 750–1258) peaks in 800s and declines after 900s dar al-Islam and "circle of justice" Sharia law Mongol Il-Khanate (mid-1200s–mid-1300s) Ottoman Empire (1299–1922) and conquest of Byzantium (1453)
Africa	Ghana (ca. 800–1200) Mali (Timbuktu, mid-1200s–1600s; Mansa Musa in 1300s) Hausa kingdoms Ethiopia Great Zimbabwe (ca. 1000–1400) Swahili city-states
East (and Central) Asia	Song dynasty (960–1279) in China mandate of heaven and bureaucracy (civil service examinations) Yuan (Mongol) dynasty in China (1271–1368) Ming dynasty (1368–1644) in China Chagatai (Mongol) khanate in Central Asia (1200s–mid-1600s) breakdown of Heian regime (794–1185) in Japan feudalism in Japan (shogun and samurai daimyo, 1100s–1500s)
South (and Southeast) Asia and Oceania	post-Gupta disunity in India (ca. 600–1200) incursions of Delhi Sultanate (1206–1526) vs. resistance of Hindu states (Vijayanagara Empire, Rajput kingdoms) Sinhalese dynasties in Sri Lanka Khmer Empire (800s–1400s) and Sukhothai kingdom (1200s–1400s) Srivijayan Empire (500s–1100s) and Majapahit (1293–1500) city-states in Southeast Asia (Malay sultanates, Melaka)
Americas	Mississippian culture (Cahokia, ca. 700–1500) city-states in Mesoamerica (legacy of Maya, ca. 250–900, and Toltecs, ca. 800s–1100s) Aztecs (Mexica) (Tenochtitlán, mid-1200s–1520) Andean city-states Chimú empire (Chan Chan, ca. 1000–1400) Incas (Cuzco, ca. 1300s–early 1500s)
Global and Interregional	Islamic expansion into Africa and Asia (600s onward) Crusades (Christian Europe vs. Islamic Middle East, 1096–1291) Mongol conquests under Genghis Khan (early 1200s) and the *pax Mongolica*

Governance

- Most forms of rulership remained nonrepresentative. Monarchies and oligarchies were the most common.
- Many states did not resemble nations in the modern sense of the world. Some were decentralized. Others were multicultural empires whose various peoples were joined only by the fact that a single authority had conquered them all.
- When classical empires collapsed, the states taking their places typically used traditional sources of legitimacy and power—such as patriarchal authority, religious backing, and the support of landowning elites—but blended them with innovative governing techniques and increasingly effective bureaucracies.
- Imperial expansion, as well as conflict and contact between civilizations, caused cultural borrowing, diffusion, and the transfer of technologies and cultural practices. Europe's Crusades against the Middle East provide one example. Others include the impact of Mongol expansion, the interchange between China and the Middle East, the regional impact of Persian culture throughout the Islamic world, and China's cultural influence throughout East Asia.
- Cities played a larger role in the political life of most civilizations.
- The invention of gunpowder technology and its diffusion throughout Eurasia began to change the balance of world power.

Cultural Developments and Interactions, 1200–1450	
Europe	Latin as regional language of religious and educated elite papal ideal of Christendom vs. "great schism" between Roman Catholicism and Eastern Orthodoxy scholasticism (partial reconciling of Christian doctrine with Greco-Roman thinkers like Aristotle and Plato) Renaissance humanism (revival of Greco-Roman learning) universities code of chivalry intellectual impact of movable-type printing press (1430s+) architecture (Romanesque and Gothic cathedrals, castle building)
Middle East	Arabic as regional language of religious and educated elite (also note cultural importance of Persian) House of Wisdom in Baghdad and golden age of Islamic culture madrasas as centers of learning *The Arabian Nights* the *Rubaiyat* of Omar Khayyám Sufi movement (Rumi's poetry) geometrical design in Islamic art
Africa	Swahili as regional language in East Africa spread of Islamic influences via war and trade oral traditions (griots in West Africa) *Sundiata* epic (Mali, 1300s+) sculpture, wood carving, weaving, metalworking architecture (Great Zimbabwe city complex, mud-and-timber mosques of Timbuktu)

Cultural Developments and Interactions, 1200–1450	
East (and Central) Asia	Mandarin Chinese as classical language diffusion of Buddhist and Daoist culture (Zen/Chan form of Buddhism) impact of Neo-Confucianism samurai culture and code of Bushido in Japan architecture (pagodas, grid layout of cities, Great Wall of China, Beijing's Forbidden City, Heian Shrine)
South (and Southeast) Asia and Oceania	Sanskrit as classical language Indian epics diffusion (and mingling) of Buddhist and Hindu cultures Bhakti movement Islam arrives in India architecture (Angkor Wat, Borobudur)
Americas	polytheism (human sacrifice and pyramid building in Mesoamerica) Mayan hieroglyphs and calendar (concept of zero) quipu (in Andes cultures) architecture (Mississippian earth mounds, Mesoamerican pyramids, Machu Picchu, Inca Temple of the Sun)
Global and Interregional	expansion of Islam's cultural influence to Africa and Asia Buddhist and Hindu influences throughout Southeast, South, and East Asia Greek and Indian mathematics transferred to Islamic world and Europe Greek science and philosophy reintroduced to medieval Europe from Muslim Spain Arab-Chinese cultural transfer European-Islamic cultural transfer during Crusades cultural transfer throughout Mongol empires interregional travel = Rabban bar Sawma (1200s), Marco Polo (1200s), Ibn Battuta (1300s), Zheng He (1400s)

Cultural Developments and Interactions

■ Distinct artistic and cultural traditions developed in all major regions. At the same time, cultural diffusion and mutual influence became increasingly common thanks to the expansion of empires, the growth of trade networks, the emergence of diasporic communities, and the sharing of religious beliefs.

■ Successful religions spread widely across regions and cultures due variously to trade, missionary activity, and conquest.

■ The civilizations possessing the greatest degree of scientific knowledge and cultural sophistication were East Asia, India, the Middle East, and Muslim Spain (al-Andalus).

■ China and India exerted tremendous cultural and religious influence over their neighbors. Buddhism, Hinduism, and art and architectural styles spread from these states to Southeast Asia, Korea, Japan, Tibet, and elsewhere.

■ In their own right and because of the knowledge they imported from China, the Middle East and Muslim Spain played a large role in spreading philosophy, science, technology, music, art, and architecture to North Africa and Europe. The Middle East's cultural influence on medieval and Renaissance Europe was indispensable.

- Europe underwent rapid cultural development at this time, especially thanks to the Renaissance, which involved the rediscovery of Greco-Roman science and philosophy or the borrowing of it from Islamic and Jewish scholars.
- Travelers and explorers created links between societies and increased geographical and cultural awareness. Examples include Marco Polo, Rabban Bar Sawma, Ibn Battuta, and Zheng He.
- In the Americas, major civilizations, such as the Toltec, Aztecs (Mexica), Chimú, and Inca, left their cultural and religious imprint on many of their neighbors.
- Certain languages, such as Sanskrit, Mandarin Chinese, and Latin, became transregionally influential because they were sacred to major religions or the official tongues of large and enduring empires.
- Certain languages attained regional and even transregional status because of their cultural or religious preeminence, their usefulness as a language of learning, or their suitability as a lingua franca for trade. Examples include Sanskrit, Mandarin Chinese, Swahili, Arabic, Persian, and Latin.

Technology and Innovation, 1200–1450	
Europe	wheeled vehicles vs. saddles and pack animals (horses, oxen) shipbuilding and navigation (cogs, carracks, caravels) movable-type printing press (mid-1400s) architecture (Romanesque and Gothic cathedrals, castle building)
Middle East	wheeled vehicles vs. saddles and pack animals (horses, oxen, camels) camel saddle improved expertise in medicine (impact of Ibn Sina's *Canon of Medicine*) expertise in astronomy (astrolabe improved 700s+) expertise in mathematics (algebra) shipbuilding and navigation (dhow and lateen sail)

Africa	wheeled vehicles vs. saddles and pack animals (camels)
	shipbuilding and navigation (monsoon winds + dhow and
	    lateen sail)
	architecture (Great Zimbabwe city complex, mud-and-timber
	    mosques of Timbuktu)

East (and Central) Asia	horse collar and stirrup spread out from China
	woodblock printing improved and movable-type concept invented
	    in China
	water mills and water clocks in China
	gunpowder invented in China (800s–900s) and spreads widely
	shipbuilding and navigation (junk, stern rudder, magnetic compass)
	architecture (pagodas, grid layout of cities, Great Wall of China,
	    Beijing's Forbidden City, Heian Shrine)

South (and Southeast) Asia and Oceania	wheeled vehicles vs. saddles and pack animals (horses and oxen) "Arabic" numerals, pi, and zero shipbuilding and navigation (monsoon winds + dhow and lateen sail) outrigger canoes (Polynesia) architecture (Angkor Wat, Borobudur)

Technology and Innovation, 1200–1450	
Americas	saddles and pack animals (llamas) Mayan hieroglyphs and calendar (concept of zero) architecture (Mississippian earth mounds, Mesoamerican pyramids, Machu Picchu, Inca Temple of the Sun)
Global and Interregional	westward transfer of many technologies from China (horse collar, compass, printing) influence of Greek and Indian mathematics on Islamic word and Europe Greek science and philosophy reintroduced to Europe from Muslim Spain gunpowder acquired from China by Middle East and Europe (1200s)

Technology and Innovation

- The systemization of rational thought—including philosophy, logic, empirical observation, and early variants of the scientific method—emerged or matured in several parts of Eurasia. In the Middle East and Europe, this largely involved the preservation and/or rediscovery of learning from the classical Greco-Roman era.
- The civilizations possessing the greatest degree of scientific knowledge and medical expertise as this era began were East Asia (especially China), India, the Middle East, and Muslim Spain (al-Andalus).
- In their own right and because of knowledge they imported from China, the Middle East and Muslim Spain played a key role in spreading science, medical skill, technology, and architecture to North Africa and Europe.
- The European Renaissance—influenced profoundly by borrowing from Islamic and Jewish scholars in the Middle East and Muslim Spain—involved significant advancements not just in the arts but in science, engineering, and architecture.
- By this time period, Arabic numerals (so called but developed in fact by mathematicians in India) had migrated westward from their point of origin, first to the Middle East and then more widely to Europe.
- The improvement of print technology allowed the faster and wider dissemination of information in Asia and Europe. Both block printing and early versions of movable-type printing emerged in China (in the 200s C.E. and 1000s C.E., respectively), and the culmination of this trend was the invention of a cost-effective, high-speed movable-type printing press in Europe by the mid-1400s. The resulting information explosion caused intellectual revolutions in many parts of Eurasia.
- Innovations in ground transport and agriculture increased the efficiency with which pack animals were domesticated and used. These included better yokes, harnesses, and saddles. (Earlier technologies, such as stirrups and horse collars, improved as well.)
- Key technologies of the era improved maritime transport, including shipbuilding refinements (such as stern rudders and deeper keels) and more advanced systems of rigging and sailing (including the shift from square sails to lateen sails).
- Previously invented navigational tools—most notably the astrolabe and the magnetic compass—improved in quality and became more widely available throughout Eurasia.
- The invention of gunpowder in China by around 900 C.E., combined with the subsequent spread of gunpowder weaponry throughout Eurasia (and especially in Europe) from ca. 1200 onward, created the potential for immense changes in military affairs and the global balance of power.

Economic Systems, 1200–1450	
Europe	revival and growth of European trade (Hanseatic League) Mediterranean trade network Crusades stimulate appetite for Asian goods (connections with trans-Saharan caravans and Silk Road) improved open-water navigation and Atlantic voyaging intensive agriculture (wheat) feudal manorialism (serfdom) guilds (artisans and craftsmen)
Middle East	trans-Saharan caravans (Arab-Berber expertise with camels) Mediterranean trade network (connections with Silk Road) (connections with Indian Ocean basin) intensive agriculture (wheat)
Africa	Indian Ocean trade network (Swahili city-states) trans-Saharan caravans (Arab-Berber expertise with camels) Mediterranean trade network salt, gold, ivory Arab trade in African slaves
East (and Central) Asia	Silk Road (briefly disrupted, then revived under *pax Mongolica*) Grand Canal in China (connections between Indian Ocean basin and Pacific trade) intensive agriculture (rice) nomadic pastoralism continues in steppe zone silk, iron, steel, and porcelain industries in China feudal landholding in Japan (serfdom)
South (and Southeast) Asia and Oceania	Indian Ocean trade network intensive agriculture (rice) cotton industry in India spices
Americas	intensive agriculture (potatoes, beans, corn/maize) chinampa, waru waru, and terracing as techniques for growing crops mit'a labor system in Andes (especially under Incan empire) pastoralism and hunting-foraging remain common in many areas
Global and Interregional	general rise in agricultural production (due to technological innovation and techniques of intensive agriculture) new trading cities and merchant classes increased craft production luxury goods fuel expansion of trade networks minting of coins and printing of paper money standardization of currencies, weights, and measures credit and banking become more common slavery, serfdom, and corvée become more common

Economic Systems

- Economic production increased globally.
- Transregional trade was practiced on a massive scale and over greater distances than before, stemming largely from innovations in overland and maritime transport.

- Such existing routes as Eurasia's Silk Roads, the Mediterranean sea lanes, the trans-Saharan caravan trails, and the Indian Ocean basin witnessed huge upswings in commercial activity. New routes expanded trade in Mesoamerica and the Andes as well.
- Trading organizations like northern Europe's Hanseatic League came into existence.
- New cities emerged as key centers for interregional trade. They included Venice, Novgorod, Baghdad, the Swahili city-states, Timbuktu, Hangzhou, Melaka (Malacca), Calicut, Cahokia, and Tenochtitlán.
- Demand for luxury goods assumed a more prominent role in interregional commerce. Textiles, porcelain, and spices from the Middle East, South and Southeast Asia, and East Asia became especially important.
- Infrastructure—which included markets, roads, harbors, and other facilities built and maintained by states—supported local, regional, and transregional trade. Tax collection and the gathering of rents became more efficient and intrusive.
- Trade was made easier and safer by the emergence of new forms of banking and monetization (credit, checking, banking houses) as well as state practices like the minting of coins and the printing of paper money. Customs agencies and standard weights and measures helped to regulate and regularize trade.
- Interregional trade was facilitated by the warmer weather of the medieval climatic optimum and then affected by the global cooling that led to the Little Ice Age.
- Technological innovation played a role in expanding trade, especially in the fields of ship design (including Atlantic cogs, carracks, and caravels; the Indian Ocean dhow; and the Chinese junk) and navigation (with the astrolabe and the magnetic compass proving crucial). Also important was the effective adaptation of environmental knowledge (such as Saharan camel herders' knowledge of the desert or Central Asian pastoralists' use of horses for steppe travel).
- Agricultural production increased worldwide, thanks partly to climate changes and partly to innovations in technology and intensive agricultural techniques (including the horse collar, better terracing, Champa rice cultivation in Asia, and waru waru and chinampa techniques in the Americas).

Social Interactions and Organization, 1200–1450	
Europe	serfdom (feudal manorialism) vs. free peasantry peasant revolts in England, France, and elsewhere (1300s) craftsmen and guilds diaspora community (Jews) and anti-Semitism money lending by Jewish diaspora (anti-Semitism) witch hunts (*Hammer of Witchcraft*, 1400s) Christian doctrine and patriarchy
Middle East	Islam and patriarchy (veiling, seclusion, polygamy) jizya tax for subject nonbelievers (dhimmi) millet system (religious communities) system in Ottoman Empire devshirme (Ottoman slave-recruiting system) military slaves (mamluks and janissaries) diaspora community (Jews)

Social Interactions and Organization, 1200–1450	
Africa	patriarchy (with some matriarchy and matrilinealism) diaspora communities (merchants from Middle East and Indian Ocean basin) Arab slavers in North and East Africa origins of Atlantic slave trade
East (and Central) Asia	diaspora communities (merchants along Silk Road) Neo-Confucianism and hierarchy (caste system) Neo-Confucianism and patriarchy (foot binding) Red Turban uprising in China (1300s) samurai nobility and feudalism in Japan (serfdom) samurai patriarchy
South (and Southeast) Asia and Oceania	diaspora communities (minorities throughout Indian Ocean trade network) Chinese merchant communities in Southeast Asia Hinduism and hierarchy (varna caste system) Hinduism and patriarchy (sati, seclusion) Islam and patriarchy (veiling, seclusion, polygamy)
Americas	mit'a labor system in Andes (intensifies under Inca) ayllu clan system in Andes
Global and Interregional	persistence of caste systems in many regions growth of artisan (craftsman) classes growth of merchant classes greater urbanization and trading cities Muslim merchant diaspora in Africa and Indian Ocean basin Jewish diaspora (Middle East, Europe, Silk Roads, Indian Ocean basin) slavery and serfdom become increasingly common patriarchy continues or deepens

Social Interactions and Organization

- Population growth continued in all parts of the world.
- Social structures in centralized states grew more complex. A wider array of social classes appeared, including peasants, laborers, artisans, merchants, clergy, and slaves. Elite and ruling classes remained small and generally hereditary.
- Class hierarchies, social stratification, and caste systems continued to function. Social mobility increased in a few places, often in urban settings where trade and commerce dominated.
- Many peoples continued to practice nomadic pastoralism as a form of labor organization.
- Of settled societies, the vast majority remained fundamentally agricultural. In the countryside, the chief forms of labor organization were free peasant production (typically owing rents to landlords or taxes to the government) and serfdom (unfree labor bound to the land and owing labor to the landowner).
- Urbanization, or the growth of cities, proceeded worldwide, although periods of decline were mixed with periods of revival and expansion. In cities, the rise of trade and commerce made merchant classes larger and more influential. Also in urban settings, a key form of labor organization was craft production, with artisans often banding together in guilds.
- Other forms of labor organization include coerced and unfree labor (especially slavery, serfdom, and the mit'a), as well as military conscription. The demand for slaves, whether for domestic labor, agricultural work, or military service, grew substantially.

- Unrest and revolts caused by unfair treatment of workers and peasants became more common in various parts of the world.

- Along far-reaching trade routes, diasporic communities and foreign enclaves formed in many ports and towns as refugees, migrants, and traders from one society made new homes far from their points of origin.

- Patriarchalism, often buttressed by traditional religions and customs, continued to be the norm. Women's roles varied from society to society, but they generally occupied a secondary status (with minimal to nonexistent political rights) and remained on the disadvantaged side of the gender division of labor. They had sharply defined occupational roles, generally confined to childbearing, homemaking, and low-status jobs such as weaving, food gathering, farm chores, and domestic servitude.

- In most places, however, women had at least some freedoms and rights (which might include the right to divorce abusive husbands, the right to a dowry, to right to at least some education, or the right to inherit and own property). They also tended to play informal but important roles as they managed households and family finances, supervised the education and upbringing of children, and influenced their husbands.

- In most societies, upper-class women lived easier lives but found themselves more constrained by religious and cultural restrictions on their behavior (such as seclusion or purdah, foot binding, and veiling). Lower-class women, whose lives were much harder, were often less bound by such restrictions because the rules of "proper" behavior applied less to them.

- In places like West Africa, Japan (during certain periods), the Mongol Empire, and parts of Southeast Asia, women enjoyed more respect than average during this period.

- Gender relations and family structure were frequently influenced by religious change, with Buddhism, Christianity, Islam, and Neo-Confucianism playing especially significant roles.

- In addition to monogamous marriage, practices such as polygamy, concubinage, and harems were permitted in certain places. Terms of divorce varied from place to place, and whether or not children born outside of marriage were recognized as legitimate likewise varied.

Humans and the Environment, 1200–1450	
Europe	environmental impact of city building and intensive agriculture (deforestation, desertification, soil erosion, silted rivers) cotton, sugar, and citrus spread through Mediterranean prevalence of disease-causing pathogens and recurring epidemics (smallpox, measles, bubonic plague) Black Death pandemic (1300s)
Middle East	environmental impact of city building and intensive agriculture (deforestation, desertification, soil erosion, silted rivers) water management systems (irrigation) migration of Mongol-Turkic horse pastoralists (East and Central Asia, Middle East) cotton, sugar, and citrus spread through Islamic world origins of coffee in Ethiopia and Yemen prevalence of disease-causing pathogens and recurring epidemics (smallpox, measles, bubonic plague) Black Death pandemic (1300s)

Humans and the Environment, 1200–1450	
Africa	environmental impact of city building and intensive agriculture (deforestation, desertification, soil erosion, silted rivers) growth of Sahara and other instances of desertification bananas spread after arrival from Middle East origins of coffee in Ethiopia and Yemen prevalence of disease-causing pathogens and recurring epidemics (malaria, yellow fever, sleeping sickness)
East (and Central) Asia	environmental impact of city building and intensive agriculture (deforestation, desertification, soil erosion, silted rivers) migration of Mongol-Turkic horse pastoralists (East and Central Asia, Middle East) spread of Champa rice prevalence of disease-causing pathogens and recurring epidemics (smallpox, measles, bubonic plague) Black Death pandemic (1300s)
South (and Southeast) Asia and Oceania	environmental impact of city building and intensive agriculture (deforestation, desertification, soil erosion, silted rivers) spread of Champa rice prevalence of disease-causing pathogens and recurring epidemics Polynesian migrations end ca. 1200 (spread of pigs and taro) + deforestation of Easter Island
Americas	environmental impact of city building and intensive agriculture (deforestation, desertification, soil erosion, silted rivers) chinampa agriculture and terrace farming continue waru waru agriculture in Andes comparative lack of domesticated animals vs. Afro-Eurasia comparative lack of disease-causing pathogens vs. Afro-Eurasia
Global and Interregional	medieval climatic optimum Little Ice Age begins continued isolation of Afro-Eurasian and American ecosystems

Humans and the Environment

- Societies and ecosystems in the Americas remained isolated from those in Afro-Eurasia.
- Nomadic and migratory populations (including the Mongols and Polynesians) continued to have a profound impact on large parts of the world.
- Innovations in overland and maritime transport permitted easier and wider travel.
- Human impact on the environment—humanity's "ecological footprint"—increased dramatically as a result of population growth and the greater capacity of advanced and urbanized societies to carry out large-scale architectural and engineering projects (such as China's Grand Canal).
- The increased scale of agricultural production and irrigation heightened the risks of soil erosion, deforestation, and other forms of major environmental damage.
- Mining, which supported the expansion of industrial production and the increased demand for metals, gems, and jewels, exerted a growing impact on the environment. Other forms of resource extraction (such as hunting and fishing) did the same.

- Increased trade activity spread plants and foodstuffs (including bananas, rice, cotton, sugar, spices, and fruits) far from their points of origin.
- Epidemic diseases, including smallpox, measles, and bubonic plague, periodically affected large parts of Eurasia. Most famous for its scope and deadliness was the Black Death, the wave of plague that swept China, the Middle East, and Europe in the 1300s.
- A global warming trend, often called the medieval climatic optimum, lasted between 800 and 1300, greatly affecting patterns of migration, agricultural life, and interregional trade.
- Between the early 1300s and the early 1500s, a cooling trend began, leading to the so-called Little Ice Age, which persisted until the early-to-mid-1800s.

QUESTIONS AND COMPARISONS TO CONSIDER

- How did the major states and empires of this era organize themselves? What state-building techniques did they use to mobilize resources, administer their lands, legitimate their power, and maintain political authority?
- How important is the nation-state, as opposed to empires and larger cultural spheres, as an object of study during this historical period?
- Consider major intellectual and cultural developments in different societies and the intellectual and cultural influences exerted by different societies on each other. Good examples include the Middle Eastern influence on medieval Europe, India's influence on Southeast Asia, the mutual influence between China and the Middle East (or between China and its neighbors), and the transfer of technology and knowledge throughout the Mongol Empire during the *pax Mongolica.*
- What roles did religions play in political development, especially in areas that attempted to create large, multinational civilizations united by religion, such as Christendom and the Islamic caliphates?
- Consider the causes and consequences of transregional communication and exchange. What new technologies and techniques enabled the freer movement of people over greater distances? What happened when different regions came into more frequent contact with each other?
- Pay attention to explorers, travelers, and diasporic communities as agents of cultural diffusion and change.
- How did new technology affect warfare during these years? Travel? Trade? Agriculture? The spread of information?
- Compare and contrast the major trade routes of the era, focusing on the Mediterranean, the Indian Ocean, trans-Saharan caravan routes, and the Silk Road.
- Think about differences and likenesses among systems of labor organization, both free and coerced.
- What roles did religion play in supporting or challenging the status quo? In legitimating political regimes or shaping social norms and gender relations?
- How did the role of women change from the preceding era? How did women's experiences vary from society to society during this era? To what degree did this depend on one's social class? How did religion affect the status of women and the dynamics of family life in various parts of the world?

- Examine major migratory movements during this period and their various effects.
- Consider the role of nomadic movement as a cause of change (environmental, social, political) during these years. Do the same for the growth of cities.
- In what ways did various states, whether centralized or less so, affect their physical environments? In what ways were they affected by their environments?
- What role did disease play in the history of this period? What about the exchange of new crops and foodstuffs?
- What roles did environmental factors such as the medieval climatic optimum and the Little Ice Age play in social and economic development?

UNIT 1

SCENIC ROUTE
(Chapters 1–6)

Governance, 1200–1450

1

IN THIS CHAPTER

→ **DIFFERING TRANSITIONS FROM CLASSICAL REGIMES (NATION-STATES VS. CULTURAL SPHERES)**

→ **EUROPEAN FEUDALISM + BYZANTINE CENTRALIZATION + ITALIAN CITY-STATES**

→ **ABBASID CALIPHATE + OTTOMAN EMPIRE**

→ **WEST AFRICAN STATES (MALI) + SWAHILI CITY-STATES + GREAT ZIMBABWE**

→ **SONG + YUAN (MONGOL) + MING DYNASTIES + CHINESE TRIBUTARY SYSTEM**

→ **HEIAN JAPAN + MEDIEVAL SHOGUNATES**

→ **DELHI SULTANATE + VIJAYANAGARA EMPIRE**

→ **MAJAPAHIT EMPIRE + KHMER EMPIRE + SUKHOTHAI + SOUTHEAST ASIAN CITY-STATES**

→ **MISSISSIPPIAN CULTURE (CAHOKIA) + MESOAMERICA (MAYA, AZTECS) + ANDES (CHIMÚ AND INCA EMPIRES)**

→ **IDEOLOGIES AND POLITICAL USES OF RELIGION (CHRISTENDOM, DAR AL-ISLAM, CIRCLE OF JUSTICE, MANDATE OF HEAVEN, NEO-CONFUCIANISM)**

→ **WARRIOR CODES (CHIVALRY, BUSHIDO, FURUSIYYA)**

→ **INTERREGIONAL CONTACT AND CONFLICT (CRUSADES, MONGOL KHANATES, FALL OF CONSTANTINOPLE)**

State-building during these years reached new levels of complexity and sophistication. Although most forms of governance remained nonrepresentative, with monarchies and oligarchies most common, states and other forms of political organization took widely varying shape in this era.

In many cases, **classical** regimes—starting in the 200s C.E. and continuing through the 1000s C.E., depending on the area in question—collapsed, leading to one of several outcomes. In some instances, new states quickly took their place, using some of the old states' traditional sources of legitimacy and power (including patriarchal authority, religious backing, and the support of landowning elites) but blending them with innovative governing techniques. Examples include Byzantium and the post-Han dynasties in China. Sometimes decentralization followed, giving rise in certain places, most famously medieval Europe and Japan, to the system of feudalism. Another alternative was for dramatically new forms of governance to appear, as in the Islamic caliphates, the Mongol khanates, and the city-state systems that emerged in East Africa, Southeast Asia, the Americas, and Italy.

On a related note, one of the central political questions of this era is whether civilizations at this time are better studied as **nation-states** (countries as formally defined political entities, in the modern sense of the word) or **cultural spheres** (defined less by political boundaries and more by ethnic similarities, shared cultural and religious traditions, or government by a larger imperial or regional power). The answer depends largely on the specific region.

As you study the states and societies listed below, pay attention to methods of rulership and administration as well as the organization of resources and labor. Also take note of how these states projected power and interacted with each other, whether peacefully or violently.

STATE BUILDING IN AFRO-EURASIA: TRADITION AND INNOVATION
Medieval Europe and Byzantium

Long after the fall of Rome in 476 C.E., the rulers of medieval Europe would attempt to live up to its political ideal of unified and centralized rule. **Roman law** (especially the Justinian law code, compiled in Byzantium during the 500s) remains a keystone of Western legal thought. **Latin** remained the common language of Europe's educated classes for centuries, and **Christianity**, legalized and adopted by Rome in the 300s C.E., persisted in Europe not just as a cultural and intellectual force but as a political one, providing a powerful sense of unity in unstable times.

Political life in medieval Europe varied depending on region and time. In the east, the state of Byzantium enjoyed wealth, cultural advancement, and a high degree of centralization. By contrast, for the rest of Europe, the Early Middle Ages (ca. 500–1000) were a time of overall backwardness, political decentralization, and perpetual military threat. During the High Middle Ages (ca. 1000–1300), an era of cultural and economic revival, nations took firmer shape. During the period between 1300 and 1500—the Late Middle Ages for most of Europe, the Renaissance in Italy—states tended toward even greater centralization, although these were also years of constant warfare, social unrest, and crises, such as the **Black Death**.

In the aftermath of Rome's collapse, no single authority emerged in Western or Central Europe to take its place. At first, small and short-lived kingdoms rose and fell. Constantly menaced by migrating barbarians and Muslim invaders, these monarchies were also weakened by decentralization: their rulers lacked the money, military strength, and administrative tools to govern their lands effectively. By the 700s, however, particularly in the Frankish kingdom that eventually spawned Charlemagne's empire, certain leaders hit upon a partial solution. This was the system of **feudalism**, in which monarchs awarded land to loyal followers, or vassals. In exchange, these vassals guaranteed that their parcels of land (fiefs) would be governed, that law and justice would be dispensed, that crops would be grown, and that the land would be protected. Those who received the largest land parcels evolved into Europe's **noble** (or **aristocratic**) **class**, and these nobles typically subdivided (or subinfeudated) their own land, becoming lords to their own vassals. The obligations owed to each other by lords and vassals were formal and contractual—a point of difference between European feudalism and feudalism elsewhere, especially in Japan, where relationships were governed by a more abstract sense of loyalty.

A Medieval Tournament

The military and political backbone of medieval Europe's feudal system was the knight. High-born and trained from youth in cavalry warfare, the knight was the state-of-the-art warrior of his era. Knights also made up Europe's noble class. Knights honed their military skills—and cultivated the arts of chivalry—at tournaments such as the one portrayed here.

A key function of the feudal nobility was military. Vassals were required to recruit foot soldiers from the land given them, and they themselves fought as **knights**, or elite armored cavalry, a style of combat that required wealth and lifelong training. In theory, the code of **chivalry**—expressed fictionally in songs and poems like those about King Arthur—was supposed to ensure that knights acted as virtuous Christian warriors, dealing fairly with the lower classes and treating women with delicacy and respect. While the code had some restraining effect in real life, it was often broken. The economic realities of feudalism were also dismal, because its **manorial system** relied on the labor of **serfs**: peasants who were not technically slaves but were tied to a feudal lord's land without the right to change profession or residence without permission. Serfs spent a certain number of days per month working directly for their lord and also owed their lord a portion of their own crops and livestock.

Feudalism remained at the heart of European politics and socioeconomic life for centuries. On the other hand, centralizing tendencies were felt in certain places as early as the 800s and 900s. Much of the need to centralize further had to do with continued struggles against Muslim forces as well as the wave of attacks launched from the north by Vikings, starting in the late 700s and lasting until approximately 1000. A prime example of an early and successful state-builder is the Frankish monarch Charlemagne (r. 768–814). Not only did he defeat Vikings, Muslims, and barbarians, but he sponsored education and culture, created a network of administrators and local officials to supervise his growing territories, and laid the foundation for the Holy Roman Empire. The very name of this state highlights two key strategies pursued by European rulers during the Middle Ages. One was to legitimate one's rule by association with the Catholic Church, and another was to hark back to Rome as a model of effective government to imitate. Charlemagne's empire was split by his grandsons, but his example was followed by later monarchs.

During the High and Late Middle Ages, European states centralized at different paces and to different extents. Even under the best circumstances, all of them had to deal with the powerful underlying tension between monarchs (who preferred centralization) and their nobles (who wished to preserve their feudal powers and privileges). Equally important, and equally complicated, was the relationship between European monarchs and the **Catholic papacy**, which exercised considerable political power during the Middle Ages. In Western Europe, the most stable states were England and France, whose royal families were intertwined for several centuries thanks to the Norman Conquest of 1066, which brought French-style feudalism to England and fused Latin-based culture with the Celtic and Anglo-Saxon traditions already present in the British Isles. Unusually, England achieved a high degree of centralization while significantly restricting the power of the king. In 1215, the **Magna Carta**, imposed on the king by his barons, guaranteed the nobility certain rights and privileges. Later in the 1200s, England's nobility won the right to form a **Parliament**, which made laws in conjunction with the king and gradually became more representative. Also during this time, England's system of **common law** began providing for jury trials and observing certain personal liberties ("a man's home is his castle," for example).

By contrast, the Capetian kings of France, who ruled from Paris, followed the more typical route to medieval state building, which was to centralize the nation by increasing their own power. The French kings' crucial task during the High and Late Middle Ages was to conquer large and economically important regions that either wished to remain independent (such as Burgundy or large parts of the south, where Paris used religious differences as an excuse to launch a brutal crusade) or were claimed by England (such as Normandy and Aquitaine). It took years of fighting to untangle England's and France's competing claims over French territory. The last and most important of these conflicts was the **Hundred Years' War** (1337–1453), which coincided with social unrest on both sides and the Black Death. While the English enjoyed the upper hand at first, the French ultimately won—thanks in large part to the warrior maid **Joan of Arc**—and victory in the 1400s vastly boosted the efforts of the French kings to centralize their power at home. Unlike their English counterparts, French monarchs were not obligated to share their power in any legally meaningful way.

Although important states formed in southern and central Europe, they were less centralized. Sprawling across the middle of the continent—especially the German-speaking parts of Europe—was the Holy Roman Empire, a multicultural monarchy founded in the 900s by Charlemagne's heirs. The emperor was supposed to work in partnership with the pope, although in actuality the two clashed more than they cooperated. Although the emperor's territory was large, his powers were comparatively weak. The position was not hereditary: each new emperor was chosen by the empire's leading noble families. The population was ethnically diverse (Germanic, Slavic, Italian, Hungarian, and more), and the empire itself was a difficult-to-administer patchwork of dozens of duchies, kingdoms, and principalities— almost two hundred of them in the 1300s. One centralizing factor near the end of this period was the **Habsburg family**, which gained permanent control over the imperial throne in 1438.

Italy—not even a country at this time—remained even more decentralized. Much of northern Italy was controlled by the Holy Roman Empire, and many parts of the south passed in and out of French, Spanish, Muslim, Byzantine, and even Viking hands. Those areas that remained free were governed as **city-states**. Italy was one of the most urbanized regions of Europe and a major player in the Mediterranean trade network, whose economic prosperity and cultural dynamism made it the birthplace of the **Renaissance** in the late 1200s and early 1300s. The chief city-states of medieval and Renaissance Italy were Florence, Milan, and Venice in the north and Naples in the south. Also important was Rome, heart of the Papal States.

As for Spain and Portugal, their medieval development was shaped above all by their conquest at the hands of the Moors, or Muslim invaders, during the 700s. On one hand, the Moorish presence benefited al-Andalus (as Islamic Spain and Portugal were known). The science, technology, and deep understanding of Greek philosophy brought to Spain by Muslim and Jewish scholars eventually spread to the rest of Europe, and the beauty of Moorish art and architecture is still evident in Spain and Portugal today. On the other hand, both countries spent most of the Middle Ages locked in a long war, the **Reconquista**, against Moorish armies. The Reconquista began in the early 1000s and lasted until 1492, although already by the late 1200s, the Moors had been pushed into Granada, the southernmost part of Spain. One of the Reconquista's legacies was the intense religious hostility shown toward Muslims and Jews by Spanish and Portuguese Catholics, both during and after the war. Another was a tradition of regional autonomy in Spain, where the existence of about half a dozen separate kingdoms, not counting Portugal, delayed full centralization until the end of the 1400s.

By far the strongest and most advanced state in medieval Europe was **Byzantium**, or the Eastern Roman Empire, whose capital, **Constantinople**, sat at the crossroads of Europe and Asia and was home to a million people at its peak. Economically, Byzantium played a role in Mediterranean trade, Silk Road commerce, and, indirectly, the Indian Ocean trade network. Politically, its emperor used **Eastern Orthodoxy** to legitimate his rulership and took advantage of a large and elaborate bureaucracy—a holdover from the days of Rome—to administer and supervise his territory. Byzantine emperors were master strategists, using complex fortifications, naval power, advanced technology, and diplomatic skill to fend off multiple enemies at once. In 1071, however, the Seljuk Turks defeated Byzantium in the pivotal battle of Manzikert, setting in process the empire's steady territorial decline. Finally, in 1453, the Ottoman Turks, thanks to effective deployment of gunpowder weaponry, **captured Constantinople** and conquered the Byzantine state.

In both Catholic Europe and Orthodox Byzantium, religion was central to political and cultural life. The relationship between church and state, however, played out differently in each half of Europe. Like the Catholic papacy, the Orthodox patriarchate strictly controlled art, music, architecture, and literature, and it strove for as much influence over politics as it could get. But the Orthodox doctrine of **caesaropapism** held the Byzantine emperor up as the supreme authority over worldly and spiritual affairs alike, leaving the Orthodox Church in a weak position on those occasions when it quarreled with the emperor. On the other hand, the Catholic Church promoted the **ideal of Christendom**: the concept of Europe as a single civilization, joined by a common allegiance to the Christian church. During the High Middle Ages, the Catholic Church argued that the pope's political authority should be higher than that of any monarch, and it gathered into its hands important worldly powers. The Catholic Church owned vast amounts of land and had the right to collect tithes from the general population. The popes determined what was **heresy** and could exclude worshippers from the Catholic Church (**excommunication**). In 1231, they established the **Holy Inquisition**, a set of special courts that sought out and punished nonconformity. The popes heavily influenced how European monarchs ruled their countries, and they had the power to declare holy wars, or **crusades**.

SPECIAL NOTE

A mix of centralization and decentralization prevailed in Eastern Europe. Much of the region was brutally Christianized and dominated by Teutonic knights from the German states, then threatened during the mid-1200s by the Mongols' westward push or, during the 1300s and 1400s, the Ottoman Turks' invasion of the Balkans. Still, places like Poland, Croatia, and Hungary flourished for a while as stable states. By contrast, the Russian lands were governed during much of this era by a loose confederation of city-states. Although the princes ruling these cities owed allegiance to the grand prince of Kiev, they feuded constantly, leaving them weak and divided when the Mongols arrived in the 1240s. For two centuries, the Russians lived under Mongol rule, after which a more centralized state took shape under the leadership of Moscow.

Interregional Contact and Conflict: The Crusades

Catholic Europe fought **crusades** for many reasons: to convert nonbelievers to Catholicism (as in the Teutonic Knights' crusades in Eastern Europe), to crush Christian sects the pope considered heretical (infamous wars of this sort enabled France's kings to tame independent regions in the south), and to combat non-Christian foreigners (Spain's anti-Muslim **Reconquista**, for example, was given the status of crusade).

TIP

Compare the Christian notion of crusade with the Islamic concept of holy war, or jihad.

NOTE

Medieval Europe's expertise in castle-building increased by leaps and bounds after 1100, as their Crusades against the Middle East exposed them to the military architecture of the Islamic world. Muslim armies had long used stone construction to build strong and complex castles, whereas European states before this time had built castles mainly with wood. European crusaders quickly imported Muslim designs for their own use at home.

The best-known crusades—the ones generally referred to as "the Crusades"—were those waged against the Muslims of the Middle East and North Africa between 1095 and 1291. The **First Crusade** (1096–1099) was sparked by Byzantine requests for military aid against the Seljuk Turks, who had smashed Byzantine forces at Manzikert in 1071 and, then gone on to capture Jerusalem and the Holy Land. Motivated by religious fervor, racial prejudice, and a hunger to gain wealth from plunder and land, thousands of crusading knights and their followers gathered in Constantinople. They then drove south to Jerusalem, which they besieged and captured during the summer of 1099, butchering numerous Muslim and Jewish civilians in the process. They then cemented their military and economic presence in the Middle East for the next two centuries by establishing a series of Latin Kingdoms on the Mediterranean's eastern shores. This threw an already politically confused Middle East into deeper chaos.

Lack of unity among Arabs, Turks, and other Muslims was a key reason for the Crusaders' initial success, since neither the weakened Abbasids nor their political rivals were capable of organizing effective resistance. Over time, the Muslims improved their efforts to expel the Europeans, and the many crusades that followed were generally European responses to major Muslim victories. For example, the Kurdish general **Saladin**, one of the most dynamic military leaders in Middle Eastern history, recaptured Jerusalem in 1187 and held back the Third Crusade (1189–1212), which followed. After 1200, the crusades lost their focus (the **Fourth Crusade** of 1202–1204 turned into a Venetian-backed trade war against Christian Constantinople, which was savagely sacked) or failed miserably (like the ill-fated Children's Crusades). The Latin Kingdoms steadily shrank during the 1200s, and the Europeans abandoned their last major outpost in 1291.

Long-term effects of the Crusades included the worsening of the relationship between European Christians and the Muslim Middle East. Also important was the greater awareness of the wider world, especially the lands of the East, that the Crusades stimulated among Europeans. Along with this came an increased knowledge of, and desire for, the economic wealth to be gained by greater interaction with the Middle and Far East. Moreover, the crusading ideal—the notion that Christian warriors were fighting on behalf of a sacred cause—contributed powerfully to the myth of knightly chivalry that emerged in Europe during the Middle Ages. There was also technology transfer, as Europeans learned much about castle architecture from their experience in the Middle East and also came into contact with some of the innovations that Middle Eastern peoples had adopted from China.

The Middle East

Prior to 600 C.E., the dominant civilizations in the Middle East were the Byzantine Empire and Persia. Suddenly, the political and religious landscape of the Middle East was transformed by the appearance of **Islam** (discussed in detail in Unit Zero).

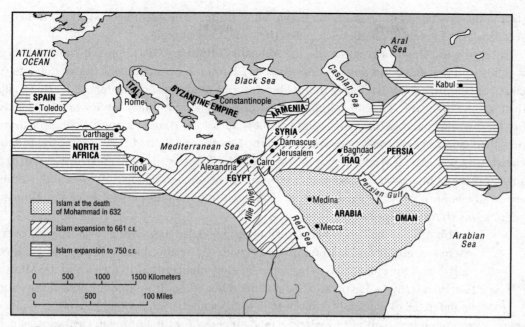

The Birth and Expansion of Islam, 632–750

Born in Arabia, the dynamic new faith of Islam triumphed throughout the Middle East, where it is still dominant. It then continued to expand, both eastward and westward.

Mohammed's new religion spread through Arabia and beyond during the 600s and 700s, destroying Persia and threatening Byzantium. A vast territory including Spain, most of North Africa, virtually all of the Middle East, and parts of Central Asia came under Islamic control during these years, and further conquests awaited.

Most people who fell under Muslim rule converted to Islam, but territorial and economic control—not conversion for its own sake—was the main aim of these wars. Islamic theology divided the world into two spheres, **Dar al-Islam** ("house of peace"), where **Sharia law** was dominant and Muslims were therefore guaranteed the ability to worship freely, and Dar al-Harb ("house of war"), where Islam was not established. In early times, Muslim authorities viewed it as their duty to expand Dar al-Islam as far as possible, but while they insisted on political submission and did not extend full rights or equal treatment to non-Muslims, they did not generally force non-Muslims to change their faith—making them arguably more tolerant than Christian authorities in medieval Europe.

The Muslim world was governed by the **caliph** ("successor"), who combined political and religious power in one person. A key political principle here was the **circle of justice**, which predated the rise of Islam but nevertheless guided the caliphates and the Ottoman Empire that followed them. According to this notion of good government, the ruler gives justice to the people, the people pay taxes to the treasury, the treasury ensures that the army receives its salary, and the support of the army allows the ruler to exercise sovereignty—and to give justice to the people, thereby continuing the cycle. The first caliphs, including Mohammed's father-in-law Abu Bakr, ruled from Medina and presided over the early expansion of Islam. After the civil war that led to the **Sunni-Shiite split** (656–661), power passed to the Umayyad Caliphate (661–750), which governed from the Syrian city of Damascus. The Umayyad caliphs continued Islam's military expansion. They also made **Arabic**, the religion's holy language, the official language of the Muslim world, and they

TIP

Compare the ideal of Christendom espoused by Europe's medieval popes with the success enjoyed by the Islamic caliphs in combining religious and political authority, and compare the Middle East's "circle of justice" concept with that of the "mandate of heaven" in China.

started the practice of imposing a tax (**jizya**) on dhimmi, or those subjects who did not convert to Islam. A series of rebellions toppled the Umayyad caliphs.

Following the Umayyad regime was the **Abbasid Caliphate** (750–1258), which established a great capital at **Baghdad** and, as described in Chapter 2, presided over the golden age of classical Islamic culture, building many libraries and **madrasas**, or centers of learning. Up through the 800s, the Abbasid caliphs were strong, applying military force when necessary but for the most part providing peace and stability across the Islamic empire. Economic unity prevailed, and Abbasid trade networks linked the Middle East with Europe, Africa, the Indian Ocean, and Asia. Abbasid commerce was stimulated by the rise of credit and the creation of a single currency. Muslim manufacturers were among the most skilled in the world at this time, especially when it came to working **steel**. The most famous and best loved of the Abbasid caliphs was Haroun al-Rashid (776–809).

NOTE

The Mongol advance into the Middle East was stopped cold in 1260, when Mamluk cavalry defeated Mongol forces at the battle of Ain Jalut (Goliath Springs) in Syria.

Abbasid political unity began disintegrating in the 900s, owing to geographic over-extension, ethnic and cultural diversity (with the Sunni-Shiite split providing added stress), and the chaos caused by nomadic movements in North Africa and the Middle East. Persia, Syria, Egypt, and Spain slipped in and out from under Abbasid rule, and Baghdad fell to the Seljuk Turks in 1055—although the Seljuks kept the caliph in place as a figurehead. Abbasid weakness made it easier for the European **Crusades**, which began in the 1090s, to wreak havoc on the Middle East. The final blow came from the **Mongols**, who captured Baghdad in 1258 and killed the last Abbasid caliph.

Political confusion prevailed in the Middle East between the 1000s and the 1300s, with the Seljuk Turks badly damaging Byzantium at the 1071 battle of Manzikert, the entire region contending with the Crusades, a **Mamluk** (elite cavalry) state arising in Egypt and Syria in the 1250s, and the Mongols arriving in force, also in the mid-1200s. None of these states proved capable of centralizing the Middle East. The region also suffered during the early 1300s as the **Black Death** arrived from China.

Not until the 1300s did a dominant power begin to emerge in the Middle East: the **Ottoman Turks**, who settled in Asia Minor and founded their own state under Osman I (r. 1299–1326). Ottoman sultans claimed the status of caliphs, eventually gaining hegemony over the Middle East and moving into southeastern Europe and the eastern Mediterranean. To ensure the trustworthiness of their soldiers and civil servants, especially in outlying areas where local autonomy threatened (as it had during the Abbasid era), Ottoman rulers relied on the **devshirme** system, which forcibly recruited boys from non-Muslim families and placed them in positions of privileged servitude—with loyalty owed directly and solely to the sultan—as bureaucrats, **janissary** troops, and even clergy.

By the 1400s, the Ottomans managed to destroy the Byzantine Empire. The armies of Mehmet II made effective use of gunpowder artillery to bring about the **fall of Constantinople** in 1453—shocking all of Europe and setting the stage for a centuries-long Ottoman-Christian struggle.

Africa

In Africa during this period, the chief distinction between major societies was whether they adopted Islam or not. The strongest and richest tended to. Some areas were incorporated into Dar al-Islam by force. In others, the conversion proceeded peacefully, in many cases facilitated by trans-Saharan trade or Indian Ocean commerce along Africa's east coast.

Most of North Africa, from Egypt to Morocco, converted rapidly, coming under the authority of the caliphates until the Abbasid collapse and under that of the Ottoman Empire in later years. The **Mamluk sultanate** in Egypt, a breakaway state founded in the 1250s by elite soldiers who had formerly served the Abbasids, was a formidable military power until its conquest by the Ottomans in the early 1500s.

By the 1000s and 1100s, Islam was taking root not just in the Sahara but in several parts of sub-Saharan Africa. The southward and westward penetration of **Arab traders** played a crucial role in this process—although an unfortunate result was a significant expansion of the **Arab slave trade**, described further in Chapter 4. In West Africa, conversion was also carried out by the **Berbers**, nomadic camel herders and hardened warriors who embraced the new faith with great enthusiasm. From Marrakesh, in present-day Morocco, Berber clans known as the Almoravids extended Muslim authority far to the south.

West Africa was home to powerful Hausa kingdoms, located between Lake Chad and the Niger River and heavily involved in the region's salt trade, but most dominant politically were the Mande-speaking states closer to the Atlantic. Most famous of these before 1200 was **Ghana**, which played a prominent role in trans-Saharan commerce thanks to large deposits of gold. Ghana welcomed Muslim traders, and many of its people adopted Islam on a personal basis, but in the late 1000s, the state's failure to officially convert triggered an invasion from the north by the zealous Berbers. Ghana survived until the 1200s, when it was succeeded by another Mande state: **Mali** (mid-1200s–1600s), which Islamized with less violence. Well positioned in the Niger River basin, an important north-south trade route, Mali was blessed with gold and other metals. Trading also in salt, ivory, animal skins, and slaves, it emerged as a key point in the trans-Saharan trade network. Mali's empire was founded by the conquering prince **Sundiata Keita** (r. 1235–1255)—whose exploits are praised in a famed epic poem named after him—and its chief commercial and cultural hub, though not its capital, was **Timbuktu**. A stopping point for caravans, Timbuktu also became a renowned center of Islamic scholarship, home to key mosques and madrasas. Mali's peaceful conversion to Islam proved beneficial, enabling good relations with Arab and Berber states and creating a community of educated scholars who served as public servants. Mali's most powerful ruler was **Mansa Musa** (r. 1312–1337), a devout Muslim who gained fame throughout Africa and Europe as one of the world's wealthiest monarchs—a Spanish map of 1375 referred to Mali as home to the "richest and noblest king in all lands." Mansa Musa centralized the government and expanded trade. In 1324–1325, his hajj, or pilgrimage to Mecca, proved an international sensation, not least because he brought so much gold from Mali that when he spent it in the Middle East, he single-handedly caused a major devaluation of gold in the region. In the 1400s and 1500s, Mali's might weakened due to foreign attacks.

On the shores of East Africa, **Swahili city-states** flourished between 1000 and 1500. Here, nearly forty autonomous, or self-ruling, urban centers were sprinkled along 1,500 miles of coastline. All were heavily involved in the Indian Ocean trade network, and all were multiethnic, with Persians, Arabs, and others migrating here and mixing with the local Africans. Also adding to these cities' populations were migrants from India and Southeast Asia. Islam, along with other religions and traditions, played a prominent role on the East African coast, and a few of these city-states came to be ruled by Arab sheiks or merchant families. Key ports included Mogadishu, Mombasa, Sofala, and **Zanzibar**. The arrival of European colonists and merchants in the early 1500s would change this region beyond recognition.

In the non-Islamic parts of sub-Saharan Africa, a handful of sizable states arose. Among these were Kongo, Benin, Mutapa, and the mighty city of **Great Zimbabwe**. In most of sub-Saharan Africa, though, large and centralized political units developed later and more slowly than elsewhere. Even with a widespread **Bantu** heritage,

NOTE

Although northeastern Africa is predominantly Islamic, pockets of Christianity have survived there to this day. The Copts form a Christian minority in Egypt and Sudan, and Abyssinia (present-day Ethiopia) is home to a well-established Christian denomination of great antiquity.

more than two thousand languages and dialects are spoken here, and this tremendous diversity encouraged the development of distinct societies by small groups. Environmental factors also limited the rise of major states: fluctuating climate and human susceptibility to insect-borne diseases (especially **malaria**, along with yellow fever and sleeping sickness) proved serious obstacles to population growth.

East Asia

After the Han dynasty's fall in 220 C.E., China alternated between periods of political unity and fragmentation. Imperial collapse in China tended not to be as traumatic as the fall of Rome was for Europe, but it did cause turmoil. Stability returned for a time after the mid-500s, especially under the Tang dynasty (618–907), which recentralized the political system, enlarged the country's borders, expanded the **Grand Canal** (a vital artery that connected the Yellow and Yangzi Rivers), and built China's **silk industry** into a global near-monopoly. Unfortunately, neglect of the common people sparked a long series of peasant uprisings and caused the Tang's collapse in 907.

Following this breakdown, China fragmented into separate states until the late 1200s. The most durable and advanced was the **Song Empire** (960–1279), which ruled east-central China from the Yellow River in the north to the Vietnamese border in the south. In the 1120s, defeat at the hands of northern rivals, the Jurchen, forced the Song to withdraw to a much smaller southern state that survived until the Mongol conquest. Despite its political troubles, Song China enjoyed steady population growth, increased urbanization, thriving trade (the port of **Guangzhou**, or **Canton**, became one of the world's busiest and most cosmopolitan), and stupendous cultural and technological advancement. It was during the Song era that key innovations, such as **gunpowder**, the **magnetic compass**, a workable form of **movable-type printing**, and **paper money**, were invented or caught on widely. Like their Han and Tang predecessors, Song rulers subscribed to the **mandate of heaven** concept, which proposed that the emperor's authority was divinely ordained, so long as he remained virtuous. As before, the hierarchical doctrine of **Neo-Confucianism**—with its argument that commoners owed obedience to their superiors, who in turn owed them just treatment—was also used to justify imperial rule, and the Song government continued to select scholar-officials according to the **civil service examination**.

Mongol armies moved into Chinese territory in the early 1200s, soon after the rise of **Genghis Khan**. (For the **Mongols** themselves, see the next section.) Most of the west and north fell by the 1230s, but the Song resisted till 1271, when **Kublai Khan**, one of Genghis's grandsons, added it to his sizable list of conquests. Establishing his capital at Khanbaliq (present-day Beijing), Kublai proclaimed the **Yuan Empire** (1271–1368), and while he called himself Great Khan of the Mongols, he can be considered the first ruler in centuries to have reunified China as a single state. Kublai reigned until 1294 and made Yuan China rich and powerful. Although he attacked Japan and Java without success, his armies forced most of China's neighbors to pay tribute. As they did elsewhere, the Mongols in China adapted themselves to local ways: Kublai embraced Buddhism and made Mandarin Chinese the official language of his court. He rebuilt China's bureaucracy and economy, repaired roads and canals, built new cities, and restored trade with the West. The **Silk Road**, which had declined somewhat, recovered as a vital trade route. **Marco Polo** visited Yuan China, and the court of Kublai himself, in the late 1200s. The Yuan state was not so lucky after Kublai's death. During the early 1300s, China experienced the first wave of the bubonic plague epidemic known as the **Black Death**, losing 30 to 40 percent of its population before the disease moved to the Middle East and Europe. Economic decline resulted, and a series of civil wars—the **Red Turban revolts**—broke out in the 1340s, leading to the final rebellion that overthrew the Yuan.

When the rebel Zhu Yuanzhang defeated the Yuan by capturing Khanbaliq in 1368, he changed the capital's name to Beijing and established the **Ming dynasty** (1368–1644), named after the Red Turban faction he had commanded. As the **Hongwu emperor** (r. 1368–1398), he, along with his sons—especially the **Yongle emperor** (r. 1403–1424)—put the new regime on a solid foundation by repairing the damage done by the recent fighting and recentralizing the administrative system. The population and the economy both rebounded but not without cost. The Hongwu emperor ruthlessly purged the government of anyone he suspected of disloyalty, killing an estimated 100,000 in the process. Also, paper money had come to be seen as unreliable during the 1300s, and so China came to rely heavily on **silver currency**—a dependency that crippled the Ming in later years.

To restore imperial legitimacy, the Yongle emperor transformed Beijing into a magnificent capital by building the **Forbidden City** as a new seat of power. The early Ming rulers used their large and mighty army to increase territory; where they did not conquer outright, the Ming followed the traditional Chinese practice of forcing neighbors into a **tributary system**, in which nearby states avoided direct takeover by allowing China to extort money from them and dictate policy to them. For a short time, the Ming navy also served as an instrument of diplomacy and intimidation. From 1405 to 1433, the admiral **Zheng He** made seven long voyages to Southeast Asia, India, the Middle East, and East Africa. He expanded trade and learned much about the outside world—and with massive ships measuring four hundred feet in length and carrying a crew and soldiers in the thousands, he compelled fifty states and cities to pay tribute to his fleet. After the Yongle emperor's death, however, Ming rulers, distracted by the land-based threat of nomads to the north, lost interest in exploration and naval expansion, even going so far as to destroy China's oceangoing fleet. This was a global turning point: had the Ming continued to exploit their power at sea, China might have begun a wave of worldwide exploration and colonization, as the nations of Europe were on the verge of doing.

NOTE

Chinese emperors did not rule under their personal names. Upon taking the throne, they adopted a regnal name that applied also to the years of their rule. Technically, Chinese regnal names function as adjectives, not proper nouns, hence "the Hongwu emperor" (meaning "vastly martial") or "the Yongle emperor" ("perpetual happiness") rather than "Emperor Hongwu" or "Emperor Yongle"—although this improper usage is not uncommon in the West. Japanese emperors follow the same custom.

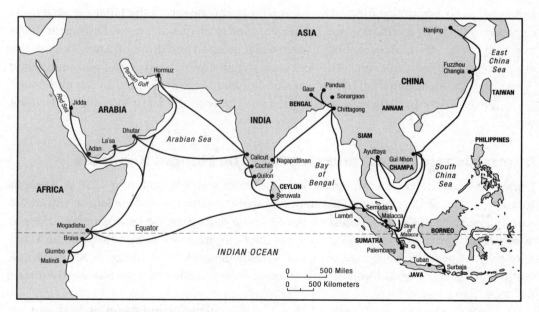

The Voyages of Zheng He, 1405–1433
China's greatest mariner, Zheng He, sailed several times from China to Arabia and East Africa. He explored, established diplomatic relations, and exacted monetary tribute from weaker states.

Japan, like other parts of the **Sinosphere**, or zone of Chinese cultural influence, was deeply affected by China in its bureaucratic methods, legal principles, and religious and artistic life. Prior to 1200, Japan had been nearing the end of its own classical era, known as the **Heian period** (794–1185), named after the emperor's capital city (present-day Kyoto). The Heian regime took an unusual shape. Although the emperor remained important as a symbolic figurehead, he lost his political power to the chancellor (*kwampaku*), whose duty it was to serve and protect the emperor. In practice, this meant keeping the emperor in seclusion and ruling in his name. In the mid-800s, the **Fujiwara clan** gained permanent control over the chancellorship, essentially making it Japan's ruling family until the mid-1100s. For years, the Fujiwara presided over a prosperous and artistically brilliant society. However, their pursuit of cultural refinement and their preoccupation with court politics caused them to neglect military affairs, which they delegated to various warrior clans. During the early 1100s, these clans quarreled among themselves and with the Fujiwara, leading to a terrible civil conflict known as the **Taira-Minamoto war** (1156–1185), in which each side supported a rival claimant to the emperor's throne. The Minamoto drove the Fujiwara from power, defeated the Taira, and created a new form of government: the shogunate.

The Minamoto victory marked Japan's transition to medieval **feudalism**. As before, the emperor retained his symbolic importance, but real power now rested with the **shogun**, or "great general." Two shogun regimes, the Kamakura and Ashikaga, ruled between the late 1100s and the late 1500s (the former gave way to the latter in the 1330s), and both coped with highly decentralized conditions. As monarchs in medieval Europe did with their knightly aristocracy, the shogun shared power with noble warlords called **daimyo**, who received control over parcels of land called *shoen*. Both the shogun and the daimyo belonged to the warrior elite known as **samurai**, who were privileged but also bound by a strict code of loyalty, honor, and bravery called **Bushido** ("way of the warrior"). Bushido was even more stringent and hierarchical than European chivalry; the most extreme penalty for violating it was ritual suicide (seppuku, or hara-kiri). Adherence to Bushido was supposed to govern the relationship between lords and vassals in the Japanese system, as opposed to the more formal contracts that were used in medieval Europe. During the 1200s and early 1300s, the Kamakura shoguns kept order in Japan and drove off Kublai Khan's two attempts to invade from China. The Ashikaga shoguns were weaker and allowed greater centralization. A combination of civil wars and peasant revolts erupted in the mid-1400s, leading to almost complete disunity by the 1500s. Only in the late 1500s and early 1600s would Japan reunify.

Interregional Contact and Conflict: The Mongol Khanates

During the early 1200s, the **Mongols**, nomadic horse warriors united in 1206 by **Genghis Khan**, burst out of the Central Asian steppes, rapidly creating one of the largest empires in world history. Their brief semiunification of Eurasia during the 1200s is known as the *pax Mongolica* ("Mongol peace"), and even after their empire broke apart into separate khanates, the Mongols facilitated the transfer of technologies, scientific and medical knowledge, cultural practices, and trade goods across Eurasia—particularly along the **Silk Road**—during the 1300s and into the 1400s.

The first wave of Mongol conquest lasted until Genghis Khan's death in 1227 and left the Mongols in charge of Mongolia, much of China, and parts of Central Asia, including the city of Samarkand. By the mid-1200s, his heirs had absorbed parts of Eastern Europe (especially most of Russia and Ukraine), portions of the Middle East, and all of China. Their westward drive was halted by Teutonic Knights and Hungarians in Eastern Europe and by Mamluk cavalry in Syria at the 1260 battle of **Ain Jalut**. They destroyed the Song Empire in China, the Abbasid Caliphate, and the Kievan city-state confederacy in Russia, among other states.

Over this massive expanse, the Mongols imposed a single political authority, revived Silk Road trade, and enforced law and order. The Mongols are frequently stereotyped as barbaric and indeed pacified enemies with great bloodthirstiness when they thought it necessary (the general who captured Baghdad in 1258 killed 200,000, many of them civilians, without hesitation). Still, they maintained rule not just by force but by a high level of administrative sophistication. They skillfully organized their army into decimally based units and quickly learned new military techniques—such as siegecraft—from neighbors and conquered peoples. In general, they were adept **cultural borrowers**. They adopted **Uighur** as a written script from Turkic neighbors; they took their paper currency and their law code (the *yasa*) from China; and they embraced Buddhism or Islam, depending on where they settled. They used their own aptitude as horse riders to create one of the premodern world's most efficient postal systems (the *yam*). From their subject peoples, the Mongols conscripted or enslaved soldiers, artisans, and others who possessed skills they needed.

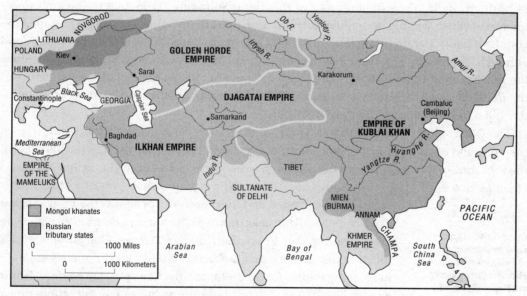

The Mongol Empires, 1294 c.e.
By 1294, the Mongols, a nomadic people, had conquered most of Asia and key portions of Europe and the Middle East. Mongol control over these territories had a major and lasting effect on many parts of Eurasia.

Even so, the Mongols were better at conquering than governing. As a Chinese official famously described the Mongols: "One can conquer an empire on horseback, but one cannot govern it from there." The last khan to rule over a united Mongol state, Genghis's grandson Mongke, died in 1260. After a brief civil war, the empire's four largest units became independent khanates. The homeland, which included Mongolia and Yuan China, went to **Kublai Khan** (r. 1260–1294 as Great Khan, from 1271 as Yuan emperor).

The Golden Horde kept Russia under its yoke until the mid-1400s. The Il-Khan Mongols converted to Islam and ruled much of the Middle East until the rise of the Ottoman Turks. The Jagatai Khanate governed Central Asia well into the 1400s, becoming Muslims like their Il-Khan rivals.

From 1370 to 1405, the Jagatai khan **Timur** (also known as Tamerlane) attempted to repeat the military triumphs of Genghis Khan, moving into Persia, southern Russia, parts of the Middle East, and northern India. This expansion ceased after Timur's death, but his descendants ruled Central Asia until the 1500s.

South Asia

As China did in East Asia, India exerted tremendous cultural and religious influence over large portions of South and Southeast Asia. Hinduism and Buddhism both spread outward from there, as did key concepts, like the wrongly named **Arabic numerals** (along with the concepts of zero and pi). One key difference from China, though, was lack of political unity, for there was no single nation called India—especially after the mid-500s C.E., with the collapse of the Gupta Empire (which itself had ruled only the north-central part of the subcontinent). Instead, for many centuries, a quiltwork of small kingdoms and city-states existed throughout India and the nearby island of Sri Lanka.

Greater consolidation came to India in 1206, when Muslim invaders, who had been battering away at the northwestern frontier since the 900s, captured Delhi and moved into much of northern India. The establishment of this **Delhi Sultanate** (1206–1526)—the key consequence of which was the permanent **introduction of Islam** to India—decisively reshaped the country's politics and culture. The first Delhi sultans imposed their new faith harshly, and although they became less severe with time, division and tensions continued to characterize the relationship between Hindus and Muslims long after the sultanate faded away. Between the mid-1200s and the mid-1300s, the Delhi Sultanate expanded to control most of modern-day India, centralizing as it did so.

The Delhi sultans' peak did not last long, as states and cities in the south began to resist their rule and break away in the 1300s. Some of these were Islamic, like the Gujarat Sultanate in the west, one of the many **Rajput kingdoms** governed by leaders—both Hindu and Muslim—claiming descent from old warrior castes. (In Sanskrit, *rajput* means "son of a king.") Most were Hindu, however, and most powerful of all was the **Vijayanagara Empire** (1336–1646), also known as the Karnata Empire. Vijayanagara monarchs rose up in southern India's Deccan Plateau and retook much of the territory that the Delhi sultans had conquered there. To make things worse for the sultanate, the Central Asian warlord **Timur** attacked Delhi from the north, capturing it in 1398 and plundering it for a year. The sultanate survived, but barely, then continued to shrink until succumbing itself to new invaders in the 1520s.

NOTE

The island of Sri Lanka and the nearby southeastern tip of India experienced their own political and religious tensions, with Tamil-speaking Hindus (prevalent mostly on the mainland) and devoutly Buddhist Sinhalese (the majority population on the island) competing for dominance throughout the region. Tamil-Sinhalese strife remains a point of friction in Sri Lanka to this day, and the more recent arrival of a Muslim minority has further complicated this mix.

What remained in India was a society very much divided by religion and culture. Even after the arrival of Islam, Hindus maintained their **caste system** and practices like the **sati** ritual (according to which women of certain castes were burned alive with their dead husbands). Where Muslims ruled, they sometimes imposed the **jizya**, or nonbeliever's tax, on the Hindu majority and other non-Muslims; in other regions, Muslim minorities were not always well-treated. Such sectarian differences have not been eliminated, even today.

Divided or not, most Indian states played vital roles in the flourishing **Indian Ocean trade network**, as described in Chapter 4. The same is true of their neighbors in Southeast Asia. Prior to 1200, two major states had exerted power there for centuries. On the mainland, in present-day Cambodia, stood the **Khmer** (or Angkor) **Empire** (800s–1450s), while the sea-borne **Srivijayan Empire** (500s–1100s) governed many of the Indonesian islands and parts of the Malay Peninsula between the 500s and the 1100s. Both were strongly influenced by Indian culture—as demonstrated by **Angkor Wat**, the Khmer Empire's architectural masterpiece— and both bore the imprint of Hinduism and Buddhism.

Between 1200 and 1500, power in Southeast Asia flowed to newer political units. The Khmer Empire declined in strength relative to neighbors like Burma, the Vietnamese states of Annam and Champa, and the **Sukhothai kingdom** (1238–1538), generally considered the ancestor of the modern Thai state, especially after its union with other Siamese states in the late 1400s and early 1500s. To the south, naval power passed from Srivijaya to the **Majapahit Empire**, founded in Java in 1293 by one of the military leaders who resisted Kublai Khan's assault on the island that year. Preeminent in the region until about 1500, Majapahit quickly conquered or forced into tribute nearly a hundred islands and cities, including virtually all of modern Indonesia, parts of the Philippines, and some of the Malay Peninsula. Its religious and cultural life was principally a fusion of Hindu and Buddhist elements—although Islam arrived in Java and Sumatra in the 1200s, and it remains centrally important in Indonesia today.

During those years, **city-states** were also an important form of political organization in Southeast Asia. The Malaysian port of **Melaka** (Malacca), which sits at a key chokepoint between the Indian and Pacific islands, is a notable example. The Sultanate of Malacca, established around 1400, found support from China as a check on the maritime and economic power of Majapahit.

In Oceania, the key development of this period was the end of the **Polynesian migrations**. This had proceeded since around 1000–900 B.C.E., slowly seeding the islands of the vast Pacific with human populations, along with new plants and animals. The settlement of the Maori on the islands of New Zealand, around 1200 C.E., is considered to have completed this long process.

STATE FORMATION IN THE PRE-COLUMBIAN AMERICAS

The geographical isolation of the Americas from Afro-Eurasia continued until the end of the 1400s, when the voyages of Christopher Columbus brought the societies of North and South America into sustained contact with outsiders. In the historiography of the Americas, the period before 1492 is referred to as the **pre-Columbian era**.

North America

In North America, most early natives tended toward nomadic lifestyles. Not counting Mexico, two regions of North America became home to more settled, agriculturally successful societies. One was the Southwest, where settlement began in the 300s B.C.E. and where **Ancestral Puebloans** (once commonly known as Anasazi), among others, inhabited the region from about 400 (perhaps earlier) to 1300. They lived in complex dwellings known as **pueblos**, sometimes built on mesas or in caves high up in the canyons, as in Chaco and Mesa Verde.

Cliff Palace Dwelling, Mesa Verde
The Cliff Palace complex at what is now the Mesa Verde National Park. Built by Ancestral Puebloans, most likely for defensive purposes, ca. 1200 C.E., it was abandoned by ca. 1300 C.E., most likely because of worsening drought conditions. Those who lived here farmed and hunted on the mesa above.

To the north and east, sophisticated societies emerged in the Ohio and Mississippi River valleys. The most advanced of these **earth mound**–building cultures was the **Mississippian civilization** (ca. 700–1500). The Mississippians also built cities, the largest of which was **Cahokia**, with a population of over 30,000 between 1000 and 1200. For unknown reasons that may include the deforestation and/or soil depletion that came with trying to support such a large number of denizens, Cahokia's people started to abandon the city after 1250; it stood virtually empty by about 1350. The Mississippian culture as a whole fell into a long decline. At around this time, Native Americans began to form smaller hunter-forager groups that evolved into the major tribes the Europeans would encounter in the 1500s and that remain familiar today.

Mexico and Mesoamerica

In Mexico and Mesoamerica, many societies emerged from the religious and cultural foundations left by the **Olmecs**, the region's "mother civilization" that faded from the scene around 400 B.C.E.

All post-Olmec civilizations had their own unique features, but most shared key characteristics as well. Among these were religious practices that centered on **human sacrifice** and the building of **pyramids**, which symbolized sacred mountains reaching to the heavens but also rooted in the underworld. Also common was an aptitude for **city-building** (with a population of 200,000, Teotihuacán ranked as one of the world's largest cities) and **intensive agriculture** to make the most of limited space. Farming methods included swamp drainage, elaborate irrigation systems, the terracing of hillsides, and, in some places, the construction of "floating islands" (chinampas) in shallow lakes. Staple crops included beans, squash, and maize (**corn**), as well as cacao, from which **chocolate** is made. The domestication of animals for food or labor was next to nonexistent.

Among the region's most noteworthy groups were the **Maya**, whose classical period lasted from 250 to 900 C.E. and whose regional relevance continued after that. The Mayan culture emerged in present-day Guatemala and spread as far north as southern Mexico. Governance of Mayan lands was divided among approximately forty city-states and kingdoms with a total population that reached at least 3 million. Conflict among these states was common, as was the enslavement of wartime captives.

The Maya practiced intensive agriculture, although most communities had little access to lakes or rivers and were forced to rely on a network of *cenotes*, or limestone sinkholes, for water management. Mayan kings served both as politicians and as priests, and they satisfied their polytheistic gods—which included jaguar deities and the winged serpent Quetzalcoatl—by means of human sacrifice. They built pyramids, the most famous of which can be found at **Chichén Itzá**. The Maya devised an elaborate **hieroglyphic script**, the most advanced system of writing in the pre-Columbian Americas. Superb astronomers and mathematicians, they understood the concept of **zero** and invented an intricate and accurate **long-count calendar**. The reasons for Mayan decline, indicated by the abandonment of many cities between 800 and 900 C.E., remain a mystery. Theories include warfare, social unrest, nearby volcanic activity, and resource depletion caused by overuse of the land. Given the fragility of the *cenote* network, drought is another plausible explanation. Although the Mayan classical era is considered to have ended after 900, several cities (including Chichén Itzá) lasted into the 1200s and beyond, and the Mayans themselves, along with their languages, have survived into the present.

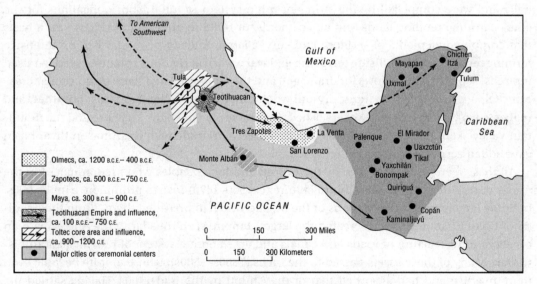

States in Pre-Columbian Central America, ca. 1200 B.C.E.–1200 C.E.
This map demonstrates that, in Central America, many civilizations developed, rose, and fell in succession. The Olmecs set the pattern for cultural development here, followed by the Maya, Toltecs, and Aztecs.

Increasingly warlike peoples filled the political vacuum left behind by the Mayans. Among these were the Toltecs, an aggressive warrior society that ruled much of central Mexico between the 800s and the 1100s. Even more powerful were the Nahuatl-speaking **Aztecs**

(1200s–1500s), or **Mexica**, who reached their military peak with a triple alliance that joined the cities of Texcoco and Tlacopan with **Tenochtitlán** on the site of what is today Mexico City. By the 1400s, the Aztecs controlled an empire encompassing more than 125,000 square miles, with an estimated population of 5 to 12 million, perhaps more. Tenochtitlán, as the chief metropolis, was home to half a million, and its marketplace alone could hold 60,000 people. Intensive agriculture, in particular the **chinampa** technique of building floating islands in shallow lakes, supported this vast populace. The Aztec economy as a whole benefited from an extensive network of roads.

The Aztecs thrived until the early 1500s, when the Spanish arrived. Like others in the region, the Aztecs adopted the cultural and religious practices of **pyramid-building** and **human sacrifice**. Subject peoples were taxed by a **tributary system** that provided the Aztecs with foodstuffs and gold. While this enriched the Aztecs, it caused deep hatred among those they had conquered, and this proved a crucial point of vulnerability against European invasion. Defeat of the Aztecs led to Spanish domination of Mexico and Central America until the 1800s.

The Andes

In South America's Andes Mountains, a number of societies achieved a high degree of centralization and advancement, beginning with the Chavin as early as 1000 B.C.E. and including the Moche from around 200 C.E. to 700 C.E.

Most of these **Andean civilizations** had certain features in common. Writing was unknown here, but most Andean peoples used the knot-tying method of **quipu** to keep records. Andean social hierarchies assigned people to clans, called **ayllu**, that owned land communally and were compelled by the stringent **mit'a** system to fulfill labor obligations for the elite—farming, tending llama and alpaca herds, or building roads and bridges—on a basis that combined elements of serfdom and corvée labor. Andean peoples relied on intensive farming techniques like **hillside terracing** and **waru waru** agriculture (planting seed in raised mounds, separated by furrows for drainage), and they domesticated **llamas** and similar creatures (alpacas, vicuñas) for transport and wool. Chief crops included quinoa, **potatoes**, and **maize** (**corn**), while coastal dwellers fished. Commerce between the seashore and the mountain valleys kept Andean economies well balanced, and trade with the Amazon River basin gave added access to fruit and other foodstuffs.

All these features were shared by the Chimú and Inca peoples who predominated in the Andes during this period. The **Chimú** culture (ca. 900–1470) rose to prominence in the 900s, building largely on the foundations of the Moche who had preceded them. From their capital of Chan Chan, the Chimú created the largest empire seen thus far in the Andes, with an excellent infrastructure of roads and canals and an elaborate system of provincial administration. Many of these assets passed to the **Incas** (1300s–1500s), whose empire became even more massive and had absorbed that of the Chimú by the mid-1400s. Having settled the **Cusco** region in the 1200s, the Incas rapidly expanded in the 1300s and 1400s until their state stretched three thousand miles from north to south and extended from the Pacific coast in the west to the upper Amazon in the east.

As with the Chimú, keys to Incan power included a road network measuring more than 13,000 miles, a complex bureaucracy, and extreme social stratification legitimized by religious belief. The ruler, known as the Great Inca, was considered the descendant of the sun god; to look at him directly was punishable by death, and he legally owned all property in the

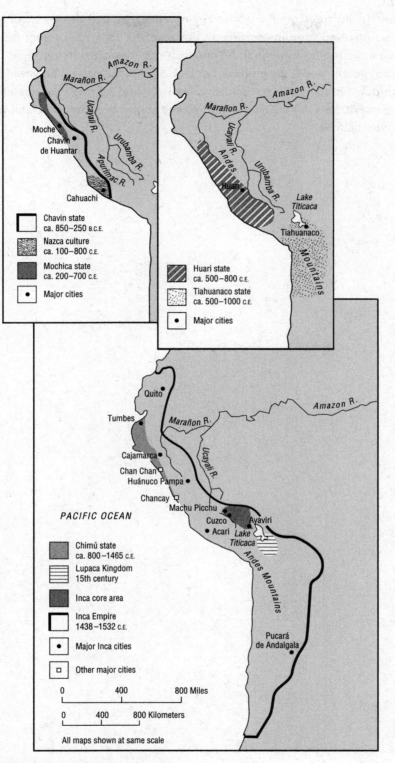

Andean Civilizations, ca. 850 B.C.E.–1532 C.E.

The earliest major civilizations of South America emerged in the Andes Mountains, on the continent's western coast. The last and greatest was the Incan Empire.

Incan state. (Incan sun worship, whose key temples included the great complex of **Machu Picchu**, also involved **human sacrifice**.) Thus justified, Inca rulers went on to make mit'a labor much more burdensome than before. Inca might reached its zenith in the 1400s, with 4 to 6 million people under the empire's control. As with the Aztecs, however, the Inca would be brought down in the 1500s by Spanish colonists—and for the Incas as well as the Aztecs, underlying resentment among their exploited subject peoples proved a fatal weakness when foreign armies arrived.

Cultural Developments and Interactions, 1200–1450

2

The level of cultural sophistication rose worldwide during this era. Much of this stemmed from the global tendency toward greater interregional connectedness. Trade, migration, empire building, and cross-cultural mixing led to the diffusion of religious practices, intellectual trends, and artistic and architectural styles.

At the same time, individual regions experienced their own cultural changes and advancements. Be aware of this balance between **cultural diffusion** and **independent innovation**. Whether they were imported from abroad or homegrown, the distinct characteristics of each of the world's major cultures should be familiar to you, as should be the general developments that caused cultures to influence each other.

CROSS-CULTURAL EXCHANGE AND CULTURAL GROWTH

Key instances of **cross-cultural exchange** shaped the art, literature, and traditions of many parts of the world during this era. As you study the cultural features of individual societies, as outlined two sections below, also remain aware of the following systems of regionwide or interregional cultural interchange:

- Chinese influence over East and Southeast Asia (the Sinosphere): especially important for spreading not just artistic and architectural styles but also systems of writing (Chinese pictographs were incorporated into Korean and Japanese scripts) and religious beliefs, including Buddhism and Neo-Confucian principles of hierarchy and filial piety.

- India's influence over South and Southeast Asia: particularly noteworthy for the fusion of Buddhism and Hinduism that radiated outward from the subcontinent and can be seen in famous places of worship like the Khmer complex of Angkor Wat and Indonesia's Borobudur temple.
- The *pax Mongolica*: established along the Silk Road by the Mongol khanates, facilitating cultural, economic, and technological diffusion.
- Islam's influence over Africa: felt with particular strength in North and West Africa but also along the eastern Swahili-speaking coast.
- Islam's influence in Asia: most evident in Central Asia but reaching as far as India and Southeast Asia, where modern-day Indonesia contains the world's fourth-largest Muslim population. Note that Persian as well as Arabic became influential in the cultural sphere that linked the Middle East with India.
- Mesoamerican and Andean cultural similarities: the many societies that rose, fell, and interacted in these areas tended to pass on common fundamental features, either as they succeeded each other or while they coexisted.

TRANSNATIONAL LANGUAGES

Throughout history, certain languages have risen up to allow communication between cultures whose native tongues are very different. The term *lingua franca* is often used to describe them. Examples include Latin; Arabic; Swahili; the sign language used by Native American tribes on the Great Plains; and, increasingly in our own time, English. A language achieves the status of lingua franca for various reasons. In some cases, it is the shared religious language of people who are ethnically different; in others, it is the tongue that most effectively facilitates trade in a multilingual region. Sometimes it is imposed by a military or imperial power (like Spanish in Latin America or English in India).

Many languages were affected by cross-cultural exchange, especially by the migration of peoples and the movement of trade goods. Silk Road commerce helped to spread **Turkic** languages throughout the Asiatic expanse between modern-day Turkey and Mongolia, particularly once the Mongol khanates adopted the **Uighur** script to provide their own language with a written form. The expansion of Islam propelled **Arabic**, the religion's holy language, even further, giving it a prominent cultural role not just in the Middle East but all the way from North Africa to the borderlands of India. (**Persian** became similarly important throughout much of Islamic Eurasia.) The migration of the **Bantu** peoples throughout sub-Saharan Africa profoundly affected linguistic development in many parts of the continent. Specifically in East Africa, trade and the mixing of ethnicities (not only African but from Arabia and the Indian Ocean basin) led to the creation of **Swahili**, the region's widely adopted lingua franca, or common tongue.

FAR FROM HOME: INTERREGIONAL TRAVELERS

Several interregional travelers from this period created important ties between distant societies or, through their writings, raised geographical and cultural awareness.

One of the first Europeans to cross the breadth of Eurasia, the young merchant **Marco Polo** traveled from Venice to Asia along the Silk Road during the mid-to-late 1200s. His journeys occupied nearly a quarter century, from 1271 to 1295, and if he is to be believed, he befriended Kublai Khan, the Mongol ruler of Yuan China. Although scholars today are not sure how far to trust his autobiography (*Books of the Marvels of the World*, better known as *The Travels of Marco Polo*), Marco Polo's writings played an enormous role in familiarizing medieval and Renaissance Europeans with the luxurious riches and cultural advancements of Asia—and in stoking the desire of Europeans to travel and trade there. Christopher Columbus was merely one of countless Europeans to read Marco Polo's descriptions of Asia with intense interest.

Venturing in the opposite direction, although roughly at the same time, was the monk **Rabban bar Sawma** (ca. 1220–1294). Of Central Asian Turkic ancestry, bar Sawma lived in Yuan China and followed Nestorian Christianity, a denomination that spread eastward and gained a certain popularity among Mongols and other Asian peoples along the Silk Road. As an emissary of the Yuan regime, he trekked to Jerusalem and then to France, seeking to form an alliance with Catholic monarchs and crusaders against the Islamic states of the Middle East. These negotiations came to nothing in the end, but they made for a fascinating encounter.

The great explorer of the Islamic world was **Ibn Battuta** of Morocco, who began a pilgrimage to Mecca in 1325 and, instead of returning, embarked on a journey lasting almost thirty years and covering over 70,000 miles. Not only did he visit most of Islamic Africa and the Middle East, he also ventured throughout Central Asia, East Asia, and South Asia, going as far as the Indonesian islands. His journal, *Travels*, reveals the remarkable diversity of customs and cultural practices among Muslim people, and Ibn Battuta was often surprised—and sometimes shocked—by how different lifestyles could be among various peoples technically joined together by allegiance to a common faith.

Another traveler to know from this era is **Zheng He**, the Chinese captain who took ships of the Ming navy on seven far-ranging voyages through the Indian and Pacific Oceans during the early 1400s. He is described in more detail in Chapter 1.

OLD AND NEW TRADITIONS: CULTURAL DEVELOPMENTS BY REGION

Medieval and Renaissance Europe

For years, it was common to view Europe's **medieval period** as the Dark Ages, an era completely lacking in culture. It is now more standard to recognize the richness of medieval culture—but it remains true that Europe (aside from Byzantium) lagged far behind the Middle East and East Asia in terms of cultural attainment and that when it did move forward, it was largely due to outside influences. Also, change over time was key: the Early Middle Ages (ca. 500–1000) were genuinely backward, and it was the High Middle Ages (ca. 1000–1300) that witnessed substantial cultural advancement. For most of Europe, the period between 1300 and 1500 is considered the Late Middle Ages, while Italy was already undergoing the cultural revival known as the **Renaissance**.

The most important factor shaping Europe's medieval culture was the Christian church. During the chaos that followed the fall of Rome, the church played an indispensable role in preserving Greco-Roman manuscripts and, at least in Western and Central Europe, promoting **Latin** as an international language of learning. The **ideal of Christendom**, according to which all European nations should be bound together by their allegiance to the church, played an important role in medieval Europe—even though the church split formally after the Great Schism of 1054, which divided **Roman Catholicism** (Latin based and governed by the Roman papacy) from **Eastern Orthodoxy** (Greek inspired and headquartered in Byzantium). Throughout the medieval period, the Catholic and Orthodox Churches provided the vast majority of employment opportunities for artists, architects, and musicians. On the other hand, both churches strictly controlled culture and severely punished art, literature, and ideas that fell out of line with church doctrine.

The writings of Aristotle on science, ethics, and politics were at the center of the medieval worldview, but there is some irony to the way Europeans learned from him during the Middle Ages. For one thing, not all of his writings met with the church's approval. More important, many of the factual errors contained in his scientific writings were unquestioningly accepted by medieval Europeans—even though Aristotle, following a logic similar to the modern *scientific method*, had argued that scientific views needed to be constantly improved and updated by means of testing and careful observation.

The dominant philosophy of the Middle Ages was **scholasticism**, an attempt to reconcile Greco-Roman learning from the past with Christian teachings. Adaptation of the former was limited for two reasons: it was dangerous to accept Greco-Roman ideas that the church objected to, and most medieval scholars were less familiar with Greek than with Latin and tended to know Greek thinkers like Plato and **Aristotle** only through Latin translations. Medieval scientific understanding was based mainly on Greco-Roman ideas that the church found acceptable. While this was of some benefit, it also encouraged mistaken ideas, especially regarding medicine and astronomy, where the church chose to adopt the **geocentric theory**, which proposed that the sun revolves around the earth.

Medieval cultural achievements include the architectural sophistication of Europe's **castles** and **cathedrals**, with the relatively simple Romanesque style giving way to the incredibly ornate Gothic style during the High Middle Ages. Icons, or religious paintings, were inspired by Byzantine styles, even in Catholic Europe, and the best-known form of church music was plainsong, or Gregorian chant. Secular music arose in the form of **troubadour poems**, which celebrated love, the gentlemanly code of **chivalry**, and adventuresome heroes like King Arthur and his knights.

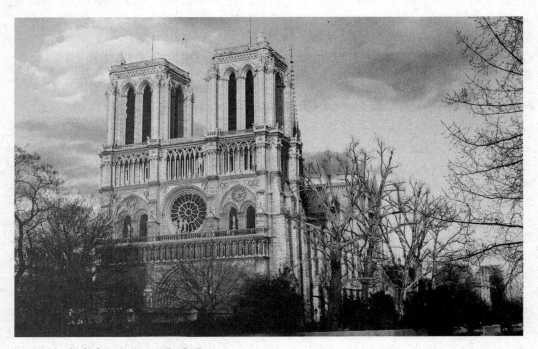

Cathedral of Notre Dame, Paris, France
One of the best-known landmarks of Paris, the Cathedral of Notre Dame provides a quintessential example of the Gothic style of church architecture.

Europe's first **universities** appeared during this time, both as centers of religious training and as places to learn law and medicine. During the Late Middle Ages, two other trends accelerated the spread of learning in Europe. One was the increased use by the 1200s and 1300s of native, or **vernacular**, languages instead of Latin by poets and other authors, including

Geoffrey Chaucer of England and Dante Alighieri of Italy. This stimulated a growth in literacy and made literature available to a wider range of people. The same is true of the second development: the invention by **Johannes Gutenberg** of the first cost-effective **movable-type printing press** during the early 1400s.

By the late 1200s and early 1300s, certain parts of Europe, particularly Italy, began to experience the cultural rebirth known as the **Renaissance**—prominent in Italy between the early 1300s and the early 1500s and prevalent in the rest of Europe between the late 1400s and the early 1600s. Italy's thriving trade-based economy, its exposure to wider cultural influences throughout the Mediterranean, and the growing familiarity of its scholars with Greek science and philosophy (thanks to cultural contacts with their Jewish and Islamic counterparts in Muslim Spain) all caused significant advancements in art, literature, architecture, and science. The cardinal principles of the Renaissance were classicism (a greater emphasis than before on Greco-Roman influences), secularism (more frequently painting or writing about nonreligious subjects, although religion remained important and Renaissance artists had to take care not to violate church dictates), and **humanism**—the conviction that to be human is something to rejoice in. This last concept, derived from Greco-Roman culture, ran counter to the prevailing medieval view that to be human was to be tainted with sin and that worldly life was less important than the heavenly afterlife. Prominent figures from the Italian Renaissance include the writers Petrarch and Boccaccio, the political theorist Niccolò Machiavelli, and the artists Leonardo da Vinci and Michelangelo.

Islam and the Middle East

Under the Abbasid Caliphate (750–1258), the Middle East enjoyed such tremendous artistic and intellectual sophistication that it is common among historians to refer to this as the **Islamic golden age**. During this time, the cultural contacts of the Middle East and North Africa with Byzantium, China, and India were extensive. Mathematical, astronomical, and scientific aptitude among Muslim scholars was great. They developed **algebra** and popularized the use of **Arabic numerals** (originally from India). The *Canon of Medicine*, by the Persian physician **Avicenna** (Ibn Sina, 980–1037), remained the most authoritative medical text in the Middle East and Europe until the 1600s.

As Christianity did in medieval Europe, Islam decisively influenced cultural life in the caliphate. Muslim authorities determined what was acceptable art or literature. Because the Qur'an forbids the worship of graven images, for example, Islamic art during these years tended to feature geometric patterns and shapes rather than human or animal figures—although this was not a hard-and-fast rule. The chief centers of learning were **madrasas**, or religious colleges, and a main thrust of Islamic philosophy, as with the scholastics of Christian Europe, was to investigate the relationship between human reason and religious faith. **Averroës** (1126–1198), a doctor from Muslim Spain, translated and analyzed the works of the Greek philosopher Aristotle, a key step in reintroducing his ideas to medieval Europe as a whole. Also from Muslim Spain and also important in refamiliarizing Europe with Aristotelian thought was the Jewish thinker **Maimonides** (1135–1204), whose *Guide to the Perplexed* attempted to reconcile the rationality of Greco-Roman thought with Jewish theology.

Key centers of learning in the Muslim world included Timbuktu, in the kingdom of Mali, as well as universities in Fez and Cairo that dated back to the ninth and tenth centuries.

NOTE

A key example of Islamic architecture from these years is the Topkapi Palace in Istanbul, built in the mid-1400s by the Ottoman sultan Mehmet II, largely in celebration of his 1453 conquest of Constantinople. In the way it was meant to impress people as a symbol of imperial might and political grandeur, it can be compared with the Forbidden City in Beijing, constructed roughly at the same time by the rulers of Ming China.

Greatest in fame was the **House of Wisdom**, founded in Baghdad during the 700s by the early Abbasid caliphs. This was a grand collection of manuscripts and a vital center for scholarly translation work. Because it was destroyed by the Mongols during their 1258 sack of Baghdad, much uncertainty unfortunately remains about its exact functions, the degree to which it was open to the public, and the size of its library.

Arabic was both the holy language of Islam and the principal language of cultural and intellectual life in the Muslim world, just as Latin was for the Christians of medieval Europe. However, starting in the 800s and 900s, **Persian** joined Arabic as a language of high status in Islamic thought and literature. Classics of Islamic writing from this period include **Ibn Battuta**'s *Travels*, described above, as well as *The Thousand Nights and a Night*, known in the West as *The Arabian Nights* and featuring the famed tales of Sinbad the Sailor, Ali Baba, and Aladdin. Also important is the *Rubaiyat* of **Omar Khayyám**, a mathematician and astronomer who composed this collection of bittersweet, meditative poems in the early 1100s. Increasingly popular during the Abbasid years was **Sufism**, a mystical strain of Islam that emphasizes union with Allah by means of spiritual exercises like chanting and dancing. The Sufi poet **Rumi** gave expression to these ideas in his verses during the 1200s.

Africa

The sheer size of Africa and its ethnic diversity make it difficult to speak briefly about African culture in general. For many centuries, non-Africans tended to view African art as primitive and to theorize that African societies advanced technologically only by borrowing from other peoples. Recent years have seen a greater acknowledgment of how skillfully produced African arts and crafts are and also of the fact that most African societies discovered advanced metalworking and architectural techniques on their own.

That said, **Islamic culture** powerfully shaped artistic and intellectual life in many parts of Africa. Most of North Africa and much of the Sahara became part of the Islamic caliphates, and Islam, if not necessarily Muslim rule, came to West African states like Mali. Islam also blended with indigenous African traditions in the **Swahili ports** along the East African coast. By comparison, the bulk of sub-Saharan Africa remained much less touched by Islamic influence.

Whether in North Africa or the sub-Saharan zones, African artists produced intricate beadwork and masterful carvings and sculptures out of wood, ivory, and metal. (The **Benin bronzes** and other metalworks from West African states are particularly renowned.) African textiles exhibited bold colors and patterns.

Architecture varied across regions owing to diverse cultural influences, both Islamic and indigenous. The **mud-and-timber constructions** of West Africa, best exemplified by the Sankore Mosque in **Timbuktu**, show a unique fusion of Islamic function with local style. The architecture of Zanzibar, on the eastern coast, is distinguished by the use of coral to decorate buildings. The vast walls enclosing **Great Zimbabwe** were constructed so sturdily that, for many years, European colonizers insisted that they must have been erected later than they actually were, because they refused to believe that Africans could have built something so precisely without learning how to do so from Europeans. For many years, Great Zimbabwe's imposing stone enclosure was the largest human-made structure in sub-Saharan Africa.

THE MOSQUE OF SANKORÉ

Sankore Mosque, Timbuktu, Mali
Built in the 1300s, during the reign of Mansa Musa, the Sankore Mosque served not only as a place of worship but also as a famed library and madrasa, or Islamic university. Its unique mud-and-stick construction demonstrates the blending of Islamic cultural influence with architectural styles indigenous to northwest Africa.

African literature of this period was preserved by **oral tradition**. Professional storytellers—best known by the West African term **griots**—chronicled history and social custom. They also acted as entertainers and advised chiefs and rulers. The most famous African epic from these years comes from Mali, dating from the 1300s. This is the *Sundiata*, named after the chieftain who founded the Mali state and relating, semifictionally, his many exploits.

Asia and Oceania

In China during the Song period and again during the Ming dynasty (1368–1644), there was a great revival of Confucius's teachings—**Neo-Confucianism**—that reinforced China's cultural tendency toward hierarchy and obedience, in line with the ideal of filial piety. During the various political crises of the Song years, Neo-Confucianism served as an important unifying factor in a politically divided China, and the Ming emperors relied on it as a tool to justify their rule. As before, most government officials gained their posts by scoring well on rigorous **civil service examinations**, which, among other things, tested knowledge of the Confucian classics. After about 600 C.E., a new form of Buddhism, **Ch'an** (known as **Zen** in Japan), emerged in China. Stressing simplicity and meditation, it became very popular, both in China and abroad.

China's emperors were generous cultural patrons. As noted elsewhere, China interacted culturally with the Abbasid Caliphate, and it heavily influenced neighbors like Korea, Vietnam, and Japan both artistically and religiously. The Ming years remain famous as a time of artistic grandeur and intellectual dynamism in China. The architectural masterpiece of the early Ming period is the **Forbidden City**, the imperial residence erected in Beijing during the early 1400s both to serve as a seat of government and to impress onlookers with the regime's power and grandeur. Key works of early Ming literature include *The Golden Lotus*, a novel about a wicked landowner. In addition to manufacturing **silk**, Ming artisans produced some of the most exquisite glassware and **porcelain** the world has ever seen. Another major art form was scroll painting, which depicted landscapes and other scenes on vertical rolls of silk and paper.

In Japan, the Heian (794–1185) period marked a time of cultural brilliance and, after about 1000, growing independence from Chinese influences. Japanese religious life had long been shaped by the importation from China through Korea of Buddhism and, to a lesser extent, Confucianism and Daoism, all of which coexisted with Shinto, Japan's native faith. The poetry, art, and architecture of China also had a profound impact on Japanese style. Chinese influence never vanished, but by the eleventh century, the Japanese had begun to develop their own more distinct artistic tradition. Heian painters reached a high degree of skill, and one of the classics of world literature, *The Tale of Genji*, a story of love and court life by **Lady Murasaki**, dates to this period. It is considered by some to be the world's first true novel.

Heian Jingu Shrine, Kyoto, Japan
Kyoto, the old capital of Japan, still contains many architectural masterpieces from the Heian era (794–1185), when the city was known by that name. Heian was a major center of Buddhist worship and scholarship, and China's cultural and artistic influence was felt heavily there.

Things changed even more dramatically after the collapse of the Heian regime in the late 1100s and the rise of the medieval shogunates. Although the code of **Bushido** ("way of the warrior") required samurai to be culturally refined as well as loyal and brave, artistic pursuits became less centrally important than during the Heian period. An epic but melancholy work of literature from this era, *Tales of the Heike*, describes the Taira-Minamoto war (1156–1185) that destroyed the Heian regime. New forms of Buddhism arrived: **Zen**, whose emphasis on self-discipline appealed to the samurai elite, while Pure Land (Jo Do) promised a heavenly afterlife and gained a large following among the lower classes. Zen's philosophical simplicity affected several important cultural practices, such as the *cha-no-yu* tea ceremony, landscaping (rock gardens and bonsai trees), and haiku poetry.

Both the Indian subcontinent and the island chains of Southeast Asia are home to many ethnic groups, dozens of different languages, and many minor and major religions. Key themes here include cultural fusion throughout the Indian Ocean basin as well as the wider regional impact of Buddhism (both from China and India) and Hinduism. Sometimes the influence of both religions intertwined, as in the fabulously ornate, forty-square-mile temple complex of **Angkor Wat**, built by Cambodia's Khmer rulers in direct imitation of architectural styles from southern India. Originally designed in the 1100s as a Hindu place of worship, Angkor Wat was converted to use by Buddhists during the 1200s. The long reach of Indian Buddhism is evident as far away as the Indonesian island of Java, where another architectural monument, the Srivijayan temple of **Borobudur**, stands. Taking the shape of a mountain over a hundred feet high, Borobudur rises in levels, each of which represents a stage on the path to enlightenment.

Religious change came to South Asia in the 1200s. Most notably, this was due to the **arrival of Islam**. Also important was the growing prominence of the **Bhakti movement** within Hinduism. Translated roughly as "spiritual devotion," this trend emerged in southern India as early as the 700s and 800s, but it was in later centuries, especially after 1400, that it swept to the north. The Bhakti outlook placed less emphasis on rigorous observance of caste (although caste remained important) and more on devotion to specific deities. This had the effect of making Hinduism more theistic, or god oriented, for many worshippers; the most popular sects are those dedicated to Vishnu (Vaishnavism) and Shiva (Shaivism).

Angkor Wat
The temple complex of Angkor Wat, built in Cambodia during the 1100s, demonstrates India's cultural and religious influence over much of Southeast Asia. Originally a site of Hindu worship, Angkor Wat became a Buddhist center during the 1200s.

Much of Oceania was populated during this period by the Polynesian peoples, who migrated throughout the Pacific in their **outrigger canoes**. The environmental impact of these migrations is described in Chapter 6. The Polynesians also blanketed much of the Pacific with a polytheistic cultural tradition that remained quite consistent over huge distances and focused on the avoidance of **taboos**—the Polynesian word for ritually forbidden behaviors. Also in Oceania were Australia's Aborigines, who followed a form of animism that involved trying to enter and understand a transcendent spiritual state known as the **dreamtime**.

The Americas

In the pre-Columbian Americas, certain core civilizations put their cultural stamp on neighboring peoples, sometimes over a wide radius. Cultural life here was unusual in that the wheel, so fundamentally important in Afro-Eurasia, was essentially unknown, and systems of writing were rare. Despite this, numerous societies reached an advanced state of civilization.

In most of North America, the principal way of life remained hunting and foraging, and the most common form of worship was animism. The most advanced society in what is today the United States was the Mississippian civilization (ca. 700–1500), whose people practiced agriculture, built cities as trading centers, and are remembered for their large **earth mounds**, which they raised for religious and ceremonial purposes.

As before, Mesoamerica was home to highly centralized and urban societies—especially the Mayans (peak period, 200s–900s) and the Aztecs (1200s–1500s)—and much of the cultural foundation laid down by earlier peoples, like the Olmecs, was still in evidence. (The Mayans' many artistic and intellectual accomplishments are related in Chapter 1.) All major Mesoamerican peoples built **pyramids**, including **Chichén Itzá**, the most famous Mayan temple, and the pyramid of the Morning Star in the Toltec capital of Tula. As the Aztecs came to dominate the region, they also built pyramids and worshipped many of the same gods as the Mesoamericans who preceded them. Key deities included the jaguar god and the feathered serpent Quetzalcóatl, but most important was the sun god Huitzilopochtli. The Aztecs believed that the sun reappeared every morning only if reenergized by human blood, so they practiced **human sacrifice** on a large scale. Victims included prisoners of war but also ordinary Aztec citizens, and victims numbered in the thousands every year.

Mayan Pyramid of Chichén Itzá
The Maya founded the city of Chichén Itzá around 250 C.E. It remains a treasure trove of archaeological evidence of how the Maya lived.

Andean societies were even more centralized and stratified, particularly by the Incan era (1300s–1500s). As in earlier times, they relied not on writing but on the knot-tying system called **quipu** to keep records and accounts. The Incas constructed large cities, including the capital, Cusco (Cuzco), and the fortress and temple complex of **Machu Picchu**. They worshipped a number of deities, chief among them the sun god. Cusco's **Temple of the Sun** was their largest place of worship: laid out in the shape of a puma, its interior was lined with gold. The temple was staffed by thousands of *acllas*, or "virgins of the sun." These were young women chosen each year from throughout the empire to serve as acolytes.

Technology and Innovation, 1200–1450

3

As with the cultural trends described in Chapter 2, the global level of technological and scientific aptitude rose considerably during these years. Indeed, many of the same factors that encouraged cultural development—trade, the movement of peoples, cross-regional conflict and cooperation—also drove scientific and technological innovation. There was much interplay between the two spheres, and sometimes it can be difficult to distinguish between them. Certain scientific insights, for example, are better categorized as abstract ideas than as practical applications. Architecture is the product of engineering, but many buildings are significant mainly as works of art. Whether to count such things as culture or technology sometimes requires judgment—whether one is studying this era or the ones to follow.

SCIENCE, MEDICINE, AND MATHEMATICS

Cross-cultural exchange during these years included pivotal transfers of technology and scientific knowledge across Eurasia. The peoples of the Americas, of course, developed their own understanding of the world in isolation.

Most scientific knowledge at this time was empirical (based on observation) and passed on as a body of received and largely unchanging wisdom. Theoretical comprehension of underlying principles was comparatively rare, and it is a matter of debate as to whether any thinker prior to the 1500s or 1600s made use of the **scientific method** in the modern sense of the term. Either way, among those from the ancient and medieval eras who can be credited with pioneering rational inquiry based on experimentation are the Greek philosopher **Aristotle** (384–322 B.C.E.), whose views on science remained enormously influential for centuries, and the Persian physician-astronomer Avicenna (see below).

Many cultures had long possessed an advanced knowledge of **astronomy** and **calendar** making, both in the Americas (notably the Mayans) and in Afro-Eurasia, where Babylonian-Egyptian-Greek astronomy provided a foundation for the expertise later gained by Islamic, European, and Indian scholars. Observational skills were high, but throughout Eurasia, astronomy was all too often linked with the fortune-telling pseudoscience of astrology. Beyond that, a fundamental error persisted nearly everywhere: the **geocentric theory**, which rested on the intuitive assumption that the sun revolves around the earth. In the European and Islamic worlds, this mistake was cemented into place by unquestioning acceptance of ancient authorities, like the eminent Greek astronomer **Ptolemy**.

Much the same pattern prevailed in the field of **medicine**. Physicians in many societies possessed a high degree of surgical skill and anatomical knowledge (although less of the latter than expected given how, in most places, dissection was illegal or forbidden on religious grounds). As with the field of astronomy, the most respected medical authority in the Western and Mediterranean worlds over many centuries was the ancient Greek scientist **Galen**, whose work, while skilled and insightful in many ways, contained many mistakes that were blindly repeated by students and followers. Only in the eleventh century did a medical thinker begin to move beyond Galen, both in terms of accuracy and a greater willingness to test his ideas by means of experiment and observation. This was the Persian scholar **Avicenna** (Ibn Sina, 980–1037), whose *Canon of Medicine* marked the most significant leap forward in medical knowledge between the Greco-Roman era and the European Renaissance. In East and South Asia, rich and important bodies of medical knowledge appeared in the form of **Chinese traditional medicine** (heavily influenced by Daoism) and, in India, various **yogic disciplines**.

Geometry and basic mathematics were known to most societies, but at least in Afro-Eurasia, **mathematical writings from India and ancient Greece** proved invaluable. During this period in particular, Muslim scholars played a vital role in popularizing the use of **Arabic numerals** (which they themselves had imported from India) and formalizing **algebra**—itself an Arabic word—as a mathematical discipline of its own.

A new wave of scientific thinking was in the making in western Eurasia, thanks to the interplay of Islamic, Jewish, and medieval Christian intellectual trends. While Greco-Roman thought was important to medieval Europeans, their access to it was limited for many years both by their comparative lack of fluency in Greek (as opposed to Latin) and by church restrictions on which ancient ideas were religiously acceptable. By contrast, Muslim and Jewish scholars were much more familiar with Greek sources. When some of them—especially in Muslim Spain, or al-Andalus—began to correspond and interact with their Christian colleagues, they exposed them more fully to **Greek philosophy and science**. This accelerated Europe's transition away from medieval scholasticism and paved the way for the intellectual revival known as the **Renaissance**.

KEY TECHNOLOGIES

By far the most technologically adept society in the world at this time was China, followed by the states of the Middle East. An array of profoundly important inventions had already flowed westward through Eurasia from China or were in the process of doing so. By the end of this period, the European Renaissance was laying the groundwork for the Western world's later technological superiority, but this was a long way off yet. As for the Americas, the level of technological advancement remained lower among most societies there for a variety of environmental and structural reasons.

Especially during the Song period, the Chinese not only demonstrated excellence in the fields described above—astronomy, medicine, and mathematics—but also turned out some of the era's most pivotal technologies, which were not only useful to themselves but influential throughout Eurasia. These included:

- accurate **water clocks** (see side note on this page)
- **paper currency** (nicknamed "flying cash" among the Chinese)
- **gunpowder**, which revolutionized warfare when it reached Europe and the Middle East in the 1200s and 1300s (ironically, the Chinese themselves were slower to adopt gunpowder weaponry, the earliest versions of which did not suit their military needs)
- the **magnetic compass** (see the section below)
- methods of **printing**, detailed in the next paragraph

Perhaps the most revolutionary technology to come out of China was **printing**, which has a long and complex history. The relatively simple technique of **block printing** originated as early as the 200s C.E., but not only was it costly and time-consuming, a block, once carved, could be used to print only one text or image, and it could not be corrected. The concept of **movable-type printing**, which allowed individual, reusable characters to be placed in a frame and then rearranged, arose during the 1000s in Song China, thanks to the inventor Bi Sheng, and was known in Korea by the 1200s.

NOTE

The most striking example of Song China's scientific and technological expertise was the celestial clock of Su Song (built in 1088), an 80-foot-tall structure that told the time of day, the day of the month, and the positions of the sun, moon, planets, and major stars. It was the first device in world history to use a chain-driven mechanism (powered by flowing water).

However, the Chinese used expensive and fragile ceramic tiles. While the Koreans developed cheaper and more durable metal tablets, Asian languages had so many characters that even this more versatile form of printing had less impact than it later did in Europe. The first easily workable and cost-effective movable-type press was designed by the German inventor **Johannes Gutenberg** in the 1430s. Especially because the small number of letters in the Latin alphabet made it easy to mass-produce texts, the Gutenberg press had an explosive effect on literacy rates, the speed at which information spread, the impact of new ideas and scientific theories, and the expansion of libraries and universities. It would also play an indispensable role in Europe's Renaissance and Protestant Reformation.

INNOVATIONS IN TRANSPORT

Trade and travel were made easier during these years by improvements in geographical knowledge, whose benefits included reliable maps and better understanding of weather patterns. They were also assisted by changes in technology.

Overland transport during the premodern era required more time and effort and was more subject to banditry and political disruption. But it was less expensive and the only way to reach places far from rivers and coastlines. Land movement of large amounts of cargo depended on **domesticated pack animals**. **Wheeled vehicles** like carts and wagons were helpful on roads and on flat ground, but rough terrain rendered them useless, so animals sometimes had to carry the loads themselves. One of Eurasia's first and most versatile pack animals was the **horse**, although it was not as strong as the **ox**, which could haul far heavier loads. In the Americas, where the horse did not exist, the most common pack animal was the **llama**, excellently suited to the Andes and other mountains. **Camels** were vital to trade in the

Sahara, the Middle East, and along the Silk Road. Large processions of pack animals and/or vehicles were called **caravans**.

Where possible, **water transport** was easier and preferable to overland transport, although it generally cost more to outfit ships than to organize caravans. During this era, changes in **maritime technology** made overseas trade more efficient than ever. Beforehand, most ships and crews were restricted to **coastal navigation** and rarely ventured far from land. This was the case in the Mediterranean, where the principal vessel was the **galley**, powered by oars and a small square sail whose rigging did not permit heading into the wind.

By contrast, the **dhow**, invented by Arab mariners in the Red and Arabian seas, was suitable for **open-water navigation**. Not only was it constructed more sturdily than the galley (its planks were not nailed together but drilled, tied with ropes, then sealed), but its tall, triangular **lateen sail** was stronger and more efficiently rigged than the square galley sail. This allowed Indian Ocean sailors to take advantage of seasonal **monsoon winds**, which were forceful enough to propel ships over long distances at great speed. The dhow style of shipbuilding caught on throughout the Indian Ocean, from East Africa to South Asia. Another ship capable of open-water navigation and of carrying large amounts of cargo was the Chinese **junk**, which often featured a **stern rudder** for improved steering and **sealed bulkheads** to prevent a single breach in the hull from sinking the entire vessel. Junks could be massive; among the largest ever built were those sailed by **Zheng He** in the early 1400s. In Europe, **sailing ships** capable of oceanic voyaging were emerging slowly, such as the single-masted, square-sailed **cog**, which would soon give way to larger and more seaworthy **carracks** and **caravels**, as discussed in Unit 2.

Certain technologies also made navigation increasingly easier. The **astrolabe**, which measured the sun's position in the sky to calculate latitude, came into wider use at sea after the 700s (it had been used on land in previous centuries). The **magnetic compass**, invented in China during the eleventh century, reached the Middle East and Europe during the late 1100s and early 1200s.

Economic Systems, 1200–1450

4

IN THIS CHAPTER

→ **MODES OF INTENSIVE AGRICULTURE**

→ **EARLY (PROTO-) FORMS OF INDUSTRIAL PRODUCTION (IRON, STEEL, PORCELAIN, TEXTILES)**

→ **GROWING DEMAND FOR LUXURY GOODS (SPICES, SILK, GEMS)**

→ **THE SILK ROAD (CARAVANSERAIS, *PAX MONGOLICA*)**

→ **MEDITERRANEAN SEA LANES (GALLEYS) + HANSEATIC LEAGUE + EARLY ATLANTIC NAVIGATION (FROM COGS TO CARRACKS AND CARAVELS)**

→ **TRANS-SAHARAN CARAVAN ROUTES (CAMEL HERDING, EXPANSION OF ISLAM)**

→ **INDIAN OCEAN TRADE NETWORK (DHOWS AND JUNKS) + LINKS TO SOUTH CHINA SEA AND PACIFIC**

→ **MAJOR TRADING CITIES**

→ **IMPROVEMENTS IN SHIPPING AND NAVIGATION**

→ **BANKING AND CREDIT + STANDARD WEIGHTS AND MEASURES**

→ **CURRENCY (COINAGE AND PAPER MONEY)**

→ **INFRASTRUCTURE (MARKETS, ROADS, CANALS)**

A central trend during this historical period was greater interconnectedness among civilizations. Afro-Eurasia and the Americas remained isolated from one another, but within each of these large spaces, steadily growing networks of exchange spun strong webs of mutual influence—cultural, economic, technological, biological, and political—among varied and often distant regions. At the heart of this interaction was trade.

At the same time, economic productivity grew in most parts of the world. Typically this was due to improved or innovative methods and technologies. The methods of **intensive agriculture** described elsewhere became more common. In addition, early forms of **industrial production** (sometimes called **cottage industry** or **protoindustrialization**) began to appear alongside traditional artisanry and craftsmanship.

TRADE NETWORKS

Trade expanded significantly during this period, with growth especially prominent along the four major **transregional trade routes** that had emerged in Afro-Eurasia in earlier centuries. Note that all of these routes were interconnected by this point, essentially binding Afro-Eurasia together into one vast economic network.

The Silk Road

Although it never fell into complete disuse, the **Silk Road** had experienced a certain amount of disruption from approximately 800 to 1200 C.E. It now flourished again through the 1400s, linking the Middle East with the rest of Asia, and, through the Middle East, touching indirectly on the economies of Europe and Africa. The Silk Road's global relevance would begin to fade once more in the 1500s and 1600s, thanks to the explosion of European maritime trade, but it would always remain central to Asian economic life.

Nearly five thousand miles long, the Silk Road stretched from the ports of the eastern Mediterranean to China's Pacific coast. Over this distance, caravans moved east and west, hauled by a variety of beasts, including horses, camels, and oxen. Stretching from the Middle East and Persia to China and the Pacific coast, the road passed through desert, steppe wilderness, and mountains, especially in Central Asia. Breaking up the journey was a network of oasis towns and **caravanserais** (roadside settlements providing safety and shelter), as well as key cities such as **Baghdad** in the Middle East, the Central Asian metropolis of **Samarkand**, and **Kashgar** in far western China. As the name suggests, silk from China remained the best-known commodity traded along this route, but many other items moved back and forth upon it. China sold porcelain in addition to silk and stepped up industrial production of iron and steel. Cotton, spices, and jewels came from India and Southeast Asia. The Middle East became a source of slaves, metalware, and glassware, with Persia specializing in textiles.

The Silk Road also served as Eurasia's principal artery for the transfer of cultural and religious practices, technological innovations, and new diseases. (Thanks to **missionary efforts** and cultural diffusion, Christianity and Islam moved eastward along the Silk Road, and Buddhism spread along it as well.) Printing, gunpowder, and navigational technology proceeded westward from China to the Middle East and Europe—but so did the **Black Death** in the 1300s. Traders and travelers of all ethnicities used the Silk Road or dominated certain sectors of it over time. After 1200, the revival of Silk Road trade owed much to the *pax Mongolica* ("Mongol peace") imposed by the Mongols as they created their empire. Muslim, Jewish, and Chinese traders also played prominent roles in Silk Road trade. In the West, the most famous description of the Silk Road came from the pen of **Marco Polo**, a Venetian merchant who traveled its length to the court of China's ruler, Kublai Khan, in the late 1200s.

The Mediterranean Sea and Europe's Economic Revival

As they had for centuries, **Mediterranean sea lanes** continued to support large-scale trade between Europe, North Africa, and the Middle East—although political disturbances, especially between medieval Europe and the Islamic states of North Africa and the Middle East, always had the potential to affect commerce. This era also coincided with a significant revival of trade within Europe itself, including the creation of new shipping routes in the Baltic and North Seas and even the larger Atlantic expanse.

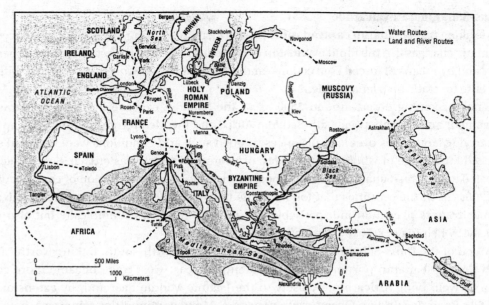

European and Mediterranean Trade Routes During the Late Medieval Period and Renaissance

European desire for more direct access to the goods of East and South Asia prompted the great wave of exploration that began during the 1400s and continued during the 1500s and 1600s.

The fall of the Roman Empire largely disrupted trade in the western Mediterranean and Europe between 500 and 1000 C.E. After that, between 1100 and 1300 C.E., Europe's **Crusades** against the Middle East had their own impact on Mediterranean economic life, increasing European access to and appetite for goods from Asia and the Middle East. Commerce in the region depended above all on **galleys**: oared ships with small square sails, well adapted to coastal navigation. (Not uncommonly, galleys were rowed by slaves or prison convicts.) Major centers of Mediterranean trade during these years include **Constantinople**, seat of the Byzantine Empire and a key crossroads point between Europe, Asia, and the Middle East; the Egyptian ports of **Alexandria** and **Cairo**; and the Italian city-states, with **Venice** as one of the wealthiest and most powerful. As before, Mediterranean commerce tied directly or indirectly into Afro-Eurasia's other leading trade networks, interacting with trans-Saharan caravan trade in northern Africa, with Silk Road traffic in the port cities of the eastern Mediterranean, and with Indian Ocean trade via Egypt and the Red and Arabian Seas.

Military concerns frequently trumped trade in the Mediterranean, especially during times of Muslim-Christian conflict. The expulsion of the Crusader kingdoms from the Middle East by 1300 put European traders at a disadvantage—for access to Silk Road traffic, they now had to rely on Muslims and Mongols as middlemen—and Muslim fleets often enjoyed naval superiority, particularly in the east and south. The 1453 **fall of Constantinople** deepened these trends further. In response, the Europeans shifted more of their economic efforts to trade routes of their own, including those along the Rhine River, in the North Sea and English Channel, and along the Baltic coastline, where the **Hanseatic League** took shape. A related impulse—the desire to find alternative routes to East and South Asia that would bypass the Middle Eastern bottleneck—led to the experiments with **sailing ships** and **Atlantic navigation** that would soon propel the European age of exploration.

> **NOTE**
>
> Economic recovery in medieval Europe after 1000 C.E. caused several trade networks to emerge outside the Mediterranean. Especially important was the formation in the 1200s and 1300s of the Hanseatic League, a trading organization that united Germanic and Scandinavian cities in the Baltic Sea and whose influence stretched from England to Russia—where the city of Novgorod, originally founded as an outpost for Viking trade with Byzantium via Russian river routes, became one of the few points of interaction between Russia and Western Europe.

Trans-Saharan Caravan Trade

Trade along **trans-Saharan caravan routes** vastly increased during this period, influenced by dramatic changes like the rapid **expansion of Islam** into North and West Africa—both peacefully and by means of forced conversion—and the formation of strong African states with an appetite for trade on a larger scale.

Since becoming desert around 2500 B.C.E., the Saharan expanse has been a barrier to movement and trade between sub-Saharan Africa and the Mediterranean. Animals capable of carrying large loads over long distances through such arid conditions were rare, and specialized knowledge of where to find **oases**, or sources of water, was crucial. Several factors boosted early trans-Saharan trade, but most crucial was the domestication of **camels** during the 200s C.E. In the centuries that followed, the trans-Saharan network expanded. **Arab and Berber traders** played an indispensable role in this—not just economically but also religiously, by helping to spread Islam throughout the region.

Much of the trans-Saharan trade of this period went north-south, linking North Africa with the sub-Saharan portion of the continent, but east-west trade became more common as well, tying Africa more closely to the Islamic Middle East and, by extension, to the Silk Road and Indian Ocean trade networks. Many commodities remained the same as in earlier years: ivory, exotic animal skins, and foodstuffs like nuts and fruits flowing northward from sub-Saharan Africa, and **salt** and manufactured goods (such as metalware, pottery, and glass) traveling southward. Two items in particular, though, took on greater importance during this period. One was **gold**, which states like Mali supplied in sizable quantities and which many Africans, ironically, found less useful than the copper and iron they received in return. As places like Europe and the Middle East adopted the practice of minting coins, the demand for African gold increased, and when Mansa Musa, the Muslim king of Mali, went on pilgrimage to Mecca in the 1300s, he brought so much gold to the Middle East that he briefly devalued it as a currency there. Sadly, the second newer element in the trans-Saharan network was the expansion of the **Arab slave trade**. Arab merchants had transported African slaves across the Sahara since the 600s but greatly increased the volume of trade by the eleventh century. The Arab slave trade caught on in eastern Africa as well and eventually resulted in the forcible removal of at least 10 million Africans.

A major hub for trans-Saharan commerce was **Timbuktu**, in Mali, a famed center for Islamic scholarship as well as a key site in the salt and gold trades. Ports on Africa's Mediterranean coast and in Egypt were also important.

The Indian Ocean

One of the world's most vibrant and culturally diverse commercial economies centered on the **Indian Ocean trade network**, in which **lateen-sailed dhows** (taking advantage of seasonal **monsoon winds**), Chinese **junks**, and other vessels plied an expanse wider than 6,000 miles from west to east. The Indian Ocean sea lanes linked East Africa and the Middle East directly with South and Southeast Asia. Land routes and straits opening into the South China Sea and the western Pacific ensured that China and Japan were part of this trading system as well.

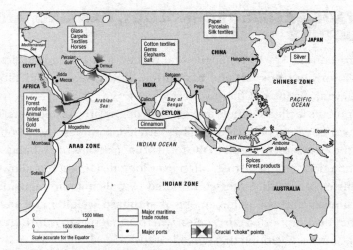

The Indian Ocean Trade Network Before 1500 C.E.
The arrival of Portuguese traders just before 1500, then the massive influx of other Europeans, changed the economic patterns of this region forever.

In the west, a zone controlled largely by Arab and Persian traders, goods came from East Africa and the Middle East—ivory, diamonds, animal hides, ebony, and gold from the former and copper, textiles, glassware, and Arabian horses from the latter. The middle zone was dominated by South Asian cities and kingdoms. India offered gems, elephants, salt, and cotton cloth. From Sri Lanka (Ceylon) came cinnamon, while other spices and exotic woods came from the East Indies (modern-day Indonesia). In the east, China traded silk, porcelain, and paper, and Japan was a major source of silver. Key points in

NOTE

An interesting site connected with Indian Ocean trade was the city of Great Zimbabwe, several hundred miles inland from the East African coast. Zimbabwe flourished from around 1200 to 1500, thanks to rich deposits of gold and diamonds. It remained relatively untouched by Islamic influence. Although it traded mainly with Swahili ports. The presence of Chinese ceramics and Persian artworks in the city's ruins shows how extensive its economic influence was.

this network included the **Swahili city-states** of the East African coast, **Mecca** in Arabia, Hormuz in Persia, the Malibar metropolis of **Calicut** in western India, and the Malaysian city of **Melaka** (Malacca), which dominated the chokepoint between the Indian and Pacific oceans. Also connected to the network were the Chinese ports of **Canton** (**Guangzhou**) and, further up the coast, **Hangzhou**, located in the Yangzi delta, at the southern end of China's **Grand Canal**. From here and other cities, ships ventured back and forth between China and Southeast Asia, India, and Persia.

The Americas

Trade routes in the Americas were not as extensive or as interconnected as in Afro-Eurasia, but they, too, expanded during this period. Cities like **Cahokia**, in Mississippian North America, arose as a center of wide-ranging exchange. The city-states of Mesoamerica traded heavily, and the Aztec capital of **Tenochtitlán** was among those that benefited the most. An elaborate system of roads and bridges made trade possible throughout the Andes, both before and after the rise of the Incas. Andean communities living on the coast fished and traded with their neighbors in the mountain valleys. Andean peoples also traded with tribal societies living along the Amazon River to the east.

MAKING TRADE EASIER: TECHNOLOGY, BANKING, AND INFRASTRUCTURE

Especially in Afro-Eurasia, key technologies and practices made trade easier and more efficient. For **innovations in transport and navigation**, which were considerable during these years, see the relevant section of Chapter 3.

Other developments facilitated trade as well, both on the private and state levels. Along the major trade networks, where political stability prevailed, commerce was boosted by the rise of **banking** and the extension of **credit** in the form of checks, bills of exchange, and loans with interest. These practices required trust, often over long distances, but allowed for the safer and simpler transfer of wealth. States contributed by policing and regulating trade routes (with **customs houses** and the enforcement of **standard weights and measures**, among other things). They also supported **currencies**, whether that meant **minting coins** or printing **paper money** (a Chinese invention that spread westward).

Good transportational and communications **infrastructure**, whether it was built and maintained privately or by the state, also enabled the expansion of trade. **Markets**, trading outposts, and port cities were all vital to the movement of goods, as were the **caravanserais**, or wayside inns and settlements that lined routes like the Silk Road. Networks of **roads** and man-made **waterways** (where rivers did not run or needed to be joined) were just as crucial. The era's most impressive waterway was China's **Grand Canal**, which ran well over a thousand miles and connected the Yellow and Yangzi Rivers. Completed by the Sui dynasty (581–618), the canal was improved in the years that followed and ran from Beijing in the north to Hangzhou in the south.

All of Eurasia's major empires helped to enable transcontinental trade during this period. Because trade flourished best under stable and predictable conditions, large empires such as Byzantium, the Islamic caliphates, the Mongol states, and China made it more viable by bringing vast territories under their authority—which typically meant consistent laws and regulations, relative safety from bandits or pirates, mutually recognized currencies, and proper care for infrastructure. Sometimes, though, rather than trading peacefully, states competed or even warred with each other over trade. In one infamous example, the authorities of Venice persuaded the armies of the **Fourth Crusade** (1202–1204) to attack and pillage Constantinople—a city of fellow Christians but also an economic rival to the city-states of Italy—instead of pursuing their original war aims against Muslim forces in Egypt.

Social Interactions and Organization, 1200–1450

5

With population growth and economic productivity rising during this era, social structures and systems of labor management grew more complicated in most parts of the world. Social stratification remained the norm, with old hierarchies and caste systems still in place and new ones emerging. The vast majority of people lived in the countryside and earned their keep by means of agriculture or herding.

On the other hand, the increased scale and importance of trade led to greater **urbanization** and sparked some degree of class diversification and **social mobility**, with trade and artisanry (craftsmanship) allowing more people to work in nonagricultural occupations and giving rise to different forms of labor organization. **Patriarchy** and **gender inequity** remained as common as before and, in some cases, worsened due to cultural or religious trends.

CITIES

As in earlier times, **cities** served as seats of power (political, administrative, and military) and as centers of cultural and economic activity. Overall, the trend worldwide was toward increased **urbanization** as existing cities grew larger and more cities came into being.

Pay close attention to the location and characteristics of the **major cities** referred to in this unit's earlier chapters as well as to the roles they played in various trade networks. The level of urbanization remained comparatively low in much of Europe and the Americas and in most of sub-Saharan Africa. The world's most heavily urbanized areas were the Middle East, the shores of the Indian Ocean basin, and East Asia—especially China, where several cities had populations exceeding a million.

The importance of cities for trade, banking, and commerce tended to make **merchant classes** larger and more influential, even if elite classes in many areas viewed trade and those involved in it with disdain. City life also fostered **specialization of labor** and created a need for artisans, laborers, and others who belonged neither to the elite nor to the rural, agricultural population.

Thanks to the enlargement of interregional trade during this period, **diasporic communities** and foreign enclaves formed in ports and cities along far-reaching trade routes. These included travelers and traders of all sorts but centered on merchant families who took up long-term residence far from home. Diasporas to be aware of from this era include Chinese merchants throughout Southeast Asia, especially in Malaysia and Indonesia; Jews throughout Eurasia; and Muslim traders throughout the Indian Ocean trade network, as far east as China's Pacific coast. Mosques in the Persian style were established in the port cities of Canton and Hangzhou during the 1300s, not just to missionize among the Chinese but to serve the community of Muslim merchants who had settled there. In all these cases, the diaspora minority introduced its traditions and practices into the host culture.

SOCIAL STRUCTURES AND LABOR MANAGEMENT

As societies grew larger, the ways they organized their labor grew more diverse. **Hunting and foraging** remained important in many parts of the world, as did **herding** and **nomadic pastoralism**. Social organization in these communities tended to be relatively egalitarian and nonhierarchical. **Settled societies**, whether urban or agricultural, had more complex class hierarchies and were more rigidly stratified.

Hierarchies and Caste Systems

Class hierarchies and caste systems continued to function. As with gender relations, organized religions and deep-rooted cultural norms were often used to justify and reinforce them.

In a typical society, **elite classes** composed 10 to 15 percent of the population. They included the royal family, if there was one, as well as aristocrats with noble status. **High-level clergy** tended to fall into this category, and the same was sometimes true of top civil servants in the **state bureaucracy**. As a rule, aristocratic elites derived their wealth from **ownership of land**. They often looked down on trade and in some cases were forbidden by religion or custom from participating in it.

A small but growing number of **commoners** worked at occupations that would today be considered **professional**: scribes, lawyers, physicians, mid- or low-level bureaucrats, and mid- or low-level clergy. Whether such jobs were open to those of low birth, they generally required **literacy**, something not easily attained during this period. In certain societies, especially in Europe, these professions helped create what would eventually be called the **middle class**.

Merchants and bankers, who also formed part of the emerging middle class, grew in size, wealth, and clout, thanks to the growing importance of trade and urbanization. What spot they occupied within the social hierarchy depended on the society in question. In many places, they sat higher than most commoners: even if elite

NOTE

China's famous *civil-service examination* system allowed entry into a desirable profession—the *mandarin class* of scholar-officials—by means of merit rather than birth. However, to qualify required a high degree of literacy and learning, so only sons from relatively privileged backgrounds stood a realistic chance of passing the exams.

classes viewed them with scorn, they earned respect by virtue of the riches they generated. However, in much of Asia, where Confucian doctrines influenced social thinking, peasants, no matter how humble their origin, were considered superior to even the richest merchant.

Others among the common classes included **artisans** and **craftspeople**, whose numbers, like those of merchants and bankers, expanded due to urbanization. In urban settings, artisans and skilled workers often banded together in **guilds**. These associations maintained a monopoly on their respective trades. They restricted membership, set prices and standards of quality, and provided pensions. Also in the cities but further down the social scale were **shopkeepers**, **unskilled laborers**, and other members of the **urban lower classes**.

The vast majority of any settled society's population lived in the countryside and worked in agriculture, although these **farmers** and **peasants** labored under a variety of conditions. Free peasants either owned land or paid rent to landlords, in addition to any government taxes. Their place in most hierarchies tended to be near the bottom, although this was not the case in Confucian parts of Asia. At the bottom of any society's hierarchy were **slaves** and other **coerced/unfree laborers**, along with the **"untouchable"** or **pariah classes** that existed in places like Japan and India.

Social Hierarchies: A Comparison

Europe	Ottoman Empire	East Asia (Confucian)	South Asia (Hindu Caste System)
royalty	royal/noble elites	royal/noble elites	royal/noble elites
aristocracy/ nobility + knights	men of the pen (scholars, civil servants)	scholars + warrior elite (samurai in Japan)	brahmins (priests)
merchants	men of the sword (warriors)	farmers	kshatriyas (warriors)
artisans and laborers	men of negotiation (merchants, artisans)	artisans	vaishyas (merchants, skilled workers, peasants)
free peasants	men of husbandry (peasants, herders)	merchants	sudras (unskilled workers, servants)
enserfed peasants	slaves	slaves (+ untouchables in Japanese caste system)	slaves; pariahs and untouchables

Social mobility tended to be limited during this era, more in some places than others. In parts of medieval Europe, for instance, cities served as pockets of relative freedom, where peasants could escape the bonds of serfdom and where trade and commerce allowed for some degree of self-advancement, regardless of birth. In certain parts of the world, **caste systems** remained in operation, eliminating any chance of social mobility and permanently condemning some members of society to pariah, or "untouchable," status. The **Hindu** (varna) **caste system** in India remains the most famous example, but caste systems existed elsewhere, including feudal Japan, which was highly regimented. Japan's own untouchable class, the *eta*, handled waste and disposed of the dead.

Coerced Forms of Labor

Although working conditions might be burdensome or even unfair, many of the forms of labor described above left those pursuing them legally free. Unfortunately, **slavery** and other forms of **coerced labor** were just as common as free forms of labor. Mesoamerican and Andean societies sometimes enslaved their neighbors. The same was true in Africa—and foreigners added to the burden here by arriving from outside to enslave Africans. The **Arab slave trade** in Africa steadily grew during these years, and with the Portuguese moving into West Africa by the early 1400s, the continent felt the first stirrings of what would soon grow into the Atlantic slave trade.

Elsewhere as well, the demand for slaves, whether for domestic labor, agricultural work, or military service, grew substantially. Where they conquered, the Mongols compelled soldiers and skilled workers to serve them, often far from home. Slavery was common in the Middle East, for military purposes as well as civilian ones. As early as the 800s, Muslim armies recruited neighboring peoples from Asia Minor as military slaves called **mamluks**. In this instance, slavery was meant less to oppress than to ensure loyalty, and not only did mamluks develop tight-knit bonds and a sense of professional pride, but they received many privileges and could attain positions of power. Mamluks were taught to observe the code of **furusiyya** ("equitation"), which involved not just military training but cultured and honorable behavior. For the same purpose of ensuring loyalty, the Ottoman Turks devised the **devshirme** ("collecting") system, in use between the mid-1300s and 1600s. This took young men from non-Muslim (typically Christian) families and groomed them to serve as privileged slaves in the civil service, the army, and sometimes the clergy. The most famous of these troops were gunpowder infantry called **janissaries**, whose status as privileged slave-soldiers was similar to that of the mamluks.

Where agricultural labor was not performed by free peasants or slaves, it fell to **serfs**, who were not technically slaves (serfs were not seen as actual property) but were legally free even though they could not change residence or profession without permission from their landowner. Serfdom was most common in feudal societies. It arose in medieval Europe during the 700s and

TIP

Compare the Mamluk code of furusiyya with chivalry in Europe and Bushido in Japan. Also compare Ming China's technique of using the civil-service examination system to foster bureaucratic loyalty to the emperor with how Ottoman sultans designed their devshirme system to guarantee similar administrative fealty.

800s, fading in Western Europe by the Renaissance but persisting in Central and Eastern Europe until the 1700s and, in the case of Russia, the mid-1800s. After Japan descended into samurai feudalism in the late 1100s, its peasants lived in serflike conditions as well. Although the conditions of serfs' lives varied, they were generally harsh. Serfs had to give a portion of their own crops and livestock to the lord, and they had to spend a certain number of days per month fulfilling labor obligations. These included not just agricultural work but also **corvée labor projects** such as building roads and cutting down forests. In addition, when knights, samurai, and other feudal landowners were called upon to raise armies for their lords, they conscripted serfs to serve as soldiers.

In the Americas, a similar form of coerced labor was the **mit'a system**, which became common practice in the Andes during the Moche period (200s–700s C.E.) and remained customary until the arrival of Europeans in the 1500s. Here, commoner clans known as **ayllu** cooperated to fulfill the labor obligations they owed their landowning warrior-priest elites. As Inca rulers came to dominate the Andes, they made the mit'a system even more burdensome. In theory, private property did not exist among the Incas, whose ruler was considered the ultimate owner of everything.

Social Unrest and Labor-Related Revolts

Whether their labor was coerced or free, most peasants and laborers faced dreary working conditions and sometimes intolerable treatment. Consequently, **labor-related unrest and revolts** became more common in various parts of the world.

Urban populations sometimes rose up in anger. A prominent example was the Wool Carders' Revolt in Florence (1378), sparked by the rage of unskilled workers who had no guild to protect them from being paid too little. Many consider this the first urban labor dispute in European history.

Peasant uprisings were more common during these years. They tended to take place either in times of famine or disaster or when taxes, rents, or military obligations suddenly increased. During the mid-1300s, China's Yuan dynasty had to contend with the **Red Turban revolt**, provoked by two main causes: the regime's unwillingness to aid peasants after disastrous floods and a sharp rise in taxes to fund military spending. It was this revolt that caused the collapse of the Yuan dynasty and the rise of the Ming emperors in 1368. During the early 1400s, Japanese peasants regularly rose up against their feudal daimyo landowners.

In Europe, the strain and stress caused by the **Hundred Years' War** (1337–1453) between France and England caused large peasant revolts on both sides. French peasants staged the Jacquerie in 1358, while Wat Tyler led the English Peasants' Revolt in 1381.

GENDER ROLES

In no part of the world did women enjoy gender equality in the modern sense of the phrase. Although gender relations varied over time, from place to place, and even between classes in a given society, **patriarchy** and **gender inequality** continued to be the norm. Organized religions and cultural traditions played a key role in shaping relations between the genders.

With respect to social status, upper-class women lived easier lives but as a rule found themselves more constrained by restrictions on their behavior. In most societies, lower-class women might endure harder working and living conditions but were often less bound by "proper" conventions of conduct.

Women's Occupations

Wherever they lived and whatever their class, women's occupational roles were more sharply restricted than those of men.

Women from elite classes might occasionally govern states, although this was rare. If they exercised political power, it was generally indirectly by informally influencing royal or noble sons and husbands. Elite women often assisted with the supervision of households and estates. They typically had access to education and sometimes distinguished themselves in the arts. (Examples include the Japanese writer **Lady Murasaki** and the German nun-composer **Hildegard von Bingen**.) Religious careers, as nuns or priestesses (but rarely in positions of real leadership), were open to women of the upper classes—but like women on lower levels of the hierarchy, elite women often found themselves occupied mainly with childbearing and homemaking.

Among commoners, women might or might not be able to inherit or own **property**, depending on time or place. Wives in merchant or shopkeeper families might help with the running of businesses, and in some cases, although far less often, women might own their own businesses. Further down the social scale, women from farming and laboring classes were generally confined to low-status jobs such as weaving, pottery, gathering food, farm chores, tending herds, and domestic servitude.

On rare occasions, women fought in wars and even led troops. In the early 1400s, the peasant girl **Joan of Arc** rallied French forces during the Hundred Years' War and defeated their English foes in several key battles. The Mongol armies of **Genghis Khan** allowed women to fight during the 1200s, and one of Genghis's own daughters commanded troops in Central Asia. And although the Chinese saga of the warrior girl **Hua Mulan** arose in the 500s C.E., poems and novels about her reached their peak popularity between the 1100s and 1300s.

Women's (Limited) Rights and Freedoms

In few cases did societies oppress women completely. Despite their secondary status, women tended to enjoy at least some rights and freedoms.

Women could generally inherit and own **property**, although not as freely as men could. These rights, although only partial, existed in Europe, the Middle East, and East Asia. They were more limited in places like the Hindu parts of India and the stratified societies of Mesoamerica and especially the Andes. They were most favorable in parts of sub-Saharan Africa.

If women received a **dowry** or **bride price**, that provided them with some economic security—although in some places and times, the woman's family had to pay a dowry to the husband-to-be, a burden that led many families to view daughters as less desirable than sons. **Divorce**, especially from abusive husbands, was possible in most places but far harder for wives than for husbands, who could typically separate for little or no cause. (Unfaithfulness was stigmatized and punished far more harshly when wives were guilty than when husbands were.) Among the upper classes, women were generally allowed to receive some **education**. Before the law and the courts, women enjoyed some **legal safeguards** but never full equality (in Islamic courts, for example, the testimony of a woman was not considered as reliable as that of a man). In medieval Europe, the cult of **chivalry** encouraged proper conduct toward women—at least those of noble birth—but was still condescending in how it regarded women as frail and weak and therefore requiring male protection.

Areas that allowed women more freedoms include sub-Saharan Africa, especially in the west, where descent was often traced **matrilineally** (through the mother) and where women's labor as farmers, working alongside their cattle-herding husbands, was highly valued. Older women in African societies were consulted for advice more frequently than elsewhere—and even where Islam penetrated, it tended to restrict women's behavior less than it did in North Africa or the Middle East. The Mongols were surprisingly more respectful of women's property and divorce rights, and gender relations among the hunter-foragers of North America appear to have been defined comparatively loosely. Japan during the Heian era, prior to 1200, afforded upper-class women a high degree of respect for their cultural and intellectual attainments—something lost after the rise of Japanese feudalism.

Restrictions on Women's Lives

Far more famous than rights during these years were the many restrictions placed on women's lives and behavior worldwide. Aside from the **secondary status** they were forced into overall, certain practices stand out as particularly repressive.

Arranged marriages—especially common in places like India and China but also widespread in other regions—worked almost always to the groom's advantage and often promised young girls as brides to older husbands.

Veiling and **seclusion** ranked among the most prominent ways to control female conduct. Both are known best for being practiced in the Muslim Middle East (where the **harem**, or women's quarters, arose, most famously in Ottoman Turkey) and among both Muslims and Hindus in India and Southeast Asia (where the custom of seclusion was referred to as **purdah**). But veiling and seclusion also had a place in Christian Europe, especially in the Byzantine and Orthodox world.

Not only did the terms of divorce vary from place to place, but so too did the basic terms of married life. **Concubinage**, the practice of taking openly acknowledged lovers in addition to a wife, was a privilege open to men in China and other parts of Asia as well as in the Middle East. **Polygamy**, the taking of more than one wife, was also practiced, most famously in the Islamic world, where up to four wives were permitted. Muslim men, however, were not supposed to marry more wives than they could comfortably support, and polygamy remained more limited in practice than in theory.

Suppression of women's equality sometimes took extreme forms. In medieval and Renaissance Europe, one manifestation of social stress was a sharp rise in the persecution of suspected witches, and due to religious and popular prejudice, a majority of those victimized by such **witch hunts** were women. In many parts of India, the ritual of **sati**, or the burning of Hindu widows on their husbands' funeral pyres, continued. In China, the subjugation of women expressed itself most obviously in the painful

WOMEN AND CHANGE OVER TIME IN ASIA

Political and religious shifts in Asia caused major change during these years in how women were treated. In India, the arrival of Islam meant that many women were no longer subject to the Hindu caste system or the sati ritual—and came to enjoy more rights than most Hindu women with respect to divorce and property. By contrast, the growing dominance of Neo-Confucianism in China led to the greater subordination of women and contributed to the growing popularity of foot binding. In Japan, the collapse of the Heian regime affected the status of upper-class women. The Heian court placed great emphasis on cultural brilliance and elaborate manners, and Heian women exerted a certain degree of social and political influence. However, the rougher warrior ethic of the feudal shogunates allowed Japanese women fewer opportunities, and unlike European chivalry, the samurai code of Bushido did little to encourage respectful treatment of women.

practice of **foot binding**, which kept women's feet tiny and dainty but in the process crippled them. Firmly established by 1200 and popular among all classes (although especially among elites), foot binding continued into the 1900s.

Organized religions played a crucial role in defining women's roles and justifying their subservience. The majority of Christian theologians, both Catholic and Orthodox, viewed women as subordinate to men, if not inherently more sinful, and refused them positions of spiritual authority. Although Islam proclaimed the desirability of treating women with respect, it also assigned women at best a secondary status relative to men. Neo-Confucianism encouraged similar thinking in China and East Asia, and Hindu women were highly restricted by the dictates of the caste system.

Humans and the Environment, 1200–1450

6

As before, human societies simultaneously adapted to their environment and sought to adapt it to their own needs and desires. Steady population growth made humanity's environmental impact dramatically heavier (and sometimes harmful or self-destructive) during this period. The same is true of humanity's increased economic productivity, which included a growing talent for engineering and construction and spurred a greater willingness to extract and deplete resources. On the other hand, environmental factors beyond human control, particularly changes in the climate and the movement of disease pathogens, affected many societies.

In keeping with this unit's central theme, much of the relationship between humans and the environment during this period was shaped by greater interregional interaction.

MIGRATIONS

Large-scale migrations regularly took place, especially in Afro-Eurasia. They were often caused by environmental factors, such as climate change, the vanishing of food supplies, or overpopulation. In turn, they had their own effects on the environment.

A prominent series of migrations had long been affecting Europe. During the late Roman and medieval periods, waves of Asiatic and Germanic peoples moved into the region from the east and north. The military threat posed by these invaders forced European states to centralize politically during the medieval era, but the invaders themselves affected the continent ethnically by settling down, founding their own states, and blending with existing European populations. Among the most influential of these were the **Vikings**. Farther to the east, the migration of **Mongol-Turkic horse pastoralists** had a similar impact on the Middle East, Central Asia, and East Asia.

In sub-Saharan Africa, the **Bantu** peoples finally completed their centuries-long, continent-wide movements. In the process, they brought with them new agricultural techniques, which increased the extent of African land under cultivation, with all the environmental impacts that entailed, such as increased reliance on water and the need to irrigate. They also spread the secret of ironworking, which encouraged mining and metallurgy and placed even more stress on African ecosystems.

The three-thousand-year **Polynesian migrations**, which had long been under way at this period, populated a 20,000-mile expanse of the Pacific. Beginning in the Indonesian and Philippine islands, these migrations led the Polynesian peoples on long eastward journeys, carried on **outrigger canoes** that allowed them to travel vast distances over water. The original Polynesians were root farmers, growing taro and sweet potatoes and supplementing their diet with pigs, chickens, and fish. They carried these foods, as well as the coconut palm, with them across the Pacific, bringing them to places as different as Hawaii and New Zealand. The arrival in New Zealand of the Maori—the largest surviving Polynesian subculture—around 1200 is considered the endpoint of the Polynesian migrations. Unfortunately, the Polynesians badly deforested some of the places they settled—most notably Easter Island, whose civilization was destroyed by environmental stress and tribal war by the 1500s c.e.

Certain trade routes opened or widened because migratory or nomadic peoples traveling upon them adapted to challenging environments. The establishment of trans-Saharan caravan routes depended upon the **camel-herding expertise of Arabs and Berbers** in the Middle East and North Africa, and the excellent **horsemanship of pastoral peoples in the steppes of Central Asia** had much to do with the development of the Silk Road. Between the 800s and the 1100s, the **Vikings**, expert mariners and fierce warrior-traders from Scandinavia, poured out of the north to Iceland, Greenland, the British Isles, northwestern France, and Sicily as well as to Russia, where, from cities like **Novgorod**, they established a trade route running all the way to **Constantinople** and the Byzantine Empire. This far-reaching influence was due to their prowess with **longboats** and their ability—extremely rare in Europe and the Mediterranean at this time—to navigate on the open ocean.

NOTE

During the time of Leif Ericsson, at around 1000 c.e., the Vikings became the first Europeans known to have reached the Americas. Although their brief time there had nowhere near the impact that the arrival of Columbus did in the 1490s, it testifies to the Vikings' navigational skills.

THE IMPACT OF MANUFACTURING, RESOURCE EXTRACTION, AND AGRICULTURE

In numerous ways, **economic productivity** rose worldwide, both in the manufacturing sphere (including cottage industry and protoindustry) and in agriculture. This increased **resource extraction and depletion** and led to a corresponding rise in the environmental impact of human economic activity.

As they grew in number, size, and political and economic importance, **cities** affected the environment by concentrating large numbers of people—and their demand for resources—into small, densely packed spaces. The environmental impact of the urban construction and engineering was likewise heavy.

In certain places, craftsmanship and artisanry approached protoindustrial levels of production. **Hunting and fishing** intensified. **Mining** and metallurgy, which supported the expansion of protoindustrial production and a heightened demand for metals, gems, and jewels, represented a particularly intrusive form of resource extraction and exerted a powerful influence on many ecosystems. Increased production of **textiles** created a greater demand for **wool** (requiring the grazing of larger number of sheep) and fibers such as **cotton** (requiring more land to be placed under agricultural production).

Whatever crops were grown, farming and water management became more efficient during these years, and more land was used for it. To handle growing populations and make the best use of space, forms of **intensive agriculture** maximized the productive potential of every square foot of a given area. Throughout Afro-Eurasia, improved versions of the **horse collar**, which originated in China, improved agricultural production, as did better plows and other farming tools. In the Americas, greater use was made of **terrace farming** (on the sides of hills and mountains) and the Mesoamerican **chinampa** technique of growing crops on "floating islands" in lakes. The **waru waru** system of interspersing raised seedbeds (where the plants grew) and ditches (which allowed for irrigation and drainage alike) arose in parts of the Andes as early as the 300s B.C.E. and was more widely adopted during this period. These and other techniques increased the risks of soil erosion and deforestation.

Afro-Eurasian trade, especially along the routes described in Chapter 4, spread plants and foodstuffs far from their points of origin. **Bananas**, originating in Papua New Guinea and Southeast Asia, reached the Middle East by the mid-600s and took root in Africa between 700 and 1500. Also from Southeast Asia, **citrus** eventually became common throughout the Islamic world and the Mediterranean. **Sugar**, first extracted from the sugarcane plant in New Guinea around 8000 B.C.E., reached the Asian mainland by 1000 B.C.E. and was being produced in crystallized form in Gupta India by the 500s C.E. Buddhist monks traveling from India brought sugar to China, and it reached Persia via the Silk Road by about 600 C.E. During their wars of expansion, Muslim Arabs encountered sugar and spread it even more widely through the Middle East and North Africa. During their Crusades in the Middle East, medieval Europeans discovered this "sweet salt" and began growing sugarcane themselves. The cultivation of **cotton** became more widespread throughout Afro-Eurasia as well. Around the 900s, important improvements in **rice cultivation** were imported from Southeast Asia to China and East Asia in the form of drought-resistant Champa rice from Vietnam. Champa rice grew fast enough to permit two harvests per year, substantially increasing food production. In Oceania, the **coconut palm** spread throughout the Pacific, largely due to the migration of Polynesian peoples.

ENVIRONMENTAL FORCES: DISEASE AND CLIMATE

In certain cases, the environment acted on humans, not vice versa. Occasionally, natural disasters such as volcanic eruptions, the diversion of rivers, and earthquakes decisively affected societies or even fatally disrupted them.

Also important were the outbreaks of disease that periodically swept over large parts of Afro-Eurasia. Already for centuries, **smallpox**, **measles**, and **bubonic plague** had moved back and forth throughout Eurasia, and they continued to do so. The deadliest epidemic to strike Eurasia in the premodern era was the so-called **Black Death** of the early 1300s. Beginning in China, this particularly virulent outbreak of bubonic plague migrated first to the Middle East and then by the 1340s to Europe via Mediterranean trade between

NOTE

Why were the Americas less susceptible to epidemic outbreaks before European contact in the 1490s? Two factors helped make this so. First, when pathogens traveled long distances, it tended to be within the same temperature zone, or in east-west directions rather than north-south ones, making Eurasia a more convenient alleyway than the Americas for the spread of illnesses. Second, domesticated animals are an important vector for transmitting certain diseases to humans; the relative lack of them in the Americas limited the exposure of societies there to pathogens that were common in Afro-Eurasia. Fatefully, this gave Native Americans no opportunity to build up natural immunity to the diseases they would eventually encounter upon the Europeans' arrival in the New World.

the Middle East and the Italian peninsula. Each region it visited lost on average a third of its population, resulting in many millions of deaths and making the Black Death one of the worst medical disasters in world history. **Tropical diseases** such as **malaria**, yellow fever, and sleeping sickness wielded their own deadly influence in Africa and elsewhere.

Climate change also affected human populations, especially in the northern hemisphere. Between 800 and 1300, a warming trend called the **medieval climatic optimum** greatly affected patterns of migration (allowing freer movement into northern regions by people like the **Vikings** and, in Arctic North America, the Inuit), agriculture (which became more productive), fishing and whaling, and interregional trade. After 1300, though, the medieval climatic optimum was followed by a general cooling that resulted by around 1400 in the **Little Ice Age**. This persisted until the early 1800s, making agricultural production more difficult in certain regions and also altering patterns of northern settlement and economic activities such as fishing, whaling, and fur hunting. The downturn in agricultural production caused by the Little Ice Age may have contributed to the wave of **peasant uprisings** that broke out in places like Europe and China during the mid-to-late 1300s.

UNIT 2

1450–1750

Unit 2: Short Cut

GENERAL REMARKS

Between 1450 and 1750, the world's civilizations became truly connected for the first time in history. The most significant trend of this era was the emergence of fully **globalized networks of communication and exchange**. Regrettably, much of this interaction consisted of warfare, exploitation, and slavery. Nonetheless, trade, discovery, cultural interchange, and the faster and easier movement of peoples brought the world's societies into greater proximity.

One of the primary causes of this greater interaction was the massive **European campaign of exploration and colonization**. Driven by scientific curiosity, the quest for power, the hope of spreading Christianity, and a desire for wealth, European explorers during the 1400s and 1500s sought out oceanic trade routes that would link them directly with China, India, Japan, and elsewhere in Asia. They also encountered the Americas: a "new world" that, for thousands of years, had lain outside the bounds of Afro-Eurasian knowledge.

Within decades, European traders, missionaries, and conquerors spread throughout the world. The Europeans were the first in history to sail around the globe, and they established a presence in many parts of coastal Africa, Southeast Asia, and East Asia. Most dramatically, European colonizers occupied and transformed North and South America. The opening of the Americas to the rest of the world was done brutally and out of greed but also tremendously shifted the world's economic, linguistic, religious, and cultural patterns. It changed forever the environments of the Americas, Africa, and Eurasia as new animals, new foods, and new diseases were passed back and forth in a phenomenon known as the **Columbian Exchange**.

Another trend of this era was the **rise of Europe**, caused by **state rivalries** and **imperial expansion**. Until the 1400s, Europe had been weak and backward compared with civilizations such as China and the Ottoman Empire. But during the 1500s and 1600s, Europe pulled even with China and the Islamic east's **gunpowder empires** (Ottoman Turkey, Safavid Persia, and Mughal India) in terms of scientific advancement, global power, and wealth. During the 1700s, Europe overtook these other cultures, becoming the strongest, most technologically adept, and richest civilization in the world. By the middle of the 1700s, Europe was poised to dominate the rest of the globe, militarily and economically—and did so in the 1800s.

Technological development and scientific knowledge increased in many parts of the world at this time. Many societies based their economies increasingly on **commerce**. In some places by the 1600s, **protoindustrial** practices were laying the foundation for fuller industrialization in the late 1700s and 1800s.

In addition, **peasant labor intensified**. In most societies, agricultural production increased, leading to a huge rise in population worldwide—from 350 million in 1400 to 610 million in 1700, the fastest rate of growth seen to that date. The bulk of this era's economic growth depended on **coerced labor** in many forms.

BROAD TRENDS

Governance, 1450–1750	
Europe	absolutist vs. parliamentary nation-states (Louis XIV and divine right theory vs. English Bill of Rights) European age of exploration (Henry the Navigator, Christopher Columbus, Vasco da Gama, Ferdinand Magellan) from Franco-Habsburg rivalry (1500s–1600s) to Anglo-French rivalry (1600s–1700s) Protestant-Catholic religious wars (1500s–early 1600s) + Thirty Years' War (1618–1648) Seven Years' War (1756–1763)
Middle East	gunpowder empires = Ottoman Empire (1299–1922) and Safavid Persia (1501–early 1700s) Ottoman-Safavid rivalry over trade and Sunni-Shiite disputes Ottoman conquest of Constantinople (1453) and campaigns of Suleiman the Magnificent (1520s) from Celali revolts (1590s–1610s) to Ottoman siege of Vienna (1683) "circle of justice" and Ottoman legal reforms (secular and Sharia law)
Africa	impact of European arrival (1410s+) Songhai (Askia Mohammed, 1400s–1500s) and military rivalry with Morocco centralized kingdoms (Kongo, Ashanti, Dahomey) Omani Arabs in East Africa (1650s+) arrival in 1600s of Dutch (Boer) colonists in South Africa (vs. Xhosa and Zulu)
East (and Central) Asia	impact of European arrival (1500s+) Ming dynasty (1368–1644) in China and Li Zicheng's revolt (1630s–1640s) Manchu conquest and Qing dynasty (1644–1912) in China mandate of heaven daimyo feudalism in Japan (late 1100s–early 1500s) reunification of Japan (late 1500s) and Tokugawa shogunate (1603–1868)
South (and Southeast) Asia and Oceania	impact of European arrival (1490s+) gunpowder empire = Mughal Empire (1500s–mid-1800s) Sikh and Maratha states (late 1600s–mid-1800s) joint-stock companies = British East India Company, Dutch East India Company Spanish colonization of Manila (1571) and the Philippines
Americas	impact of European arrival (1490s+) and colonies conquistadors defeat Aztecs and Incas (early 1500s) piracy in the Caribbean (1500s–1700s) joint-stock company = Hudson's Bay Company
Global and Interregional	greater political centralization and new bureaucratic elites global impact of European age of exploration = trading-post and maritime empires (1400s+) Dutch and English rivalry with Portugal and Spain over trade routes and colonies (1500s–1600s) Omani-European competition over East Africa and Indian Ocean basin (1650s+) global impact of Seven Years' War, especially in Canada and India (1756–1763)

Governance

- During the 1500s and 1600s, global might was concentrated in China and the Islamic world's gunpowder empires: Ottoman Turkey, Safavid Persia, and Mughal India.
- The nations of Europe grew more powerful. By the early 1700s, they were overtaking the civilizations listed above in terms of military, scientific, and technological aptitude.
- The most dramatic development of the era was the European campaign to explore (and, where possible, colonize) the rest of the world. Numerous European states—Portugal, Spain, the Dutch Republic, England, and France, for example—created trading-post empires and maritime empires with a truly global reach.
- European colonization of the Americas, the African coast, and parts of Asia set the stage for a massive burst of imperial activity during the 1800s. It also sparked military competition among European powers for global dominance, including the Seven Years' War (1756–1763), which raged not only in Europe but also in North America and India and can be considered one of history's first "world wars."
- Several states, including Russia, Ottoman Turkey, Mughal India, and China under the Manchus, created expansive land empires.
- In addition to multicultural and multiethnic land empires, nation-states in the contemporary sense of the word emerged. These were political units with relatively fixed borders, a sense of national unity, and populations that were largely (though never completely) homogeneous in terms of language and ethnicity.
- State consolidation in many regions led to greater political centralization and sophistication. Features of modern government—such as bureaucracies, treasuries, and state banks—became more commonplace. Rulers devised more reliable means to collect taxes and conscript soldiers.
- At times, state consolidation sparked rebellions and other episodes of resistance to centralized authority.
- State-building techniques included impressive displays of architecture and art as well as continued reliance on religious concepts to legitimate the authority of the regime.
- Most monarchies remained traditionally autocratic or absolutist, but some nations experimented with forms of government that were more representative, including parliamentary monarchy.
- The increased importance of gunpowder weaponry meant that from this time forward, military strength depended even more on technological aptitude than before.

Cultural Developments and Interactions, 1450–1750	
Europe	Renaissance continues and spreads through Europe (1300s–early 1600s) baroque style (1600s) Enlightenment begins (1700s) Protestant Reformation (1500s) architecture (St. Peter's, 1500s; Versailles, 1600s)
Middle East	widening of the Sunni-Shiite split miniature painting in Persia and Ottoman Turkey carpet weaving architecture (Suleiman Mosque, 1500s; Blue Mosque, 1600s; Great Plaza of Isfahan, 1600s)

Cultural Developments and Interactions, 1450–1750	
Africa	sculpture and carving (Benin and Oyo bronzes) textile weaving and basketry oral tradition (griots) *Sundiata* epic (1300s+) *The Epic of Askia Mohammed* (1500s+)
East (and Central) Asia	porcelain Qing imperial portraits *Journey to the West* (1500s) kabuki theater ukiyo-e woodblock prints architecture (Beijing's Summer Palace, 1700s)
South (and Southeast) Asia and Oceania	Sikhism (1500s) miniature painting in Mughal India Indo-Persian cultural fusion architecture (Taj Mahal, Red Fort, both 1600s)
Americas	religious syncretism (vodun, Latin American cult of saints) creole, mestizo, and other "mixed" traditions Florentine Codex and other Mesoamerican codices (1500s) architecture (Mesoamerican pyramids; Machu Picchu and Incan sun temple in Andes)
Global and Interregional	growing impact of the printing press increased availability of culture to nonelite classes cultural impact of Europe's age of exploration global spread of Christianity

Cultural Developments and Interactions

■ After the European encounter with the Americas, networks of communication and exchange moved beyond the level of transregional and became truly global. The Atlantic basin in particular became a gigantic cauldron of economic, cultural, religious, ethnic, political, and military interaction.

■ Most major societies possessed well-defined artistic and literary traditions. Increased technological aptitude enabled the production of arts and crafts of high quality.

■ The increased influence of the printing press led to the rapid spread of information and new ideas. By creating more materials to read—and more incentive to read—the printing press helped to boost literacy rates.

■ Art, literature, and drama became more accessible to popular audiences among wider segments of society—including the emerging middle classes and, in some cases, the lower classes—not just to elite classes.

■ Architecture and art continued to be used for political purposes, especially to show off the power and grandeur of various rulers and regimes.

■ New and syncretic religions appeared during this era, including vodun (voodoo) in the Caribbean, the cult of saints in Latin America, and Sikhism in India.

- Within established religions, schisms appeared or widened. The Sunni-Shiite split in Islam grew more pronounced during this era, as did the influence of Sufism within Islam. Europe experienced a religious earthquake, the Protestant Reformation, that profoundly affected not just matters of faith but cultural life, military and political affairs, and the way Europeans spread Christianity to other parts of the world.
- The movement of Europeans and Africans (mainly enslaved) altered the patterns of North and South American ethnicity, religion, language, art, and music.
- Buddhism and Christianity spread particularly far during these years, thanks to missionary activity, trade, and colonization.

Technology and Innovation, 1450–1750	
Europe	impact of Renaissance and printing press on growing scientific awareness heliocentric theory (Copernicus and Galileo) Scientific Revolution (scientific method) and Newtonian physics improvements in navigational and marine science and technology (magnetic compass, sailing ships) innovations in gunpowder weaponry
Middle East	innovations in gunpowder weaponry (janissary musketeers) astronomical expertise
Africa	importation of European technology and gunpowder expertise
East (and Central) Asia	stagnation in China's use of gunpowder weaponry limited influence of "Dutch learning" (European scientific knowledge) in Japan
South (and Southeast) Asia and Oceania	innovations in gunpowder weaponry
Americas	importation of European technology and gunpowder expertise
Global and Interregional	shift in balance of scientific and technological expertise from Middle East and China to Europe growing impact of printing press in spreading scientific and technological expertise gunpowder revolution in Eurasian states

Technology and Innovation

- The level of scientific knowledge and technological achievement was especially high in civilizations such as China, Ottoman Turkey, Mughal India, and Safavid Persia.
- Europe made exceptional strides in terms of scientific knowledge and technological achievement. The Renaissance, Scientific Revolution, and Enlightenment all furthered the intellectual growth of Europe to the point that, during the late 1600s and 1700s, it overtook the civilizations listed above.
- The increased influence of the printing press led to the rapid spread of scientific knowledge, especially in Europe and North America.

- The global impact of gunpowder weaponry grew steadily throughout this era.
- Advances in maritime and navigational science and technology—including adoption of the magnetic compass and the crafting of sailing ships like the carrack, caravel, fluyt, and galleon—helped to alter the balance of world power in Europe's favor.

Economic Systems, 1450–1750	
Europe	mercantilism joint-stock companies (including Dutch East India Company, Hudson's Bay Company, British East India Company) investment disasters ("bubbles"): tulipmania, Mississippi Bubble, South Sea Bubble silver glut and inflation cottage industry and protoindustrialization
Middle East	relative decline of Silk Road Omani-European rivalry in Indian Ocean and East Africa Ottoman-Persian competition over Indian Ocean trade carpets and textiles silver glut and inflation
Africa	arrival of European traders and trading-post empires Omani-European rivalry in Indian Ocean and East Africa Arab slave trade continues Atlantic slave trade begins and intensifies
East (and Central) Asia	relative decline of Silk Road appearance of European traders Chinese and Japanese restrictions on European traders porcelain and tea silver glut and inflation
South (and Southeast) Asia and Oceania	appearance of European traders and trading-post empires Omani-European rivalry in Indian Ocean Ottoman-Persian competition over Indian Ocean trade cotton and spices
Americas	European piracy and privateering in Caribbean rise of plantation and cash-crop agriculture increased reliance on slavery and coerced labor sugar, cotton, tobacco, coffee, silver
Global and Interregional	global circulation of trade goods (finished products and raw materials) piracy, privateering, and state competition over trade routes triangular trade in the Atlantic influx of New World silver into world economy increased agricultural production (plantation agriculture) increased manufacturing and the emergence of protoindustrial production increased resource extraction (mining, fishing, hunting)

Economic Systems

- The incorporation of the Americas into existing networks of exchange led to the emergence of a truly global economic system, complete with the worldwide circulation of raw materials and finished products.

- The emergence of a "triangular" Atlantic trade system, combined with the Europeans' ability to circumnavigate the globe, disrupted and altered traditional trade routes, particularly land routes such as the Silk Road.

- Competition over trade routes, especially maritime ones, affected state relations in several parts of the world, including the Atlantic Ocean, the Caribbean Sea, and the Indian Ocean.

- Agriculture remained dominant as a mode of economic production and as the form of labor practiced by the vast majority of people worldwide. Even so, trade and manufacturing became steadily more important during these years.

- The rise in global productivity and wealth rested on a foundation of coerced labor, which took many forms. The Atlantic and Arab slave trades were extensive. Serfdom was common in Europe (especially Russia) and other parts of the world. Plantation and cash-crop agriculture in the Americas was based on unfree labor.

- Mercantilism became the dominant economic principle of colonizing states that formed maritime or trading-post empires. Joint-stock companies and monopolies with royal charters financed and carried out much of this era's exploration and colonization. These included the Dutch East India Company, the Hudson's Bay Company, the Company of New France, and the British East India Company.

- During the 1500s and 1600s, Spanish and Portuguese extraction of precious metals, especially silver, from the Americas affected economies around the world. This huge and sudden influx of coinage into so many economies created a harmful glut, leading to severe inflation in places as diverse as China, Europe, and the Ottoman Empire.

- In several civilizations, primarily Europe, protoindustrial modes of production began to appear, especially during the 1700s. By the late 1700s, the concept of capitalism was emerging as well. Both of these trends would have a profound impact on economic life in the 1800s.

- Interregional trade was affected by the global cooling that led to the Little Ice Age.

Social Interactions and Organization, 1450–1750	
Europe	serfdom (declining in Western Europe, increasing in Russia)
	German Peasants' War (early 1500s) + Russian serf and Cossack uprisings (1600s–1700s)
	rise of the burgher and bourgeoisie (middle) classes
	elite adjustments for European nobles (nobility of the sword vs. nobility of the robe; Russia's Table of Ranks)
	Protestant-Catholic religious strife
	anti-Semitism
	patriarchy continues, with slightly improved opportunities for women of middle and upper classes

Social Interactions and Organization, 1450–1750	
Middle East	elite adjustments (janissaries and devshirme civil servants) devshirme (Ottoman slave-recruiting system) Celali revolts (1590s–1610s) Arab slave trade jizya tax for subject nonbelievers (dhimmi) mudarra ("moderation") policy and the millet (Ottoman system for religious minorities) Islam and patriarchy (veiling, seclusion, polygamy, the harem)
Africa	Arab slave trade in North and East Africa growth of Atlantic slave trade (1400s–1800s; Middle Passage, triangular trade) matrilineal social organization in certain areas impact of Arab and Atlantic slave trades on family structure
East (and Central) Asia	intensification of peasant labor (silk) elite adjustments (mandarin bureaucrats in China; salaried samurai in Japan) Li Zicheng's peasant revolt and the fall of China's Ming dynasty (1630s–1640s) serfdom and social stratification in Tokugawa Japan Neo-Confucianism and patriarchy (foot binding) samurai patriarchy and geisha courtesans
South (and Southeast) Asia and Oceania	intensification of peasant labor (cotton) elite adjustments (zamindar landowners) tolerance and tensions among India's Hindus, Muslims, and Sikhs (Akbar the Great vs. Aurangzeb) Hinduism and patriarchy (sati, seclusion) Islam and patriarchy (veiling, seclusion, and polygamy) role of Southeast Asian women in early encounters between European traders and Asian populations
Americas	encomienda system (1500s) Spanish adaptation of mit'a system plantation monoculture (sugarcane, cotton, tobacco) Atlantic slave trade (1400s–1800s, Middle Passage, triangular trade) indentured servitude in North America creole and mixed populations (República de Indios and race-based hierarchies in Latin America) role of women in encounters between European arrivals and native populations (Malinche, Pocahontas)
Global and Interregional	increased agricultural production and greater tax and conscription burdens on peasants urbanization and class diversification growth of artisan (craftsman) and urban working classes growth and ambiguous status of middle and merchant classes political and economic adjustments for elite classes coerced labor and chattel slavery become increasingly common patriarchy continues

Social Interactions and Organization

- Agriculture remained dominant as the form of labor practiced by the vast majority of people worldwide. Most people lived in rural settings.

- As the centralizing power of the state expanded, especially its power to gather taxes and conscript soldiers, pressure on peasant communities increased, occasionally leading to peasant revolts and rebellions.

- New forms of peasant labor, including plantation farming and cash-crop monoculture, arose to take their place alongside traditional methods.

- The rise in global productivity and wealth rested on a foundation of coerced labor, which took many forms, including chattel slavery, or the direct ownership of human beings. The Atlantic and Arab slave trades were extensive. Serfdom was common in Europe (especially Russia) and other parts of the world. Plantation and cash-crop agriculture in the Americas was based on unfree labor.

- Social diversification resulted from the increased importance of banking, commerce, trade, shopkeeping, artisanry, and manufacturing. Growth in these sectors led to the creation of middle and urban working classes. These were small to begin with but grew in numbers and in cultural and social influence.

- Urbanization continued. This trend was often related to an increase in social mobility.

- Elite classes in many regions faced new challenges either because of political centralization on the part of their monarchs or because of greater importance being placed on trade and money-based wealth rather than on land—which, for centuries, had been the source and measure of power and riches for traditional elites.

- In more societies, merit became important as a criterion for social advancement and even for entry into the elite classes.

- Diasporic communities and foreign enclaves continued to form in many towns and ports due to the expansion of interregional and global trade.

- Colonization, particularly in the Americas, created mixed populations, such as mulattos, mestizos, and creoles. New hierarchies emerged in Europe's New World colonies.

- Ethnic and religious minorities were treated differently in various parts of the world. In some cases, they enjoyed freedom and equal status. More often, though, they were persecuted, treated as second-class citizens, or restricted in various ways.

- Family and gender relations underwent restructuring. In Europe, for example, families tended to grow smaller.

- In most parts of the world, women continued to occupy a secondary status in terms of social roles, economic opportunities, and political influence. In parts of Europe, a limited awareness that the treatment of women was unjust began to develop.

- Individual women from small but important segments of society—from the aristocracy or emerging middle class, for example—gained educations, became active in business, made scientific discoveries, and became artists and writers.

- Local women often played crucial roles during economic or political encounters between their own people and European colonizers and traders.

Humans and the Environment, 1450–1750	
Europe	arrival of corn/maize, potatoes, and other crops via Columbian Exchange fur hunting increases (especially in Siberia)
Middle East	coffee spreads throughout region (1400s–1500s)
Africa	arrival of corn/maize, manioc, and other crops via Columbian Exchange enlargement of Sahara Desert due to Little Ice Age
East (and Central) Asia	arrival of corn/maize, potatoes, and other crops via Columbian Exchange
South (and Southeast) Asia and Oceania	arrival of corn/maize, potatoes, chili peppers, and other crops via Columbian Exchange
Americas	arrival of horses, pigs, cattle, and other animals via Columbian Exchange arrival of sugarcane, cotton, okra, rice, coffee, and other crops via Columbian Exchange Afro-Eurasian diseases (smallpox, measles, and influenza) kill at least 50 percent of indigenous Americans plantation and monoculture agriculture (sugarcane, cotton, coffee, tobacco) silver mining (Potosí) fur hunting in North America
Global and Interregional	Little Ice Age reaches its peak (ca. 1500–mid-1800s) environmental impact of mining, manufacturing, and urbanization increases in many regions environmental impact of fishing and whaling increases, especially in the Atlantic environmental impact of fur hunting increases

Humans and the Environment

- The European age of exploration brought the Americas into contact with Afro-Eurasia at the end of the 1400s. The transmission of foodstuffs, animal species, and disease pathogens between these geographical areas is known as the Columbian Exchange.

- The introduction of Afro-Eurasian diseases (especially smallpox, measles, and influenza) into the Americas caused a massive demographic crisis, killing at least one-half of the indigenous population and perhaps much more.

- The importation of corn (maize), potatoes, and manioc from the Americas dramatically altered the diets and agricultural practices of Europe, Africa, and eventually Asia. Tomatoes had an impact as well, and American-grown crops like tobacco and cacao (from which chocolate is made) were highly desired by Europeans. Populations rose significantly throughout Europe, Africa, and Asia as a result of the new foods.

- To the Americas, Europeans and Africans brought horses, pigs, and cattle. Afro-Eurasian crops transplanted to the Americas included okra, rice, citrus, bananas and other fruits, sugarcane, coffee, and cotton.

- The introduction of European modes of economic production into the Americas, especially plantation agriculture and the cultivation of cash crops like sugar and tobacco, radically altered North and South American ecosystems.

- Fishing, whaling, and the hunting of fur-bearing animals—activities with a significant environmental impact—became increasingly important to the economies of European nations, especially as they intensified their efforts to explore and colonize larger parts of the world.
- Manufacturing and mining increased in importance, leading to greater resource extraction and a heavier environmental impact.
- The movement of peoples between Afro-Eurasia and the Americas, whether voluntary or involuntary, ranks as one of the most important migrations in history.
- After a gradual cooling during the 1300s and 1400s, the Little Ice Age hit its peak between the early 1500s and the early-to-mid-1800s.

QUESTIONS AND COMPARISONS TO CONSIDER

- Consider various forms of state consolidation during this era as well as the state-building techniques (use of religious concepts, improvements in bureaucracy and infrastructure, better tax gathering, displays of art and architecture, and so on) they used to maintain, expand, and legitimate power.
- How were states in Africa and the Americas similar to and different from those in Europe and Asia? Also compare European monarchies with Asian states.
- Compare the emerging Atlantic slave trade with other systems of coerced labor, such as serfdom in Russia, the Arab slave network in Africa and the Mediterranean, the encomienda and hacienda systems in Latin America, and the Ottoman devshirme.
- What technologies and innovations facilitated exploration and imperial expansion? What made European exploration different from earlier campaigns of exploration and long-range oceanic navigation?
- Examine the emergence of gunpowder weaponry, the way it spread, and the consequences of its invention, both military and political.
- Compare elite classes, such as Europe's noble class, zamindars in Mughal India, mandarin civil servants in China, and the daimyo in Japan. What other elites existed or emerged? Did the criteria for elite status include wealth, birthright, or merit? What challenges did traditional elites face during this era, whether because of the increased centralization of states or because of the rising economic importance of trade, commerce, and manufacture?
- What were the consequences of the rise of trade and commerce in different regions? How did trade and commerce enrich and/or disrupt existing social, political, and cultural practices?
- How did elites in non-European regions interact with European traders and colonizers?
- What were the environmental effects of the European encounter with the Americas? The economic effects? What were the social and cultural consequences? What mixed populations came into being as a result?
- Examine the development of popular and more easily accessible forms of culture, such as drama, poetry and the novel, and painting.
- Where did literacy improve most quickly? What impact did the printing press have on this development? What were the implications?
- Compare religious developments in various parts of the world. To what degree did religious schisms and disputes affect social and political life more widely? How did interregional interactions affect religion?
- Contemplate the restructuring of gender and family relationships during this era.
- Consider key state rivalries during this period. Also consider the way competition over trade affected the global balance of power and patterns of international commerce.

UNIT 2

SCENIC ROUTE
(Chapters 7–12)

Governance, 1450–1750

7

IN THIS CHAPTER

→ EMERGENCE OF NATION-STATES

→ POLITICAL AND ADMINISTRATIVE CENTRALIZATION (BUREAUCRATIC ELITES)

→ LAND EMPIRES VS. MARITIME EMPIRES AND TRADING-POST EMPIRES

→ EUROPE'S AGE OF EXPLORATION (VASCO DA GAMA, CHRISTOPHER COLUMBUS, FERDINAND MAGELLAN)

→ CONQUISTADORS AND THE ENCOMIENDA SYSTEM IN THE AMERICAS

→ JOINT-STOCK COMPANIES (DUTCH EAST INDIA COMPANY, BRITISH EAST INDIA COMPANY, HUDSON'S BAY COMPANY)

→ ATLANTIC SLAVE TRADE AND COLONIAL-ERA FORMS OF COERCED LABOR

→ GLOBAL COMPETITION OVER TRADE ROUTES AND OVERSEAS COLONIES

→ ABSOLUTISM AND PARLIAMENTARISM IN EUROPE

→ ISLAMIC GUNPOWDER EMPIRES = OTTOMAN TURKEY + SAFAVID PERSIA + MUGHAL INDIA

→ SONGHAI VS. MOROCCO; KONGO AND ASHANTI; ZULU VS. BOER COLONISTS

→ MING AND QING DYNASTIES IN CHINA

→ JAPANESE UNIFICATION AND THE TOKUGAWA SHOGUNATE

→ IDEOLOGIES AND POLITICAL USES OF RELIGION (DIVINE RIGHT, DAR AL-ISLAM, CIRCLE OF JUSTICE, MANDATE OF HEAVEN)

→ MILITARY REVOLUTION THESIS

→ MAJOR CONFLICTS AND BATTLES (FALL OF CONSTANTINOPLE, EUROPE'S RELIGIOUS WARS AND THIRTY YEARS' WAR, 1683 SIEGE OF VIENNA, OTTOMAN-SAFAVID COMPETITION, SONGHAI-MOROCCO CONFLICT, OMANI-EUROPEAN RIVALRY OVER EAST AFRICA AND INDIAN OCEAN TRADE, SEVEN YEARS' WAR)

During the first centuries of this era—the 1500s and 1600s—global might was concentrated mainly in states like China and the Islamic world's gunpowder empires: Ottoman Turkey, Safavid Persia, and Mughal India.

However, in a major geopolitical development, the nations of Europe grew steadily more powerful. By the early 1700s, they were overtaking the civilizations listed above in military, scientific, and technological aptitude. Much of this change had to do with the European campaign, starting in the 1400s, to explore the rest of the world. Between the 1500s and 1700s, numerous European states—including Portugal, Spain, the Dutch Republic, England, and France—created trading-post empires and maritime empires with a truly global reach.

Another key development of this period involved the incorporation of gunpowder weaponry into warfare as it was practiced by a number of Eurasian states. Both state building at home and imperial expansion in both hemispheres depended on skill in deploying gunpowder in the infantry, cannons, and gunships as well as on the ability to build new fortresses and fortified cities capable of defending against gunpowder artillery.

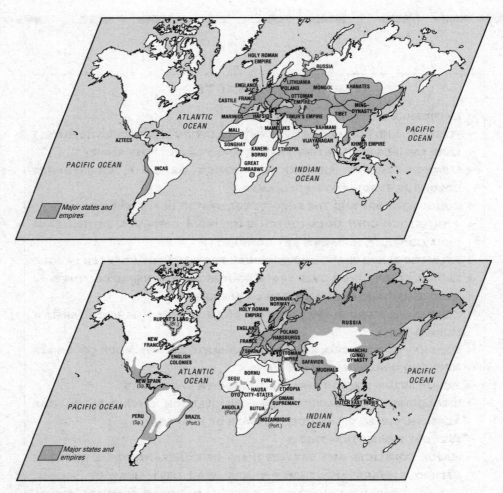

World Boundaries in 1453 and 1700

In 1453, major states and empires were concentrated in Eurasia and small territories in Africa and the Americas. By 1700, large civilizations had spread into Russia, into more portions of the Americas, and deeper into Africa.

STATECRAFT: OLD AND NEW TECHNIQUES OF GOVERNANCE

In addition to multicultural and multiethnic land empires, **nation-states**, in the contemporary sense of the term, emerged. These were political units with relatively fixed borders, a sense of national unity, and populations that were largely (though never completely) homogeneous in terms of language and ethnicity.

In many parts of the world, **political and administrative centralization** became more sophisticated and led to a higher degree of state organization and efficiency. Features of modern government—such as bureaucracies, treasuries, and state banks—were more commonplace. Rulers devised more reliable and more efficient means to collect taxes and conscript soldiers.

As in earlier eras, **state-building techniques** included impressive displays of architecture and art. Regimes also continued to rely on religious concepts to legitimate their authority. As detailed in Chapter 11, states grew more adept at placing ethnic and religious minorities more firmly under their control while keeping them economically productive. Examples include the Ottoman Empire's treatment of non-Muslim subjects, the exercise of Manchu authority over ethnic Chinese during the Qing dynasty, and the Spanish treatment of native populations in their New World colonies. Many states also depended on larger and more modern **bureaucratic elites**. Examples include the civil servants recruited by the Ottoman **devshirme system**, the **Chinese mandarins** who arose thanks to the Confucian examination system, and various nobles who adapted to civil service in several places—such as Russia (the **Table of Ranks**), Japan (**salaried samurai**), and Europe (see France's **nobles of the robe** during the 1600s and 1700s).

Most monarchies remained autocratic or absolutist, but some nations experimented with more representative forms of government, including parliamentary monarchy. While many states established new **land empires** or expanded existing ones, the nations of Europe, as described below, took the lead in building **trading-post empires** and **maritime empires** across the globe.

EMPIRE BUILDING: THE AGE OF EXPLORATION AND COLONIZATION

Between the early 1400s and the mid-1700s, the nations of Europe accomplished what no other civilization had done. They explored the wider world around them, discovered how to sail around the globe, and mapped the planet's major oceans and landmasses.

With this knowledge came great power and wealth, but the legacy of European exploration and colonization is mixed. Europe eventually became the planet's dominant civilization but paid a steep moral price in exchange. Colonization went hand in hand with war, greed, racial and religious intolerance, and slavery. Many parts of the world remained under European rule for centuries, and even now, the tensions left over between Western nations and their former colonies continue to affect international relations.

Motivations and Capabilities

Why and how did the Europeans become the first to explore the world? For centuries, European states were less technologically and scientifically advanced than those in the Middle East and Far East, and their geographical knowledge was limited until the 1400s. As noted earlier, it was China that invented several key **navigational and maritime technologies**, such as the astrolabe, the magnetic compass, and the sternpost rudder. And with the voyages of **Zheng He** in the early 1400s, China had the potential to lead the way in world exploration—although it turned its back on that opportunity.

Early on, Europe's primary motivation for exploring was economic. Throughout the Middle Ages, **Mediterranean trade**, greater awareness of the Middle East gained during **the Crusades**, and tales told by travelers like **Marco Polo** whetted European appetites for the wealth of eastern locales like China, the Indies, and Japan. Rather than rely on the **Silk Road** and Middle Eastern middlemen, Europeans increasingly wanted their own direct access to Asiatic goods such as **silk**, **spices**, and other luxury items.

As the Europeans' interest in exploring grew, so did their ability to voyage farther and more safely. By the 1300s and early 1400s, the Europeans were adopting from Asia key navigational and maritime technologies: the **astrolabe**, the **magnetic compass**, and the **sternpost rudder**. At the same time, Europeans were developing **sailing ships** capable of long-range oceanic voyaging, with deep keels for stability and advanced rigging systems that permitted ships to sail where they needed to despite the direction of the wind. The most important model was the nimble, three-masted **caravel**, in extensive use by the 1400s, but the Dutch fluyt and the larger carrack played roles as well.

Gunpowder weaponry, which the Europeans began to use in the 1300s and 1400s, also had an impact on the age of exploration. Wherever they went, European sailors and soldiers came equipped with muskets and cannons. Used against less technologically advanced natives, these weapons allowed for faster and easier colonization. By the 1500s and 1600s, the Europeans had invented **galleons** and other large **gunships** that allowed them to project even greater quantities of firepower.

The Iberian Wave: Portugal and Spain

The first European nations to systematically explore the wider Atlantic world were Portugal and Spain, on the Iberian peninsula.

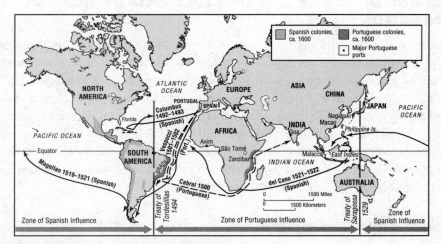

Spanish and Portuguese Exploration, 1492–1529
The first European nations to colonize the wider world were Spain and Portugal. Their successes are attested to in this map. The north-south lines of demarcation were established by the papacy, to whose authority both nations, being Catholic, submitted.

Portugal's exploring efforts, encouraged by **Prince Henry the Navigator**, began around 1410 with voyages to the west and south. The Portuguese claimed several Atlantic island groups, including the Azores, as well as ports along Africa's west coast. In 1488, Bartholomeu Díaz reached the southern tip of Africa, which the rulers of Portugal named the **Cape of Good Hope**, recognizing this as an important step on the way to India. Over the next decade, the Portuguese made their way into the Indian Ocean basin, capturing East African ports and cities and then crossing the ocean to India itself. The first European to reach India by sea was Portugal's **Vasco da Gama**, who landed in Calicut in 1498, earning an immense profit upon returning home. The Portuguese quickly took steps to enlarge their presence in Africa and Asia.

In the meantime, the Spanish, distracted by anti-Muslim reconquest in southern Spain, fell behind Portugal when it came to exploring. Blocked from following Portugal's African-Indian Ocean route to Asia, Spain's monarchs—Ferdinand and Isabella—turned to the unusual proposal made in 1492 by the Italian captain **Christopher Columbus**: to sail west to reach the Far East. The boldness of Columbus's plan lay not in the idea that the world was round (a fact known to educated Europeans) but in his erroneous belief that the globe was small enough that an expedition would be able to sail from Spain to Asia before running out of food or water or without being barred by some other landmass. Columbus set sail in August 1492 and reached the Caribbean's Bahama islands in October.

Columbus himself was convinced that he had found the Indies—hence the mistaken term "Indians" for indigenous Americans—but others quickly realized that he had found something completely unknown to Europe. Spain and Portugal turned to the pope to determine who could claim which parts of this "New World." In **lines of demarcation** agreed to between 1492 and 1529, the pope gave most of South America and all of North America to the Spanish. The Portuguese received Brazil, which was discovered in 1500. The pope similarly defined Spanish and Portuguese spheres of influence in Asia. In the 1520s, all of the two countries' earlier efforts were tied together by **Ferdinand Magellan**, a Portuguese mariner sailing on behalf of Spain. Leader of the first **circumnavigation of the globe**, Magellan left Europe in 1519, traversed the Atlantic, and rounded the tip of South America. His ships crossed the Pacific and returned to Europe in 1522, although he himself died along the way, in the Philippine islands.

The Portuguese and Spanish now established a commercial or colonial presence wherever they could. In the Far East and Southeast Asia, most states were too strong or advanced for the Portuguese to conquer, and for the most part, the Portuguese settled for trade. Still, they took over certain areas. In addition to their West African outposts, they gained control over East African cities like Mombasa and **Zanzibar** and even the port of **Muscat** (1507) in the Arab state of **Oman**. They also seized the Indian port of Goa (1510), the thriving commercial center of **Melaka** (Malacca, 1511), and the island of Sri Lanka. Portugal opened up ties with China in the 1510s and with Japan in the 1540s, and while the Chinese granted it the port of Macau in 1557 as a reward for fighting pirates, the Portuguese had no hope of actual conquest here. What they built in this part of the world is generally referred to among historians as a **trading-post empire**. In the 1600s, Portugal lost many of these colonial and commercial assets to the Dutch, English, and Omani Arabs.

> **NOTE**
>
> Spain's colonial presence in Asia remained quite limited relative to its vast holdings in the Americas. Of key importance, though, was its control over the Philippines, especially the port of Manila, which Spain took in 1571. Strategically vital as a naval asset, Manila also became a crucial link in the global silver trade: a transfer point through which precious metals mined in South America were shipped across the Pacific to ports in South and East Asia, especially to China.

In the New World, by contrast, the Portuguese and Spanish founded **maritime empires**, or overseas colonies fully under their control. Portugal moved into Brazil, while Spain built up power in the Caribbean, using islands such as Cuba, Puerto Rico, and Hispaniola (today Haiti and the Dominican Republic) as bases. The mainland fell to **conquistadors**: generals who received permission from the crown to bring huge parts of North and South America under Spanish control and to profit themselves while doing so. Florida fell to Juan Ponce de León in 1513. The Mayans first encountered the Spanish around 1502, and various Mayan communities and city-states were conquered between the 1520s and 1590s. Spain's most dramatic victories involved **Hernán Cortés**, who carried out the brutal **conquest of the Aztecs** (1519–1521), and **Francisco Pizarro**, who accomplished a similar **conquest of the Incas** in the 1530s. The Aztec capital of Tenochtitlán, renamed Mexico City, became the headquarters for all of **New Spain**, and Cortés's success opened the way to Spanish domination of Mexico, Mesoamerica, and most of what is now the U.S. Southwest along with California. Pizarro opened the way to the Spanish takeover of South America.

Several factors aided these conquests. **Horses**, metal armor, and **gunpowder weapons** gave the Spanish and Portuguese sizable military advantages, making up for their small numbers (Cortés brought only a few hundred Spaniards to fight the Aztecs, while Pizarro led barely over a hundred). European arrivals also proved adept at **divide-and-conquer tactics**, whereby they stirred up rivalries among native groups and allied with some against others. This proved especially effective against the relatively new Aztec and Incan Empires, many of whose conquered subjects deeply resented their masters and embraced the Spanish as potential liberators. This allowed Cortés to enlarge his forces to a total of 200,000 before moving against Moctezuma II of the Aztecs. (As noted in Chapter 11, local women provided invaluable diplomatic guidance and contacts, the most notable example being Cortés's Nahua mistress **Malinche**, or Doña Marina.) By far the most important reason for Spain's and Portugal's triumph over the New World was the grimmest: as part of the **Columbian Exchange** discussed in Chapter 12, diseases like **smallpox** and **measles**, brought from Afro-Eurasia by European colonizers, killed indigenous Americans in massive numbers. Most historians now estimate that at least half of the Americas' original population perished (some believe that up to 90 percent died)—and the survivors were left all the more vulnerable to European conquest.

The conquistador Cortés famously stated that he came to the Americas for "God, gold, and glory." Although the conversion of Native Americans to Catholicism was considered important, particularly to offset the loss of European worshippers to Protestant churches, economic exploitation was the highest priority for Spain and Portugal in the New World. The most important activities were **mining** (especially for **silver** near Mexico City and at **Potosí**, Bolivia's "mountain of silver") and **plantation monoculture**—with **sugarcane** the most prized and most labor-intensive cash crop. At first, conquistadors governed the land they took over on the crown's behalf, sending one-fifth (*la quinta*) of their profits back to Spain. Starting in 1535, New Spain was placed under more direct government control as a **viceroyalty** ("in place of the king"), with all colonial economic activity run by the **House of Trade** in Seville. By the 1700s, three new viceroyalties—Peru, New Granada (northern South America), and La Plata (southern South America)—had been added. A similar pattern prevailed in Brazil.

A direct consequence of Spanish and Portuguese colonization in the New World was **coerced labor**. Initially, the **encomienda** ("grant") **system** gave conquistadors and their agents the right to enslave American natives, who were declared against their will to be subjects of Spain. The natives' continued vulnerability to Euro-African diseases lessened their usefulness as a labor force, and many Catholic clergy—including Bartolomé de las Casas, author of the influential *Account of the Destruction of the Indies* (1542–1552)—judged encomienda slavery to be too inhumane, so it was abolished in the early 1540s. This did not stop the Spanish from exploiting "free" native workers in other ways, including low pay and dreadful working conditions. Also, in the Andes, the Spanish took the **mit'a system**, the form of coerced labor used previously by the Incas, and adapted it for their own purposes. Worst of all, the Spanish came to rely increasingly on the importation of slaves

NOTE

The Europeans' growing presence in the Americas sometimes sparked episodes of native resistance. Between 1680 and 1692, the Pueblo Revolt temporarily drove Spanish colonists out of the Santa Fe province of what is now New Mexico. In New England, competition over land and hunting grounds, as well as the encroachment of English laws on native life, convinced the Wampanoag chief Metacomet, son of the once-friendly Massasoit, to fight English settlers. This conflict, King Philip's War (after Metacomet's English nickname), lasted from 1675 to 1678 and raged from Rhode Island up to Maine. Throughout the Caribbean and parts of South America, so-called Maroon communities—consisting of Africans who escaped from slavery and indigenous refugees from colonial rule—lived outside state authority and engaged in various acts of resistance during the 1600s and 1700s.

from Africa, a practice that the Portuguese had begun in the 1400s and had brought to Brazil and the Caribbean by the 1510s. Having been long exposed to the diseases that felled Native American workers, Africans proved a more durable labor source, and racism caused them to be viewed as less worthy of salvation and protection. The first direct shipments of captive Africans to the New World began in the 1520s, and the resulting **Atlantic slave trade** continued well into the 1800s. Over time, Brazil became by far the largest importer of African slaves, and it was the last country in the Americas to outlaw slavery—not until 1888.

The Northern Wave: The French, Dutch, and English

During the 1500s, other European nations began to explore and colonize, the most important being France, the Dutch Republic, and England. From the start, Spain and Portugal were anxious to lock these "northern wave" countries out of Atlantic exploration. At stake were immense wealth, military power, and, except in the case of France, Catholic-Protestant rivalry.

Originally, the only places open to new exploration were those farther north, which the Spanish and Portuguese cared little about. Hoping that a **Northeast Passage** (along Russia's northern coast) or a **Northwest Passage** (through Canada's northern waters) might provide an alternative route to Asia, French, Dutch, and English mariners turned to Arctic and North Atlantic voyaging. These expeditions brought them no closer to Asia, but they did discover rich **fishing** and **whaling grounds**, and they developed an interest in the northern coast of North America. Moreover, by the late 1500s, the French, Dutch, and English had grown strong enough and sufficiently skilled at seafaring to challenge the Spanish and Portuguese for control over Caribbean, Indian Ocean, and Pacific sea routes—and even ports and colonies.

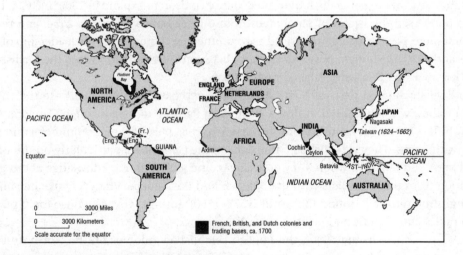

French, English, and Dutch Colonization by 1700
By 1700, France, England, and the Netherlands had gained many imperial footholds in the Americas, the Caribbean, Africa, and Asia.

The French colonial presence in North America began in Canada, in the 1530s, when Jacques Cartier charted the St. Lawrence River. It was during the early 1600s that France established its first cities in Canada—among them Quebec, founded by Samuel Champlain in 1608—and it created the **Company of New France** in the 1620s. Later in the 1600s, the French moved southward, claiming the vast Louisiana territory, which included the Great Lakes and the Mississippi basin. Their highest priority in these areas was the **fur trade**. In the south and along the Gulf of Mexico, the French challenged the Spanish; they seized Caribbean islands as well, such as Martinique and Saint-Domingue (today Haiti), where they grew sugarcane and coffee. Also in the 1600s, the French, like other northern nations, elbowed their way into the Indian Ocean, competing with the Portuguese for trade. The 1700s were less kind to France's colonial efforts. Its principal enemy by this time was England, which took Canada from France as a result of the **French and Indian Wars** (1756–1763), an offshoot of the **Seven Years' War** in Europe. Although the province of Quebec retained its French heritage, French-speaking Acadians were driven out of eastern Canada and forced to resettle in Louisiana, where their descendants are still known as Cajuns. Also during the Seven Years' War, English troops defeated Mughal states allied to the French, ensuring that England, not France, would go on to gain colonial mastery over India.

NOTE

French hunters and trappers were more adept than other Europeans at cooperating with Native Americans (especially the Hurons and Algonquins), adapting themselves to local customs and environments. One factor reducing friction here was that French colonists were less numerous and more interested in fur hunting than farming, which meant less competition over land ownership. By contrast, the agricultural interests of English settlers drew them more directly into conflict with Native Americans.

Exploration by the Dutch was closely tied to their long war of independence against Spain, which lasted from 1568 to 1648. Dutch mariners disrupted Spanish trade and attacked Spanish-controlled ports worldwide, and they did the same to the Portuguese. By 1600, they had begun to seize colonies from both: the port of **Melaka**, the island of Sri Lanka, much of West Africa, and a number of Caribbean islands. In 1619, they captured the Javanese city of Jakarta, renaming it Batavia and using it as a capital from which to colonize the East Indies (modern-day Indonesia). The Dutch controlled the East Indies for centuries, running pepper and spice plantations. Operations here were administered by the **Dutch East India Company**, a joint-stock enterprise founded in 1602. In 1621, a Dutch West India Company was established to oversee Caribbean colonies. For a time, the Dutch also controlled the New York region, which they hired Henry Hudson to explore in 1609. In 1624, Dutch settlers purchased the island of Manhattan from a local Native American tribe, and the city they built there, New Amsterdam, thrived as a commercial center under the leadership of Peter Stuyvesant. New Amsterdam became New York between 1664 and 1674 when the English took it for their own after a series of Anglo-Dutch wars.

The English claimed parts of North America as early as the 1490s thanks to the voyages of John Cabot, who attempted to find a Northwest Passage to Asia through Canada's Arctic waters. In the 1500s, they moved into the New World as part of their commercial and naval rivalry with Spain. They established a presence in the Caribbean, particularly on the islands of Barbados and Jamaica, where they grew sugar, and gained much knowledge about global navigation from their conflicts with the Spanish and Portuguese. Francis Drake became the first Englishman to sail around the world (1577–1580) during a voyage whose main purpose was to raid Spanish ships and ports.

In the 1600s, the English established colonies on the North American mainland. Their first successful settlement was Jamestown, Virginia, founded in 1607 and led by John Smith. Soon after, religious minorities came to North America to flee persecution in England. The *Mayflower* Pilgrims landed at Plymouth Rock in 1620, and Puritans founded the Massachusetts Bay Colony in 1628. Pennsylvania owed its existence to the Quaker William Penn. Economics mattered as well. From the New World, the English took sugarcane, timber, corn, potatoes, and tobacco. They also searched for furs, and the **Hudson's Bay Company**, incorporated in 1670, intruded into Canada and other French colonies for that purpose. As in other parts of the New World, **coerced labor** was part of life in English

NOTE

Pocahontas proved indispensable in forging relations between the Jamestown colony and the local Native Americans. She saved the life of John Smith from her father, the chief, and later married one of the colonists. Like Malinche with Cortés in Mexico, she illustrates the vital role that local women often played in the first encounters between Europeans and native populations.

settlements. Many colonists paid for their passage by means of **indentured servitude**, and English planters came to rely on Africans brought over by the **Atlantic slave trade**.

The English also ventured into the Indian Ocean basin and South Asia. Their first expedition to the Indies came in 1591. Like the Dutch, they interfered with Portuguese trade and forced Portugal to abandon some of its outposts and ports. In 1600, they founded the **British East India Company** to manage economic and military relations with South and Southeast Asia. The English had gained a presence in northwestern India by 1608 and eventually took over more of the subcontinent. They seized the key port of **Melaka** from the Dutch in 1795.

A final observation: it should be noted that indigenous populations in eastern North America fell victim to Afro-Eurasian diseases brought by the English, French, and Dutch (especially **smallpox**) in much the same way that native groups did in the Portuguese- and Spanish-controlled territories to the south and west.

Russia in Siberia and America

Russia, which established a **land empire** in Siberia during the 1500s and 1600s, also extended its reach to North America. After reaching Siberia's Pacific coast in the 1600s, the Russians set their sights on Alaska and other parts of North America. In the 1730s and 1740s, the **Bering Expedition**, a scientific venture organized by the Russian government, surveyed the waters separating Siberia from North America. Afterward, Russian missionaries and hunters moved into the Aleutian Islands and Alaska. The **fur trade** stimulated Russian settlement of Siberia and North America. The Russians established a colony in Alaska in the late 1700s, administered by the **Russian-American Company**. They moved down the Pacific coast, building fortresses as far south as northern California. They sold all their American possessions, Alaska included, to the United States in 1867.

Native Siberians were subjected to the coerced-labor system known as the **yasak**, which required them to pay tribute and hunt fur-bearing animals for the Russians. In Alaska, the Russians fought bitter wars against the indigenous populations. Most notably, at least 80 percent of native Aleutians are said to have perished from Russian colonization due to violence, the spread of disease, and alcoholism.

> **NOTE**
>
> What the conquistador Cortés was to the Aztecs, the Cossack leader Yermak was to the native peoples of Siberia. In the mid-1500s, on contract from the merchant family that had been chartered by the tsar to develop the Russo-Siberian frontier, Yermak led the armies that began the long process of conquering all of Siberia.

MAJOR STATES AND EMPIRES

The world's geopolitical balance was hugely altered in favor of Europe during this era. By the late 1700s, it was the world's most powerful region, having outstripped militarily and technologically advanced states like Qing China, Ottoman Turkey, and Mughal India. Its might would only increase in the 1800s.

Europe

During this era, most European nations became **nation-states** in the modern sense of the word: **politically and administratively centralized** units with fixed borders, a sense of national unity, and mostly homogeneous populations in terms of language and ethnicity. Centralization allowed European monarchs to abandon the weak institutions of medieval feudalism and assert their power with more confidence. Frequently this meant competition between monarchs and noble aristocracies, who were anxious to hold on to the feudal privileges their ancestors had been granted during the Middle Ages.

Two major forms of government emerged in Europe: **absolutism** and **parliamentarism**. In the former, the monarch was theoretically all-powerful, with no legal restrictions on his or her power. (In real life, absolute monarchs could be handicapped by weak personalities, uncooperative nobles, or unreliable armies.) Absolutism in Europe was typically justified by the doctrine of **divine right**, according to which the monarch reigns by the will of God. Europe's archetypal absolute monarch was **Louis XIV** of France, the Sun King, who ruled from 1661 to 1715. In his youth, Louis was profoundly influenced by the **Fronde** (1648–1653), a civil war led by powerful nobles who resented the crown's growing power. With Louis's father dead and his mother governing as regent, the throne seemed vulnerable for these aristocrats to strike, and while they were defeated in the end, the event traumatized Louis enough that he determined as an adult to force noble obedience at all costs.

Accordingly, Louis centralized the French bureaucracy and broke the power of stubborn aristocrats by shifting administrative power from traditionally powerful families (nobility of the sword) to civil servants that he himself ennobled and who therefore owed him loyalty (nobility of the robe). He turned Paris and his palace of **Versailles** into impressive centers of power, and he built the largest army and navy Europe had seen since the fall of Rome. In many ways, Louis illustrates the strengths and weaknesses of absolute monarchy. He was intelligent and capable, but he also persecuted Protestants, even though they had been granted religious freedom in the late 1500s, and he involved France in too many wars, accumulating a national debt that would worsen during the 1700s and eventually help cause the French Revolution.

Most other nations in Europe, among them Austria, Prussia, and Russia, attempted to build absolute monarchies. Noteworthy absolutists included **Peter the Great**, who westernized Russia in the late 1600s and early 1700s and forced his nobles to serve the state according to a strict Table of Ranks, and **Frederick the Great** of Prussia, a skilled general who, during the mid-1700s, made his kingdom vastly more efficient but also more autocratic. Censorship and restrictions on social mobility were the rule in absolute monarchies. In Central and Eastern Europe, especially in Russia, **serfdom** remained in place much longer than in Western Europe, where it faded away for the most part following the Renaissance.

A smaller number of European states chose **parliamentarism**, in which the ruler governed with a lawmaking body appointed by the aristocracy or elected by some or all of the people. As they freed themselves from Spanish rule in the late 1500s, the Dutch developed a parliamentary system in which there was not even a king but an executive official—the *stadtholder*—who shared power with a large council called the States General. Several minor powers, including the city-state of Venice, created similar systems, but the most famous arose in England. Here, monarchs had been compelled to share power with Parliament since the 1200s—even strong-willed ones like **Henry VIII** and his daughter **Elizabeth I** during the 1500s. In the 1600s, the balance of power shifted decisively in favor of Parliament. The English Civil War (1640–1649) led to the execution of the king by Parliamentary forces and to a temporary assumption of power by the Puritan parliamentarian Oliver Cromwell. When the royal family returned in 1660 and resumed the rivalry between monarch and Parliament, the latter overthrew the king once again in the Glorious Revolution of 1688. Parliament then invited the Dutch prince William of Orange to become king but with conditions. William had to agree to the **English Bill of Rights**, which curtailed the powers of the monarch and made Parliament dominant in the English political system. Parliament grew increasingly stronger, while the monarchy steadily weakened.

Nations with parliamentary systems enjoyed certain advantages. Both the Dutch and the English, for example, developed strong commercial economies, powerful navies, urbanized societies, and intellectual and cultural outlooks that were relatively open and free from religious persecution. Although poverty and inequality existed, social mobility tended to be greater than in absolutist states.

The Middle East

The unity of the Abbasid Caliphate as a single Islamic state crumbled during the Middle Ages and vanished in the 1200s. Decades of political confusion followed as Mongol warriors invaded and the Seljuk and Ottoman Turks rose up as regional powers. Afterward, strong political units emerged in the Middle East: the Ottoman Empire, centered in present-day Turkey, and the Safavid Empire in Persia. Both were highly centralized, technologically advanced, and militarily powerful. With the Mughal Empire in India, the Ottoman and Safavid states are referred to as **gunpowder empires** because of their mastery of new weaponry and their effective use of it—at least during the 1500s and 1600s—in accumulating regional might.

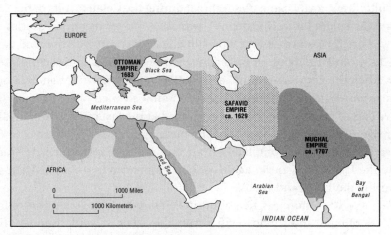

The Islamic World's Gunpowder Empires, ca. 1629–1707

Nomads from Central Asia, the Ottoman Turks established their own state in the 1290s. In the late 1300s and 1400s, they gained hegemony over most of the Middle East, restoring central authority to the region. Making effective use of gunpowder artillery, they accomplished the **conquest of Constantinople** in 1453, and a further wave of expansion in the early 1500s, led by Suleiman the Magnificent, carried the Ottomans deep into southeastern Europe and across most of North Africa (with only Morocco remaining free). The Ottoman presence lingered in both areas until the late 1800s and early 1900s.

The Ottoman sultans borrowed many state-building techniques from the past. In the early 1500s, Selim I claimed religious authority as well as political power, equating the Ottomans' right to rule with that of the bygone Arab caliphates. The sultans also adopted the centuries-old **circle of justice** ideology. They ruled with an elaborate bureaucracy, headed by the grand vizier and staffed by lesser viziers and provincial governors called pashas and beys. Key Ottoman institutions included the **devshirme** system of recruiting civil servants and elite troops—musketeer infantry known as **janissaries**—by enslaving sons from Christian families and placing them in positions of privileged servitude. Also important was the **millet** system, which sorted and administered non-Muslims according to their religious categories. These subjects, known as dhimmi, included Jews and Christians of several denominations and paid the **jizya**, or unbelievers' tax.

The Ottomans' last gifted sultan was **Suleiman the Magnificent** (r. 1520–1566), whose talents as a lawmaker and domestic ruler matched his above-mentioned abilities as a general. Although religious experts—the *ulema* ("learned ones")—continued to wield legal and political influence, Suleiman began a trend of asserting the sultan's right to shape the law, blending secular dictates with Sharia, or Islamic law. This was part of building royal power, but it also had the effect of softening some of the fundamentalist aspects of Muslim tradition.

Many of Suleiman's successors were mediocre or worse and coped ineffectively with key problems in the late 1500s and 1600s. As the empire grew, so did regional autonomy, which threatened to pull away far-flung territories and even provinces closer to home. Like Europe and China, the Ottomans suffered runaway inflation as New World silver flooded the economy, and environmental change—the Little Ice Age—caused terrible famines. Military efforts in the early 1600s, both against the Habsburg Empire to the west and the Safavid Persians in the east, went poorly. Worst of all, political and military elites became less interested in state service and more so in guarding their own privileges, sometimes to the point of defying the sultan. The sultan's authority came under threat during the Celali revolts of the 1590s through the 1610s, and the sultan himself, Osman II, was assassinated by his janissaries in 1622.

Stability was briefly restored by the Köprülü clan, which provided several capable viziers between the 1650s and the 1680s. However, the empire entered a long decline after the pivotal year of 1683, when the Ottomans launched their last major offensive against Europe, driving deep into Austrian territory. The **1683 siege of Vienna** seemed likely to open the way for a full-scale invasion of Europe, but the city was saved at the last minute by a massive Catholic counteroffensive. The Austrians responded by pushing back far to the east, and though the Ottomans were not expelled completely from Europe, they lost much territory to Austria and Russia in the 1700s. They never again seriously menaced Europe, and their global power weakened during the 1700s and 1800s.

NOTE

Existing on the periphery between Russia and the Middle East were Cossack hosts, made up of Russians and Ukrainians living semiautonomously on the frontier—free from serfdom—and intermarrying with local populations. Skilled cavalry warriors, they clashed often with Turks and Persians, sometimes on their own behalf, sometimes in alliance with the Russian state. Although several Cossack revolts troubled Russia in the 1600s and 1700s, they came firmly under Russian control during the 1800s, and many served as the tsar's most loyal troops.

The Ottomans' neighbors in Persia, which had been controlled by various Mongol and Turkic regimes from the 1200s onward, regained their independence during this era. In 1501, Ismail I rose to power, took the ancient title of shah, and proclaimed the Safavid Empire. Devoted to the Shiite form of Islam, the Safavid shahs converted the majority of Persians to that denomination and warred with their Sunni neighbors in the Ottoman Empire. Safavid Persia was economically vibrant, and Isfahan, its chief commercial center, was a hub for the production of silk, ceramics, and Persian rugs. Thanks to Abbas the Great (r. 1587–1628), the Safavids made effective use of gunpowder weaponry and military slavery, much like their Ottoman rivals. Unlike the Ottomans, the Safavids fell in the early 1700s due to a series of famines and plagues. Not only did these disasters cause population loss and tax shortfalls, but they left Persia open to external attacks by Uzbeks from Central Asia and Cossacks from Russia.

Africa

While North Africa came to be ruled by the Ottomans in the 1500s, the rest of the continent was governed in a variety of ways. The biggest changes experienced during this era were the establishment of a long-term European presence along Africa's coasts and the ravages caused by the horrific **Atlantic slave trade**.

Africa's most powerful states arose in the west. As the empire of Mali faded, the Muslim kingdom of **Songhai** took its place in the mid-1400s, asserting control over **Timbuktu** and the region's key trade routes. Songhai's most famous ruler was **Askia Mohammed**, a general who came to the throne by overthrowing the previous monarch (*askia*, his adopted name, means "usurper"). Between 1493 and 1528, Askia expanded Songhai's boundaries and created a complex bureaucracy to centralize his power. A builder of many mosques, he used Islam to justify his rule. He expanded trade, and Songhai's growing merchant class generated wealth by exchanging salt for gold. A fictional account of his reign, *The Epic of Askia Mohammed*, is a classic of the West African oral tradition, performed by **griot** storytellers since the 1500s. Songhai prospered until civil war and invasion by Moroccan forces destroyed it in the 1580s and 1590s. **Morocco**, once ruled by the Berbers, now distinguished itself as the one North African state to remain free from Ottoman rule. Its invasion of Songhai was motivated largely by the need for funds to pay for wars against Christian forces from Portugal and Spain.

After the 1400s, the advent of the Portuguese and other Europeans profoundly shaped the development of West African states. Several of these attained or maintained power by cooperating with the outsiders at the expense of their neighbors. One example is **Kongo**, a Bantu state that took shape around 1400 on the western edge of the modern Congo. The Portuguese arrived in 1483, and though they did not conquer Kongo outright, they took hostages and compelled it to enter a long and coercive partnership. Kongo's monarchs converted to Catholicism, took European names, and gave Portugal favorable trade terms and the right to use their ports. Kongo had little choice, but in many ways, its ties with Portugal enriched and strengthened it. Kongo acquired gunpowder weapons from the Portuguese, using them to defeat fellow Africans, thousands of whom were promptly sold to the Portuguese as slaves. With Dutch help, Kongo expelled the Portuguese in the mid-1600s but fell into disunity and later suffered recolonization. In the 1600s and 1700s, other West African societies likewise warred on and imprisoned their neighbors, then sold the captives to European slavers. In particular, the **Ashanti** (Asante) **kingdom**, founded by Osei Tutu in 1680, grew immensely powerful because its leaders sold gold and slaves to Europeans in exchange for muskets and gunpowder.

NOTE

The arrival of Europeans politically affected West Africa by causing certain states to centralize as a way to avoid being taken over. This centralizing trend was further reinforced by the labor mobilization need to clear land for growing corn, which the Europeans had brought from the Americas and which proved enormously helpful in offsetting the agricultural downturn caused by the Little Ice Age. In addition to Kongo and the Ashanti kingdom described in the main text, Benin, Oyo, and Dahomey consolidated during this era.

Sketch of Queen Nzinga (1582–1663)
Ruler of Angola's Mbundu people, **Nzinga** eventually signed treaties that allowed Portugal access to her country. Before that, however, she stoutly resisted Portuguese domination, accepting aid from Portugal's Dutch enemies and occasionally commanding forces in the field.

In South and East Africa, just as in the west, Portugal established itself as a colonial and trading-post power. This changed significantly in the mid-1600s. Control of South Africa passed to Dutch colonists called **Boers**. Also known as Afrikaners, the Boers enslaved the African herding tribes nearest them, including the peaceful Xhosa, and then encountered a stronger group, the **Zulu**. Many wars broke out between the Zulu and the Boers, and also the English, who arrived on the scene somewhat later. Portuguese power in East Africa was broken during the 1600s and 1700s, both by other Europeans—particularly the Dutch and English—and by **Omani Arabs**, who rose up against Portuguese rule in the 1650s. After expelling the Portuguese from their home port of Muscat, the Omanis proceeded down the East African coast, starting in the 1690s and continuing into the early 1700s, pushing the Portuguese out of many cities, including Zanzibar and Mombasa. Despite this, Portugal maintained a colonial presence in parts of East Africa for a long time to come.

East Asia

Through the early 1400s, Ming China was politically and militarily dynamic. Thanks to the voyages of **Zheng He**, it also had an opportunity to engage in its own campaign of global exploration. But although the Ming kept up their tradition of cultural brilliance and although economic prosperity continued for a while, China grew bureaucratically and strategically stagnant in the late 1500s and early 1600s. The Ming also opened China up to the European traders and Christian, especially Jesuit, missionaries who began arriving in the 1500s: first the Portuguese (who received the port of Macau as a gift for driving away local pirates) and then the Spanish and Dutch.

For the Ming, the 1600s were a time of rapid decline. Government control decentralized. The massive **influx of silver** with which the Portuguese and Spanish paid for trade goods triggered inflation and economic breakdown. New crops from the Americas sparked population growth, but the land's capacity to support that growth was limited, especially because of the general cooling brought on by the **Little Ice Age**. Famines recurred regularly, and the effort to put more land under cultivation led to deforestation, which led in turn to devastating floods.

The Ming state's inability to solve these problems prompted **Li Zicheng's peasant revolt** in the 1630s and early 1640s. This toppled the Ming regime, which ended with the suicide of the last emperor and opened the door for external conquest by the **Manchus**, a Turkic people living to China's northeast. The new dynasty was called the **Qing** ("pure") and lasted from 1644 to 1912. Skilled warlords, the early Qing rulers spent the late 1600s consolidating their rule over southern China and expanding it to the island of Formosa (now Taiwan). They gained control over Mongolia, Tibet, and much of Central Asia, and they forced many neighboring areas into their **tributary system**. For many years, the Manchus, who made up a tiny fraction of the population—1 million ruling over 250 million—subjugated their Chinese subjects by enforcing the ethnically based system of social stratification mentioned in Chapter 11.

Starting in the 1690s, the Qing traded with European nations but regulated trade tightly and limited foreign contacts as much as possible. Christianity was banned in 1724, and by the 1750s, foreign trade was funneled through a handful of ports and border cities, the most important of which was **Canton**, on the Pacific coast. While Qing China sold a high volume of **tea**, **silk**, and **porcelain**, it allowed few imports. This policy of **trade protectionism** made China wealthy but also angered its European trading partners—a growing problem whose consequences were felt in the 1800s.

During the late 1600s and early 1700s, the Qing emperors were capable administrators and strong centralizers. The **Kangxi emperor** (r. 1661–1722) is widely considered one of China's greatest rulers: an adept general, a just lawgiver, and a sponsor of culture and learning. He bolstered Qing authority by claiming to have the **mandate of heaven** and also by patronizing Confucianism, with its emphasis on respect for authority. Unlike many of the rulers who followed him, he appreciated the importance of the West's growing technological aptitude. In the late 1700s, as Qing rulers grew more complacent with respect to scientific and technological advancement, they left the country open to foreign domination in the 1800s.

Japan had been ruled since the end of the 1100s by **shoguns**, military rulers who wielded power on behalf of the symbolically important but politically powerless emperor. A feudal system from the beginning, in which the shoguns shared power with landholding **daimyo** of the **samurai** class, the regime grew increasingly decentralized during the 1300s and 1400s to the point that civil war, banditry, and economic breakdown became the norm during the late 1400s and 1500s. This disunity left Japan open to European influence when the Portuguese arrived in the 1540s, followed by Spanish and Dutch traders and missionaries. The Europeans also introduced gunpowder weapons into Japan.

The **reunification of Japan**, which lasted from 1560 to 1615, was completed by three warlords. The first two relied on gunpowder weapons and an increasingly harsh system of social stratification to defeat their rivals and restore civic order. Finishing the process was **Tokugawa Ieyasu**, a brilliant, ruthless commander who declared himself shogun in 1603 and brought the entire country under his control by 1615. The shogunate he founded lasted until 1868, and the Tokugawa era is often referred to as the "great peace." Peace, however, came at the price of increased autocracy and social hierarchy. Ieyasu moved Japan's capital to the city of Edo (modern-day Tokyo), but the emperor remained a figurehead as before. Japan's **caste system**—samurai, peasants, artisans, and merchants, with *eta* "untouchables" at the bottom—was justified by **Confucian ideology** and became more rigid than before. Although samurai retained the privilege of owning swords, ordinary citizens were forbidden to possess weapons or serve as soldiers, and the Tokugawa maintained a monopoly on gunpowder technology. **Salaried samurai**, now that their warrior function was no longer needed, served the regime as bureaucrats and civil servants.

Another feature of Tokugawa policy was **isolationism**, a trend from the late 1500s. Like their predecessors, the Tokugawa feared the influence of foreign ideas and the further importation of gunpowder weapons. Christianity was officially discouraged, and the **national seclusion policy**, instituted in the 1630s, restricted foreign access to an artificial island, Dejima, off the port of **Nagasaki**. Despite such restrictions on trade, Japan's economy flourished under the Tokugawa. (Japan's biggest trading partner by far was the Dutch East India Company, and what little Western scientific knowledge did make its way into the country was popularly known as "Dutch learning.") The population grew rapidly. Rice production more than doubled between 1600 and 1720. Tokugawa Japan became highly urbanized, and the government built an elaborate network of roads and canals. During this era, the Japanese became great producers of lacquerware, pottery, and steel. The merchant class gained much economic and social clout in the 1600s and 1700s, despite the low status it occupied in the Japanese caste system.

South Asia

In the late 1400s, India was still ruled by the Delhi Sultanate, which had been weakening for decades. In 1520, the Central Asian warlord Babur, a descendant of Timur, invaded the sultanate from the north. This led to the 1526 establishment of the **Mughal Empire**, which eventually conquered the rest of India and ruled for the next several centuries. (Its name comes from the Persian word for "Mongol," and its alternative spelling, "mogul," is still used to describe a rich or powerful individual.)

Like the Delhi sultans, the Mughals were Muslims. They turned India into one of the Islamic world's three **gunpowder empires**. Bureaucratic centralization transformed the previously autonomous landowning **zamindar** class into regional governors and tax collectors. The economy thrived, thanks to a boom in India's **cotton trade**. Mughal rule reached its peak under **Akbar the Great** (r. 1556–1605), who used gunpowder weaponry to complete the conquest of India. Not only did he centralize, as described above, and also reform taxes and the law code, but he gained fame for his religious tolerance. He abolished the **jizya** tax paid by non-Muslims and encouraged friendly relations among Muslims, Buddhists, Hindus, and Sikhs. He ensured that a minimum percentage of government officials were Hindu, and he married a Hindu princess. Without success, he attempted to outlaw the Hindu funeral custom of **sati**. Akbar's grandson, **Shah Jahan**, also a benevolent ruler, left behind a great architectural legacy that includes the beloved **Taj Mahal**. Mughal rulers remain famous for having sponsored a rich artistic and literary style based on **Indo-Persian cultural fusion**.

NOTE

The Mughal Empire's struggle to control rebellious states can be compared to the difficulties experienced by the Ottomans with outlying regions in their own empire—although religious differences mattered more in India and more states successfully broke away there as well.

The Mughals' fortunes took a downward turn under Akbar's great-grandson, **Aurangzeb** (r. 1658–1707), a militant Muslim who abandoned the policy of religious flexibility, reimposed the jizya tax, and began forcing non-Muslims to live under **Sharia** and Muslim dietary restrictions. Aurangzeb's intolerance stirred up civil strife and affected the economy adversely. He militarized India's Sikhs by putting their leader, or guru, to death in 1675, and he provoked the secession of the **Maratha Empire**, a Hindu state founded by the warrior-sovereign Shivaji in west-central India.

The Mughal state declined during the 1700s as religious struggles continued and as many provinces joined the Sikh and Maratha states in declaring independence. European interference also disrupted economic and political life in the Indian Ocean basin. During the 1500s and early 1600s, Mughal India was advanced enough to keep European traders in their place. During the 1600s, the balance of power shifted. The English built textile factories near Calcutta and Madras. The western gateway port of Bombay (now Mumbai) was ceded to the **British East India Company** in 1661. The **Dutch East India Company**—also the master of Indonesia (having taken Jakarta in 1619) and **Melaka** (seized from Portugal in 1670)—established bases in Ceylon (now Sri Lanka). The French created a garrison and trading center at Pondicherry, on the east coast. During the 1700s, European control over India increased. At first, the European presence was concentrated mainly on the coastline, but by the 1740s, large numbers of French and British troops were clashing for the "right" to colonize more of the interior. In the 1750s, during the **Seven Years' War**, the English defeated key Indian allies of the French, after which they turned to the domination of India itself. The English easily triumphed, although they kept many Mughal rulers in place as puppets. In a short time, one of the world's mightiest empires would be transformed into a weak colonial possession.

Spanish control over the Philippines, cemented in the 1570s, is also worth remembering, especially because of the role played by **Manila** in the **global silver trade**.

The Americas

As described earlier, most of the Americas fell under European control in the 1500s. Despite episodes of indigenous resistance, various colonial regimes and joint-stock companies came to exert power over both continents.

War and State Rivalries

A number of Eurasian states experienced what many historians refer to as the **military revolution**: the process by which nations fully incorporated gunpowder weaponry into their way of war, roughly between 1500 and 1700. This did not mean simply adopting cannons and muskets but completely readjusting one's military methods. It also meant replacing medieval castles with gunpowder fortresses and learning how to safely install cannons on ships. Just as important, it entailed the development of bureaucracies capable of conscripting larger numbers of soldiers, training them, and supplying them. Ironically, China, which invented gunpowder, was slowest to undergo this process and only did so partially. The **gunpowder empires** of Ottoman Turkey, Safavid Persia, and Mughal India started off strong in the 1500s but stagnated in the 1600s and 1700s. It was Europe where military modernization played out most thoroughly and most efficiently—a major cause of its rise to global dominance in the 1700s and 1800s.

Major conflicts of the era erupted over several issues: religious disputes, competition over trade routes, and long-standing territorial rivalries. Franco-Habsburg hostilities divided Europe in the 1500s and early 1600s, as did the **Catholic-Protestant religious wars**, which culminated in the **Thirty Years' War** (1618–1648). These wars weakened Spain and Austria but strengthened France, which now engaged in an **Anglo-French rivalry** that lasted from the late 1600s to the early 1800s. The global ramifications of this rivalry were profound: the **Seven Years' War** (1756–1763) raged not only in Europe but across the globe. A true "world war," it shifted control of Canada and India to Great Britain but also set into motion the chain of events that led to the American Revolution by increasing the costs of defending the American colonies.

Other major rivalries include the **Ottoman-European conflict** that played out in southeastern Europe and in the Mediterranean. The advantage here belonged to the Turks during the **1453 conquest of Constantinople** and the campaigns of **Suleiman the Great** in the 1520s. However, the balance tipped permanently in the other direction after the Ottomans' failed **1683 siege of Vienna**. In West Africa, **Songhai-Moroccan conflict** led to the destruction of the former after the crucial battle of Tondibi in 1591. The Indian Ocean basin was the scene of an **Ottoman-Safavid competition** over trade and religious differences (Sunni Islam vs. Shiite Islam) as well as the **Omani-European rivalry** for influence over the East African coast. European powers competed with each other over trade routes worldwide. This involved **piracy in the Caribbean** as well as French, Dutch, and English sparring with the Portuguese and Spanish (and with each other) in many parts of the globe.

Cultural Developments and Interactions, 1450–1750

8

IN THIS CHAPTER

→ **AVAILABILITY OF CULTURE TO WIDER SET OF SOCIAL CLASSES (PRINTING PRESS, RISING LITERACY)**

→ **RELIGIOUS SCHISMS (WIDENING OF SUNNI-SHIITE SPLIT, PROTESTANT REFORMATION)**

→ **MISSIONARY ACTIVITY AND THE GLOBAL SPREAD OF CHRISTIANITY**

→ **RELIGIOUS SYNCRETISM (VODUN, LATIN AMERICA'S CULT OF SAINTS, SIKHISM)**

→ **POLITICAL USES OF ART AND ARCHITECTURE (VERSAILLES, GREAT PLAZA OF ISFAHAN, SUMMER PALACE, RED FORT, BLUE MOSQUE)**

→ **RENAISSANCE AND ENLIGHTENMENT IN EUROPE**

→ **MIMAR SINAN AND OTTOMAN MOSQUE BUILDING + ISLAMIC MINIATURE PAINTING**

→ **GRIOT STORYTELLING (EPICS OF ASKIA MOHAMMED AND SUNDIATA) AND BRONZE SCULPTURES IN AFRICA**

→ *JOURNEY TO THE WEST* **(WU CHENGEN)**

→ **KABUKI THEATER AND UKIYO-E PAINTING**

→ **INDO-PERSIAN CULTURAL FUSION IN INDIA (MINIATURE PAINTING, TAJ MAHAL)**

→ **CREOLE AND MESTIZO TRADITIONS IN THE AMERICAS + MESOAMERICAN CODICES**

Cultural sophistication rose worldwide during these years. Artistic and literary traditions took deeper root in their respective states and regions, in some cases building on older traditions and in other instances taking advantage of new styles and innovations.

Other—and less gradual—departures from the previous era included the colossal effects of the encounter between Eurasia and the Americas. Especially in the Atlantic, new interactions led to a profound fusing and mixing of cultures. Also, significant religious changes occurred in several parts of the world, involving either the appearance of new syncretic faiths or major schisms and conflicts within established ones. Finally, the widening impact of the printing press and a corresponding growth in the infrastructure by which knowledge was spread (publication of books and newspapers, schools and other educational institutions, and so on) meant that general levels of literacy rose and also that art and ideas exercised much greater practical influence than ever before.

PRINT CULTURE AND THE IMPACT OF IDEAS

One of the most transformative inventions of this era was the **movable-type printing press**. It came into its heyday after the 1430s, when Johannes Gutenberg developed a cost-effective, easy-to-use version of the press in the German city of Mainz.

Starting in Europe and eventually throughout Eurasia and the Americas, the printing press disseminated information over ever-greater distances and to increasingly large audiences. Literary works, religious debates, and new ideas in general—including the scientific theories and discoveries discussed in the next chapter—spread more rapidly and more widely. By creating more materials to read and more incentive to read, the printing press elevated literacy rates—quickly among the upper and middle classes but gradually among the lower classes as well. The press's spin-off effects, which typically included the expansion of libraries, publishers, schools, universities, and museums, further boosted the power of ideas and new knowledge to affect historical events.

RELIGIOUS DEVELOPMENTS

TIP

For a refresher on the origins and principles of major religions, review the "Cultural Developments and Interactions" section of Unit Zero.

Although religious beliefs and practices diversified during this period—even including publicly declared atheism—religion remained central to the lives of most people. It also served as the cause of numerous conflicts, and it continued to be used for political purposes, mainly to justify regimes and rulers.

Divisions: New Sects and Denominations

Within established religions, several major schisms appeared or widened. As Buddhism spread throughout Asia, the rift grew larger between older **Theravada**, or Hinayana, schools of thought—which emphasized simplicity and meditation and were more popular in South Asia—and newer **Mahayana** denominations, which predominated in East Asia and in some cases put more of a premium on rituals, deities, and concepts of an afterlife. And even among Mahayana traditions, approaches like **Zen** (Ch'an in China) differed greatly from sects like Pure Land. **Tibetan Buddhism**, with a sizable following among the Turkic and Mongol peoples of Central Asia, developed its own traditions as well.

In the Muslim world, existing divisions deepened. **Sufism**, the mystical strain within Islam that emphasized communion with Allah over doctrinal strictness, continued to flourish after taking root between the 900s and the 1300s. Especially disruptive was the hardening of the **Sunni-Shiite split**, which, since the mid-600s, had divided most Muslims from the minority who viewed Mohammed's son-in-law Ali, not the Umayyad caliphs, as Mohammed's rightful successor. Due to how it took hold in Safavid Persia, Shiism's differences from the Sunni majority became more pronounced than before. Shiite Muslims, who form a majority in what is now Iran—and a sizable minority in other places—believe that correct interpretations of Islamic doctrine and Sharia law flow from the teachings of twelve religious authorities called **imams** (a term also used by Sunnis but in a different sense). This now-standard version of Shiism is often referred to as Twelver Shiism. The imams include Ali and the eleven leaders who followed him until the mid-800s. The Twelfth Imam is considered by Shiites not to have died but to have entered a hidden spiritual state, from which he is someday supposed to return as a messiah known as the Mahdi. Tensions between Sunnis and Shiites persisted throughout this era, paralleling the ongoing conflict between the Sunni Ottoman Empire and Shiite Persia.

NOTE

Protestants conducted their services in their own languages, as opposed to Latin. Unlike Catholics, they were encouraged to read scripture for themselves. This resulted in the translation of the Bible into numerous languages, and it prioritized education and literacy among many Protestant populations.

Europe experienced its own religious earthquake: the **Protestant Reformation**, which affected not just matters of faith but culture, politics, and the spread of

Christianity to other parts of the world. Prior to the 1500s, two established denominations wielded religious authority over Europe: Eastern Orthodoxy, which prevailed in and around Byzantium, and Roman Catholicism, which dominated the central and western parts of the continent. During the 1300s and 1400s, both churches suffered a series of grave crises. In the east, Byzantium's gradual decline, followed by its destruction in 1453, left Orthodoxy politically weakened and confined mainly to Europe's Slavic and Balkan periphery. In Catholic Europe, the power and prestige of the papacy waned, thanks first to its forced transfer from Rome to the French city of Avignon for most of the 1300s and then to several decades of confusing and painful rivalry between two papacies, each of which claimed allegiance from all Catholics. Even after the restoration of a single pope to Rome, the situation worsened during the 1400s due to growing corruption within the Catholic hierarchy. Church offices were sold, not earned by merit, and certificates of forgiveness for sins (indulgences) were granted in exchange for money. All this caused many to view the church as hypocritical and overly concerned with wealth and power. Much of this willingness to address church problems had to do with the questioning spirit of the **Renaissance**. Until the early 1500s, however, Catholic authorities were able to crush any opposition.

This changed in 1517, when a German monk, **Martin Luther**, protested the sale of indulgences. In his Ninety-Five Theses, Luther launched a general attack against church abuses and certain parts of Catholic doctrine. When he refused the pope's order to retract his criticisms, he was excommunicated and threatened with arrest and death. Now a fugitive, Luther took shelter with sympathetic political figures and, in the 1520s, founded a new church: Lutheranism, the first of Europe's major Protestant denominations.

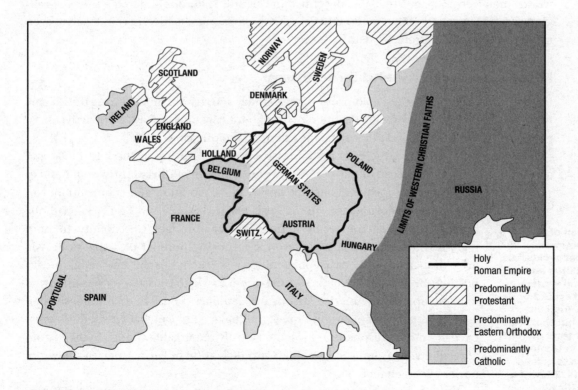

Religious Divisions in Europe, ca. 1600
For centuries, Christianity had been divided into two large denominations, Eastern Orthodoxy and Roman Catholicism. In most of Europe, the latter had predominated. Starting with the Protestant Reformation in 1517, new religious rifts began to appear. By the end of the 1500s, western and northern Europe were divided into Catholic and Protestant camps, as shown in this map.

With the **Protestant Reformation** under way, other movements soon emerged, with the **printing press** playing a key role in spreading new religious ideas. The French scholar **John Calvin** established a theocratic community in the Swiss city of Geneva and preached an even stricter form of Protestantism. Calvinist denominations caught on in France (the Huguenots, an oppressed minority), the Dutch Republic (the Reformed Church), parts of England (the Puritans), and Scotland (the Presbyterians). In England, Henry VIII formed the Protestant **Church of England**, also called the **Anglican Church**. Many beliefs and practices separated Protestants from Catholics. The former favored institutional simplicity, in contrast to the bureaucracy of the Catholic Church, and sacraments were less important to them. Protestants did not venerate the saints or the Virgin Mary the way Catholics did, and they allowed their clergy to marry. Most important was the concept of **salvation by grace**, the belief that only God's forgiveness—not good works, observance of rituals, or the power of the pope—could bring a worshipper to heaven. (Calvin's doctrine of predestination took this idea further, arguing that whether a person would be saved or not was known to God from the beginning of time.)

In the mid-1500s, in response to the Protestant Reformation, the Catholic Church subjected itself to a process of change called the **Catholic Counter-Reformation**. On one hand, it eliminated the worst of its corruption. On the other, it reaffirmed the authority of the pope, gave new powers to the Holy Inquisition, and created an Index of Forbidden Books that remained in place until the 1960s. The Counter-Reformation also saw the use of art and architecture to impress worshippers with Catholicism's might and grandeur. (This included the construction of **St. Peter's Basilica**—still the largest Christian church building in the world—between 1506 and 1626.) As described in Chapter 7, Europe suffered a series of **religious wars** between the 1520s and the 1640s as Catholic monarchs tried in vain to stem, even reverse, the spread of Protestantism.

Missionary Activity and Syncretism

In conjunction with trade and colonization, **missionary activity** did much during these years to spread certain faiths over wide distances. Throughout Asia, this was a time of active proselytization of Buddhism, and other religions extended their reach as well.

Christianity experienced the era's most massive growth. Starting in the late 1400s and continuing throughout the rest of this period, the **global spread of Christianity** went hand in hand with Europe's campaign of worldwide exploration and colonization. Not long after the Portuguese and Spanish reached South and East Asia, Catholic priests—including the Jesuit **Francis Xavier**—brought Christianity to both regions. Christian missionaries won a surprising number of converts in Asia even though in some cases political leaders reacted to the new religion with hostility. Even more dramatic was the extent to which Christianity was imported to North and South America, first by the Catholic Spanish and Portuguese, then also by French Catholics and Protestant English and Dutch. Christianity's presence in both hemispheres represented a truly remarkable change in the history of religions. The almost monolithic **Catholicization of Latin America** shows the power of this change.

Another prominent trend was the development of new **syncretic religions**, or faiths that emerged from the blending of two or more religions traditions. Many of these arose from Europe's colonization of the New World as well as the forcible transfer of enslaved Africans. One example is **vodun** (popularly known as "voodoo"), which developed among African-descended populations throughout the

NOTE

In Asia, the spread of Christianity sometimes provoked political backlashes. During the late 1500s and early 1600s, Japan's rulers occasionally persecuted or even executed Christians and essentially shut the religion out with their national seclusion policy in the 1630s. China's emperors tolerated Christianity until 1724, when they banned it officially. By contrast, in places like the Philippines, which was colonized by the Spanish, large segments of the population became devout Christians.

Caribbean due to the mixing of spirit worship from West Africa with animistic practices native to the Americas and also with elements drawn from Christianity. Similarly, native traditions in Latin America combined with Catholicism to create a **cult of saints**, in which indigenous worshippers came to identify their own polytheistic deities with the array of saints venerated by Catholics. Encouraging or at least tolerating this logic made it easier for European missionaries to win converts in the Americas. In Mexico, for example, Aztecs and other Nahuatl-speaking natives equated Mary, the mother of Jesus, with their own mother goddess, giving rise in the 1500s and 1600s to stories and icons of the **Virgin of Guadalupe**—a much-loved depiction of Mary as a native girl and even today a symbol of central importance in Mexican Catholicism. (An identical process can be seen in the Andes, where icons of the Virgin of Cerro Rico portrayed Mary as the spirit goddess who embodies the "silver mountain" of Potosí—no doubt as a way to appeal to the indigenous laborers who toiled in the Potosí mines.)

The Virgin of Guadalupe

As Catholicism came to Mexico, tales arose in the 1500s and 1600s of a peasant boy who witnessed a vision of the Virgin Mary in the form of a young girl who spoke Nahuatl—the indigenous language—and had native features. The location of her sighting happened to be a key place of worship for the Nahuatl mother goddess. The emergence of a distinctly New World version of an Old World Catholic figure is a classic instance of religious syncretism.

While many consider **Sikhism** an independent tradition, it is categorized by others as syncretic, joining certain aspects of Hinduism with a monotheism perhaps inspired by Islam. Whatever label one gives it, Sikhism was founded in the late 1400s, in India's Punjab region, by **Guru Nanak**. The early Sikh gurus, who led the religion until the death of the tenth in 1708, taught that meditation and virtuous behavior would help worshippers penetrate the veil of maya, or worldly illusion, and thereby come to know Waheguru, the one true god. Originally pacifistic, Sikhism embraced a warrior culture during the 1600s because of growing persecution, particularly after the Mughal emperor Aurangzeb killed the guru and provoked the creation of a powerful Sikh army called the Khalsa. Over time, Sikhism has grown into one of the world's largest organized religions, with almost 30 million followers.

TRENDS IN ART, LITERATURE, AND ARCHITECTURE

General Developments

By this point in time, societies worldwide had well-defined artistic and literary (or oral) traditions. Increased technological aptitude enabled the production of arts and crafts of high quality. Where the printing press was adopted, the availability of written works expanded.

Cultural interaction continued as in previous centuries but received an extra boost during these years from Europe's campaigns of exploration, especially from the movement of Europeans and Africans to North and South America. Most dramatic was the **transatlantic impact on the Americas**, whose languages, religions, artistic traditions, and music were profoundly reshaped by the importation of European and African culture.

The **political use of art and architecture** likewise continued. Impressive artworks and buildings showed off the grandeur of various regimes and helped to legitimate their power. Cultural patronage, the organizing of elaborate court dances, and the staging of musical or dramatic performances contributed to the same goals. Key examples from this era include the French palace of **Versailles** (built by Louis XIV to demonstrate his power as an absolute monarch and avidly imitated by other European rulers), China's **Summer Palace** (an exquisite garden complex constructed near Beijing by the Qing emperors), the **Grand Plaza of Isfahan** (a grand display of Persian might, featuring the Shah Abbas Mosque), the **Blue Mosque** in Istanbul (built to distract attention from Ottoman military defeats at the hands of Persia), and the **Red Fort** in Delhi (the residence of the Mughal emperors, erected by Shah Jahan, who also commissioned the Taj Mahal).

Palace of Versailles, ca. 1688
Built by Louis XIV of France, the stunning palace of Versailles, with acres of gardens and its famous Hall of Mirrors, communicated wealth and majesty to all onlookers. Intended by Louis as an architectural embodiment of his political might, Versailles served as a model for other European monarchs of the era, who built their own palaces to convey the same message.

The **availability of culture** steadily widened. Not just elite members of society but merchant and middle classes—and in some cases the lower classes—enjoyed greater access to art, literature, and musical and dramatic performances. Prosperity and merchant-generated profits expanded the cultural marketplace. Print technology made written works easier and cheaper to produce, and literacy increased as a result. With the passage of time, genres of art and literature specifically targeting popular audiences began to appear.

Cultural Innovations by Region

In Europe, the **Renaissance**, which had begun in Italy during the late 1200s and early 1300s (as described in Chapter 2), spread to the rest of Europe and continued until the early 1600s. By the late 1400s and early 1500s, Italy was in the midst of the High Renaissance—the era of Michelangelo and Leonardo da Vinci—while the **Northern Renaissance** featured the Dutch philosopher Erasmus (known for his religious debates with Luther as well as his satirical novel *In Praise of Folly*), the English scholar Thomas More (who invented the term "utopia" in his book of the same name and lost his life as a Catholic resisting Henry VIII's Anglicanism), the Spanish novelist **Miguel de Cervantes** (author of *Don Quixote*, the tale of an aged knight bewildered by Europe's transition from the medieval period), and the English poet and playwright **William Shakespeare**. Novels like Cervantes's and theatrical productions like Shakespeare's are prominent examples of art forms that catered to all classes, not just the elite. So are the paintings and other artworks commissioned by increasingly prosperous **merchant and middle-class patrons** both during the Renaissance and afterward.

The cultural style that followed the Renaissance was the baroque, which dominated European painting, architecture, and music from the early 1600s through the early 1700s. Baroque culture emphasized the bold and the colorful and was often used by political and religious elites to impress the public and to legitimize their policies, especially during the struggles of the Reformation.

During the 1700s, Europe, as well as its American colonies, experienced what came to be known as the **Enlightenment**: a philosophical and intellectual movement that put full confidence in the power of rational thought to solve social and political problems and to understand the wider world. Inspired by the Scientific Revolution (detailed in Chapter 9) and by certain philosophers from the late 1600s—particularly **John Locke** of England—Enlightenment thinkers prided themselves on logic and progressive ideas, and they provided much of the intellectual justification for the American and French Revolutions in the late 1700s. The Enlightenment is discussed further in Chapter 14.

Although the leading states of the Middle East—Ottoman Turkey and Safavid Persia—allowed their technological and scientific edge over Europe to slip away, they both displayed cultural brilliance. During this period, Islamic culture was dominated by a synthesis of Arabic, Turkish, and Persian elements. Ottoman architectural innovation reached its peak in the 1500s and 1600s due mainly to **Mimar Sinan**, a military engineer who designed more than eighty mosques. Sinan's masterpiece was the stunning Süleymaniye Mosque—commissioned by Suleiman the Magnificent in the 1550s to surpass the glory of the Hagia Sophia mosque, which had originally been built as a Christian cathedral—and it was one of Sinan's students who built Istanbul's renowned **Blue Mosque** in the early 1600s.

Both in Turkey and Persia, **carpet weaving** stood out as a key art form and as a profitable enterprise. Also distinctive was the tradition of **miniature painting**, which arose in Persia during the 1300s and 1400s and then spread to the Ottoman Empire and Mughal India in the 1500s. These vibrantly colored illustrations, collected in albums called *muraqqas*, featured many subjects, including portraits, because Islam's traditional disapproval of depicting human subjects had always been weaker in Persia than in Arabia. Despite their exceptional skill, Ottoman and Persian miniaturists did not strive for the level of exact realism that Renaissance artists in Europe did, nor did they apply the laws of perspective as rigorously. This was due to their religious-philosophical conviction that the physical world was imperfect and that art should present a more idealized version of reality. The most famous miniatures were produced at the Herat and Tabriz workshops in Persia and in the Topkapi Palace in Istanbul. The best-remembered Ottoman painters are Nakkas Osman (late 1500s) and Levni (early 1700s).

The Blue Mosque, Istanbul, Turkey
Officially the Sultan Ahmed Mosque, this masterpiece was built for Ahmed I between 1609 and 1618 by Sedefkar Mehmed Aga, largely for the political purpose of drawing public attention away from embarrassing military losses against Persia. It is unusual in having six minarets.

The diversity of traditions in Africa makes it difficult to generalize about art and culture there, but **sculpture** and **carving** remained dominant. Many materials were used, including wood, metal, and ivory; among the best-known collections are the **Benin** and **Oyo bronzes** produced in West Africa. Much African art was **abstract**—deliberately avoiding the replication of visual reality—long before the concept of abstraction gained popularity among European artists. **Textile arts** and **basketry** were also prominent, featuring highly complex geometric patterns. African architecture came to be gradually influenced by Arabs and European colonists, who built fortresses and residences along the coasts of East and West Africa. Where tales, songs, and poems were concerned, the **oral tradition** overshadowed written works. Professional storytellers—known in West Africa as **griots** (and elsewhere by other names)—acted as entertainers, historians, musicians, and, in some cases, advisers to kings. The ***Epic of Askia Mohammed*** glorified (and somewhat fictionalized) the deeds of the Songhai state's founder, and still popular in this period was the ***Sundiata***, an earlier saga that did the same for the chieftain who ruled Mali in the 1200s.

In East Asia, the cultural dynamism of China's Ming dynasty (1368–1644) continued. The Ming remain famous for their fine **porcelain** as well as literary masterpieces like Wu Chengen's ***Journey to the West***. This much-loved novel, published in the late 1500s, narrates the travels of the seventh-century monk Xuanzang to India in the form of an adventure fantasy starring the mischievous half-beast Monkey King as Xuanzang's companion. Part of *Journey*'s appeal was that its author, rather than imitate old-fashioned prose from earlier dynasties, wrote in a style that matched how people in his own time spoke. This made *Journey* accessible to the middle classes, not just elite audiences. As China moved into the Qing era, its cultural attainments included the construction in the mid-1700s of the beautiful **Summer Palace** outside Beijing.

Also in East Asia, Japan's transition to unification under the Tokugawa shogunate (1603–1868) brought about certain cultural changes. On one hand, Japan's samurai class maintained many of the traditions and styles mentioned in Chapter 2. On the other, new art forms arose in response to the growing wealth of merchants and the urban classes. Especially popular was **kabuki theater**, which featured acrobatics, swordplay, and scenes of city life—and contrasted greatly with the older, more elegant Noh drama favored by the upper classes. Thanks to woodblock printing, **ukiyo-e painting** became affordable and, like kabuki, was driven largely by urban, middle-class tastes.

Ukiyo-e Print of an Actor, by Kiyotada (early 1700s)
Literally meaning "pictures of the floating world," ukiyo-e woodblock prints were easily mass-produced and increasingly affordable to middle-class and urban audiences. They featured portraits of actors and geisha courtesans, scenes of city life, landscapes, and similar subjects.

The highlight of South Asian culture in the 1500s and 1600s was the **Indo-Persian cultural fusion** that took place under India's Islamic Mughal emperors. As in Ottoman Turkey and Safavid Persia, **miniature painting** caught on here as a dominant art form. This was also an age of architectural magnificence in India. In the 1580s, for both artistic and political purposes, Akbar the Great transformed the northwest city of **Lahore** into a sumptuous capital and palace complex. Agra, where the Mughals relocated their capital in the 1590s, is also home to Mughal landmarks—most famously the **Taj Mahal**, the white marble mausoleum built by Shah Jahan in memory of his wife. It was likewise on Shah Jahan's initiative that the mammoth **Red Fort** was constructed as a royal residence in Delhi.

In countless ways, the arrival of European conquerors and colonists—and the slaves they brought from Africa—affected cultural life in the Americas. This blending of European,

African, and indigenous elements gave rise to **creole and mestizo traditions**, along with other "mixed" cultures, with a powerful impact on language, religion, music, and art. In addition, the Europeans' arrival caused literature and writing to assume widespread importance for the first time in a region where written scripts had been extremely rare over the course of many centuries.

This was not without negative impact. A sense of racial and religious superiority prompted European colonizers to alter or destroy the customs and beliefs of indigenous Americans, and much native culture was forever lost as a result. Between the 1540s and 1580s, for example, Spanish priests burned nearly every existing manuscript that contained Mayan writing, erasing an entire literary legacy. Inscriptions on pottery and stone survived but would take centuries to decipher. The Aztecs fared somewhat better, thanks to the **Mesoamerican codices** of the 1500s, an interesting example of interchange between native and European literary practices. Approximately five hundred of these texts survive, produced by Aztec converts to Catholicism, often in conjunction with Spanish priests. Most famous is the **Florentine Codex** (also known as *The Universal History of New Spain*), assembled by the Spanish Franciscan friar Bernardino de Sahagún between 1545 and 1590. Written partly in Nahuatl, partly in Spanish, and partly in Latin, they combine the pre-Columbian practice of codex painting and the European emphasis on writing, and most are richly illustrated. The codices address many subjects, including translations of Aztec pictograms, explanations of Aztec beliefs and customs (religious practices, folk medicine, the calendar system), and occasionally complaints about Spanish abuses.

A similar text from the Andes, although produced exclusively by a native and far more critical of the Spanish, is *The First New Chronicle* (1600–1615), an eleven hundred–page document written and illustrated by the high-born Quechua Felipe Guamán Poma de Ayala, largely in protest of Spanish policy in the decades following the conquest of the Inca.

Technology and Innovation, 1450–1750

9

In parallel with the overall rise of political centralization, economic productivity, and cultural sophistication during this era, scientific knowledge and technological expertise increased virtually everywhere between the 1400s and 1700s.

It was in Europe, however, where the difference between starting point and endpoint turned out to be greatest, and by a sizable margin. Building on the age of exploration and the experience of the Renaissance, European thinkers and inventors found themselves engaged in a process that historians have labeled the **Scientific Revolution**. This began in the mid-1500s and culminated with the career of Isaac Newton in the late 1600s and early 1700s.

The Scientific Revolution went beyond the simple absorption of new technologies and the discovery of isolated scientific concepts. It revived the scientific method and yielded a comprehensive understanding of fundamental scientific principles. In so doing, it laid the groundwork for European industrialization and the remarkable rise in global power—the so-called rise of the West—that Europe would undergo in the 1800s.

NOTE

Just as it contributed to the wider and faster spread of literature, thought, and culture, the movable-type printing press produced by Johannes Gutenberg in the 1430s accelerated the dissemination of scientific theories and technological insights— most directly in Europe but also wherever else the printing press exerted influence.

MARINE/NAVIGATIONAL TECHNOLOGY: CONTINUED INNOVATION

Advances in marine and navigational technology had a tremendous global impact during this period, especially in the way it facilitated the **European age of exploration**.

In Europe during these years, homegrown innovations combined with others that had arrived from China via the Middle East. By now, key navigational instruments, originally imported from Asia, were in regular use. Among these were the **astrolabe**, which measured latitude (one's position on the globe in a north-south direction), and the **magnetic compass**, which determined one's direction of travel. During the Renaissance, the Europeans improved their knowledge of cartography and the movement of the stars, gradually producing ever more **precise maps** and **astronomical charts**. (The Mercator projection used commonly on maps today was devised in the mid-1500s.)

One navigational problem that went unsolved until the mid-1700s was the calculation at sea of **longitude** (one's position on the globe in an east-west direction). This requires a device that can simultaneously measure one's own local time and the time at one's place of origin; only by knowing the time difference and the physical distance between both points could one figure out longitudinal position. For centuries, though, no clock existed that was both accurate and portable enough to be used on board a ship for long periods of time. Solving this dilemma was such an urgent issue that the British Admiralty offered a huge cash prize to whoever could do so. The prize was eventually claimed by John Harrison, whose **marine chronometer** appeared in 1761.

Shipbuilding technology improved in Europe as well, again with help from innovations that had been borrowed earlier from Asia. After centuries of relying on oared galleys in the Mediterranean and relatively clumsy sailing vessels that were incapable of venturing far from shore, the Europeans learned to build sturdy and maneuverable **sailing ships** that could travel far into the open ocean. These vessels had deeper keels for greater stability and **stern-post rudders**, a steering system first used on Chinese junks. They also moved beyond the simple practice of using square sails on a single mast, instead adopting a mix of square sails and **lateen sails**, all on several masts and with complex systems of rigging. This allowed boats to sail in the direction they needed to even in unfavorable winds.

During the 1400s and 1500s, the new model that first enabled true oceanic exploration was the **caravel**, largely invented by the Portuguese, who combined square and lateen sails for better control over direction. Larger, multimasted ships, like the carrack and **galleon**, that were capable of carrying cannons as well as cargo quickly followed. The Dutch **fluyt** sacrificed the protection of heavy guns to maximize cargo space while remaining nimble and swift.

GUNPOWDER AND THE MILITARY REVOLUTION THESIS

Although **gunpowder weaponry** had originated in China during the 1000s and 1100s and spread to the Middle East and Europe during the 1200s and 1300s, it was not until the 1400s and afterward that it fundamentally changed warfare. Ironically, China was one of the places where this process worked itself out most slowly.

Several parts of Eurasia—most notably Europe but also the so-called gunpowder empires in Ottoman Turkey, Safavid Persia, and Mughal India—experienced what some historians refer to as a **military revolution**. Originally focused on changes in Europe between the mid-1500s and mid-1600s, this concept now refers to a more global trend lasting roughly from 1500 into the early 1700s and arguably beyond. The "military revolution" thesis deals not just with the technological changes themselves but also with the social and political developments they caused or accelerated. To varying degrees and at different paces, states during this period learned to deploy gunpowder artillery and handheld weapons like muskets in sieges and battles. Because medieval castle walls proved unable to withstand gunpowder attacks, engineers built new fortresses—geometrically ornate and very expensive—to provide more effective defense. In the case of Europe, navies designed oceangoing ships capable of traveling vast distances and carrying heavy guns.

Because armies now relied more on gunpowder infantry (relatively easy to train and supply) and less on cavalry (difficult to train and supply and increasingly old-fashioned), they grew much larger than ever before. Tearing down medieval walls and replacing them with gunpowder fortresses took tremendous amounts of money, as did the creation of gunship navies. All these changes—not to mention the impact of conscripting more men into military service and paying for their equipment—vastly increased the social and economic burdens of war. The enormous costs involved with converting to the new style of warfare gave many states the crucial incentive they needed to modernize their bureaucracies and tax-gathering systems. In this way, supporters of the military revolution thesis argue, not only did the state make war but war—or at least the need to adapt to new forms of war—made the state.

This process happened most quickly and most thoroughly in Europe even though European states were far from the first to incorporate gunpowder into their way of war. Over time, many hypotheses have been put forward to explain Europe's success with gunpowder. Older arguments attributed it to Europe's supposedly greater hospitality to entrepreneurship and scientific innovation, but these are generally seen now as resting on outdated stereotypes. A key political difference between Europe and other regions was the lack in Europe of a single dominant state that easily eliminated all nearby military rivals. Having used gunpowder to pacify all opposition in their domains, regimes like the Ottoman sultan's or the Tokugawa shogun's had less incentive to devote resources to the constant improvement of gunpowder technology. In Europe, by contrast, near-constant warfare among numerous neighboring states created a persistent need to experiment and innovate.

In addition to this more competitive environment, Western and Central European states found themselves fighting specific kinds of war that made even the most primitive gunpowder weapons worth investing in. Useful handheld muskets and pistols took a long time to appear, and the first artillery pieces were so heavy, unreliable, and slow to fire that in most circumstances—especially in a fast-moving battle or when pursuing a mobile enemy—their inefficiency outweighed any advantage that might be gained by their firepower. The one exception was siegecraft, where lack of speed mattered less and explosive power helped immensely. More so than in other regions, warfare in medieval and Renaissance Europe revolved mainly around siege action, making cannons and other forms of artillery immediately useful—and immediately worth expending money and brainpower on to improve. Contrast this with China, where the most dangerous military threat came from frontier nomads on horseback, easily able to avoid any military force armed with heavy gunpowder weapons. Viewed this way, China's decision not to invest heavily in developing gunpowder's potential seems less a mistake—as many in the West have traditionally viewed—and more a logical choice based on the needs of the day. (The same can be said of naval gunships: other states that already possessed material wealth and luxury goods had no need to develop the oceangoing ships that a relatively impoverished Europe needed for exploration and then turned into platforms for heavy guns.)

EUROPE'S SCIENTIFIC REVOLUTION

Relative to other civilizations during this era, Europe enjoyed the most explosive increase in scientific and technological aptitude. Already during the Renaissance, certain scholars were moving away from the intellectual orthodoxy of the Middle Ages, in which a fixed set of ideas taken from certain ancient Greek and Roman thinkers—especially **Aristotle**—were combined with Catholic doctrine.

During the mid-1500s, despite the Catholic Church's continued control over much of Europe's intellectual life, individuals such as the Polish astronomer **Nicolaus Copernicus** began to cross important scientific boundaries. In his 1543 book *On the Revolution of the Heavenly Spheres*, Copernicus provided mathematical proof for the **heliocentric theory**,

NOTE

Europe was not alone in clinging to a geocentric understanding of astronomy. Ptolemy, geocentrism's originator, was just as respected among Muslims as in pre-Copernican Europe. Astronomers elsewhere, including China and India, likewise concluded that the sun, stars, and planets revolved around the earth.

according to which the earth and other planets revolve around the sun. This ran counter to long-held standard wisdom in which the earth sat at the center of the universe. Handed down by the Greek scientist Ptolemy, this **geocentric theory** found favor with Europe's religious authorities, especially the Catholic papacy, because it placed human beings—God's greatest creation in the Christian view—at the heart of all existence. It took more than another century after Copernicus published his findings for the heliocentric theory to become more widely accepted throughout Europe.

The mid-1500s are commonly seen as the beginning of a **Scientific Revolution** in Europe, continuing into the 1600s and early 1700s. Also in the 1540s, the Flemish scholar Andreas Vesalius revolutionized the study of medicine: his new textbooks on anatomy—based on the dissection of corpses, then a controversial and often illegal practice—corrected many of the errors of the ancient Greek authority Galen (just as Copernicus was correcting Ptolemy at the same time) and even improved on the work done by the Persian physician Avicenna in the eleventh century. In all scientific fields, the pace of discovery accelerated with every passing year.

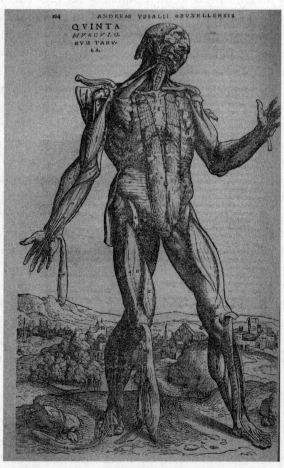

Illustration of Human Musculature, from Andreas Vesalius, *On the Fabric of the Human Body* **(1543)**

Published the same year that Nicolaus Copernicus released his mathematical proof of the heliocentric theory in *On the Revolutions of the Heavenly Spheres*, Vesalius's masterwork corrected errors in the study of anatomy that had persisted since the days of ancient Greece and Rome—just as Copernicus did for the science of astronomy—and represents a major early step forward in Europe's Scientific Revolution.

Momentum picked up in the 1600s. Thinkers such as René Descartes of France and Roger Bacon of England laid the groundwork for formal logic and the modern **scientific method** in which observation and experimentation are used to prove theoretical hypotheses. The mode of scientific thinking that had arisen among the ancient Greeks, especially in the writings of Aristotle, was revived but in a more systematic way. Also in the 1600s, the German astronomer Johannes Kepler and the Italian physicist **Galileo** confirmed and popularized Copernicus's theories. (Kepler also proved the elliptical orbits of the planets, while others had envisioned circular orbits.) Those who promoted Copernican thought continued to run afoul of the Catholic Church. Galileo was tried by the Inquisition and forced to reject his own scientific conclusions in public; his scientific writings remained on the church's index of forbidden books for centuries. Although some Protestant clergy rejected the new science, Protestant nations such as England and the Dutch Republic became relatively safe havens for scientific pioneers. Only in the 1700s did it become less risky for those in Catholic countries to challenge church doctrine.

Many of the ideas behind the modern understanding of science were discovered or proved during the Scientific Revolution. They include the states of matter (liquid, gas, or solid), the question of whether light consists of waves or particles, the fact that living creatures are made of cells, the concept of the vacuum, and the science of statistics. Zoological and botanical taxonomy—the modern system of classifying animals and plants—began during the early 1700s; the system of classification still used today was devised in the eighteenth century by the Swedish botanist and zoologist **Carl Linnaeus**. Among the scientific instruments invented or perfected during the 1600s and 1700s were the telescope, the microscope, the pendulum clock, the thermometer, and the barometer.

Isaac Newton (1642–1727) of England represents the Scientific Revolution at its peak. Newton is famous for the laws of motion, for his thoughts on the concept of gravity, and as one of the two mathematicians who invented the system of calculus. Just as important is the fact that Newton, more than any other figure of the era, understood scientific thought as a totality. He took the discoveries of his day and tied them together into a single system of thought—Newtonian physics—backed up by mathematical proof. Newton's book *Principia* (1687) is considered one of the most influential scholarly texts ever written, and not until Einstein's theory of relativity in the early 1900s would Newton's fundamental principles be seriously challenged or altered.

Economic Systems, 1450–1750

10

IN THIS CHAPTER

→ **THE IMPACT OF EUROPE'S AGE OF EXPLORATION ON EXISTING TRADE ROUTES**

→ **THE INDIAN OCEAN BASIN AND ASIAN TRADE**

→ **ECONOMIC EFFECTS OF THE COLUMBIAN EXCHANGE**

→ **EMERGENCE OF THE ATLANTIC SYSTEM (TRIANGULAR TRADE)**

→ **INFLUX OF PRECIOUS METALS (SILVER) FROM THE AMERICAS INTO THE WORLD ECONOMY**

→ **FISHING, WHALING, SEA MAMMAL HUNTING, FUR HUNTING**

→ **MONOPOLY CHARTERS AND JOINT-STOCK COMPANIES (DUTCH EAST INDIA COMPANY, BRITISH EAST INDIA COMPANY, HUDSON'S BAY COMPANY)**

→ **PIRACY AND STATE COMPETITION OVER TRADE (OTTOMAN-SAFAVID COMPETITION, SONGHAI-MOROCCO CONFLICT, OMANI-EUROPEAN RIVALRY)**

→ **INCREASED AGRICULTURAL PRODUCTION**

→ **THE RISE OF MANUFACTURING AND PROTOINDUSTRIALIZATION**

→ **MERCANTILISM VS. CAPITALISM**

→ **ECONOMIC RELIANCE ON COERCED LABOR**

The incorporation of the Americas into Afro-Eurasia's existing networks of exchange led to the emergence, for the first time in history, of a truly global economy. Raw materials and finished products now circulated to meet a growing worldwide demand.

Modes of production. Among the world's settled societies, the vast majority of people worked as agriculturalists and lived in rural settings. This continued to be the case until well into the industrial era, and agricultural production increased. At the same time, other sectors of the economy expanded. Trade, banking, and manufacturing generated a great deal of wealth and encouraged significant growth among urban populations.

Interregional trade and agricultural production were both affected during these years by the global cooling that caused the **Little Ice Age**.

THE EARLY GLOBALIZATION OF ECONOMICS

By extending Europe's physical and commercial reach directly to Africa and Asia and also by bringing Afro-Eurasia into permanent contact with the Americas, the **European age of exploration** made it possible to speak of an early stage of economic globalization.

Changing Trade Routes and New Trade Goods

Europe's encounter with the Americas, combined with its newfound ability to voyage to Asia and the Indian Ocean basin, reshaped existing patterns of interregional trade. Certain trade routes became less relevant. The most notable example was the **Silk Road**, which never fell into complete disuse but, because of the relative slowness and expense of overland transport compared to overseas transport, declined in importance after the 1500s.

Seaborne trade in the **Indian Ocean basin** (and the Pacific regions closest to it) increased in volume and was also restructured by the Europeans' arrival in the 1400s and 1500s. The Portuguese came first, establishing a **trading-post empire** that consisted of ports along the African coast and wherever in Asia they were strong enough to conquer or persuasive enough to negotiate territorial concessions. Key possessions included **Oman** on the Arabian peninsula, **Zanzibar** and Mombasa in East Africa, Goa in India, **Melaka** (Malacca) on the Malay peninsula, and Macau in China. Following and sometimes replacing the Portuguese in the late 1500s and 1600s were the Dutch, English, and French, all of whom were firmly entrenched in Asia by the early 1700s. Spain controlled the Philippines, using **Manila** as a transit point for the shipment of silver from the New World to Asia.

Europe's colonial presence in Asia and, for the most part, its economic role involved moving goods from one Asian market to another or of pumping silver into Asian economies in exchange for goods to sell back home. These activities—especially the **influx of silver**, which caused inflation—had a noticeable impact on the region. Just as important was the precedent set by Europeans as, early on, they worked to gain thorough control over Indian Ocean sea lanes—at first to combat piracy, then to compete against one another as well as against Muslim fleets. No state had ever attempted this before, and naval escalation of this sort paved the way for a larger European military presence in Asia and eventually full-scale colonization.

More quickly than in the Pacific, a full-fledged **Atlantic system of trade** came into being. The **Columbian Exchange**, whose environmental impact is described in Chapter 12, introduced a large assortment of trade goods to the global economy—whether they were extracted from the New World or transplanted to it. Aside from staple foodstuffs taken from the Americas (like **manioc**, **corn**, and **potatoes**), cacao and **tobacco** became desirable luxury goods. Of the crops introduced by Europeans to the Americas, several had a mammoth impact on world trade: the arrival of **coffee** in the 1700s was noteworthy, but most important were **cotton** and **sugarcane**. Immensely profitable, both crops required backbreaking labor to cultivate, and the lightning rise of the **Atlantic slave trade** was due primarily to growing demand for these goods.

Two other aspects of Atlantic trade had global consequences. First, during the 1500s and 1600s, Spanish and Portuguese extraction of precious metals—especially silver—from the Americas affected economies around the world. The huge and sudden **influx of silver** and gold bullion into so many places at once created a harmful glut of precious metals throughout Afro-Eurasia. Severe **inflation** resulted not just in Europe but in places as diverse as the Ottoman Empire and China; in several cases, it caused social and political disruption, up to the point of rebellion.

Second, during the 1600s and 1700s, the expansion of European wealth depended increasingly on the Atlantic network known as the **triangular trade system**. Here, European manufactured goods (metalware, cotton textiles, firearms, gin, and rum) would be brought to Africa's west coast and exchanged for gold, ivory, and slaves. The voyage would continue to the Americas, where the slaves were sold in exchange for sugar, tobacco, furs, cotton, and other raw materials. These, along with the gold and ivory from Africa, would be shipped back to Europe. The centrality of the Atlantic slave trade to this system should be noted.

Another economic by-product of European exploration was a rise in the harvesting of animal products over vast distances. **Fishing** and **whaling** led European ships to venture throughout the Atlantic and into Arctic waters where possible. **Sea mammal hunting**—for walrus ivory and for the oil and pelts of seals—escalated, as did **fur hunting**, which played an enormous role in the settlement of remote regions like Canada and Siberia.

Controlling Trade: Companies and Competition

The exploration and exploitation of newfound lands was expensive and represented an extremely risky investment. Governments rarely paid for it, at least not directly.

Instead, mariners, merchants, explorers, and investors tended to operate under **monopoly charters** awarded by the state. Those given the charters assumed the costs and risks of exploration or trade that required long voyaging. In return, they enjoyed exclusive rights to profit from new territories or markets—although all discoveries were considered to belong to the charter-granting nation and a share of earnings might be owed to the government. Early Spanish conquistadors handed over to the state a portion of their New World wealth, and all goods and resources extracted from there had to pass through the state-run **Board of Trade** in Seville. In Russia, the mapping and settlement of Siberia was begun by merchant clans authorized by the tsars to search eastward for precious metals and fur-bearing animals.

Elsewhere in Europe, a common way to share the expenses and risks involved with overseas exploration and trade was to form **joint-stock companies**. These forerunners of the modern corporation allowed investors to pool their funds and receive a share of the profit based on the size of their investment. Among the first was the Muscovy Company, founded in England during the mid-1500s to carry out trade with Russia via the Arctic. During the 1600s, nations such as Britain, the Netherlands, and France founded numerous joint-stock companies to oversee commercial and colonial interests in the West Indies, North America, and the East Indies. Among the most famous were the **British East India Company** (1600), the **Dutch East India Company** (1602), the Company of New France (1664), and the **Hudson's Bay Company** (1670). Not only did these act as business entities, they often became chiefly or solely responsible for exerting their home nation's political and strategic will overseas.

> **NOTE**
>
> At its peak, the Dutch East India Company controlled a fleet of over 250 ships. For a time, the British East India Company maintained an army in South Asia that was larger than Britain's actual army. Imagine Facebook or McDonald's with its own air force or squadron of nuclear submarines.

Competition over trade routes led to tension and even armed conflict among both Europeans and non-Europeans. **Piracy** was common, whether in the Caribbean, the Indian Ocean, or Asia's Pacific and southeastern waters. In the Atlantic and the Caribbean, European states relied not just on their navies but also on the practice of **privateering**, or the licensing of captains who owned their vessels privately to capture enemy ships or raid enemy ports. (The line between piracy and privateering was very thin.) In Asian waters, Malay and Japanese pirates were a particular concern, and when the Chinese government allowed the Portuguese to establish themselves in Macau, it was to reward them for suppressing piracy in the region.

There are several important trade- and colony-related rivalries to be aware of. In Africa during the 1500s, Morocco's desire to increase its share of the gold and salt trades helped to provoke its war against the Songhai Empire. In the Atlantic, there was Anglo-Dutch and Anglo-French competition over parts of North America—New York in the case of the former, Canada in the case of the latter—both won by the English in the 1600s and 1700s. Also, most European powers quarreled over island colonies and shipping lanes in the Caribbean, or "West Indies." Southeast Asia and India became an arena of competition during the late 1500s and 1600s as the Spanish and Portuguese, who had inserted themselves into these economies earlier in the 1500s, were elbowed aside by the Dutch, French, and English. The Dutch cemented their presence in the "Spice Islands" (in and around present-day Indonesia), while the English, during the 1700s, enlarged their presence in India at the expense of the French.

The Indian Ocean as a whole witnessed a great deal of trade-related rivalry during the 1600s and 1700s. Aside from their concern about European encroachments, the Ottoman Empire and Safavid Persia dueled for economic influence here. Also important was the **Omani-European rivalry** that erupted in the mid-1600s as the Arab state of Oman rebelled against Portuguese colonial rule. Not only did the Omanis expel the Portuguese from their own territory, but they pushed the Portuguese out of Swahili ports such as Zanzibar and ruled those ports as their own for many decades. Also for a time, the Omani Empire competed with the British East India Company and other European commercial entities attempting to break into Indian Ocean markets during the 1600s and 1700s.

FROM MERCANTILISM TO CAPITALISM AND PROTOINDUSTRIALIZATION

Agriculture remained the world's dominant mode of economic production. Even so, this era witnessed profound changes with respect to how crops were grown and goods produced.

In the agricultural sphere, production vastly increased during these years, even though much of the world, especially in the northern hemisphere, was affected by the **Little Ice Age**. Many factors caused this rise in production. Crops transplanted as a result of the **Columbian Exchange** flourished in their new homes, especially the **corn**, **potatoes**, and **manioc** brought to Afro-Eurasia from the Americas. More land was brought under cultivation during this period. The **improvement of agricultural methods** also played a role: better fertilizers came into wider use, and the scientific rotation of crops and fields—which kept soil from becoming depleted too quickly or easily—was practiced more commonly.

Growth was just as dramatic in other sectors of the economy. **Trade** and **banking** became more important, with **merchant classes** earning great wealth and rising to positions of social, cultural, and political prominence. **Manufacturing** expanded as well, with artisan and craftsman classes growing in size and importance. Worldwide, most manufacturing continued to be done by hand and on a small scale. Still, by the 1600s and 1700s, especially in Europe, there was a noticeable rise in machine-assisted production and cottage industry. This **protoindustrialization** lay the groundwork for actual industrialization in the late 1700s and 1800s. It also began to stimulate a greater global demand for raw materials such as cotton (from Egypt and India), silk (from China), and wool and linen (from Europe).

Whether or not they used the term, the dominant economic philosophy in most advanced societies tended to be **mercantilism**. Mercantilist states assumed a fixed and finite quantity of wealth in the world. Consequently, they viewed all other nations as rivals and aimed for self-sufficiency. They believed in state control of economic activity. If they possessed colonies, they viewed them as economic extensions of the homeland: as a source of raw materials and a market for manufactured goods. By contrast, a new economic concept was catching on in Europe by the second half of the 1700s. This was **capitalism**, which emphasized free trade and argued for less state control of the economy. Hand in hand with industrialization, capitalism would soon revolutionize economic life worldwide.

ECONOMIC BUBBLES

The boom-and-bust nature of commercial economies became apparent during the 1600s and 1700s when several financial disasters resulted from optimistic overinvestment in corporate schemes whose potential profitability turned out to be wildly overvalued. Many of these bubbles involved investment in foreign trade or exploitation of colonies. Most infamous during this era were the tulipmania of the early 1600s when Dutch merchants purchased huge quantities of tulips from Ottoman Turkey, causing a terrible crash of the tulip market in 1637; the Mississippi bubble of 1720, which involved overvalued shares in the Mississippi Company, meant to reap profits from France's New World colonies; and Great Britain's South Sea Bubble, also in 1720, and due to similar overinvestment in Pacific territories.

Unfortunately, the global rise in productivity and wealth rested on a foundation of **coerced labor**, which took many forms. The **Atlantic slave trade** was extensive (and formed the heart of the Atlantic world's **triangular trade**), and so were the Arab slave trade and the market for slaves in Southeast Asia. **Serfdom** was common in Europe, especially in eastern regions like Russia. In the Americas, **plantation** and **cash-crop agriculture**—particularly the cultivation of **sugarcane**, **cotton**, and **coffee**—was based on unfree (or badly treated and poorly paid) labor.

Social Interactions and Organization, 1450–1750

11

IN THIS CHAPTER

→ **INCREASED AGRICULTURAL PRODUCTION AND HEAVIER BURDENS ON PEASANT POPULATIONS (TAXATION, CONSCRIPTION)**

→ **PLANTATION MONOCULTURE AND ITS EFFECTS ON PEASANT LABOR AND SLAVERY**

→ **FOOD RIOTS AND PEASANT UPRISINGS**

→ **URBANIZATION AND CLASS DIVERSIFICATION**

→ **RISE OF URBAN WORKING CLASS, MIDDLE CLASS, AND MERCHANT CLASS**

→ **ADJUSTMENTS MADE BY ELITE CLASSES TO POLITICAL CENTRALIZATION AND ECONOMIC CHANGES (EUROPEAN NOBLES, JAPANESE DAIMYO, INDIAN ZAMINDARS)**

→ **NEW BUREAUCRATIC ELITES (NOBLES OF THE ROBE, CIVIL SERVANTS RECRUITED BY OTTOMAN DEVSHIRME, CHINESE MANDARINS, SALARIED SAMURAI)**

→ **FORMS OF COERCED LABOR (SERFDOM, DEVSHIRME, ENCOMIENDA, SPANISH ADAPTATION OF MIT'A, INDENTURED SERVITUDE)**

→ **CHATTEL SLAVERY (ARAB SLAVE TRADE, ATLANTIC SLAVE TRADE)**

→ **PROTESTANT-CATHOLIC RELIGIOUS TENSIONS**

→ **EUROPEAN ANTI-SEMITISM**

→ **OTTOMAN MUDARRA POLICY (MILLET, JIZYA TAX)**

→ **HINDU-MUSLIM-SIKH TENSION IN INDIA**

→ **CREOLE AND MIXED POPULATIONS + RACE-BASED HIERARCHIES IN THE AMERICAS**

→ **PATRIARCHY AND GENDER INEQUALITY**

→ **FORMS OF GENDER DISCRIMINATION (WITCH HUNTS, SECLUSION, HAREMS, SATI, FOOT BINDING)**

→ **ROLE OF LOCAL WOMEN IN ENCOUNTERS WITH EUROPEAN TRADERS AND EXPLORERS**

Many of the main social trends from the previous era continued. These included a high degree of **social stratification**, a steady move toward greater **urbanization**, continued reliance on **coerced labor**, and the perpetuation of a **secondary status for women**.

Certain changes were afoot as well. The new economic complexities described in Chapter 10 led to greater **class diversification**. This, along with a general tendency toward political centralization, forced **elite classes** to adapt to new realities or risk losing their power. **Literacy rates** improved, especially in urban settings, as did greater accessibility of art and culture. Unfortunately, more varieties of coerced labor appeared during this period, and the number of people forced into it increased significantly.

SOCIAL CLASSES IN FLUX

Agriculture

Agriculture remained the dominant form of labor worldwide, and most people continued to live in rural settings.

Nonetheless, changes came to the countryside. For one, new forms of peasant labor arose. **Plantation agriculture** and **cash-crop monoculture**, which prevailed especially in Europe's overseas colonies, were extremely labor-intensive. They placed immense strain on peasant populations and typically involved **coerced labor** if not outright **slavery**. Peasant labor intensified in other places as well. Examples include the expansion and greater systemization of **cotton production in India** as well as the similar enlargement of **silk production in China**. Also falling in this category is the imposition or continuation of **serfdom** in certain areas. Most notably, serfdom arose in Russia during the 1400s and 1500s—and was exported to the Siberian frontier in the 1600s and 1700s—just as many parts of Europe were abandoning the practice or relying less heavily on it. Serfdom also became increasingly important in Japan.

Another source of pressure was the expansion of state power. As governments centralized, their power to affect peasant communities grew. Along with the imposition of **serfdom**, the most common ways for states to intrude into peasants' lives were **taxation** (which grew more efficient and therefore more burdensome) and **conscription** (as states centralized, larger armies drafted more serfs and peasants). Sometimes states proved unable or unwilling to assist rural populations when floods or bad harvests caused **food shortages**.

Increasingly often, conditions in the countryside caused enough frustration and desperation to trigger **food riots** and **peasant uprisings**. The largest social disturbance in Europe prior to the French Revolution was the **German Peasants' War** of the 1520s in which 300,000 rebelled against landowners and aristocrats in central Europe. The Ottoman sultans struggled against the **Celali revolts** of the late 1500s and early 1600s. Japan was rocked from the late 1400s through the mid-1500s by the Ikko-ikki revolts and again in the 1630s by the Shimabara rebellion. Both pitted peasants against samurai landowners and high taxes. Russia experienced numerous **Cossack and serf uprisings** in the 1600s and 1700s, including that of Stenka Razin—popularly remembered as a Robin Hood–style figure—in 1670 and the Pugachev revolt in the 1770s, which shook the regime of Catherine the Great to its foundations. In China, the Ming dynasty was brought down by a peasant war launched in the 1630s by the shepherd and ironworker **Li Zicheng**, who called for the abolition of grain taxes and the redistribution of land from the upper classes to the farmers. He ruled briefly as China's "Dashing King" until the Manchus toppled him in 1644 and established the Qing dynasty.

Urban and Merchant Classes

In most parts of the world, **urbanization** continued. This nearly always encouraged greater **social mobility** and **class diversification**.

The growing importance of artisanry, manufacturing, shopkeeping, unskilled labor, and domestic servitude to middle- and upper-class households led to the enlargement of **urban**

working classes and servant classes. Like peasants, they tended to be near the bottom of the hierarchy in most societies, and many of them suffered poverty and related hardships.

It was also in urban settings that the size of what later came to be known as the **middle class** grew. These included highly skilled artisans, professionals such as lawyers and physicians, and **merchants** and **bankers**. The middle classes placed a high premium on hard work and education. Where they stood in a given social hierarchy depended on which part of the world they were from. (As a reminder of this, consult the table "Social Hierarchies: A Comparison," in Chapter 5.)

Frequently, the middle classes, especially merchants, found themselves in an ambiguous situation. On the one hand, the economic importance of merchants greatly increased during this era, and they often commanded as much wealth— and sometimes as much informal power—as member of the elite classes. On the other hand, in most societies, elite classes looked down at merchants, scorning trade and the earning of money as somehow beneath them. Also, in most places, merchants were categorized as commoners, meaning that no matter how hard they worked or how much wealth they amassed, they found it difficult or impossible to gain the prestige that many elites simply inherited. Also, in societies where commoners paid taxes and elites did not, merchants ended up making valuable contributions to society without ever gaining society's full respect.

NOTE

In medieval and Renaissance Europe, merchants and other prosperous city dwellers were typically known as burghers, a Dutch and German term. Its French equivalent—the bourgeoisie—became famous during the industrial era when Karl Marx adopted it as a label to describe businessmen, factory owners, bankers, and others belonging to the higher levels of the middle class.

Merchants fared best in places with a high degree of social mobility. They played influential social and political roles—and sometimes moved into the elite classes—in England, the Netherlands, the Italian city-states (especially Florence and Venice), and the Swahili city-states. In much of Europe, they experienced difficulty entering the top levels of society. In many parts of Asia, their status remained low, and where Confucianism prevailed—as in China and Japan—they ranked below artisans and peasants, at least in theory.

Middle-class frustrations with existing social orders increased throughout this period. While they remained bottled up for the most part during these years, they would prove an enormous force for change in the late 1700s and 1800s.

Elite Classes

Most elite classes held onto their power and privileges, although political centralization and changing economic circumstances forced them to make adjustments. In many societies, new elites arose to coexist alongside traditional ones and in some cases replaced them or threatened to do so.

Political centralization deeply affected aristocrats and nobles, whose authority depended on inherited status and landownership. Traditionally, these elites provided military leadership and local governance in decentralized or feudal systems. This meant that, while they were theoretically subject to their monarchs, they in fact wielded a great deal of power in their own lands. They could not always be dictated to, and there were often clashes between the will of the monarch and that of the nobility.

Centralization altered this equation. In many places, power shifted decisively to the monarch, who compelled nobles and aristocrats to serve their state more actively. **European nobles**, due to monarchical pressure, served as officers in their nations' rapidly expanding armies and navies and as civil servants in their governments' growing bureaucracies. As the Mughal Empire strengthened its hold over India, landowning **zamindars**, who had previously enjoyed much local autonomy, were incorporated into the Mughal system as local officials and regional governors. Similarly, the **daimyo**, Japan's samurai landowning nobility, were masters of their own domains during the feudal disunity of the 1400s and 1500s but were forced into loyalty and service by the Tokugawa shogunate in the 1600s and 1700s.

Another political reality that traditional elites had to cope with was the tendency of modernizing states to create or elevate new **bureaucratic elites** and **military professionals**, sometimes based on skill or merit instead of hereditary status. There was already a long history of this in China, where the **Confucian examination system** continued to produce a **mandarin class** of bureaucrats. Also in Asia, **salaried samurai** took up administrative posts in a Japan that had been made more peaceful by unification after 1600 and no longer required traditional warrior skills. The Ottoman **devshirme system**, which recruited boys from the empire's Christian populations and converted them to Islam, provided the sultan's government not just with **janissary gunpowder troops** but also **civil servants**. In theory, this ensured loyalty to the sultan, although friction resulted whenever Ottoman elites felt the sultan was causing too much change or threatening their privileged status—especially in 1622 when janissary units went so far as to assassinate the sultan. In Europe during the 1600s, as a deliberate way to centralize at the expense of his powerful traditional aristocrats—known as "nobles of the sword" in honor of the military roles they had played since the Middle Ages—Louis XIV of France transferred many of his state's increasingly important (but less glamorous) bureaucratic jobs to **nobles of the robe**: civil servants who were ennobled by Louis himself and therefore owed their aristocratic status to the king rather than to their family tree. This ensured their loyalty to and continued dependence on the king.

Traditional elites also faced new economic challenges. Because their wealth depended so much on landownership profits, the rising importance of trade and commerce—which they tended to disdain—did not work in their favor. In an era where merchants, bankers, and urban entrepreneurs were generating more wealth and gaining more social and political influence (at least unofficially), traditional elites had to adapt and work harder to remain relevant. Those who failed to do so would fall behind or suffer serious consequences—if not during the 1700s, then in the 1800s or later.

SLAVERY AND COERCED LABOR

Forms of **coerced labor** increased in variety during this era, as did the number of people who fell under its yoke. **Chattel slavery**—the outright ownership of human beings as personal property—was commonly practiced throughout the world.

Miscellaneous Forms of Coerced Labor

Serfdom, or the binding of peasant laborers to the land in a way that left them unfree although not technically enslaved, was practiced in medieval Europe and elsewhere, mainly in feudal conditions. In many areas, it now faded away, but it remained important in places like Japan and the eastern half of Europe—especially in Russia, where serfdom formed the bedrock of social and economic life until after the mid-1800s.

Other forms of coerced labor that continued from the previous era were the Ottoman Empire's **devshirme system** (which recruited scribes, civil servants, and **janissary gunpowder troops** from non-Muslim communities, converted them to Islam, and placed them in conditions of privileged servitude) and the **Arab slave trade** (which exported African captives throughout the Middle East and the Indian Ocean basin). As Russians expanded into Siberia between the 1500s and 1700s, they forced native populations to work for them and provide them with a yearly quota of fur pelts and other goods. This combination of labor obligations and tribute payments was called the **yasak**.

Change was most apparent in the Atlantic region and the Americas, where European colonization radically altered labor conditions. During the late 1400s and early 1500s, Spain exploited its New World possessions by means of the **encomienda system**, which declared all American natives to be Spanish subjects and used many of them as slaves in mines and on plantations. However, not only did the vulnerability of indigenous Americans to European-borne diseases make them unreliable as a supply of slaves, but Catholic clergymen protested the cruelty caused by the encomienda system. *A Short Account of the Destruction of the Indies*, a book by the monk Bartolomé de las Casas, did much to sway Spanish opinion, and the encomienda was abolished by the New Laws of 1542–1543.

Unfortunately, this did not end coerced labor in the Americas. In South America, the Spanish adapted the **mit'a system** that Inca rulers had previously used in the Andes to harness labor in a manner similar to serfdom. The rise of **plantation monoculture**, both in Spain's New World colonies and in Portuguese Brazil, involved the intensive cultivation of a single crop on large estates known as **haciendas** and latifundias. As with **mining**, this sort of agriculture required an immense amount of labor and encouraged the employment of native workers on harsh terms and for little pay. Even more ominously, it persuaded the Spanish and Portuguese to rely heavily on **slave labor from Africa**. Plantation monoculture spread to North America, where French and especially English colonists practiced it and also resorted to slave labor. The crops most directly connected with this trend were **sugarcane** in the Caribbean and South America and **cotton** and **tobacco** in North America.

NOTE

One institution that brought labor to North America, especially to English colonies, was a form of debt bondage called indentured servitude. Would-be colonists who could not afford passage across the Atlantic agreed to work for a period of time for the families who paid their way. In addition, English criminals were often punished by transportation, or exile, to the Americas.

The Atlantic Slave Trade

Once started, the **Atlantic slave trade** became a central part of the European economy and a primary factor in Europe's ability to generate such great wealth. By the 1440s, the Portuguese had begun to enslave Africans, taking them to Portugal and selling them in Europe. This number was relatively small. But in the 1500s, when the Portuguese and Spanish started shipping slaves to the Americas and the Caribbean for mining and plantation monoculture (especially sugarcane production), numbers grew and conditions became harsher.

Europeans enslaved roughly 1,000 Africans per year in the late 1400s and more than 2,000 per year in the 1500s, for an estimated sum of 325,000 during these two centuries. During the 1600s and 1700s, the Atlantic slave trade mushroomed far beyond this: more than a million Africans were transported in the 1600s and at least 6 million in the 1700s. In total, approximately 12.5 million Africans were forced into New World slavery between the mid-1400s and the late 1800s. Thirty-seven percent went to Brazil (the largest slaveholding country), 15 percent to Spanish America, 41 percent to non-Spanish parts of the Caribbean, and 5 percent to the southern colonies of British North America, where they grew crops such as cotton and tobacco.

Africans were captured and shipped to the Americas under notoriously appalling conditions. Many were captives or prisoners of war, conveyed to Africa's west coast and sold to European slavers by Africans from enemy tribes, and many were separated from families or mixed in with other tribes with unfamiliar languages and customs. They were then loaded onto ships to make the infamous **Middle Passage** across the Atlantic. The more slaves a ship could carry, the greater the profit, so captives were packed into boats as tightly as possible. Chained, lying on their backs, surrounded by hundreds of other bodies, all in darkness, they endured a nightmarishly claustrophobic sea journey that lasted for weeks. Upon arrival, they would be taken to slave markets and sold. In the early years, up to 25 percent of captives perished during the Middle Passage. During the 1700s and 1800s, slavers cut the average death rate to 10 percent or less—not for humane reasons but because each dead slave was a financial loss. The shipment of enslaved Africans via the Middle Passage was an integral part of the **triangular trade** that made Europe rich during this era.

GENDER AND ETHNICITY

Religious and Ethnic Differences

Ethnic and religious minorities—or, on occasion, populations governed by an ethnic or religious minority—were treated differently in various parts of the world. In some cases, they enjoyed freedom and equal status. More often, they were persecuted, treated as second-class citizens, or restricted in other ways.

In Europe, **Protestants and Catholics** regularly persecuted each other, and **anti-Semitism** was rampant throughout the continent. Jews were stereotyped by European Christians as greedy because of their success since the Middle Ages in fields like banking and commerce. Jews were further resented because of the popular but misguided belief that they bore responsibility from biblical times for the death of Jesus. Due to tensions stirred up by the Spanish Reconquista and the Ottoman Empire's campaigns against Constantinople and the Balkans, **anti-Islamic tendencies** prevailed among European Christians as well.

Middle Eastern states imposed their own restrictions on non-Muslims. Although violence and persecution were not unknown, both Ottoman Turkey and Safavid Persia officially operated according to a policy of relative religious tolerance, referred to among the Ottomans as **mudarra**, or "moderation." As under the earlier caliphates, non-Muslims were allowed to convert to Islam if they wished but were not forced to do so. Dhimmis, or nonbelievers, did not have equal rights. They could not serve in the military, their testimony in trials was given less weight than that of Muslims, and as before, they paid a special tax called the **jizya**. The devshirme system of taking boys from Christian families to serve the Ottoman regime was generally disliked—although some families saw this as an opportunity for their sons to rise up in the world. To administer its non-Muslim subjects, the Ottoman Empire organized each religious minority into a unit called a **millet** ("nation"). Three millets existed before the 1700s: one for Jews, one for Armenian Christians, and one for Greek Orthodox Christians.

Treatment of non-Muslims remained relatively mild until the 1800s when nationalist aspirations among the Ottomans' subject peoples began to heighten tensions.

NOTE

As before, but now on a greater scale, due to the expansion of global trade, diasporic communities formed in many towns and ports. The desire for profits often trumped ethnic or religious prejudice, or at least blunted it. Not always, though: in some places, the presence of foreign traders was highly restricted, as in China and Japan, where, by the 1600s and 1700s, outsiders were confined to specific port cities, such as Canton and Nagasaki.

In Mughal India, where a Muslim minority ruled a Hindu majority as well as a growing population of Sikhs, religious policy varied. It ranged from the tolerant benevolence of **Akbar the Great**, who abolished the jizya tax for Hindus in the late 1500s and encouraged friendly relations among those of all faiths, to the Islamic militancy of **Aurangzeb**, who imposed Sharia law on India's Hindus in the late 1600s and whose persecution of the Sikhs caused them to revolt and to establish their own state in the Punjab.

Colonization and conquest led to the formation of new **race-based hierarchies**. For many years after the 1644 establishment of the Qing dynasty in China, the ruling Manchus, who composed a tiny percentage of the population, stratified society according to race. They forced their Chinese subjects to wear certain clothes and to braid their hair into long queues. Males had to shave their foreheads, as reflected in the classic proverb, "lose your hair or lose your head." In the Americas, colonization created **mixed populations** as Europeans had children with Native Americans or transplanted Africans and as Africans had children with Native Americans. **Mestizos** and **métis** (Spanish and French for "mixed") were common names for the offspring of Europeans and American natives. Those of European and African descent were known as **mulattos**, while **zambo** described someone of mixed African and Native American heritage. The word **creole**—the French equivalent of the Spanish *criollo*—eventually came to mean someone of mixed descent, but it originated from the Portuguese term *crioulo* (from the verb *criar*, "to raise") as a way to describe a person of European descent who happened to be born in the colonies.

In the long run, the emergence of creole cultures and mixed populations hugely enriched the cultures of the New World, especially in Latin America and the Caribbean. Unfortunately, during the centuries of Portuguese and especially Spanish rule, these groups were organized into a rigid social hierarchy. Pure-bred Spanish who settled in the New World were known as *peninsulares* and remained at the top, with *criollos* (creoles according to the original definition of the word) alongside them enjoying elite status. Those of mixed blood and native ancestry were nearer the bottom, and slaves occupied the lowest rung of the social ladder. For a time, Spanish colonial authorities set natives apart by forming a **República de Indios**, an administrative unit that resembled the Ottoman millet in that it kept natives under Spanish jurisdiction (and harnessed their labor and taxes) but allowed a certain degree of social and cultural autonomy.

Restructuring of Gender and Family Relations

In most parts of the world, women continued to occupy a secondary status in terms of social roles, economic opportunities, and political influence. In some places and some ways, conditions for women improved. Individual women from small but important segments of society—such as the aristocracy and the emerging middle class—gained educations, became active in business, and worked as artists and writers. Improvements were limited, though, and not all changes were positive.

In Europe, women of the upper classes enjoyed more access to education and took a more active role in intellectual life. Many in the middle classes also became more educated and assumed a greater economic role as operators of businesses or partners in them. Those of all classes gained more control over when and whom they married as well as over issues like divorce, childbirth, and inheritance. Particularly in urban settings, where the labor of children was needed less than on a farm, women opted to have fewer children, causing a decline in the average size of European families. Progress in cultural life was significant as well. Many Catholic nuns achieved a high level of education, and Protestantism's emphasis on literacy led upper- and middle-class women to attain at least some learning. A number of baroque and eighteenth-century painters were women, and women also turned to writing, philosophy, and scientific research—although they were not allowed to become university faculty. Important monarchs from this period of European history were women, including Isabella of Castile, Elizabeth I of England, Maria Theresa of Austria, and in the late 1700s, Catherine the Great of Russia.

In no sense, however, were women in Europe treated as equal to men. Legally and economically, they remained subservient. Rates of death during childbirth were still high. Women made up about 75 percent of the victims of the witch hunts of the 1500s and 1600s, and both Catholicism and the new Protestant faiths used scripture to justify the view that women were inferior to and more sinful than men. Even during the Enlightenment of the 1700s, few among Europe's otherwise more liberal thinkers were willing to entertain the notion of women's equality—despite the crucial role women played in shaping Enlightenment culture.

A similar ambiguity prevailed in the Muslim world, both in the Middle East and South Asia. Among the elite classes, women played informal but influential roles. In Ottoman Turkey, the sultan's mother ran the household, controlled marriage alliances, and sometimes conducted diplomacy. Among both the Ottomans and the Persian Safavids, the **harem** was not simply a collection of concubines for the ruler's pleasure, as is popularly thought. Instead, it was a complex social network that included most female members of the imperial family—relatively few of whom were used for any sexual purpose—and involved itself with the raising of children and pursuit of the arts. **Polygamy** was also rarer in the Muslim world than is generally believed. On the other hand, the **seclusion of women** was practiced consistently throughout the Muslim world and among most classes. And while Muslim women had certain rights with respect to owning and inheriting property, they had few rights within marriage or when it came to divorce. Although they could testify in court, their testimony was not counted as equal to a man's.

In India, the impact of Mughal rule on women was mixed. By and large, Muslim women had more rights than their Hindu counterparts, who remained subject to the **caste system** and, depending on their status, the funeral practice of **sati**, or ritual burning. On the other hand, the **seclusion of women** applied both to Muslim women and Hindu women of high caste, and when Mughal rulers chose in the 1600s to impose **Sharia law** on non-Muslims, these restrictions fell on Hindu women, not just Muslims. In China, **foot binding** became more widespread, and Confucian doctrine continued to justify a secondary status for women. The stratification of Japanese society by the Tokugawa shogunate placed heavier restrictions on the behavior of women, especially if they belonged to the samurai class. Obliged to obey their husbands or face death, women in Tokugawa Japan had little authority over property and received less education than men, even if artistic and cultural pursuits were encouraged among elite women. In both China and Japan, girl children, as in earlier eras, were less valued and sometimes put to death or sold into prostitution or servitude. In Japan, some women gained status and fame as **geishas**, special courtesans valued not just as sex objects but for their musical, artistic, and conversational skills.

As before, several African societies, especially in the west, were **matrilineal** and relatively willing to accept female leadership, as in the famous case of **Queen Nzinga** of Angola during the late 1500s and early 1600s. Throughout the continent, gender and family relations were affected by Islam's deepening presence, which led to more veiling and seclusion, and also by the arrival of Europeans and Arabs along the coasts. The escalation of the Arab and Atlantic slave trades had the effect of breaking apart many families, even in the interior, beyond the direct reach of foreigners.

As European colonizers and traders spread their influence to Africa, Asia, and the Americas, **local women** often played crucial roles during the economic and political encounters that unfolded between outsiders and their own people. For instance, the Portuguese and other Europeans who arrived in Southeast Asia found themselves heavily dependent—for cultural orientation and social connections—on the local women they took as mistresses or wives. In the Americas, Hernán Cortés's success in conquering the Aztecs was due at least in part to the guidance and diplomatic skills provided by his Nahua mistress Doña Marina, or **Malinche**. The story of **Pocahontas** and her helpful interactions during the early 1600s with English colonists in Virginia—saving the life of John Smith from her own people and later marrying John Rolfe—is the most famous illustration of this trend.

Humans and the Environment, 1450–1750

12

IN THIS CHAPTER

→ **THE COLUMBIAN EXCHANGE**

→ **AFRO-EURASIAN ANIMALS TO THE AMERICAS (HORSES, PIGS, CATTLE)**

→ **AFRO-EURASIAN CROPS TO THE AMERICAS (SUGARCANE, COTTON, OKRA, RICE, COFFEE)**

→ **AMERICAN CROPS TO EURASIA (MANIOC, CORN/MAIZE, POTATOES)**

→ **IMPACT OF AFRO-EURASIAN DISEASES ON INDIGENOUS AMERICAN POPULATIONS**

→ **PLANTATION AND MONOCULTURE FARMING**

→ **MINING AND MANUFACTURING**

→ **FUR HUNTING, FISHING, AND WHALING**

→ **THE LITTLE ICE AGE**

Because of technological advances and the worldwide expansion of trade, human impact on the environment increased substantially. Reinforcing this trend was the intensification of certain economic activities, including new forms of agricultural production, the rise of manufacturing, and resource extraction on a greater scale than ever before. Worldwide population growth added to this impact.

Even more dramatically, the ecosystems of Afro-Eurasia and the Americas were brought into contact with each other at the end of the 1400s by the European campaigns of exploration. The environmental impact of this encounter on both hemispheres was monumental, and the resulting two-way transmission of foodstuffs, animal species, disease pathogens, and human populations is known as the **Columbian Exchange**.

With respect to climate, the **Little Ice Age**—after a gradual cooling during the 1300s and 1400s—hit its peak between the early 1500s and the mid-1800s. This affected agricultural practices, trade routes, and patterns of animal migration and human settlement, especially in the northern hemisphere.

Thanks in large measure to the arrival of new foodstuffs from the Americas, the populations of Europe, Africa, and Asia underwent significant growth from the 1500s onward.

THE COLUMBIAN EXCHANGE: PLANTS AND ANIMALS

Europe's encounter with the Americas—truly a "new world" from the perspective of the European arrivals—led to one of the greatest ecological and demographic transformations in world history, known commonly as the **Columbian Exchange**.

The exchange of animals, plants, and foods shaped the environments of Old World and New World alike. From Afro-Eurasia came sheep, goats, cattle, and pigs, which increased the supply of meat and milk in the Americas. Europeans also brought the **horse**, which provided labor and transport and radically changed the lifestyle of Native Americans who lived and hunted on plains and grasslands.

Columbus himself introduced **sugarcane** to the Americas, where it would eventually be produced in massive quantities—a crucial factor in the emergence of the Atlantic slave trade. The southeastern part of North America joined Egypt and India as one of the world's great sources of **cotton**, yet another development that encouraged the use of slaves in the Americas. **Okra** and **rice** from Africa, along with wheat, olives, grapevines, citrus, and other fruits and grains, were brought to the Americas as well. Later, during the 1700s, **coffee** (which originated in northeast Africa and spread to the Middle East and Europe between the 1400s and 1600s) was found to flourish in the Caribbean and South America.

From the Americas came crops that were eventually adopted as staple foods by populations throughout Afro-Eurasia. **Manioc** and **corn** (maize) displaced many traditional foods in Africa, and in Asia, corn grew readily in areas that were too dry to grow rice but too wet to grow wheat. **Potatoes** had an equally large impact on Europe and Asia. All three crops were relatively easy to grow and yielded many calories per acre. They sparked a general growth in Afro-Eurasian populations, and they also helped to offset the negative effects that the Little Ice Age had on agricultural production in many parts of the northern hemisphere.

Other plants that traveled from the Americas to Afro-Eurasia included squash, sweet potatoes, chili peppers, beans, peanuts, and vitamin-rich tomatoes. **Tobacco** and cacao (for making chocolate) became eagerly sought luxury goods in Europe.

THE COLUMBIAN EXCHANGE: DISEASES AND POPULATIONS

Tragically, the Columbian Exchange also involved the movement of diseases, almost exclusively in a one-way direction: from Afro-Eurasia to the Americas. Tropical diseases such as yellow fever and **malaria** came from Africa, taking hold especially in the Caribbean but also South America and warmer parts of eastern North America. Even deadlier in their effect were **smallpox**, **measles**, and **influenza**. Because of their centuries-long environmental isolation from Eurasia and Africa, the inhabitants of the Americas had no immunity to these new illnesses. The one disease the Europeans may have brought back from the New World is the sexually transmitted disease syphilis (although scholarly debate continues about the origins of this malady).

Most historians think that the death rate among American natives caused by their first encounters with Afro-Eurasian diseases could run to at least 50 percent of the pre-Columbian population. Recently, an increasing number of estimates have gone even higher, reaching as high as 80 or 90 percent. Here, the principal research difficulty is the scarcity of evidence that would provide a reliable estimate of how many people lived in the Americas prior to European contact. Either way, European arrival spelled medical disaster for indigenous Americans.

NOTE

The arrival of Afro-Eurasian diseases in the Americas is the most attention-getting medical story of this era. Even so, remember that in Afro-Eurasia itself, many diseases—whether well established or newer—continued to have a recurrent and lethal impact on large numbers of people until the discovery of germ theory and the development and widespread distribution of vaccines. Bubonic plague flared up periodically until the late 1700s and early 1800s, and smallpox, influenza, and measles remained deadly killers. The growing trend toward urbanization helped certain diseases to spread quickly and widely, especially among the poor. Along with the diseases already listed, these included cholera, typhus, tuberculosis, and polio.

Another demographic change associated with the Columbian Exchange was the **mass transfer of populations**. Trade and traffic back and forth across the Atlantic increased steadily during this period, touching off a huge series of **migrations**, both voluntary and involuntary. Millions of slaves and hundreds of thousands of colonists came from Africa and Europe to the New World. Once in the Americas, their interaction with the indigenous peoples—and with each other—led to rich and complex ethnic and cultural mixing.

MONOCULTURE AND RESOURCE EXTRACTION: ECOLOGICAL EFFECTS

Nearly every economic activity pursued by major societies during this period placed a greater burden on the environment. In and of itself, human population growth did the same.

Agriculture remained the dominant form of production in most parts of the world. With greater numbers of people practicing it in more parts of the world, it increased in scale and intensity. Especially striking and especially harmful to the environment was the European introduction to the Americas of **plantation monoculture**. Whether in the Americas or elsewhere, overexploitation of the land typically led to **soil depletion** (as nutrients were exhausted) and **deforestation** (as woods were cleared to make room for farms), and it could cause **water shortages** as well. Monoculture also increased dependency on a single staple crop for food, heightening the risk of food shortages or **famine** if something went wrong with that one crop. In areas where herding and pastoralism were still practiced, the risk of **overgrazing** was always present.

With the emergence of manufacturing as a larger sector of the economy in places like Europe, the Middle East, and Asia—and with urbanization generally accompanying this trend—other stresses on the environment became more severe. The number of **water mills** and **windmills** grew. For metallurgy and for protoindustrial production and also to heat a growing number of homes and buildings, the **burning of coal and wood fires** vastly increased in scale. This led to a gradual rise in **pollution** that would only grow worse with the advent of modern industrialization in the late 1700s and early 1800s.

> ### EFFECTS OF CASH-CROP AGRICULTURE
>
> Certain cash crops had a particularly profound impact during this period. These included sugar in the Caribbean and tobacco in the Americas as well as cotton, the cultivation of which spread to the Americas and was intensified in places like India. Coffee from Ethiopia, which was adopted by Sufi Muslims in southern Arabia during the mid-1400s, spread throughout the Middle East during the 1500s. Over the course of the next century, as the Europeans grew fond of coffee, they imported it from the Middle East but also transplanted it to Southeast Asia in the mid-to-late 1600s and then, starting in the early 1700s, to the Caribbean and Brazil. The production of cash crops by means of plantation monoculture placed huge strains on the environment and accelerated the rise of slavery and other forms of coerced labor.

The extent of **resource extraction** also grew in all parts of the globe during this period. Wood—needed both for fuel and for the making of houses, furniture, and ships, among other things—was one of the many **raw materials** for which manufacturing created a greater hunger. The growing appetite for metals and minerals—whether for currency, for the production of gunpowder weaponry, or for the manufacture of trade goods—caused **mining** to become more significant and more environmentally damaging than ever before. (The extraction of gold and particularly **silver from the Americas** had an especially pronounced impact during these years.) Expansion of the **textiles trade** required larger quantities of cotton, silk, linen, and wool.

Other forms of resource extraction similarly intensified, especially as European mariners, merchants, and colonizers extended their reach to the Americas and throughout the Atlantic and Pacific. Large-scale **fishing** became more important, as did the **hunting of whales** for meat and oil, used mainly to light lamps. The quest for **furs**—often referred to as "soft gold"—fundamentally shaped the course of European expansion into places like North America and Siberia, and it drastically reduced the numbers of dozens of animal species, including seals, beavers, otters, sables, and others. The killing of walruses and elephants for **ivory** ramped up during these years as well.

THE LITTLE ICE AGE

As noted before, a warming trend known as the **medieval climatic optimum** (ca. 800–1300) gave way to a gradual cooling in the 1300s and 1400s. This in turn culminated in a period of sharper cold called the **Little Ice Age** by environmental historians and that lasted from the late 1400s and early 1500s to the mid-1800s. It mainly affected the northern hemisphere but was not without influence farther to the south.

Whatever its causes, the Little Ice Age had predictable physical effects, including the lowering of agricultural yields and the shifting of sea routes and of hunting and fishing grounds. The enlargement of the Sahara Desert during these years is attributed to the Little Ice Age; cooling there increased rather than decreased aridity.

Beyond that, in more unexpected ways, the Little Ice Age exerted a powerful influence on the political and social fortunes of many societies. Food shortages and other disruptions to agriculture, along with the general harshness of the climate, helped to cause or worsen events such as the German Peasants' War, the religious wars in seventeenth-century Europe, the Ottoman Empire's Celali revolts, and the rebellion that ended Ming rule in China.

NOTE

One theory gaining currency among archaeologists and environmental historians is that the peak effects of the Little Ice Age may have been sparked—or at least made more extreme—by the massive die-off of indigenous Americans after the arrival of Afro-Eurasian diseases. The logic here is that the near-complete devastation of so many native communities led to rapid reforestation (and a decline in pollution) on such a scale that the world's climate was affected.

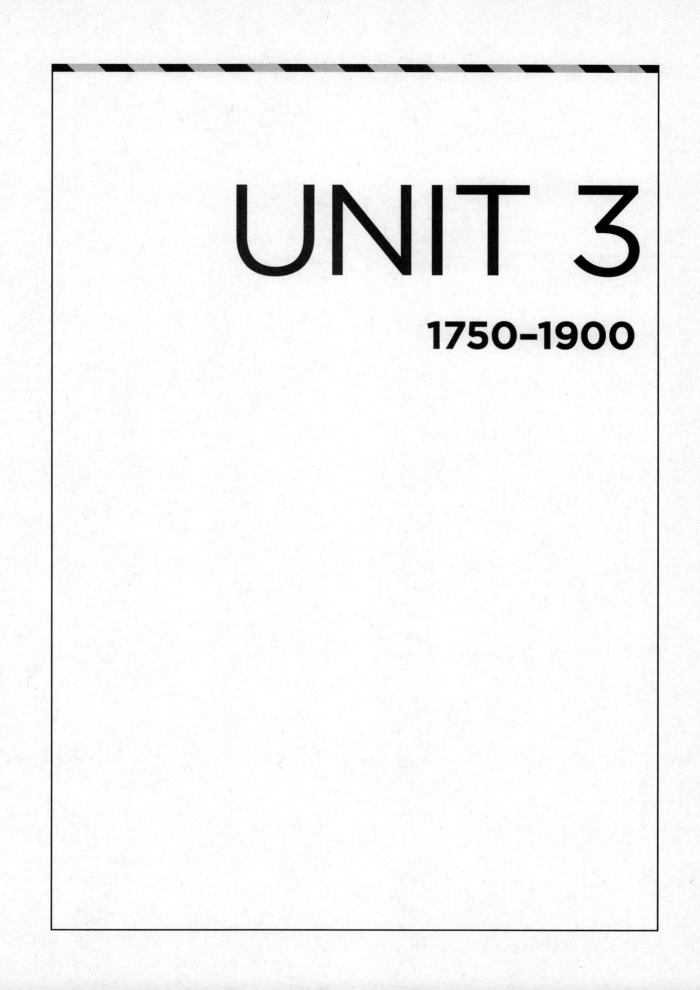

UNIT 3

1750–1900

Unit 3: Short Cut

GENERAL REMARKS

During the 1750–1900 period, the world entered the modern age.

What defines **modernity** is a question of debate among historians. In popular terms, the word *modern* is used as a synonym for "contemporary" or as a way to describe one's own times. In historical terms, it describes an era characterized by certain features. Different scholars identify these in different ways, but most agree on the following.

- In politics, there is a move from traditional monarchy toward greater political representation. The end result in most societies is some form of democracy or at least the appearance of democracy.
- In economics, industrialization becomes a driving force. A shift occurs from feudalism and mercantilism to capitalism. Economies are based increasingly on industry and commerce rather than primarily on agriculture.
- In society, there is class transformation and the breakdown of traditional hierarchies, as hereditary aristocracies fade away in favor of new elites whose status derives from wealth. New classes expand or emerge, especially the middle class and industrial working class. As agriculture gives way to industry, societies urbanize. Population growth accelerates, and large-scale migration becomes easier and more prevalent.
- In culture, a scientific, secular worldview becomes dominant. Artistic and literary styles change more rapidly and radically than ever before.

In all these things, Europe, with the United States, moved forward first. Great political upheavals such as the **American Revolution** and the **French Revolution** began the long process of giving more people a greater voice in politics. It was in Europe that the **Industrial Revolution** began, and it was there that **capitalism** emerged (as well as alternative economic visions, such as **socialism**). These changes transformed the economies of the world. Population growth, class diversification, and urbanization were hallmarks of Western social development during the late 1700s and 1800s. The foundations for modern cultural and intellectual life were laid in Europe during the 1700s thanks to the Scientific Revolution and the **Enlightenment**.

To varying degrees, modernization reached the rest of the world in the 1800s and early 1900s. A few non-Western nations adapted quickly, such as Japan. Some, including the Ottoman Empire, China, and the nations of Latin America, modernized slowly or partially. Others lagged further behind. No matter the pace, however, change came to all these regions. **Coerced** and **semicoerced labor** remained common worldwide, although antislavery sentiment grew steadily more powerful.

Another overarching development was the **rise of the West** as the world's dominant civilization. Not only did industrialization and modernization make the West prosperous and technologically advanced, they enabled it to control a vast percentage of the world's habitable territory. Many areas that had originally been colonized during the Age of Exploration—such as North and South America—became free during the late 1700s and early 1800s. However, a **new imperialism** swept over Asia, the Middle East, the Pacific, and Africa during the 1800s and early 1900s. Seeking markets and raw materials and armed with industrial-era weaponry, the nations of the West subjugated an unprecedented portion of the globe. But as impressive as imperialism was as a practical accomplishment, it carried a steep moral and ethical price. It was inextricably bound up with warfare, racial prejudice, economic rapacity, and slavery. Many of its harmful effects are still felt to this day.

By the end of the nineteenth century, Europe had reached the peak of its power but would soon fall from that pinnacle. The young United States was overtaking Europe in economic and military strength. New philosophies, scientific theories, and cultural movements were calling into question the traditional certainties and values of the Western world. Most important, diplomatic tensions were leading Europe toward the devastation of World War I (1914–1918), which decisively hastened the process of European decline.

BROAD TRENDS

Governance, 1750–1900	
Europe	French Revolution (1789–1799, Declaration of the Rights of Man and the Citizen) and Napoleonic Wars (1799–1815) Congress of Vienna (1814–1815) and reactionary politics (1815–1848) revolutions of 1848 reform and widening of political representation (1848–1914) women's suffrage movements anti-Semitism wars of Italian and German unification (Franco-Prussian War) geopolitical conflict (from balance of power to European alliance system; competition over empire)
Middle East	Tanzimat reforms and Ottoman constitution of 1876 (vs. janissaries and Islamic traditionalism) from Ottomanism (Young Turks) to Turkish nationalism Balkan nationalism (Greek War of Independence, Balkan Crisis of 1876–1878) French colonization of Algeria (1830s–1840s) Muhammad Ali's revolt (1805) in Egypt and construction of Suez Canal (1850s–1860s) geopolitical conflict (Eastern Question, Great Game) millenarian revolts (the Mahdi)
Africa	continuation and decline of Atlantic and East African slave trades African states (Wassoulou Empire, Sokoto Caliphate, Zulu and Ashanti kingdoms) vs. European imperialism (Berlin Conference, South Africa, Belgian Congo, Herero Wars) geopolitical conflict (Scramble for Africa, Boer War) millenarian revolts (Xhosa cattle killing, the Mahdi, Maji Maji) training of native elites and native troops by imperial powers

Governance, 1750–1900	
East (and Central) Asia	Qing China's positive balance of trade vs. technological stagnation Opium Wars and "unequal" treaties (foreign concessions) self-strengthening movement vs. Qing conservatism Taiping Rebellion (1850–1864) and Boxer Rebellion (1900) Tokugawa isolationism vs. Perry's "opening" of Japan (1853) Meiji Restoration (1868) and industrial modernization of Japan geopolitical conflict (foreign concessions, Open Door policy, Russo-Japanese War) millenarian revolts (Taiping Rebellion)
South (and Southeast) Asia and Oceania	fracturing of Mughal Empire (Marathas, Sikhs) British East India Company and Indian Revolt (1857–1858) colonization in Southeast Asia (Dutch East Indies, Singapore, French Indochina, U.S. annexation of Philippines) colonization of Australia (Aborigines) and New Zealand (Maori) U.S. annexation of Hawaiian kingdom geopolitical conflict (battle of Plassey, Anglo-Russian Great Game) training of native elites and native troops by imperial powers (sepoys) national-liberation impulses (Indian National Congress, from Filipino Propaganda Movement to Emiliano Aguinaldo)
Americas	American Revolution (1775–1783, Declaration of Independence) U.S. expansion (Louisiana Purchase, "manifest destiny," Mexican-American and Spanish-American wars, Hawaiian kingdom) U.S. suppression of Native Americans (Tecumseh, Cherokee Nation and Trail of Tears, Indian wars, Wounded Knee, reservation system) slavery in the Americas (Maroon societies, U.S. Civil War, Brazil) Haitian Rebellion (1791–1804, François Toussaint L'Ouverture) Latin American wars of independence (1810–1825, Simón Bolívar's Jamaica Letter) failure of constitutional rule in Latin America (caudillos) economic imperialism in Latin America geopolitical conflict (Monroe Doctrine, Spanish-American War) millenarian revolts (Ghost Dance and Wounded Knee) national-liberation impulses (Tupac Amaru II in Peru, Mayan Caste War, José Martí in Cuba)
Global and Interregional	increased prominence of the nation-state global impact of "new" imperialism (white man's burden, *la mission civilisatrice*, social Darwinism) and economic imperialism nationalist impulses indigenous revolts and national-liberation movements (including millenarian revolts)

Governance

- With every passing decade, the nation-state emerged as the leading form of political organization in more parts of the world.
- Modern political and economic ideologies—including conservatism, liberalism, nationalism, and socialism—emerged.

- The hallmark of modern political life is greater popular representation, as subjects challenged national and imperial regimes in reformist and revolutionary ways. This trend first got underway in the West, beginning in the late 1700s with the American and French Revolutions.
- Other parts of the world were slower to move away from traditional autocracies or monarchies. A few, such as Japan and the Ottoman Empire, developed parliamentary monarchies by around 1900. Latin American nations developed parliamentary governments in theory, but many slipped into dictatorial or military rule.
- The technological, economic, and military rise of the West—Europe and the United States—altered the balance of global power. World affairs were increasingly determined by foreign-policy and military developments in Europe, especially in the 1800s.
- The United States broke away from English rule during the late 1700s. In the 1800s, it achieved dominance over the North American continent and became a world power.
- The Spanish and Portuguese colonies of Latin America freed themselves from European rule during the early 1800s, another alteration of the global balance of power.
- In North Africa and the eastern Mediterranean, the gradual collapse of the Ottoman Empire presented Europe and the Middle East with a troubling and destabilizing diplomatic issue known as the Eastern Question.
- European and U.S. imperialism—the "new imperialism" of the mid-to-late 1800s—gave the nations of the West unprecedented global dominance. In 1815, the nations of the West controlled roughly 35 percent of the world's habitable territory. By 1914, that figure had risen to approximately 85 percent.
- The one non-Western nation that developed a modern colonial empire in the late 1800s and early 1900s was Japan.
- By the end of the 1800s, diplomatic tensions, nationalism, and competition over colonies made it increasingly likely that the nations of Europe would go to war. An alliance system formed, and the level of aggression rose steadily until the outbreak of World War I in 1914.

Cultural Developments and Interactions, 1750–1900	
Europe	Enlightenment (1700s; Locke, Montesquieu, Voltaire, Rousseau) romanticism, realism, and modernism (late 1700s–early 1900s) conservatism (and reaction) vs. liberalism capitalism (Adam Smith) vs. socialism and communism (Karl Marx) nationalism + social Darwinism secularization of culture + Western crisis of faith
Middle East	cultural Westernization in Ottoman Empire during Tanzimat reforms (mid-1800s) from Ottomanism to Turkish nationalism Islamic traditionalism revival of Arabic culture
Africa	oral tradition and griot storytelling nonrepresentational art and impact on Western modernism influence of Christian missionaries national-liberation impulses (Maji Maji revolt)

Cultural Developments and Interactions, 1750–1900	
East (and Central) Asia	*Dream of the Red Chamber* (late 1700s) influence of Christian missionaries in China ukiyo-e woodblock painting (Hokusai, early-to-mid-1800s) "Goodbye Asia" and Japanese ideologies of nationalist-racial superiority (late 1800s) national-liberation impulses (Boxer Rebellion)
South (and Southeast) Asia and Oceania	"Company" style in India (Gateway to India arch) influence of Christian missionaries national-liberation impulses (Indian National Congress, Filipino Katipunan)
Americas	Enlightenment (1700s; founding figures) romanticism, realism, and modernism (late 1700s–early 1900s) conservatism (and reaction) vs. liberalism capitalism vs. socialism and communism nationalism + social Darwinism national-liberation impulses (José Martí) secularization of culture + Western crisis of faith
Global and Interregional	rising literacy rates increased westernization of non-Western cultures (colonial educational systems) nationalism and national-liberation impulses

Cultural Developments and Interactions

- In eighteenth-century Europe and America, the Enlightenment prompted rational inquiry into the nature of politics and society. By questioning social hierarchies and traditional forms of monarchy, it paved the way for massive political changes, including key revolutions.
- Access to public education became an increasingly normal part of life in North America and most parts of Europe. Literacy rates rose as a result. The same became true for many other parts of the world during the late 1800s.
- Modern political and economic ideologies—including conservatism, liberalism, nationalism, and socialism—emerged.
- Nationalism became a powerful political and cultural force in Europe and then elsewhere. By the end of the 1800s, nationalist and national-liberation movements became prevalent in non-Western parts of the world dominated by foreign colonial rule.
- Ideologies of racial superiority, in some cases based on pseudoscientific concepts like social Darwinism, arose in many quarters.
- The non-Western world began to adopt many of the artistic, architectural, and literary forms of the West. Conversely, styles from Asia, Africa, and the Middle East had an influence on Western culture, particularly in painting, sculpture, and decor.
- In Europe and the Americas, the pace of cultural change sped up. By the end of the 1800s, new artistic and literary trends were emerging at a rapid rate. Increasingly, these were about breaking rules and defying older conventions.

Technology and Innovation, 1750–1900	
Europe	impact of Scientific Revolution and Enlightenment steam engine and machine power mining and metallurgy (coal, iron, steel) electricity and petroleum as new power sources communications technology (telegraph, radio, telephone) transportation (steamboats, rail, internal combustion) vaccination + germ theory + treatments for tropical disease geological theories Linnaean taxonomy evolution and natural selection (Charles Darwin) relativity (Albert Einstein) and early atomic physics psychology (Sigmund Freud)
Middle East	partial importation of industrial-era science and technology
Africa	minimal (and colonial) importation of industrial-era science and technology
East (and Central) Asia	partial importation of industrial-era science and technology
South (and Southeast) Asia and Oceania	colonial importation of industrial-era science and technology
Americas	full-scale development and/or importation of industrial-era science and technology in North America partial to high degree of importation of industrial-era science and technology in Central and South America
Global and Interregional	varying and uneven adaptations to industrial-era science and technology

Technology and Innovation

- In eighteenth-century Europe and America, the Enlightenment built on the recent insights of the Scientific Revolution and jump-started an unceasing wave of scientific discovery and technological innovation that gained even greater momentum in the 1800s.

- Starting in the West, a scientific, secular worldview became increasingly paramount, thanks initially to the Scientific Revolution and the Enlightenment and then additionally to the technological and scientific advancements of the industrial era.

- Technological change was profound, rapid, and thorough in those parts of the world affected by industrialization. National economies and personal lives alike were influenced by constant and increasingly affordable innovations and inventions.

- Innovations in steam-driven machine power were central to the Industrial Revolution and the early industrial era. Key sectors of development during these first years included mining (iron and coal) and textile production (cotton).

- The later industrial era (or Second Industrial Revolution) witnessed the emergence of newer technologies associated with steel, electricity, petroleum, rubber, and chemicals.

- Transportation and communications were revolutionized during the industrial era, starting with the steamboat, the locomotive, and the telegraph during the first part of the century and moving on to the internal combustion engine, the radio, the telephone, and just after 1900, the airplane.
- Modern medical knowledge and techniques emerged in the West.

Economic Systems, 1750–1900	
Europe	from protoindustrialization to Industrial Revolution (ca. 1780s–1840s; steam engine, coal, iron, textiles) Second Industrial Revolution (late 1800s; steel, electronics, chemicals, petroleum) factory system free-market vs. state-sponsored industrialization industrial-era communications and transport free-market capitalism (classical economists = Adam Smith, John Stuart Mill) vs. state capitalism trade-unionist and socialist (Karl Marx) reactions to capitalism limited-liability corporations and other financial instruments (central banks, stock exchanges, gold standard) Panic of 1873 and Long Depression (1870s–1890s) rise of middle and industrial working classes
Middle East	state-sponsored and limited industry (Muhammad Ali in Egypt, Tanzimat reforms in Ottoman Turkey) construction of Suez Canal (transnational company = Suez Canal Company) resources (cotton, petroleum)
Africa	economic imperialism by Western powers continued reliance on African coerced labor by Western economies construction of railroads by Western powers (+ Suez Canal) transnational company = early components of Unilever resources (gold, diamonds, rubber, ivory, palm oil)
East (and Central) Asia	economic imperialism by Western powers in China (Opium Wars, foreign concessions and treaty ports) transnational company = Hong Kong and Shanghai Banking Company state-sponsored and limited industrialization in China (self-strengthening movement) state-sponsored and full industrialization in Japan (Meiji Restoration of 1868, zaibatsu)
South (and Southeast) Asia and Oceania	economic imperialism by Western powers construction of railroads, telegraphs, and infrastructure by Western powers British industrialization of Indian cotton trade transnational company = British East India Company resources (cotton, coffee, metals, rubber, petroleum)

Economic Systems, 1750–1900	
Americas	Industrial Revolution (ca. 1780s–1840s) and Second Industrial Revolution (late 1800s) in the United States factory system free-market capitalism in the United States limited-liability corporations and other financial instruments (central banks, stock exchanges, gold standard) rise of middle and industrial working classes (trade unionism) state-sponsored industrialization and limited industrialization in Latin America (late 1800s) economic imperialism in Latin America (transnational company = United Fruit Company) resources (metals, petroleum, guano, rubber, fruit, coffee, sugar)
Global and Interregional	widespread protoindustrialization international impact of industrialization (importation by colonial powers, state-sponsored imperialism) economic imperialism by Western powers (raw materials, consumer markets, transnational corporations, "banana republics") population growth and urbanization oceanic whaling and sealing in search of oil

Economic Systems

- Economic life was transformed by industrialization, which displaced agriculture as the most influential sector of the economy. New patterns of global trade emerged as well.

- Industrialization began in England and spread to parts of Europe during the late 1700s and early 1800s—the era of the Industrial Revolution. During the late 1800s, a period often referred to as the Second Industrial Revolution, industrial practices matured and spread further, expanding to include steel, electricity, chemical industries, and petroleum. Gradually and to varying extents, industrialization spread to other parts of the world.

- The non-Western world adopted industrialization in different ways. Sometimes European imperial powers introduced it to their colonies. In other cases, non-Western rulers imposed industrialization from above or at least attempted to do so.

- In many non-Western parts of the world, native manufacturers and cottage industries were crowded out by colonial and foreign industrial interests as well as other aspects of Western economic imperialism.

- Capitalism became the dominant mode of economic organization in the industrial-era West. Over time, its influence became global.

- Reactions to the stresses of early industrialization and to the more exploitative aspects of early capitalism included trade-union activism, utopian socialism, Marxism, and anarchy.

- Commerce and banking—the foundations of a money-based economy, as opposed to a land-based one—grew in importance. Banks, stock markets, and other modern financial instruments became more solidly established.

- Limited-liability corporations and transnational companies became increasingly central to modern economic life.

- See "Social Interactions and Organization" below for the relationship between economic growth during this era and reliance on coerced and semicoerced forms of labor.

Social Interactions and Organization, 1750–1900	
Europe	class diversification (impact of revolutions and industrialization; growth of industrial working class, rise of middle class) serfdom in Russia (uprisings, emancipation) Siberian exile and prison labor migration to the Americas (Irish Potato Famine, anti-Jewish pogroms) emergence of modern feminism and suffragette movements (Mary Wollstonecraft, Olympe de Gouges, Emmeline Pankhurst) industrialization and women (domestic sphere, cult of domesticity)
Middle East	millets Tanzimat reforms and limited social liberalization corvée labor (Suez Canal) veiling of women
Africa	racially segregationist policies in Western-controlled colonies (native elites) East African slave trade Atlantic slave trade Indian migration to East and South Africa imperialism's impact on women's roles
East (and Central) Asia	social stratification and increased tensions in Qing China (opium addiction, Taiping Rebellion) social stratification in Tokugawa Japan Meiji restoration in Japan: rise of merchants, samurai privilege abolished indentured servitude (coolie labor) Chinese migration throughout Southeast Asia missionary efforts against Chinese foot binding
South (and Southeast) Asia and Oceania	racially segregationist policies in Western-controlled colonies (native elites) British undermining of Hindu caste system indentured servitude (coolie labor) transportation to Australia Indian migration throughout Southeast Asia, East Africa, and South Africa Chinese migration throughout Southeast Asia reaction to migration (White Australia Policy) British struggle against sati; veiling of women
Americas	class diversification (impact of revolutions and industrialization; growth of industrial working class, rise of middle class) trade unions and labor movement continued reliance on African slavery migration from Europe and Asia (Chinese Exclusion Act) emergence of modern feminism and suffragette movements (Susan B. Anthony, Seneca Falls Convention) industrialization and women (domestic sphere, cult of domesticity)
Global and Interregional	urbanization expansion of resource extraction and cash-crop monoculture as forms of labor persistence, then gradual fading, of slave systems seasonal and permanent migration (Europe and Asia to the Americas, Chinese and Indians in Indian Ocean basin) anti-immigrant sentiment

Social Interactions and Organization

- Politics in Europe and the West became gradually more representative, although women could not yet vote. Even in less representative states, bureaucracies and parliaments became increasingly important relative to the will of individual monarchs.
- Hierarchies and caste systems tended to break down or weaken, and if they remained in place, they heightened social discontent. Revolutions and rebellions broke out more frequently.
- Industrialization transformed class structures. Traditional aristocracies, with their status based on land and family prestige, faded. The proportion of peasants and farmers shrank. The middle class (bourgeoisie) expanded, gained wealth, and diversified. A new lower class, the industrial working class (proletariat), was born.
- Industrialization led to urbanization. Cities grew in size, and more of them were established.
- For any society, the first decades of industrialization were typically painful for the lower classes. Working conditions were poor, and wages low. Over time, industrialization raised the average prosperity of a society's population, and even the lower classes benefited after some time.
- Coerced and semicoerced forms of labor persisted. Along with slavery, indentured servitude (common in places like India and China) and migrant labor (technically free but poorly paid) were common. Africa was the primary victim of slave trading. The East African and Atlantic slave trades continued well into the 1800s, as did Russian serfdom.
- There was a tremendous migration of peoples, both permanent and seasonal. Massive waves of emigrants moved from Europe and China to the Americas during the 1800s and early 1900s. The United States was the preferred destination, but Canada, Argentina, and Chile took in many immigrants as well, as did Australia. Anti-immigration sentiment was common, both on a popular and official level.
- Diasporic communities and foreign enclaves remained common, thanks to expanding commercial ties or overcrowding at home.
- Although in most societies the status of women remained secondary, this period saw great changes in gender relations. In the West, a keener awareness of the unequal treatment of women began to spread. This was stimulated largely by Enlightenment philosophy as well as by the active role played by women in the American and French Revolutions.
- The Industrial Revolution altered the conditions under which families worked. It shifted the workplace away from the farm, where both men and women worked, to mines, factories, and similar places, creating separate domestic and working spheres.
- In Europe and North America, lower-class women entered industrial workplaces during the early 1800s but left again after the mid-1800s when wages for industrial workers rose (making such jobs more desirable to men) and new laws restricted the number of hours that women and children could work. A cult of domesticity, stressing that a woman's place was in the home and a man's in the workplace, dominated Western society, especially among the middle and upper classes, during the mid-to-late 1800s.
- Vigorous women's movements appeared in Europe, Canada, and the United States. They agitated for suffrage, equal opportunities, and other causes. A handful of places—but no major nations—granted women the right to vote before World War I.

■ The move toward women's equality tended to be slower in non-Western societies. In some, however, the educational level of women rose as did the extent of property rights. As in the West, women worked, especially in certain occupations, such as agricultural labor, domestic service, and nursing. As non-Western parts of the world industrialized, lower-class women tended to enter the workplace.

Humans and the Environment, 1750–1900	
Europe	industrial-era pollution (carbon-based and fossil-fuel emissions) industrial-era resource extraction (mining) earth shaping (major canal systems, road and rail networks) vaccination (late 1700s) and germ theory (mid-1800s) severity of cholera and tuberculosis worsened by industrial-era living conditions resources (coal, metals, timber)
Middle East	earth shaping (Suez Canal) resources (cotton, petroleum)
Africa	industrial-era resource extraction by colonial powers (mining and cash-crop monoculture) treatments for tropical diseases like malaria allow Western penetration of African interior resources (gold, diamonds, ivory, rubber, fruit, palm oil) species endangerment (elephants)
East (and Central) Asia	industrial-era resource extraction by colonial powers (mining and cash-crop monoculture) species extinction and endangerment (sables, otters) resources (tea, silk, cotton)
South (and Southeast) Asia and Oceania	industrial-era resource extraction by colonial powers (mining and cash-crop monoculture) treatments for diseases like malaria allow Western penetration of tropical interior resources (cotton, rubber, spices, coffee, metals, petroleum)
Americas	industrial-era pollution (carbon-based and fossil-fuel emissions) industrial-era resource extraction (mining and cash-crop monoculture) earth shaping (Erie and Panama Canals, road and rail networks) species extinction and endangerment (passenger pigeon, bison) treatments for diseases like malaria allow Western penetration of tropical interior (coal, metals, petroleum, timber, meat, fruit, sugar, coffee, rubber, guano)
Global and Interregional	Little Ice Age ends (mid-1800s) permanent and seasonal migrations (Eurasia to the Americas; regional movements within Indian Ocean basin) species extinction and endangerment (whales, fur seals, walruses)

Humans and the Environment

- Industrialization vastly increased humanity's impact on the environment. Rising levels of pollution were one result. Carbon-based and fossil-fuel emissions began an upward spike that has increased ever since, all the way to the present day.
- The hunger of industrializing economies for natural resources (metals, minerals, guano for fertilizer, petroleum, rubber, foodstuffs, and cotton) led to extractive practices that hugely strained the environment. Mining and cash-crop monoculture tremendously damaged ecosystems.
- Industrialization permitted major earth-shaping engineering projects such as the Erie Canal and the Suez Canal (and, in the early 1900s, the Panama Canal).
- Human-caused extinction or endangerment of animal species became increasingly common.
- Industrial-era forms of transportation contributed to the widespread distribution of diseases.
- Diseases such as tuberculosis and cholera spread easily amid the overcrowded living conditions created by industrialization and rapid urbanization.
- The development of effective treatments for tropical diseases such as malaria enabled imperial powers like Europe and America to penetrate deeper and more efficiently into Africa and Asia.
- A global wave of migration (discussed in more detail under "Social Interactions and Organization") caused millions of people to travel vast distances—most famously from Europe and Asia to the Americas but in other directions and to other places as well.
- The Little Ice Age came to an end during the early-to-mid-1800s.

QUESTIONS AND COMPARISONS TO CONSIDER

- What distinguishes the nation-state from other forms of political organization? Why did it become increasingly prevalent during these years?
- What factors contributed to the rise of industrial production and global capitalism, both in Europe and elsewhere?
- What distinguished the initial Industrial Revolution from the second one that is said to have occurred during the late 1800s? What impact did industrialization have on transportation, communications, society, and labor?
- Discuss new patterns of global trade, including the exploitation of raw materials. How did these new patterns affect international politics? Systems of labor?
- What socioeconomic visions alternative to capitalism appeared during this era? What were their strengths and weaknesses?
- How were gender and family dynamics affected by industrialization (or failure to industrialize), whether in Europe or elsewhere?
- What impact did the Enlightenment of the 1700s have on the political and social changes of the late 1700s and 1800s?
- Compare the nature and content of major political philosophies, including nationalism.
- Compare various acts of resistance against colonial and Western imperialism. Examples include Tupac Amaru II's rebellion, Japanese modernization, the Indian Revolt, the Boxer Rebellion, African wars against the French and English in West Africa, the Filipino war against U.S. occupation, the Xhosa cattle-killing movement, and Wounded Knee.

- What challenges were posed by subjects to national and imperial regimes? Compare two or more of the following: the American Revolution, the Haitian rebellion, the Latin American wars of independence, the Indian Revolt, and the Taiping Rebellion. Compare key revolutionary documents such as the Declaration of Independence, France's Declaration of the Rights of Man and the Citizen, and the Jamaica Letter.
- Discuss the response of non-Western parts of the world such as China, India, Japan, and the Ottoman Empire to imperial encroachments and foreign pressures during this period.
- What factors caused such widespread migration during the 1800s? Where did it generally take place? What forms did those migrations take?
- Compare the status of women in the West and in other parts of the world. Compare the roles and conditions of upper- and middle-class women with those of the peasant and working classes.
- Describe the approaches taken by various Western powers to colonization. Also, what caused the late-nineteenth-century wave of imperialism (the "new" imperialism), and how did this compare to earlier waves of colonization?
- Discuss how non-Western states attempted to modernize and adopt industrial practices. How important is the question of whether industrialization was imposed on a society from above, by the ruler, or emerged from below?
- Compare Japanese industrialization and European modernization.
- Compare Western intervention in Latin America with Western intervention in Africa during the 1750–1900 period.
- Examine nationalist and anticolonial movements in non-Western parts of the world. Compare and contrast their methods and their successes and/or failures.

UNIT 3

SCENIC ROUTE
(Chapters 13–18)

Governance, 1750–1900

13

IN THIS CHAPTER

→ GROWING PROMINENCE OF THE NATION-STATE

→ ATLANTIC REVOLUTIONS + REVOLUTIONARY DOCUMENTS
(U.S. DECLARATION OF INDEPENDENCE, DECLARATION OF THE RIGHTS
OF MAN AND THE CITIZEN, JAMAICA LETTER)

→ "NEW" IMPERIALISM AND WESTERN POWER VS. ACTS OF ANTI-IMPERIAL
RESISTANCE

→ DOCTRINES OF RACIAL SUPERIORITY (SOCIAL DARWINISM, WHITE MAN'S
BURDEN, *LA MISSION CIVILISATRICE*, "GOODBYE ASIA")

→ BALANCE OF POWER VS. COMPETITION OVER EMPIRE AND JINGOISTIC
NATIONALISM

→ GEOPOLITICAL CLASHES (MONROE DOCTRINE, EASTERN QUESTION,
GREAT GAME, SCRAMBLE FOR AFRICA, EUROPEAN ALLIANCE SYSTEM)

→ REACTION IN EUROPE (CONGRESS OF VIENNA) VS. REVOLUTIONS OF 1848
AND POLITICAL REFORM

→ TANZIMAT REFORMS AND YOUNG TURKS VS. OTTOMAN DECLINE AND
TERRITORIAL LOSSES

→ AFRICAN STATES VS. SCRAMBLE FOR AFRICA (BERLIN CONFERENCE)

→ OPIUM WARS + QING DECLINE ("UNEQUAL" TREATIES VS. SELF-
STRENGTHENING MOVEMENT)

→ TOKUGAWA SHOGUNATE VS. MEIJI RESTORATION

→ BRITISH EAST INDIA COMPANY (SEPOY TROOPS AND INDIAN REVOLT)

→ SPANISH-AMERICAN AND PHILIPPINE-AMERICAN WARS

→ "MANIFEST DESTINY" AND SUPPRESSION OF NATIVE AMERICANS IN THE
UNITED STATES

→ ECONOMIC IMPERIALISM AND CAUDILLO RULE IN LATIN AMERICA

During this era, the **nation-state**—a state-level community united in theory by a common ethnic, linguistic, religious, and cultural heritage—emerged as the leading form of political organization in more parts of the world, particularly in the West.

The hallmark of modern political life became greater popular representation. This trend began in the West during the late 1700s with the **American** and **French Revolutions**. Afterward, Western nations followed various paths—revolutionary or reform oriented, faster or slower—toward greater democratization. **Industrialization** drove these changes as well.

Other parts of the world were slower to move away from traditional regimes. A few, such as Japan and the Ottoman Empire, did so, developing parliamentary forms of monarchy by the start of the twentieth century. The nations of Latin America developed parliamentary governments in theory, but many slipped into dictatorial or military rule. **Revolutions** were periodically sparked in these parts of the world, whether because of middle- or lower-class discontent or as a form of protest against Western imperial influence.

The global balance of power changed profoundly, thanks to the technological, economic, and military rise of Europe and the United States. World affairs were increasingly determined by Western foreign policy. Moreover, the "**new imperialism**" of the mid-to-late 1800s gave Europe and North America unprecedented global dominance. In 1815, the nations of the West controlled roughly 35 percent of the world's habitable territory. By 1914, that figure had risen to approximately 85 percent. By that time, however, **nationalism** and competition over colonies made it increasingly likely that Western nations would go to war. The **European alliance system** formed in the late 1800s, and the level of aggression rose steadily until the outbreak of World War I in 1914.

THE ATLANTIC REVOLUTIONS AND THE BIRTH OF MODERN POLITICS

Early in this era, the political order in Europe and the Americas changed dramatically. In the mid-1700s, all of Europe's major powers were monarchies in which the ruler shared power with aristocratic nobles who, despite their small numbers, controlled most of the country's wealth and land and enjoyed virtually all influence over politics. (Even parliamentary monarchies like Great Britain allowed comparatively little popular representation at this time.) Latin America and the Caribbean, along with much of North America, lived under European colonial authority.

This state of affairs was shaken apart by a wave of **Atlantic revolutions** between the 1770s and the 1810s. These include the **American Revolution**, the **French Revolution**, the **Haitian Rebellion**, and the **Latin American wars of independence**. Though not all their goals were met, they dealt a death blow to absolute monarchy in most of Europe, and they ended European colonial rule over most of the Americas. Another legacy of the Atlantic revolutions was that an ever-increasing number of people began to dream of—and fight for—social and political systems that gave them more voice in government. (Another factor changing ordinary people's social and economic aspirations at this time was the **Industrial Revolution**, which coincided with the Atlantic revolutions and is detailed more fully in Chapter 16.)

THE CAUSES OF REVOLUTION

Understanding how and why revolutions take place is a daunting task for any historian. Social stress and class differences, economic inequality and poverty, incompetent or oppressive political leadership, and intellectual and cultural forces (religion, nationalism, doctrines, ideologies) are almost always at the root of any major revolution. Studying and comparing revolutions involves trying to figure out which of these is more or less important in any given case. Another important distinction has to do with whether forces causing revolution come *from above* (top-down), *from below* (bottom-up), or, as is often the case, both. Who are the actual revolutionaries? Do they continue to cooperate after the initial seizure of power, or do they disagree and quarrel among themselves, leading to further struggle?

The American Revolution and the Birth of the United States

Several trends combined to spark the **American Revolution** (1775–1783) that swept the thirteen British colonies of New England and the mid-Atlantic coast. One was a growing sense of **nationalism**. Another was increased resentment of Britain's economic mastery. The taxes Britain levied to pay for the army it maintained in North America angered many colonists, especially because the colonists lacked representation in Britain's Parliament. The spirit of **capitalism** was catching on among colonial merchants, who believed that free trade—something not permitted by Britain's

mercantilist policy (which required the colonies to trade only on British terms)—would create greater wealth. Also important was the influence of **Enlightenment philosophy**, which Chapter 14 describes in more depth. Most of those who carried out the American Revolution and wrote the Constitution followed the intellectual lead of Enlightenment thinkers such as **John Locke** and the Baron Charles de **Montesquieu** about social contracts and civil liberties guaranteed by natural rights. The **Declaration of Independence** (1776), authored chiefly by Thomas Jefferson, is a classic Enlightenment text.

The revolution itself broke out in 1775. At first, the poorly trained and poorly equipped American forces, led by George Washington, struggled against Britain's professional armies and superior navy. In 1777, the tide began to turn. Although so-called Tories remained loyal to the British, popular support for the revolution grew. The Americans had the advantage of fighting on their home territory. Also, late in the year, France—Britain's mortal enemy—decided to lend the Americans money and military aid. The French fleet's assistance against Britain's Royal Navy was helpful, as was the military training provided by French officers (and other Europeans) at Washington's Valley Forge encampment in 1777–1778. By 1781, the British war effort was failing. When the Americans surrounded the main British force at Yorktown, the war was effectively over, although peace talks dragged on until 1783.

After victory, the next step was to devise a form of government. This process involved much disagreement and lasted until the Constitutional Convention of 1787 and the ratification of the **United States Constitution** in 1789. The resulting system was a democratic republic in which a federal government shared power with governments in each of the thirteen states. It was also the first attempt by a major state to base a political system on the philosophy of popular sovereignty and other rights-oriented concepts drawn from the Enlightenment. To ensure that political authority was not concentrated too much in any one office or body, power at the federal level was shared among three branches—executive (president), legislative (Congress), and judicial (Supreme Court)—according to a concept borrowed from the Enlightenment thinker Montesquieu.

However, democracy in the early American case was not all-inclusive. Elections were indirect, favoring the upper and middle classes. Women and Native Americans could not vote, and neither could men who failed to fulfill certain property requirements. Free blacks could vote in some states but not all and lost many of their voting rights in the early 1800s. Most glaringly, the U.S. Constitution did not outlaw slavery, with vast long-term implications for race relations in America.

Despite its initial flaws, the U.S. Constitution, largely because of the adaptability built into it, has remained one of the most successful political documents in world history. It should also be remembered as both the product and the cause of an international philosophical exchange: just as European Enlightenment ideals inspired the American Revolution, the revolution and the constitution that sprang from it inspired political action in Europe during the 1780s and 1790s—notably in France. The impact of the American Revolution can also be seen in Haiti and Latin America during the 1790s and early 1800s.

The French Revolution and the Napoleonic Era

As in America, it took a complex mix of political, social, economic, and intellectual causes to touch off the **French Revolution** (1789–1799).

Long-term factors included the yawning **socioeconomic gap** between ordinary citizens (Third Estate) and the country's elite, which consisted of the Catholic clergy (First Estate) and the aristocracy (Second Estate). France's blatantly **unfair tax system** exempted the wealthy First and Second Estates. Members of the middle class—who possessed wealth and education but were barred from social advancement (and forced to pay heavy taxes) because they belonged to the Third Estate—grew increasingly frustrated. Added to this were the political ineptitude of France's kings and the **long-term debt** the state had piled up since the late 1600s. (This was worsened in the 1770s by France's financial support for the American Revolution.) Also, just as it did in the American colonies, **Enlightenment philosophy** inspired a growing number of people with its powerful arguments in favor of fair government, popular sovereignty, social contracts, and civil liberties guaranteed by natural rights.

The immediate cause of the French Revolution was the impending bankruptcy of the government. Saddled with debt, unable to tax the rich First and Second Estates, and burdened with a wife, Marie Antoinette, who spent lavishly, **Louis XVI** (r. 1774–1792) could not solve France's financial crisis. In 1787 and 1788, inflation, unemployment, and food shortages tormented the entire country. While searching for a solution, Louis XVI summoned the **Estates General**, a national assembly of delegates from each estate, to meet with him at Versailles in May 1789. The delegates elected by the Third Estate—mainly middle-class lawyers—expected to negotiate seriously about changing the tax system and treating all classes more equitably. By June, however, it was clear that neither Louis XVI nor most delegates from the other Estates were prepared to compromise. This clash of wills set off ten years of revolution.

In late June, the delegates of the Third Estate, with liberal members of the First and Second Estates, formed a new governmental body, the National Assembly, and vowed not to leave Versailles until the king granted them a constitution. In July, climaxing with the **storming of the Bastille**, the people of Paris and other cities rose up in support of the assembly, as did peasants in the countryside. Over the summer, the assembly assumed power in Paris.

During the first three years of the revolution, Louis XVI was allowed to remain king but with reduced powers. Guided by Enlightenment ideals and the American Declaration of Independence, the assembly guaranteed civil liberties in the **Declaration of the Rights of Man and the Citizen**—the writing of which was overseen by the Marquis de **Lafayette**, a liberal noble who had fought at Washington's side during the American Revolution and now took advice directly from Thomas Jefferson. Future assemblies were to be elected by popular vote. Aristocratic status and privileges, especially the exemption from taxes, were done away with, and church and state were separated. Policy was guided by the motto "Liberty, Equality, and Fraternity."

There were, however, problems. At first, the rights proclaimed by the revolution, including the vote, applied only to white Catholic adult males. Only with time did Jews, Protestants, and blacks gain those rights, and women did not until well into the 1900s. Slavery was not ended in France's colonies until 1794. Also, the assembly failed to solve worsening economic problems. Louis XVI, encouraged by Marie Antoinette, secretly plotted **counterrevolution**, as did many former aristocrats. Worst of all, the victorious revolutionaries could not agree on how to change France. Liberal nobles and clergy, with much of the middle class, were satisfied with parliamentary monarchy and moderate change. The rural population, happy to have equal rights and to limit the power of the king, wanted economic relief but not deeper social change. The urban lower classes (known as sans-culottes) and certain middle-class idealists were more radical. They wished to end the monarchy altogether, drive out or persecute former aristocrats (even liberal nobles), change society more thoroughly (some favored abolishing Catholicism), and export their revolution to other countries by force. Resolving all these desires would prove impossible.

From the spring of 1792 through the summer of 1794, the French Revolution took a sharply radical turn. In April 1792, France went to war with Austria and Prussia. Other countries, including Britain, joined in, and France would be at war for almost the next quarter century. The economy worsened, and early military failures caused mass hysteria. Remaining aristocrats and political moderates—even heroes from the early years, such as Lafayette—fell under suspicion, as did the royal family. Radical parties became more influential.

In the fall of 1792, a new constitution stripped the king of all powers and proclaimed the French Republic. Elections to a new legislature brought radicals to power, the most important of whom were the **Jacobins**, led by **Maximilien Robespierre**, a fanatically idealistic lawyer. In January 1793, Louis XVI was executed for treason; Marie Antoinette followed in October. The Jacobins created an executive body, the **Committee of Public Safety**, which assumed dictatorial powers and attempted the radical transformation of French society. It expanded the war effort, mobilized the economy for combat, and carried out modern Europe's first nationwide draft. Civil war erupted in the countryside as peasants rebelled against conscription and the radicals' efforts to do away with Catholicism.

Between the summer of 1793 and the summer of 1794, Robespierre and the Committee, supported by the urban sans-culottes, carried out a **Reign of Terror**, searching for traitors and counterrevolutionary foes. In this panicked, witch hunt atmosphere, civil liberties were largely ignored. More than 300,000 people were arrested without warrant and tried without jury or appeal. Between 30,000 and 50,000 were killed, many beheaded by the guillotine. In July 1794, a coup within the Committee executed Robespierre, ending the Terror.

For five years, a more moderate regime, the Directory, presided over the revolution, stabilizing the military situation and attempting to heal the wounds caused by the Terror. However, it proved unpopular, and its 1799 overthrow brought an end to the revolution.

Among those who ousted the Directory was a talented general, **Napoleon Bonaparte**, who quickly seized power for himself. Napoleon claimed to be a man of revolutionary ideals, but in reality he created a new dictatorship, going so far as to crown himself emperor in 1804.

Napoleon is best known for his military career. After rising to power, he continued the wars France had begun during the revolution. From 1805 to 1811, his victories made France the most powerful country in Europe; the only major nations not under his direct or indirect control were Britain and Russia. After this, several factors brought about Napoleon's downfall: his inability to counter British naval power, bloody guerrilla resistance to his authority in Spain, and his famously overambitious invasion of Russia in 1812. He was defeated and exiled in 1814. In 1815, he escaped and had to be beaten again at the Battle of **Waterloo**. Peace was restored at the **Congress of Vienna** (1814–1815). Napoleon died in captivity in 1821.

> **NOTE**
>
> Evaluating Napoleon's reign is difficult. He was arrogant and autocratic but also charismatic and popular. His wars cost untold amounts of money and killed hundreds of thousands but, until near the end, made France rich and mighty. He modernized France and created institutions that still exist today, such as the Bank of France and the internationally influential Civil Law Code (Napoleonic Code), still the foundation for modern law not just in France but wherever France's colonial influence extended.

What made the French Revolution so important, especially considering its many short-term failures? For one, it did away with absolute monarchy in Europe. Kings and emperors continued to rule (even in France, where the royal family was restored), but in no major country were they all-powerful, and as time passed, monarchs yielded more of their authority to ministries and legislatures. Also, the French Revolution, like the American Revolution, inspired future uprisings. As detailed in Chapter 14, the emergence of modern political ideas—including the use of the terms "left" and "right" and the formation of **conservatism** and **liberalism** as coherent movements—had much to do with the French Revolution. Finally, the greatest legacy of both the American and French Revolutions was to cause people to demand greater popular participation in government and to force nineteenth-century leaders to be more attentive to their desires. The story of modern politics is primarily *this* story.

Haiti and the Latin American Wars of Independence

Revolutionary influence catapulted back across the Atlantic as the impact of events in France spread far beyond Europe's borders, especially to Haiti and Latin America.

Prior to independence, the sugar- and coffee-producing colony of Haiti was called Saint-Domingue by the French and Santo Domingo by the Spanish, with each country occupying half the island and relying heavily on slave labor imported from Africa. After 1789, revolution in France threw Saint-Domingue into turmoil, largely because the "rights of man and the citizen" were not extended to everyone living in French colonies. Revolutionary freedoms went automatically to Frenchmen and Creoles (those of French descent but born in the colonies) but were not extended to free blacks and mulattos until May 1791. Because France's revolutionary government decided at that point not to end slavery, the half-million slaves of Saint-Domingue revolted in August. This began the **Haitian Rebellion** (1791–1804), the only large-scale slave revolt to succeed in the New World.

By 1793, **François Toussaint L'Ouverture**, a talented commander known as the "black Washington," had come to lead the revolt. Although the French government finally abolished slavery in 1794, L'Ouverture's goal was now full independence and the liberation of slaves on the Spanish side of the island, which he invaded in 1798. For several years, France debated the question of whether to let Haiti go free and establish friendly relations with it (the outcome L'Ouverture hoped for) or to retake it by force. In 1802, Napoleon—who, ironically, as a junior officer in the 1790s had admired L'Ouverture—sent a large force to end the rebellion. Although L'Ouverture fell into French captivity and died in prison, the French proved unequal to tropical warfare and lost 40,000 soldiers to yellow fever. They went home in disgrace, and the independent nation of Haiti was born in 1804. Not only did the Haitian Rebellion lead to further uprisings in Latin America, but it convinced Napoleon that maintaining major colonies in the New World was strategically wasteful. In 1803, he sold the vast Louisiana territory, stretching from the Great Lakes to the Mississippi delta, to the United States at a bargain price. This **Louisiana Purchase** significantly boosted the young country's chances of eventually mastering the entire continent and can be seen in hindsight as a major shift in global power.

> **NOTE**
>
> Anticolonial resentments were nothing new in Latin America. In addition to the Pueblo War of the 1600s in New Mexico, a massive revolt shook Spanish rule over the Andes in the 1780s. This was the Túpac Amaru II Rebellion (ca. 1780–1782), led by a Quechua—or perhaps mestizo—of high social rank who adopted the name of the last Incan king. Over 100,000 natives and mestizos rose up, largely to protest unjust racial policies, and nearly captured the city of Cuzco. The revolt ended with violent Spanish reprisals, including the execution of Túpac, his wife, and most of his family. The event shows how ripe the region was for political change as the 1800s approached.

In the meantime, revolutionary impulses were gathering force in Mexico, Central America, and South America, where the **Latin American wars of independence** would rage from 1810 to 1825. Underlying factors here included a growing sense of nationalism and local resentment of Spain's and Portugal's restrictive economic policies. Also important was the frustration that the *criollo* ("creole"), or European-descended, upper and middle classes felt at being barred from upward mobility by the rigid social hierarchy that prevailed in Latin American colonies. For clear examples of how political action could achieve decisive results, discontented Latin Americans had the American Revolution and the Haitian Rebellion close at hand.

It was Napoleon, between 1807 and 1809, who toppled the colonial order in Latin America by invading Spain and Portugal. With the Spanish king under house arrest and Portugal's royal family forced to flee to Brazil, rebellions sprang up throughout Central and South America.

The most influential of these revolutionaries was **Simón Bolívar** (1783–1830), known as the Liberator. A member of Venezuela's *criollo* upper class, Bolívar was inspired by Enlightenment ideals, frustrated by the inefficiency and injustice of Spanish rule, and personally ambitious.

In 1810, he took control of the independence movement sweeping across the northern parts of Spanish South America. Unlike many others of the creole elite, who rebelled against Spain for their own narrow interests, Bolívar realized that no revolt could succeed unless it attracted all classes. In a bold stroke, he promised to fight for the rights of mixed-race Latin Americans and the emancipation of slaves—harnessing much of the anger that had driven the failed **Túpac Amaru II Rebellion** of the 1780s. These principles, elaborated in documents like Bolívar's 1815 **Jamaica Letter**, turned a small and unsuccessful upper- and middle-class rebellion into a mass war of independence. The military turning point of Bolívar's wars came in the years 1819–1821 when he gained control over present-day Venezuela and Colombia. At this juncture, Bolívar joined forces with another freedom fighter, José de San Martín, a general turned revolutionary. Between 1816 and 1820, San Martín freed southern areas such as Argentina, Chile, Uruguay, and Paraguay. Despite political differences—San Martín was more conservative—the two decided to cooperate, with Bolívar as leader. By 1825, royalists had been cleared out of Bolivia, Ecuador, and Peru, and Spanish South America was free.

Mexico and Central America liberated themselves as well. The **Mexican War of Independence** (1810–1823) was complicated by the inability of various social classes to cooperate. It began when the priest **Miguel Hidalgo**, unfurling the flag of the Virgin of Guadalupe, called for freedom from Spain. Hidalgo was killed in 1811, but his fight was carried on by another priest, José María Morelos. Both fought not just for national independence but also for constitutional rule, equal rights for Indians and mestizos, and the liberation of slaves. Their platform gained mass support from the lower classes but angered many upper-class Mexicans, even those who wanted independence. In 1815, Morelos was killed, like Hidalgo before him, but by conservative Mexicans, not the Spanish. In the end, Mexico's revolt was completed by the elite, not the lower classes. A right-wing colonel, Agustín de Iturbide, overthrew Spanish rule in 1821. He tried to establish himself as a dictator but was quickly ousted. A Mexican republic was proclaimed in 1823, the same year that the nations immediately to the south established the United Provinces of Central America.

As discussed below, the constitutional arrangements that followed the Latin American wars of independence, although based on similar principles, did not prove as successful as the one established in the United States. Most regimes in the region also failed to reduce their socioeconomically and environmentally harmful dependence on plantation monoculture.

NOTE

In 1820, the king of Portugal went back to Europe to reclaim his throne. He left his son, Prince Pedro, to govern Brazil, but gave him this advice: "My son, if Brazil starts to demand independence, make sure you are the one to proclaim it. Then put the crown on your own head." This is exactly what happened in 1822 when Brazil became a free constitutional monarchy. Pedro was supported by local elites who feared that the alternative to his rule would be a more comprehensive and more disruptive slave revolt.

WESTERN IMPERIALISM AND GLOBAL CONFLICT

Western colonial expansion, pursued since the 1400s, had become normal policy. From the mid-1800s to the early 1900s, however, it took on a more aggressive and systematic character, referred to by many as the **new imperialism**. As a practical undertaking, this domination of the world was an impressive military feat, and it brought Europe and America great power and wealth. On the other hand, it was inseparable from bloodshed, racial prejudice, and slavery. As the English-Polish author Joseph Conrad wrote in the novel *Heart of Darkness*—one of the classic literary depictions of European imperialism—"The conquest of the earth, which mostly means taking it away from those who have a different complexion or slightly flatter noses than ourselves, is not a pretty thing when you look into it too much." Moreover, Euro-American imperialism left deep political scars around the globe, many of which have not yet healed in the twenty-first century.

Causes and Motivations

A variety of factors enabled and motivated the new imperialism. Industrialization made Western economies hungry for **raw materials**—including timber, industrial and precious metals, coal, rubber, and various chemicals—which could be wrested from less powerful societies by force, and for **overseas markets**. Industrial-era weaponry lent Western armies and navies **military superiority**, and because modern ships powered by coal (and then petroleum) required repair bases and refueling depots, Western **sea power** depended on control over islands and ports around the world.

Also prompting imperialism was Europe's rapid **population growth**, which caused **migration** not just to the Americas but also to **settler colonies** far from the homeland. **Geographical and scientific aptitude** allowed for easier penetration of the African and Asian interior. In particular, medical advances—such as the antimalarial treatment **quinine**—made it possible for Westerners to establish themselves in tropical zones where illnesses like sleeping sickness, yellow fever, and **malaria** had previously kept them from gaining footholds.

Finally, a complex set of cultural factors motivated empire building. A sense of **racial superiority**, buttressed in many cases by the doctrine of **social Darwinism** discussed in Chapter 14, was widespread among white Europeans and Americans. Beyond that, many Westerners became convinced that they had a duty to teach and modernize the peoples of Africa and Asia. The English poet Rudyard Kipling famously labeled this the **white man's burden**, and the French spoke of their civilizing mission, or *la mission civilisatrice*. This attitude could be well-meaning, and Euro-American missionaries, doctors, scientists, and colonial officials sometimes did much useful work. However, they did so as much out of condescension as out of goodwill, and they often trampled on or eradicated native cultural practices and beliefs.

NOTE

When Japan emerged as an imperial power, social Darwinism and ideologies of racial exceptionalism became increasingly popular there. The influential 1885 essay "Goodbye Asia" (discussed at greater length in Chapter 14) shows how many Japanese were coming to believe that their rapid modernization made them inherently superior to other Asians.

Forms of Imperialism

Empires took different forms during this era and were governed with different degrees of severity. Individual empires are dealt with on a region-by-region basis in the following section, but some generalizations are possible here. **Overseas empires** and **settler colonies** were the best known. By far the largest was Britain's, on which "the sun never set," as expressed in a famous motto of the time. France gradually accumulated the era's second-largest empire, and countries like Spain, Portugal, and the Netherlands, which had been more active during the Columbian age of exploration, continued to hold on to certain overseas possessions. After 1870, new countries such as Germany and Italy began to build overseas empires in an attempt to catch up with more established imperial powers. **Land-based empires** expanded as well. Austria, not commonly thought of as a colonizing power, maintained one in eastern and southeastern Europe, colliding with the empire ruled by the Ottoman Turks. Russia conquered Siberia, much of Central Asia, and for a time, parts of North America. At the end of the century, Japan extended its imperial reach to the Asian mainland, a short distance away.

Economic imperialism, which typically involved pressuring weaker nations to offer favorable trade terms rather than outright colonization, was practiced as well. Prominent targets during this century included Latin America and Qing China, and arguably Egypt during and after the construction of the **Suez Canal**.

Geopolitical Tensions and Rising Conflict

As the century passed, wherever imperial expansion was pursued, it caused a steady rise in global conflict. Campaigns of conquest were violent in their own right, and in the late 1800s, with fewer desirable territories left to be claimed, Euro-American **competition over empire** became increasingly bitter. Tensions were heightened further by specific geopolitical conflicts, including the **Eastern Question** (how to fill the power vacuum caused in the Balkans and the eastern Mediterranean by the Ottoman Empire's steady decline), the **Great Game** (the collision of British and Russian spheres of influence in Central Asia), and the **Scramble for Africa** (the rush to subjugate the entire continent between the 1880s and the 1910s). The growing intensity of **nationalism** in Western nations added to the problem.

All this made it increasingly harder for Western states to maintain their **balance of power**. Between Napoleon's defeat in 1815 and the outbreak of the Crimean War (1853–1856), the settlement devised at the **Congress of Vienna** (1814–1815) preserved peace among the European powers. After midcentury, armed conflict became more common in Europe—including the **Franco-Prussian War** (1870–1871), which created the modern German state, and the wars of Italian unification. While such wars were short and limited, they encouraged a growing spirit of belligerent patriotism (nicknamed **jingoism** by the British press). On the surface, relative stability prevailed among the Western powers between 1871 and 1914, a period in European history known as the Long Peace. Underneath, however, the potential for a major conflict grew with every year, especially after 1890 when the German chancellor **Otto von Bismarck**—a cautious diplomat and a key architect of the European balance of power—was dismissed by Germany's rash and impatient emperor, Wilhelm II.

During the 1890s and early 1900s, the **European alliance system** divided the great powers into two armed camps. Germany and Austria were already aligned with Italy in the Triple Alliance (formed in 1881, although Italy would drop out in 1914). In the mid-1890s, France, bitter about defeat in the Franco-Prussian War, allied with Russia, which viewed Austria as a threat in the Balkans. Geographically, France and Russia now had their rivals surrounded. As long as possible, Britain remained uncommitted: thanks to the Great Game in Central Asia, it viewed Russia as an enemy, and it had little affection for France. But after 1900, Britain grew increasingly alarmed by Germany's aggressive empire building, especially in Africa, and its rapid naval expansion, which threatened Britain's sea power, the root of Britain's global might. In 1907, Britain informally partnered with the Franco-Russian alliance, forming the Triple Entente. From this point forward, any crisis between two countries could potentially involve all of Europe's major powers—significantly increasing the likelihood of a major war.

NATIVE ELITES

One technique commonly used by imperial powers was the Western-style training of native elites to serve as officials and bureaucrats, and of native troops—such as sepoys in India and askaris in Africa—to fill the ranks of overseas forces. The aims here were to economize on labor and to ensure loyalty. The educational system in British India, in the words of one of its architects, was to create elites who were "Indian in blood and color, but English in taste, in opinion, in morals, and in intellect." Likewise, the reasoning behind America's sponsorship of the pro-U.S. Federalista Party in the newly acquired Philippines was that "these picked Filipinos will be of infinite value as the chief agents in securing their people's obedience." In the economic sphere, compradors were native merchants, particularly in East and South Asia, who cooperated with Western colonists and corporations as commercial agents and middlemen.

NOTE

Southeastern Europe—the Balkans—became one of the world's most unstable regions during the late 1800s and early 1900s. The imperial ambitions of Russia, Austria, Italy, and the Ottoman Empire all centered on it. Many of the states there, most famously Serbia, were newly independent and fiercely nationalistic. The Balkans earned the label "powderkeg of Europe" during the turn of the century as several short wars broke out there, even before World War I.

POLITICAL DEVELOPMENTS BY REGION

Europe

Following the French Revolution and as the Industrial Revolution progressed, European governments had to decide how to respond to the shock waves caused by both events. The political philosophies and ideologies discussed in Chapter 14 were a product of those decisions.

Between 1815 and 1848, most governments, convinced that even the slightest liberalism would lead to renewed political chaos, attempted to minimize change or even undo what had transpired during the years of revolution. This archconservative stance, known as **reaction**, was the guiding principle of the **Congress of Vienna** (1814–1815), which not only ended the Napoleonic wars but forged an informal agreement among Europe's major regimes to preserve order and prevent change. Monarchies were no longer absolute, but royal families were restored wherever possible, including France. Civil liberties were restricted, censorship was heavy, and secret police forces were common. Trade unions were illegal, as were political parties in many countries. Repression lightened somewhat in parliamentary states like Britain, where the 1832 Reform Act slightly expanded the vote and where the worst industrial-era working conditions began to attract Parliament's attention, and France, where the 1830 revolution further limited the power of the monarch. In Central and Eastern Europe, the level of repression was greater: if voting systems existed at all, they were limited, and Russia not only remained an absolute monarchy but still continued the practice of **serfdom**.

A key turning point came with the **revolutions of 1848**, whose underlying causes included popular impatience with reactionary rule, socioeconomic stress caused by industrialization, and a series of bad harvests (like the Irish Potato Famine) that caused the decade to be known as the "hungry forties." The revolution began in France, where the king was deposed and Napoleon's nephew appointed president. Uprisings then spread to much of the rest of Europe, although they spared England and Russia. These were crushed by the summer of 1849 but had lasting effects nonetheless. They compelled Austria and German states like Prussia to grant constitutions, and since many of them had involved ethnic revolts against Austrian rule, they demonstrated the growing political importance of **nationalism**. They inspired **Karl Marx** and Friedrich Engels to write *The Communist Manifesto*. Most of all, they hammered home for good the lesson of the French Revolution: the demands of ordinary people had to be taken seriously.

Therefore, during the second half of the century, most European governments expanded **political representation** and legislated the **improvement of working conditions**, although whether they did so by means of **reform** or **revolution** varied.

> **NOTE**
>
> Britain did not undergo actual revolution during the early 1800s (though it was attempted in Ireland), but it faced popular discontent that was potentially revolutionary. Most influential was the Chartist movement—named for the People's Charters it presented to Parliament in 1838, 1842, and 1848—which agitated for political and economic improvements, especially an expansion of the vote. The Chartists failed to get their demands met formally, but the pressure they placed on the government helped lead to reform.

In Victorian Britain, Parliament gradually extended the vote to middle- and lower-class males by means of the **Second** (1867) and **Third** (1885) **Reform Acts** and also granted economic concessions and fairer labor laws to the lower classes. Britain by the late 1800s possessed the world's largest empire and was extremely prosperous. It wrestled, however, with the questions of **women's suffrage** and Irish nationalism.

France's progress toward democracy was less gentle. After 1848, all adult males could vote in France, but in 1851, the president, Louis Napoleon, staged a coup and crowned himself Napoleon III. Not an absolute dictator, he helped to modernize Paris and industrialize the country, but his humiliating defeat during the **Franco-Prussian War** (1870–1871) caused his abdication. After a short but bloody revolution, a new democratic republic arose in 1871 and lasted until 1940. Democracy did not solve all of France's problems. Women remained without the vote. Corruption and financial scandals rocked France, and worst of all was the **Dreyfus Affair** (1894–1906), in which the army and government falsely blamed a Jewish officer for the leaking of military secrets to Germany. This controversy divided the left (which maintained Dreyfus's innocence) from the right (which was convinced of his guilt) and exposed the ugly streak of **anti-Semitism** in modern European society.

NOTE

Economic concessions desired by the working class in any given country generally included all or most of the following: higher wages, shorter workdays and workweeks, safer working conditions, insurance in case of injury, and pensions for retirement. The right to form trade unions and go on strike was considered crucial as well.

Nationalism profoundly affected politics in Italy, Germany, and Austria. The **unification of Italy** as a parliamentary monarchy took place in the 1860s (although less than 5 percent of the population received the vote). The **unification of Germany** was spearheaded by Prussia in a series of three short conflicts culminating in the **Franco-Prussian War** of 1870–1871. The new German emperor shared power with a legislature called the Reichstag, and all adult males technically had the vote—although the electoral system was heavily stacked in favor of the upper classes. With **Otto von Bismarck** serving the emperor as chancellor (and also as Europe's most skilled diplomat), Germany rapidly modernized thanks to a policy of **state-directed industrialization**. Despite his staunch conservatism, Bismarck craftily offered the lower classes substantial economic concessions—the most generous in Europe at the time—to keep them from becoming attracted to trade unions or socialism. In Austria, post-1848 liberalization led to the creation of a parliament in 1861 and various concessions to the empire's many minority populations, whose nationalist aspirations were rising. The **Ausgleich** ("compromise") of 1867 granted equal status to Austria's largest minority, the Hungarians, and the state was renamed the Austro-Hungarian Empire. (In total, the empire had eleven official languages, although German and Hungarian remained most important.) As in other parts of Europe, **anti-Semitism** became a major part of political life here.

Even autocratic Russia was forced to change. Shaken by his country's embarrassing loss in the Crimean War (1853–1856), the moderately liberal Alexander II modernized Russia with a series of "great reforms," chief of which was his 1861 **emancipation of the serfs**. However, Alexander was assassinated by radical terrorists who believed he had not gone far enough, and the conservative tsars who succeeded him undid many of his changes. Nicholas II, who met with a terrible defeat during the **Russo-Japanese War** (1904–1905), almost lost his throne during the 1905 Revolution. This compelled him to share power with a new and popularly elected legislature, the Duma—but once the danger passed, Nicholas weakened the Duma and avoided cooperating with it. **Anti-Semitic persecution** escalated in late tsarist Russia, and **pogroms**, or anti-Jewish raids, became distressingly common.

The Middle East and Central Asia

This was a time of decline for the Middle East as the glory days of the once-mighty "gunpowder empires" faded away. Safavid Persia had disappeared in the early 1700s, and although the Ottoman Empire survived into the early 1900s, it lost territory at an alarming rate during the 1800s and came to be derided as the "sick man of Europe."

Not only did the Ottoman Empire lose a number of wars to Austria and Russia during the 1700s, internal troubles plagued it. The chief dilemma was that sultans and reformers who wished to modernize met with resistance from Islamic traditionalists or influential elites with a vested interest in preserving old ways. A key example

NOTE

Technically governed by the Qajar dynasty between 1794 and 1925, Persia suffered a fate similar to that of Qing China. It was dominated by foreign powers in the 1800s without being formally colonized. Although they kept the Qajar rulers in place, Russia and Britain divided the country into northern and southern spheres of influence—an arrangement that lasted until after World War II.

involved the armed forces, where the once-innovative **janissaries**, now privileged but woefully outdated, blocked any attempt to improve the military, to the point of assassinating the sultan in 1807.

Reformers had better luck between the 1820s and the 1870s, although not enough in the long run. Janissary power was broken in the 1820s, and the army and navy were upgraded and westernized. From 1839 to 1876, in a series of changes known as the **Tanzimat reforms**, the government promoted religious tolerance and equality before the law for non-Muslims, introduced Western science and technology into the educational system, boosted industry and built railroads and telegraphs, and liberalized and secularized the law code and legal system. Sultan **Abdul Hamid II** even proclaimed the **constitution of 1876** and agreed to share power with an elected legislature.

Unfortunately, in 1878, the sultan suspended the constitution for twenty years, and the Tanzimat effort fizzled. Internally, Abdul Hamid was caught between traditionalists who opposed any changes at all and a growing number of modernizing politicians and military officers—the so-called **Young Turks**—who wanted more change than he was willing to deliver. By the early 1900s, the Young Turks would play a decisive role in ending his rule.

In the meantime, the Tanzimat effort, as well as Ottoman domestic policy in general, was handicapped further by a cascade of rebellions and wars that threatened the empire with disintegration. The **Greek War of Independence** (1821–1832) inspired future nationalist uprisings among other Balkan Christians, and by persuading Britain and Russia to intervene out of sympathy for the Greeks, it stoked a decades-long anti-Turkish prejudice in Europe. At the same time, the rebellion of **Muhammad Ali** (who transformed Egypt into an autonomous principality in 1805), along with the **French colonization of Algeria** (taken from the Turks in 1830 and brutally pacified by the end of the 1840s), demonstrated the Ottoman state's structural vulnerability. Before Ali's death in 1839, he created a Western-style military and industrialized the production of Egyptian cotton. Visionary in certain ways, he governed autocratically as khedive (hereditary prince) and subjected cotton growers and textile workers to oppressive labor conditions.

The Ottomans' external problems worsened after midcentury. Russia's sudden annexation of Ottoman provinces on the Danube provoked the Crimean War (1853–1856), in which Britain and France stepped in to aid the Turks against Russia. Balkan nationalism intensified, as illustrated by the **Balkan Crisis** of 1876–1878, when Bulgarians, Serbs, and others revolted against economically harsh policies. In lashing back, Ottoman troops committed terrible anti-Christian atrocities, undermining the Tanzimat reforms' modernizing spirit and triggering widespread anti-Turkish revulsion in Europe. Russia warred against the Ottomans on the rebels' behalf and imposed a punitive treaty. Although other European powers, not wishing the Ottomans to be fatally destabilized, negotiated a more lenient treaty, the rebel nations went free.

Ottoman control over North Africa likewise weakened. Egypt remained outside the Ottoman orbit, ruled by the khedives (Muhammad Ali's descendants) and then, after the 1850s, falling increasingly under European influence. The construction of the **Suez Canal** (1854–1869), financed by the French-dominated **Suez Canal Company** and overseen by the French engineer Ferdinand de Lesseps, gave France huge economic leverage over the khedive. That leverage passed in the 1870s and 1880s to Britain, which

The Ottoman Empire's seemingly unavoidable collapse presented Europe with the geopolitical challenge known as the Eastern Question. Although they had been enemies since the 1300s, the Ottomans were predictable. If they fell, chaos or a stronger foe might arise in their place. Also, if European nations let themselves be tempted into seizing too much of the crumbling empire at one time, it might upset Europe's fragile balance of power. European powers therefore agreed to manage the empire's decline carefully and even to prop it up if it seemed in danger of immediate collapse.

purchased shares in the canal and then stepped in militarily to save the khedive from an 1881 revolt. That same year, the British established a protectorate, the Anglo-Egyptian Administration, which left the khedive on the throne but placed real control in British hands. To the west of Egypt, the Ottomans had already lost Algeria to the French. They now watched helplessly as Tunisia fell to France, Morocco to the French and Spanish, and Libya to Italy.

As the new century began, the sultan's days were numbered, thanks to the pro-Western **Young Turks** who had coalesced during the late 1800s around an agenda of rapid modernization. Led by the army officer **Enver Pasha**, the Young Turks deposed Abdul Hamid II in 1908–1909, installed a figurehead sultan, and restored the **constitution of 1876**. The Young Turks pursued a program of industrialization, secularization, and socioeconomic reform. However, they continued to lose territory in North Africa and the Balkans, and their decision to forge close ties with Germany led them to support the losing side in World War I—the final step in the empire's ultimate demise.

As for Islamic Central Asia, home to the Silk Road khanates, Russia waged long wars of imperial conquest here in the 1800s. The Russians fought to gain natural resources (Central Asia is a great cotton-producing center), secure their open southern frontier (a long-standing strategic concern), and further their dream—never realized—of winning warm-water ports on the Indian Ocean coast. As noted above, Russia's ambitions in this region brought it into diplomatic conflict with the British, who feared any possible interference with their lines of communication to India. The resulting **Great Game** caused bitter Anglo-Russian rivalry until the early 1900s.

NOTE

One of the Ottoman reformers' most tragic failures was their inability to develop a form of patriotism that included all subjects, regardless of ethnicity or religion. The ideology of "Ottomanism," meant to forge this common sense of citizenship, did not inspire Muslims and was viewed by non-Muslims with suspicion. In the late 1800s, a more aggressive form of Turkish nationalism took wider hold—even among some reformers—and the persecution of minorities, especially Armenian Christians, became more common.

Africa

Paradoxically, Africa, which had been victimized by foreign colonists and slave traders for hundreds of years, remained comparatively free of direct outside influence until well into the 1800s. The Ottoman Empire controlled North Africa. Omani Arabs ruled most of the East African shore and Swahili ports (after displacing the Portuguese), and the European presence on the continent was restricted to selected spots on the coast.

In other words, many African societies were strong enough in the late 1700s and early 1800s to resist foreign domination. Others were cooperative enough that foreigners found it useful to work with them rather than fight them. Several of them, such as Benin, Dahomey, Kongo, and the Ashanti (Asante) kingdom, played significant roles in the Atlantic slave trade; in exchange for gold and guns, they took prisoners from enemy peoples and sold them to Euro-American slavers. Among this era's most powerful and unified African states were the following:

NOTE

The Atlantic slave trade continued to ravage Africa—approximately two million Africans were forcibly taken to the Americas during the 1800s—but it was made illegal and eventually shut down. The East African slave trade ended as well during the late 1800s.

■ The **Barbary states** of Islamic North Africa (present-day Morocco, Algeria, Tunisia, and Libya), which were technically ruled by the Ottomans but increasingly autonomous. Piratical **corsairs** from these states threatened European and American shipping and enslaved captives. Their raids embroiled the young United States in the Barbary Wars (commemorated in the line from the U.S. Marine hymn, "to the shores of Tripoli") and partly provoked the **French colonization of Algeria**, starting in 1830.

- The **Ashanti** (Asante) **kingdom** in West Africa's Gold Coast (present-day Ghana), which engaged in a dramatic military buildup during the late 1700s, financed by its participation in the Atlantic slave trade. The Ashanti threatened European outposts and trade routes along the Gold Coast and resisted Euro-American attempts to destroy the slave trade. Starting in 1823, Britain found itself locked in a long series of wars with the Ashanti, who kept up their fight for independence until 1902. (The nearby **Sokoto Caliphate**, an Islamic state founded in present-day Nigeria during the Fulani revolt of 1809, likewise resisted the British until 1903.)
- The **Zulu kingdom**, which existed on the edge of Dutch and British possessions in South Africa. Before 1800, the Bantu-speaking Zulu were organized into small, relatively peaceful clans, but from 1816 to 1828, a new chieftain, **Shaka**, united them into a single warlike tribe. Their rapid expansion caused a large wave of tribal migration throughout southern Africa, and they also clashed with Dutch Boers and British settlers. Only after several conflicts, especially the **Zulu War of 1879**, were they pacified.
- **Zanzibar**, which produced spices, sugar, and cloves for the Indian Ocean trade network and served as a key hub for the **East African slave trade**. Ruled by the Arab sultanate of Oman after 1698, it became the Omani capital in 1840 and was promoted to the status of sultanate in 1861. It controlled the Zanj, a large portion of the East African coast.
- **Ethiopia**, which remained Coptic Christian in predominantly Muslim East Africa. Ethiopia existed largely in isolation between the mid-1600s, when it expelled the Portuguese, and the mid-1800s, when Theodore II, a pro-Western but mentally erratic king, began a process of military modernization. This policy, continued by his successors, allowed Ethiopia to ward off European invasion. Its 1896 victory over Italian forces at Adowa ranks as one of the most embarrassing setbacks suffered by a nineteenth-century European power.

As the century progressed, nearly every part of Africa lost its freedom to European states. Coastal areas were the first to fall. **South Africa**, colonized by Dutch **Boers** (also known as Afrikaners) in the mid-1600s, saw an influx of new settlers after the Napoleonic Wars, when the

NOTE

In 1856 and 1857, British settlement in South Africa touched off the Xhosa cattle-killing movement, an example of the many millenarian rebellions, or religiously inspired episodes of resistance, that occurred during the era of new imperialism. Here, the Xhosa came to believe that if they killed their own livestock, who were already falling ill, the spirits would expel the British from their lands.

British assumed control over the region. Displaced by the British, the Boers made a **Great Trek** to the north during the 1830s and founded their own states on the border of British South Africa. The Boers and British periodically clashed with each other and more regularly with the local Xhosa and Zulu until the capitulation of the latter in the **Zulu War of 1879**. The discovery of **South African gold mines** and **diamond fields** heightened military tensions there and led to the cruel exploitation of African laborers. Far to the north, the **French colonization of Algeria** was carried out during the 1830s and 1840s with scorched-earth devastation and frightful violence against local civilians.

Leading the resistance was the Sufi scholar Abd al-Qadir, internationally respected, even after his defeat, for the dignity and bravery with which his forces fought. The French became particularly attached to Algeria, viewing it as their most important possession in the way Britain regarded India. The economic and political domination of Egypt from the 1850s onward, thanks to the construction of the **Suez Canal**, is described above.

Despite all this, only about 10 percent of African territory fell under European control before 1880. At that point, the so-called **Scramble for Africa** began, lasting until the eve of World War I and rapidly subjugating the entire continent. Thanks to geographical knowledge gained by explorers between the late 1700s and the mid-1800s and also to industrial-era weaponry and effective medical treatments for tropical diseases, Westerners were now able to press fully into the African interior. Civil and intertribal conflict made numerous parts of Africa vulnerable to European takeover, and African states that had benefited from the slave trade found themselves economically weakened when that commerce came to an end. (A sad paradox about the end of slavery was that, even where African economies remained free, they now turned to forms of **plantation farming** and **resource extraction** that were barely less brutal as systems of labor.) The Europeans themselves were motivated by a combination of greed (**gold**, **diamonds**, **ivory**, **rubber**, and **palm oil** were just a few of the resources they coveted), belief in their own racial superiority (reinforced by the doctrine of **social Darwinism**), and their condescending **white man's burden** conviction that they had a duty to "civilize" what they thought of as "the dark continent." Moreover, the century's-long antislavery campaigns accustomed Westerners not just to taking military action in Africa but to thinking of intervention there as morally justified.

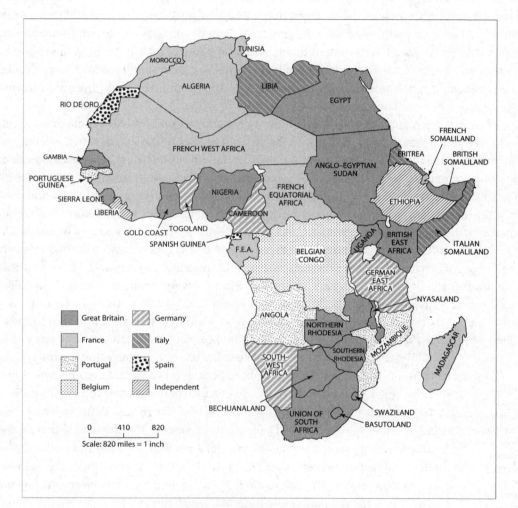

European Imperialism in Africa, 1914

A pivotal moment in the Scramble for Africa was the **Berlin Conference** (1884–1885), convened by the German statesman **Otto von Bismarck** to defuse diplomatic tensions stirred up by Europe's headlong rush to carve up Africa. Boundaries were agreed upon, as were guidelines for further expansion, but long-term harm was done to Africa by the fact that the lines drawn on the map during and after Berlin reflected only European desires. They bore no relation to the traditional territorial demarcations used by Africans themselves, and even today many African ethnic groups remain divided by European-drawn borders or forced by those borderlines into close proximity with their enemies.

Europe's colonial policies varied widely in Africa. Britain controlled several colonies in the west, including the Gold Coast and Nigeria (after their defeat of the Ashanti kingdom and the Sokoto Caliphate), but even more extensive was its nearly unbroken chain of possessions in the east, gained at the expense of the Omani Arabs. This ran from South Africa to Egypt, or "from Cape to Cairo," as the imperialist Cecil Rhodes put it.

As in India, the British governed with a blend of exploitative selfishness, racist sentiment, and well-meaning condescension. They trained native elites and troops in the Western style and brought with them new science, medicine, and industrial technology. Much the same can be said of France, which (after its initial brutality in Algeria) acted mainly in accordance with its *mission civilisatrice*. In addition to the island of Madagascar off the southeast coast, France dominated much of the Saharan north and vast portions of the west. French West Africa and French Equatorial Africa were among the largest colonies on the continent. French victory over the Wassoulou Empire founded by **Samory Touré** (r. 1878–1898) in the region of modern Guinea, Sierra Leone, and Côte d'Ivoire—the so-called Mandingo War—was crucial in establishing French power here. (Years later, Touré's grandson would become the first president of independent Guinea.)

By contrast, Portuguese rule in its colonies Angola and Mozambique was quite harsh. Even worse were the Belgians and Germans. In the 1870s, **Leopold II**, the Belgian king, established a private company (later bequeathed to the Belgian nation) for the economic development of the **Congo**, and its claim to the colony was recognized at the Berlin Conference of 1884–1885. Belgian-owned **rubber plantations** brutally forced Congolese laborers to meet production quotas, often allowing overseers to chop off the right hands of harvesters who fell short and sometimes massacring them as punishment. Before the Belgians' arrival, Congo had a population of around 20 million, but that number fell to 8.5 million by 1911. Germany moved aggressively into Tanganyika, near Zanzibar in the east, and several small areas in the west. However, these were unprofitable leftovers, and the Germans also faced several costly uprisings. They killed over a quarter million to suppress the **Maji Maji revolt** (1905–1907) in German East Africa— where the rebels believed that drinking blessed water would keep them safe from European bullets. (Compare this with similar beliefs among the Boxer rebels in China.) Germany's infamous **Herero Wars** (1904–1907) involved the use of **concentration camps** against civilians and killed nearly 80 percent of Southwest Africa's Herero natives. Some scholars consider this conflict an early instance of twentieth-century genocide.

NOTE

Starting in 1882, the British were opposed in the Sudan by a millenarian rebellion led by the Mahdi—Arabic for "one who is rightly guided"—the title of the messianic figure foretold in Islamic prophecy. In 1885, the Mahdi's army, driven by religious fervor and anticolonial fury, massacred a British force at Khartoum, one of Britain's most stunning imperial defeats. Not until 1898, when they crushed the Mahdi at Omdurman, did the British gain revenge.

Within three decades, all of Africa—except for Liberia and Ethiopia—had been brought under Europe's sway. However, the Scramble for Africa backfired on the Europeans by rousing their combative passions and contributing to the diplomatic tensions that helped cause World War I. In 1896, France and Britain almost came to blows because of the Fashoda Incident, in which French troops moving eastward into the Nile valley encountered British forces who regarded the region as theirs. German interference with French and Spanish plans for northwestern Africa led to a Morocco Crisis in 1906 and another in 1911.

Also destabilizing was Germany's public support of Dutch Afrikaners in their **Boer War** (1899–1902) against Britain. Although the British had a more powerful army, the Boers were skilled sharpshooters fighting on their home territory. The war grew painfully vicious, with the British using **concentration camps** to keep 120,000 civilians— over 20,000 of whom died—from supporting Boer guerrillas. Germany's open sympathy for the Boers worsened Anglo-German relations (already strained by the two countries' naval race), with profound implications for the **European alliance system** that took shape prior to World War I.

East Asia

Largely isolated from the wider world during the late 1700s and early 1800s and highly self-satisfied with the cultural splendor of bygone days, both China and Japan were confronted by Western imperial pressures in the mid-1800s. To China's loss and Japan's gain, they reacted in diametrically opposed ways.

Qing China in the late 1700s still enjoyed immense wealth, artistic and intellectual grandeur, and firm political and military sway over the states in its **tributary system**. The **Qianlong emperor** (r. 1763–1795) is remembered as the Qing dynasty's last truly capable ruler. Unfortunately, even during his reign and more so afterward, **Confucian-based social stratification** remained rigid, and the cost of defending China's northern and western frontiers—combined with too-rapid population growth (from 300 million in 1799 to 400 million a century later)—burdened the economy. Popular discontent erupted in violent uprisings like the **White Lotus Rebellion** (1796–1804), and the government grew even more corrupt and incompetent after the Qianlong emperor's death.

At the same time, the Qing badly mishandled relations with the West. In the late 1700s and early 1800s, Europeans and Americans were allowed to trade with China only in a handful of designated cities (most famously **Canton**, on the southern coast). Also, while the Chinese sold silk, porcelain, and increasingly large quantities of **tea** to Western nations, they accepted only silver in exchange, refusing to allow any more than a tiny selection of Western goods to be sold in their country. For years, this lopsided balance of trade angered Westerners, but when the **Macartney mission** petitioned the Qianlong emperor in 1793 for permission to open a British embassy and sell more goods in China, the emperor replied dismissively that "your country has nothing we need." While this refusal to bargain was partly tough business sense, it also reflected an imprudent sense of superiority. Based on past glories, the Qing continued to believe that China was the **Middle Kingdom** and that all outsiders were barbarians. What they failed to recognize was that they had already fallen behind the West when it came to science and technology and could not hope to match the stronger navies, better weapons, and more effective armies that would be pitted against them in the 1800s.

Tea Harvesting in China
For hundreds of years, silk, then porcelain, had been China's chief trade commodities. During the 1600s and 1700s, however, tea overtook both in importance. The tea trade played a great role in global economics during the 1700s and 1800s. During those centuries, "all the tea in China" became the most popular slang phrase to describe unimaginable wealth.

In the meantime, the British, followed by other Western nations, including the United States, embarked on a campaign of **economic imperialism** by flooding China with a highly potent variety of opium from British India. This **opium trade** overwhelmingly reversed the economic balance of power: instead of flowing into China, silver bullion now flowed out at an alarming rate. Also, opium addiction became so widespread during the early 1800s that on any given day, millions of farmers and workers were too incapacitated to work. In 1839, the Qing trade commissioner **Lin Zexu** protested to the British, begging Queen Victoria herself to end the trade. He then confiscated a huge quantity of opium from British warehouses in Canton and cast it into the ocean—a stunning financial blow that incensed British merchants and sparked the **First Opium War** (1839–1842). The fighting, easily won by the technologically advanced British, ended with the Treaty of Nanking, the first of many "**unequal treaties**" forced on nineteenth-century China by Western powers. The Qing had to open more ports to foreign trade, lower tariffs on British goods, and surrender **Hong Kong** to Britain. Further trade conflicts in the 1850s and 1860s, including a Franco-British assault on Beijing, resulted in more unequal treaties, which legalized the opium trade, opened additional ports, and allowed Americans and Europeans to set up **foreign concessions**—large coastal districts where Western, not Chinese, law prevailed. By 1898, foreign vessels were allowed to sail as far up Chinese rivers as they pleased.

MILLENARIAN REBELLIONS

A number of millenarian rebellions during the 1800s were motivated in part by religious and apocalyptic thought. In addition to the Taiping Rebellion and the revolt of the Mahdi, examples include the Xhosa cattle-killing Movement of the mid-1850s and the Ghost Dance revival that led to an 1890 massacre of Sioux. In the former, a female prophet foretold in 1856 that, if the Xhosa of South Africa slaughtered their cattle, spirits would wipe out the British settlers. With many of their animals already dying from a sickness probably brought to Africa by European cattle, the Xhosa began killing their cattle in early 1857, leading to a vast famine. In the case of the Ghost Dance, the Paiute visionary Wovoka—ironically a preacher of peace—popularized the ritual among many western Native Americans. It became a rallying point for the Sioux, many of whom were killed by U.S. forces at Wounded Knee.

Internal crises dogged the Qing at the same time. Worst was the **Taiping Rebellion** (1850–1864), which claimed between 20 million and 30 million lives, making it possibly the second deadliest war in history, next to World War II. The uprising was led by Hong Xiuquan, a Cantonese clerk educated partly by Protestant missionaries. Shocked by failing his civil service examination, Hong experienced visions that convinced him he was Jesus Christ's younger brother, destined to establish a "heavenly kingdom of supreme peace"—the meaning of *taiping*—in China. An extraordinarily magnetic leader, Hong organized an effective modern army and appealed to millions of ordinary Chinese who resented the Qing's high taxes and oppressive rule. The rebels also opposed practices like the binding of women's feet. At their peak, the Taiping controlled a third of China, but Qing forces, assisted by foreign military units, recovered by the early 1860s. Hong committed suicide in 1864, and the rebellion collapsed.

Reacting to the Taiping chaos, elements within the Qing government attempted a reform campaign, the **self-strengthening movement**, starting in the 1860s and pursued sporadically over the next few decades. It was of limited impact because it confined itself to economic and military modernization without meaningful social change. It was also opposed by the leading figure in Chinese politics, the dowager empress **Cixi**, who governed as regent for her nephew, the Guangxu emperor, beginning in 1878, and controlled him even after he grew to adulthood. Conservative and oppressive, Cixi resisted all change and even placed her nephew under arrest when he launched a short-lived "Hundred Days' Reform" in 1898. (His reformist advisors were executed.)

The price of Cixi's stubbornness was internal decay and economic decline as well as continued humiliation on the diplomatic front. Outlying possessions and parts of China's tributary system gained autonomy or fell into foreign hands. France seized Indochina after a short conflict with China in 1883. Even more embarrassingly, tiny Japan thrashed China in the **Sino-Japanese War** (1894–1895) and occupied Korea and Taiwan. In 1899, the United States' **Open Door Policy** arranged equal access to Chinese markets for all Western nations, further increasing foreign intrusion.

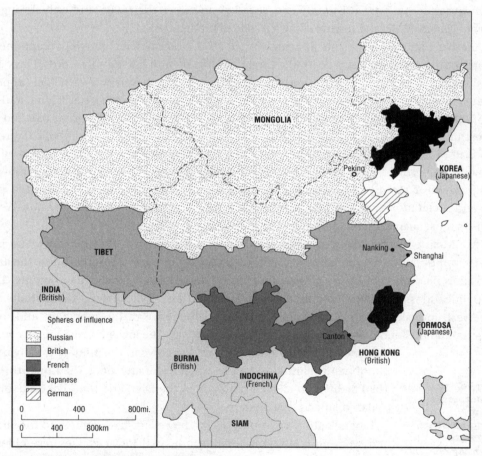

Western Spheres of Influence in China, 1910
Starting in the early-to-mid-1800s, Great Britain, then other Western nations, pressured China into opening its markets and yielding up economic and political control over much of its coastline and riverways. These concessions grew in size and number during the 1800s and early 1900s, reaching their peak just before the Qing dynasty's collapse in 1911.

NOTE

Like the Maji Maji rebels in German East Africa only a few years later, many of China's Boxer rebels believed that certain rituals would prevent Western bullets from harming them.

In late 1899, Chinese anger at foreign influence burst out of control, worsened by severe drought and high unemployment. What followed in the summer of 1900 was the Yihetuan revolt ("Militia United in Righteousness"), nicknamed the **Boxer Rebellion** because many of the rebels were martial artists. Qing authorities initially tried to put the rebels down, but when Cixi realized she could unleash their rage against Western occupiers, she encouraged them. Months of violence and destruction threatened foreign concessions, even in key cities like Beijing, and only in the fall of 1901 did Western forces manage to quash the uprising. In revenge, Western powers burned a number of Chinese temples and forced the Qing to pay heavy reparations. Even Cixi now recognized the need for change and formed a committee to consider writing a constitution. She and the Guangxu emperor both died in 1908, leaving Henry Puyi, China's last dynastic ruler, to take up the reform effort. Unfortunately for him, revolution destroyed the Qing regime in 1911–1912, as described in Chapter 19, leading to the rise of the Chinese Republic.

As for Japan, the **Tokugawa shogunate** tried in the late 1700s and early 1800s to enjoy the fruits of urbanization and protoindustrialization, all while keeping in place its dictatorial rule and its rigid social stratification, which favored the **samurai** elite. It had also sealed itself off from the wider world: Christianity had been banned since the 1600s, and only through the port of **Nagasaki** did the regime allow a trickle of foreign trade.

All this changed with the appearance in 1853 of American gunships captained by **Commodore Matthew Perry**. With the threat of force behind his friendly words, Perry asked the Japanese to open up to trade, and once the shogun agreed, other Western fleets appeared with similar demands. It appeared that Japan might suffer the same fate as China, and so in 1867–1868, a coalition of samurai clans, angered by the shogun's unwillingness to stand up to foreign intimidation, abolished his office and restored the emperor—a symbolic figurehead since the 1200s—to a position of full authority. The **Meiji Restoration** of 1868, named after the new emperor (r. 1868–1912), began Japan's modern age. In a revolution from above, the Meiji emperor rapidly industrialized Japan's economy and thoroughly modernized political and social life. Japan even emerged as an imperial power, making this the non-Western world's most successful adaptation to the industrial era.

The Meiji emperor swept away the feudal social hierarchy of the Tokugawa era. In the 1870s, samurai lost their hereditary privileges, including immunity from taxation, the annual subsidies paid to them by the government, and their right to wear swords in public. Access to political positions depended increasingly on merit and civil service examinations. As in the West, industrialization increased the size and influence of the merchant and middle classes, and the feudal prejudice against trade faded away. The lower classes gained access to public education and were allowed to serve in the military after centuries of not being allowed to handle weapons of any kind. The **Constitution of 1890** created an elected parliament, the Diet, and the Civil Code of 1898 updated Japan's legal system.

NOTE

To build popular allegiance, the Meiji emperor and his successors turned to Japan's ancient indigenous faith, creating an Office of Shinto Worship in 1872. All priests became state employees and emphasized the veneration of the emperor as a descendant of the gods. By the 1930s and 1940s, this form of "State Shinto" was used to justify a sense of Japanese racial superiority and blind obedience to government.

Liberalization went only so far, however. Taxes increased for farmers, and working conditions for the industrial lower classes resembled the ghastly ones that had characterized Europe's early Industrial Revolution. Owing to property qualifications and other restrictions, only about 5 percent of the population could vote for the Diet, and the emperor exercised a great deal of control over it. The civil code also made little room for the rights of women, who were largely confined to a secondary status.

The Meiji regime excelled at westernization, economic efficiency, and militarization. The new tax system of 1872 funded a national educational system, and Japan imported Western science and technical know-how at an astonishing rate. The elite and middle classes adopted Western dress and manners, the Western calendar, and the metric system. From Britain and Germany, the Japanese navy and army adopted not just industrial-era technology but also Western tactics and organizational methods.

With this new military machine, Japan began to expand in the 1870s. A resource-poor island, Japan needed raw materials to feed its industrial growth, and nationalist sentiment swelled as the century wore on. From China in 1879, it took the Ryukyu Islands, which include Okinawa, the most cherished of Japan's possessions. It joined the Western powers in forcing China to grant it **foreign concessions**, and more success followed in the **Sino-Japanese War** (1894–1895), which allowed Japan to occupy Taiwan and Korea. Even more impressive was the **Russo-Japanese War** (1904–1905), the first large-scale conflict of the modern era in which a non-Western state defeated a European power. Russia's imperial and railroad-building ambitions in eastern Siberia, Mongolia, and Manchuria collided with Japan's plans for expansion. Instead of negotiating spheres of influence with the Japanese, the tsar pushed ahead with foolish overconfidence. Equipped just as well as the Russians were and fighting close to home—while the Russians struggled to supply their war via the Trans-Siberian Railway, several thousand miles long—the Japanese shocked their foes. Victory gave them the Kurile Islands and southern Sakhalin, and Japan strengthened its position in Korea and mainland China. It entered the new century as an empire on the rise and as a regional power to be respected. Unfortunately, its militaristic streak and its imperial ambitions continued to widen.

South Asia, Southeast Asia, and Oceania

In eighteenth-century India, the centralizing authority of the once-mighty **Mughal Empire** fractured. During the late 1600s, the Islamic militancy of the emperor Aurangzeb had provoked the creation of a **Sikh** state in the Punjab and the breakaway of the Hindu **Maratha Empire**. Muslim states like Mysore won their freedom as well. The Maratha princes, who belonged to the warrior caste and demonstrated a willingness to innovate with gunpowder weaponry, were formidable leaders.

Another threat was the steadily growing European presence in South Asia: first the Portuguese and Dutch and then the French and British, who emerged as the main competitors for influence over India. Britain's victory over France during the **Seven Years' War** (1756–1763)—particularly its 1757 defeat of France's Mughal allies at the battle of **Plassey**, in Bengal—ensured British superiority on the subcontinent and confined France's colonial presence to the southeastern port of Pondicherry.

Until the mid-1800s, the **British East India Company** carried out the colonization of India. In 1800, it controlled only a small part of the country, mainly around Bombay (now Mumbai, the gateway port of the west coast), Madras (a textile-producing center on the southeast shore), and Calcutta (in the Bengal northeast). One initial interest was the **cotton industry**, although the company also traded in tea, spices, and opium. During the early 1800s, it expanded through a combination of diplomacy, warfare, and the training of **native elites**. Many Mughal rulers surrendered bureaucratic authority to the British in exchange for being allowed to keep their thrones. Company armies defeated the Mysore sultanate, the Maratha princes, and the Sikhs, extending British authority into the interior, along the vital Ganges River valley, and up to the northwest frontier. To save on humanpower, the company relied as much as possible on native personnel.

For administration and tax gathering, the British turned to native officials and **zamindar** landowners. (This decision caused trouble in the late 1700s when many zamindars overtaxed their countrymen and seized land from peasants who could not pay. Resulting famines killed one-third of the rural population under British control, after which the company reformed its tax-gathering system.) The most famous native personnel were the **sepoys**, or Indian soldiers trained and equipped in Western style. This practice, begun by the French in the mid-1700s, was used on a huge scale by the British, who stationed a surprisingly small number of their own officers and soldiers in India.

After their missteps in the 1700s, the British came to administer India more efficiently, with the combination of self-interest and well-meaning but condescending "**white man's burden**" thinking that typified their approach to imperial rule. They made no secret about their feelings of racial superiority or their hunger for profits. Native artisanry and cottage industry (much of it female-run) was displaced by British economic interests. When the British built schools, railroads, and telegraphs or when they improved the food-distribution network to prevent famines, it was more for their own benefit than for that of native Indians. The costs and benefits of British rule in India continue to be debated.

A key change in Britain's handling of India came in the years 1857–1858 with the traumatic **Indian Revolt**. Here, underlying resentment of British rule was inflamed by growing sepoy anger at changes to their terms of service made by the company to save money. This existing tension exploded into open violence due to false rumors that new cartridges issued to sepoy riflemen had been greased with cow and pig fat, deliberately to undermine Hindu and Muslim religious practices. Groundless though it was, these fears caused great outrage and spread quickly. The initial disturbances grew into a massive wave of nationwide revolt, and sepoy units in Delhi proclaimed the aged Mughal sultan the new emperor of India. Savage massacres of British civilians, especially at Cawnpore (where the butchered remains of women and children were cast into a dry well to rot), incensed the British, who responded with devastating reprisals and mass executions. With their Western training and anticolonial zeal, the sepoys gravely threatened British rule in India, but they had no clear plan or single leader, and Muslim and Hindu rebels often failed to cooperate. In 1858, the British, with native troops who remained loyal, put down the rebellion and formally ended the Mughal dynasty. Several hundred thousand people, most of them Indian, perished. The last rebel leader, the Rani of Jhansi, is remembered in India as a female freedom fighter in the style of Joan of Arc.

After the Indian Revolt, the British crown took over from the British East India Company as India's colonizing authority. Under direct rule, India became the British Empire's proverbial "jewel in the crown": by the late 1800s, one-quarter of the wealth generated by the empire came from there, making it an indispensable asset. At the same time, Britain's strategy of educating Indian elites began to backfire. Many were exposed to liberal or radical ideas and concluded that the British, with their long tradition of civil rights, were treating their nonwhite subjects hypocritically. Many became attracted to **national-liberation movements**, including the **Indian National Congress**, which formed in 1885.

Southeast Asia—rich in rubber, petroleum, and metals like copper, tin, chrome, and aluminum ore (bauxite)—also came under Western dominance. The Dutch East Indies, known today as Indonesia, had been administered by the **Dutch East Indies Company** since the 1600s, although the Dutch government itself stepped in after 1799 when the company went bankrupt. The British, as they tightened their grip on India, made parallel advances into Southeast Asia. In 1819, the British established the outpost of **Singapore** at the tip of the Malay Peninsula. This strategically placed naval base and trading center became one of Britain's most prized possessions in Asia. Nearby Burma fell to Britain in 1826.

The French developed their own interest in Southeast Asia, gradually detaching **Indochina**—the region that comprises Vietnam, Cambodia, and Laos—from China's tributary system and, then colonizing it in the 1880s and 1890s. More so than the British, the French emphasized religious conversion, and so their native elites were almost exclusively Catholic. In other respects, the French imperial model was similar to Britain's.

NOTE

Mongkut and his son Chulalongkorn, who ruled until 1910, are widely remembered in the West because of the literary and movie adaptations of the memoirs of Anna Leonowens, the English educator and antislavery activist hired in the 1860s to tutor Mongkut's children. Best known is the (grossly inaccurate) musical *The King and I*.

The one mainland state in Southeast Asia to avoid European colonization in the 1800s was Siam, or Thailand, due to good leadership and good luck. Like the Meiji emperor in Japan, King Mongkut, who ruled from 1851 to 1868, saw industrialization and Western-style reform as the key to continued freedom. Siam's geographic setting was also fortunate: it served as a convenient buffer zone between British-controlled Burma and French Indochina.

The last major acquisition in Southeast Asia was the **U.S. annexation of the Philippines**, a Spanish colony since the early 1500s but forfeited to the United States in 1898 after the **Spanish-American War**. During the 1880s and 1890s, the Filipino Propaganda Movement tried to persuade Spanish authorities to enact reforms, while the **Katipunan** national-liberation society struggled more directly against Spanish rule. With Spain defeated, most Filipinos initially welcomed the Americans as liberators. But then the United States, fearing that the Philippines would fall into Japanese hands (and realizing what a superb naval base the islands would make), proclaimed a policy of "benevolent assimilation" and took possession of them in 1899. Tragically, this led to a **Philippine-American War** of occupation in which a guerrilla force led by the Katipunan rebel **Emilio Aguinaldo** resisted the U.S. takeover until 1902. Over 200,000 Filipinos died during this conflict.

NOTE

The English poet Rudyard Kipling wrote "White Man's Burden," the era's most famous literary justification of imperialism, to commemorate the Americans' victory over the Spanish and to encourage them to take the Philippines for their own.

Thanks to explorers like Britain's **James Cook**, the Pacific became increasingly familiar to Europeans and increasingly subject to their colonial authority. Cook charted and claimed Australia's east coast in 1770; the nearby islands of New Zealand, home to the Polynesian **Maori**, came under English control as well. Britain took formal possession of eastern Australia in 1788 and extended its authority to the entire island in 1830, transforming an outpost of roughly a thousand soldiers and colonial officials into a settler colony whose English-speaking population grew to 1.2 million by the 1860s. Many of the new arrivals were English and Irish convicts punished with **transportation** (a sentence that, in the 1700s, sent prisoners more commonly to New England and the Caribbean), but miners and **sheep farmers** came here in large numbers as well. Free or unfree, the settlers overwhelmed Australia's roughly 300,000 **Aborigines**, dispossessing them, often with violence, and driving them into the bush. In New Zealand, the Maori gained access to gunpowder weapons during the "musket wars" of the early 1700s, and it took another round of combat, the Land Wars of 1845–1872, for the British to bring them fully under control.

NOTE

The late 1800s witnessed the arrival of the French and Germans in the Pacific as colonizers of Tahiti, Samoa, the Marshalls, the Marianas, and other islands.

The United States expanded its Pacific presence in 1867 by purchasing the Russian colony of Alaska. It also extended its reach to the **Hawaiian kingdom**, founded in 1795 by Kamehameha I, who used Western weaponry to conquer the islands and forge them into a European-style absolute monarchy. Hawaii evolved into a constitutional monarchy and a noteworthy producer of fruits and sugar (many immigrants from China and Japan arrived to work in these industries). However, it was attacked several times by France and other powers, leading it to seek American protection in the 1840s. Although the United States recognized Hawaii as an independent nation, it gained much influence over Hawaiian affairs in the late 1800s, and in 1893, when Queen Liliuokalani proposed to amend the constitution in ways contrary to U.S. interests, she was overthrown. With the monarchy ended, the United States annexed Hawaii in 1898, just prior to its occupation of the Philippines.

The Americas

The domestic history of the United States is largely beyond the scope of the AP World History: Modern exam. A few comparative notes, however, as well as some points about the United States' effect on global affairs, should be made:

- *Inspiring freedom*: Democratic government and respect for civil liberties (despite racial and gender inequality) made America an example during the 1800s for those in other countries who wished to bring about similar changes.
- *Sphere of influence*: The **Monroe Doctrine** (1823), in which the U.S. government warned Europe against intervening in the western hemisphere's political affairs, was the first step in creating a sphere of influence. The United States quickly became the dominant power in the Americas, practicing **economic imperialism** in much of Latin America and gaining ownership of or protection over Caribbean (and Philippine) territories after the **Spanish-American War** (1898).
- *Expansion*: The United States' rapid growth, which altered the balance of world power, began with the **Louisiana Purchase** (1803) and continued with the **Mexican-American War** (1846–1848), numerous "**Indian wars**," the 1867 purchase of Alaska, and the 1890s annexation of the **Hawaiian kingdom**. The ideology of **Manifest Destiny** arose in the 1840s to promote the belief that America was naturally entitled to expand.
- *Native American policy*: U.S. handling of Native Americans vacillated between assimilationist attempts to "civilize" them and military campaigns of expulsion or pacification—the so-called **Indian wars**. Key steps in this process were the 1811 battle of Tippecanoe (a huge setback for the Shawnee chief Tecumseh's rebellion of 1810–1813) and Andrew Jackson's **Indian Removal Act** of 1830, which pushed many tribes west of the Mississippi. Treaties typically arranged for Native American tribes to be placed on **reservations** with some degree of autonomy, but even when the U.S. government negotiated in good faith, farmers, ranchers, and miners often broke the peace, leading to more forced resettlement. For example, the **Ghost Dance** resistance that led to the 1890 massacre of Native Americans at **Wounded Knee** was precipitated by the U.S. desire for the gold discovered in the Black Hills territory sacred to the Sioux.

THE CHEROKEE NATION

Even "civilizing" along American lines was not enough to save the Cherokee Nation, which formed in the late 1700s as a confederation of related tribes in Georgia and its environs, from abuse. Early adopters of new technology and farming techniques from the Americans, the Cherokee also devised their own written script—Sequoyah's alphabet—and a sophisticated political system, later adapted to U.S. constitutional norms (including the right to own slaves, which many Cherokee did). In 1820, the U.S. government asked the Cherokee to move west to Arkansas and Oklahoma on a voluntary basis, but this became mandatory with the passage of the 1830 Indian Removal Act, and thousands died of starvation and disease on the Trail of Tears that led to their new homes. The Cherokee Nation continued to exist as a sovereign entity on the periphery of the United States until 1906, when the U.S. government dismantled it.

- *Slavery*: The persistence of **slavery in the American South** was a key factor in allowing the Atlantic slave trade to continue for so long. It was the underlying cause of the **U.S. Civil War** (1861–1865), and race relations are still affected by its legacy today. Prior to the Civil War, several slave revolts were attempted, most famously by **Nat Turner** in 1831 and the abolitionist **John Brown** at Harpers Ferry in 1859.
- *Industrial and commercial growth*: During the last two-thirds of the 1800s, the United States equaled, then surpassed, Europe as an industrial power. Many of the era's key innovations came from here. In addition, New York joined London as one of the world's most important hubs of banking and commerce.
- *Immigration*: Political freedom and economic opportunity drew huge quantities of **immigrants**—an estimated 17 million between the 1830s and the 1890s—from Europe and Asia. **Anti-immigration sentiment** was common.

As for Latin America, **Simón Bolívar** drafted constitutions for more than a dozen nations after the wars of independence, influenced by the Napoleonic law code and the ideals of the American and French Revolutions. But good constitutions did not by themselves bring about good government, social justice, or healthy economies, and even Bolívar, before his death in 1830, mourned that "we have achieved our independence … at the expense of everything else." Latin American democracy was frequently subverted by political strongmen known as **caudillos**, who ruled by means of personal charisma, military force, or oppression.

One important exception to caudillo rule was Mexico's president **Benito Juárez**, descended from Zapotec natives and a determined supporter of land reform, separation of church and state, and equal treatment for all races. A member of the Liberal Party, Juárez served as president several times between 1858 and 1872. His first election took place during an armed conflict with Mexico's Conservatives—the Reform War (1857–1861)—and he also led the war of resistance against France's 1864 to 1867 attempt to install Maximilian of Austria as Mexico's emperor. Juárez's onetime ally, the general **Porfirio Díaz**, reverted to the caudillo mode, securing his hold over the presidency from 1876 to 1911, when the **Mexican Revolution** (1910–1920) forced him out of office.

Also problematic in Latin America was the persistence of **racial inequality**. Although constitutions theoretically did away with rigid colonial-era hierarchies, Indians, blacks, and those of mixed race still experienced much prejudice. As in the United States and Canada,

Resistance to slavery took an interesting form in the Caribbean, the Gulf of Mexico, and mainland South America: runaways and natives called Maroons (from the Spanish *cimmarón*, a colloquial term for "fugitive") formed communities on islands or coastlines on the periphery of larger states. They preserved not just their independence but also their African and indigenous heritages. Several—especially in Jamaica and Dutch-controlled Suriname—grew sizable enough during the 1700s and early 1800s to force colonial officials to sign treaties recognizing their right to exist freely.

Indian wars were common throughout Latin America, particularly in Mexico's Yucatán Peninsula (where a Mayan rebellion raged from 1847 to 1901), the Argentinian pampas, and Brazil's Amazon basin. The **Atlantic slave trade** continued to bring Africans against their will to Latin America and the Caribbean, and **slavery** remained legal in Cuba and Brazil until the 1880s.

Moreover, Latin America contended with **economic backwardness**. Centuries of colonial rule had geared Latin American economies toward an overreliance on **resource extraction** (guano for fertilizer, Mexican copper and other precious metals) and **plantation monoculture** (sugar, coffee, fruits, rubber, beef from Argentina and Uruguay). Both damaged the environment and hindered industrialization until late in the 1800s. Moreover, these practices, which depended on slaves or poorly paid peasants and migrant laborers, also fostered **social inequality**. (Rubber harvesting in the Amazon, for example, especially in Peru's **Putumayo** region, was revealed by investigators to be nearly as abusive as in the Belgian Congo.) Profits went overwhelmingly to the elite classes and their foreign-investor partners, leaving a wide gap between rich and poor. A certain measure of industrialization occurred in some parts of the region by the late 1800s, with countries like Mexico and Argentina leading the way.

Slavery in Brazil
From the mid-1500s to the end of the 1800s, Brazil was the largest single importer of slaves from Africa. In particular, the sugar industry depended on slave labor. Not until the 1800s did Brazil's government make slavery illegal. Shown here are scenes of the work and punishment of slaves in Brazil.

Foreign influence over Latin America remained heavy even after independence. The United States seized vast amounts of territory from Mexico during the Texas rebellion of the 1830s and the **Mexican-American War** (1846–1848). France under Napoleon III sponsored the ill-fated attempt to install the Habsburg prince Maximilian as emperor of Mexico (1864–1867). British and American **economic imperialism**—exemplified by the actions of the **United Fruit Company**—became more rampant. Spain maintained a presence in Cuba and

Puerto Rico, which received harsh treatment. A **national-liberation** movement led by the Cuban poet **José Martí** sparked a war of independence during which opponents of Spanish rule were placed into **concentration camps**, the modern world's first such prisons (soon to be borrowed by the British during the Boer War and the Germans during their campaign against the Hereros of Southwest Africa). Events in Cuba led directly to the **Spanish-American War** (1898), which ended Spain's influence in the Caribbean but handed dominance over to America, which annexed Puerto Rico and established a protectorate in Cuba. The United States went on to build the **Panama Canal** in the early 1900s, another sign of its regional influence.

NOTE

Illustrating further the concept of economic imperialism, Western companies invested heavily in the building of Latin American roads and railroads. Although it did not lead to the same degree of political control as U.S. involvement with the Panama Canal (or Franco-British involvement with Egypt's Suez Canal), British funding played a massive role in the construction of Argentina's Port of Buenos Aires—the largest in Latin America—between the 1880s and the 1920s.

Cultural Developments and Interactions, 1750–1900

14

IN THIS CHAPTER

→ THE ENLIGHTENMENT (JOHN LOCKE, MONTESQUIEU, VOLTAIRE, JEAN-JACQUES ROUSSEAU)

→ SOCIAL CONTRACT, NATURAL RIGHTS, POPULAR SOVEREIGNTY, SEPARATION OF CHURCH AND STATE

→ ROMANTICISM, REALISM, AND MODERNISM

→ VARYING DEGREES OF CULTURAL WESTERNIZATION IN NON-WESTERN REGIONS

→ CONSERVATISM (AND REACTION) VS. LIBERALISM

→ CAPITALISM (ADAM SMITH) VS. SOCIALISM AND COMMUNISM (KARL MARX)

→ NATIONALISM

→ IDEOLOGIES OF RACIAL SUPERIORITY (SOCIAL DARWINISM)

→ NATIONAL-LIBERATION MOVEMENTS

In Europe and America during these years, the pace of cultural change sped up. In contrast to long-lasting movements like the Renaissance and even the Enlightenment, trends and styles in the 1800s and 1900s changed constantly. Such rapid evolution has been a hallmark of modern Western culture. Also characteristic were greater access to culture, the formation of modern political philosophies, and a more scientific and secular worldview. (For more on the last point, including the Western crisis of faith, see Chapter 15.)

Elsewhere, the non-Western world began to adopt many of the artistic and literary forms of the West, especially print culture and writing styles, as well as architecture. Conversely, styles from Asia, Africa, and the Middle East had an influence on Western culture, particularly in painting, sculpture, and decor.

Greater access to **public education** became a normal part of life in North America and most parts of Europe throughout the 1800s. **Literacy rates** rose as a result. The same became true for certain other areas of the world in the 1800s.

ART AND CULTURE IN THE MODERN ERA

In the Western world, cultural modernization is considered to have begun with the **Enlightenment** of the 1700s, also commonly referred to as the Age of Reason, the name given to it by the American revolutionary Thomas Paine.

Enlightenment thinkers put faith in the power of human logic and in the recent discoveries of the Scientific Revolution. They also pondered how to make society and government more efficient and humane. The sociopolitical philosophies of the Enlightenment—as articulated by individuals like **John Locke**, the Baron

> **NOTE**
>
> Immanuel Kant, the principal spokesman of the German Enlightenment, described the 1700s as the time when humanity had grown out of its "self-imposed immaturity" to proclaim a new motto: "Dare to Know!"

NOTE

Women shaped Enlightenment culture in many ways, whether by organizing the salons at which philosophical debate took place or—like Mary Wollstonecraft of England and Russia's Catherine the Great—by participating directly as authors, activists, and political actors.

Charles de **Montesquieu**, **Voltaire**, and **Jean-Jacques Rousseau**—are detailed further in the next section, but they generally opposed tyranny, or arbitrary exercise of monarchical power, and favored greater respect for individual rights. Freedom of opinion and religion was also important to Enlightenment thinkers, some of whom remained devoutly Christian, some of whom adopted vaguer religious stances like **deism** (belief in a divine being but not the literal truth of a specific doctrine), and some of whom became atheistic. Enlightenment circles and salons appeared throughout the Western world during the 1700s and helped to inspire the **American and French Revolutions**.

Moving from the late 1700s into the 1800s, the principal cultural movement in the West was **romanticism**. A backlash against the rational Enlightenment, romanticism emphasized emotion, individuality, and the imagination. As summed up by the English poet Samuel Taylor Coleridge, romantics considered the "creative faculty" to be superior to the "calculating faculty." Around the 1840s, romanticism, while it did not die away, yielded its place of prominence to **realism**. Realists were concerned with everyday life, social problems, and the psychology of their characters.

Both romanticism and realism reacted strongly to the process of industrialization in Europe and America. As illustrated by William Blake's poetic contrast of England's "green and pleasant land" with the "dark Satanic mills" of industry, romantics idealized nature and viewed industrialization as a blight upon it. In their best-known novels, authors like Victor Hugo and Charles Dickens disapprovingly portrayed the social miseries of the industrial era. Realist painters and writers regularly addressed themes of poverty and inequality.

Romanticism and Nature

The Wanderer Above the Mists (ca. 1818), by the German painter Caspar David Friedrich, exemplifies the trend among romantic artists and writers to portray the natural world not just as picturesque but as embodying sublime qualities.

The culture of the late 1800s and early 1900s was characterized by diversity and innovation. Turning away from realism in the 1870s onward, **modernist** artists and writers (including Vincent van Gogh and a young Pablo Picasso) broke the rules of traditional culture and experimented with a dazzling array of new styles: impressionism, postimpressionism, cubism, and abstraction. Asian and African art powerfully influenced this generation of artists.

Aristide Bruant at Les Ambassadeurs (1892), by Henri de Toulouse-Lautrec
French painter and poster artist Henri de Toulouse-Lautrec (1864–1901) was one of many artists who, during the late 1800s, departed from the strictly realist styles of the early and middle nineteenth century. Like many of France's impressionist and postimpressionist painters, Toulouse-Lautrec was influenced by foreign art, most particularly Japanese prints.

In other parts of the world, Western forms of art and writing often blended with indigenous styles, whether because of voluntary adoption or because they were imposed by colonial masters as they trained **native elites** according to Western norms. In the Middle East, for example, especially during the **Tanzimat reforms** of the mid-1800s, Ottoman authors adopted European styles like romanticism and realism. At the same time, partly in opposition to westernizing trends, a resurgence of Arabic culture—which had long been overshadowed by Turkish and Persian art and literature—made itself felt in the region.

In Africa, the **oral tradition** remained dominant, as witnessed by the continued popularity of **griot storytelling** and other forms of poetic and epic recitation. As more of the continent fell under imperial control, foreign colonists and Christian missionaries imported Western culture on a larger scale. In turn, Western artists tiring of traditional realism found themselves energized by Africa's **nonrepresentational art**, which inspired innovative **modernist** styles, such as primitivism and abstraction, in Europe and America.

East Asia continued its tradition of cultural grandeur. One of the greatest novels in Chinese literature appeared during the late 1700s: Cao Xueqin's ***Dream of the Red Chamber***, which narrates the tragedy of two young lovers caught up in the decline of a wealthy and powerful clan. In Japan, the **ukiyo-e** style of woodblock painting reached its highest peak of development during the early 1800s, thanks to artists like **Hokusai** and Hiroshige, both of whom influenced impressionist and postimpressionist painting in Europe. Throughout the region, though, westernizing tendencies were increasingly evident.

The Great Wave off the Coast of Kanagawa (ca. 1831)
Arguably the most internationally recognized painting to come out of Asia, this scene—part of Katsushika Hokusai's "Thirty-Six Views of Mount Fuji"—illustrates the delicacy and refinement of Japan's ukiyo-e style as well as the blend of realistic and nonrepresentational elements that made Asian painting so fascinating to Westerners in the late 1800s.

South and Southeast Asia experienced an even higher level of westernization, thanks to the influx of missionaries and colonial authorities. In India, Mughal culture did not fade completely but yielded much of its preeminence to the "**Company style**": art and architecture conditioned by admixtures brought to the subcontinent by the British East India Company. Such cultural fusion can be seen in monuments like the **Gateway to India** arch, built in Bombay (Mumbai) to celebrate British imperial control over India. Catholicism and the French language were imported into Indochina during the late 1800s, and Siam (modern-day Thailand)—much like Japan under the Meiji emperor—westernized thoroughly as a way to avoid foreign conquest and colonization.

The Gateway to India
Erected between 1911 and 1924 by the British government to welcome visitors to the port of Bombay (now Mumbai), the "Gateway to India" arch symbolizes British colonial authority. It also demonstrates the fusion of Western and South Asian architectural styles during the era of "new" imperialism.

POLITICAL THOUGHT: NEW PHILOSOPHIES AND IDEOLOGIES

The Enlightenment

In eighteenth-century Europe and America, the **Enlightenment** prompted rational inquiry into the nature of politics and society. As described above in Chapter 13, Enlightenment thinkers, by questioning social hierarchies and traditional forms of monarchy, paved the way for massive political changes—including key revolutions—in Europe and the Americas.

Among the earliest Enlightenment thinkers was England's **John Locke** (1632–1704), who argued that a government's power should depend on the consent of the governed. He favored freedom of religion and opinion and the protection of private property. Owing largely to Locke, concepts such as **popular sovereignty**, **natural rights**, the **social contract** (mutual obligations owed to each other by governments and their people), and **separation of church and state** became cornerstones of Enlightenment thought. Other influential Enlightenment figures include:

- Baron Charles de **Montesquieu**: French author of *The Spirit of Laws* (1748), which proposed the **separation of powers** (executive, legislative, and judicial) to avoid tyranny.
- **Voltaire**: Versatile playwright, novelist, and philosopher from France. Best remembered as a champion of **freedom of expression** and as a fierce enemy of organized religion, which he viewed as corrupt and hypocritical.
- **Jean-Jacques Rousseau**: Swiss-born French author who felt more strongly than many of his fellow thinkers that ordinary people deserved political power, as expressed in his 1762 book *The Social Contract*, a forceful continuation of Locke's thinking on the subject.
- America's **founding fathers**: Thomas Jefferson, George Washington, Benjamin Franklin, Thomas Paine (who coined the term "Age of Reason"), and others who led the American Revolution and designed the U.S. Constitution. These were the first to establish an entire political system (however imperfectly) on Enlightenment principles.

Revolutionary documents on both sides of the Atlantic, including the **Declaration of Independence**, France's **Declaration of the Rights of Man and the Citizen**, and Simón Bolívar's **Jamaica Letter**, belong squarely within the Enlightenment tradition.

New Ideologies: Reacting to Revolution and Industrialization

Most modern forms of political thought were born in the West, either during the Atlantic and Industrial Revolutions or in reaction to them.

Conservatism regarded the changes brought about by the Atlantic revolutions as completely undesirable or as having taken place too quickly and with too much violence. It also feared the social and political effects of industrialization. The most uncompromising form of conservatism, **reaction**, was typified by a leader at the **Congress of Vienna** like Austria's Klemens von Metternich. A more moderate form of conservatism, which argued for gradual reform rather than sudden change, is associated with a thinker like the Anglo-Irish philosopher **Edmund Burke**. Political **liberalism** favored the extension of political privileges and individual freedoms, at least to the middle class but not always to the lower classes or to women. It tended to favor the **free-market capitalism** preached by **Adam Smith** and other **classical economists** (see Chapter 16). The century's most famous liberal philosopher was **John Stuart Mill** of England.

Liberal optimism about industrialization and capitalism was not uniformly shared by members of the industrial working class or by certain thinkers who came to see capitalism as

> **NOTE**
>
> Even the use of "left" and "right" as political terms emerged during the early days of the French Revolution when radical members of the National Assembly sat on the left-hand side of the building and conservative opponents of the revolution took places on the right.

unfair and exploitative. Especially after the **1848 revolutions** in Europe, it became clear that pure capitalism, in its original dog-eat-dog form, could not remain as it was without causing severe, if not unbearable, socioeconomic stress. But how should it be changed? Liberals and reformers, along with conservatives who felt there was no choice, worked to keep capitalism in place by gradually eliminating the worst of its abuses and sharing its benefits more fairly. From the other end, many members of the working class turned to **trade-union activism** to gain concessions like pensions, better hours, safer working conditions, and higher wages. (Taken for granted now as normal parts of working life, such improvements were won at the time only after great struggle.)

NOTE

In the countryside, a prominent non-Marxist form of socialism was agrarian socialism (sometimes known as populism, though this term has many different political meanings). This ideology, especially influential in Eastern Europe, viewed downtrodden peasants as a potentially revolutionary force and saw their communally organized villages as possible models for the ideal society of the future. Russia's agrarian socialists, the Socialist Revolutionary Party, were major contenders for power during the revolutions of 1917.

Because of the slow pace of liberal and reformist change, other alternatives arose as well. Most extreme was **anarchism**, which rejected all forms of government. More widespread was **socialism**, which appeared in many forms, ranging from moderate to radical, but all sharing the belief that economic competition is inherently unfair and eventually leads to injustice and inequality. The **utopian socialists** of the early 1800s believed that governments and business owners should forgo maximum profits to pay workers better and care for them properly. Many of their demands and suggestions became standard policy during the late 1800s and early 1900s. The most practical of the utopian socialists, the Welsh businessman **Robert Owen**, founded a number of factory-based communities along these cooperativist lines in both the British Isles and the United States.

A more radical form of socialism was **communism**, originated by the German philosophers **Karl Marx** and Friedrich Engels and most famously outlined in *The Communist Manifesto* (1848) and *Das Kapital* (1867–1894). Marx and Engels argued that all historical development was driven by a **class struggle** between the upper class (which controls capital, or the means of economic production) and the lower class (which is forced to labor for the

NOTE

Even the Catholic Church stepped into the debate about workers' treatment under capitalism. In 1891, Pope Leo XIII issued the encyclical *Rerum Novarum* (also known as "The Rights and Duties of Capital and Labor"). While Leo condemned communism, he called for legalizing trade unions and criticized unfettered capitalism for the "misery and wretchedness" it caused many workers.

upper class). They predicted that the age of industrial capitalism, with its struggle between the bourgeoisie and the working-class proletariat, was the final stage of human history before the realization of socialism. Society would then move on to communism, which Marx and Engels described as an economic state of perfect justice, equality, and prosperity. To achieve socialism, however, Marx and Engels believed that **revolution** would most likely be needed, so they advocated force as potentially necessary to overthrow capitalism.

The boldness with which Marx proclaimed the impossibility of fixing capitalism and the inevitability of socialist revolution made communism appealing to many—more so than most other varieties of socialism. His confidence, however, turned out to be misplaced (or at least premature), and already during the late 1800s, many who agreed with Marx's critique of capitalism began to question whether violent revolution was desirable or even necessary as a way to achieve Marxism's goals. These **revisionists** began to seek legal ways to bring about socialism, such as trade-union activism and parliamentary politics. They founded **social democratic parties**, which gained large followings in countries like France and Germany before World War I and which sometimes opposed communists who remained more radical. The quarrel between Russia's Mensheviks (communists who favored gradual change and working within the system) and Lenin's Bolsheviks (communists who favored faster change and revolutionary action) is typical of this split.

International Socialism vs. Capitalism

The attempt to coordinate socialist and communist movements throughout Europe can be seen in these nearly identical propaganda posters, dating from the turn of the century. Both portray rigidly stratified social orders, with the industrial working class at the bottom, their labor enriching the prosperous middle class; an army that serves as a tool of oppression; a clergy that deceives ordinary people into being content with their situation (inspired by the Marxist dictum that "religion is the opiate of the masses"); and a ruling class at the top of the structure. The poster on the left was distributed in Russia, while the one on the right is from England.

Nationalist Strains of Thought

Although patriotism had not been absent from Western political life in earlier eras, it was not as prominent as it became in the modern era. The late 1700s and early 1800s witnessed the advent of **nationalism**—a feeling of shared identity defined by ethnicity, language, traditions, and territory—as a powerful political force.

Much of this had to do with the rise of the **nation-state** as a dominant form of political organization. In addition, the Enlightenment ideal of the **social contract**, which was put into political action during the **American and French Revolutions**, fostered the growing sentiment that, just as an individual owed certain obligations (such as obedience, taxes, and military service) to his or her nation, the individual was owed certain things in return *by* the nation—making it worth belonging to and feeling pride in.

Not only was nationalism felt more strongly in existing states, it also burned with great intensity among groups that did not have a nation of their own but were divided or ruled by others. Nationalism flared up especially among the Germans and Italians (each of whom would unify during the 1800s), the Irish, the Poles, and the Eastern European and Balkan peoples who lived under Austro-Hungarian or Ottoman rule.

In the right circumstances, nationalism manifests itself as patriotism and no more. Unfortunately, as the era progressed, nationalism frequently encouraged aggressive **militarism** and can be seen as a contributing factor to Europe's armed conflicts of the late 1800s—especially the wars of Italian and German unification—and to its overseas campaigns of imperial conquest. It also aroused feelings of **ethnic and racial superiority**, which were further reinforced by pseudoscientific notions regarding racial differences and the interaction of peoples. The most famous of these was **social Darwinism**, a misguided interpretation of Darwin's insight that, in nature, the better-adapted are more able to compete for scarce resources. Among those who popularized the application of Darwin's thinking to human relations—something Darwin himself strenuously opposed—was the English intellectual Herbert Spencer, who coined the phrase "survival of the fittest." Based on the false premise that white races had progressed further along the evolutionary scale than nonwhite ones, social Darwinism and similar strains of thought were used to justify numerous forms of inequality, including ethnic prejudice and colonial domination. At home, social Darwinists regarded women as the provably "weaker sex" and felt that lower-class poverty was a "natural" product of human competition.

By the late 1800s, nationalist tendencies were spreading to non-Western parts of the world. The modernizing **Young Turks** in the Ottoman Empire were ardent nationalists trying to keep their country on a technological par with Europe. Hoping to create a sense of unity among all citizens, regardless of religion or ethnicity, most Young Turks promoted **Ottomanism** as a shared imperial identity during the mid-to-late 1800s. When this failed to take hold—and as the empire suffered more rebellions and territorial losses in the late 1800s and early 1900s— many of them (though not all) turned to a narrower form of **Turkish nationalism**. All too often, this took the form of prejudice against non-Muslim minorities, with particular harshness toward Armenian Christians, both before and especially during World War I.

Where foreign colonists ruled, nationalist sentiments often produced **national-liberation movements**, which would grow increasingly potent in the twentieth century. These sought to protest imperialism's abuses or overturn it altogether. Before his death in battle, the poet-philosopher José Martí used his eloquence to awaken Cuba's nationalist movement against Spain and to launch its 1895–1898 war of independence. The **Katipunan**, the Filipino national-liberation society, fought against Spanish colonization in the 1890s, only to face U.S. occupiers after Spain relinquished control over the Philippines in 1898. In India, one paradox of greater colonial centralization after the 1850s was that it created a stronger sense of "India" as a single country, with a single national identity, as opposed to a quiltwork collection of many different peoples with different languages and traditions. This impulse helped give birth to the **Indian National Congress**, which formed in 1885 (mainly on the initiative of British-educated native elites) to demand more rights for natives in British India and eventually to end colonial rule there. The **Boxer Rebellion** can be seen as a national-liberationist backlash against the West's growing domination of Chinese coastal territories, and the **Maji Maji revolt** against German colonizers demonstrated much the same trend in Africa.

The non-Western country that came closest to adopting Western-style nationalism, complete with a social Darwinist outlook, was Japan after 1868. As Japan industrialized, militarized, and defeated neighbors like Korea and China—not to mention Russia (1904–1905)— many Japanese became convinced that they were not just more technologically advanced than their fellow Asians but innately superior to them. This sentiment is communicated in the influential 1885 essay "**Goodbye Asia**," which foreshadowed the "master race" thinking Japan later adopted by proclaiming that "We do not have time to wait for the enlightenment of our neighbors. . . . It is better for us to leave the ranks of Asian nations and cast our lot with the civilized nations of the West. . . . [We are] no different from the righteous man living in a town known for foolishness and lawlessness."

Technology and Innovation, 1750–1900

15

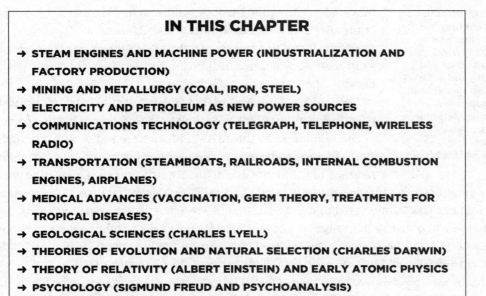

IN THIS CHAPTER

→ **STEAM ENGINES AND MACHINE POWER (INDUSTRIALIZATION AND FACTORY PRODUCTION)**

→ **MINING AND METALLURGY (COAL, IRON, STEEL)**

→ **ELECTRICITY AND PETROLEUM AS NEW POWER SOURCES**

→ **COMMUNICATIONS TECHNOLOGY (TELEGRAPH, TELEPHONE, WIRELESS RADIO)**

→ **TRANSPORTATION (STEAMBOATS, RAILROADS, INTERNAL COMBUSTION ENGINES, AIRPLANES)**

→ **MEDICAL ADVANCES (VACCINATION, GERM THEORY, TREATMENTS FOR TROPICAL DISEASES)**

→ **GEOLOGICAL SCIENCES (CHARLES LYELL)**

→ **THEORIES OF EVOLUTION AND NATURAL SELECTION (CHARLES DARWIN)**

→ **THEORY OF RELATIVITY (ALBERT EINSTEIN) AND EARLY ATOMIC PHYSICS**

→ **PSYCHOLOGY (SIGMUND FREUD AND PSYCHOANALYSIS)**

→ **RELIGIOUS REACTIONS AND THE WESTERN CRISIS OF FAITH**

Between 1750 and 1900, the industrial era ushered in the greatest age of invention the world had seen to date—a cascade surpassed only by the unending process of innovation and reinvention that has followed since. This wave of advancement originated in Europe and North America during the Industrial Revolution and primarily benefited those regions, but it spread to other parts of the world as well during the nineteenth century.

Scientific knowledge likewise expanded enormously. Building on the foundations created in the 1600s and 1700s by the **Scientific Revolution** and the **Enlightenment**, scholars, physicians, engineers, and others—again, principally from Europe and North America—made innumerable discoveries and proposed new theories and ideas in every field of inquiry. For the nations of the West, economic prosperity, military might, and imperial power were tightly intertwined with this growing scientific and technological superiority.

TECHNOLOGY IN THE INDUSTRIAL ERA

With rare exceptions, power as late as the 1700s was produced exclusively by wind, water, or muscle, just as it had been from humanity's earliest days.

This state of affairs changed in the 1780s when the Scottish engineer James Watt patented a **steam engine** that was both cost-effective and sufficiently strong to pump out coal and iron mines and drive new machines in the textile industry. The steam engine quickly unlocked the broader potential of **machine power** and **factory production**, giving rise to the **Industrial Revolution** in the late 1700s and early 1800. As the century progressed, new machines and new power sources were integrated into all aspects of economic and practical life, leading to the decades of industrialization described in Chapter 16.

Machines and processes based on **coal** and **iron** dominated the early industrial years. During the so-called **Second Industrial Revolution** of the mid-to-late 1800s, newer building blocks of industrial technology emerged. Among these were the **Bessemer process** (1850s), which enabled the cost-effective production of **steel** (stronger and more reliably workable than iron); the rise of **electricity** as a feasible power source from the 1830s onward; and the commercial use of **petroleum** after 1859. **Chemical** industries advanced in the second half of the century, and the process of **vulcanization** (which prevented rubber from melting when hot or growing brittle when cold) was perfected between the 1830s and 1880s.

NOTE

Even after the midcentury introduction of petroleum as a lubricant and fuel source, oil from marine mammals continued to be extensively used and highly valued for industrial and lighting purposes. Sealing and whaling continued on a large scale throughout the 1800s and early 1900s, causing much environmental stress. Another lucrative alternative was palm oil, especially from West Africa, where it was produced by means of plantation monoculture.

Technological innovation transformed the field of **communications** with the invention of the **telegraph** in 1837, followed by the appearance of the **telephone** in the 1870s and wireless **radio** between 1895 and 1901. **Transportation** was similarly revolutionized, with the effect of seeming to shrink the world, thereby making travel easier and enabling the long-distance shipping of trade goods and farm produce. Key inventions include the **steamboat** (1807), which led to rapid transatlantic voyaging by the 1850s; **railroads** (1820s), which, for the first time in history, put ground transport on a par with water transport for speed and cost-effectiveness; the **internal combustion engine** (1860s–1880s), which led to the **automobile**; and just after the turn of the century, the **airplane** (1903).

Many aspects of everyday life were affected by industrial-era technology. The first workable lightbulbs (1879), especially Thomas Edison's version, are often held up as a symbol of this trend. Canning and refrigeration changed the patterns of food consumption. Concrete-and-steel construction enabled the building of high-rise structures in major cities (skyscrapers were pioneered in Chicago in the 1880s) as well as engineering projects like the Suez and Panama Canals. Systems of public transport, including buses and subways, appeared late in the century. Warfare industrialized as well, with modern rifles, better artillery, the machine gun, and steam- and petroleum-driven warships. In the countryside, the tractor helped cause an agricultural boom. National economies and personal lives alike were influenced by constant and increasingly affordable innovations that involved machine power and fossil-fuel energy.

SCIENTIFIC ADVANCEMENTS

Scientific advancement kept pace with technological innovation during this era, and each reinforced the other in many ways. As with industrialization and engineering, progress was fastest and most comprehensive in Europe and North America.

NOTE

Whether Catholic or Protestant and whether from Europe or North America, Christian missionaries proved immensely important as transmitters of Western scientific, medical, and technological medical knowledge to Africa, India, China, Southeast Asia, and other places.

Medical expertise improved tremendously. Knowledge of **germ theory** helped prevent the spread of common diseases, especially those that spread easily due to poverty and urban overcrowding. **Vaccinations**, pioneered in the 1790s to combat smallpox, became more common in the 1800s. Nursing techniques—especially as developed in wartime by Clara Barton of the United States and Florence Nightingale of Great Britain—and surgical procedures became steadily more modern, particularly as methods of **antiseptic sterilization** and

anesthesia were adopted more widely. **Childbirth** became less risky, at least for women of means, and **infant mortality** decreased. Treatments for **tropical diseases** (most notably quinine for malaria) became more readily available.

The earth and life sciences were both enriched by key insights. In the 1830s, the Scottish geologist **Charles Lyell** used meticulous fieldwork to prove two fundamental points about the earth: first, that it was not a fixed creation altered by periodic catastrophes but a planet constantly changing due to the action of geological forces; and second, that it was millions of years old at the least—orders of magnitude older than commonly thought. The system of **Linnaean taxonomy** allowed botanists and zoologists to categorize living creatures more precisely, and mounting evidence from the **fossil record** caused a growing number of scientists to embrace the **theory of evolution** in the late 1700s and early 1800s. The basic idea behind evolution occurred to many scholars at the time, but the difficulty lay in devising a convincing model for how it operated.

Answering this challenge was the English naturalist **Charles Darwin**, who explained the process of evolution with his **theory of natural selection**. In *On the Origin of Species* (1859), Darwin caused a scientific and cultural storm by arguing that evolution is a random process in which physical changes that increase an animal's chance for survival are passed on to that animal's offspring. In *The Descent of Man* (1871), he applied the principles of natural selection to human beings and postulated that humans and apes share a common evolutionary ancestry. (Alfred Russel Wallace, also of England, hit upon the notion of natural selection independently and simultaneously but had the bad luck of publishing his findings after Darwin did.)

NOTE

Among Darwin's intellectual inspirations were the geologist Charles Lyell (a friend and mentor, though he never fully accepted the implications of Darwin's research) and the population expert Thomas Malthus, whose ideas about competition for scarce resources led Darwin to ponder how that process worked in the wild. What Darwin failed to explain was *how* naturally selected mutations are passed on from parent to offspring. The answer required an understanding of genetics, but the early research done in this field by the Austrian monk Gregor Mendel in the 1800s remained unknown until the 1900s.

Around the turn of the twentieth century, the field of physics, dominated since the early 1700s by the Newtonian system of thought, changed forever. Developed in the 1890s and early 1900s by **Albert Einstein**, the **theory of relativity** established the speed of light as a maximum velocity in the known universe and demonstrated that, when considered on an astronomical scale, the mathematics behind Newtonian physics began to break down in paradoxical ways. The new field of **atomic science**, including **quantum physics**, likewise tested the limits of Newtonian physics on the microscopic level.

Another field in its relative infancy as this era ended was **psychology**. Although many scholars and doctors contributed to the development of this science, the most influential work was done by the Austrian physician **Sigmund Freud**. While Freud attained his greatest fame in the years following World War I, he had developed his fundamental principles of **psychoanalysis**—including his understanding of the personality as influenced by the unconscious mind and divided into three components (id, ego, and superego)—by 1900, the year he published his most important book, *The Interpretation of Dreams*.

SECULARISM AND RELIGION IN A SCIENTIFIC AGE

During this era, a **scientific, secular worldview** became increasingly paramount, at least in the Western world. This did not mean that religions lost their political and social importance or that people ceased to follow them. However, in a growing number of countries, **separation of church and state** became the norm, and less risk and scandal was attached to openly professing unconventional beliefs like **deism** or **atheism**. In the public sphere, religion became less convincing to many as a justification for keeping certain rulers in power or maintaining social or gender-based hierarchies.

Numerous discoveries in the late 1700s and early 1800s accelerated the rise of secularism relative to religion in the West. Archaeological and linguistic research in the Middle East and Asia—including the decoding of hieroglyphs by means of the **Rosetta Stone**, unearthed by Napoleon's armies in Egypt—revealed that certain cultures and ancient languages, such as Sanskrit, predated even the oldest described in the Judeo-Christian Bible. The use of fossils to prove the **extinction of species** (including dinosaurs, a category defined in the 1840s), combined with the findings of the geologist **Charles Lyell** (as described in the section above), indicated that the planet was many millions of years old. At a time when many still believed that the Earth was roughly 10,000 or so years old—based on the time accounted for in the Bible—this basic fact was both revolutionary and unsettling.

This was even more the case when **Charles Darwin** outlined his theories of **evolution** and **natural selection** in *On the Origin of Species* (1851) and added human beings to the mix in *The Descent of Man* (1871). These ideas, along with discoveries in other sciences, did much to erode faith in traditional religion and encouraged more secular worldviews. (See Chapter 14 for the impact of Darwinian theory on social and economic thinking—the so-called **social Darwinism** of which Darwin himself disapproved.)

Western feelings about the century's scientific and technological developments were mixed. On the one hand, scientific and techno-logical progress and the rising economic prosperity that accompanied it infused Western culture with excitement and confidence. For the most part, especially among the general public, this sense of optimism continued until the eve of World War I. On the other hand, particularly among intellectuals and artists, this was a time of growing uncertainty and anxiety. As scientific insights like Darwin's made it harder to sus-tain a literal belief in the Christian Bible, a **crisis of faith** shook the

Western mind-set during the late 1800s and early 1900s. The German philosopher Friedrich Nietzsche proclaimed famously that "God is dead" and argued that all systems of morality were valueless in the materialistic modern age. Quantum physics and Einstein's **theory of relativity** opened up new and mathematically unsettling questions in the fields of physics for the first time since the days of Newton. The **psychoanalytical theories** of **Sigmund Freud**, which demonstrated how poorly most individuals understood even the workings of their own minds, made many people uneasy. These feelings of distress would grow even stronger dur-ing and after World War I.

Economic Systems, 1750–1900

16

Until the end of the 1700s, the world's economies were principally agricultural. Over the centuries, manufacture, trade, and commerce had become increasingly important but, compared with agriculture, remained relatively minor.

In Europe and North America, this state of affairs changed dramatically. In the late 1700s and early 1800s, the mass production of goods by means of machine power—**industrialization**—became a key part of Western economies. Trade and commerce skyrocketed, and masses of people moved from rural areas to the city. **Capitalism** became the dominant economic system. Taken together, these changes formed the **Industrial Revolution**, whose first stage coincided roughly with the political revolutions taking place in America, France, and the Atlantic world.

Although industrialization was a "revolution" only in a metaphorical sense—it lasted decades and had no clear-cut beginning or end—it changed life in Europe and the rest of the world as thoroughly as its political counterparts. It placed new machines and inventions at the disposal of ordinary people. It affected old social classes and created new ones. It changed the way millions worked, where they lived, and how they understood political problems. By 1900, the United States and most of Europe had industrialized and urbanized. Many other parts of the world were starting to follow suit.

INDUSTRIAL REVOLUTIONS IN THE WEST

Background to Industrialization

The Industrial Revolution is considered to have begun in England in the 1770s and 1780s with the successful application of the **steam engine** to two sectors of the economy: **mining** and **textiles**.

NOTE

One global effect of early industrialization involves the 1793 invention of the cotton gin by the American Eli Whitney. This, the final step in mechanizing the textile industry, phenomenally boosted international demand for raw cotton, especially in England. Along with Egypt and India, a key source of cotton was the U.S. South, where the crop was grown and harvested by slaves. Slavery in the U.S. had been growing less profitable by this time and might have died away relatively easily, but many historians agree that the cotton gin's invention revived and prolonged it for decades.

Many things combined to spark industrialization in Britain. Already from the 1600s, **protoindustrial practices**, methods more productive than traditional artisanry and craftsmanship, had been in place. Machines such as the flying shuttle and the spinning jenny, which sped up the manufacture of cotton, were invented as early as 1733 and 1764. England was already relatively urbanized, and a set of harsh agricultural laws, the **Enclosure Acts**—which, in favor of wealthy landowners, fenced off large pieces of farmland that had once been common property—impoverished many farmers and forced them to relocate to the cities, creating a pool of available labor. Environmental change played a role as well: the depletion of forests (timber was used both for fuel and to build ships for the Royal Navy) increased dependency on coal, and efficient coal mining required machine power, especially to pump water out of mine shafts. Other factors working in Britain's favor were its location in the Atlantic, an excellent system of **roads** and **canals**, large supplies of **iron** and **coal**, and a strong tradition of trade and commerce, which allowed investors to accumulate capital.

Steam Power and Beyond: The Industrial Era Begins and Matures

What was needed by the end of the 1700s was a power source greater and more reliable than wind, water, or muscle to drive new machines in factories and mines. In 1782, the Scottish inventor **James Watt** patented a steam engine that was both powerful and cost-effective. The first stage of the Industrial Revolution involved the integration of Watt's steam engine into the textile and coal-mining industries.

The next stage of the Industrial Revolution, which lasted roughly until the middle of the 1800s, involved the universal application of steam power—and, more slowly, electricity—to all areas of economic activity. Industrialization also spread to other parts of Europe as well as North America. Key trends include

- The modernization of transport, thanks to **steamships** (1807) and **railroads** (the 1820s)
- The modernization of communications, beginning with the **telegraph** (1837)
- The **factory system**, which systematized, mechanized, and increased the scale of production
- The concept of **interchangeable parts**, pioneered by two Americans, the inventor Eli Whitney and the gunsmith Samuel Colt

Although the Industrial Revolution is generally said to have ended in the mid-1800s, the **industrial era** continued over the rest of the century and birthed a huge wave of invention. Crucial innovations during the second half of the 1800s—often referred to as the

Second Industrial Revolution—include the **Bessemer process** (1850s), which made **steel** production cheaper and easier; concrete-and-steel **construction**, which enabled high-rise building in urban cores and key engineering projects like the Suez and Panama canals; the widespread use of **electricity** and **petroleum**; the birth of chemical industries and the increased use of **rubber**; the **internal combustion engine** and vehicles like the automobile; the **telephone** and **radio**; and the **airplane**. Industrialization affected warfare as well, giving rise to engine-driven warships, rifles instead of old-fashioned muskets, accurate and fast-firing artillery, and machine guns.

NOTE

Industrialization caused something of a "food revolution" in the 1800s. Not only did mechanization (including the tractor) and guano-based fertilizers boost agricultural yields, innovations in canning and refrigeration, not to mention industrial-era transportation, allowed this growing quantity of foodstuffs to be shipped and sold far from their farms of origin.

Industrialization occurred first and most thoroughly in Western Europe (especially Britain, the Low Countries, France, and Germany), as well as in the United States. Southern and Eastern Europe lagged behind. Britain led the world in industrial production for most of the 1800s, as measured by key indices like railroad building and output of iron, steel, coal, and textiles. By the end of the century, Germany and the United States were catching up to, then surpassing, Britain.

As industrialization spread, two models took hold. One was the **free-market industrialization** that arose in Britain and was dominant in most of Western Europe and North America. Its fundamental assumption was the laissez-faire principle that government involvement in and regulation of industrialization should be kept to a minimum. In some places, **state-sponsored industrialization** prevailed. Here, governments either directed industrialization from above or, following an approach sometimes described as **state capitalism**, set nationwide industrial priorities and contracted with certain favored private firms to achieve those goals. Germany and Japan used this approach most successfully, and elements of it were visible in Egypt under Muhammad Ali.

The Social Impact of Industrialization

The Industrial Revolution and its aftermath transformed Western society. Especially for the lower classes, the industrial era's birth pangs, suffered between the 1780s and 1840s, were as traumatic as they were important.

The economic clout of the traditional aristocracy, with wealth based primarily on land, was diminished by industrialization. The class that benefited most was the **middle class**, particularly the bankers, merchants, and factory owners who came to be known as the bourgeoisie.

The Industrial Revolution astronomically expanded the size of the **working class**, or proletariat. During the first decades of industrialization, this class bore the heaviest economic burden. Their labor allowed the Industrial Revolution to move forward, but until the second half of the 1800s, they were badly treated and barely compensated. Workers received low wages, lived in squalid and crowded housing, worked long shifts (fourteen hours a day, six days a week, was not unusual), coped with unsafe working conditions (risk of fire, dangerous machines, exposure to poisonous or harmful substances), and had no pensions, safety laws, or insurance. Child labor was common.

In the countryside, industrialization caused new social divisions. More land came to be owned by well-off farmers and homesteaders who were essentially middle class. Under them were poor agricultural laborers who formed a rural working class of sorts.

NOTE

During the early industrial era, as machines came to play a larger role in economic production, workers used to traditional forms of labor sometimes reacted with technophobia. Most famous were the Luddites: English textile artisans who, during the 1810s, rioted and wrecked power looms and other industrial devices they felt were destroying their livelihood. Their name is still used to describe anyone who reacts to new technology with reflexive fear. A similar revolt by weavers erupted in the Prussian province of Silesia in 1844.

Only after the 1840s did industrialization bring meaningful improvements for larger numbers of Americans and Europeans. Especially after the **1848 revolutions** (caused partly by the socioeconomic stress of early industrialization), various laws and measures began to give relief to the working class—although truly fair treatment and full political equality were still distant goals, achieved only after much hard effort and mainly in the following century. The overall standard of living rose during the second half of the 1800s, even for the lower classes. At least in major cities, many features of modern life became available after midcentury, including bus service, streetlights (gas, then electric), citywide sewage systems, icebox refrigeration, indoor plumbing, steam heating, canned food, and medical advances (vaccination, antiseptic surgery, anesthesia).

Related social trends are massive population growth and urbanization. Europe's population grew from an estimated total of 175 to 187 million in 1800 to 266 million in 1850 and 423 million in 1900. Similar growth took place in the United States. European cities that existed grew larger; in 1800, London reached the 1 million mark, as did Paris in the 1830s. Many new cities sprang up, such as Liverpool and Manchester, precisely because of the Industrial Revolution. By the mid-1800s, England and Wales were urban societies, meaning that 50 percent or more of the population lived in cities. At the time, the level of urbanization reached 25 percent in France and the German states, and it grew as well in the Low Countries and the United States.

Urbanization is generally associated with social advancement, but it had its seamier side during the industrial era. Cities were typically polluted and crowded, and the lower classes lived in slums or shantytowns where sewerage was primitive or nonexistent. Diseases such as **cholera**, **tuberculosis**, and typhoid ran rampant in such conditions. Crime was pervasive.

Industrialization went hand-in-hand with the rise of **capitalism**. (For more on this, as well as forms of **socialism** as a reaction to it, see Chapter 14 and the section directly below.) Other reactions included the fairer labor laws and social welfare measures passed, mainly by liberals and reformers, in the mid-to-late 1800s. For workers, a more radical option (by the standards of the day) was the **trade union** movement. In the early 1800s, unions were illegal in Europe and the United States, and workers risked injury and arrest if they joined unions or went on strike. Still, the union movement gave them a way to struggle for political rights and better treatment in the workplace (higher wages, five-day workweek, shorter hours, safety regulations, pensions, and employee insurance). In the late 1800s and early 1900s, unions earned legal status in most countries and gained greater economic and political strength. Political parties dedicated specifically to workers' needs and interests, such as Labour in Britain, France's Radicals, and Germany's Social Democratic Party, were formed.

CAPITALISM AND COMMERCE

Capitalism and the Classical Economists

The Wealth of Nations, by **Adam Smith**, appeared in 1776, just as the Industrial Revolution began. Smith's brand of economic thinking, later associated with **free-market capitalism**—also called laissez-faire ("let it alone") capitalism—encouraged free trade and political liberalism, at least for the middle classes. In the long term, as with industrialization, capitalism led to the creation of great wealth in the Western world. On the other hand, it was based on competition and, left unregulated, could be cruel to those on the losing end—such as the working class in the early 1800s.

Smith and the other **classical economists** who favored capitalism argued that the laws of supply and demand—the "**invisible hand**," to use Smith's metaphor—should operate freely, with minimal government intervention. The **state-directed capitalism** pursued by economic powerhouses like Germany and Japan yielded its own successes and had its own weaknesses.

Although Smith himself insisted that governments should take measures to fight extreme poverty—a point often forgotten today—other classical economists maintained that little could be done for the poor. Thomas Malthus of England wrote in his influential *Essay on Population* (1799) that poverty was one of the inevitable consequences of population growth. David Ricardo's "**iron law of wages**" was just as pessimistic: employers, he said, will naturally pay workers no more than what is needed for them to survive. To force them to pay higher wages, Ricardo predicted, would cause them to fire workers, who would then starve. Such theories caused economics to be nicknamed the "dismal science" and were used for a long time by middle- and upper-class industrialists to justify oppressive labor practices.

In the mid-1800s, the English liberal thinker and economic theorist **John Stuart Mill** continued to favor free-market capitalism. However, Mill—having observed the abuses of early industrialization, and sensitive to political disturbances like the **1848 revolutions**—came to favor at least some government regulation of capitalist and industrial practices. Also by this time, alternative visions to capitalism were emerging in reaction to the severe socioeconomic strains caused by it. Among these were various forms of **socialism**, including **communism** as preached by **Karl Marx**; they are detailed in Chapter 14.

Commerce and Banking

The rise of capitalism and industrialization coincided with an equally steep rise in the global importance of **commerce** and **banking**.

To protect and expand the growing wealth of merchants and investors, new financial instruments appeared or became more sophisticated. Governments formed **central banks** to house national reserves of precious metals to back their currencies and to determine economic policy. (The Bank of England had existed since the 1690s, but it was in the 1800s, starting with Napoleon's establishment of the Bank of France, that most other Western nations followed suit.) Limited liability **corporations** grew in number and size. Not only did this allow investors to pool their resources, it also allowed them to further minimize risk by separating their personal assets—which could not be touched in case of disaster or bankruptcy—from the assets they invested in the corporation. **Stock exchanges** emerged to regularize the buying and selling of corporate shares. The century's most dominant were the London Stock Exchange, founded in 1801 after decades of less formal trading, and the New York Stock Exchange, established in 1817. Also during the 1800s, **insurance** became more common as a way to protect personal property, corporate assets, and even one's life and health. (Lloyd's of London, perhaps the world's most famous insurance company, took shape in the 1770s and formally incorporated during the 1800s.)

A key economic debate during the 1800s involved the question of whether or not governments should adopt the **gold standard**: the practice of tying the value of a country's currency (and its rate of exchange with other currencies) to gold rather than the more traditional silver. Britain moved in this direction in the 1810s, but other countries stayed with silver or attempted bimetallism (working with both silver and gold) until late in the century.

NOTE

The Wizard of Oz, which appeared in book form in 1900, is thought by many to have been an allegory of the gold-standard crisis, with the yellow brick road and the name Oz (the abbreviation for "ounce") signifying gold. In the book, as opposed to the movie, Dorothy returns to Kansas thanks to her *silver* slippers.

A major shift occurred after the Franco-Prussian War (1870–1871), when the newly united Germany moved from silver to gold, vastly debasing the value of silver. Other European nations made the transition as well. The United States adopted the gold standard in 1900 after a bitter debate that featured one of the most famous speeches in American history, the "cross of gold" address ("you shall not crucify mankind upon a cross of gold") by Democratic presidential candidate and silver advocate William Jennings Bryan.

The crisis that shocked Western economies the most during the 1800s was the **Panic of 1873**, caused mainly by Germany's conversion to the gold standard. The sudden drop in silver's value negatively affected mining enterprises, railroad building, and a myriad of industrial efforts worldwide. This caused a global slump, the **Long Depression**, lasting from 1873 to the mid-1890s.

Transnational Businesses

Also during these years, especially with the spread of the West's "new" imperialism, **trans-national businesses** came to dominate the economic landscape. Some of the **joint-stock companies** from earlier centuries, such as the Hudson's Bay Company, survived into the 1800s. (Others folded beforehand, like the Dutch East India Company, and the British East India Company was dismantled after the Indian Rebellion of the 1850s.) New companies emerged to fund railroads and other major building projects in far-off regions. Among these was France's **Suez Canal Company**, opened in 1858 to oversee construction of the Suez Canal. After the canal's 1869 completion, the company remained in Egypt to oversee its operation. However, while the French owned the majority of shares, their influence waned in 1873, when Egypt sold its shares to Britain, and was lost altogether in 1888, when Egypt's ruler placed the canal under Britain's protection in exchange for military aid against internal rebellion.

One successful transnational (still thriving today) was the **Hong Kong and Shanghai Banking Company** (HSBC), opened in 1865 by British merchants who received special privileges for consolidating Britain's commercial interests in Hong Kong (a British colony after the Opium Wars) and Shanghai (where Britain enjoyed economic concessions). The HSBC assumed responsibility for issuing banknotes—official currency—in British possessions like Hong Kong and Singapore and did the same even in independent states like Thailand. It quickly established branches throughout Asia, and its widespread presence gave Britain informal economic influence over much of the continent.

NOTE

One of today's largest transnationals, the British-Dutch food conglomerate Unilever, grew out of companies that formed in the 1870s and 1880s—including Dutch margarine producers and soap-making Lever Brothers from England. They were heavily involved in the monoculture harvesting of palm oil from West Africa and the Belgian Congo. Unilever itself incorporated in 1929 with the merger of Lever Brothers and Margarine Unit.

Even more influence was exercised over Latin America by the **United Fruit Company**, a U.S. corporation formed in 1899. Starting in Costa Rica, then spreading throughout Central America, Ecuador, Colombia, and the Caribbean, United Fruit monopolized the **cash-crop monoculture** of many fruits, with a special emphasis on **bananas**. It also involved itself in large infrastructure projects such as railroad building and the expansion of shipping. United Fruit used mutually profitable relationships with local business and political elites to gain a tremendous amount of sway over Latin American economies and governments. (The derisive slang term "**banana republic**," which describes monoculture-based economies in the tropics, first arose to describe the nations that fell under United Fruit's influence.) Historians consider the actions of United Fruit and of corporations like it to have been *economic* imperialism.

INDUSTRIALIZATION AND CAPITALISM IN GLOBAL PERSPECTIVE

Few places industrialized during the 1800s to the same extent as Europe and North America, and capitalist economies were rare outside the West. Still, the effects of both trends were felt worldwide, thanks to the expansion of **global capitalism** and the growing imperial influence of Western nations. As during the age of mercantilist colonization but even more intensely, Western economic growth depended heavily on both the acquisition of **raw materials** from non-Western regions and the transformation of those non-Western regions into new **consumer markets** for Western manufactured goods.

NOTE

By placing new weapons—gunboats, machine guns, faster and more accurate rifles and artillery—in the hands of Westerners, industrialization made it easier to acquire new imperial conquests at the expense of primitively armed Asians and Africans. Also, the growing importance of industrial-era warships, powered by coal and petroleum, required Western nations to maintain naval bases around the world, a key way in which industrialization motivated imperialism in addition to making it more feasible.

Even in parts of the world that Europe and America did not conquer or colonize, industrialization and industrial-era capitalism had a profound effect. In Africa, Asia, and Latin America, Western industrialists—often on behalf of **transnational businesses** like the ones described above—struck deals with local elites to extract **cash crops** or **natural resources**. Such practices retarded the development of a healthy, diverse economy. They also exploited native workers in non-Western nations: foreign payments ended up in the pockets of the upper class rather than adding to the national well-being, and the workers themselves typically labored under harsh or **(semi)coerced conditions**. The extraction of **gold**, **diamonds**, ivory, **rubber**, and **palm oil** from Africa was a classic example of direct exploitation, as was the extraction of rubber, tin, aluminum ore (bauxite), oil, and **cotton** from Southeast Asia, Indonesia, and India by the Dutch, French, and British. The industrialized West's relations with Latin American nations and Qing China—which were technically free but dealt with on economically unequal terms—was more indirectly exploitative.

In the long term, most non-Western parts of the world came to imitate industrial methods of production. Western colonizing powers exported industrial practices to their imperial possessions or created industrial-era infrastructures in the form of railroads, canals, and telegraphs. In one example, Britain brought industry to India, although with varying motives and results. To make their own lives in India more comfortable and to maximize profits—and also because they thought it would be better for native Indians—British colonizers modernized the country in many ways. They created roads and railways (which reduced the number of famines by improving food distribution), a telegraph network, and a postal service. On the other hand, the profits generated by Indian raw materials went to Britain rather than benefit the local economy. In addition, the size and efficiency of British enterprises tended to drive local ones out of business. This happened in India's textile trade (where women had previously played important roles), as well shipbuilding and ironworking there.

Also spreading industrialization to the non-Western world were political leaders in free nations, who in some cases came to see industrialization as a way to gain wealth and power. Here, industrialization was typically imposed from above by the ruler and/or encouraged by members of the elite. In Latin America, mining for copper and **guano**—newly desirable for the manufacture of fertilizer—along with the cash-crop monoculture of fruits, coffee, and rubber, was generally carried out by local elites in conjunction with **transnational businesses** like the United Fruit Company. Near the end of the 1800s, countries like Mexico and Argentina were starting to industrialize more sectors of their own economies.

In the Middle East, industrializing initiatives came overwhelmingly from above. Muhammad Ali, the breakaway ruler of Egypt, modernized the textile trade and imported

Western doctors and engineers. The Ottoman Empire's **Tanzimat reforms** involved an attempt to import industrial methods, but this effort depended on the determination of the regime, which gave up on it prematurely. Also, the Tanzimat program was bitterly opposed by Islamic traditionalists, who resisted modernization. A similar pattern unfolded in Qing China, where the **self-strengthening movement** of the late 1800s brought about only limited industrialization and also aroused the wrath of traditional-minded foes, who undermined its effectiveness.

The one place in the non-Western world to fully industrialize was Japan after the **Meiji Restoration** of 1868. Here, too, the impetus for change came from above, although with much greater success than in China or the Ottoman Empire. The Meiji emperor altered the economy beyond recognition. Young members of the upper class were sent to visit or study in Europe and America to learn engineering, economics, and military science. The regime created a ministry of industry in 1870 as well as state banks to finance Japan's industrial campaign. New railroads, steamships, ports, and canals were constructed. Huge corporations, called **zaibatsu**, sponsored largely by the state, carried out large-scale industrial efforts, but the government also encouraged private enterprise, spurring the growth of a middle class. At the same time, Japan's lower classes experienced many of the same travails that Europe's workers had gone through in the early 1800s. Sweatshop environments, low wages, and unsafe labor practices prevailed, especially in textile mills and coal mines. In one mine near Nagasaki, workers toiled in temperatures of up to 130 degrees Fahrenheit and were shot if they tried to escape. Unions of any type were forbidden.

In the twentieth century, industrialization was adopted on a much greater scale worldwide. This process continued throughout the century and is still ongoing.

Social Interactions and Organization, 1750–1900

17

IN THIS CHAPTER

→ **URBANIZATION AND CLASS DIVERSIFICATION IN THE WEST (MIDDLE AND INDUSTRIAL WORKING CLASSES)**

→ **NON-WESTERN CHANGES IN SOCIAL CLASSES (TANZIMAT LIBERALIZATION, MEIJI ABOLITION OF SAMURAI STATUS, BRITISH UNDERMINING OF INDIAN CASTE SYSTEM)**

→ **RACIALLY SEGREGATIONIST POLICIES IN WESTERN-CONTROLLED COLONIES (NATIVE ELITES)**

→ **INDENTURED SERVITUDE, COOLIE LABOR, AND SERFDOM**

→ **THE EAST AFRICAN AND ATLANTIC SLAVE TRADES**

→ **SEASONAL AND PERMANENT MIGRATION (EUROPE AND ASIA TO AMERICAS, CHINESE AND INDIANS IN INDIAN OCEAN BASIN)**

→ **MIGRATION AND ANTI-IMMIGRATION SENTIMENT**

→ **EARLY FEMINIST WRITERS**

→ **WESTERN SUFFRAGETTE MOVEMENTS**

The 1750–1900 era witnessed tremendous change in how societies worldwide were composed and organized. These changes resulted from a combination of political transformation and economic industrialization.

On the political front, revolutions strove to make governments more representative and more responsive to people's needs, and in a number of cases they succeeded. Industrialization and urbanization transformed class structures, and while systems of coerced and semicoerced labor did not disappear, the most extreme forms of slavery were gradually done away with. Whether they were based on class or ethnic/religious/gender identity, hierarchies and caste systems tended to break down or weaken, and if they remained in place, they heightened social discontent.

Migration took place on an epic scale during these years for both economic and political reasons. The best-known examples of migration are the mass movements from Europe and China to the Americas, but it occurred in other areas as well. The roles of women also changed in many societies, although most notably in Europe and the Americas.

THE TRANSFORMATION OF SOCIAL CLASSES

Class Diversification in Europe

One of the modern era's hallmark social developments is **class diversification**. This was most striking in Europe and North America. Here, Enlightenment philosophy and the Atlantic revolutions—followed in the 1800s by the gradual expansion of political representation—called into question the fairness and efficiency of old social hierarchies. At the same time, industrialization and **urbanization** exerted their own influence on social relations.

Consequently, in most of the Western world, traditional aristocracies, with their status based on land and hereditary noble status, saw their political power and social clout weaken (in certain cases, as in revolutionary France, noble privileges were formally abolished). Urbanization and increased agricultural efficiency meant that rural populations decreased. New social divisions appeared in the countryside: more land came to be owned by well-off farmers and homesteaders who were essentially middle class. Under them were poor agricultural laborers, renters, and sharecroppers who formed a rural working class of sorts.

If the proportion of rural folk among the lower classes shrank, this was more than made up for by the mammoth expansion of the **industrial working class** (or **proletariat**, in the term popularized by Karl Marx). This newer working class included factory workers, miners, and wage laborers of any kind, skilled or unskilled, in urban and industrial settings. It was this working class that shouldered the burden of early industrialization without enjoying many of its benefits until several decades into the process. It spent most of the century struggling for greater political representation, better working conditions, and the right to form unions.

An equally dramatic change involved the rising prosperity and prominence of the **middle class**. This class expanded and diversified, including in its ranks landowners, well-off farmers, master artisans and craftsmen, professionals such as doctors and lawyers, and many others. Its most influential members were the bankers, merchants, and factory owners who increasingly controlled the means of generating wealth and drew direct profits from industrial and commercial growth. (The term popularized by Marx for this segment of the middle class was the **bourgeoisie**.)

The middle class stood out for its industriousness, its commitment to education and literacy, and its generally liberal outlook, which favored the expansion of political rights and economic opportunity—at least for itself. When it came to the plight of the lower classes or to issues such as slavery and women's rights, middle-class liberalism sometimes sympathized with them but surprisingly often did not. The political role of Europe's and North America's middle classes—in leading revolutions and helping to widen political representation, whether through revolt or reform—proved immense during this era.

There were variations and exceptions to this pattern throughout Europe. Aristocratic privilege lessened at a faster or slower pace depending on the country. Societies remained more agrarian and had smaller middle classes the farther east and south they were, especially in Russia.

Social Classes in Non-Western Societies

In non-Western parts of the world, class diversification came more slowly.

In Latin America, middle-class ambitions did much to motivate the wars of independence of the early 1800s, and the frustrations of the lower classes, especially those of mixed, black, or indigenous background, turned those wars into mass movements. However, even though Spanish and Portuguese colonial hierarchies were overthrown and new constitutions written, inequality persisted. Indians, blacks, and those of mixed race still suffered prejudice. The economic gap between a small, wealthy landowning and business elite, on the one hand, and the lower-class masses, on the other, not only continued but grew wider.

In the Ottoman-dominated Middle East, the **Tanzimat reforms** of the mid-1800s ushered in a degree of liberalization and secularization and also emphasized greater religious toleration for non-Muslim **millets** (administrative units categorized by religion). Still, these changes were limited, and the reforming impulse died away after the 1870s.

Africa, the region least touched by industrialization, underwent little of this class diversification. As the continent fell steadily under colonial domination, social dynamics there were shaped more by foreign imperial powers, most of which enacted **racially segregationist policies** of varying severity.

The record in Asia was mixed when it came to social change. Social stratification in Qing China remained rigid, with heavy taxes levied on the impoverished masses—a prime reason for uprisings like the White Lotus Rebellion (1796–1804) and the **Taiping Rebellion** (1850–1864). Another social crisis for China during these years was widespread **opium addiction**, which one Qing official despairingly described as "a disease which will dry up our bones, a worm that gnaws at our hearts, and a ruin to our families and persons." As in Africa, South Asia experienced **racially segregationist policies** at the hands of Western imperial powers. In some cases, imperial rule brought about a measure of social modernization as colonizing powers like Britain in India and France in Indochina imported industrial practices and educated **native elites** according to Western norms. In India, the British authorities also strove to undermine the most abusive aspects of the **Hindu caste system** and to reduce **Hindu-Muslim religious strife**.

The non-Western part of the world that came closest to following the Western model of social diversification was Japan after the mid-1800s. Prior to the Meiji Restoration of 1868, the Tokugawa shogunate did its best to preserve its **samurai**-dominated system of **social stratification**, with low social mobility for the lower orders. However, partial modernization during the late 1700s and early 1800s placed the shogun and the samurai classes in a dilemma: although it added to Japan's prosperity, modernization undermined the power and land-based wealth of the aristocracy by encouraging urbanization and lending more influence to the **merchant class**—which technically occupied one of the lowest spots in the **Japanese caste system** despite its growing socioeconomic importance.

During the 1870s, the Meiji emperor took things even further with the **abolition of samurai status** and hereditary privileges (including the exclusive right to wear swords). The old prejudice against trade and artisanship died away, and an increasingly **westernized middle class** appeared in Meiji Japan. As in Europe, the farming population decreased relative to a new industrial working class. Also as in Europe, working-class conditions during Japan's early industrialization remained harsh. Commoners of all types received better, nationally funded educations and were now eligible to serve in the military, whereas during the Tokugawa years they had been forbidden to handle weapons under any circumstance.

LABOR AND MIGRATION

The prevailing trend with respect to labor was the steadily rising impact of industrialization on the ways people worked. In addition to factory work and other forms of **manufacturing**, forms of **resource extraction**, especially **mining**, were made increasingly important by industrialization. Also prominent was **cash-crop monoculture**.

In all these fields, even **free laborers** experienced oppressive conditions until the advent of **labor laws** and **trade unions**, which came into effect at different points during the 1800s and early 1900s, depending on the country in question. Harshest of all was the long persistence of **coerced** and **semicoerced forms of labor** in many parts of the globe, even as popular sentiment against them was growing.

Indentured Servitude and Serfdom

In Asia, an oppressive form of **indentured servitude** arose during the late 1700s and 1800s, popularly known as **coolie labor** (from the Hindi word *kuli*, later adopted in China as well). To pay off debts or because they were deceived into thinking that good jobs awaited them, large numbers of Asian workers—particularly from India and China—signed labor contracts that placed them under the near-complete control of their employers. This often involved being shipped abroad over great distances to the Pacific islands, to the Americas, or to the Caribbean, where they were exploited as cheap labor on plantations, in mines, and on construction projects. They planted and harvested sugar, collected guano and rubber in South America, and worked on some of America's and Canada's western railroads.

> **NOTE**
>
> **Other forms of coerced labor prevailed. In many non-Western parts of the world, corvée labor—the forcing of people to work on large-scale projects against their will—was still practiced. Egypt's Suez Canal was built largely in this fashion between 1859 and 1869. Prison labor was equally common. Russia sentenced serf rebels and political dissidents to hard labor in Siberia. Britain relied on transportation—banishment to underpopulated colonies like Australia—to get rid of unwanted criminals.**

In parts of Central and Eastern Europe, the system of **serfdom** lasted until about 1800. It was mostly done away with thanks to Enlightenment-era reform (as in Austria) or the influence of the French Revolution and Napoleon's conquests (as in Prussia and other German states). However, **Russian serfdom** not only continued but remained central to economic and social life. Even with the number of **serf uprisings** growing yearly during the early 1800s, noble landowners were reluctant to surrender what was a near-limitless supply of cheap labor. Finally, in the mid-1850s, Russia's defeat in the Crimean War made it clear that serfdom was holding back economic and industrial modernization—to the point of jeopardizing Russia's military security—and the system was discarded. Alexander II presided over the **emancipation of Russia's serfs** in 1861.

African Slave Trades

Ending the **East African** and **Atlantic slave trades** proved complicated and required long international efforts. The former, run largely by Arabs, flourished throughout most of the 1800s, fueled by a growing demand for East African cloves and sugar. By the 1870s and 1880s, just before the slave trade ended, over 40 percent of the population in the East African plantation zone was enslaved. Abolition here took decades and came about as a result of popular outrage in the West, military action on the part of Western governments, and missionary activity (a key figure was the Scottish explorer and humanitarian **David Livingstone**). A major step in the process was the closing of the great slave market in the center of **Zanzibar**.

Western nations benefited more directly from the **Atlantic slave trade**, and they took a long time to stop it. During the late 1700s and early 1800s, mining, **sugar cultivation**, and plantation agriculture in Latin America and the Caribbean depended heavily on African slave labor. Slaves were also used in the southern United States as domestic servants and agricultural laborers, especially for **cotton production**, made internationally important by the Industrial Revolution. Over 12 million Africans were victimized by the Atlantic slave trade between the mid-1400s and the late 1800s. Approximately 2 million were transported during the nineteenth century, with most going to Brazil, Cuba, and the Caribbean and a comparatively small number smuggled into the United States.

In other words, the Atlantic slave trade declined in scale during the 1800s but also lasted a regrettably long time. Its gradual demise resulted partly from practical economic considerations: as the century progressed, it became more difficult and more expensive to obtain slaves. The **Haitian Revolution** (1791–1804) set a monumental precedent for possible slave rebellions in the future. Equally important was the growing political, religious, and ethical revulsion for slavery that arose among Western populations in the wake of the Enlightenment and the Atlantic revolutions. In the 1790s and the first decade of the 1800s, countries like revolutionary France, the Netherlands, and Denmark made slavery illegal.

A major turning point came in 1807 when Britain's Parliament declared the slave trade illegal in all parts of the empire (slavery itself would not be banned there until 1833–1834). During the peace talks that settled the Napoleonic wars, Britain convinced nearly all of Europe and the Americas to outlaw the slave trade. Spain and Portugal refused, and Russia continued its system of serfdom. In the Americas, the longest holdouts were Cuba and Brazil, which did not end slavery until 1883 and 1888. The United States, split between the slaveholding South and the nonslave North, agreed to outlaw the international slave trade but not slavery itself. The painful debate and failed compromises over where and how to permit slavery in the United States—especially as the country expanded—formed the root cause of the U.S. Civil War (1861–1865). Only at the end of that conflict did slavery become illegal in the United States.

With slavery surviving so long in the Americas, the Atlantic slave trade, illegal though it was, continued into the second half of the century. The fact that a number of West African states, as described in Chapter 13, enriched themselves by cooperating with the Atlantic slave trade helped to keep it going. Foreign pressure against the slave trade included not just official legislation but also the efforts of **abolition movements**, especially in Britain and the northern United States. Canada served as a haven for slaves escaping from the southern United States. European and American **missionaries** campaigned against slavery, both in West and East Africa. Starting in the early 1800s, Britain dispatched the Royal Navy to blockade the West African shoreline, hunt down slave ships, and bombard the coastal forts of West African kingdoms that supported the slave trade. Less enthusiastically, France and the United States joined in these expeditions.

Both slave trades took an immense toll on Africa. Obvious effects included human suffering, population loss, and the disruption of traditional trade networks. Local collaboration with foreign slavers stirred up wars and long-term animosities among African peoples. The benefits of ending slavery are equally obvious—but there were unforeseen consequences as well, not all of them positive. One was a financial slump suffered by the African states that had profited from slavery. In turn, that economic weakness left African states more vulnerable to foreign takeover. Also, however well intentioned, antislavery interventions gave the British, French, and other Europeans a pretext for involving themselves in Africa's affairs and thinking of military action there as legitimate. This helped pave the way for conquering almost all of Africa near the end of the century.

Migration and Immigrant Communities

Another great trend of the era was a tremendous **migration of peoples**, both permanent and seasonal, that began during the 1800s and never truly ceased.

Excluding the involuntary relocation of slaves across the Atlantic or coolie laborers across the Pacific, nineteenth-century migration was mostly driven by a combination of overcrowding at home and economic opportunity abroad. In other instances, political persecution or violent unrest at home provided people with an incentive to emigrate. Another key reason for migration during this period was Western imperialism as colonial officials, settlers, and others seeking opportunity or adventure traveled far from home to new places. As they grew more commonplace and more affordable, industrial-era modes of transport, such as railroads and steamships, made migration more feasible than ever before.

NOTE

Three examples of mass emigration to North America illustrate the variety of factors that caused it. The Irish potato famine of the 1840s precipitated the movement of hundreds of thousands of Irish to the United States. In the Russian Empire, persecution of religious minorities—including anti-Jewish pogroms and the harassment of non-Orthodox Christians like Mennonites—led to a massive outmigration of Jews to the United States and elsewhere and of many Ukrainians to central Canada. In China, the economic ruin and violence caused by the Taiping Rebellion convinced large numbers of Chinese to move to North and South America, often as coolie laborers in mines, on plantations, and on railroads.

Most famously, huge numbers of Europeans and Asians relocated to the Americas during the 1800s. The United States' reputation as a land of freedom and economic opportunity drew an estimated 17 million immigrants between the 1830s and 1890s, and more continued to arrive in the 1900s. Canada, Argentina, and Chile also took in many immigrants from both Europe and Asia. Migration throughout Southeast Asia and the Indian Ocean basin was common as well, with Chinese merchants and laborers spreading throughout Malaysia and with large numbers of Indians traveling to East and South Africa because of commercial ties. Australia also received a number of immigrants from Asia.

In some cases, these migrations were permanent. In others, they were temporary or seasonal as migrants relocated for work and either returned home or sent wages back to their families. This sort of work tended to involve agriculture or resource extraction. Typically, it was men who migrated and women who assumed new burdens and leadership roles at home and in the family.

Among the diasporic communities to be aware of from this era are Asians in Australia, Japanese agricultural laborers throughout the Pacific (especially in Hawaii and on the Americas' western coasts), Chinese railway workers and guano harvesters in the Americas, Lebanese merchants in the Americas, Italians throughout North America and also Argentina, the Irish in North America, the Chinese diaspora throughout Southeast Asia, and the large presence of Indians in East Africa and South Africa and even as far away as the Caribbean.

Anti-immigration sentiment was common on both a popular and official level. It arose for several reasons, including ethnic or religious prejudice and the alarmist tendency to view new arrivals as potential economic competitors. Jews and nonwhites were rarely well received in their new societies, but neither were groups like the Irish or Italians. Countries hosting large numbers of immigrants typically imposed **quota systems**, limiting the quantity of people they would let in per year from a given country. Other regulations were common as well. In the United States, feverish racial fears about a rising "yellow peril," combined with concerns about jobs for white Americans, motivated the **Chinese Exclusion Act** of 1882. This suspended Chinese immigration for ten years and was then renewed into the 1900s. A similar logic inspired the **White Australia Policy**, which involved a number of laws, including the Immigration Restriction Act of 1901. These were intended to give every possible advantage to white immigrants from Britain as opposed to potential arrivals from China, the Pacific islands, and continental Europe, all seeking jobs in Australian mines or sugar plantations.

Anti-Immigration Sentiment during the 1800s and Early 1900s
On the left, a message that all too often confronted Irish immigrants in the United States after the 1840s, when they began arriving in large numbers due to the Irish potato famine. On the right, a poster unabashedly praising the White Australia Policy that discouraged non-British migration to the island in the late 1800s and early 1900s.

GENDER AND FAMILY ISSUES

Women's Rights Movements Emerge in Europe and North America

Although in most societies, the status of women remained secondary, the 1750–1900 period saw many changes in gender relations. In the West, a greater awareness of the unequal treatment of women was stimulated largely by the theories of Enlightenment philosophy as well as by the active role played by women in the American and French Revolutions.

In her 1792 treatise, *A Vindication of the Rights of Women*, English author **Mary Wollstonecraft** insisted that women, like men, possessed reason and were therefore entitled to equal rights. During the French Revolution, the playwright **Olympe de Gouges** argued in her "Declaration of the Rights of Woman and the Citizeness" that women should have the same rights granted to men by the Declaration of the Rights of Man and the Citizen. The government dismissed her proposal, and she died during the Reign of Terror.

During the late 1800s and early 1900s, women engaged in activities even more radical than the struggle for votes. The campaign for birth control and reproductive rights, which featured the American nurse Margaret Sanger, proved extremely difficult. Also, in Russia and other countries, where few chances for within-the-system political action existed, many female activists turned to the far left in order to advance feminist agendas.

Larger women's rights movements emerged in the 1830s in Europe and North America. They first focused on reforming laws to allow women to own property and file for divorce. This initial effort did not reap quick results as women did not gain full property rights in Britain until 1870, Germany until 1900, and France until 1907.

Soon female activists were seeking better access to higher education and jobs as well as equal pay. The first professions open to women, beyond domestic servitude, were teaching and nursing. Women also led the way in campaigning against slavery and in favor of aid for orphans and the poor.

By the mid-1800s, women began to seek political rights, most notably suffrage, or the right to vote. As a rule, European and North American **suffragette movements** were led by women of the middle and upper classes. The most vocal women's movement was Britain's, led by Emmeline Pankhurst. Major figures in the U.S. movement were Susan B. Anthony and Elizabeth Cady Stanton. Not only did American and Canadian women call for the right to vote at the **1848 Seneca Falls Convention**—which based its "Declaration of Sentiments" on the U.S. Declaration of Independence—they agitated for better working conditions for women and for child welfare and temperance. Almost no countries gave women the vote until late in World War I or afterward. Norway, Finland, Australia, New Zealand, and a handful of U.S. states were exceptions.

Marching Toward Women's Rights

On the left, Nikolai Yaroshenko's *Female Student* (1880) depicts the awakening of a feminist spirit in tsarist Russia, connecting it with the power of education. The "Women Are Persons" Monument on Ottawa's Parliament Hill, on the right, celebrates a court decision that carried the suffragette impulse to its logical conclusion. Although Canadian women had received federal voting rights in 1918 and could serve in many political offices, it was not decided until 1929 that they were "persons" legally able to serve in Canada's senate. Here suffragette and politician Nellie McClung displays the proclamation declaring them eligible to do so.

Women and Industrialization

The Industrial Revolution profoundly altered the conditions under which women and families worked.

Industrialization shifted the workplace away from the farm—where both men and women worked—to mines, factories, and other places away from the home. This created a **domestic sphere** separate from the workplace. In Europe and the United States, women of the lower classes were generally compelled to take up work, most frequently in textile factories, where women made up 50 percent of the workforce until 1870. These women bore the double burden of serving as their families' primary homemakers and caregivers.

A **cult of domesticity**, stressing that a woman's place was in the home and a man's in the workplace, dominated Western culture—especially among the middle and upper classes—during the mid-to-late 1800s. Certain occupations were open to women, such as child care (governesses), teaching, domestic household work (servants and maids), and nursing.

NOTE

After the mid-1800s, the number of working women in Europe and North America declined. Women of the middle and upper classes had rarely worked to begin with. As wages for industrial workers rose, making such jobs more desirable to men, and as new laws restricted the number of hours women and children could work, the number of lower-class working women fell.

Non-Western Developments

The move toward women's equality tended to be slower in non-Western societies.

In some places, the educational level of women rose, as did the extent of property rights. As in the West, women worked, especially in occupations such as agricultural labor, domestic service, and nursing. As non-Western parts of the world industrialized, lower-class women tended to enter the workplace, as in the industrial West. Also, the arrival of Western colonists often affected gender roles and family relations.

In the Middle East, one effect of the Tanzimat reforms was to give women greater access to education. Public schools were founded for them, and more women, though still a small number, began to enter public life in the late 1800s. Countering this trend were strict forms of Islamic traditionalism, including Wahhabism from Arabia, that opposed modernization in general. **Veiling** remained common.

As Africa came increasingly under colonial control, many families were broken up. Husbands worked in mines or on plantations or served in native military units, while wives stayed in villages to grow food and care for children. When Western employers and colonial officials gave out jobs and introduced new property laws, they tended to favor male heads of household. This left women with fewer economic opportunities and, in many ways, undercut matrilineal authority in those parts of Africa where it had prevailed.

In Qing China, Confucian traditionalism continued to place women in a secondary social position. **Foot binding** continued, although this was increasingly opposed by foreign missionaries as well as by the Taiping rebels of the mid-1800s. In Japan, the Meiji Restoration ended the Tokugawa regime's strict social stratification, but even the 1890 Constitution made little room for the rights of women, who remained largely confined to a secondary status. Industrialization in Japan created jobs for lower-class women, but these were low-paying, low-prestige positions. The **Hindu caste system**, complete with its traditional patriarchalism, remained in place in South Asia, although in British India, colonial authorities combatted many of its excesses, including the **sati ritual**. Islam also affected the place of women in South Asia.

Most Latin American nations based their legal systems on the **Napoleonic civil code**, which concerned itself even less with women's rights than laws in North America. Also, industrialization progressed more slowly in Latin America, so nonagricultural working opportunities were limited. Still, over time, countries such as Argentina, Uruguay, and Chile made it possible for women to gain educations; in Chile, they could earn degrees in high-status professions such as law and medicine.

Humans and the Environment, 1750–1900

18

Arguably, the period 1750–1900 can be described as the era when human beings consistently began to influence their environment more than they were influenced by it. There is no doubting the fact that industrialization and technological advancement exponentially increased human impact on the environment. This trend continued into the twentieth century and has shown no signs of stopping in the twenty-first.

In a macroscopic development that affected agriculture, patterns of human settlement, and the ability to explore and exploit the polar regions, the **Little Ice Age**, which had persisted since around 1500 (with steady cooling even before that), finally ended during the mid-1800s.

INDUSTRIALIZATION AND THE ENVIRONMENT

Industrialization provided societies not just with new abilities to affect the environment but with new incentives to do so.

Population growth and **urbanization**, each going hand in hand with industrialization, placed greater strains on local ecosystems. Without proper planning, the higher concentration of human beings in a given area led to greater resource consumption and worsening environmental stress. Mass **deforestation** arose as a growing problem in many parts of the world during this era. Not only were forests cleared to make room for farms, factories, and settlements, but timber became a much-needed commodity for fuel, construction, and the manufacture of paper.

Technology hugely multiplied the **earth-shaping capacity** of industrialized societies, allowing them to leave deeper and more noticeable marks on the environment. **Road networks** and **railroads** quickly expanded over great distances. New and growing cities, along with the ever-larger buildings that appeared in them—such as factories and skyscrapers—spread across more of the landscape. **Large-scale agricultural enterprises**, in the form of plantations and other sizable farming units, encouraged major manipulations of the environment. Perhaps the most visible earth-shaping endeavors of this era involved the construction of dams and **canals** by industrializing nations that wished to facilitate shipping and transport. Most famous during the 1800s were the **Erie Canal** (1825) in the United States and the strategically and economically vital **Suez Canal** (1869) in Egypt, which linked the Mediterranean with the Indian Ocean basin via the Red Sea. In 1914, the **Panama Canal**, a project pursued by several nations since the late 1800s, was completed by the United States and revolutionized global shipping by connecting the Atlantic and Pacific Oceans.

Resource extraction dramatically increased during the industrial era, severely depleting resources and causing higher levels of environmental damage. **Cash-crop monoculture** intensified, both in colonies governed by Western nations and in countries where Western nations and corporations invested heavily. As textile industries expanded during the era, so too did the growing and harvesting of **cotton** in the U.S. South, Egypt, Central Asia, and India. Other monocultural crops included **palm oil** (West Africa), **silk** (China), **coffee** (Latin America, Africa, South Asia), **tea** (China and India), **fruit** (Africa and Latin America), and **rubber** (extracted from trees in Africa, Southeast Asia, and South America until blight ended the industry there). Aside from its environmentally harmful nature, cash-crop and plantation monoculture lent itself to **coerced** and **semicoerced labor practices**, including the worst forms of **slavery**.

Another environmental impact was the escalation of **mining** and **fossil-fuel extraction**. Industrializing nations developed a voracious appetite for **coal** and **iron**, and a host of other metals became crucial as well. **Gold** and **diamonds** were precious for luxury purposes but also because of their industrial uses. They were avidly sought wherever possible, from Africa to Arctic regions like the Yukon, Alaska, and northeastern Siberia. Already in the late 1800s and more so after 1900, the quest for **petroleum** began, both as a manufacturing lubricant and as a source of energy—with deposits discovered initially in the Americas, in the Middle East, and also in parts of Southeast Asia.

Two forms of environmental damage made themselves increasingly obvious. One was the **pollution** of air and water, which reached unprecedented levels. Unlike today, there were few laws to combat pollution, and scientists have traced the first stages of **human-caused climate change**, or global warming, to the carbon-based fossil-fuel emissions of the early industrial era. Second was the **endangerment** or **extinction of species** as overhunting and the destruction of habitats became more common. The population of fur-bearing creatures like sables, otters, and fur seals dwindled dangerously, as did North America's once-massive herds of bison. Oil from whales and seals served as lamp fuel and as lubricants for industrial production until the shift to petroleum. These mammals hovered perilously close to extinction, as did walruses hunted for ivory. Notorious extinctions of the era included the great auk, the Carolina parakeet, the passenger pigeon, and in the North Pacific, the Steller's sea cow.

NOTE

One of the earliest examples of modern extinction, is that of the dodo, whose very name is a synonym of the process. Indigenous to the island of Mauritius (east of Madagascar in the Indian Ocean), the dodo came to the notice of Dutch travelers in the late 1500s. It took only till the mid-1600s for foreign overhunting to drive the bird to extinction. This grimly foreshadowed the greater waves of human-caused species depletion to come in the 1800s and beyond.

As noted in earlier chapters, imperialism and industrialization both spurred extraordinarily large waves of **migration**, both permanent and seasonal. Aside from redistributing human populations over great distances on the order of millions, these migrations had the long-term environmental effect of transferring large numbers of people to regions that had previously been sparsely populated. In addition, new arrivals typically brought with them industrial-era economic practices that burdened local ecosystems far more heavily than the preindustrial modes of production pursued by indigenous peoples.

 NOTE

Migrants and colonists also brought new species from far away. Consider the importation of sheep to Australia, where the animals now vastly outnumber the humans living there. Strawberries and apples, also alien to Australia before the 1700s, regularly grow there today.

DISEASE IN THE MODERN ERA

For the first time in history, a truly scientific understanding of diseases—and how to combat them—emerged. Experiments with **vaccination** during the late 1700s proved effective in the treatment and prevention of smallpox, one of the deadliest killers in medical history. The practice spread during the 1800s and 1900s, slowly but eventually leading to the complete eradication of many diseases. Also helpful was a proper understanding of **germ theory** and **medical sterilization**, which was achieved in Europe and North America during the mid-to-late 1800s. Not just medical procedure profited; thanks to scientists like Louis Pasteur, so did the handling and processing of food. Overall, this understanding led to a new level of human mastery over the environment and contributed directly to **population growth**.

NOTE

Deaths of women during childbirth decreased where modern medical knowledge was available, as did infant mortality.

Also by the mid-1800s, Europeans and Americans grew adept at developing cures (or at least symptom-relieving treatments) for **tropical diseases** like **malaria**, yellow fever, and sleeping sickness. Medical innovations of this sort played a significant role in enabling the exploration and colonization of previously difficult-to-access parts of Africa and Asia.

On the other hand, disease was not yet entirely conquered. Certain illnesses proved resistant to vaccines or adaptable to them. Also, where treatment was lacking or too expensive to afford, diseases continued to kill large numbers of people. Paradoxically, while industrial-era science played a role in the nineteenth century's medical breakthroughs, industrial-era living conditions—which included overcrowding, air pollution, and unprotected water supplies—worsened the severity of certain diseases. Smallpox, where untreated, remained deadly, but the most infamous of the industrial-era maladies were **cholera** and **tuberculosis**.

UNIT 4

1900 to the Present

Unit 4: Short Cut

GENERAL REMARKS

The twentieth century ranks as one of the most tumultuous eras ever. It was a time of paradox and contradiction, leading the eminent historian Eric Hobsbawm to label it the "age of extremes." Democratic forms of government were adopted more widely than ever before (and women gained the vote in large parts of the world), but history's most oppressive dictatorships appeared as well. The 1900s were a time of unprecedented prosperity but also of striking socioeconomic polarity as the gap between rich and poor widened. There were tremendous cultural and scientific advancements but also the worst wars—including the modern form of violence known as **genocide**—and the greatest arms buildups in human history.

The first half of the century was dominated by two mammoth military conflicts: **World War I** and **World War II**, "total" wars characterized by improved military technology and new tactics, comprehensive mobilization of resources, and immense devastation. World War I destroyed several of the nineteenth century's great empires and sapped Europe's strength. World War II, the bloodiest conflict humanity has ever experienced—especially in combination with the **Holocaust**—dislodged Europe completely from its position of global mastery.

The interwar years were marked by economic crises, culminating in the **Great Depression**, which emanated outward from the United States. This period also saw the rise of powerful dictatorships, such as Soviet Russia, Fascist Italy, and Nazi Germany, and it appeared for a time that **totalitarianism**, not democracy, might be the wave of the future. Starting with the establishment of the Soviet state, **communism** became an influential—although, in the end, seemingly unworkable—alternative to **capitalism**.

During the century's second half, sweeping trends affected the entire world. One, following the collapse of Europe's global dominance, was **decolonization**. From the 1940s through the 1970s, parts of Africa, Asia, and the Pacific that had been under European (and U.S.) imperial control became free. This wave of **national liberation** created dozens of new nations. In some cases, decolonization proceeded peacefully. In others, it was attained by force or disintegrated into political chaos.

Another effect of World War II was a new geopolitical alignment, the **Cold War**. In the previous century and a half, world affairs had been determined by the workings of the European balance of power, but political and economic might was now concentrated in the hands of two evenly matched **superpowers**: the United States and the Soviet Union. This bipolar equilibrium persisted for four and a half decades, dividing most of the globe into two hostile camps—although the rise of China as a communist power opposed to the USSR and the attempt of certain nations to form a **nonaligned movement** provided diplomatic alternatives.

The twentieth century was an era of rapid modernization. Societies already industrialized when the 1900s began—North America, Europe, and Japan—became even more adept at scientific and technological innovation and shifted toward **postindustrial** (or **service**) economies during the post–World War II era. Such societies are generally referred to as belonging to the **developed world**. A number of other countries, especially in Asia, have similarly modernized. The **developing** or **nondeveloped world** (or in Cold War terms, the **Third World**) includes most other regions, which remain in a less advanced stage of economic and technological progress. In global terms, a wide economic gap—the **north-south split**—opened between richer societies above the equator and poorer ones below it.

POSTMODERN ERA

With respect to historical labels, it is common to speak of the modern period (ca. 1800–1945) as ending after World War II, at least in the developed West. The years following are generally referred to by historians as the contemporary or postmodern era and are characterized by postindustrial and global forms of economic organization, multiculturalism, the blurring of national lines, and extreme individualism. To what degree this label fits less developed societies in Africa, Asia, and elsewhere is a matter of debate.

The 1980s and 1990s saw the collapse of communism in Europe and the USSR and, with that, the end of the Cold War. The same decades witnessed a wave of democratization in many parts of the world as well as the increased **globalization** of the world economy. The greater ease with which ethnicities and traditions mix has stimulated a high degree of **multiculturalism**, and mass communications and transport have, metaphorically speaking, eliminated geographical distance, making the world a much more connected place. This is especially due to the proliferation of computer technology, which has caused an **information** (or **digital**) **revolution**. Entities other than **nation-states**—such as **multinational corporations**, **nongovernmental organizations**, and **regional trade alliances**—have had an increasingly large impact on world affairs.

The world's general direction in the twenty-first century remains unclear. Many trends, such as the end of the nuclear arms race, economic globalization, and the spread of popular culture, mass communications, and computer technology, seem to be drawing the world closer together. Other developments threaten to pull the world further apart, including ethnic violence and genocide, extreme forms of **nationalism**, **religious fundamentalism**, proliferation of **weapons of mass destruction**, potential tensions between China and the West, and ongoing tensions between the West and Islamic states. The same is true of **terrorism**, most notably in the aftermath of the al-Qaeda attacks of September 11, 2001. On the planetary level, all modern societies, developed or undeveloped, have had an immensely greater impact on the environment. The most noticeable and most dangerous effect today is **climate change**, popularly known as global warming.

BROAD TRENDS

Governance, 1900 to the Present	
Europe	World War I (1914–1918, trench warfare) and Paris Peace Conference (1919, Treaty of Versailles) Russia's October Revolution (1917, Vladimir Lenin) weakness of interwar democracies (effects of Great Depression) vs. rise of totalitarian dictatorships (Soviet Russia, Fascist Italy, Nazi Germany) civilian involvement in war (Guernica, Battle of Britain, strategic bombing and Dresden) collective security vs. appeasement in 1930s diplomacy (Munich Agreement) World War II (1939–1945, blitzkrieg, aerial warfare) genocide (Holocaust, ethnic cleansing in Yugoslav wars) Cold War rivalry (arms race and MAD, containment and domino principle, détente, fall of Berlin Wall) "Iron Curtain" division of Europe (NATO vs. Warsaw Pact, Berlin Wall) social welfare systems and economic union in Western Europe (EU) East European dissidents (Solidarity) and Gorbachev's perestroika in USSR collapse of European communism (1989–1991) and postcommunist "shock therapy" (1990s)
Middle East	World War I (1914–1918, Gallipoli) genocide (Armenians in Ottoman Empire) Paris Peace Conference and the mandate system interwar modernization under Mustafa Kemal Ataturk and Reza Shah Pahlavi Arab-Israeli conflict (Balfour Declaration, partition of Palestine, Arab-Israeli wars, PLO and Hamas, Camp David and Oslo accords, First and Second Intifadas) OPEC and the geopolitical importance of Middle Eastern oil Gamal Nasser (pan-Arabism) and nationalization of Suez Canal Iranian Revolution (1979, Shah of Iran vs. Ayatollah Khomeini) Iran-Iraq War and Gulf War (Desert Storm) al-Qaeda attacks of 9/11/2001 and U.S.-led "war on terror" (Iraq, Afghanistan) Arab Spring + Syrian civil war + ISIS
Africa	civilian involvement in war (Italian terror bombing of Ethiopia, child soldiers, Boko Haram abductions) negotiated vs. violent decolonization in Africa (Ghana and French West Africa vs. Algeria, Congo, and Biafra) Kwame Nkrumah and pan-Africanism (Organization of African Unity) authoritarianism in Africa (Joseph Mobutu, Idi Amin, Muammar Gaddafi) apartheid in South Africa (African National Congress, Nelson Mandela) genocide (Rwanda, Darfur) impact of HIV/AIDS on society and politics

Governance, 1900 to the Present	
East (and Central) Asia	Chinese Revolution (1911–1912, Sun Yat-sen, Chiang Kai-shek, and KMT) Japanese invasion of China (1931+) and World War II (1939–1945, East Asian Co-Prosperity Sphere) civilian involvement in war (Nanjing, Tokyo firebombing, Hiroshima) Japan's economic resurgence and Asia's "little tigers" Mao Tse-tung and People's Republic of China (1949+, Great Leap Forward, Cultural Revolution) Korean War (1950–1953) Deng Xiaoping (economic reform in China, Tiananmen Square protests) economic growth and potential superpower status for Communist China nuclear weapons in North Korea
South (and Southeast) Asia and Oceania	national liberation in India (Indian National Congress, Mohandas Gandhi and nonviolence) World War II (1939–1945, East Asian Co-Prosperity Sphere) Indochina and Vietnam wars (1945–1975, Ho Chi Minh) Indian and Pakistani independence (1947, Jawaharlal Nehru) Indonesian war of independence (1945–1949, Sukarno) genocide (Khmer Rouge in Cambodia) Indo-Pakistani rivalry and nuclear weapons
Americas	U.S. sphere of influence in Latin America Mexican Revolution (1910–1920, PRI) Cold War rivalry (arms race and MAD, containment and domino principle, détente, fall of Berlin Wall) authoritarianism in Latin America (Juan Perón, Augusto Pinochet, death squads) genocide (Mayans in Guatemala) Cuban Revolution (1959, Fidel Castro, Bay of Pigs, Cuban Missile Crisis) Nicaraguan Revolution (1979, Sandinistas vs. Contras)
Global and Interregional	international organizations (League of Nations, United Nations, GATT/WTO, International Criminal Court) total wars (civilian casualties, economic mobilization, conscription, restrictions on civil liberties) ethnic violence and genocide World War I and World War II global impact of Cold War (proxy wars and brushfire conflicts) decolonization and national liberation rise of terrorism (Black Hand, PLO, IRA, FLQ, Weather Underground, Hamas, al-Qaeda, ISIS) asymmetrical warfare (WMDs and RMA vs. low-intensity and guerrilla wars) nuclear proliferation ("nuclear club" vs. Israel, India, Pakistan, North Korea, Iran)

Governance

- During the first half of the 1900s, two world wars reshaped global affairs. Europe's position of world dominance was weakened by World War I, and the United States became the world's richest and most powerful nation. World War II completed the dismantling of Europe's global dominance. Both were total wars that required near-complete mobilization of human and economic resources.

- For four and a half decades after World War II, most of the world was divided into hostile camps led by two superpowers, the United States and the USSR, in a geopolitical struggle known as the Cold War. This involved a nuclear arms race, the largest weapons buildup in world history, and the creation of huge military-industrial complexes.

- From the 1940s through the 1970s, a mass wave of decolonization deprived the European powers of their empires. Sometimes through peaceful negotiation, sometimes through violent separation, former colonies in Asia, Africa, and the Pacific became free. Dozens of new nations were formed.

- Countries that were neither Western nor Soviet bloc came to be seen as belonging to the so-called Third World. These nations, many recently decolonized and most relatively backward in terms of economic and technological development, experimented with a variety of political and economic systems. During the Cold War, some sided with the United States or the USSR, while others attempted to remain neutral or even to join together in a nonaligned movement. Some were attracted to Communist China, whose emerging rivalry with the USSR complicated the bipolarity of the Cold War.

- During the late 1980s and 1990s, communism in Eastern Europe and the USSR collapsed, ending the Cold War. The only remaining superpower since has been the United States, with China—which remained communist—as a rising power.

- The terrorist attacks of September 11, 2001, by al-Qaeda began a new global struggle, the U.S.-led war on terror. This sharpened tensions between the West and the Islamic world and sparked wars in Iraq and Afghanistan. Terrorism in general (carried out by groups such as the ETA, the IRA, the PLO, Hamas, and others) played a significant role in international politics in the 1900s and continues to do so in the 2000s.

- New weapons and tactics were constantly developed. Wars became increasingly destructive and caused greater numbers of casualties, especially among civilian populations. They also created larger numbers of displaced persons and refugees.

- Warfare became increasingly connected with racial hatred and campaigns of ethnic violence such as the Holocaust. The term "genocide" was coined during World War II to describe such crises. Conversely and largely because of this trend, a greater concern for human rights and wider recognition of the need to safeguard them arose.

- By the 1990s and early 2000s, the gap between high-tech and low-level warfare had grown wider than ever before. The most advanced armed forces possess weapons of mass destruction, precision-guided ("smart") weapons, and—thanks to what strategists call the revolution in military affairs—digitally integrated systems. Much of the rest of the world fights low-intensity or guerrilla wars, using only small arms and hand-to-hand weapons.

- Domestically, the level of popular representation in national governments grew in many countries. Women gained the vote in most Western nations in the early twentieth century and later elsewhere.

- Between the world wars, democracies tended to be politically weak and economically depressed. The interwar states that seemed to enjoy the greatest political momentum were dictatorships, including totalitarian regimes which aimed to control as many aspects of their subjects' lives as possible.

- After World War II, the primary form of political and economic organization in the West (Canada, the United States, and Western Europe) was the democratic state with a capitalist system, although capitalism was modified to varying degrees by social welfare systems.

- A number of regimes, led by the Soviet Union and China, adopted communist economic systems. Their political systems tended to be dictatorial.
- Military and authoritarian dictatorships proliferated throughout the Third World during the Cold War, some of them pro-Soviet, some of them pro-U.S., and some of them neutral. Many have democratized during the 1990s and early 2000s, although with varying degrees of success.
- Entities other than nation-states, including regional trade organizations (such as the European Union and NAFTA), nongovernmental organizations (such as Amnesty International and the Red Cross), and multinational corporations (such as Coca-Cola, Shell Oil, and McDonald's), began to exert greater influence over world affairs.
- Unofficial actors, including antiwar protesters, civil-rights and freedom activists, and proponents of nonviolent resistance (most famously Mohandas Gandhi and Martin Luther King Jr.), affected political events on numerous occasions.

Cultural Developments and Interactions, 1900 to the Present	
Europe	uncertainty and anxiety in high culture (impact of world wars, Freudian thought) mass media (high culture, entertainment, propaganda) digitization and social media sports professionalized and politicized existentialism synthetic spirituality (new age, Hare Krishna)
Middle East	adoption and adaptation of Western high culture mass media (high culture, entertainment, propaganda) digitization and social media sports professionalized and politicized Americanization and Westernization of global culture ("coca-colonization") religious fundamentalism
Africa	adoption and adaptation of Western high culture mass media (high culture, entertainment, propaganda) digitization and social media sports professionalized and politicized Americanization and Westernization of global culture ("coca-colonization")
East (and Central) Asia	adoption and adaptation of Western high culture mass media (high culture, entertainment, propaganda) digitization and social media sports professionalized and politicized Americanization and Westernization of global culture ("coca-colonization") synthetic spirituality (Falun Gong)
South (and Southeast) Asia and Oceania	adoption and adaptation of Western high culture mass media (high culture, entertainment, propaganda) digitization and social media sports professionalized and politicized Americanization and Westernization of global culture ("coca-colonization") religious fundamentalism

Cultural Developments and Interactions, 1900 to the Present	
Americas	uncertainty and anxiety in high culture (impact of world wars, Freudian thought) mass media (high culture, entertainment, propaganda) digitization and social media sports professionalized and politicized existentialism Americanization and Westernization of Latin American culture ("coca-colonization") synthetic spirituality (new age, Hare Krishna) religious fundamentalism liberation theology
Global and Interregional	modernity vs. postmodernity multiculturalism (Marshall McLuhan's "global village," Bollywood, manga) impact of global conflict on mass culture (James Bond, video games) social media sports professionalized and politicized (modern Olympics)

Cultural Developments and Interactions

- Mass media and mass communications technology transformed the cultural sphere. Cinema, radio, television, and other electronic media have been used to create high art.
- Mass media have also been used to create popular (or mass) culture: music, literature, and other forms aimed at a popular audience for purposes of entertainment.
- Governments increasingly used mass media to create propaganda, or art with political messages.
- The high art of the twentieth century was characterized by bold experimentation and the distortion, even abandonment, or traditional norms and conventions.
- During the first two-thirds of the 1900s, largely because of Europe's decline, Freudian thought, and the two world wars, Western high art was marked by uncertainty and pessimism—in contrast to the exuberance and energy of popular, or mass, culture.
- After World War II, Western culture began to move beyond the "modern" period into a newer "postmodern" era.
- Global cultures have mixed, interacted, and blended to an unprecedented degree. The celebration and acknowledgment of different traditions and styles is generally referred to as multiculturalism.
- Computer digitization and social media have shaped the production of art and culture worldwide.
- New forms of spirituality, many of them synthetically combining elements of old religions with new beliefs, appeared. Whether old or new, religious beliefs were in many cases used to advance political agendas. Religious fundamentalism has proved influential in many places throughout this period.

Technology and Innovation, 1900 to the Present	
Europe	fastest and most thorough progress in new scientific fields
Middle East	ongoing progress in new scientific fields
Africa	ongoing progress in new scientific fields
East (and Central) Asia	fast and thorough progress in new scientific fields (mainly in postwar period)
South (and Southeast) Asia and Oceania	ongoing progress in new scientific fields (fast and thorough in certain places)
Americas	progress in new scientific fields (fastest and most thorough in North America)
Global and Interregional	varying degrees of progress in new scientific fields theoretical physics (relativity and quantum theory) nuclear power + renewable energy (wind, solar, geothermal) agricultural science and technology (Green Revolution) aviation + rocketry and space science new weaponry medical advances + genetic science (discovery of DNA) consumer electronics + mass media + social media computers and the digital (information) revolution

Technology and Innovation

- Scientific and technological advancement proceeded on a breathtaking scale, accelerating even beyond the rapid pace set during the industrial era of the 1800s.
- Breakthroughs in the field of physics included the theory of relativity and quantum theory, both of which disrupted Newtonian physics and probed questions on the astronomical and subatomic levels.
- New sources of power became available, including nuclear energy, improved wind power, solar energy, and geothermal energy.
- Innovations in agricultural science and technology boosted food production and, in parts of Latin America and Asia, led to a so-called Green Revolution between the 1940s and 1970s.
- Advancements in military technology, spurred on by both world wars and the subsequent Cold War, vastly increased the destructive capabilities of military forces worldwide.
- New discoveries and inventions were pioneered in the fields of aviation, rocketry, and space science.
- Medical, pharmaceutical, and biotechnological advances—including the discovery of DNA—have extended human life expectancy and created the potential for genetic engineering.
- Consumer electronics and mass media have become central to modern life worldwide.
- Since the 1990s, the proliferation of personal computer technology—combined with the rise of the Internet, the World Wide Web, and social media—has led to a digital revolution in how modern societies work, communicate, and process information.

Economic Systems, 1900 to the Present	
Europe	impact of Great Depression (low exports, mass unemployment) economic intervention: Soviet nationalization (five-year plans) + state capitalism (syndicalism) in fascist nations + democracies' relief and welfare programs (Keynesian theory) Bretton Woods system (World Bank, IMF, GATT) Marshall Plan vs. Soviet economic zone in Eastern Europe economic union in Western Europe (European Coal and Steel, European Economic Community, European Union) 1970s economic crisis (gold standard, oil embargo, stagflation) 1980s free-market reform and economic liberalization (Margaret Thatcher and theories of Milton Friedman; Mikhail Gorbachev and perestroika) globalization in 1990s and 2000s G7/G8 the EU and the euro ("eurozone") 2007 economic crisis + 2016 Brexit vote
Middle East	Bretton Woods system (World Bank, IMF, GATT) state intervention: Nasser's nationalization of the Suez Canal OPEC 1970s economic crisis (gold standard, oil embargo, stagflation) globalization in 1990s and 2000s north-south split 2007 economic crisis and aftereffects
Africa	Bretton Woods system (World Bank, IMF, GATT) 1970s economic crisis (gold standard, oil embargo, stagflation) globalization in 1990s and 2000s African Free Trade Zone north-south split 2007 economic crisis and aftereffects
East (and Central) Asia	economic intervention: state capitalism (zaibatsu) in imperial Japan impact of Great Depression (low exports, mass unemployment) Bretton Woods system (World Bank, IMF, GATT) + Asia's economic "tigers" 1970s economic crisis (gold standard, oil embargo, stagflation) G7/G8 (Japan) economic intervention: Mao's Great Leap Forward 1980s free-market reform and economic liberalization (Deng Xiaoping's limited capitalism in China) Asia-Pacific Economic Cooperation group globalization in 1990s and 2000s some nations afflicted by north-south split 2007 economic crisis and aftereffects
South (and Southeast) Asia and Oceania	Bretton Woods system (World Bank, IMF, GATT) 1970s economic crisis (gold standard, oil embargo, stagflation) globalization in 1990s and 2000s north-south split 2007 economic crisis and aftereffects

Economic Systems, 1900 to the Present	
Americas	U.S. origins of Great Depression (Smoot-Hawley Tariff Act) economic intervention: New Deal (Keynesian theory) + Cárdenas's nationalization of Mexico's oil industry impact of Great Depression on Latin America (low exports, mass unemployment) Bretton Woods system (World Bank, IMF, GATT) 1970s economic crisis (gold standard, oil embargo, stagflation) G7/G8 1980s free-market reform and economic liberalization (Ronald Reagan, Augusto Pinochet, and theories of Milton Friedman) globalization in 1990s and 2000s NAFTA + Mercosur 2007 economic crisis and aftereffects
Global and Interregional	partial or widespread industrialization of nondeveloped and developing world dominance of postindustrial and service economies in developed world observance of Bretton Woods system by majority of noncommunist world growing importance of multinational corporations rise of regional economic associations and free-trade zones transition from GATT to WTO

Economic Systems

- During the first half of the 1900s, most of Europe, Canada, and the United States fully industrialized. Certain other parts of the world achieved significant degrees of modernization and industrialization, including Japan, parts of Latin America, and China.
- During the 1930s, the Great Depression, emanating from the United States, negatively affected the economies of most of Europe and Latin America as well as Asia and Africa.
- Fascist and authoritarian regimes typically relied on state-directed forms of capitalism to regulate their economies with varying degrees of heavy-handedness.
- A number of countries experimented with communist economies: the Soviet Union, some Eastern Europe nations, China, North Korea, Cuba, Vietnam, and others.
- After World War II, the primary form of political and economic organization in North America and Western Europe was the democratic state with a capitalist system, although capitalism was modified to varying degrees by social welfare systems. During the Cold War, a wide split separated these economic systems from those of the communist blocs led by the Soviet Union and China.
- A different split emerged between the developed world, whose prosperity steadily grew (with some regressions, as during the 1970s), and the nondeveloped or developing world (or Third World), which lagged behind. Because so many nondeveloped and developing nations are located near or south of the equator, this disparity is sometimes referred to as the north-south split.
- Also after World War II, an elaborate system of international economic organizations appeared, influential mainly in the West and in the Third World, including the General Agreement on Trade and Tariffs (GATT), the World Bank, and the International Monetary Fund (IMF).

- After the 1950s and 1960s, Western economies began to move from industrial production to postindustrial production, based less on manufacturing and more on service, high-tech fields, and computers. This trend continues.
- During the 1970s, a general economic crisis, characterized by oil shortages, recession, and unemployment, struck the capitalist West. A general rise in prosperity—associated with an emphasis on free-market economics but not necessarily equitably distributed throughout society—took place in Western economies during the 1980s and 1990s. The same was true in China. The Soviet bloc experienced a severe economic downturn.
- The 1980s and 1990s were an era of greater economic globalization as international trade, economic regionalization (as typified by NAFTA and the European Union), and the clout of multinational corporations became increasingly important. This trend continues.
- A worldwide financial crisis, arguably the worst since the Great Depression, struck in 2007. Its effects still linger.

Social Interactions and Organization, 1900 to the Present	
Europe	features of Western and developed societies (transition to postindustrial and service-oriented lifestyles) rise of BRIC nations social activism: 1968 global protests + Solidarity and Eastern European anticommunist protests ethnic violence and anti-immigration sentiment (anti-Semitism and the Holocaust, persecution of Roma, former Yugoslavia, animosity toward "guest workers" and Muslim refugees) migration from former colonies and spheres of influence (India, Pakistan, Caribbean, Indonesia, Africa) extension of vote to women (near total) feminism and significant progress toward gender equality (Simone de Beauvoir) emerging gay and lesbian rights
Middle East	partial transition to industrial or postindustrial lifestyles ethnic violence and anti-immigration sentiment (Turkish massacre of Armenians, Arab-Israeli conflict) extension of vote to women (limited to partial) limitations on gender equality
Africa	partial transition to industrial or postindustrial lifestyles social activism: antiapartheid movement in South Africa ethnic violence and anti-immigration sentiment (Rwanda, Darfur) extension of vote to women (partial) limitations on gender equality
East (and Central) Asia	partial transition to postindustrial and service-oriented lifestyles rise of BRIC nations social activism: Tiananmen Square protests extension of vote to women (widespread) many limitations to gender equality removed

Social Interactions and Organization, 1900 to the Present	
South (and Southeast) Asia and Oceania	partial transition to postindustrial and service-oriented lifestyles rise of BRIC nations ethnic violence and anti-immigration sentiment (Indo-Pakistani violence) Indian caste system weakened end of White Australia policy social activism: self-immolation of Thich Quang Duc extension of vote to women (widespread) some limitations on gender equality
Americas	features of Western and developed societies (transition to postindustrial and service-oriented lifestyles; full in North America, partial in Latin America) rise of BRIC nations social activism: Jim Crow laws vs. civil rights movement in United States + 1968 global protests ethnic violence and anti-immigration sentiment (Mayans in Guatemala, U.S. "melting pot" ideal vs. nativist impulses) migration from former colonies and spheres of influence (Puerto Rico, Philippines) extension of vote to women (near total) feminism and significant progress toward gender equality (Gloria Steinem, Betty Friedan, NOW) emerging gay and lesbian rights
Global and Interregional	rapid population growth social equality vs. hierarchy urbanization and suburbanization undeveloped vs. industrial vs. postindustrial lifestyles (north-south split) growing importance of social activism (national liberation, civil rights and racial equality, opposition to war, 1968 global protests, feminism) ethnic violence and anti-immigration sentiment extension of vote to women (widespread) uneven progress toward gender equality

Social Interactions and Organization

- In the West, labor unions grew in power during the first half of the century. During the 1920s and especially during the Great Depression of the 1930s, many capitalist societies adopted social welfare policies (the British "dole," the U.S. New Deal, Scandinavia's "third way") to provide a social safety net.
- The middle class became more dominant and numerous in developed societies by World War II, and this trend deepened during the postwar era. In communist societies, class divisions were minimized, at least in theory. In the developing world, class divisions between the elite and the rest of society were very wide.
- Gender equality made great strides during the twentieth century in the developed world. Most women there received the right to vote after World War I. Job opportunities increased, partly due to the world wars, especially World War II.

- The postwar development of reliable contraception, especially birth-control pills, gave women unprecedented control over pregnancy and sexuality. The gradual legalization of abortion, while controversial, did the same.
- During the 1960s and 1970s, a powerful feminist movement agitating for women's liberation and equal rights swept Canada, the United States, and most of Europe. Since then, women's movements have sought to achieve more than simple legal equality and the right to vote. Their goals have been full cultural and economic equality and deeper changes in social norms and behaviors.
- Progress toward equal treatment of women has been uneven in other parts of the world.
- Migration has remained as much a global reality in this era as during the 1800s. Work opportunities continue to motivate migration, but refugees and displaced persons have migrated in huge numbers because of war. In addition, many Western nations have allowed significant levels of migration from their former colonies. Anti-immigrant sentiment remains common.
- Racial tensions divided many communities and nations. Racial segregation and ethnic violence—official and unofficial—plagued societies throughout this era.
- The collapse of communism in Eastern Europe and the USSR forced a number of countries to make painful social and economic transitions from communism to free-market capitalism.
- Many parts of the West, including the United States, experienced a general rise in prosperity from the 1980s through the financial collapse of 2007. However, this was accompanied by a growing split between rich and poor and increased burdens on the middle class.
- Globally, the world still struggles with a north-south split, meaning that economic prosperity and access to cutting-edge technology, medical care, and social stability tend to be concentrated in the developed world, with many parts of the developing world lagging behind and still impoverished.

Humans and the Environment, 1900 to the Present	
Europe	comprehensive vaccination (eradication of polio and smallpox) diseases associated with lifestyle and longevity (diabetes, Alzheimer's) famine in Stalin's USSR modern environmentalism (recycling, NGOs, green parties) strongest environmental regulations environmental disasters (Chernobyl)
Middle East	oil industry and environmental impact of fossil fuels agricultural impact of Green Revolution Aswan High Dam
Africa	Ebola HIV/AIDS (origination and particular severity) famine in Ethiopia and elsewhere Green Belt movement
East (and Central) Asia	diseases associated with lifestyle and longevity (diabetes, Alzheimer's) famine in Mao's China agricultural impact of Green Revolution Three Gorges Dam environmental disasters (Fukushima)

Humans and the Environment, 1900 to the Present	
South (and Southeast) Asia and Oceania	Spanish flu pandemic (particular severity) famine in India agricultural impact of Green Revolution environmental disasters (Bhopal incident, Southeast Asian tsunami)
Americas	comprehensive vaccination in North America (eradication of polio and smallpox) diseases associated with lifestyle and longevity (diabetes, Alzheimer's) "dust bowl" crisis in United States and Canada agricultural impact of Green Revolution (Latin America) modern environmentalism (John Muir, Rachel Carson, Earth Day, Greenpeace, recycling) strongest environmental regulations (North America) environmental disasters (dust bowl crisis, Three Mile Island, *Exxon Valdez*, Hurricane Katrina, Deepwater, Superstorm Sandy)
Global and Interregional	vaccination campaigns Spanish flu pandemic HIV/AIDS pandemic rapid population growth (fastest in nondeveloped and developing worlds) environmental impact of fossil-fuel dependency pollution and ecosystem destruction + ozone depletion species endangerment global warming (Kyoto and Paris agreements vs. climate-change denial)

Humans and the Environment

- Population growth, caused above all by improvements in medicine and public health, reached unprecedented levels and continues to accelerate.
- Medical innovations lengthened life spans in many parts of the world.
- Escalating industrialization, increased fossil-fuel and resource consumption, massive engineering projects, and the production of toxic, chemical, and nuclear wastes have exponentially increased humanity's impact on the environment.
- Diseases associated with poverty, such as malaria, tuberculosis, and cholera, persisted in many parts of the world.
- Better and faster transportation hastened the global spread of new epidemic diseases such as Ebola, HIV/AIDS, and many new strains of influenza, starting with the "Spanish flu," which killed millions at the end of World War I.
- Diseases associated with sedentary lifestyles and new dietary habits, including heart disease, diabetes, and obesity, became more common. Extension of longevity placed larger numbers of people at risk of diseases associated with old age, such as Alzheimer's.
- Periodic famines, both natural and human-caused, struck various parts of the world, including the USSR in the 1930s (caused by Stalin's collectivization of agriculture), India in the early 1940s, China during the 1950s (caused by Mao's Great Leap Forward), and Ethiopia in the 1980s.
- In Canada and the United States during the 1930s, the "dust bowl" crisis—which caused thousands of square miles of fertile soil to be lost to aridity and giant windstorms—severely affected agriculture and added to the stress of the Great Depression.

- Between the late 1940s and the 1970s, a Green Revolution spread advanced agricultural techniques around the world, leading to a huge rise in the production of food. Mexico, where it is considered to have originated, played a key role in this development, and its impact spread not just through Latin America but to India, China, and other regions that had previously suffered damaging famines. However, the environmental impact of agriculture increased as a result of the Green Revolution thanks to greater water consumption, the clearing of more land, and the extensive use of pesticides.

- Habitats like wetlands, rain forests, and polar ecosystems have been badly threatened during this era. Large numbers of species in these and other ecozones faced extinction or endangerment.

- Environmental awareness in the West grew steadily but slowly during the early 1900s and then expanded after World War II. Green movements and nongovernmental organizations (NGOs) devoted to environmental issues have grown in size and influence.

- Climate change, or global warming, dramatically increased throughout the twentieth century and is considered by overwhelming scientific consensus to have been caused by the human-produced emission of greenhouse gases (especially carbon dioxide). It reached unprecedented levels in the 1990s and early 2000s. The best-known international efforts to reverse this trend are the Kyoto Protocol (1997) and the Paris Agreement (2015).

- Warfare in the twentieth and twenty-first centuries has had a growing impact on the environment. Examples include radiation from nuclear-weapons testing, biological and chemical warfare between Iran and Iraq during the 1970s, the defoliation of forests during the Vietnam War, and the destruction of oil wells during times of armed conflict.

- Natural disasters (Hurricane Katrina, the Southeast Asian tsunami, Superstorm Sandy) and energy-related crises (Chernobyl, Three Mile Island, the Bhopal incident, *Exxon Valdez*, the Fukushima nuclear disaster, the Gulf of Mexico oil spill, the melting of Arctic ice) demonstrate how contemporary societies can still be affected by the environment and how technology now allows them to affect the environment more deeply than before.

QUESTIONS AND COMPARISONS TO CONSIDER

- Discuss the ways different nations and regions modernized during the twentieth century. Were they industrialized before the 1900s? Did modernization efforts come from the population at large, or were they instituted by the government? Did they have to be put into place by force? Has modernization by force proved effective?

- In what ways did war evolve during this period? Consider tactics, new technologies and weapons, and impact on population.

- What impact did the world wars have on the non-Western world? Compare different regions, such as Africa and Asia. How did the wars affect women?

- Compare two or more of the twentieth century's major revolutions, such as the Russian, Chinese, Mexican, Cuban, or Iranian. Alternatively, compare one or more of these with revolutions in previous centuries. Compare how each affected women and/or ethnic minorities.

- Examine the process of decolonization as it played out in various parts of the world. Be sure to address cases that involved negotiation (India, the Gold Coast) and those that involved violent separation (Vietnam, Algeria, Angola).

- Focus on specific national-liberation, civil-rights, antisegregation, and antiwar movements. How did they achieve their goals? To what degree did they rely on force (or the threat of force) or nonviolent resistance?

- How has the legacy of colonialism affected cultural identity and patterns of economic development in Africa, Asia, and Latin America?
- How has nationalism in Europe differed from nationalism in decolonizing and decolonized parts of the world in both character and its political effects? Be sure to consider xenophobia, anti-immigration sentiment, and Christian-Muslim tension since 9/11.
- How has the rise of Western consumerism and economic globalism affected different societies outside the West?
- How have twentieth- and twenty-first-century technologies and agricultural techniques affected social structures? The environment?
- How have epidemics and other medical crises affected states and societies during this era? How have medical innovations lengthened human life spans?
- How does ethnic violence in the 1990s and early 2000s compare with the Holocaust?
- What effects have major scientific breakthroughs (genetics, quantum physics, the digital revolution) had on society, politics, and culture during this era? How have they reduced the impact of geographical distance on human affairs and economic relations? How have certain scientific programs (the space race, for example) interacted with global political and military affairs?
- How have family and gender relations been affected by new social trends? By new technological and medical developments?
- What social trends restricted or increased access to education, career choices, and professional or political roles?

UNIT 4

SCENIC ROUTE
(Chapters 19–25)

Governance, 1900–1945

19

IN THIS CHAPTER

→ TOTAL WARS (INCREASED CIVILIAN CASUALTIES)

→ GENOCIDE (ARMENIAN MASSACRE, THE HOLOCAUST)

→ WORLD WAR I (ALLIES VS. CENTRAL POWERS, TRENCH WARFARE)

→ PARIS PEACE CONFERENCE (FOURTEEN POINTS, TREATY OF VERSAILLES)

→ LEAGUE OF NATIONS

→ THE GREAT DEPRESSION AND INTERNATIONAL REPERCUSSIONS

→ DEMOCRATIC WEAKNESS IN EUROPE VS. TOTALITARIAN STATES

→ THE MANDATE SYSTEM AND THE BALFOUR DECLARATION

→ MIDDLE EASTERN MODERNIZERS (MUSTAFA KEMAL ATATURK, REZA SHAH PAHLAVI)

→ THE CHINESE REVOLUTION (SUN YAT-SEN, KMT, CHIANG KAI-SHEK)

→ MAO TSE-TUNG AND THE CCP

→ ZAIBATSU INDUSTRIALIZATION AND MILITARISM IN JAPAN (RAPE OF NANJING)

→ INDIAN NATIONAL CONGRESS (MOHANDAS GANDHI)

→ U.S. SPHERE OF INFLUENCE IN LATIN AMERICA

→ THE MEXICAN REVOLUTION AND THE PRI

→ COLLECTIVE SECURITY VS. APPEASEMENT IN 1930S FOREIGN POLICY

→ WORLD WAR II (ALLIES VS. AXIS POWERS)

→ OFFENSIVE CAPABILITIES IN WORLD WAR II (BLITZKRIEG, STRATEGIC BOMBING, HIROSHIMA)

→ WAR CRIMES, GENOCIDE, AND THE HOLOCAUST

→ NUREMBERG AND TOKYO TRIALS (CRIMES AGAINST HUMANITY)

Dramatic political changes have characterized the 1900s and 2000s. During the first half of the 1900s, two **world wars** reshaped global affairs, weakening Europe's position of global dominance after 1914 and dismantling it altogether after 1945. Both conflicts were **total wars** that required near-complete mobilization of human and economic resources. During the interwar years, the future of democracy seemed doubtful with the seemingly inexorable rise of dictatorships, including **totalitarian regimes** like Soviet Russia and Nazi Germany.

Throughout the twentieth century, new weapons and tactics made warfare steadily more destructive and increased its impact on civilian populations. It also gave rise to new categories of violence, such as **genocide**. Consider the following factors as underlying sources of conflict during the first half of the 1900s: (1) aggressive expansion of empires by Europe and Japan; (2) Anglo-German geopolitical rivalry; (3) ethnic tensions and racial hatred; (4) nationalism; (5) competition for resources; and (6) international economic stress caused by the **Great Depression**.

WORLD WAR I AND THE PARIS PEACE CONFERENCE

World War I began in the summer of 1914 and lasted until the fall of 1918. In many ways, it marks the true beginning of the twentieth century.

Background and Combat

The long-term causes of World War I include a potent cocktail of **nationalism**, **competition over empire**, and an unstable **European alliance system** (France and Russia, informally aligned with Britain against Germany and Austria, which was weakly tied to Italy) that had the potential to draw all the continent's powers into conflict in the event of a crisis.

That crisis came in Sarajevo, the capital of Bosnia: a Balkan province under Austrian authority but with a large Serb population and coveted by the intensely nationalistic state of Serbia. On June 28, 1914, Bosnian Serbs affiliated with the **Black Hand**, a terror group supported informally by influential parties in Serbia, carried out the **assassination of Franz Ferdinand**, heir to the Austrian throne. The Austrian government was genuinely outraged but also decided cynically to use the event as a pretext to humble its troublesome neighbor— even though its own police concluded that Serbia's government was not to blame. During the **July crisis**, Austria issued a list of humiliating demands and threatened war if Serbia did not accept. Russia, Austria's rival in the Balkans, supported Serbia, but Germany persuaded Austria not to back down—the infamous **blank check**—even if Russia intervened militarily. When Austria declared war on Serbia on July 28, the alliance system went into motion.

Russia and Germany mobilized in the east, and because Germany's strategy for avoiding a long two-front war—the Schlieffen Plan, described below—required lightning speed, the Germans moved quickly against France and neutral Belgium. Britain supported its French and Russian partners. Except for Italy, which remained neutral for the moment, Europe's major powers were all at war by August 4.

NOTE

To catch France off guard in 1914, the Germans moved their main attack force through neutral Belgium, an illegal action that killed numerous civilians and enabled Allied propaganda to convincingly depict the Central Powers as villains and aggressors.

Germany opened with the **Schlieffen Plan**, a daring gamble which sent 75 percent of its army into France, with the aim of taking Paris in six weeks. The other 25 percent, with Austrian help, would defend against Russia, on which the Germans intended to focus after France's defeat. The Germans drove into northern France and came within reach of Paris. However, during the first week of September, the Allies' determined stand at the **First Battle of the Marne** foiled the Schlieffen Plan and dashed any hope of a quick end to the war.

The war proved so surprisingly long principally because of the tactical stalemate that resulted when evenly matched sides deployed the latest in industrial-era technology against each other—instead of against the comparatively backward forces they had defeated in Asia and Africa during their wars of imperial conquest. Modern artillery and rifles, along with machine guns, made the battlefield so deadly that traditional tactics, which had climaxed in mass charges against the enemy, were no longer feasible. With military technology disproportionately favoring the defensive, **trench warfare**, one of history's most horrific styles of combat, resulted in three years of bloody deadlock—especially on the **Western Front**, the 500-mile chain of trenches, bunkers, and barbed wire that stretched from the English Channel to the Swiss border. Here, until late in the war, combat operations such as the **Verdun Offensive** and the **Battle of the Somme**, both in 1916, brought about no useful outcome and virtually no movement, despite costing hundreds of thousands of casualties. This futility, combined with the horrors of **poison gas** and the ever-present miseries of mud, filth, and vermin, made the trench-warfare experience maddeningly terrible, as attested to in the Erich Maria Remarque novel *All Quiet on the Western Front* and other works of antiwar art described in Chapter 21. Trench warfare was also the norm in the south, where the Italians clashed with their Austrian foes.

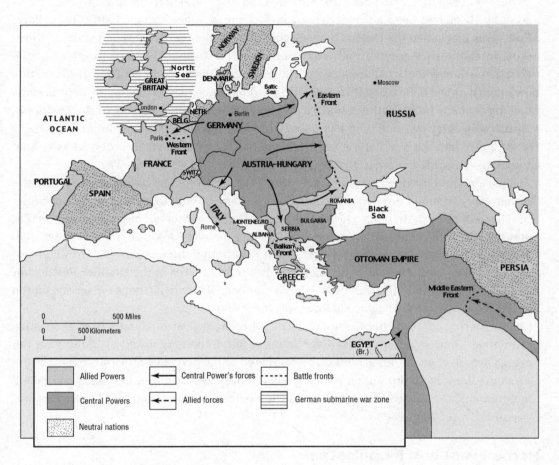

World War I in Europe, 1914–1918
In Western Europe, the basic dynamic of the conflict was determined quite early. Then, thanks to the stalemate of trench warfare, it changed very little until the last months of war. In the east, fighting conditions were much more fluid.

Combat on the longer and less entrenched **Eastern Front** was more fluid but still catastrophically deadly—especially for the Russians, who sustained crushing defeats at Germany's hands and who found themselves cut off from their allies when Ottoman Turkey sided with the Central powers, denying Russia access to the Mediterranean. Fighting spread far beyond Europe. Britain and France moved against Germany's possessions in Africa, while Japan and Australia seized its Pacific colonies. The most important non-European theater was the Middle East. In 1915, the British, with large numbers of Indian,

Not until 1917 and 1918 did improved tactics (including the use of precisely targeted artillery to pin down enemy forces in their trenches while one's own troops charged across "no man's land") and new weaponry—such as tanks and airplanes—start to end the painful stalemate of trench warfare.

Australian, and New Zealand troops, tried to knock the Ottomans out of the war by landing at **Gallipoli**. This months-long campaign proved an utter disaster, resulting in an embarrassing retreat and 50 percent casualties. More successful were British support for the **Arab revolt** against Ottoman power and the Russian thrust through Ottoman defenses on the Caucasus frontier. It was on the Russo-Turkish front that one of the war's worst tragedies unfolded. In 1915, the Ottoman state perpetrated the **Armenian massacres**, systematically killing somewhere between 500,000 and 1.5 million men, women, and children in an episode most historians consider an instance of **genocide**.

The war at sea took an ironic turn. Although the **Anglo-German naval race** of the 1890s and early 1900s had been an underlying cause of the war, few surface battles took place. Allied fleets blockaded the Central powers, constricting their economies and starving thousands. In response, Germany mastered **submarine** (or **U-boat**) **warfare** to intercept the transatlantic movement of Allied supplies and troops. It discovered in 1914 and 1915 not only how much damage U-boats could do but also the diplomatic risks of destroying neutral ships or killing civilians from neutral countries. In May 1915, Germany's **sinking of the *Lusitania***, a British ship carrying more than a hundred American passengers, nearly brought an angry United States into the war. For the next year and half, Germany sharply curtailed its U-boat campaign—but with great reluctance.

Exhaustion and turning points characterized 1917. Frustrated by the stalemate at sea, the German navy resumed unrestricted submarine warfare, hoping to starve Britain out of the war. This reduced Britain to a six-week food supply by the spring but also provoked the **U.S. entry into the war** in April. At the same time, Russia was collapsing. The tsarist regime fell in the spring, and while the new government tried to continue the war, Russia's army suffered mass desertions and several defeats. Communists seized power in the **October Revolution** and pulled Russia out of the war, freeing large numbers of German troops for service on the Western Front, where the balance of force was razor thin.

In the spring of 1918, the Germans, faced with the arrival of hundreds of thousands of Americans and a severe disadvantage in tanks and airplanes, staked everything on the **Spring Offensive**, an all-out assault on Paris. Halted at the **Second Battle of the Marne**, the Germans were forced into full retreat by August. Strikes and mutinies in the fall compelled the Ottomans, the Austro-Hungarians, and the Germans to cease fighting in October and November. World War I ended on November 11, 1918.

Home Front and Mobilization

World War I was a **total war**, requiring the near-complete mobilization of populations and resources. The **home front** became a crucial part of every combatant nation's war effort as entire economies were geared for war. The procurement of raw materials—steel, coal, petroleum, rubber, cloth, and more—was centralized, as was agricultural production and the manufacture of uniforms, weapons, and other military necessities. The **rationing** of food, fuel, and consumer goods became increasingly strict—painfully so by late 1916 and early 1917 when all European belligerents were suffering terrible material shortages.

Another home-front effect of the war was the **restriction of civil liberties**, even in the democracies. All combatants censored the press and the mail. Special laws allowed anyone suspected of espionage or treason to be arrested and tried without due process. Trade unions and socialist parties were supervised and their activities curtailed. Even pessimism or an insufficient show of patriotism could get one in trouble. Men who sought conscientious-objector status were often denied and harassed or ridiculed if they succeeded.

The war required mass **recruitment** and then **conscription**, the involuntary drafting of soldiers. Most combatant nations began with armies of 1 to 2 million, but these did not suffice, and eventually 70 million personnel were called up for service. Especially in countries with traditions of all-volunteer armies, like Britain and Canada, the move to conscription caused much social stress, including protests and riots. Imperial powers mobilized large numbers of colonial troops. Over 2.5 million Africans fought, mainly on their own continent, although the French brought Moroccan, Algerian, and Senegalese soldiers to the Western Front (in a classic instance of racial stereotyping, the Germans feared the Senegalese as cannibals). Soldiers from French Indochina also served on the Western Front. Britain relied on major contingents of Canadians, Australians, and New Zealanders but also used almost a million Indian, Sikh, and Nepalese Gurkha troops in theaters ranging from Europe to the Middle East.

Especially striking was the **role of women** in World War I. Some women served on the lines: a portion as uniformed auxiliaries, most as nurses. On the home front, they stepped up in huge numbers to take the place of men on farms and in factories. These jobs mostly went back to men when the war ended, but women's wartime contributions played a significant role in their being granted the right to vote in many countries after the war.

The Paris Peace Conference and Long-Term Consequences

After the war, terms were decided at the **Paris Peace Conference**, which lasted from 1919 to 1920 and drew up treaties for each of the five Central powers. The most important was the **Treaty of Versailles**, imposed on Germany in June 1919.

The peacemaking was marked by conflict on all sides. The defeated nations were allowed no meaningful role in the negotiations, and they believed that all European powers, not just Germany and Austria-Hungary, were equally to blame for the war. Not only did they consider the final terms too harsh, Germany in particular saw them as illegitimate.

Quarrels also divided the Allied leaders: Woodrow Wilson of the United States, David Lloyd George of Britain, and Georges Clemenceau of France. All three held the Central powers responsible for the war and deserving of punishment. But Wilson's idealism differed starkly from Lloyd George's and Clemenceau's emphasis on national self-interest. Arriving with his famous **Fourteen Points**, Wilson hoped to prevent all war in the future. He called for freedom of the seas, arms reduction, an end to secret treaties, **decolonization**, the rearrangement of borders according to the **self-determination** of national groups, and the establishment of an international dispute-resolution body called the **League of Nations**. By contrast, Lloyd George and Clemenceau (and the Belgians and Italians) were anxious to make the Central powers pay as much as possible for the wartime damage they had caused. Both also feared a future resurgence of Germany and sought to keep it militarily weak.

NOTE

Black soldiers who served in Europe as part of the American Expeditionary Force were segregated from their white counterparts and used mainly as labor battalions. When they did fight, it was typically alongside French, not American, troops. The United States and Canada were slow in both world wars when it came to integrating black, Asian, and Native American troops but eventually did so following World War II.

NOTE

In addition to the Armenian massacre, the Central Powers committed a significant number of wartime atrocities, although these paled in comparison to what followed in World War II. In occupied territories like Belgium and Poland, the Germans and Austrians killed many civilians, destroyed or confiscated civilian property, and illegally used thousands of civilians as forced labor. Because these real crimes were exaggerated by Allied propaganda during the war, they were taken less seriously afterward—and this had the unfortunate long-term effect of making it easier for people in the 1940s to dismiss early reports of the Holocaust as a new round of anti-German propaganda.

The resulting treaties were the product of bitter debate and compromise. At the cost of bargaining away several of his Fourteen Points, Wilson won approval for the **League of Nations**. (Ironically, because Congress did not ratify the Treaty of Versailles, the United States never joined the League, weakening the new organization from the start.) Other main points included the **dismantling of Austria-Hungary** into two states; the creation of new nations according to the principle of self-determination (Yugoslavia, Czechoslovakia, Poland, Finland, Latvia, Lithuania, and Estonia were carved out of lands lost by Germany, Austria-Hungary, and Russia); and the establishment of a complex **mandate system** to administer the Central powers' former imperial possessions.

NOTE

The mandate system categorized former colonies according to their readiness for independence. They were then placed by the League of Nations under the long-, medium-, or short-term "supervision" by nations like Britain and France. In theory, supervising nations were meant to guide their mandates to freedom, but in practice, this was colonization under a new name and in a form that allowed the Europeans to avoid offending Woodrow Wilson's anticolonial sensibilities.

The mandate system affected Africa and the Pacific but had its heaviest impact on the Middle East, where the **Arab lands** once under Ottoman rule became British and French mandates—even though the disappointed Arabs had expected independence in exchange for their military aid against the Ottomans. One of these mandates was Palestine, where the British, in the **Balfour Declaration** of 1917, agreed to help create a Jewish "national home." Intended to redress a set of grave injustices—the historical dispossession of the Jews and modern anti-Semitism in Europe—this policy, although not acted on right away, set the stage for an equally grave conflict between Jews (both local and returning) and Palestinian Arabs.

Directed against Germany, the **Treaty of Versailles** contained a **war-guilt clause** that blamed the war on Germany and its partners. Germany suffered **loss of territory** (approximately 13 percent) and **population** (approximately 10 percent) as Alsace and Lorraine—which Germany had seized from France in 1871—were returned and as other pieces of land went to Belgium, Czechoslovakia, Denmark, and Poland. **Loss of African and Pacific** colonies followed. **Disarmament** restricted Germany to a token army of 100,000 and forbade all tanks, military aircraft, warships, and submarines. Most controversially, Germany was required to pay **reparations** of over $32 billion (the other Central powers owed reparations as well). Initially, Britain, France, and Belgium wanted reimbursement not just for damage done but for the entire cost of the war, a vastly higher amount. Wilson insisted on a more limited approach—not that this was appreciated by the Germans, who felt any demands for payment were unjust.

NOTE

Germany's indignation at the supposed unfairness of Versailles is worth contrasting with its willingness to force the even harsher treaty of Brest-Litovsk, one of the most punitive settlements in history, on Russia in the spring of 1918. A generation before, after defeating France in 1871, Germany had gleefully stripped away the provinces of Alsace and Lorraine and demanded a fortune in gold. These facts were studiously ignored by most interwar Germans.

The Paris Peace Conference produced flawed results. Greed and revenge dictated many of the terms and much of the redrawing of the world map, especially concerning former colonies. Ignorance about places like Eastern Europe, Africa, and the Middle East left ethnic tensions unresolved and created new regimes that looked stable on the surface but were weak at the core. The League of Nations, particularly without the United States to lead it, proved too feeble to keep peace in the future. While one can debate the fairness of the *terms* of the Treaty of Versailles, the high-handed *way* the treaty was foisted on the Germans guaranteed that the overwhelming majority of them would *perceive* it as unfair—a significant factor in (though not the *direct cause* of) Hitler's later rise to power.

The immediate consequences of World War I were obvious: 9 to 10 million soldiers killed, another 2 to 7 million civilians dead, and 28 to 30 million people wounded. The genocidal massacre of Armenians by the Ottoman Empire marked a new level of military atrocity, foreshadowing the Holocaust of World War II. Millions of people, particularly in Eastern Europe, with its constantly shifting borders, were made homeless or stateless. Adding to this pain, a global epidemic of **Spanish flu** struck during the closing months of World War I, lasting until late 1920 and killing at least 25 to 40 million, perhaps many more.

Long-term consequences are discussed throughout this unit. Geopolitically, they include the **destruction of four empires** (Imperial Germany, Habsburg Austria, tsarist Russia, and the Ottoman Empire, which collapsed shortly after the war), a **general decline in European global power** (even the victor nations were badly drained, and their overseas empires became increasingly difficult to control), and **instability in Central and Eastern Europe** (where German resentment of Versailles would simmer, where Soviet expansionism threatened, and where political inexperience made new nations vulnerable). Far-reaching social and economic changes were unleashed or sped up by the war, including the **continued decline of hereditary aristocracies**, the **growing clout of the middle and lower classes** (especially "white-collar" professionals), the granting of **women's suffrage** in most Western nations (although France and Italy held out until the 1940s), and the **fuller industrialization of Western economies**. The war also encouraged a greater **sense of uncertainty and anxiety in European culture**.

DOMESTIC POLITICS, 1900–1939

Many have argued that the world wars were two halves of the same conflict, separated by twenty years of temporary armistice. Whatever the truth of that, the peace of the **interwar period** rested on a shaky foundation, both in Europe and throughout the globe, and was destabilized by the **Great Depression** that began in 1929.

Fragile Peace and Political Extremism in Europe

Peace prevailed in Europe during the 1920s but was fragile at best. Political violence and civil war rocked Germany, Soviet Russia, and Eastern Europe until 1922, and even afterward, it was exhaustion rather than true amity that preserved peace on the continent. The **League of Nations** resettled refugees and carried out famine relief, but with few powers of enforcement, it soon proved an inadequate peacekeeper. European economies struggled, even during the comparatively stable 1920s, and then plunged into free fall during the 1930s as the effects of the **Great Depression** spread outward from the United States.

Democracy did not flourish in interwar Europe. In 1919, twenty-three governments there could be considered democratic. By 1939, half of those had become dictatorial (although to varying degrees of severity). Italy slipped into fascism as early as 1922, and the Depression helped drive Germany to Nazism in 1933. Even well-established democracies like Britain and France experienced political weakness and economic sluggishness. Only U.S. investment and German reparations kept the British and French economies afloat during the 1920s, and even then, unemployment, deficits, and strikes were the norm. The Depression made things worse, and both political systems suffered: British elections returned weak-willed coalition governments, whereas the French government lurched from left to right and back again in frequent elections. On the foreign-policy front, economic frailty and political indecision made it difficult for Depression-era France and Britain to cope with the growing threat of Nazi Germany. One bright light is that most interwar democracies—including France and Britain—found some relief by

NOTE

Another source of interwar stress for France and Britain was the growing difficulty of holding on to empires. All but the northern fragment of Ireland freed itself from Britain after World War I, and national liberation movements were increasingly restless in colonies like French Indochina and British India. Hoping to make imperial rule seem less burdensome, Britain—starting with the 1931 Statute of Westminster—began the long transformation of its empire into the more egalitarian British Commonwealth, which exists today.

putting into place the earliest elements of the **social welfare systems** that most Western states enjoy today.

The general crisis of democracy meant that political momentum in interwar Europe seemed to belong to dictatorships, several of which attained **totalitarian** levels of control over their people. The first new dictatorship was the Soviet Union, the communist regime that took power in Russia in the fall of 1917. Russia underwent two revolutions that year, with the tsarist regime collapsing in February due to repeated World War I disasters, the political incompetence of Nicholas II, and dire food shortages. After this **February Revolution**, a liberal provisional government attempted to repair the dismal economy and build democracy, all while continuing to fight Germany. Its good intentions, however, did not satisfy the desire of the vast majority of Russians for economic stability, land reform (about 80 percent of the population were peasants), and an end to the war at any cost. As popular discontent grew during the summer and early fall, those who benefited most were the **Bolsheviks**, the most radical of Russia's communists, led by **Vladimir Lenin** and his second in command, Leon Trotsky. The **October Revolution** of 1917 brought them to power.

The Bolsheviks struggled for survival between 1917 and 1921, pulling out of World War I and then defeating their anticommunist enemies—the Whites—in the terrible **Russian Civil War**, which resulted in the death of millions from disease, starvation, and persecution and the emigration of hundreds of thousands more. Lenin quickly created a one-party dictatorship and a **secret police** (originally the Cheka, eventually the KGB) and tried to modernize the country along Marxist lines. His main challenge was that while Marx had spoken of communism succeeding first in a mature capitalist society with a large industrial working class, economically backward Russia had a huge peasantry but only a tiny working class. In 1921, Lenin compromised with this reality by instituting the **New Economic Policy** (**NEP**), a more gradual approach to socialist development that allowed for limited private trade. This lasted until 1928, although Lenin died in the meantime, in 1924.

In 1928, after a half-decade succession struggle against Trotsky, **Joseph Stalin** gained control of the Soviet government and became one of the most oppressive dictators of all time. Immediately overturning NEP, Stalin returned to the revolutionary policy of overnight modernization with his **Five-Year Plans** (complete centralization of the economy to bring about rapid industrialization) and the **collectivization of agriculture** (the forced transfer of peasants from villages to state-run farms, both to control them more tightly and to confiscate their grain more efficiently in order to pay for the Five-Year Plans). Although the USSR indeed modernized under Stalin, the price was steep. The Five-Year Plans combined the social and economic trauma of a state-sponsored industrial revolution with ruthless police brutality. Millions of peasants who opposed collectivization were imprisoned or executed, and 4 to 6 million more died in the **Great Famine** (1932–1933) caused by Stalin's grain confiscations in southern Russia, Kazakhstan, and Ukraine (which suffered the largest losses and where the famine is remembered as the Holodomor, or "extermination by hunger"). From 1936 to 1938, Stalin used the secret police to carry out a series of mass arrests and show trials, called the **Purges**, executing approximately a million people and exiling millions more to labor camps called **gulags**. Like other modern dictators, Stalin used propaganda to indoctrinate his subjects and glorified himself by means of an extravagant **cult of personality**. His state-directed form of modernization brought the country far more torment than benefit.

In Italy, dictatorship came from the right. After World War I, Italy's constitutional monarchy was undermined by economic downturn and political chaos. The upper and middle classes, fearing social breakdown and communist revolution, sought a strong leader to restore stability.

In October 1922, **Benito Mussolini** led his newly founded Fascist Party in a **March on Rome** to display the strength of his movement. Viewing the Fascists as a less dangerous threat than the communists, the king placed Mussolini in charge of the government for the next twenty-one years. **Fascism**, Mussolini's invention, is best described as right-wing radicalism (as opposed to right-wing conservatism, which seeks to prevent change). It was anticommunist but also anticapitalist and antidemocratic and characterized by **militaristic nationalism**. Mussolini killed and arrested few people compared to Stalin and Hitler, and he modernized Italy with new highways, literacy campaigns, and the industrial development of backward regions. He was well regarded, both at home and abroad, during the 1920s. On the other hand, he imposed censorship, used propaganda to create a lavish **cult of personality**, and suppressed trade unions and political parties. His foreign-policy aggression, plus his decision to ally with Hitler, damaged his international reputation during the 1930s, and the Depression undercut his modernizing efforts at home.

NOTE

Most modern dictatorships are categorized as authoritarian, with the ruling elite concerned mainly with the enforcement of obedience. Totalitarianism is more extreme—both in the level of control and in the number of people killed or imprisoned. In some cases, the difference between the two can be debated, but Stalinist Russia, Maoist China, and Nazi Germany are clear-cut examples of totalitarianism. George Orwell's *1984* is the classic fictional depiction of totalitarianism in its ultimate form.

Germany's road to dictatorship was longer than Italy's, and the results were infinitely worse. From 1919 to 1933, Germany was governed by the democratic **Weimar Republic**. Dogged during the early 1920s by **hyperinflation** (which caused several years of nightmarish poverty) and political unrest from the left (a communist uprising in 1919) and the right (several assassinations and coup attempts, including one by the fledgling Nazi Party in 1923), the Weimar regime managed to restore economic and political order between 1924 and 1929. In 1930, however, the **Great Depression** ended this temporary calm, causing **mass unemployment**—nearly 40 percent of the workforce by 1932—and boosting the popularity of Germany's most extremist movements: the communists and the **Nazi Party**, led by **Adolf Hitler**, originally from Austria, but a fierce pan-German patriot. A conscious imitator of Italian fascism, Hitler despised communism and democracy in favor of **militaristic nationalism**. He embraced racial hatred of many groups, especially a virulent form of **anti-Semitism**—all expressed in his infamous memoir *Mein Kampf*.

During the relative stability of the late 1920s, the Nazis enjoyed little political appeal. But when the Weimar regime failed to cope with the Depression, ordinary Germans began heeding Hitler's rhetoric. They remembered their resentment of the Treaty of Versailles. Many came to believe the Nazis' anti-Semitic conspiracy theories about how Jews had supposedly sold Germany out during World War I or were enriching themselves while the rest of Germany suffered through the Depression or were responsible for international communism. During the Weimar electoral crisis of the early 1930s, as vote after vote failed to produce a clear majority, the Nazis emerged as Germany's largest party. The Communists also gained in popularity, reflecting the country's political polarization. In January 1933, Germany's president—the conservative war hero Paul von Hindenburg, who had little love for the Nazis but feared the Communists even more—appointed Hitler chancellor of Germany.

Within months, Hitler established himself as an absolute dictator. In February 1933, the Reichstag building, seat of the German government, was set ablaze by a communist arsonist, allowing Hitler to declare a state of emergency and to pass the **Enabling Act** in March. This suspended the Weimar constitution and gave Hitler the power to rule by decree. He soon outlawed all political parties, banned trade unions, and turned the press and mass media into instruments of Nazi propaganda (relying on a **cult of personality** similar to Mussolini's and Stalin's). In 1934, he assumed the presidency when Hindenburg

NOTE

Fascist and authoritarian economies typically follow the principles of syndicalism, a form of state capitalism in which business leaders, rather than practicing free trade, cooperate directly with the government. In exchange for obedience, they receive preferential treatment, and the regime ensures that labor unions pose no challenge to them. This approach prevailed in Fascist Italy, Nazi Germany, Japan, and many minor dictatorships.

suddenly died, and he violently purged remaining rivals within the Nazi Party in the "night of the long knives." To control dissidents and opponents, the Nazis built **concentration camps** like Dachau and created a secret police, the **Gestapo**. Hitler's system of **state capitalism**, similar to Mussolini's, reduced German unemployment with a giant program of public works and highway building coupled with mass **military conscription** and renewed **arms production**—both of which required the renunciation of the Treaty of Versailles. Hitler's belligerent foreign policy was a key reason for the erosion of European and global peace during the 1930s.

The Nazis also acted on their notorious obsession with racial purity, believing as they did in the **Aryan myth**: the misguided notion that Germans and other northern Europeans were the "truest" descendants of the earliest Indo-Europeans. Hitler's regime targeted several races as "undesirable," including Slavs, Africans, and Roma (Gypsies)—but from the Nazi perspective, the worst of these "subhumans," the source of all of Germany's troubles, were the Jews. In this way, the Nazis added extra malevolence to a streak of anti-Semitism that had long existed throughout Europe. Although the Nazis eventually resorted to genocide, their prewar **anti-Semitic policies** emphasized official discrimination and physical harassment. Jewish writings and artworks were banned or burned, Jewish businesses were boycotted, and Jews were forced out of professions like law, medicine, civil service, and university teaching. The **Nuremberg Laws** of 1935 deprived Jews of their civil rights and forbade intermarriage between them and non-Jews. Sporadic violence, including the 1938 pogrom called *Kristallnacht* ("night of broken glass"), ramped up during the late 1930s as the regime tried to pressure Jews into leaving the country. Many stayed, either because places like Britain, Canada, and the United States refused them entry or because European Jews did not anticipate how much worse Nazi rule would become.

Nationalism and Modernization in the Middle East

Even before World War I, the Middle East was on the threshold of great change, with modernization finally coming to—and ultimately destroying—the Ottoman Empire and nationalism arising throughout the region.

WHAT ABOUT INTERWAR AFRICA?

Most of Africa remained firmly under European colonial control. Exceptions include South Africa, which formed a union of British and Boer provinces in 1910 and gained dominion status within the British Empire in 1931. Liberia, founded in the 1800s by freed slaves from the United States, remained independent. Ethiopia, the only state other than Liberia to escape colonization during the Scramble for Africa, was conquered by Fascist Italy in the mid-1930s. Although not yet as potent as in Asia or the Middle East, national liberationist impulses started to awaken in Africa. Jomo Kenyatta mobilized Kikuyu nationalism against British colonial rule, and French colonies in Morocco and West Africa were convulsed by strikes, protests, and even rebellion. On a positive note, Blaise Diagne of Senegal became, in 1914, the first black African to be elected as a delegate to France's National Assembly.

The Ottoman Empire resumed its path toward reform in 1908 and 1909 when the westernizing **Young Turks**, led by **Enver Pasha**, replaced Abdul Hamid II with a figurehead sultan and restored the constitution of 1876. But even the Young Turks' program of modernization could not save the empire, especially once the Ottomans entered World War I and shared in the Central powers' defeat in 1918. Disgraced by its military failures and having lost its imperial possessions to revolt or to the Paris Peace Conference, the Ottoman Empire was threatened after the war with the seizure of even more territory by Greece. Into this crisis stepped **Mustafa Kemal**, a heroic World War I commander who now repelled the Greeks and, forming a new government, negotiated a more favorable treaty with the Allies. In 1923, the last Ottoman sultan vacated the throne, and Kemal proclaimed the Turkish Republic—appointing himself president and taking the name **Ataturk**, or "father of all Turks."

From 1923 to his death in 1938, Ataturk governed as a secularizing modernizer, promoting industrialization,

Western dress, Western education, and the use of the Roman alphabet for written Turkish. Church and state were separated, with a European law code replacing Islamic Sharia. Women, no longer required to wear the veil, received the right to vote in 1934 and were encouraged to get educations and jobs. Although he wrote a constitution and kept up a democratic pretense, Ataturk tolerated little opposition and began a long tradition of authoritarian rule in Turkey.

A similar change took place in Persia, which became the modern state of Iran in the 1920s. Ruled in theory by the Qajar dynasty since 1794, Persia had in fact been divided into British and Russian spheres of influence during the 1800s. Drawn by Persia's oil reserves, Britain increased its presence there after World War I, causing a nationalist backlash. In 1921, an officer named Reza Khan mutinied against the Qajar and expelled the British, gaining control of the country by 1925. Taking the name **Reza Shah Pahlavi**, he established a new royal dynasty and became an authoritarian westernizer like his neighbor Ataturk. Although less inclined than Ataturk to make a show of democracy or to clash as hard with Muslim clergy, the new shah industrialized Iran, boosted education, and did away with the veil for women.

Islamic North Africa remained in British, French, and Italian hands. Britain continued to dominate Egypt, even though Egypt technically gained independence in 1922. Nationalist sentiment grew here, often taking the form of Islamic traditionalism as in the 1928 formation of the **Muslim Brotherhood** in Cairo. Initially, the Ottomans retained the Arabian Peninsula, but the other Arab lands once under their rulership were placed into the **mandate system** and administered by France and Britain under the League of Nations' supervision. (Syria and Lebanon were assigned to France, and Iraq, Jordan, and Palestine fell to Britain.) This arrangement angered the Arabs, who had believed during World War I that the Allies would grant them complete freedom as a reward for their anti-Ottoman revolt. They were further enraged by the **Balfour Declaration** of 1917. This pledged British support for a Jewish "national home" in Palestine, which was 90 percent Arab before substantial Jewish immigration—faster and larger in scale than the British had intended—in the 1920s and 1930s.

The one Arab state to achieve full independence during these years was Saudi Arabia, formed in 1932 by the prince **Ibn Saud**, who spent the 1920s driving the Turks out of the Arabian Peninsula and uniting its many tribes. An authoritarian monarchy attracted to **Wahhabism**, a strictly fundamentalist form of Islam, the Saudi state modernized little—except to industrialize its huge **oil reserves**, whose discovery in 1938 made it instantly wealthy and strategically vital.

Militarism and Revolution in Asia

Huge upheavals came to interwar Asia, beginning in China, where the **Chinese Revolution** of 1911–1912 had swept away the Qing regime. The revolution's leading figure was **Sun Yat-sen**, who spent the 1890s and early 1900s promoting Western-style modernization and constitutional rule based on three "**people's principles**": nationalism (opposition to Manchu rule and Western imperialism), democracy (including universal suffrage for women as well as men), and livelihood (a semisocialist concern for people's welfare). When anti-Qing uprisings broke out in the fall of 1911, Sun was in America but quickly returned and became president of the new Chinese Republic. His movement renamed itself the **Nationalist Party**, or **Kuomintang** (KMT).

Unfortunately, Sun's idealism was no match for the civil war and anarchy that followed. In 1912, the authoritarian general Yuan Shikai seized power, which remained in his hands until his death in 1916 and then passed to other right-wing officers until 1928. Opposed to this military regime were warlords and bandits, who established control over vast stretches of China, as well as

FACT

The Chinese Republic banned foot binding and began preparations for allowing women to vote. However, when Yuan Shikai took power from Sun Yat-sen, he canceled suffrage for women. Only in 1947 did Chinese women receive the right to vote.

intellectuals and students, whose Western-oriented progressivism clashed with the regime's attempt to revive traditional Confucian values. Popular discontent with the military government became clear on May 4, 1919, when thousands of students gathered in **Tiananmen Square**. Although they gathered mainly to protest the regime's willingness to allow Japan to annex Shantung Province (a German concession awarded to Japan by the Treaty of Versailles), the other goal of this May Fourth Movement was democratic reform.

Also clashing with the military regime were the Kuomintang, still led by Sun and now running a revolutionary effort in the south, based in Canton, and the **Chinese Communist Party** (CCP), founded in 1921. In the mid-1920s, both cooperated to combat unruly warlords and to unseat the military government. In 1925, Sun died of cancer, passing KMT leadership to **Chiang Kai-shek**, a Western-educated officer who leaned further to the right than Sun had. By early 1927, the KMT-CCP alliance had won control of all China south of the Yangtze River. Then, in April, Chiang turned against the Communists, murdering thousands in Shanghai and driving the rest far to the north. In 1928, Chiang took Beijing and founded a Kuomintang regime that professed allegiance to Sun's principles and attempted a certain degree of modernization but soon grew corrupt, inefficient, and authoritarian. Chiang governed China until 1949 but faced two deadly threats. First was the CCP, kept alive by **Mao Tse-tung** (**Mao Zedong**), who led the CCP to its new northern base of Yenan during the arduous **Long March** of 1934–1935 and from there continued the anti-KMT struggle. Second was Japanese expansion, which began in 1931, worsened after 1937, and never ceased until the end of World War II.

Like Lenin in Russia, Mao confronted the awkward fact that Marxism was theoretically poorly suited to nonindustrial societies with few proletarian workers. He radicalized China's peasant masses and made communism appealing to them.

Japan began the interwar period with democratizing potential but veered in the end toward authoritarian militarism. Through the late 1920s, the powers of the Diet increased, freedom of the press expanded, and a 1925 bill of rights granted universal male suffrage and other civil liberties. On the other hand, Japan continued its policy of **state-directed industrialization**, with a small number of powerful corporations, or **zaibatsu**, benefiting from government favoritism. Not only did this system concentrate wealth in a tiny oligarchy of influential industrialists, but it kept trade unions weak and did little to improve working conditions. Even before the Depression, strikes and riots were common, and social stress was building to a dangerous level.

In the 1930s, the Great Depression and Japan's foreign-policy aggression derailed further liberalization. The Depression caused Japanese exports to plummet more than 50 percent. Resulting economic stress gave rise to left-wing extremism, including communist agitation, and this was met by conservative backlash. Two prime ministers were assassinated, one in 1930 by leftists, the other in 1932 by radical rightists. A steady political crackdown resulted in military control of the government by 1937, climaxing with the 1941 elevation of **Hideki Tojo**, head of Japan's army, to the prime ministership. At the same time, **militaristic nationalism** skyrocketed. Starting in 1931, the Japanese put their nationalistic feelings into action, seizing Manchuria from China and withdrawing from the League of Nations. They resumed their war against China in 1937, committing dreadful atrocities like the **Rape of Nanjing** that December when Japanese troops butchered 200,000 to 300,000 noncombatants, including thousands of women who were first sexually assaulted. Before the end of World War II, the Japanese would spread this campaign of xenophobic imperialism throughout much of East and Southeast Asia, euphemistically naming their sphere of influence the **Greater East Asian Co-Prosperity Sphere**.

Nationalism in interwar Japan was bolstered by the ideology of *State Shinto*, which propagandistically perverted Japan's indigenous faith to foster a sense of racial superiority and unquestioning loyalty to the state. Anti-Western feelings sharpened, and the slogan "Asia for the Asians" called for the expulsion of colonizing powers like Britain and France.

In South and Southeast Asia, **national liberation movements** became increasingly influential. Anticolonial agitation escalated in the Dutch East Indies (now Indonesia), Burma, and Indochina (especially among the Vietnamese). Such efforts were typically led by Western-educated elites and middle-class intellectuals and students, and they tended to involve uneasy alliances between liberal modernizers and radical communists—much like that between the Nationalists and Communists in China and often breaking apart in the same way.

The most successful of these movements appeared in India, spearheaded by the **Indian National Congress**. Because they had supported Britain loyally during World War I, Indians hoped for greater autonomy after the war. Aggrieved by the lack of change, they began staging mass protests, one of which, at **Amritsar** in 1919, resulted in the killing or wounding of more than 1,400 unarmed demonstrators by British troops. During the 1920s, India balanced on a political knife edge and could easily have erupted into bloody revolution.

That it did not was due mainly to the guidance of **Mohandas Gandhi**, a leading figure in the Congress since 1915, known to his followers as Mahatma, or "great soul." Imprisoned several times by the British, Gandhi combined political activism and Hindu religious principle to devise the policy of **nonviolent resistance**, which he called *satyagraha* ("hold to the truth"). An example of *satyagraha* in action came in 1930 after the British imposed a punitively high tax on salt. Rather than protest violently, Gandhi led 5,000 people on a two hundred–mile march to the seashore, where they made salt illegally by drying out seawater. When the British arrived, Gandhi allowed himself to be arrested peacefully.

Freed in 1931, Gandhi continued to work with the Congress but more as a spiritual leader than a political one. The latter role fell to the lawyer **Jawaharlal Nehru**, a secular modernizer. Gandhi and Nehru now pressed for full independence, and even after Britain granted a constitution in 1935 that promised eventual self-rule, the Congress responded with its "Quit India" campaign. Britain realized that it would have to accelerate its plans for withdrawal—although these were delayed until 1947 by the advent of World War II.

The Congress, which chiefly represented Hindu interests, was not the only force agitating for Indian freedom. In 1930, **Muhammad Ali Jinnah** ended many years of cooperation with the Congress and founded the **All-India Muslim League**, which aimed not just for independence but for the creation of a separate Islamic state. The failure of the Muslim League and the Congress to resolve their differences peacefully led to great bloodshed and decades of Indo-Pakistani rivalry.

> **NOTE**
>
> **Influences on Gandhi included the American Henry David Thoreau, especially his *On Civil Disobedience* (1849), and the Russian novelist Leo Tolstoy, who embraced spiritual pacifism. Gandhi himself shaped the outlook of Martin Luther King Jr., who adopted nonviolent resistance in the African-American struggle for civil rights.**

Authoritarianism in Latin America

During the interwar years, Latin America coped as before with Western **economic imperialism**—the **United Fruit Company** was merely the best known of the many corporations that influenced politics there—and the diplomatic weakness that came with being part of the **U.S. sphere of influence**. The Cuban-American Treaty of 1903 authorized the United States to intervene in Cuba's foreign policy (and gave it the option, still active, to lease the Guantánamo naval base). The Americans also occupied Haiti in 1915 to protect U.S. sugar companies, established a long-term military presence in Panama after opening the **Panama Canal** in 1914, and invaded northern Mexico in 1916, although this was a response to repeated raids on U.S. soil by the rebel leader Pancho Villa. The only attempt to *reduce* U.S. influence in Latin America was Franklin Roosevelt's **Good Neighbor Policy** (1935), which included the withdrawal of troops from Haiti.

Latin American economies modernized unevenly during these years, largely because it remained advantageous for economic elites and foreign investors to continue **plantation monoculture** and the extraction of a handful of **raw materials** rather than industrialize or diversify. Also, after 1929, the **Great Depression** devastated Latin American economies by wiping out international demand for nearly half their exports. Most farmers and laborers, especially those of mixed or native race, worked under oppressive conditions and enjoyed few political rights.

The region did not escape its long tradition of authoritarian rule, a trend made worse by the Depression. Three examples—Mexico, Brazil, and Argentina—show the varying degrees to which dictatorship prevailed. Mexico was the mildest, after the convoluted **Mexican Revolution** (1910–1920), which followed a pattern not unlike China's. In 1910–1911, the liberal democrat **Francisco Madero** overthrew **Porfirio Díaz**, a general who had ruled since 1876, modernizing the country but growing corrupt and abusive over time. Like Sun Yat-sen in China, Madero was not destined to govern for long. From the left, he was pressured by rural radicals like **Francisco "Pancho" Villa** and **Emiliano Zapata**, who initially supported him but led uprisings against him when he did not deliver agrarian reform—the breakup of large plantations unfairly acquired by wealthy owners and the redistribution of that land to village communities—as rapidly as he had promised. From the right, Madero faced opposition from conservative military officers, who staged a coup in 1913 and executed him. Madero's liberal ally Venustiano Carranza took back power in 1914 and enacted the **Constitution of 1917**, which guaranteed universal suffrage (including women), the separation of church and state, and the right to strike. Unfortunately, like Madero before him, Carranza was caught between Zapata's and Villa's radical insurrections on one side and military disloyalty on the other. Although he defeated Zapata in 1919, he was removed in 1920 by the general Álvaro Obregón and soon killed.

Emiliano Zapata
Zapata, commander of the Liberation Army of the South and famed for his slogan "better to die on your feet than live on your knees," perished in battle in 1919. Like his ally Pancho Villa (assassinated in 1923), Zapata was derided by his enemies as a bandit. However, he is widely regarded as a hero in Mexico, and many throughout Latin America revere him as an icon of grass-roots activism and principled popular revolt.

Although violence continued into the early 1930s, Obregón fundamentally restored order in Mexico, and Carranza's death is considered the revolution's endpoint. Obregón eliminated Villa in 1923, began substantial land redistributions, and instituted a number of labor and educational reforms. He stepped down in 1924, only to be assassinated in 1928. In 1929, Obregón's successors founded the **National Revolutionary Party** (PNR), which renamed itself the **Institutional Revolutionary Party** (PRI) in 1946 and ruled until the late 1980s. Like Napoleon in France, the PNR/PRI claimed to govern in the revolution's name. In reality, it created a durable oligarchy in which the party chose a president every six years and arranged a "democratic" election that guaranteed victory to its candidate. Under this mild form of authoritarianism, the upper classes prospered and the country modernized. However, the lower classes—workers and peasants—lagged far behind the elite, and the middle class remained small. Conditions improved under **Lázaro Cárdenas**, president from 1934 to 1940, who carried out a massive **land reform**, transferring 40 million acres from the upper classes to the peasantry. Cárdenas also stood up to the United States with his **nationalization of the oil industry**. Because Cárdenas compensated U.S. investors for their losses, Franklin Roosevelt abided by his **Good Neighbor Policy** and did not intervene, allowing Cárdenas to form PEMEX, Mexico's state-run oil enterprise.

More so than Mexico, Brazil descended deep into dictatorship in 1930 when an oligarchy dominated by wealthy landowners gave way to the despotic presidency of the cattleman Getúlio Vargas, who ruled from the far right until 1945. Vargas freed Brazil from its economic overdependence on coffee exports and turned it into Latin America's most industrialized nation, and he cleverly generated popularity by granting limited concessions to minorities and the poor. But as an admirer of Mussolini and Hitler, Vargas also censored the press and authorized his secret police to torture prisoners. Likewise, Depression-era Argentina became a dictatorship, also in 1930, when the military ousted radical president Hipólito Yrigoyen, who had spent the 1920s antagonizing the army and elite classes with pro-union and pro-worker policies. Argentina's "**infamous decade**" of dictatorship lasted until 1943, when a new series of coups paved the way for the 1946 rise of another strongman, the charismatic general **Juan Perón**.

WORLD WAR II AND THE HOLOCAUST

World War II (1939–1945) was and remains the largest and deadliest conflict in human history. It involved more than sixty nations, cost several trillion dollars, and killed approximately 60 million people. **Civilian deaths** account for half that figure, owing largely to **destructive tactics and technologies** (including **terror bombing** and **strategic bombing**) and even more to campaigns of **genocide**—a new term coined during the war—which included the Nazi **Holocaust**. World War II completely shifted the balance of global strength, toppling the European powers from their position of geopolitical superiority and ushering in the U.S.-Soviet **Cold War** and a massive wave of postwar **decolonization**.

The war's principal actors included:

- The **Axis powers**: Nazi Germany, Fascist Italy (joined the war in June 1940; left in July 1943), and Japan
- Major **Allied powers**: Great Britain, France (left the war in June 1940), Canada, Australia, New Zealand, the USSR (joined the war in June 1941), the United States (joined the war in December 1941), and Nationalist China

Origins and Interwar Foreign Policy

Compared to the complex origins of World War I, the causes of World War II are straightforward. Aggression during the 1930s on the part of Japan, Italy, and Germany went unchecked by a feeble **League of Nations** and was repeatedly answered by the Western democracies with the policy of **appeasement**—letting a belligerent party have what it wants in the hope that it will ask for no more.

Foreign-policy destabilization began in 1931 when Japan invaded the Chinese province of Manchuria and left the League of Nations. In 1933, Hitler pulled out of the League; in 1935, he began rearmament and conscription in open violation of the Treaty of Versailles. Fearing Hitler's anticommunist rhetoric and his talk of *Lebensraum* ("living space") in Eastern Europe, the USSR attempted a policy of **collective security** with the West, securing a seemingly reliable alliance with France and Czechoslovakia. Britain, distrusting the Soviets, distanced itself from this partnership.

Several factors explain the democracies' passivity in the face of fascism during the 1930s. U.S. isolationism did not help, and neither did British antipathy for the USSR. The Great Depression kept the democracies economically timid, and the memory of World War I bloodshed made them reluctant to risk a new round of fighting. Also, Britain and France put too much faith in defensive barriers to keep them safe: the English Channel in the case of the former and the Maginot Line, a long chain of border fortifications, in the case of the latter.

Events quickly proved the hollowness of collective security. In 1935, Italy brutally invaded Ethiopia, and when the League of Nations tried to sanction it, Italy abandoned the League and drew closer to Germany. In the spring of 1936, Hitler defied France and Britain by sending troops into the Rhineland, which the Treaty of Versailles had demilitarized, and the democracies' failure to respond emboldened him. That summer, Mussolini and Hitler joined forces to intervene in the **Spanish Civil War** (1936–1939), aiding the military rebellion led by the right-wing general Francisco Franco against Spain's recently elected coalition of liberals and leftists. The Soviets sent assistance to the Spanish government—but when the French, who also promised to help, were persuaded by Britain to remain neutral, they disappointed Stalin and undermined collective security. The Germans and Italians tested new tanks, airplanes, and tactics in Spain, and with their help, Franco marched to victory in 1939, ruling as Spain's dictator until his death in 1975. Things grew worse in 1937 as Japan resumed its war in China—committing the horrific **Rape of Nanjing** that December—and forged friendly ties with Germany and Italy.

Interwar Conflicts: Laboratories of Destruction
The conflicts of the interwar period served as a test case for many of the destructive tactics and technologies unleashed more notoriously during World War II. Italy's 1935–1936 conquest of Ethiopia and Japan's war in China both included the use of **poison gas** and **terror bombing**, the deliberate targeting of civilians to demoralize an enemy population. Japan's **Rape of Nanjing** in 1937 foreshadowed worse atrocities to come. In addition to experimenting in Spain with the tank-airplane coordination that made **blitzkrieg warfare** possible, Germany pursued terror bombing. Pablo Picasso's renowned *Guernica*, pictured above, stands as an immortal artistic protest against the Germans' aerial destruction of the Spanish city of the same name.

Collective security's final collapse soon followed. In 1938, Germany annexed Austria and, that summer, threatened war against Czechoslovakia over the **Sudetenland**, a border region given to the Czechs by the Treaty of Versailles even though it contained a large German-speaking population. Because of France's and the USSR's treaties with Czechoslovakia, war seemed unavoidable. Then, at September's **Munich Agreement**—the century's most woeful example of **appeasement**—the British prime minister, Neville Chamberlain, and the French premier agreed to let Hitler take the Sudetenland in exchange for his promise to expand no further. The Czechs and Soviets, both uninvited, were outraged, and Stalin, already upset about the Spanish Civil War, lost faith in collective security.

In the spring of 1939, Hitler exposed Chamberlain's foolishness by invading the rest of Czechoslovakia and staking loud claims to Polish territory. The British and French now decided to stand firm over Poland, but in August, Stalin, no longer trusting the democracies, negotiated a nonaggression treaty with Hitler. This **Nazi-Soviet Pact** kept the USSR neutral and allowed Hitler to invade Poland without worrying about a two-front war. Germany's invasion of Poland on September 1, 1939, began World War II.

World War II: A Combat Overview

Between 1939 and the end of 1941, the Axis powers enjoyed great triumphs. New technology and tactics gave armed forces tremendous offensive capacity, making World War II far more mobile and faster paced than World War I—but also far more destructive, especially where civilians were concerned.

Germany immediately exploited this new offensive potential with its innovative **blitzkrieg** ("lightning war"), which used tanks and airplanes to penetrate quickly and deeply into enemy territory. Poland fell to Germany in six weeks in the fall of 1939, and when Hitler turned against Norway, Denmark, Belgium, the Netherlands, and France in the spring of 1940, his forces defeated them all between April and June. From the summer of 1940 through the spring of 1941, Germany focused its attention on Britain, trying—but failing—to bomb it into submission from the air. The Royal Air Force defended England's skies in the **Battle of Britain**, and Britain held on thanks to control of the seas, the skill of its pilots, its use of radar, and economic aid from Canada and the United States. (Although the latter was neutral, Franklin Roosevelt sympathized with the Allies and began his **Lend-Lease program** of economic assistance to Britain, and later the USSR, in the spring and summer of 1941.)

The war expanded in 1941 to Africa, where German tank forces drove toward the British-controlled Suez Canal, and also to Eastern Europe, as Hitler began a surprise invasion of the USSR—a fateful decision since he had not yet finished off the British. **Operation Barbarossa** began in June, and from this point forward, between 60 to 75 percent of all German forces fought on this Soviet front. At first, it looked as though blitzkrieg would topple the USSR as quickly as it had France: the Germans surrounded Leningrad, the country's second largest city, placing it under the worst siege in modern times, and reached the outskirts of Moscow in October. But a last-ditch defensive effort halted the German advance in December.

At this point, events in Asia further complicated the war. Earlier in 1941, the Japanese, extending their imperial reach from China to Southeast Asia, had occupied French Indochina, a bold move that also threatened Britain's Asian colonies and the U.S.-controlled Philippines.

> **NOTE**
>
> **World War II was so dynamic because of new or improved technologies. At sea, aircraft carriers appeared alongside battleships to give navies an airborne punch, and long-range submarines extended offensive reach. On the ground, tanks combined the power of artillery with excellent mobility, allowing maneuvers like Germany's nimble sidestepping of France's mammoth but ineffectual Maginot Line. Heavy bomber aircraft dropped unheard-of quantities of explosives on dozens of cities from London and Rotterdam to Dresden and Tokyo. Among the wartime innovations that deeply affected postwar life were radar, jet aircraft, rocketry, atomic bombs, and computers.**

Repeated U.S. trade embargoes heightened diplomatic tensions and convinced the Japanese to launch a massive naval and air assault throughout the Pacific, beginning with the December 7, 1941, surprise attack on **Pearl Harbor**. By the late spring of 1942, the Japanese were masters of the South Pacific and Southeast Asia, having captured Hong Kong, Thailand, Burma, Britain's mighty naval base at Singapore, the Philippines, and the Dutch East Indies (modern Indonesia). However, Pearl Harbor, while devastating, was not a knockout blow, and by bringing the United States into the war—just as the Soviets stalled the Germans outside Moscow—Japan had roused a gigantic enemy that neither it nor Germany could come close to matching in terms of industrial production or humanpower reserves. Although they were still winning major victories, the Axis powers had made the war far more strategically and economically challenging for themselves.

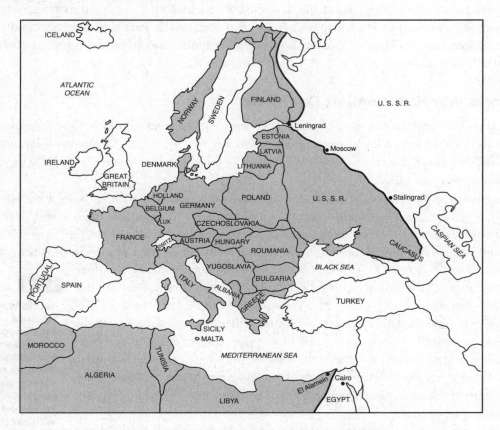

The European and Mediterranean Theaters of Combat, World War II, 1942
From September 1939 until the autumn of 1942, the Axis powers—Germany, Italy, and Japan—succeeded in seizing the military initiative and keeping it. By the middle of 1942, Nazi Germany had reached the height of its power. The areas shaded in gray mark territory that was controlled directly by Germany before the war, belonged to its allies, or had been conquered by it during the war. Not long after this point, primarily because of defeats at El Alamein and Stalingrad, the tide of war turned against the Germans and their partners.

This fact became clear in the summer and fall of 1942 when three turning-point battles completely reversed the war's tide. Had the Axis won them, their short-term advantages in skill and speed might have forced an end favorable to them before the Allies' long-term economic and population advantages overpowered them. The three battles were **Midway** (June 1942), a Pacific clash in which the U.S. Navy destroyed the bulk of Japan's carrier fleet;

El Alamein (July–November 1942), where the British turned back the German tanks driving toward the Suez Canal; and **Stalingrad** (August 1942–February 1943), a savage showdown on the Volga, where a huge German force nearly pushed the Soviets across the river en route to the USSR's oil reserves but was instead encircled and captured.

In 1943 and 1944, U.S. forces in the Pacific moved west toward Japan in a strategy of **island hopping**, while Allied armies and guerrilla uprisings in China and Southeast Asia pinned down Japanese forces on the mainland. In Europe, the Allies invaded Italy from North Africa in 1943, deposing Mussolini's government. At sea, they neutralized Germany's submarines—the only truly dangerous threat still at Hitler's disposal—in the **Battle of the Atlantic** (1942–spring 1943). From the east, the Soviets pushed the Germans out of the USSR, into Eastern Europe, and toward Berlin. In June 1944, Operation Overlord, or the **D-Day invasion**, landed more than 170,000 British, Canadian, and American troops on the beaches of Normandy in northern France. By this point, the Allies also had complete control of the skies. Having been bombed so mercilessly in 1940 and 1941, they now carried out the **strategic bombing** of German-held Europe at will, seeking to disrupt military and economic efforts and to break the civilian population's morale. By the summer of 1944, U.S. forces were within range to do the same to Japan. Strategic bombing killed hundreds of thousands of civilians and remains one of the most controversial aspects of the Allies' war effort.

The Axis collapsed in 1945. With the Soviets storming Berlin, Hitler committed suicide on April 30, and Germany ceased hostilities in early May. Japan continued to fight, despite constant firebombing and the steady approach of U.S. naval forces. America's new president, Harry Truman, who took office after Franklin Roosevelt's death in April, feared that an invasion of Japan's home islands would cost hundreds of thousands of casualties. He hoped to win from the air, but conventional bombardment did not appear to be denting the Japanese leadership's resolve. So in mid-July, when Allied scientists completed the first successful atomic bomb test, Truman elected to use the new weapon to hasten Japan's surrender. On August 6, the B-29 *Enola Gay* dropped an atomic bomb on **Hiroshima**, killing an estimated 80,000 initially, with tens of thousands dying later from burns or radioactive fallout. Japan still refused to yield, but a second bomb, released over Nagasaki on August 9 and killing another 80,000 in total, forced Japan's capitulation. Formal surrender followed in September.

War Crimes and the Holocaust

Violence in World War II was unprecedented, both in scale and type. Half of the approximately 60 million people killed by the war were civilians, and the **war crimes** were of unprecedented cruelty. It was during World War II that **genocide** was formally defined as a crime.

The Allies were not blameless when it came to brutality. The Soviet army raped as many as 2 million women and girls as it advanced through Germany toward Berlin. The Allies' **strategic bombing** campaign killed over 600,000 in German-held Europe and at least another 500,000 in Japan, and some historians and legal commentators—albeit a minority—have argued that Allied bombing should be considered a war crime. Similarly, the question of whether it was proper or necessary to drop the atomic bombs on Japan, especially the second one, remains a matter of controversy.

Allied bombing proved especially devastating to certain cities, including Hamburg in 1943 and **Dresden** in early 1945, where firebombing killed approximately 25,000 to 35,000 (this figure was inflated to 200,000 by early but inaccurate German reports that continue to confuse the record today). Dresden remains notorious because it took place when the war was essentially over and because it is debatable whether the city was militarily important enough to warrant targeting. The author Kurt Vonnegut was present in Dresden with a number of other U.S. prisoners of war and portrays the event in his novel *Slaughterhouse Five*. The U.S. firebombing of Tokyo in March 1945 killed approximately 100,000 people—more than either atomic bomb did in its initial blast.

Nonetheless, the Axis committed atrocities more systematically and on a larger scale. Both Japan and Germany killed large numbers of civilians, executed or mistreated prisoners of war, and pressed several million enemy noncombatants into forced labor. Japan plundered its occupied territories, the so-called Greater East Asian Co-Prosperity Sphere. It used prisoners as human subjects to test biological and chemical weapons, and Japan's army forced thousands of women from mainland Asia to serve as "comfort women," or military prostitutes.

Most heinous were the German campaigns of **genocide**, a crime defined in 1943 by the Polish-Jewish lawyer Rafael Lemkin as the premeditated attempt to annihilate a group based on its identity. As noted above, Nazi policy singled out several racial groups as "subhumans" who could not be allowed to "contaminate" the Germans' "pure Aryan" blood. These included Slavs, those of African descent, Roma (Gypsies), and especially Jews. Others considered "undesirable" were homosexuals, the mentally disabled, and people with venereal or incurable diseases. Before 1939, treatment of these groups—particularly **anti-Semitic persecution**—had grown steadily worse, but the war triggered an escalation of systematic violence, culminating in the mass exterminations popularly known as the **Holocaust**. Nazi officials estimated that 11 million Jews in Europe would have to be expelled or eradicated—the so-called Jewish problem—and Roma were to be eliminated as well. Slavic peoples were to be conquered with brute force and the survivors enslaved.

In 1939 and 1940, as much of Europe came under German control, Nazi authorities began detaining Jews in **concentration camps** and city neighborhoods called **ghettos**. In the spring of 1941, as Germany readied its invasion of the USSR, special **task groups** (*Einsatzgruppen*) were formed to accompany the German army and execute Soviet Jews by shooting. In July, moreover, an order to prepare a "**final solution** of the Jewish problem" was handed down to Nazi security forces, and though it was not signed by Hitler, it came from Nazi leader Hermann Goering, certainly on Hitler's orders. Firing-squad executions proved too slow for the Nazis, and by late 1941, they were seeking more efficient means of mass killing. Inspired by how Nazi doctors had been clinically "euthanizing" the mentally and physically ill since 1939, key officials decided—principally at the **Wannsee Conference** of January 1942—to use special **extermination camps**, already under construction in German-held Poland, to kill victims on a truly industrial scale. At these camps, which included the infamous **Auschwitz-Birkenau**, victims were gassed, their bodies plundered for hidden loot, and their remains cremated. Also at these camps, numerous victims, especially Jews, Roma, and Soviet prisoners of war, were used for medical and scientific experiments to the point of mutilation and death.

In the end, the "final solution" killed approximately 6 million Jews. Another 5 to 6 million non-Jewish victims—including an estimated 200,000 to 1.5 million Roma—perished as a result of nonmilitary killings carried out by the Germans. It was to punish these atrocities that the Allies organized the **Nuremberg Trials** (1945–1946), where Nazi leaders were prosecuted and the concept of **crimes against humanity** was codified. (A series of Tokyo Trials followed in the years 1946–1948.) In 1948, in a collective effort to avoid such barbarities in the future, the United Nations adopted the **Universal Declaration of Human Rights**.

Governance, 1945 to the Present

20

For almost five decades after World War II, most of the world was divided by the **Cold War** into hostile camps led by the United States and the USSR.

Domestic developments worked themselves out in myriad ways during the postwar years. Geopolitical struggle resulted in a nuclear arms race and the creation of massive military-industrial complexes that still operate today. Warfare continued to harm large numbers of civilians. Also during the Cold War, a mass wave of **decolonization** deprived the European powers of their empires. Sometimes through peaceful negotiation, sometimes through violent separation, dozens of new nations were formed in Asia, Africa, and the Pacific.

During the late 1980s and 1990s, communism in Eastern Europe and the USSR collapsed, ending the Cold War, and a number of other dictatorships democratized as well. This left the United States as the world's sole superpower, with China—which remained communist—as a rising power. The **al-Qaeda terrorist attack of September 11, 2001**, began a new global struggle, the U.S.-led war on terror, which sparked wars in Iraq and Afghanistan and generally sharpened tensions between the West and the Islamic world. Although the end of the Cold War removed the threat of superpower-caused nuclear annihilation, heightened geopolitical instability and recurrent instances of **genocide** and **ethnic cleansing** have prevailed ever since.

THE UNITED NATIONS AND OTHER INTERNATIONAL ORGANIZATIONS

Compared to the League of Nations, the United Nations has greater powers of enforcement, including a wide variety of sanctions and the ability to call up peacekeeping forces and to intervene in crises and conflicts. The 15-member Security Council, not the larger and more unwieldy General Assembly (which includes all members), theoretically provides streamlined leadership. On the other hand, five permanent members of the Security Council—the United States, Russia, China, Britain, and France—possess automatic veto power, sometimes blocking effective action. Famous branches of the United Nations include UNICEF (children's relief), the World Health Organization, and UNESCO (cultural preservation). Also during the postwar era but separate from the UN, a variety of nongovernmental organizations and humanitarian groups have arisen to promote important causes or carry out relief efforts outside the nation-state framework. Famous examples include the Red Cross and Doctors without Borders (medical relief), Greenpeace (environmental activism), and Amnesty International (human rights).

COLD WAR AND DECOLONIZATION: FOREIGN POLICY SHIFTS, 1945–1991

During the final years of World War II, the "Big Three" among the Allies—Britain, America, and the USSR—settled key questions about the postwar peace, including how to occupy German- and Japanese-held territories. They supported the creation of a new international body, similar to the defunct League of Nations, to arbitrate disputes and preserve the peace. This **United Nations** (UN) came into being at war's end and was designed to be stronger and more durable than its predecessor.

However, tension proved the rule after World War II. Disagreements quickly arose between the Soviets and the Anglo-Americans over a host of issues, especially Stalin's intention—made clear at the **Yalta Conference** in early 1945—to transform Eastern Europe into a Soviet sphere of influence. The Soviets also refused to take part in the **Bretton Woods system** created to facilitate free trade after the war. The Allies divided Germany and Austria into occupation zones, with the Soviets in charge of the east. The capitals, Berlin and Vienna, were similarly divided, although this was complicated by the fact that Berlin lay within the Soviet zone. Austria's occupation ended in 1955, but Germany remained divided until 1990. In Asia, the Korean peninsula was likewise split into a communist northern zone and a pro-Western southern one—a state of affairs that persists today.

The Early Cold War, 1945–1949

Thus began the **Cold War**, the **superpower** rivalry between the United States and the USSR. From 1945 to 1991, the Cold War divided the world into hostile camps, although its bipolar nature was complicated by the eventual breakup of the alliance between Communist China and the USSR. Postwar **decolonization** in the so-called **Third World** interacted with the Cold War because, while some of the era's new nations attempted to preserve neutrality by forming a **nonaligned movement**, many found themselves compelled to ally with one superpower or the other. The Cold War gave birth to the largest **arms race** in history, complete with nuclear arsenals, and while the United States and USSR never went to war with each other, an estimated 50 million people—more than half of them civilian—died in the dozens of smaller conflicts that were fought worldwide during the Cold War.

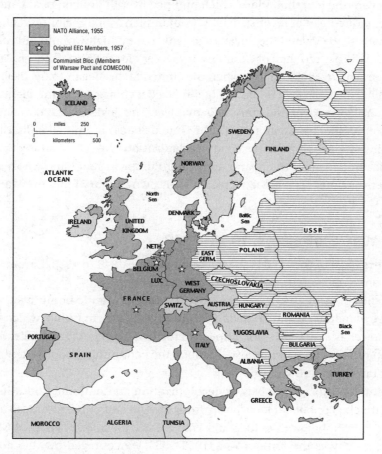

The Cold War Division of Europe, 1957

From 1945 until 1989, the Cold War divided the nations of Europe—with only a few exceptions—into two camps, one dominated by the Soviet Union, the other led by the United States and its European allies. By the mid-1950s, the so-called Iron Curtain had descended over Europe. A number of Western nations were united by the North Atlantic Treaty Organization, a military alliance, and many also joined in the European Economic Community. The Eastern bloc was held together by the Soviet-imposed military alliance known as the Warsaw Pact, as well as COMECON, an economic union led by the USSR.

The first stage of the Cold War lasted from 1945 to 1949 and mainly involved the division of Europe by what Winston Churchill poetically referred to in 1946 as the "**Iron Curtain**": the descent of Soviet power over Poland, Czechoslovakia, Hungary, Romania, Bulgaria, Albania (until 1961), and the eastern half of Germany. (Yugoslavia became communist as well, but its stubbornly independent leader, Josip Broz Tito, broke with the Soviets in 1948.) The Soviet bloc also appeared poised to expand into Iran, Turkey, and Greece, which would have brought the USSR closer to the oil fields of the Middle East and the vital waterways of the eastern Mediterranean.

The U.S. responded with **containment**, a strategy devised by the diplomat George Kennan, who predicted that the USSR would expand as far as it could, as long as it did not have to fight, and could therefore be halted not by combat but by "firm and vigilant" support for countries targeted by the Soviets. In 1947, the United States committed politically to containment with the **Truman Doctrine**, which pledged assistance to Greece and Turkey—and more generally to "any and all countries whose political stability is threatened by communism"—and economically with the **Marshall Plan**, which pumped over $13 billion of aid and investment into a Europe in dire need of reconstruction. Containment's first major test came during the **Berlin Blockade** of 1948 when the Soviets suddenly cut off highway and rail traffic between West Berlin and the western half of Germany. It was easy for the Soviets to stop ground transport without provoking violence, but when the United States began to fly airplanes through Soviet-controlled airspace to West Berlin, Stalin faced a choice: allow the flights to continue or shoot the airplanes down and start an actual war. The Soviets backed down, seeming to validate the containment strategy. In 1949, the United States committed militarily to the Cold War by forming the **North Atlantic Treaty Organization** (NATO), a strategic alliance that bound America to Canada, Britain, and nine other European states and whose membership steadily grew over time. (The Soviets created their own military bloc, the **Warsaw Pact**, to oppose NATO.)

The Cold War Globalizes, 1949–1968

During the next stage of the Cold War, which lasted from 1949 to 1968, Europe ceased to be the conflict's only—or even primary—battleground.

The watershed year of 1949 witnessed the **first Soviet atomic bomb test**, which erased America's edge in military technology, and **communist victory in China**, which brought **Mao Tse-tung** to power as a new ally—for a time—of the USSR. China's Nationalist regime fled to Taiwan, which remains noncommunist, although the communist People's Republic of China (PRC) claims Taiwan as its own.

By this point, the process of postwar **decolonization** and **national liberation** was under way, shifting much geopolitical focus away from Europe and outward to Asia and Africa. In other words, the Cold War quickly globalized, an early sign of which was the **Korean War** (1950–1953). Encouraged by Mao and supported in a more limited way by Stalin, the communist northern half of Korea attempted to conquer the southern half, which was defended by a UN army led by the United States. This was **containment** once again but for potentially higher stakes than in Berlin. Despite fears that the Korean War might spark a larger superpower conflict, the fighting was confined to the peninsula—although it caused more than a million deaths and left the country divided exactly where it had been before.

NOTE

America's involvement in Korea and Vietnam, as well as its other anxieties about communism's global expansion, were based on the domino principle: the belief that if one country in a region "fell" to communism, the rest would too.

This increasing global dimension made the Cold War more complex and stretched U.S. containment to new limits during the 1950s and 1960s. Although a number of the less developed and/or newly decolonized nations in the **Third World** sought to remain neutral or unaligned, most were open to superpower influence, as were national-liberation movements worldwide. As the Soviets and their allies labored to spread communism in these areas, the United States responded with its own interventions. These diplomatic struggles often led to **proxy wars**. Unfortunately, America came to choose its Third World allies based principally on how anticommunist they were, not how democratic. It thus supported many authoritarian regimes. After Korea, key Cold War events in the Third World included the **Cuban Revolution** (1959), which heightened tensions by placing a communist state and Soviet ally less than 100 miles off the U.S. coast. The **Vietnam wars** (1945–1975) began with the liberation of Indochina from French colonization and continued with the division of Vietnam. After France's defeat in 1954, America, prompted by domino-principle logic, attempted to prop up the unpopular southern government against invasion by the communist north. The U.S. effort took a sharp turn for the worse in 1968 and ended with withdrawal in 1973, opening the way for communist victory in 1975.

NOTE

Among the dictators whose anticommunism earned them U.S. support during the Cold War were Francisco Franco in Spain, Fulgencio Batista in Cuba (overthrown in 1959), Ferdinand Marcos in the Philippines, Augusto Pinochet in Chile, Joseph Mobutu in the Congo, and the Shah of Iran (ousted in 1979).

As for the superpower duel, it heated and cooled during the 1950s and 1960s. The death of Stalin in 1953 and his replacement by the less hard-line Nikita Khrushchev appeared to create the potential for better relations. During the **Suez Crisis** of 1956, when Britain, France, and Israel reacted to Egypt's nationalization of the Suez Canal with a military invasion, the Americans—seeking to avert a wider Middle Eastern war—cooperated with the Soviets against their own allies, forcing them to withdraw from Egypt. Even so, Khrushchev quickly showed the limits of his goodwill. In 1956, when Hungary attempted to reform its communist regime and restore ties with the West, the USSR intervened, sparking a **Hungarian uprising** that Khrushchev brutally suppressed. Encouraged by the Cuban Revolution of 1959 and angered by the flight of American U-2 spy planes over the USSR, Khrushchev pursued an aggressive and unpredictable foreign policy in East Germany and Cuba. The Soviets built the **Berlin Wall**, the most tangible embodiment of the Iron Curtain, in 1961. A more dangerous showdown came in 1962 when Khrushchev attempted to install nuclear missiles in Cuba. This led to the **Cuban Missile Crisis** in October when U.S. President John Kennedy successfully countered Khrushchev's move with a naval blockade of Cuba. This moment brought the superpowers the closest they would come to nuclear war, and it played a key role in the forced retirement of Khrushchev in 1964 and his replacement by the more authoritarian but less erratic Leonid Brezhnev. In 1968, Brezhnev reaffirmed the Soviet sphere of influence in Europe by sending Warsaw Pact troops into Czechoslovakia to put down the pro-reform "**Prague Spring**" movement. He justified this invasion by asserting the USSR's right to "protect communism" in Eastern Europe, a stance known as the **Brezhnev doctrine**. Proxy struggles in the Third World continued, and the U.S. involvement in Vietnam escalated.

By the end of the 1960s, the superpowers were deeply enmeshed in their **nuclear arms race**. The United States had maintained a sizable edge through the 1950s, but the Soviets achieved **strategic parity** by the mid-1960s. Each had roughly the same quantity of weapons, and each had developed the **nuclear triad** (the ability to drop nuclear bombs from airplanes, launch nuclear warheads on intercontinental ballistic missiles, or ICBMs, and fire nuclear missiles from submarines). Nuclear weapons made traditional military thinking obsolete: too destructive to contemplate deploying except under extreme circumstances, they became most useful for their **deterrence** value. In theory, as long as each side remained convinced that rash action would destroy it as well as its enemy, both

Cold War diplomacy grew more complicated with the Sino-Soviet split, which began in the 1960s and continued until the collapse of the USSR. The United States began to exploit this split in the 1970s.

sides would avoid doing anything that might trigger a serious crisis. This logic, referred to as **mutually assured destruction** (MAD), was viewed paradoxically—or perversely, depending on one's point of view—as a way to preserve peace between the superpowers. The economic costs of the arms race were enormous, leading President Dwight Eisenhower to warn of the permanent domination of the U.S. economy by a **military-industrial complex** and causing Khrushchev in the USSR to complain about weapons as "metal-eaters" devouring resources that could be put to better use. By the 1960s and 1970s, a vigorous **antinuclear movement** had formed in Europe and North America to protest the expense of nuclear weapons, the inherent dangers they posed, and the environmental and human damage caused by nuclear-weapons testing.

NOTE

Major antinuclear actors include the Committee for Nuclear Disarmament (CND) and Greenpeace (founded as a result of antinuclear activism). The *Bulletin of the Atomic Scientists*, while not strictly antinuclear, has striven since 1945 to educate the public about dangers like nuclear weapons. Every issue features a "doomsday clock" to show how close to "midnight" (global destruction) the world is at any given point.

With U.S. assistance, Britain and France built small nuclear arsenals during the 1960s. China developed its own in 1964. Israel secretly gained nuclear weapons during the Cold War, and South Africa briefly had them but voluntarily decommissioned them. Because rocket technology was so tightly connected with the manufacture of nuclear missiles, the superpower arms race was closely paralleled by the **space race**, associated with hyperpatriotic pride and military rivalry. The USSR put the first human-made object into space (1957) and launched the first successful human space flight (1961), but the United States accomplished the first moon landing in 1969.

The Late Stages of the Cold War, 1969–1991

The late stages of the Cold War encompassed the 1970s and the 1980s, with the final collapse of Eastern European and Soviet communism occurring between 1989 and 1991.

Between 1969 and 1979, the conflict entered a more peaceful phase known as **détente** (French for "relaxation"). The USSR was motivated by fears that America would befriend China, which President Richard Nixon visited in 1972, deliberately exploiting the **Sino-Soviet split**. The United States was wearied by the Vietnam conflict and weakened by the global recession of the 1970s. Both were eager to scale back hostilities. They cooperated in enforcing the **Nuclear Nonproliferation Treaty** (1968–1969) and signed substantial arms-control agreements, such as the Strategic Arms Limitations Treaty (1972). They even joined forces in space during the joint Apollo-Soyuz mission of 1975.

Animosity resumed, however, in 1979. That year, the **Soviet invasion of Afghanistan**, whose purpose was to safeguard against Islamic fundamentalism but which seemed to threaten the oil supplies of the Middle East, damaged Soviet relations with the West. Another point of tension was the **Sandinista revolution in Nicaragua** (1979), which the Soviets supported. Soviet distress at growing unrest in Eastern Europe—especially the 1980 emergence of the dissident trade union **Solidarity** in Poland—made the USSR more edgy, and the election of leaders like **Margaret Thatcher** in Britain (1979) and **Ronald Reagan** in the United States (1980) swung NATO foreign policy to the right. Between 1979 and 1985, the arms race accelerated, Third World brushfire wars worsened, and both superpowers expressed mutual contempt by boycotting each other's Olympic Games (Moscow in 1980, Los Angeles in 1984). Because the weaponry of the 1980s was faster, more accurate, and more powerful than before, the danger of a civilization-destroying nuclear exchange became greater than at any time since the Cuban Missile Crisis.

The Cold War pendulum started swinging the other way in 1985 with the accession of **Mikhail Gorbachev** as leader of the USSR. A liberal reformer, Gorbachev was unwilling to prop up Eastern Europe's communist regimes by force, and he realized that the inefficient Soviet system could no longer afford to keep up with the arms race or continue fighting in Afghanistan, which had turned into a Vietnam-like quagmire for the Red Army. In 1987, Gorbachev resumed arms talks with the United States. His regime allowed Solidarity and other anti-Soviet movements to arise in Eastern Europe, joking that the USSR was replacing the Brezhnev Doctrine with the Sinatra Doctrine, letting Eastern Europeans do things "their way."

The climactic year was 1989. That summer, for the first time since before World War II, Poland held free elections, which gave victory to noncommunist candidates backed by Solidarity. Other communist regimes collapsed as well, culminating in the **fall of the Berlin Wall** that November and the reunification of Germany in 1990. In the opinion of most, the fall of the wall marked the end of the Cold War. It also hastened the end of the USSR. With Gorbachev's economic reforms rapidly failing and with **anti-Soviet nationalism** surging among the USSR's non-Russian ethnic minorities, the Soviet Union itself collapsed in late 1991. Only the United States remained as a true superpower.

Decolonization: General Patterns

Decolonization and **national liberation** deserve to be considered on their own, although specific cases are discussed in the geographical sections that follow.

Between the 1940s and the 1970s, dozens of new nations that attained freedom from their imperial masters came into being. This represented an astounding shift in the balance of global power away from Europe, although many painful legacies of colonization are still felt. Whether a newly liberated nation succeeded in building a healthy political and socioeconomic system depended largely on the answers to the following questions.

- Did it have to fight a war to become free, or did it separate peacefully?
- Had the colonizing power educated a native elite that included trained civil servants and professionals? Did the colonizing power assist actively with the transition to freedom, or did it leave the new country on its own?
- Did serious ethnic, cultural, or religious divisions exist? In some places, the colonizing power had kept such tensions under control. Decolonization sometimes released them, leading to violence.
- Did a country have natural resources to exploit, and did the new government exploit them efficiently and fairly? Many new regimes failed to diversify their economies, and others proved corrupt, hoarding profits for the elites and leaving large gaps between rich and poor.
- Did a newly liberated country take sides in the Cold War? Befriending a superpower could attract technological and economic assistance but could also involve a new country in a Cold War proxy conflict. It could also mean superpower intervention in a country's policy making or the propping-up of an authoritarian or unpopular leader by a superpower "ally."

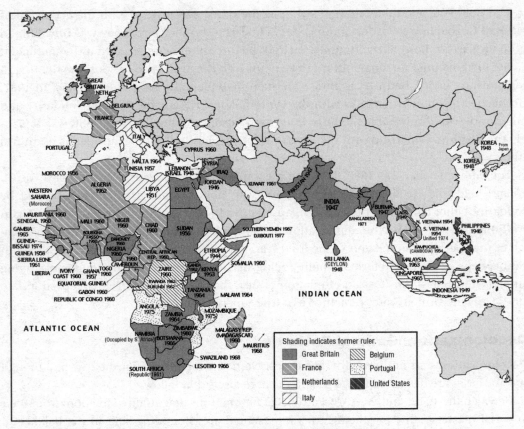

Decolonization and National Liberation in Africa and Asia After 1945
World War II dealt the final blow to Europe's ability to maintain control over colonial empires.
From the 1940s through the 1970s, a great wave of decolonization and national liberation swept
Africa and Asia. Freedom was attained in a variety of ways—sometimes peacefully, sometimes
by force.

In 1955, the **Bandung Conference**, hosted by Indonesia, brought together 29 nations—
most of them recently decolonized—that were interested in staying neutral during the Cold
War and opposing imperialism or neocolonialism of any kind. The conference helped give
birth in 1961 to the **Nonaligned Movement (NAM)** thanks to major players like Gamal Nasser
of Egypt, President Sukarno of Indonesia, India's Jawaharlal Nehru, and Kwame Nkrumah of
Ghana. The NAM eventually came to include 120 states, although formal cooperation among
them was not extensive. Also, many members eventually aligned with one superpower or
another anyway.

DIVERGENT FORMS OF DOMESTIC DEVELOPMENT, 1945–1991
Europe

Postwar Europe found itself in a paradoxical situation. On the one hand, World War II and
global decolonization ended its global dominance, and the superpowers divided it into a Cold
War battleground. On the other hand, once it repaired its wartime damage, it came to enjoy
unprecedented levels of prosperity and modernization—even in the east and especially in
the west.

The **sovietization of Eastern Europe** followed quickly after World War II, consisting of the industrialization and nationalization of the economy, the collectivization of agriculture, and the installation of secret police forces and prison camps. Both Eastern Europe and the USSR recovered from the war surprisingly quickly, and the region enjoyed substantial economic growth between the early 1950s and early 1970s. **Social welfare systems** provided education, medical care, pensions, and other basic services to all citizens. However, Eastern European production was characterized by poor quality, and consumer goods were constantly in short supply because of the priority given to the Cold War arms race. Moreover, the environmental damage caused to Eastern Europe by half a century of careless industrialization has proved nothing short of catastrophic, with the **Chernobyl disaster** of 1986 the most famous of countless examples.

Politically, Soviet-style communism was maintained by repression. Even though Soviet leader Nikita Khrushchev began **de-Stalinization** with his "**secret speech**" of 1956 (which criticized Stalin's purges), reforms were sporadic and limited, and they were scaled back by Khrushchev's more dictatorial replacement, Leonid Brezhnev. The price of going beyond what the USSR was willing to allow was demonstrated by Soviet invasions during the **Hungarian uprising** of 1956 and the 1968 "**Prague Spring**" in Czechoslovakia. In the 1970s, as Western Europe suffered through its own economic crisis, the Soviet bloc entered an economic and administrative decline known as the **Brezhnev stagnation**. At the same time, **dissident movements** arose throughout the region but were kept firmly under control. Only in the 1980s would real change make itself felt.

Recovery was more dramatic in Western Europe, thanks initially to the European Recovery Plan, better known as the **Marshall Plan** (1948). This infusion of more than $13 billion helped to rebuild the war-torn nations of Europe and, by reducing economic desperation, made the spread of communism less likely. Industrial growth and high-tech innovation proved phenomenal during the 1950s and 1960s. With this newfound prosperity, most Western European nations put into place **social welfare systems** or improved on the ones created during the interwar era. Their blending of capitalism and elements of socialism was frequently referred to as the "**middle**" or "**third way**." At times, this involved **nationalizing** sectors of the economy seen as crucial to public well-being—typically transport, communications, and utilities.

One way Western Europeans made up for their loss of global clout was **economic union**, a long process that began with the 1952 birth of the European Coal and Steel Community (Belgium, Luxembourg, the Netherlands, France, and West Germany). It took firm shape in 1957 and 1958 when the same nations formed the **European Economic Community** (EEC), or Common Market, to eliminate tariffs and allow the freer movement of goods and services.

NOTE

Britain, Ireland, and Denmark joined the EEC in 1973, and Greece, Spain, and Portugal were admitted in the 1980s. By the mid-1990s, when the EEC reconstituted itself as the European Union (EU), it had 15 members and has even more now.

Many members of the EEC also participated in the NATO alliance. Not all developments were positive. Europe was caught in the crosshairs of the superpowers' nuclear arms race, and **decolonization** was demoralizing, especially when countries fought unsuccessful wars in an attempt to keep their possessions, as France did in Indochina (1945–1954) and Algeria (1954–1962). Generational change, combined with discontent over the Cold War and wars of decolonization, rendered many parts of Europe vulnerable to the global wave of **1968 protests**, which included **Paris riots** by students and workers and the Soviet bloc's Prague Spring. Authoritarian rule persisted until after the mid-1970s in countries such as Portugal, Greece, and Spain (where Francisco Franco, dictatorial victor of the Spanish Civil War, continued to rule). **Terrorism** also became persistent in the 1960s and 1970s, sometimes as a form of left-wing extremism (as in Italy's Red Brigades, who killed the prime minister in 1976), sometimes as a strategy pursued by separatist movements (including the Basque ETA, fighting to be rid of Spanish rule, and the **Irish Republican Army**, or IRA, a Catholic paramilitary faction trying to wrest mostly Protestant Northern Ireland from British rule and unite it with the Republic of Ireland). Thanks to the shock of the U.S. abandonment of the **gold standard** in 1971 and the **OPEC oil embargo** of 1973, Europe suffered the same **global economic crisis of the 1970s** that most of the developed world did, complete with **stagflation** (slow growth combined with inflation). The soaring costs of Europe's social welfare systems became harder to sustain.

To escape the malaise of the 1970s, many Western European nations moved economically and politically to the right in the 1980s with the election of conservatives like **Margaret Thatcher** in Britain and Helmut Kohl in West Germany. Leaders like these pursued **free-market policies**, retreating in part from the social welfare systems of the past, defying labor unions, and **privatizing** many state-run sectors of the economy. This approach—paralleled by Ronald Reagan's in the United States—led to a recovery of overall wealth but also caused social stress in the form of strikes and layoffs. One key legacy has been a long-term, upward redistribution of wealth from the middle class to the very rich.

Meanwhile, in Eastern Europe, the 1980s saw communism's general collapse. Brezhnev-era stagnation, the rising cost of the arms race, the USSR's ill-fated **invasion of Afghanistan** (1979–1989), the general inefficiency of the system, which led to terrible disasters like the nuclear meltdown at **Chernobyl** in 1986, and the increasingly active **dissident movement** all undermined stability in the Soviet bloc. Unrest was especially apparent in Poland, where the trade union **Solidarity**, led by Lech Walesa, spearheaded a protest movement that united workers, intellectuals, and Catholic clergy. (Pope **John Paul II**, originally from Poland, did much to support anti-Soviet agitation in Eastern Europe.)

Real change here was impossible until 1985 when **Mikhail Gorbachev**, a reform-minded politician, rose to power. Keenly aware that the USSR could no longer pay for the Cold War arms race or its Eastern European sphere of influence, Gorbachev launched a twin reform effort: **perestroika** ("restructuring" the economic system and allowing limited capitalism, similar to what Deng Xiaoping was attempting in Communist China) and **glasnost** ("openness," meaning greater freedom of opinion and the media). He ended the war in Afghanistan, entered into arms talks with the United States, and allowed freedom movements, especially Poland's Solidarity, to reemerge in Eastern Europe. He permitted the **fall of the Berlin Wall** in late 1989, thus helping to end the Cold War.

Unfortunately for Gorbachev, his reforms failed in the USSR, primarily because he did not pursue economic change aggressively enough and because glasnost allowed public discontent to undermine him when things went wrong. Also, **anti-Soviet nationalism** spiked among the USSR's non-Russian ethnicities, who wanted the same freedoms that Eastern Europeans had just gained. By 1990 and 1991, Gorbachev found himself isolated between democratizers (who thought he was not changing enough) and communist hard-liners (angry about the limited changes he had already made). Almost overthrown by a failed coup attempt in the summer of 1991, Gorbachev agreed to the disbandment of the USSR that December.

Population (in millions)

Estonia, Latvia, Lithuania	8.0
Georgia	5.5
Armenia	3.3
Turmenistan	3.5
Moldova	4.3
Kyrgyzstan	4.3
Tajikstan	5.1
Azerbaijan	7.0
Belarus	10.2
Kazakhstan	16.5
Uzbekistan	19.9
Russia	147.4
Ukraine	51.7

Ethnic Groups

Other	8.2%
Russian	50.8%
Ukrainian	15.4%
Kyrgiz	0.9%
Turkmen	1.0%
Lithuanian	1.1%
Moldovan	1.2%
Georgian	1.4%
Tajik	1.5%
Armenian	1.6%
Azeri	2.4%
Tatar	2.4%
Kazakh	2.8%
Belarusian	3.5%
Uzbek	5.8%

Republics Joining Commonwealth
Not Joining

The Fall of the Soviet Union and Formation of the Commonwealth of Independent States, January 1992

In late 1991, Mikhail Gorbachev was forced to dissolve the USSR. At that time, leaders of the former republics of the Soviet Union, with the exception of Estonia, Latvia, Lithuania, and Georgia, chose to form the Commonwealth of Independent States as a way to maintain ties and attempt a smooth transition from Soviet rule.

The Middle East

During the 1950s, Middle Eastern states that were not already free threw off the mandates and protectorates that Europe had established after World War I. Islamic North Africa decolonized as well.

Turkey and Iran continued the programs of secularism and modernization they had begun during the interwar period. The new state of Israel, founded as a Jewish homeland in 1948, did the same and also democratized. Regional developments as a whole were dominated by several factors. Foremost was the Middle East's strategic and economic importance as the world's key source of oil: the **Organization of Petroleum Exporting Countries** (OPEC), founded in 1960, consists largely of states from there. Another was the role of **Islamic fundamentalism** (including Saudi Wahhabism), which hindered modernization and democratization, negatively affected the status of women, and increased tensions between Sunni and Shiite Muslims. The seemingly intractable **Arab-Israeli conflict** diplomatically divided the entire region and gave rise to persistent violence and **terrorism**. Domestically, **authoritarian rule** and human rights abuses were prevalent.

Independence and oil-based wealth made the states of the Middle East more assertive in the 1950s and 1960s, and their geopolitical importance during the Cold War allowed them to bid for superpower patronage as the Soviets and Americans competed for their allegiance. The most prominent example of this new Arab nationalism appeared in Egypt, where military officers overthrew the pro-British king in 1952, bringing Colonel **Gamal Nasser** to power in 1954. An authoritarian modernizer, Nasser defied the West by seizing control of foreign-owned industries; his boldest step came in 1956 with the **nationalization of the Suez Canal**.

This prompted the **Suez Crisis**, in which British, French, and Israeli troops tried to retake the canal but were forced to withdraw by the United States and USSR—an embarrassing demonstration of how the Cold War had diminished European power. Nasser temporarily strengthened ties with the USSR, whose advisers brought technology and weaponry to Egypt and assisted with construction of the monumental **Aswan High Dam**. But when the Soviets became too controlling, Nasser's successors expelled them. Nasser died in 1970. Those ruling after him, Anwar Sadat and Hosni Mubarak, drew closer to the United States and—first among Arab leaders—recognized Israel in 1978. Unfortunately, both men's concerns about rising Islamic fundamentalism persuaded them to continue Nasser's tradition of authoritarian rule.

NOTE

Nasser and certain other leaders promoted the ideology of pan-Arabism, the notion that Arab identity transcends national boundaries left over from Ottoman and European imperialism. Nasser tried to form a United Arab Republic with nations like Iraq and Syria, but except in the case of the tiny United Arab Emirates, such schemes have always collapsed. However, many states—currently more than twenty—have been joined since 1945 in the Arab League, an influential regional association.

Among the most dramatic developments in the postwar Middle East was the **establishment of the state of Israel** (1948) and the resulting **Arab-Israeli conflict**. The British, who took custody of Palestine after the collapse of Ottoman power, had announced their support for a Jewish homeland in the **Balfour Declaration** of 1917. Knowing, however, that keeping this promise would displace Palestinian Arabs and cause local unrest, the British held off on actual implementation during the 1920s and 1930s. After World War II, the question could no longer be delayed due to international sympathy following the horrors of the Holocaust. In 1947, the United Nations took responsibility for the mandate and handed down terms for the **partition of Palestine** the following year. When the partition went into effect, many Palestinian Arabs refused to comply and, with support from surrounding Arab states, launched a war to drive the Israelis away (1948–1949). Not only did this fail, but it scattered many Palestinians to Jordan, Lebanon, and elsewhere as long-term refugees. Military action on the part of Arab states repeatedly fell short, most notably during the Six-Day War in 1967 and the Yom Kippur War in 1973. Each time, Israel, with strong backing from the United States, defeated Arab forces and gained new territories beyond what the UN had granted in 1948. Some Palestinians turned to **terrorism**, especially after 1964 when **Yasser Arafat** founded the **Palestinian Liberation Organization** (PLO). PLO attacks increased in frequency; the most infamous was the assassination of Israeli athletes at the Munich Summer Olympics in 1972.

Hopes for peace blossomed with the **Camp David accords** of 1978 when Anwar Sadat of Egypt, encouraged by U.S. President Jimmy Carter, agreed to recognize Israel in exchange for the return of the Sinai Peninsula, which Israel had seized in 1967. Other moderate Arab states followed Egypt's lead. However, throughout the 1980s, the Palestinian population of Israel staged a continuous uprising called the **(First) Intifada**, protesting discriminatory treatment that they likened to apartheid but which Israeli authorities regarded as self-defense. Intifada-related violence and stepped-up terrorism by the PLO, the Palestinian radical group **Hamas**, and the Shiite movement Hezbollah placed Israel in a difficult position. Its democratic values have not always sat comfortably with harsh occupation policies and the force Israeli authorities have used against civilian agitators in the name of security. The **Oslo Accords** of 1993 held out the promise of a **two-state solution**, but they foundered in 2000–2001, leading to a **Second Intifada** and continued strife.

The most powerful dictatorships in the Cold War Middle East were those of Iran and Iraq. Since the 1920s, Iran had been ruled by the Pahlavi shahs. The last shah, **Mohammad Reza Pahlavi**, governed from 1941 to 1979. Like his predecessors, he used oil wealth to industrialize the country. He opposed Islamic fundamentalism, encouraging Western dress, Western education, the unveiling of women, and the eradication of Sharia law. A U.S. ally, the shah was also ruthlessly authoritarian, relying on torture and secret-police repression. Although he tried to package his modernization policy as a "**White Revolution**" in favor of ordinary people, the shah grew increasingly unpopular. In ill health by 1979, he left the country to seek medical treatment and died of cancer in 1980. The **Iranian Revolution** began in the meantime, and while it first moved in a secular, left-wing direction, control quickly passed to the fundamentalist Shiite cleric **Ayatollah Khomeini**, whom the shah had exiled years before. Khomeini transformed Iran into an anti-Western theocracy in which an elected government came to coexist with authoritarian clerics who held real power and decided ahead of time which candidates could run for office. The new regime stormed the U.S. Embassy, leading to the **Iran hostage crisis** (1979–1981), which damaged American prestige and permanently soured U.S.-Iranian relations. It also became enmeshed in the **Iran-Iraq War** (1980–1988), which caused more than half a million total deaths and devastated both nations.

Iraq's ruler at this time was **Saddam Hussein**, whose Sunni Baath party came to power in 1979. Originally sponsored by the United States because of his opposition to Iran and the USSR, Hussein turned his brutality against his own people and his neighbors. During the Iran-Iraq war, he used poison gas, drafted teenagers for combat, and targeted civilians. He persecuted Iraq's Kurdish minority. In 1990, he also invaded the oil-rich state of Kuwait and appeared ready to move against Saudi Arabia. In the first major conflict of the post–Cold War era, the **Gulf War** (1991), a U.S.-led coalition launched **Operation Desert Storm** to push Hussein out of Kuwait. Between 1991 and Hussein's overthrow in 2003, the international community strove to contain Iraq and prevent its development of weapons of mass destruction.

Africa

Decolonization began in Africa during the 1950s and 1960s. Transitions to freedom varied wildly, depending on whether the colonial power pulled out peacefully or had to be expelled by force and also on whether the new state was able to avoid ethnic violence.

The Islamic states of North Africa became free during the 1950s: Egypt and Sudan from Britain, Libya from Italy, and Morocco and Tunisia from France. The **Algerian war of independence** from France (1954–1962) proved agonizingly violent because the French regarded Algeria not merely as a colony but as part of the actual homeland. Both sides resorted to torture and violence against civilians, and total deaths exceeded 300,000. The bloodshed in Algeria notwithstanding, North African states had several advantages over sub-Saharan ones when it came to decolonization. They had existed earlier as meaningful political units, making the transition to nation-state status easier, and they were more homogeneous (though not completely so) in terms of religion, ethnicity, and language. Their colonizing powers also left behind useful industrial, economic, and infrastructural assets.

NOTE

The anticolonial writer Frantz Fanon, who fought for Algerian independence, justified anti-French violence in his 1961 book *The Wretched of the Earth* on the grounds that Western imperialism had begun the cycle of violence and deserved to be opposed by force. His views resembled those of fellow Marxist Che Guevara, a leader of Cuba's revolution, but contrast greatly with those of Gandhi and Martin Luther King Jr.

In other parts of Africa, Britain and France presided over relatively smooth transitions to freedom, training native elites and working to minimize the possibility of interethnic conflict. French Equatorial Africa and French West Africa—where France had been courting black subjects by gradually expanding their right to vote—separated gradually and without strife between 1945 and 1960, each splitting into smaller states (including Mali, Niger, and Senegal). The Gold Coast's negotiation of freedom from Britain in 1957 and its transformation into the state of Ghana was a key success story. Ghana's leader **Kwame Nkrumah** dreamed idealistically of a peaceful and prosperous continent united by **pan-Africanism**.

Unfortunately, such optimism was not justified. All too many decolonization efforts were plagued by violence. Although Jomo Kenyatta pursued nonviolence on the path to Kenyan independence from Britain in 1963, the radical Mau Mau movement killed almost 2,000 people there during the 1950s. Angola and Mozambique fought bitter wars of independence from Portugal—a notoriously exploitative imperial master—and both of these struggles (1961–1975 and 1969–1975, respectively) gave way to lengthy civil wars between communist and noncommunist forces. In Angola, the U.S.-backed UNITA movement raised $3.5 billion for its war effort by selling diamonds, prompting the first outcries against the global trade in "**blood diamonds**" (also called "conflict diamonds"). Diamonds extracted under slavelike conditions in Liberia and Sierra Leone caused further distress in the 1990s and 2000s.

Violence or the potential for violence also arose between ethnic groups after the colonists withdrew (much as Indians and Pakistanis did when Britain left India in 1947). By the time Belgium pulled out of Rwanda in 1962, its divide-and-conquer tactics had artificially exacerbated hatred between two tribes, the **Hutu** and **Tutsi**, and the potential for bloodshed between them simmered. Muslims and Arabs in North Africa suppressed minorities like the desert Berbers and the **Darfurians** of southern Sudan. When Belgium freed the Congo, postindependence violence was so pervasive from 1960 to 1964 that the United Nations had to intervene, and the democratically elected prime minister, **Patrice Lumumba**, was executed by rebels in 1961—most likely on orders from the Belgian and U.S. governments, which feared his Marxist sympathies. America adopted his dictatorial successor, Joseph Mobutu, as an ally.

White-black tensions persisted longest in **South Africa**. On the one hand the most prosperous, most industrialized, and most technologically advanced country in Africa—and one of the world's richest sources of gold and diamonds—South Africa was also the continent's most deeply racist. In 1948, as an autonomous dominion within the British Commonwealth, South Africa adopted its notorious **apartheid policy**, segregating blacks and "coloureds" (other nonwhites, including a sizable Indian minority) and depriving them of the vote. A broad **antiapartheid movement**—including the Zulu Confederation, the **African National Congress** (ANC), and other groups—arose in the 1950s and called for an end to discrimination in the 1955 Freedom Charter. The killing of almost seventy unarmed protesters during the **Sharpeville massacre** of 1960 further galvanized the movement, and ANC president Albert Luthuli won the Nobel Peace Prize that year. However, the South African government struck back with a series of treason trials, imprisoning leaders like the ANC's **Nelson Mandela**, who remained in jail between 1964 and 1990. In 1961, South African whites voted to withdraw from the British Commonwealth and proclaimed the Republic of South Africa, largely in response to British criticism of their racial policies. Resistance continued, although the ANC and other groups were divided by debates about whether to embrace radicalism and armed struggle or to pursue less violent means. Major figures included Mandela's spouse Winnie and the Anglican bishop **Desmond Tutu** (another Nobel Peace Prize recipient). Finally, during the 1980s, internal unrest, combined with worldwide revulsion and the threat of economic sanctions and divestment, convinced the white government that apartheid could not be maintained. Nelson Mandela was released in 1990, and the government prepared for free election—which, in 1994, resulted in ANC victory and Mandela's election as president.

To generalize about postwar Africa is difficult, but it can be said that few nations managed to build democratic regimes, open societies, and equitably prosperous economies. Several key problems hampered modernization efforts in much of Africa.

- **DICTATORSHIP AND CORRUPTION:** Many of Africa's governments degenerated into strongman regimes. Among the most notorious were those of **Joseph Mobutu** in Congo/Zaire (1965–1997) and **Idi Amin**, who ruled Uganda from 1971 to 1979 and killed 300,000 people, many from rival tribes. Political elites often milked profits from natural resources like gold, diamonds, and oil rather than use them for the betterment of the country. Bribery, nepotism, and tribal favoritism ran rampant.

- **LACK OF CULTURAL AND ETHNOLINGUISTIC UNITY:** Most of Africa's boundary lines were drawn by European colonizers with no regard for tribal or ethnic territorial claims, leaving most new states with a confusing variety of cultures, languages, and religions. This made governance difficult even if groups were not hostile toward each other.

> **NOTE**
>
> **Ethiopia fell victim to dictatorship in 1977 when a Soviet-backed general, Mengistu Haile Mariam, ousted the monarch Haile Selassie I. Mengistu killed political rivals and ethnic minorities, launched war against Somalia, and mishandled the 1983–1985 Ethiopian famine (even using it as a weapon against regions that opposed him). Before losing power in 1991, Mengistu caused between 1 and 2 million deaths.**

- **ETHNIC VIOLENCE AND CONSTANT ARMED CONFLICT:** Warfare in Africa was near-constant during these years, although most conflicts were fought within national boundaries, not between different countries—a testament to the prevalence of ethnic violence. Sometimes the Cold War restrained such violence in places where a strongman supported by one of the superpowers kept order. In other cases, African nations—or rival factions within nations—became pawns in the global chess game between the United States and the USSR. By the end of the Cold War, Africa was awash in the uncontrolled flow of light weapons, and the horrific practice of conscripting **child soldiers** was well under way.

- **HEALTH-RELATED CRISES:** From the 1980s onward, the **HIV/AIDS** virus, which originated in Africa, killed millions. Funding for treatment is perennially low, and unprotected sex has caused the virus to spread among heterosexuals as well as homosexuals. Older diseases like **malaria** and sleeping sickness are still widespread. Population growth has outstripped economic growth and agricultural production, and **famines** remain common. Among the worst were those in Somalia and Ethiopia during the 1980s.

East Asia

Much like West Germany in Europe, Japan was forced by defeat in World War II to rebuild completely, and therefore its emergence as an economic powerhouse was a surprise. The United States occupied Japan during the 1940s, demilitarizing and democratizing it, although the emperor kept his place on the throne as a symbolic figurehead. Viewing Japan as an anchor of its Cold War policy in Asia, America invested in it heavily and maintained a large military presence on the island of Okinawa. Japan's moderately conservative **Liberal Democratic Party** (LDP) promoted economic growth by fostering a culture of hard work and selfless discipline. **Zaibatsu corporations** still played a significant role in Japan. At its peak during the 1980s, Japan's economy—the **"tiger"** of Asia—was the third most productive, and its social welfare and educational systems were top-notch. Economic downturn after the early 1990s broke the LDP's near-monopoly on power, but even in a weakened state, Japan remains economically important in the post–Cold War era.

Joining Japan in prosperity were the so-called **little tigers** of Taiwan (home to Chiang Kai-shek's Nationalist regime) and South Korea. Both developed high-tech, productive economies but remained mildly authoritarian until Chiang's death in 1975 and South Korea's liberalization in the 1980s. Both were staunch anticommunist allies of the United States, even after the U.S. government established diplomatic ties with Communist China. Other little tigers included Hong Kong (a British colony until its return to mainland China in 1997) and Singapore.

The People's Republic of China (PRC), established in 1949 by **Mao Tse-tung** (Mao Zedong), has been the most populous communist nation on earth for more than half a century. Appealing to China's vast peasant populace instead of relying solely on proletarian support, Mao defeated Chiang Kai-shek after World War II and drove his Nationalist government to Taiwan, which still remains politically separate from the mainland. China was ruled by Mao until his death in 1976. At the start, Mao seemed satisfied with pragmatic social and economic reforms. His New Democracy of the early 1950s was greeted with enthusiasm, as were his initial land reforms. His first Five-Year Plan (1953–1958), which imitated the Soviet model, led to industrial growth. Collectivization of agriculture began in 1955 but was (at first) carried out more gradually than in Stalin's USSR.

On the other hand, Mao's radical transformation of society, which included persecution of dissenters and so-called class enemies (members of the bourgeoisie or aristocracy), was harsh. At the end of the 1950s, he pressed too quickly for further modernization. In 1958, his **Great Leap Forward** industrialized on a more grandiose scale than the Five-Year Plan, and it intensified the collectivization of agriculture, calling for an unrealistic increase in food production. Stress and confusion led to chaos, industrial breakdown, and agricultural collapse. The resulting famine killed millions in 1959 and 1960 (the best estimate is 15 to 20 million).

Mao halted the Great Leap Forward in 1960 but embarked on another radical program in 1966: the **Great Proletarian Cultural Revolution**, which lasted until 1976. Generally interpreted as a way for Mao and his wife, Jiang Qing, to strike at their political enemies, the Cultural Revolution sought to instill absolute revolutionary purity within Chinese culture. Censorship was crushingly heavy, and young communist activists, known as Red Guards, rampaged through the country, denouncing anyone—professors, managers, artists—they considered untrue to revolutionary ideals. Victims were demoted, often sent to labor camps for "reeducation," and sometimes executed. Even members of the communist elite were not immune; among those arrested was Mao's future successor, Deng Xiaoping.

The Cultural Revolution ended with Mao's death in 1976. In 1978, **Deng Xiaoping**, having defeated Mao's widow and her radical allies (the "Gang of Four"), rose to power. Deng was a modernizer like Mao but also a pragmatist more concerned with China's well-being than abstract Marxist ideals. (He expressed this view by commenting that it makes no difference whether a cat is black or white as long as it catches mice.) In contrast to Mao's strict anticapitalism, **Deng's economic reforms** returned a measure of collectivized land to the farmers and allowed limited capitalism—much like Gorbachev's perestroika program in the USSR but faster and more permissive. Deng allowed certain levels of private trade and created **special economic zones** where communist regulations did not apply. As a result, China experienced huge economic growth through the 1980s, including rising wages and an improved standard of living. This trend has continued since.

However, with greater prosperity came the desire for greater freedom, a luxury Deng was not prepared to allow. Unlike his fellow reformer Gorbachev, whose glasnost policy allowed more democracy in the USSR, Deng maintained authoritarian control. The clearest sign of this came in May 1989 when Chinese students gathered at **Tiananmen Square** in Beijing and demanded political freedoms to match their newfound economic ones. Deng refused to grant any concessions, and when the students disobeyed orders to disperse, he crushed the demonstrations by sending in tanks. To this day, China's communist authorities have pursued this same combination of political strictness and economic liberalization.

South and Southeast Asia

As in Africa, decolonization in these parts of Asia proceeded along two lines. In some cases, it was negotiated peacefully. In others, it was achieved by means of armed struggle.

Examples of the former approach include **the Philippines**, which was promised independence by the United States during World War II and received it in 1946. Even more noteworthy was the separation from Britain that led in 1947 to **independence for India and Pakistan**, although bloodshed quickly followed in freedom's wake. During World War II, national-liberationist pressures from the **Indian National Congress** (the party of **Mohandas Gandhi** and **Jawaharlal Nehru**) and the **All-India Muslim League** (led by **Muhammad Ali Jinnah**) made it obvious that the British could no longer hold on to India. Riots and violent clashes between Muslims and Hindus sped up the British timetable for withdrawal, and independence was granted in August 1947. Unfortunately, Hindu-Muslim conflict over the terms of **Indo-Pakistani partition** cost at least a million lives over the next months, created numerous refugees, and resulted in the assassination of Gandhi in 1948—ironically, by a Hindu extremist who opposed his rhetoric of toleration between the two faiths.

Despite their difficult beginnings, both nations survived. Under Jinnah and his successors, Pakistan became a modern Islamic republic and a major regional power. However, it became mired in corruption and military authoritarianism during the Cold War, and it has spent decades locked in a costly and dangerous rivalry with India. (Occasional border wars have broken out over the Kashmir frontier zone, and the development of nuclear-weapons capability by both nations has made this conflict even tenser.) Unlike India, Pakistan decisively chose sides during the Cold War, pursuing alliance with the United States.

As for India, it transformed itself into the world's largest democracy but also suffered administrative inefficiency, great difficulty in balancing economic growth with population growth, and interethnic and interfaith strife. (Even after partition from Pakistan, one-sixth of India's population remained Muslim; other minorities include Sikhs, Parsees, and Buddhists.) The dominant political force in free India was the Congress Party, led by **Jawaharlal Nehru**, who served as India's prime minister from 1947 until his death in 1964. Unlike Gandhi, who had favored traditional values and economic simplicity, Nehru worked to secularize and industrialize India. Diplomatically, he negotiated a tightrope: neighbor to a hostile China and an even more hostile Pakistan but not wishing to be a client of the Soviets, the British, or the Americans, Nehru stayed on friendly terms with the USSR without falling into the Soviet camp. He was a leading figure in the **Nonaligned Movement**.

From 1966 to 1977 and again from 1980 to 1984, Nehru's daughter, **Indira Gandhi**, was prime minister. She continued her father's policies of modernization and diplomatic

NOTE

Women received the vote in India after independence in 1947. India's 1949 Constitution also outlawed discrimination by caste, and its policy of "reservation" allowed for the "special advancement" of castes and ethnic groups that had traditionally received poor treatment. Sadly, informal prejudice against groups such as Dalits (former "untouchables") still persists.

nonalignment but also ruled high-handedly, suspending the constitution during the "Emergency" of 1975–1977. Religious strife brought her down: her actions against the Sikh minority of Punjab provoked her Sikh bodyguards to assassinate her. From 1984 to 1991, her son, Rajiv Gandhi, succeeded her; he was killed by Sri Lankan separatists.

NOTE

After freeing India, Britain let go of its other colonies in the region. Burma (now Myanmar) became independent in 1948, Malaysia in 1957, and Singapore in 1965.

Elsewhere, it took violence to end European rule. In the Dutch East Indies, the charismatic **Sukarno** began a war of nationalist liberation in 1945 and, with the Dutch gone, founded the new nation of Indonesia. Although 80 percent Muslim—giving it the world's largest Islamic population—Indonesia is a sprawling archipelago consisting of 18,000 islands, and its ethnic and linguistic diversity makes it challenging to govern. Sukarno governed democratically at first but grew more authoritarian. He helped establish the **Nonaligned Movement** by hosting the **Bandung Conference** of 1955 and went much further than Nehru in India or even Nasser in Egypt in calling for the Third World to defy the West. He drew closer to the Indonesian Communist Party until 1965 when the army, allied with conservative Muslims, staged a coup against him that killed as many as half a million people—mainly communists—and forced his resignation in 1967. From then until 1998, Indonesia was governed by the military strongman **Suharto**, an anticommunist dictator who promoted economic growth and alliance with the United States but frequently abused human rights.

Violence proved even more devastating in **Indochina**, the French colony composed of Vietnam, Laos, and Cambodia. Having lost Indochina to the Japanese in World War II, the French hoped to reimpose their authority in 1945 but were foiled by a national-liberation war led by the Vietnamese communist **Ho Chi Minh**. The French, with U.S. support, tried until 1954 to keep Indochina but were defeated by Vietnamese expertise in guerrilla warfare and the relative popularity of Ho Chi Minh's policies, which included land reform and appeals to anti-French nationalism. Laos and Cambodia went free in 1953, and Vietnam was temporarily divided into a northern communist zone and a southern noncommunist zone.

NOTE

In Cambodia during the 1970s, the ultraradical Khmer Rouge, under Pol Pot, combined Marxism with an ideology of racial superiority and a bizarre notion that "corrupt" city dwellers should be relocated to the countryside. Before Pol Pot was driven from power in 1979, famine and genocide killed approximately 2 million Cambodians.

Vietnam's two halves were to be united under a single government chosen by free election as soon as possible. However, Ngo Dinh Diem—the French-educated, Catholic, U.S.-backed leader of South Vietnam—kept delaying the election, fearing that the Buddhist anti-French peasant masses would vote against him. Tensions rose steadily, with war breaking out by 1959. Throughout the 1960s, the United States, following the Cold War **domino principle**, stepped up its military support for South Vietnam, paying insufficient attention to the unpopularity of the regime. (A clear sign of opposition to Diem came in 1963 when the Buddhist monk Thich Quang Duc committed suicide by **self-immolation**, burning himself to death publicly in the capital.) By the end of the decade, antiwar opposition was mounting in the United States and elsewhere, playing a significant role in the global wave of **1968 protests**. In 1968, the communists caught the Americans and South Vietnamese badly off guard with their Tet Offensive, and although U.S. forces withstood that blow, war weariness caused America to scale back its war effort and withdraw completely in 1973. Communist victory over the entirety of Vietnam followed in 1975. The severity of communist rule tempered somewhat during the 1980s, especially with the implementation of the **doi moi** ("renovation") **reforms** of 1986, which allowed for limited capitalism along the lines of Deng Xiaoping's reforms in China.

As in other parts of the world, regional associations formed in Southeast Asia. Most important was the **Association of Southeast Asian Nations** (ASEAN), founded in 1967 by Indonesia, Malaysia, Singapore, Thailand, and the Philippines to boost economic and security cooperation. It has since taken in other members, including Vietnam.

The Americas

Despite some temporary progress toward economic modernization and democratization in the late 1940s and early 1950s, many Latin American nations reverted to exploitative economies and dictatorial government from the late 1950s through the early 1980s. By the mid-1970s, only a tiny handful of countries in the region could be considered democratic. The **Organization of American States** (OAS), founded in 1948 and headquartered in Washington, D.C., fostered economic and diplomatic cooperation in the region—although cynics saw it as a tool for enforcing the **U.S. sphere of influence** in the western hemisphere.

Military governments and right-wing dictatorships predominated. Because of their anticommunism, many of these were Cold War allies of the United States despite their human-rights abuses and their tendency to gear their economies for the benefit of the elite instead of tending to the needs of the population at large. Indigenous populations—Indians, Mayans, Amazon tribes, and so on—were often badly treated. Key examples of Latin American governance follow.

TIP

Domestic politics in Canada and the United States will not receive much attention on the AP exam. Focus instead on socioeconomic and cultural issues. Note that terrorism played a role in North American politics as well. U.S. radicals like the Weather Underground resorted to violence in their opposition to the Vietnam War. In Canada, the separatist group FLQ carried out more than a hundred bombings between 1963 and 1970 in a failed attempt to detach Quebec from Canada.

- **ARGENTINA:** Military rule was established there during World War II. In 1946, the charismatic officer **Juan Perón** came to dominate the government by appealing to the poor. In this, he was aided by his wife, **Eva Perón**, who enjoyed popularity among the lower-class *descamisados* ("shirtless ones"). His modernization program of the 1950s borrowed heavily from Mussolini's brand of fascism and state capitalism. Overthrown by his army in 1955, Perón fled to Spain; he returned in 1973 and served as president until his death in 1974. A brutal military regime, the National Reorganization Process, ruled from 1976 to 1983, ruthlessly purging leftists and dissidents in the "**dirty war**" and causing the deaths of perhaps 30,000, including numerous *desaparecidos*, or "disappeared ones": people who were secretly arrested and never seen again.

- **CHILE:** In 1973, General **Augusto Pinochet**—backed by the U.S. Central Intelligence Agency—led a coup against Salvador Allende, a Marxist who had been democratically elected in 1970. Like Argentina's military rulers, Pinochet arrested thousands of leftists and other opponents, torturing 30,000 and killing or "disappearing" over 3,000. Economically, he began **free-market reform** (similar to Ronald Reagan's policy in the United States and Margaret Thatcher's in Britain) on the advice of economists known as the "**Chicago boys**" because of the influence exercised over them by **Milton Friedman** of the University of Chicago. Pinochet stepped down in favor of a democratically elected government in 1990. He left the country but was later arrested; he was on trial for human-rights abuses and corruption when he died in 2006.

- **GUATEMALA:** In 1954, nearly a decade of democratically elected reformist rule came to an end with a CIA-supported coup that brought the general Carlos Castillo Armas to power. A succession of military dictators followed until the mid-1990s, each of them suppressing leftist rebels and ethnic minorities with brute force. In particular, the regime perpetrated an **anti-Mayan genocide** in the 1980s.

- **MEXICO:** An example of mild authoritarian oligarchy as opposed to extreme dictatorship, Mexico maintained a nominally democratic system that ensured an unbroken string of electoral victories for the **Institutional Revolutionary Party** (PRI). Oil-based wealth during the 1950s and most of the 1960s kept the economy healthy and the population reasonably satisfied. However, by the late 1960s and 1970s, economic downturn, growing awareness of government corruption, and anger among Indians and Mayans because of popular and official prejudice all increased general discontent with the regime. Mexico City was hit hard by the global wave of **1968 protests**, and emigration to the United States, both legal and illegal, accelerated in the 1970s and 1980s. The PRI regime gradually reformed during the 1980s and 1990s.

NOTE

Latin America's right-wing dictators enforced their will in the countryside with secret police units and paramilitary forces known as death squads. On the other end of the spectrum, left-wing insurgents engaged in guerrilla violence and terrorism. Among these were the Maoist Shining Path, which operated in Peru during the 1980s, and the Leninist FARC, active in Colombia since 1964 and guilty of hostage taking and cocaine trafficking on a massive scale.

Dictatorship also arose as a result of the **Cuban Revolution**, this time from the left. In 1959, a guerrilla force led by **Fidel Castro** ousted the dictator Fulgencio Batista. Even the United States was glad to see Batista gone, and Castro initially governed as a nonaligned modernizer who nationalized industry, carried out land reforms, and combatted illiteracy and socioeconomic inequality. But he also regarded U.S. influence in Latin America as "Yankee imperialism," and prompted by his Marxist second-in-command, the Argentine intellectual **Ernesto "Che" Guevara**, Castro declared himself a communist and turned to the USSR for assistance. Because of its proximity to the United States, Cuba's pro-Soviet alignment made it a Cold War hot spot from 1961 onward, as demonstrated by moments like the **Cuban Missile Crisis** of 1962. Domestically, the Castro regime's record is mixed. Cuba modernized and narrowed the gap between rich and poor. However, Castro's government became rigidly dictatorial, restricting civil liberties and committing human-rights abuses of its own.

Adding to Cold War tension in Latin America was the **Nicaraguan Revolution** of 1979 when the Marxist **Sandinista movement** overthrew the Somoza clan that had ruled since the mid-1930s. Professing commitment to social democracy instead of dictatorship, the Sandinistas began with a program of land reform and wealth redistribution but were soon distracted by Cold War geopolitics. Nicaragua's new friendliness with the USSR unnerved Ronald Reagan in the United States, which was already abandoning détente over the Soviet invasion of Afghanistan. Against the wishes of the U.S. Congress, Reagan's administration attempted to destabilize the Sandinistas by illegally funding right-wing guerrillas known as **the Contras**. This bloody conflict persisted until the end of the Cold War.

NOTE

Cuban troops supported communist movements throughout Latin America—increasing U.S. anxiety about any sort of leftist activism in the region—and took active part in Cold War brushfire conflicts in Africa, including Angola's civil war and the Ethiopian war against Somalia started by the pro-Soviet Mengistu Haile Mariam.

A wave of **Latin American democratization** occurred in the late 1980s and early 1990s. Much of this was tied to economic improvements, but just as much was due to the cooling down of the Cold War, which reduced superpower concerns about influence in the region. Pinochet gave up power in 1989–1990, Argentina moved from dictatorship to democracy between 1983 and 1989, and Mexico's PRI loosened its monopoly on power beginning with the national elections of 1988. Peace and democracy returned to Nicaragua in 1990; an anti-Sandinista candidate, Violeta Chamorro, was elected as the country's first female president, although the Sandinistas have since returned to office via the ballot box. Such transitions, of course, were not complete. The Castro dictatorship retained power in Cuba and remains communist even after Castro's death. The Sandinistas have not governed in a fully democratic manner since regaining power. Corruption, resurgent authoritarianism, and dependence on illegal **drug trafficking** have continued elsewhere.

GLOBALISM IN THE 1990s AND 2000s

In 1990, U.S. President George H. W. Bush proclaimed confidently that the collapse of the Cold War was bringing about a "**new world order**" based on the worldwide triumph of democratic capitalism. The end of the nuclear arms race lowered the risk of mass annihilation, and new freedoms improved lives in many parts of the world. However, the superpower conflict had been predictable and had also kept in check various ethnic and religious tensions around the globe. It soon became clear that the geopolitics of the post–Cold War era would be far more complex than many had expected.

One key issue is that **U.S. unilateralism** as the world's remaining superpower has turned out to be limited, not just by its finite resources but also by the "**cold peace**" arising between it and former Cold War foes like Russia and China. The former, weakened during the 1990s by **Boris Yeltsin**'s chaotic mishandling of Eastern Europe's "**shock therapy**" transition to democratic capitalism, has entered a more belligerent phase under the "managed democracy" of the authoritarian, nationalistic **Vladimir Putin**. No longer a superpower, Russia has nonetheless regained much of its strength since 2000. It has sought to reassert its sphere of influence in the former Soviet Union—as illustrated by the **Chechen wars** of the 1990s and early 2000s—and to counter American geopolitical ambitions. The **Russian seizure of Crimea** from Ukraine in 2014–2015 and its support of pro-Russian rebels in eastern Ukraine are part of this pattern. So are its **cyber operations** against neighbors like Estonia and Georgia in 2007–2008 and against foes like the United States during its 2016 presidential election.

As for China, its rise to superpower status seems all but inevitable, an impression it conveyed with its grandiose hosting of the **2008 Beijing Olympics**. With the world's largest population and a huge economy enjoying thunderous growth, China is already in a position to assert military power regionally and will soon be able to do so Pacific-wide, if not globally. Its influence on international trade and finance is titanic. Key questions related to China are whether its authoritarian communist regime can muster the right combination of strength and flexibility to maintain order in a large, diverse country undergoing the stresses of rapid growth and whether China will flex its military and diplomatic muscles peacefully or aggressively. China's reabsorption of **Hong Kong** in 1997 (when Britain's colonial lease expired by treaty) went smoothly, but its abuses in **Tibet** and against the **Muslim Uighurs** on its western frontier are well documented. How long China will continue to tolerate the independence of **Taiwan**—which it regards as a renegade province, not a free nation—remains a matter of concern, as does China's insistence on claiming islands and waterways in the **South China Sea** that most of the world considers to belong to no one.

Another fact of the present day is that the very nature of war has changed. Thanks to trends from the Cold War that gained traction in the 1990s and 2000s, the gap between high-tech forces and low-level military capability has grown wider than ever before. Only a very few states possess meaningful stockpiles of **weapons of mass destruction** (nuclear, biological, and chemical weapons). The post–World War II period has witnessed many **asymmetrical wars** in which jet aircraft, third-generation tanks, helicopter gunships, aircraft carriers, and global airlift capacity—available only to the superpowers and a small group of other nations—have been pitted against the small arms (assault rifles, grenade launchers, hand-to-hand weapons) that are all most armies and paramilitary groups can afford. After the Cold War, computer technology widened this gap even further. During the 1990s and early 2000s, the United States and a handful of other nations underwent the so-called **revolution in military affairs,** or the full integration of computer technology, satellite communications, and precision-guided ("smart") weapons into military operations. Technological superiority carries with it many advantages, especially in straight-up conventional combat, but it is no guarantee of success (as demonstrated to the superpowers during the Vietnam War and the Soviet invasion of Afghanistan and to the United States in its ongoing wars in Iraq and Afghanistan). In particular, **low-intensity** ("brushfire") **conflict** and **guerrilla insurgency** offered (and continue to offer) many ways for weaker, more poorly equipped forces to frustrate larger, high-tech armies.

Adding further to post–Cold War instability is the weakening of restraints on the capacity for large-scale devastation. Of greatest concern is access to **weapons of mass destruction**. Although Russia and the United States have significantly reduced their nuclear arsenals, concern about "**loose nukes**" (warheads or weapons-grade radioactive material) disappearing from the former USSR and ending up in the wrong hands has been a persistent worry. Despite the overall success of the **Nuclear Nonproliferation Treaty** (1968–1969), **nuclear proliferation** expanded during the 1990s and 2000s and threatens to worsen in the near future. **Biological** and **chemical weapons** (infectious pathogens like Ebola and anthrax, gases, toxins) have become easier to manufacture and weaponize—not just for national governments but potentially for nonstate actors—making such weapons harder to monitor and control. **Terrorism** has remained central to post–Cold War geopolitics and has achieved new levels of destructiveness, as illustrated most infamously by the **al-Qaeda attacks on September 11, 2001**, and more recent killings by groups like **ISIS**. At the same time, **genocide** has proved distressingly easy for even small, crudely armed forces to commit—most notoriously in **Rwanda** and **the former Yugoslavia** in the 1990s but also elsewhere.

Looking more broadly at this unpredictable period, a central question is whether **global integration** has predominated over **global fragmentation** or vice versa. One trend encouraging the former is the growing importance of **international organizations** and **regional associations**, both existing and new. The **United Nations**, the **World Trade Organization** (WTO), formed in 1994 from the GATT system, and the **International Criminal Court** (ICC), signed into being in 1998 and operating in The Hague since 2002 to prosecute genocide and other crimes against humanity, all foster international cooperation and dispute resolution. The **European Union** (EU) was formed in the 1990s from the European Economic Community and expanded immensely after the collapse of Eastern European communism. Most of its states adopted the **euro** as a common currency in 2002.

On the other hand, the integrating strength of such organizations is not always evident. More capable than the interwar League of Nations, the United Nations has still sometimes shown impotence in the face of conflicts and humanitarian crises. Over 150 nations have signed the ICC charter but not all have ratified it, and some, like Russia, China, Israel, and the United States, have chosen not to fully recognize its authority. How effective the WTO will be in regulating trade in times of crisis remains to be seen. The 2016 **Brexit** vote deeply weakened the EU.

Likewise, a region-by-region glance makes it difficult to guess whether integration or fragmentation will prevail as the century progresses. Europe's **transition from communism**, for instance, has met with mixed results. The "**shock therapy**" method of moving as quickly as possible to free-market capitalism proved painful even where it seemed to work well (as in East Germany, Poland, the Czech Republic, and the Baltic states) and disastrous in places like Russia, which suffered hyperinflation and the sudden collapse of once-reliable social welfare systems.

The sudden rush of Eastern European nations to join **NATO** and the **EU** angered a Russia that was already smarting from the loss of its superpower status. **Ethnic tensions** in Europe have heightened, even in the most democratic states. **Populist discontent with globalization** has crested from the mid-2010s onward, evident in **anti-immigrant senti- ment**, protests like the **Brexit** vote of 2016 and the "yellow vest" strikes of 2018–2019 in France and rightward voting shifts in several democracies.

NOTE

Anti-immigrant sentiment has been directed at Turkish guest workers and other Muslim communities, especially refugees fleeing North Africa and Syria's civil war. Anti-Roma (Gypsy) prejudice remains widespread throughout Eastern Europe.

The most terrible manifestations of ethnic violence in post–Cold War Europe came during the **Yugoslav wars** (1991–1995, 1998–1999) when tensions among South Slavs, kept under control by the authoritarian Titoist regime, broke loose after the collapse of communism. As the various states that made up Yugoslavia declared independence, opportunistic politicians, especially **Slobodan Milosevic** of Serbia—which controlled most of Yugoslavia's armed forces—exploited nationalist fervor to seize territory from Croatia and the multiethnic state of Bosnia, home to Orthodox Serbs, Catholic Croats, and Muslim Bosniaks: all Slavs but now bitterly divided. Serbian forces and Bosnian Serb paramilitaries committed mass rape, massacred civilians (most infamously at Srebrenica, where more than 8,000 Bosniaks were killed in 1995), besieged and shelled the Bosnian capital of Sarajevo for over three years, and carried out forced deportations euphemistically called **ethnic cleans- ings**. At least 100,000 were killed and 2 million more made refugees before the UN and NATO intervened to impose the **Dayton Accords** in late 1995. Another round of fighting followed in 1998–1999 as Serbia attempted to remove ethnic Albanians from the province of Kosovo, requiring a NATO bombardment of Serbia to end the hostilities.

Most of Latin America has generally stayed on track, although economic inequalities remain in many states and **illegal drug trafficking** causes politically destabilizing violence in places like Colombia and along the Mexican border. Strongman authoritarianism reemerged in certain countries—most notably in oil-rich Venezuela under the bombastic socialist **Hugo Chávez**, who ruled from 1999 to 2013 by building solid support among the poorer masses but also by tightly controlling elections and the mass media. Venezuela under Chávez and his successors is part of a "**pink wave**" bloc that includes Nicaragua, Ecuador, and Bolivia, all opposing what they see as U.S. imperialism. They support Cuba, which remains communist.

In Asia, the economic dynamism and high-tech innovation found in places like China, Singapore, and parts of India (such as Bangalore, the Silicon Valley of South Asia) contrasts with the geopolitical perils posed by ongoing Indo-Pakistani border skirmishes, the perpetual instability of Afghanistan, the possibility of clashes between Communist China and Taiwan or Japan, and the increasingly erratic bellicosity of a nuclear-armed North Korea.

Stability has proved even more elusive in Africa. Some areas have made headway with socioeconomic development and open politics, and the **truth and reconciliation process** in South Africa healed some of the race-relations damage caused by apartheid. Unfortunately, religious and ethnic differences, combined with competition over resources like oil, gold, and diamonds, have ensured that civil war and the recruitment of **child soldiers** remain depress- ingly common. In 1994, the **Rwandan genocide** resulted in the deaths of 800,000 members of the **Tutsi** minority at the hands of their **Hutu** rivals. Hatred between the two groups had been fostered by Rwanda's Belgian colonizers but had been kept mainly in check since the early 1970s. Between 1996 and 2003, the **First and Second Congo Wars**, sparked by the crumbling of **Joseph Mobutu**'s repressive regime in Zaire/Congo, drew nine Central African nations into combat and killed more than 5 million, if one counts deaths by famine and disease.

Between 2003 and the creation of a separate state of South Sudan, Sudanese persecution of the non-Arab **Darfur minority** killed more than half a million people and created millions of refugees.

Most volatile of all has been the Middle East, combined with Islamic North Africa. The **Arab-Israeli conflict** has ebbed and flowed since the end of the Cold War. In 1993, **Yasser Arafat** of the **PLO** signed peace accords with Israel's Yitzhak Rabin, ending the **First Intifada** and creating a Palestinian National Authority as a first step toward a **two-state solution**. U.S. mediation helped preserve a fragile truce until 2000–2001, when extremists on both sides sabotaged negotiations and triggered a **Second Intifada**. Arafat died in 2004, and Rabin was assassinated by an Israeli opponent of the peace process. Since then, Arab and Israeli moderates alike—including the Palestinians' **Fatah** leadership—have struggled with Palestinian terrorists like **Hamas** (which uses violence deliberately to disrupt the peace process), hard-right Israeli politicians (who have used Palestinian terror as the pretext to quarantine nonviolent Palestinians in apartheid-like conditions, further inflaming Palestinian opinion against Israel), and Israeli religious fundamentalists determined to build **illegal settlements** on Palestinian land (which they regard as their own biblical inheritance).

NOTE

In Nigeria, religious fundamentalism motivated the 2014 abduction of almost 300 young women by Boko Haram, an Islamic extremist group that has killed over 10,000 civilians and made over a million homeless.

Desert Storm, the U.S.-led response to **Saddam Hussein**'s 1990 invasion of Kuwait, brought war to Iraq in 1991. For the next twelve years, the United Nations monitored the possibility that Hussein might be amassing a large store of **weapons of mass destruction**. When **Osama bin Laden** and **al-Qaeda** carried out the **September 11, 2001, bombings** against the United States, President George W. Bush used the attacks as the occasion to extend his "**war on terror**" not just against Afghanistan (whose Taliban government, made up of rigid Islamic fundamentalists, provided al-Qaeda with safe haven) but also against Iraq, which in fact had not been involved in the al-Qaeda assault. American operations against Afghanistan began in 2001 and are not yet complete although Osama bin Laden was killed in 2011. The war in Iraq began in 2003 and immediately deposed Saddam Hussein (captured and killed in 2006) but plunged the country into political anarchy. Most U.S. forces withdrew in 2011, and much of the country fell in 2013–2014 to the fanatical Sunni terror group known as **ISIS** (the Islamic State of Iraq and Syria.)

NOTE

One catalyst for the Arab Spring was the self-immolation of a Tunisian fruit seller, Mohamed Bouazizi, who had been abused by the police. His gesture was highly reminiscent of Thich Quang Duc's suicide by burning during the Vietnam War.

Adding recent drama to Middle Eastern affairs is the ongoing **Iranian nuclear effort**, which has not yet yielded a weapon (and may have been forestalled by an important treaty in the spring of 2015, even though the United States abandoned the agreement in 2018). Also key is the so-called **Arab Spring**, which began in December 2010. The latter politically transformed the region by deposing a number of longtime authoritarian regimes, starting with the Tunisian monarchy and continuing with the strongman government of Hosni Mubarak in Egypt and the dictatorship of Muammar Gaddafi in Libya. The terrible **civil war in Syria**, between dictator Bashar al-Assad and various rebel forces, began in 2011 as part of this trend (by 2014, this conflict had killed 400,000 and displaced 12 million). It was initially tempting to view the Arab Spring as a triumph of "people power" against oppression, but the principal result appears to have been steadily worsening instability, with the deadly prolonging of the Syrian civil war (and the resulting global refugee crisis), the expansion of ISIS, and the growing influence of Iran among the region's many Shiite Muslims.

Cultural Developments and Interactions, 1900 to the Present

21

IN THIS CHAPTER

→ **THE MODERN AND POSTMODERN PERIODS**

→ **HIGH CULTURE VS. MASS (POPULAR) CULTURE**

→ **UNCERTAINTY AND ANXIETY IN WESTERN HIGH ART (INFLUENCE OF FREUDIAN THOUGHT)**

→ **EXISTENTIALISM**

→ **NON-WESTERN ADAPTATION OF WESTERN HIGH CULTURE (NEGRITUDE)**

→ **MASS MEDIA AS HIGH CULTURE (CINEMA, JAZZ)**

→ **MASS MEDIA AS ENTERTAINMENT (DISNEY, HOLLYWOOD, SPORTS)**

→ **MASS MEDIA AS PROPAGANDA**

→ **AMERICANIZATION AND WESTERNIZATION OF GLOBAL CULTURE ("COCA-COLONIZATION")**

→ **MULTICULTURALISM (MARSHALL MCLUHAN'S "GLOBAL VILLAGE," BOLLYWOOD, REGGAE, MANGA)**

→ **THE INFORMATION (DIGITAL) REVOLUTION + SOCIAL MEDIA (FACEBOOK, TWITTER)**

→ **SYNTHETIC FORMS OF SPIRITUALITY**

→ **RELIGION AND MODERN POLITICS (ETHNIC CONFLICT, RELIGIOUS FUNDAMENTALISM, LIBERATION THEOLOGY)**

The hallmarks of twentieth- and twenty-first-century thought and culture have been rapid change and incredible diversity. After World War II, high art in the West began its transition from the **modern period** (considered in cultural and intellectual terms to have lasted roughly from the 1870s through the 1940s) to the **contemporary era**, also referred to as the **postmodern era**.

Other major trends, both in the West and beyond, have included **multiculturalism**—the interaction and fusion of the world's various ethnic, artistic, and intellectual traditions—and the effect of **mass media technology** on culture and the arts. The **information** (or **digital**) **revolution** caused by the widespread availability of computers and the invention of the **World Wide Web** has vastly altered cultural life in the 1990s and beyond.

HIGH ART AND CULTURE

High art in the West during this era was characterized by bold experimentation and the distortion, even abandonment, of traditional norms and conventions.

During the first half of the 1900s, Western art was marked by uncertainty and pessimism. Even before World War I, the prevailing faith in progress that had characterized Europe's cultural life during much of the 1800s had waned (see Chapter 15). Despair caused by World War I brought an even greater sense of anxiety to the forefront. Eloquent accounts of the wartime experience can be found in literary works such as Erich Maria Remarque's novel *All Quiet on the Western Front*, which describes the dehumanizing effects of trench warfare, and the verses of Britain's war poets (Siegfried Sassoon, Wilfred Owen, and others), who questioned traditional patriotism as an adequate justification for the war's mindless butchery. The avant-garde artists of the **Dada movement**, which exhibited in Europe and New York during the war, used shock and absurdism to push the boundaries of what should be considered art and to highlight the irrationality of World War I, which they opposed. The best-known Dadaist artwork is *Fountain*: the bowl of a urinal irreverently turned into a sculpture by Frenchman Marcel Duchamp.

NOTE

Alternative literary approaches to World War I included satire (Czech author Jaroslav Hašek's novel *The Good Soldier Svejk*), sentimentality (the poem "In Flanders Fields," by Canadian doctor John McCrae, commemorating soldiers killed by poison gas), and, in a sharp contrast to antiwar works like *All Quiet on the Western Front*, patriotic adventurism (*Storm of Steel* by Germany's Ernst Jünger, who saw World War I as a grand cause and an ennobling experience).

Gloom deepened during the interwar period due to Europe's political and economic comedown and the unsettling philosophical implications of recent scientific insights, including the theory of relativity, quantum physics, and the psychological theories of **Sigmund Freud**. All these called into question whether anything was fully knowable or whether any objective truths existed. The prose and poetry of T. S. Eliot and Franz Kafka dealt with dehumanization in an industrialized, bureaucratized era. Experiments with **stream-of-consciousness prose** by Virginia Woolf, Marcel Proust, and James Joyce attempted to capture, almost in Freudian style, the workings of the human mind on the written page. **Abstract painters**, such as Pablo Picasso, distorted reality to demonstrate that things could be seen from a variety of perspectives. **Surrealists** like Salvador Dalí and others placed realistic objects in unrealistic situations to confuse the viewer's sense of reality.

After World War II, the philosophical and literary school of **existentialism** rose to prominence, although it had existed since the interwar years. Championed by the Irish playwright Samuel Beckett and the French philosophers Albert Camus and Jean-Paul Sartre, existentialists proposed that humanity was not guided by any deity, special destiny, or objective morality. Alone in the universe, the individual must learn to create a worthwhile, ethical existence for himself or herself without the benefit of religion or the hope of any life beyond the earthly one. At the same time, Western culture entered the **postmodern era**, which has been characterized by even more unpredictability, relativism, and unconventionality than before. The notion of an artistic and literary canon—a universally agreed-upon body of "great" works—has been called into doubt by postmodern thinking in keeping with its rejection of the notion that any standards can be objectively valid.

In the non-Western world, the twentieth and twenty-first centuries have seen artistic and literary traditions gain the same degree of respect and prestige once reserved for works from the West. In addition to maintaining indigenous styles, non-Western authors and artists have adopted Western forms of writing, painting, and composing—often modifying them with elements from their own culture.

Prior to World War II, the Indian poet Rabindranath Tagore, the first non-Westerner to win the Nobel Prize for literature, dazzled readers worldwide with lyrical verses inspired by

Hindu mysticism. China's Lu Xun (Hsun) wrote hard-hitting stories about his country's economic domination by outside powers and his own government's lack of concern for lower-class commoners. Starting in the 1930s, the **negritude movement**, inspired by the African American poets of the Harlem Renaissance and the Marxism percolating in interwar Paris, encouraged African and Caribbean writers from French colonies to express their opposition to European imperialism and their own pride in being black. The Mexican artist **Diego Rivera** created powerful murals expressing the plight of the working poor as well as that of Mayans and other indigenous peoples. His wife, the painter **Frida Kahlo**, remains famous in her own right for her feminist themes and her bold use of color.

Frida Kahlo (1907–1954) and Diego Rivera (1886–1957)
Married, briefly divorced, and married again, Frida Kahlo and Diego Rivera remain Mexico's best-known painters. *The Two Fridas* (1939) shows Kahlo divided between a genteel European identity and a Mexican peasant identity; the twins' exposed hearts are linked by a single artery. Rivera's *The Flower Carrier* (1935) depicts a poor mestizo worker burdened by the flowers that he will attempt to sell as luxuries to the upper classes.

Non-Western voices arose more frequently and outspokenly in the artistic world after World War II. Common themes included the growing pains associated with decolonization, the difficulty of resisting Western (especially U.S.) cultural hegemony, and opposition to politically repressive regimes. **Chinua Achebe** looked backward to the impact of British imperialism and missionary activity on Nigeria's Ibo (Igbo) people in *Things Fall Apart* (1958), one of the first African novels to gain an international audience. Japan's **Yukio Mishima**, a prolific novelist and traditional nationalist, bitterly opposed what he saw as the destruction of Japan's cultural values. His ritual, samurai-style suicide in 1970 elevated him to cult status. In Latin America, authors such as **Gabriel García Márquez** and Isabel Allende pioneered magical realism, a richly textured style featuring intricately detailed storytelling. In the Islamic world, novelist Naguib Mahfouz won the Nobel Prize for his *Cairo Trilogy*, a vibrant portrait of postwar Egypt. The Indian-born, English-speaking Salman Rushdie came to world attention in 1988 with *The Satanic Verses*, an irreverent treatment of Islamic orthodoxy. Both Mahfouz and Rushdie fell afoul of Muslim traditionalists. Mahfouz was stabbed by an Islamic extremist in 1984. Rushdie was declared a heretic by Iran's Ayatollah Khomeini, who openly called for his assassination and forced him into hiding for years.

MASS CULTURE AND MULTICULTURALISM

During the 1900s, **mass media** (such as radio, film, and television) came into their own, vastly transforming the cultural sphere. In many ways, their exuberance and energy contrasted with the anxiety and uncertainty expressed by most high art.

The dividing line between **high culture** and **mass** (or **popular**) **culture** has become increasingly difficult to define in the 1900s and 2000s. All the new media of this era have been used to create great artworks that belong in the former category. Film directors such as Russia's Sergei Eisenstein and Germany's Fritz Lang dominated **high-art cinema** during the interwar years. The postwar era has seen masterpieces by Sweden's deeply existential Ingmar Bergman, by Italy's Federico Fellini, noted for his extravagance and fondness for farce, and by Japan's Akira Kurosawa, popularizer of the samurai epic. **Jazz**, which flourished in early twentieth-century America, particularly during the **Harlem Renaissance**, crossed the line between mass culture and high art. The same is true of the **cabaret culture** that flourished in Weimar Germany before 1933 and featured jazz music and witty social commentary in musical dramas cocreated by Kurt Weill and the Marxist playwright Bertolt Brecht.

On the other hand, mass media have been used mainly to create products aimed at a popular audience for purposes of entertainment, and critics of mass/popular culture argue that it tends to cheapen or "dumb down" art by catering to the tastes of the lowest common denominator. Whether this is an elitist viewpoint or a valid one, there is no denying the perennial popularity of **Disney**, **Hollywood** films, rock and roll and popular music, and the press coverage related to popular technologies like aviation and rockets (featuring heroes like Charles Lindbergh and U.S. astronauts or Soviet cosmonauts) and automobiles (car racing, popular on both sides of the Atlantic).

Mass media also gave rise to the international popularity of **sporting events**. From the start, these were intertwined with national pride and political agendas. The **modern Olympic Games**, created in 1896 to foster peace, have been used to make statements of strength (Hitler's Berlin Olympics in 1936, Beijing's summer Olympics in 2008) or to wage symbolic battles (the U.S. and Soviet teams throughout the Cold War). **World Cup soccer tournaments**, active since 1930, galvanize audiences worldwide every four years. Another game exported from Europe to wider parts of the world is **cricket**, played wherever the British established colonies. It is a great point of pride for teams from South Asia and the Caribbean that they routinely beat the British themselves in international competition—similar to how Cubans, Puerto Ricans, and other Latin Americans often beat baseball teams from the United States, which taught them the game in the first place.

Another criticism of mass culture is how it has been used for political and corporate purposes. Dictatorships have freely employed mass media as mouthpieces for **propaganda** and indoctrination, or "brainwashing." In Nazi Germany, the filmmaker Leni Riefenstahl boosted support for Hitler's regime with visually impressive but thoroughly propagandistic movies like *Triumph of the Will* (1935). Stalinist Russia used mass media to churn out relentlessly optimistic artworks in the style of socialist realism, which featured heroic images of productive peasants, tireless factory workers, and stalwart soldiers and pilots, all toiling happily under Stalin's supposedly benevolent leadership. In free societies, critics say, people are brainwashed less for political purposes than for the advertisement of goods and the earning of profits, with mass media functioning as powerful tools in the hands of business interests.

Propaganda in the Age of Mass Media

The 78-foot-tall *Worker and Collective Farm Woman* (1937), completed by Vera Mukhina and praised at numerous international exhibitions, is an iconic example of socialist realism, bursting with the heroic grandeur that the Soviet regime wished the style to convey. A similar monumentalism is communicated throughout *Triumph of the Will* (1935), by Leni Riefenstahl, who dedicated her considerable talents to the dubious cause of glorifying the Nazi Third Reich.

Other effects of mass media have included the **westernization**, even **Americanization**, of global popular culture *and*, somewhat contradictorily, the boosting of a **multiculturalism** that blends cultural traditions from all over the globe and sometimes influences Western and U.S. culture.

Even before World War II, the lure of American jazz and Hollywood movies was globally seductive. Afterward, when America dominated world markets and mass-media technology, Disney, McDonalds, and Coca-Cola, among others, became economic and cultural symbols recognizable not just in the United States but in every corner of the planet. Some, particularly non-Western intellectuals, have expressed concern about the corporatizing and Americanizing effects of mass culture; the Japanese novelist Yukio Mishima angrily condemned it as "**coca-colonization**." (Along similar lines, several Muslim states in the 2000s have created toy dolls—including **Sara** in Iran and Fulla in Egypt—to compete with American products like Barbie. The competitors come complete with clothing and features that more closely match local standards of appearance.)

Others, however, have spoken of mass media's potential to draw people closer together. In the 1960s, Canadian sociologist Marshall McLuhan gained fame for his argument that modern communications technology would create a **global village**—a prediction that seems to have been partly realized thanks to the Internet. McLuhan's vision also appears to have been fulfilled by the mixing and interaction of global styles and traditions known as multiculturalism. Not only have Western and U.S. influences gone abroad, non-Western influences have mutually affected Europe and the United States. Examples include **reggae music**, with its Afro-Caribbean roots; the global popularity of **Bollywood films** (produced in India, where Bombay/Mumbai serves as the equivalent to Hollywood); and Japan's **manga comics** and its anime style of film animation. Global cuisine has long been influenced by multicultural trends, especially with the movement of once-colonized peoples to the countries that formerly ruled them. Indian, Indonesian, and Georgian dishes, for example, have added extra variety—and spice—to the cuisines of Britain, the Netherlands, and Russia, respectively.

Discussed further in Chapter 22, the **information** (**digital**) **revolution**, generated since the 1990s by the ongoing proliferation of personal computers and smart phones as well as the invention of the **World Wide Web**, has greatly amplified all the above trends. The availability of mass and high culture alike has expanded beyond expectation. Consumer culture and ways of working have been reshaped by online entities such as **Amazon**, eBay, Uber, and in China, **Alibaba**. The cultural, socioeconomic, and political ramifications of **social media**—especially platforms like **Facebook** and **Twitter**—are still being measured. As shown by events like the Arab Spring, the Brexit vote, and the 2016 U.S. presidential election—all affected profoundly by social media—their impact is heavy indeed and likely to grow even more so over time.

RELIGION IN THE MODERN ERA

Religion continued to play significant historical roles in the twentieth and twenty-first centuries.

In many ways, religions adapted to what was, overall, an increasingly secular era—when literal belief in traditional scriptures was harder to sustain and when many dictators, especially in the communist world, sought to ban worship altogether. Numerous **synthetic forms of spirituality** appeared, combining elements of old religions with new beliefs. Examples include the Hare Krishna movement (arising in New York in the mid-1960s and borrowing chants and scriptures from Hinduism), Falun Gong (a meditative and martial arts–oriented practice originating in China in the 1990s and, much to the displeasure of the communist regime, reviving aspects of Daoist and Buddhist worship), and the many varieties of "new age" faiths in the West (alternative spiritualities that incorporate whatever they choose from Buddhism, Hinduism, yoga, shamanism, or paganism).

Old or new, religious beliefs were also used to advance political agendas. **Religious differences** frequently aggravated or contributed to ethnic and political disputes, as in the Turkish massacre of Christian Armenians, the Arab-Israeli conflict, Indo-Pakistani violence, the Catholic-Protestant "troubles" in Northern Ireland, Sunni-Shiite rivalries in the Middle East, and the Yugoslav wars of the 1990s. **Religious fundamentalism** has proved politically influential in many places during the 1900s and 2000s. Christian fundamentalism in North America has systematically advanced right-wing voting preferences in electoral politics, and in the form of evangelical Protestantism, it has made major inroads into Africa and Latin America, the latter long monopolized religiously by the Catholic Church. Islamic fundamentalism has driven political trends in the Middle East, generally in opposition to westernization and, at times, to modernization in general. In South Asia, it has caused tensions between Hindus and Muslims and also between Hindus and Sikhs. In recent years, Hindu nationalism, in the form of Hindutva ("Hindu-ness," a term originating in the 1920s), has widened these fissures.

NOTE

Presently, 10 to 15 percent of Muslims worldwide are Shiite, although Shiites enjoy large majorities in Iraq (65–70 percent) and Iran (over 90 percent). In India, roughly one-sixth of the population is Muslim.

Another instance of how religious belief has been applied to politics involves **liberation theology**, a concept that arose during the 1950s and 1960s among Catholic priests in Latin America (the term itself was not coined until the early 1970s). Arguing that Christ's teachings mandated a "preferential option for the poor," liberation theologists felt it was their duty to support impoverished communities against oppressive governments and elite classes, even if doing so meant opposing the church hierarchy or cooperating with radical or Marxist activists. In the mid-1980s, under the fiercely anticommunist pope **John Paul II**, the Vatican cracked down on liberation theology, but the notion of combining liberal Christianity (of whatever denomination) with social-justice activism remains alive thanks to the movement's influence.

Technology and Innovation, 1900 to the Present

22

IN THIS CHAPTER

→ **THEORETICAL PHYSICS (RELATIVITY, QUANTUM PHYSICS) + NUCLEAR POWER**

→ **RENEWABLE ENERGY SOURCES (WIND, SOLAR, GEOTHERMAL)**

→ **AVIATION + ROCKETRY (NEW WEAPONRY)**

→ **ASTRONOMY AND SPACEFLIGHT**

→ **INCREASED AGRICULTURAL OUTPUT (GREEN REVOLUTION)**

→ **MEDICAL ADVANCES (VACCINES, ANTIBIOTICS) + GENETIC SCIENCE (DNA, BIOENGINEERING)**

→ **CONSUMER ELECTRONICS + MASS MEDIA**

→ **COMPUTERS AND THE INFORMATION (DIGITAL) REVOLUTION + SOCIAL MEDIA**

Scientific and technological advancement during the twentieth and twenty-first centuries has been unceasing and spectacular. At breathtaking speed, even beyond the rapid pace set during the industrial era of the 1800s, each invention and insight has sparked new and related innovations. Scientific discoveries have built upon each other in similar fashion, vastly expanding intellectual frontiers.

Although cutting-edge technology and science can be found on every part of the planet, great diversity persists when it comes to the question of how thoroughly they have been adopted or how widely available they are. The advantage possessed here by Europe, North America, and parts of Asia is part of the **north-south split** discussed in other chapters.

PHYSICS AND ENERGY

The field of physics was revolutionized at the beginning of the 1900s. As mentioned in Chapter 15, **Albert Einstein** developed the **special and general theories of relativity** between 1905 and 1916, proposing—among other things—the equivalency of mass and energy ($E = mc^2$) and establishing the speed of light as the maximum attainable speed in the universe. In so doing, Einstein became the first to push beyond the synthesis of mathematics and physics achieved by Isaac Newton's laws of motion in the late 1600s and early 1700s.

Also in the early 1900s, the field of **quantum physics** was born, helped largely by Einstein's insights, even though he did not accept all of its implications. Major figures here included Max Planck, Niels Bohr, Werner Heisenberg, and Enrico Fermi, all of whom were keenly interested in questions on the atomic and subatomic levels. Just as Einstein had shown that Newtonian laws broke down when considered on an astronomical scale, quantum physicists demonstrated—by means of Heisenberg's uncertainty principle—that, at a certain microscopic point, one can know a particle's location or its momentum but not both at the same time. Such breakthroughs enabled decades of new progress in astronomy, astrophysics, and atomic science. In the realm of technology, they also made **atomic weaponry** and **nuclear energy** possible.

Other pioneers of the atomic frontier include Wilhelm Roentgen of Germany, who detected the phenomenon of atomic radiation (and learned how to photograph it in the form of X-rays) and the Polish-French researcher Marie Curie, who discovered radium and polonium and remains the only woman to win two Nobel Prizes (physics in 1903, chemistry in 1911).

Although the production of energy still depends above all on the burning of fossil fuels, new sources of energy have emerged in the post–World War II era. **Wind power** is actually anything but new, but advanced technology has greatly improved the ability of wind turbines to generate electricity. **Solar power** has also advanced tremendously, from a novelty half a century ago to a major—and steadily improving—source of renewable energy. Where circumstances permit, **geothermal energy**, which harnesses the heat of the earth itself, works as an alternative source of power. **Nuclear power** is the longest and most thoroughly established of energy sources not reliant on fossil fuels, but it remains controversial. Nuclear power plants produce highly toxic waste that is difficult to store and remains dangerous for centuries, and the potential for contamination by fallout over a wide range if something goes wrong with a plant—as at **Chernobyl** in 1986—is dire in the extreme.

AVIATION AND SPACE

The new fields of **rocketry** and **space science** emerged in the 1900s. Progress here went hand in hand with simultaneous developments in **powered flight**, which was achieved in 1903 with the Wright Brothers' invention of the **airplane**.

Pioneers of rocket science included the American Robert Goddard and Russia's Konstantin Tsiolkovsky. This field matured during World War II thanks largely to the efforts of German scientists like Wernher von Braun, who developed the V-1 and V-2 rockets for use against Britain late in the war. The United States and the USSR proved eager to use the expertise of German rocket scientists after the war for the purposes of both building intercontinental missiles and developing space programs. (Despite his dubious history of working for the Nazi regime, von Braun was instrumental in work done in the United States by NASA.)

NOTE

World War II and the early Cold War years witnessed rapid and massive advances in aviation. These include the development of large, high-altitude aircraft (strategic bombers and cargo planes in war, passenger and freight airliners in civilian life), jet planes, and supersonic flight. Navigational and guidance systems, for both airplanes and spacecraft, became remarkably sophisticated over a few short decades.

The nuclear arms race between the United States and the USSR spurred a parallel **space race**. The Soviets were the first to put a human-made object into space (the satellite *Sputnik* in 1957), and they launched the first human being into space as well (Yuri Gagarin in 1961). Although the Soviets landed an unmanned spacecraft on the moon in 1959, the Americans succeeded in carrying out the first crewed moon landing in 1969 (the Apollo 11 mission, led by Neil Armstrong).

Apollo 15 Mission to the Moon, August 1971
To this date, the United States is the only nation that has landed crewed spacecraft on the moon. The first moon landing came on July 20, 1969. The Apollo 15 mission, pictured here, was one of the several landings that followed.

The move toward a permanent presence in space was encouraged by the USSR's work in developing orbital laboratories and the United States' development of the space shuttle program. Rocket science has also made **satellite telecommunications** and **telemetry** possible. Emerging trends since the end of the Cold War have included the deployment of unmanned probes (into deep space and to neighboring planets) and increasingly powerful radio telescopes. Private spaceflight may also become a reality in the near future.

BIOLOGICAL AND MEDICAL FRONTIERS

Medical, pharmaceutical, and biological advances have extended life expectancy and improved public health in many ways. They have also created the potential for biological engineering in ways that may change the nature of what it means to be human. On the other hand, benefits from these changes are unevenly distributed between developed and nondeveloped societies—and even in developed societies, class and wealth create deep divisions where access to health care is concerned.

Carrying over from the 1800s, **vaccinations** have been at the center of important medical triumphs. The same is true of **antibiotics**, which fight harmful bacteria (development here began with the 1928 discovery of **penicillin** by Scotland's Alexander Fleming). Thanks to both, once-fatal infections can be more easily countered, and certain diseases that routinely killed millions—such as smallpox and measles—have been all but eliminated. The **polio vaccine** (developed by Jonas Salk in the 1950s, followed in the same decade by Albert Sabin's oral vaccine) eradicated another serious threat. Heart transplants began in 1967 thanks to Christiaan Barnard in South Africa, and the first successful implant of an artificial heart took place in 1982. Aside from unequal access to medical care, one set of recent concerns has been the emergence of new bacteria capable of resisting antibiotics and new disease strains that defy vaccines. The tendency of some groups and individuals—so-called anti-vaxxers—to refuse vaccinations also compromises the effectiveness of public health programs.

NOTE

Biological and botanical advancements boosted agricultural production worldwide and, in certain regions, gave rise to the Green Revolution of the 1940s–1970s. For more, see Chapter 25.

A related field of special significance is **genetics**, which came into being during the late 1800s thanks to the work of the Austrian monk Gregor Mendel. The field's greatest breakthrough came with the deciphering of the **molecular structure of DNA** in 1953—a feat attributed to James Watson and Francis Crick but due also to the work of Rosalind Franklin, whose contributions were not properly acknowledged until recently. Since then, scientists have gained an unprecedented wealth of knowledge about how living organisms work at the cellular level. Gene mapping and bioengineering (including the potential for human cloning) are within grasp—with ramifications that are simultaneously exciting, terrifying, and ethically complex.

Since the 1990s, **neurology** has made astounding progress in gaining previously unimaginable insights into the workings of the brain.

MASS MEDIA AND COMPUTER TECHNOLOGY

Much of the twentieth century witnessed the full incorporation of **mass media** and **consumer electronics** into the workplace and ordinary life.

From the 1990s onward, a similar but even more powerful transformation connected the **computer** to nearly every aspect of human existence. The machines that anticipated the computer as we know it today were invented during and shortly after World War II thanks to the efforts of many individuals but notably the British mathematician Alan Turing. (One early purpose was to break German codes for the Allied war effort.)

Beginning in the 1980s, the availability and affordability of the **personal computer**—brought about by innovators like Bill Gates, Steve Wozniak, and Steve Jobs—caused an **information** (or **digital**) **revolution** that altered the way people work, communicate, entertain themselves, and process information. Key to this development was the invention and expansion of the **Internet**, originally created in the 1960s for U.S. defense purposes. By the end of the 1990s, a **World Wide Web**—brought into being by Tim Berners-Lee—had connected millions of users, and it continues to grow, particularly with the rise of **wireless technology** and **mobile communications**, which allow access to the Internet and to **social media** via handheld devices like cellphones. Although a "digital divide" exists between those in the developed world, who have better access to computer technology and reliable cellphone networks, and those in the less developed world, who have less access, the worldwide trend is toward more access for all.

Economic Systems, 1900 to the Present

23

IN THIS CHAPTER

→ BOOM-AND-BUST BUSINESS CYCLE

→ FREE-MARKET CAPITALISM (UNREGULATED VS. REGULATED)

→ "MIDDLE" OR "THIRD WAY" ECONOMIES AND SOCIALIST POLICIES

→ STATE-DIRECTED CAPITALISM (SYNDICALISM, CORPORATISM)

→ COMMUNISM AND ECONOMIC CENTRALIZATION (FIVE-YEAR PLANS, GREAT LEAP FORWARD)

→ FREE TRADE VS. PROTECTIONISM

→ GREAT DEPRESSION (SMOOT-HAWLEY TARIFF ACT, INTERNATIONAL EFFECTS, NEW DEAL)

→ BRETTON WOODS SYSTEM (WORLD BANK, IMF, GATT/WTO) VS. ECONOMIES IN THE COMMUNIST WORLD

→ ORGANIZATION OF PETROLEUM EXPORTING COUNTRIES (OPEC)

→ ECONOMIC CRISIS OF THE 1970S (OPEC EMBARGO, STAGFLATION)

→ FREE-MARKET REFORMS AND ECONOMIC RECOVERY IN THE 1980s AND 1990s

→ MULTINATIONAL CORPORATIONS

→ REGIONAL ECONOMIC ASSOCIATIONS (EEC/EU, NAFTA, MERCOSUR)

→ ECONOMIC GLOBALIZATION (G7/G8; WORLD TRADE ORGANIZATION)

→ 2007 GLOBAL ECONOMIC CRISIS

→ DIGITIZATION + CONSUMER CULTURE + KNOWLEDGE ECONOMIES (AMAZON)

The twentieth and twenty-first centuries have witnessed experiments with many forms of economic organization. There has been a steady march toward the **globalization** of economic affairs and a more recent one toward the **digitization** of economic exchange and consumer culture.

These developments have presented both costs and benefits, and their full impact has yet to be measured. Immense wealth has been created in the aggregate during this era—more than the world has ever seen before—but it remains very unevenly distributed, both within societies and between them. Moreover, economies the world over remain vulnerable to **business cycles** of periodic **boom and bust**, and the more integrated they become, the more vulnerability they share.

DIVERGENT APPROACHES TO THE ECONOMY

Throughout this era, while most states attempted economic modernization, they adopted widely divergent approaches to economic organization.

The primary approach in the West—and gradually in other places—was capitalism, typically paired with electoral democracy. Capitalism, however, could be modified to varying degrees. While **free-market capitalism** could be left mostly **unregulated**, it could also be more heavily **regulated** by means of government intervention. Proponents of minimal regulation favor the laissez-faire spirit of the nineteenth-century classical economists and argue that the unfettered operation of the **market forces** of **supply and demand** is the surest way to generate wealth for the greatest number of people. Those favoring more regulation counter that even early capitalist thinkers like Adam Smith warned about dangerous levels of poverty and the formation of **monopolies** if governments did not intervene sufficiently. They also maintain that a stronger government hand is necessary to correct downward fluctuations in the market, to provide a **social safety net** to shield citizens from the harshest effects of capitalist competition, and to ensure a sufficient **infrastructure** for the good of the state and the smooth functioning of the economy.

The unregulated approach to capitalism prevailed in most of Europe before World War I and in the United States during the 1920s, and it was aggressively pursued again in these places during the 1980s. The regulated approach is exemplified by the U.S. New Deal of the 1930s and also by the approach taken by most European democracies, with their highly developed **social welfare systems**, during much of the post–World War II era.

Modern economic theories regarding capitalism have focused primarily on this question of government intervention. The dominant thinker in favor of regulation is **John Maynard Keynes** of Britain, author of *The General Theory of Employment, Interest and Money* (1936)—the century's classic text on macroeconomics—and an adviser to or influence on many governments from the 1920s onward, including Franklin Roosevelt's during the Great Depression. Keynes argued that booms and busts proceed from the waxing and waning of consumer confidence (the "animal spirits," to use his terminology) and that, in times of crisis, governments should invest in public works, relief efforts, and stimulus programs to keep confidence high, even if it means running deficits for a time. The best-known opponent of Keynesian theory is the American economist **Milton Friedman**, whose influence on governments in the 1980s and 1990s—especially in Britain, the United States, and Latin America—equaled that of Keynes in earlier decades. An advocate of austerity and privatization, Friedman proposed that governments should intervene as little as possible in the workings of the free market.

More centralized approaches also prevailed. Fascist and authoritarian regimes generally favored **state-directed capitalism** with varying degrees of heavy-handedness. Such systems were based on partnerships between political leaders and economic elites like landowners and industrialists. Economic elites were allowed to own their enterprises and pursue profits as long as they accepted priorities set for them by the state. In exchange for obedience, the state refrained from outright nationalization or centralization, and cooperative parties were rewarded with preferential treatment and state contracts. As an added bonus for economic elites, the state also limited workers' rights and weakened or outlawed trade unions. Such practices were pursued most famously in Nazi Germany, Fascist Italy, and Japan but also in a host of dictatorial and oligarchic regimes.

NOTE

Fascist forms of state capitalism are typically referred to as corporatist or syndicalist.

Socialist economies leaned toward centralization and government intervention: some central planning, the nationalization of certain sectors of the economy, and a willingness to balance respect for private property with the needs of society as a whole. Communist economies committed more fully to central planning, maximal nationalization of the economy, and active hostility toward the principle of private property. The most successful **socialist** or **social democratic** systems—especially in Europe—have been voted into power and have tended to be mild. Many of these have injected enough elements of capitalism that they fall into the category of "**middle**" or "**third way**" economies described above. In the less-developed world (often in recently decolonized nations), quasi-socialist or temporarily socialist measures have been carried out as a way to encourage development or build wealth quickly. Examples include Lázaro Cárdenas's 1938 formation of the state-owned **PEMEX** conglomerate, following his nationalization of Mexico's oil industry, and Gamal Nasser's **nationalization of the Suez Canal** in 1956.

Countries that went **communist** during the 1900s included the Soviet Union, most of Eastern Europe, mainland China, North Korea, Cuba, and Vietnam. Centralization here is greatest, with communism explicitly aiming—at least in theory—to eradicate the profit motive, eliminate private trade, and nationalize economic life as completely as possible. Although communist regimes often claim to be "people's democracies," they nearly always come to power by means of revolution and keep themselves in place by means of dictatorship. They typically pursue ambitious modernization projects, including **state-sponsored industrialization** and the **collectivization of agriculture**. Stalin's **First Five-Year Plan** (1928–1932) and Mao's **Great Leap Forward** (1958–1961) are the most prominent examples, each causing astounding levels of social and economic stress, each relying heavily on **prison-camp labor**, and each linked to notorious famines that killed millions. On the other hand, not all communist regimes have pursued such extremist policies, and many have shown themselves capable of effective reform, such as China under Deng Xiaoping, following Mao's death in 1976, and Vietnam with its *doi moi* ("renovation") reforms in the mid-1980s onward. However, even these reformist regimes remain politically authoritarian.

BOOM AND BUST: TOWARD THE GREAT DEPRESSION AND BRETTON WOODS

As described in Chapter 16, trade and commerce were highly internationalized before 1900, especially between Europe and North America—London and New York had already emerged as the world's leading centers of banking and commerce. Western imperialism drew the rest of the globe into this system as well.

On the eve of the twentieth century, the Western world experienced a bad turn of the **boom-and-bust business cycle**: the **Long Depression** of the early 1870s through the mid-1890s, complete with **protectionist trade policies**. Economic recovery and the resumption of **free trade** caused a rebound between the late 1890s and World War I. The war badly weakened the economies of Europe, but it enriched North America, paving the way for the "**roaring twenties**" in the United States. During and after World War I, all nations in the West industrialized more fully, as did Soviet Russia. Some other parts of the world, such as Japan,

China, and certain parts of Latin America, achieved significant degrees of modernization and industrialization. The scope and volume of international trade remained high during the 1920s, but trade, along with the world's economic health in general, depended heavily on U.S. investment and U.S. willingness to import goods from abroad.

It was for this reason that the **Great Depression**, caused by the wild overvaluation of stocks in the United States and the resulting crash of the New York Stock Exchange in October 1929, had such an adverse effect on the global economy. (The agricultural downturn caused at the same time by the U.S. and Canadian **dust bowl crisis** added to these problems.) The initial reaction of the U.S. government was to institute austerity measures, which depressed consumer confidence, caused runs on banks (as depositors sought to withdraw their money all at once), and led to **mass unemployment** (eventually reaching 25 percent). The Depression also sparked one of the most rashly protectionist measures in U.S. history, the **Smoot-Hawley Tariff Act** of 1930, which attempted to shield U.S. industries and farms by imposing high tariffs on other nations' goods but almost immediately destroyed the ability of Europe, Latin America, and Asia to export their products—in effect spreading the Depression to all these regions as well. Because the USSR's economic connections with the West were so limited, it remained essentially untouched by the Depression. Indeed, because Stalin's five-year plans created virtually 100 percent employment and because propaganda hid their unpleasant realities from public view, some in the West became convinced that Stalinist communism was superior to democratic capitalism.

Political reactions to the Depression are recounted in Chapter 19. Economic reactions generally included some combination of **public works projects** (large-scale construction, dam or highway building, electrification), **social welfare** (soup kitchens, farm relief, unemployment insurance), and in some cases, **military conscription** and **arms buildup**. Franklin Roosevelt's **New Deal**, begun in 1933, attempted the first two, while Nazi Germany, Fascist Italy, and Japan relied mainly on the first and third. European democracies like Britain and France turned to the second alternative, foreshadowing the even more elaborate **social welfare systems** they would put into place after World War II.

World War II shattered most economies besides those of America and the Soviet Union, and even the latter lost a full third of its economic capacity to the fighting. The United States therefore took the lead in rebuilding the global economic system. Franklin Roosevelt, guided by the economic principles of John Maynard Keynes and the post–World War I convictions of Woodrow Wilson, believed that free trade was the key not only to economic prosperity but also to lasting world peace. In July 1944, he met with Allied delegates at Bretton Woods, New Hampshire. It was here that the **World Bank** and the **International Monetary Fund** (IMF) were created, with the goals of rebuilding Europe and aiding countries in Asia, Africa, and Latin America. Plans were also laid for a **General Agreement on Tariffs and Trade** (GATT), which was signed by twenty-three countries in 1947 and met regularly until 1994, when it became the World Trade Organization. Most currencies measured themselves against the U.S. dollar, which in turn based its value on the **gold standard**. The Soviet Union and its Eastern European bloc refused to join this **Bretton Woods system**, as did Communist China.

REGIONALIZATION AND GLOBALIZATION AFTER WORLD WAR II

During the 1950s and 1960s, growing prosperity came especially to the United States but also to Canada, Japan, and the nations of Western Europe.

One way Western Europe staged its economic recovery was through **economic union**, forming the precursors to the present-day European Union: the six-nation European Coal and Steel Community in 1952 and then the **European Economic Community**, also known as the **Common Market**, in 1957. Most European nations, along with Canada, invested heavily in **social welfare systems** that provided for some combination of universal health care, cheap or free higher education for those who qualified academically, generous pensions, and unemployment insurance. The reconstruction of war-torn Western Europe, assisted at the outset by the **Marshall Plan** (1948), was nothing short of incredible. The same was true of Japan.

The rest of the world developed unevenly. In Latin America and Africa, many governments still relied on the export of a narrow assortment of natural resources or crops, just as they had in the 1800s. The Middle East benefited from its dominance in oil production. The **Organization of Petroleum Exporting Countries** (OPEC), formed in 1960 and still one of the most influential cartels in economic history, consists largely of Middle Eastern countries. The economies of the Soviet Union, its Eastern European allies, and Communist China tended to remain largely but not completely isolated from those of the Western world. Parts of Asia, such as Japan, the continent's economic "tiger," along with the so-called **little tigers** (Taiwan, South Korea, Hong Kong, and Singapore), quickly adapted to global capitalism and industrialization. Many Asian nations joined regional economic associations; the **Association of Southeast Asian Nations** (ASEAN), formed in 1967 to promote regional security, strengthened economic ties among its member states.

In the 1970s, Western economies began a long transition from industrial production to **postindustrial production**, based less on manufacturing and more on service and "knowledge economies" (which include white-collar work, high-tech fields, and computer expertise). At the same time, a general economic crisis struck much of the developed world and lasted most of the decade. In 1971, Richard Nixon rocked the international community by taking the U.S. dollar off the gold standard. OPEC's 1973 **oil embargo** severely affected the energy-dependent economies of the West. A curious combination of recession and inflation (which generally occurs in times of economic growth) called **stagflation** plagued North America and Western Europe, and those nations with costly social welfare systems found them difficult to maintain. Although the USSR had its own oil reserves and was safe from OPEC's embargo, inefficiency, food shortages, the cost of the arms race, and governmental corruption sapped Eastern European economies. In the mid-1970s, largely to combat these negative trends, the countries with the seven largest noncommunist economies—Great Britain, France, West Germany, Italy, Japan, Canada, and the United States—formed the **Group of Seven** (**G7**) to coordinate policies to mutual economic benefit.

> **NOTE**
>
> The Western world's transition from industrial production to service and knowledge economies went hand in hand with a gradual relocation of industrial production to previously less-developed parts of the world. This took place first in places like Asia's little tigers and later in countries like Mexico, Bangladesh, Vietnam, and Honduras.

During the 1980s, most economies outside the Soviet bloc recovered. In the West, the shift from industrial to postindustrial/service modes of production continued. To one degree or another, most governments pursued **free-market reforms**, which involved **privatization** of previously nationalized sectors of the economy (typically transport and energy), trimming or elimination of social-welfare benefits, and **austerity** (the sharp reduction of government spending). The economic theories of **Milton Friedman** were followed most eagerly by Ronald Reagan in the United States, Margaret Thatcher in Great Britain, and the dictator Augusto Pinochet in Chile. Such policies led to an overall rise in economic growth but also caused great social stress, in the form of layoffs and the weakening of unions, and began a thirty-year trend of shifting the distribution of wealth upward from the middle class and toward corporate elites. Debate also continues as to whether free-market policies caused the economic recovery or simply coincided with it.

The 1990s brought about a high tide of **economic globalization**, which has shown no signs of receding in the 2000s. A major factor was the growing influence of **multinational corporations**, starting in the 1980s and continuing to the present. These large conglomerates, technically "from" a single country, maintain factories and subsidiaries around the world and employ many foreign workers. Examples include Coca-Cola and McDonald's, originally from the United States; carmakers like Japan's Toyota; Royal Dutch Shell, with fossil-fuel interests worldwide; Nestlé (Swiss-based, the largest food company in the world) and the Anglo-Dutch Unilever; and electronics and computer giants such as Sony (originally Japanese) and Microsoft, Facebook, and Apple from the United States.

While corporations like these generate massive wealth, critics contend that their profit seeking weakens societies and challenges state power in many ways. Multinationals engage in **tax sheltering** (shifting assets out of a home country to places with lower tax rates or no tax at all) and regularly **relocate** or "**outsource" jobs** from city to city or country to country, causing sudden layoffs or firings in the process, in their search for the most lenient environmental regulations, the most favorable tax breaks, and most important, the cheapest labor. The impact of multinationals on the developing world is also mixed: even though they provide jobs and invest in local infrastructure, they often exploit labor (in some cases turning a blind eye to dreadful **sweatshop conditions**), harm local ecosystems, and put homegrown industries and craft production out of business.

NOTE

A sense that globalization mainly benefits corporate and high-tech elites has driven powerful protests and political reactions in several forms. These include anti-G7 and anti-IMF demonstrations, the Occupy Wall Street movement, France's "yellow vest" strikes, and the Brexit vote of 2016. On the left, a World Fair Trade Organization arose in 1989 and contrasts directly with the World Trade Organization. On the right, populist and nationalist electoral shifts in the 2010s have been prompted largely by desires for a less globalized world.

The growing extent of globalization is reflected in the increased importance of **international economic organizations** and **regional economic associations**, which foster economic cooperation and provide for freer trade. Throughout the 1990s and 2000s, the **Group of Seven** (**G7**)—renamed the **Group of Eight** (**G8**) between 1997 and 2014, when Russia was accepted as a member—met more frequently and more formally. In 1994 and 1995, the GATT accords were upgraded and strengthened by the formation of the **World Trade Organization** (WTO), whose purpose is to regulate the economic interactions of the more than a hundred nations that belong to it (these now include Russia and Communist China). In 1994, the United States, Mexico, and Canada created a zone of free movement of money, goods, services, and labor by means of the **North American Free Trade Agreement** (NAFTA), which, as of 2019, is still in the process of being renegotiated. Other regions have tightened economic ties as well. In 1989, Pacific Rim nations formed the **Asia-Pacific Economic Cooperation Group** (APEC), which now includes more than twenty members. In Latin America, the Southern Common Market, or **Mercosur**, was established in 1991; it consists of Argentina, Brazil, Paraguay, Uruguay, Venezuela, and Bolivia. A number of trading blocs from the 1980s and 1990s joined together in 2008 to create the **African Free Trade Zone** (AFTZ).

By far the boldest experiment in economic integration has been Europe's. In 1991, the nations of the **European Union**, or EU (formerly the European Economic Community), signed the Maastricht Treaty, which provided for the creation of the **euro** as a single currency and for the free movement of money, goods, and labor. The euro went into circulation in 2002 and was adopted by most EU members (Britain was a major holdout). The viability of the euro was called into question in the wake of the **2007 global economic crisis**, and while the "eurozone" has so far survived, anti-immigration sentiment in the 2010s and the 2016 **Brexit** vote have seriously weakened the EU.

The costs and benefits of economic globalization are mixed. It has generated great wealth, at least in a broad sense and in certain parts of the world. With some justification, proponents of globalization argue that free trade helps to preserve peace. On the other hand, the above-mentioned practices of multinational corporations may lead to a constant state of economic instability, and agriculture is greatly affected by globalization, as farmers in one country compete with cheap food imported from other parts of the world. The fact that so many nations' economies influence one another means that negative trends in one region can adversely affect larger parts of the world—the financial crises in Mexico in 1994, Asia in 1997, Russia and Brazil in 1998, and the U.S. collapse in 2007 are all examples. Finally, it remains questionable how far all nations will be willing to go in subjecting their economic policies to the dictates of the EU, the WTO, or other regional and international bodies.

To this date, globalization has not healed the **north-south split** that continues to divide the developed world from the nondeveloped and developing nations located near or south of the equator. In addition, the effects of the **2007 global economic crisis**, which began in the United States and emanated outward, still linger.

NOTE

Economic reform was pursued in the communist world during the mid-1980s but with varying results. Both Deng Xiaoping in China and Mikhail Gorbachev in the USSR allowed limited degrees of private trade and free-market activity. Deng's reforms put China on the path toward rapid and sizable growth. Gorbachev's perestroika program destabilized the Soviet system and ultimately failed. The difference seems to be explained by the fact that Gorbachev moved too slowly with economic change and weakened his position by simultaneously pursuing political liberalization. Deng moved quickly on the economic front but tolerated little political opposition.

Social Interactions and Organization, 1900 to the Present

24

IN THIS CHAPTER

→ **GLOBAL POPULATION GROWTH**

→ **SOCIOECONOMIC FEATURES OF THE DEVELOPED WORLD (MIDDLE CLASS, URBANIZATION, SOCIAL WELFARE SYSTEMS) VS. THE COMMUNIST STATES**

→ **INDUSTRIAL VS. POSTINDUSTRIAL (SERVICE, HIGH-TECH, AND KNOWLEDGE) ECONOMIES**

→ **THE DEVELOPING WORLD (THIRD WORLD) AND THE NORTH–SOUTH SPLIT**

→ **SOCIAL ACTIVISM AND PROTEST MOVEMENTS**

→ **ETHNIC VIOLENCE AND GENOCIDE**

→ **ETHNIC PREJUDICE AND SEGREGATION (JIM CROW LAWS, APARTHEID)**

→ **MIGRATION (MIGRANT AND ILLEGAL LABORERS, GUEST WORKERS) + MOVEMENT OF REFUGEES**

→ **ANTI-IMMIGRATION SENTIMENT, NATIVISM, XENOPHOBIA**

→ **WOMEN'S SUFFRAGE**

→ **WOMEN'S LIBERATION AND THE FEMINIST MOVEMENT (SIMONE DE BEAUVOIR, BETTY FRIEDAN, GLORIA STEINEM)**

→ **GENDER EQUALITY (EQUAL PAY, REPRODUCTIVE RIGHTS, EQUALITY IN MARRIAGE) + LGBTQ RIGHTS**

Different parts of the world have experienced social transformations differently. As a rule, the changes of the 1900s and early 2000s proceeded along four basic tracks:

■ In Western Europe, the United States, and Canada—the West—as well as in Australia and New Zealand, movement (although in some cases slow or nonexistent before the end of World War II) was toward stable democratization, social equality and individual rights, economic prosperity, the creation of social welfare systems, the shift from industrial to postindustrial production, and rapid scientific and technological development.

■ Prosperous nations in Asia—first Japan, then others like Taiwan, South Korea, Indonesia, and Singapore—made great strides toward economic and technological modernization, especially after World War II. They urbanized, built social welfare systems, and developed postindustrial, high-tech economies. However, they were (and in some cases remain) slower to embrace democracy and tolerate the individualism that had come to characterize Western societies in the 1800s and 1900s.

- The Soviet Union and Eastern Europe modernized economically. They urbanized and developed social welfare systems, and technological and scientific advancement was considerable. However, political systems were repressive, and not only were economies here overly centralized, but they remained industrial rather than postindustrial and were cruder in terms of technological finesse than in the West. Even after the collapse of communism, it has been difficult for this region to move toward democracy and prosperity.

- To one degree or another, the developing nations of Asia, Africa, the Middle East, and Latin America are striving to create advanced economies, modern societies, and representative forms of government. Some have made progress, attaining a high level of prosperity or a functioning democracy or both. Others are mired in backwardness, poverty, civil strife, and dictatorship. Most are somewhere in between. Perhaps the most distinctive case is the People's Republic of China, which has the geography, population, and military capacity of a major power and whose economy has grown considerably since the 1980s. But China's government is still authoritarian, and social and economic progress remains uneven. Some economists use the acronym **BRIC** to refer to Brazil, Russia, India, and China, countries whose socioeconomic development does not yet match that of the West but which have been rapidly modernizing and gaining global clout.

LABOR AND LIFESTYLES

The most dramatic changes in these spheres have been felt in Europe and North America and to a lesser extent elsewhere.

NOTE

In 1900, the world population was 1.6 billion. By 2000, it had reached 6 billion, and it has since topped 7.5 billion. Most historians contend that this growth has been caused primarily by improvements in medicine and public health as opposed to the eradication of hunger.

A cluster of social trends that began in the West during the 1800s sped up significantly in the 1900s and was accelerated in many ways by World War I. Legal distinctions between social classes were eliminated. **Equal political rights** and **equal treatment before the law** were provided to all adult citizens, including women and minorities (a slow process and still ongoing in many places). Aristocratic social elites were replaced by a professional and meritocratic **white-collar class** whose status depended on education, skills, and earned wealth. Developed societies created a large, stable **middle class** and provided access to at least a **minimum standard of living** and an adequate level of well-being, even among the lower classes. Other developments included:

- The growing power of **trade unions**.
- The creation of **universal educational systems**.
- The growing availability and affordability of **transportational** and **energy infrastructures** along with the mobility that came with **mass transit** and the **automobile**.
- **Urbanization** throughout the 1900s, with **suburbanization** increasingly common in the postwar era.
- The adoption of **social welfare systems**, either as a way to cope with the economic pain of the interwar years and the Great Depression (such as the British "dole" or Franklin Roosevelt's New Deal in the United States) or because of the new possibilities opened up by post–World War II prosperity. These generally included some combination of unemployment insurance, pensions, and health care (at least for the elderly and poor if not the entire population). In capitalist societies, they required a willingness to place a "safety net" under the workings of the free market or even to blend capitalism with some elements of socialism—the so-called "**middle**" or "**third way**."

During and after the Cold War, the Western world experienced a gradual transition from industrial economies, still dominant in the 1950s and 1960s, to **postindustrial economies**, more the norm since the 1980s and 1990s. These tend to emphasize **consumerism** and **service industries** rather than manufacturing, as well as the creation of "**knowledge economies**" focused on **computerization and cutting-edge technologies**. (Among the countries leading the way here are the United States, Japan, Finland, and South Korea.) This change is associated with many innovations and opportunities. As with the shift from agriculture and craftsmanship to industrialization during the 1800s, it has also caused stress, with many jobs made obsolete by new machines or lost to cheaper labor overseas. Moreover, even the economic boom of the 1980s and 1990s was accompanied by a growing divide between the wealthiest members of Western societies and the less well-off, with increased burdens falling on a noticeably **shrinking middle class**. The economic collapse caused by the **global financial crisis of 2007** has only worsened these trends.

In communist Europe, many of these same trends played out during the Cold War but somewhat differently. Social welfare and universal education were at the heart of the state system, and class divisions were minimized, at least in theory. In reality, a communist elite—comprising about 10 percent of a given society and denounced by the Yugoslav intellectual Milovan Djilas as a corrupt and self-important "**new class**"—enjoyed enormous privileges. For everyone else, the social welfare system provided what cynics referred to as "equality of poverty" or, at best, "equality of adequacy." Industrial manufacturing was strong, but the production of consumer goods was weak, and high-tech innovation outside the military sphere lagged. When communism finally collapsed in Eastern Europe and the USSR, a wrenching social and economic transition to free-market capitalism followed.

In developing regions, the so-called **Third World**, social divisions between the elite classes and the rest of society tended to remain wide, with a small middle class (if any) separating the very wealthy from the poor masses. Where social and economic modernization did take place, it was generally directed from above—sometimes in opposition to traditional religious outlooks or value systems, as in Turkey and pre-1979 Iran. On a global basis, both during the Cold War and afterward, the world has struggled with a pronounced **north-south split**, meaning that economic prosperity, social stability, and access to food, clean water, medical care, and cutting-edge technology have tended to be concentrated in the developed world, with many parts of the developing world running behind and still impoverished.

Social activism has been part of modern social life since the days of the American and French Revolutions but has brought about particularly tremendous changes during the 1900s and early 2000s. It played a leading role in **national liberation movements** worldwide and in the struggle for **racial equality** in places as diverse as South Africa (the **antiapartheid movement**) and the United States (the **civil rights movement** versus **Jim Crow laws**). It clashed with existing social and political orders, as during the various **1968 protests** that rocked city streets and college campuses from Paris and Prague to Mexico City and New York, and it gave voice to those who opposed nuclear weapons, Cold War conflicts like Vietnam, and damage to the environment. Social activism advanced the cause of **women's liberation** and **gay rights**, and it has defied dictatorial regimes—unsuccessfully but bravely during the **Tiananmen Square protests** in China in 1989 and with more decisive results during the **Solidarity strikes** against Poland's communist government during the 1980s and in the related "people's power" movements that brought down communism in Eastern Europe more widely in 1988 and 1989. Social activism sparked the **Arab Spring** of 2010–2011, and as noted in Chapter 23, **anti-G7** and **antiglobalization** protests were common in the 1990s and 2000s.

ETHNICITY AND RACE RELATIONS

Racial tensions divided many communities and nations throughout this era. **Ethnic violence**, **persecution of minorities**, and **segregation**—official and unofficial—plagued societies worldwide and continue to do so.

Ethnic tensions took their most extreme form in the **genocides** and **mass killings** described in Chapters 19 and 20, such as the Armenian massacres of World War I, the extermination of Jews and Roma during World War II, the Guatemalan murder of Mayans in the 1980s, the Rwandan genocide and the Yugoslav ethnic cleansings of the 1990s, and the Arab killing of African Darfurians in Sudan during the early 2000s. There are also certain regions where long-term ethnic tensions and sporadic violence persist, such as the Indo-Pakistani animosity in South Asia, the Israeli-Palestinian conflict in the Middle East, intertribal rivalries in Africa, and Greek-Turkish hostility on the island of Cyprus, divided since 1975.

Segregationist schemes existed in many places to restrict the rights of unfavored ethnic groups or to keep them apart from those groups favored by the authorities. Certainly in no colony did the imperial power allow natives to mix freely with whites. Prior to the revolutions of 1917, Jews in Russia were not allowed to live outside the **Pale of Settlement**, a special zone in western Russia, Ukraine, and Belarus, without a permit. In the United States, **Jim Crow laws**—enforced by lynching and other forms of legal or semilegal violence—perpetuated antiblack segregation in the south until protests and demonstrations by **civil rights activists** like **Martin Luther King Jr.** helped to bring about passage of the **Civil Rights Acts** of 1964 and 1968.

Indigenous Americans of all types struggled against secondary status and racial prejudice, whether in the United States and Canada or throughout Latin America. In addition to being forced onto reservations, many were taken from their families as children, either to be adopted by white families or to be educated in residential schools, where abuse was rampant and native traditions discouraged. One of the most deeply entrenched forms of segregation was the South African system of **apartheid**, instituted in 1948 by white Afrikaners and rigidly enforced until the 1990s. Not only did apartheid earn South Africa decades of world disapproval, but it provoked determined opposition on the part of groups like the **African National Congress**, led most famously by **Nelson Mandela**, jailed for his activism between 1964 and 1990. Throughout Eastern Europe, **Roma** (Gypsies) continue to be treated as distinctly second-class. In the Middle East, Kurds struggle against marginalization and seek freedom from governments like Turkey's, Iraq's, and Syria's.

Migration has remained as much a global reality in this era as during the 1800s, and so have **xenophobia** and **anti-immigration sentiment**. Migration continued to be motivated by **work opportunities** (including migrant and illegal labor), but warfare has done its share to prompt it as well, creating **refugees** and **displaced persons** by the millions. The movement of peoples intensified after World War II. During the late 1940s and 1950s, refugees from Eastern Europe, where Nazi genocide and Soviet occupation caused massive population transfers, moved to Western Europe or North America or in some cases to the recently founded state of Israel. During the postwar period, economic opportunity, violence in the developing world, and political repression led millions to leave Asia, Africa, the Middle East, and Latin America for Western Europe and North America.

> **NOTE**
>
> **Compare the various struggles waged by American civil rights activists, the Indian National Congress, and the antiapartheid movement. The principle of nonviolence guided leaders like Gandhi and Martin Luther King Jr. but was less relevant to the African National Congress, many of whose leading figures, including Nelson and Winnie Mandela, embraced guerrilla action and Marxist radicalism. Even in the United States, King's nonviolence was counterbalanced by the more extremist and revolutionary approaches espoused by those like Malcolm X and the Black Panthers.**

> **NOTE**
>
> **Certain castes and ethnic groups were heavily discriminated against in India, although this was legally forbidden by the Constitution of 1948. In the Pacific, note how anti-immigration White Australia policies were dismantled between the 1940s and 1970s.**

Such migrations increased in scope during and after **decolonization** as countries that dismantled their empires allowed **former colonial subjects** to live and work in the metropole, or "home" country. Indians, Pakistanis, and Caribbean islanders traveled in large numbers to Britain, Indonesians migrated to the Netherlands, and Algerians and Moroccans came to France. (The migration of Filipinos and Puerto Ricans to the United States can be considered part of this phenomenon as well.) The late Cold War saw an increase in legal and illegal immigration of Latin Americans to the United States and Canada. The admission of **guest workers** to Western Europe amounted to 15 million by the 1980s, many of them Turks living in Germany. The collapse of communism in the Soviet bloc and the rise in ethnic conflict in places like the former Yugoslavia caused new waves of migration. Since 2011, the Syrian civil war has forced millions of refugees to flee the country.

Migration has typically provided a much-needed labor force (if not always a well-treated one), and it has enriched the cultural diversity of host nations. However, especially when economic times are tight, it has stirred up **anti-immigration sentiments** that involve varying degrees of prejudice and discrimination. At their worst, they involve **race riots** or the formation of **skinhead movements** or **nativist political parties** that call for an end to immigration.

Wartime can also trigger anti-immigrant sentiment if a country is home to a large immigrant population originally from a nation it is fighting. Distrust of German Americans and German Canadians ran high during World War I, for example. During World War II, both Canada and the United States took the drastic step of rounding up tens of thousands of Japanese Canadians and Japanese Americans without cause and confining them against their will to "relocation centers." The largest and most infamous of these was **Manzanar**, near California's Sierra Nevada.

GENDER ISSUES

One of the most important trends of the twentieth and twenty-first centuries has been the march toward **gender equality**. Progress here came most quickly in the Western world, although other regions moved forward as well, if slowly and partially.

In Europe and North America, the **women's suffrage movements** that had arisen during the late 1800s continued their agitation during the early 1900s. They scored major successes during and after World War I when large numbers of women took jobs as farmhands and factory workers, especially in munitions plants. Women also served as nurses and uniformed auxiliaries, and their contributions to their countries' war efforts earned them much respect. It was largely because of this that women received the **right to vote** in many Western nations between 1917 and 1920, with Spain, France, and Italy standing out as noteworthy exceptions. (The **right to hold office** generally came as well.)

NOTE

Mexico's 1917 constitution granted women the right to vote, and much of Latin America did the same in the 1920s and 1930s, including Brazil in 1932. Turkey gave women the vote in 1934, but this was a rarity in the Middle East and Islamic North Africa. (Morocco, for example, followed suit only in 1963.) Japan established universal suffrage in 1945, and India and China did so in 1947. (Although the Chinese Republic was late in giving women the vote, it did outlaw foot binding in 1912.)

Except in the USSR, where rapid industrialization required as large a workforce as possible, the rate of female employment decreased in Europe and North America during the 1920s as men returned from World War I. It declined further in the 1930s when during the mass unemployment caused by the Great Depression, it was considered "wrong" for women to have jobs if men were out of work.

The interwar dictatorships differed sharply in their treatment of women. In the USSR, Marxist ideology called for gender equality, and while the Soviets observed this ideal imperfectly (especially under Stalin), women made up a large part of the workforce. By contrast,

Italian fascism, German Nazism, and Japanese traditionalism were explicitly hostile to the notion of gender equality. In all three countries, women were expected to be principally mothers and homemakers. Non-Western parts of the world that afforded educational or workplace opportunities to women during the interwar years were rare, although they included Turkey, Iran, and certain parts of Latin America.

Famously, World War II brought women into the workplace in even greater numbers than World War I had. The image of "Rosie the Riveter" became a potent symbol of the role of women in U.S. wartime production. In the Soviet Union, women made up nearly 40 percent of the national workforce. Large numbers of American, Canadian, Australian, New Zealand, and British women served as war nurses and military personnel (although not as combat troops). In the USSR, women served in the military and, in some limited but important cases, saw active duty in combat—mainly as pilots and snipers. Although there was a temporary dip in female employment afterward, World War II served the purpose of permanently cementing a place for women in the working world—at least in North America and Europe. In addition, more countries, including holdouts like France and Italy, gave women the vote after the war.

During the postwar years, women in the developed world assumed an increasingly larger role in the workplace and in public life. Even so, during the late 1940s and 1950s, it was still generally considered that a woman's main roles were that of homemaker and childbearer. Even women who worked were subjected to widespread **gender discrimination**: sexual harassment, unequal wages, and lack of access to positions of leadership (the "**glass ceiling**"). French philosopher **Simone de Beauvoir** analyzed the place of women in modern society in *The Second Sex* (1949), which investigated the deep-seated cultural and biological reasons for male domination of women.

A great step toward equality was taken by women in the Western world during the 1960s and 1970s when the modern **feminist movement** began to press for **women's liberation**, which meant not just legal equality and the right to vote but the elimination of cultural stereotypes of women as the "weaker sex" and of social barriers that still blocked the way toward full equality. Major figures here came from the United States and included **Gloria Steinem**, a founding figure in the **National Organization for Women** (**NOW**), and **Betty Friedan**, whose book *The Feminine Mystique* (1963) joined *The Second Sex* as part of the feminist movement's intellectual foundation. NOW organized a major event, the Women's Strike for Equality, in 1970, although it failed in its larger goal of passing an Equal Rights Amendment to the U.S. Constitution. Throughout the Western world, achievements of the women's movement include better and more varied career opportunities, higher pay, equal access to higher education, greater respect for women's athletics, a greater role in political life, and the right to equality in marriage and divorce. **Reproductive rights** have also proved crucial. The postwar development of reliable contraception, especially birth control pills, gave women unprecedented control over pregnancy and sexuality. The gradual legalization of abortion, while controversial, did the same.

Progress toward equal treatment of women has been uneven in non-Western parts of the world. In many societies, women are still relegated to traditional and secondary roles. Although it is an overgeneralization to say that women are not treated equally in *all* parts of Asia, Africa, the Middle East, and Latin America, the fact remains that Islamic fundamentalism, conservative Catholicism, machismo, and old-fashioned views of women as inferior (or of wives as servants or property) constrain women more commonly in these regions than in the West. In sub-Saharan Africa, rates of HIV/AIDS infection among women are unusually high owing to the reluctance of many African men to engage in safe-sex practices. The custom of clitoridectomy (female circumcision) is still practiced in certain parts of Africa. On the other hand, the vast majority of societies allow women more rights and legal protections than they once did.

Momentum has also been gained in recent years by **LGBTQ rights movements** in Europe and North America. In the United States, the contemporary gay rights movement is considered to have begun with the **Stonewall riots** of 1969 in New York's Greenwich Village. But despite gay pride parades and protests since the 1970s and despite growing awareness of gay, lesbian, and transgender relationships, wider acceptance and the formalization of equal rights have been a longer time in coming. **Same-sex marriage** became legal only in the 2000s—in over two dozen countries as of this date, including the United States.

Humans and the Environment, 1900 to the Present

25

At no other point in history has human activity had such an overpowering **environmental impact** as it has had during the twentieth and twenty-first centuries. **Population growth,** due principally to improvements in medicine and public-health programming, has exploded.

THE ENVIRONMENT

It is common to think of pollution and environmental crisis as modern problems. In fact, societies have affected—and been affected by—the environment from the Stone Age onward. Resource extraction and consumption, as well as pollution, have always been part of the human past. The downfall of civilizations like those of the Indus Valley and Easter Island has been linked directly to environmental disaster or, in the latter case, mismanagement. In countless ways, the industrial era has made humanity's footprint on the environment heavier than ever before. Societies consume more, rely more on machine production and fuel-driven transport, and possess engineering skills that can change the earth in ways unimaginable to preindustrial societies. Currently, climate change (global warming) serves as the clearest demonstration of how profoundly human action has affected the environment.

That, combined with ever-increasing reliance on energy-dependent technology, has led to unprecedented and continually mounting levels of **resource extraction** and **consumption**. **Pollution** and **species extinction** threaten the well-being of the environment as never before, and humanity's **earth-shaping capacity** now operates quite literally on a planetary scale—with consequences such as widespread flooding, deforestation, desertification, and **climate change** in the form of **global warming**.

DISEASE, HEALTH, AND POPULATION IN THE CONTEMPORARY ERA

Diseases associated with poverty, such as malaria, cholera, and tuberculosis, persisted in many parts of the world. On the other hand, **vaccination campaigns** and other public-health initiatives, both in developed countries and internationally as part of relief efforts, have in many cases reduced or even eliminated certain diseases. **Polio** and **smallpox**, formerly huge killers, are among the illnesses that have been all but eradicated, and treatments for formerly incurable venereal diseases, such as syphilis, have been developed as well.

Conversely, **new epidemic diseases** have emerged during this era, their global spread made easier by better and faster transportation. Some of them lasted only briefly, while others proved to be of greater duration. The era's first—and by far the deadliest—was the influenza outbreak of 1918, popularly known as the **Spanish flu**; it infected 500 million people between early 1918 and late 1920 and killed anywhere from 40 million to 100 million. Despite its name, the Spanish flu's origins are unknown. (The earliest reports of it came from Spain, where wartime censorship did not apply, but it may have arisen in Asia, where the vast majority of deaths seem to have occurred.) The global movement of soldiers and supply shipments during the final months of World War I, not to mention the displacement of peoples and demobilization of troops afterward, helped to spread Spanish flu to all quarters of the globe.

Other strains of **influenza** repeatedly threaten to reach pandemic status, such as the H1N1 virus that caused great panic in 2009. Since its identification in the mid-1970s in Africa, the **Ebola virus**, which causes severe internal bleeding and kills a high percentage of its victims, has threatened several times to erupt as a major disease beyond Africa's borders. **HIV/AIDS**, also originating in Africa and identified in 1981, has killed over 30 million people worldwide. Spread via blood or sexual transmission, HIV/AIDS quickly became a global phenomenon and remained highly fatal until the development of effective treatments in the late 1990s and early 2000s. Still incurable, HIV/AIDS is a chronic disease for those with access to treatment but deadly to those without. Rates of infection are especially high in Africa, where it is a particular scourge.

The contemporary era has also seen the proliferation of diseases associated with sedentary lifestyles and increased longevity. Diets high in sugar and processed foods—common in

DISEASES AND WORLD HISTORY

From humanity's earliest days, disease has played an enormous role in how societies interact with each other. Pandemics in the form of bubonic plague (which swept from China to Europe in the 1300s and plagued Eurasia for centuries) devastated numerous societies. The demographic impact of the spread of smallpox and measles to the Americas by European explorers and conquerors in the 1400s and 1500s was nightmarish. Rampant urbanization and overcrowding in the 1700s and 1800s caused massive outbreaks of cholera and tuberculosis. Until the mid-1800s, illnesses like malaria and sleeping sickness prevented European imperial powers from penetrating too deeply into the interiors of Southeast Asia and especially Africa. The modern age has brought with it a better understanding of disease, but it has also given rise to much greater global mobility, a factor that makes the widespread outbreak of epidemics and pandemics faster and more likely than before. The Spanish influenza after World War I, the emergence of AIDS (acquired immune deficiency syndrome), and the recent appearance of SARS (severe acute respiratory syndrome), Ebola, and avian flu are good examples.

North America but also in other regions where American food habits have caught on—have caused a rapid increase in **diabetes** worldwide. **Heart disease** and **obesity** are more common for the same reason. Paradoxically, medical advances in developed societies and the resulting extension of average human life spans into the eighties rather than the six-ties or seventies have placed larger numbers of people at risk of **Alzheimer's disease** and other ailments associated with old age.

Also on the topic of public health, **population growth** during this era has been breathtaking. In 1900, the world population was 1.6 billion. That figure had risen to 3 billion by 1960 and to 6 billion by 2000. It exceeds 7.5 billion today. Even in the developed world, where birthrates have tended to decline, population has increased. In the developing and less developed worlds, birthrates are climbing. China and India each have populations of more than a bil-lion. A great concern for the twenty-first century is whether the earth can support continued growth on this scale. **Overconsumption** of food and energy, **overproduction** of waste and pollution, and sheer **overcrowding** are all possible consequences of unchecked growth.

THE MODERN ENVIRONMENTAL MOVEMENT

Ever since the Industrial Revolution, there has been a spirit of environmentalism, striving to prevent the natural world from overdevelopment or destruction. The romantic movement's love for nature sparked popular concern about the effects of industrialization, and figures such as Henry Thoreau and Ralph Waldo Emerson promoted environmentalist ideals during the 1800s.

Modern conservation efforts date back to the creation of **national parks** (the first in the world being Yellowstone in 1872) and **national park services** (Canada leading the way in 1911, followed by the United States in 1916). Activism by figures such as the Scottish-American naturalist **John Muir**, cofounder of the Sierra Club, and President Theodore Roosevelt, an avid outdoorsman, were crucial at the turn of the century.

If environmental awareness grew during the first half of the 1900s, it hugely expanded after World War II with the rise of the contemporary **environmental** (or **green**) **movement**. This arose with growing evidence that pollution, species extinction, and unregulated industrial-ization posed undeniable threats to the earth's ecological well-being. Under the United Nations, the **International Union for Conservation of Nature** (IUCN, founded in 1948), began maintaining a "red list" of **endangered species** and continues to monitor the issue today. Many green groups and organizations took shape in the 1960s and 1970s in both North America and Western Europe. A major inspiration came with the 1962 publication of *Silent Spring*, by **Rachel Carson**, who warned of the dangers connected with the insecticide DDT. The first celebration of **Earth Day**—now an annual event on April 22—also popularized the environmental movement.

Nongovernmental organizations (**NGOs**) working on behalf of the environment have become globally influential. These include the World Wildlife Fund (1961) and **Greenpeace**, founded in the years 1969–1972 out of protests against atomic testing in Alaska. Arguably the world's most famous eco-activist group, Greenpeace is also one of the most interventionist, with a policy of "direct action" to impede industrial, hunting, and fishing efforts of which it disapproves. The **World Fair Trade Organization**, founded in 1989, strives for environmental sustainability as well as economic justice. Also renowned is Kenya's **Green Belt Movement**, established in 1977 by Wangari Maathai, the first African woman to win the Nobel Peace Prize. A prominent example of ecofeminism, the Green Belt Movement trained large numbers of women to fight deforestation by planting trees and engaging in ecotourism.

In certain countries, especially in Western Europe, **green parties** play an important role in electoral politics. Contemporary environmental efforts are largely focused on the problem of **climate change**.

POLLUTION, EARTH SHAPING, AND GLOBAL WARMING

The **earth-shaping capacity** of human societies has dramatically increased during this era, thanks to escalating industrialization, greater scientific aptitude, and massive engineering projects. An important example of this trend is the so-called **Green Revolution**: an immense campaign from the 1940s through the 1970s to improve agricultural production, especially in the developing world, by clearing more land, relying on new scientific techniques, and using new fertilizers and insecticides. Most consider the Green Revolution to have begun with improvements in corn production in Mexico during the 1940s; it then spread throughout Latin America. From there it was exported to places like India, China, and the Middle East, where famine had previously threatened populations on a regular basis. Although the Green Revolution improved food production—and can be said to have saved many lives—it also had a large and not entirely positive impact on the environment as it resulted in greater deforestation, increased water consumption, and the extensive use of pesticides.

Prior to the Green Revolution, **famine** and other forms of agricultural downturn periodically occurred. Human-caused famines struck the USSR in the 1930s and China in the 1950s. Natural famines blighted India in the 1940s and Ethiopia in the 1980s. In the United States and Canada, the "**dust bowl**" crisis of the 1930s—during which thousands of square miles of fertile soil were lost to a disastrous combination of aridity and huge windstorms—drastically lowered agricultural output and added extra stress to the Great Depression.

Dam building and the **diversion of rivers** constitute another form of earth shaping, one increasingly frequent during the 1900s and 2000s. Projects like the Hoover Dam in Depression-era America, the Dnieprostroi hydroelectric complex in Stalinist Russia, Egypt's **Aswan High Dam**, and China's mammoth **Three Gorges Dam** have all left gigantic ecological footprints. Sizable bodies of water—such as the Aral Sea, between Kazakhstan and Uzbekistan—have dried up or suffered irreversible damage due to the rerouting of rivers. When taken on a large enough scale, the **environmental impact of warfare** can be considered its own form of earth shaping. Examples of how war has affected the environment include radiation from **nuclear-weapons testing** (in the Pacific, off Alaska, in Central Asia, and in the Soviet Arctic), biological and chemical warfare between Iran and Iraq during the 1970s, the use of napalm and **Agent Orange** to wipe out forests during the Vietnam War, and the destruction of oil wells during times of armed conflict, especially in the Middle East.

Pollution has been and remains an ever-present threat, whether on the ground or in the air and water. In both the developed and developing worlds, communities continue to generate more trash and toxic waste, burn more fossil fuels, and release more emissions into the air and water with every passing year. Habitats like wetlands, rain forests, and polar ecosystems have been especially harmed. In numerous urban settings—Tokyo, Los Angeles, Mexico City, Delhi, and many cities in China and Russia—air quality reaches noxious levels on a routine basis. Certain **environmental disasters** have proved particularly devastating, including the Bhopal incident of 1984 (when a Union Carbide pesticide factory killed thousands in India with an accidental release of poison gas), the 1989 wreck of the oil tanker *Exxon Valdez* off the Alaskan coast, the 2010 Deepwater oil platform blowout in the Gulf of Mexico, and the nuclear incidents described below. Before the elimination of chlorofluorocarbons (CFCs) in spray form, deep concerns arose during the 1980s and 1990s that the atmosphere's protective **ozone layer** would become dangerously depleted.

A serious failure here has been the inability or unwillingness to move faster and more completely toward adopting sources of clean, sustainable energy. Continued **reliance on fossil fuels** such as coal and petroleum leads not only to periodic shortages and economic dilemmas but also to continued pollution. Hydroelectric generation of electric power has its limits, and the dams required for it create huge ecological stress. Increased development of wind, solar, and geothermal power—potentially the cleanest sources possible—is still in many cases inadequately supported by governments or corporations. (At times, the latter, whose profits depend on fossil-fuel technologies, have actively opposed such experiments.) The only alternative source of energy that has met with any success is nuclear power. This, however, carries with it serious risks as was demonstrated by **nuclear accidents** at Three Mile Island in Pennsylvania (1979), **Chernobyl** in Ukraine (1986), and Fukushima in Japan (2011).

The most dangerous environmental issue of the present day is **climate change** in the form of **global warming**. This trend, built gradually over the course of the industrial era, is caused, in the opinion of a vast scholarly majority, by the human-produced emission of carbon-based **greenhouse gases**. The resulting rise in average temperatures became steadily more noticeable during the 1900s and then spiked upward in the 1980s and 1990s. Its effects, especially the catastrophic melting of Arctic, Antarctic, and glacial ice, are unmistakably apparent. The combination of a thinner ozone layer, which allows more of the sun's heat to enter the atmosphere, and greater quantities of greenhouse gases, which keep that heat trapped in the atmosphere, makes the problem doubly acute.

On the whole, international efforts to combat climate change have met with limited success. Prime examples include the Kyoto Summit (1997), where over 150 nations gathered to discuss the dangers of global warming, and a similar gathering in Paris in 2015. Although a **Kyoto Protocol** was hammered out in the 1990s, many countries, including the United States, did not ratify it. The 2015 **Paris Agreement** was more widely embraced, but its terms are voluntary and nonbinding. A particular point of conflict when it comes to international cooperation on climate change is the question of whether industrializing countries in the less developed world should be compelled to abide by the same clean-air regulations as the richer nations of the developed world. In addition, a wave of **climate-change denial** has arisen during the 2000s, sponsored by corporate and political interests with the goal of convincing the public to disregard the scientific consensus that climate change is indeed an urgent matter for concern. America's 2017 decision to opt out of the Paris Agreement has also weakened efforts to combat climate change.

NOTE

The world's most damaging nonmilitary nuclear event, the Chernobyl disaster of 1986 exposed the systemic weaknesses of the crumbling Soviet Union. It killed 8,000 in the short term, and thousands more—the number is in dispute—fell ill or died afterward. Fallout spread far beyond the USSR's borders, poisoning fish and reindeer as far away as Scandinavia, and a large exclusion zone in Ukraine and Belarus is still off-limits.

NOTE

Recent natural disasters such as Hurricane Katrina, the Southeast Asian tsunami, and Superstorm Sandy clearly demonstrate how contemporary societies can still be affected by the environment, regardless of their mastery of technology. They are also thought by many scientists to indicate the erratic effects that global warming appears to be having on planetary weather patterns.

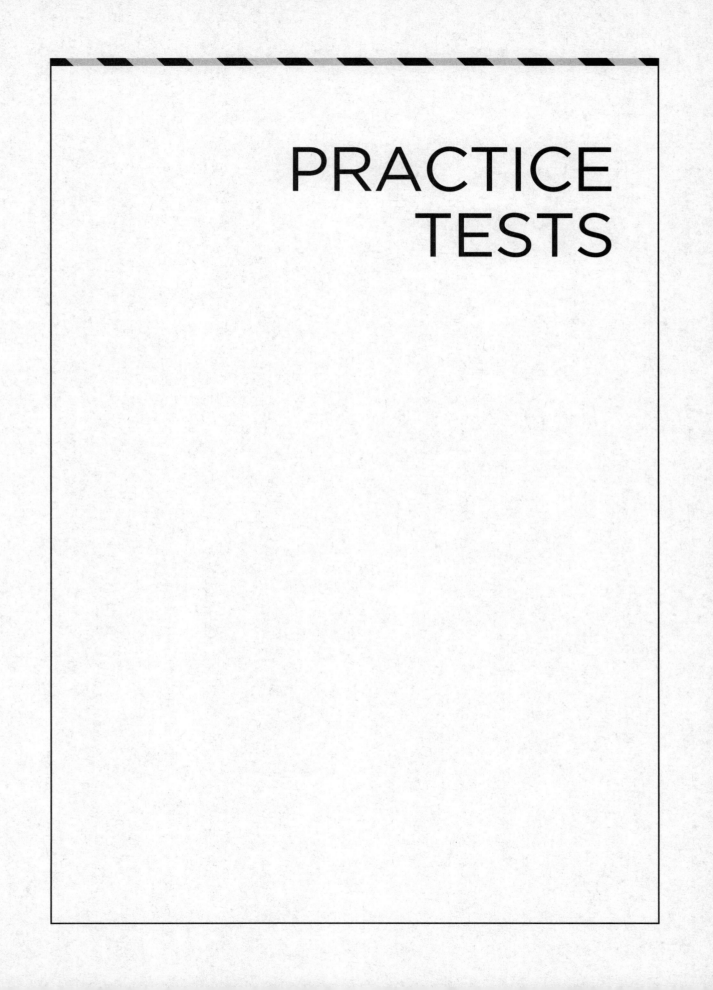

PRACTICE TESTS

ANSWER SHEET
Practice Test 1

SECTION I

Part A

1. Ⓐ Ⓑ Ⓒ Ⓓ   21. Ⓐ Ⓑ Ⓒ Ⓓ   41. Ⓐ Ⓑ Ⓒ Ⓓ
2. Ⓐ Ⓑ Ⓒ Ⓓ   22. Ⓐ Ⓑ Ⓒ Ⓓ   42. Ⓐ Ⓑ Ⓒ Ⓓ
3. Ⓐ Ⓑ Ⓒ Ⓓ   23. Ⓐ Ⓑ Ⓒ Ⓓ   43. Ⓐ Ⓑ Ⓒ Ⓓ
4. Ⓐ Ⓑ Ⓒ Ⓓ   24. Ⓐ Ⓑ Ⓒ Ⓓ   44. Ⓐ Ⓑ Ⓒ Ⓓ
5. Ⓐ Ⓑ Ⓒ Ⓓ   25. Ⓐ Ⓑ Ⓒ Ⓓ   45. Ⓐ Ⓑ Ⓒ Ⓓ
6. Ⓐ Ⓑ Ⓒ Ⓓ   26. Ⓐ Ⓑ Ⓒ Ⓓ   46. Ⓐ Ⓑ Ⓒ Ⓓ
7. Ⓐ Ⓑ Ⓒ Ⓓ   27. Ⓐ Ⓑ Ⓒ Ⓓ   47. Ⓐ Ⓑ Ⓒ Ⓓ
8. Ⓐ Ⓑ Ⓒ Ⓓ   28. Ⓐ Ⓑ Ⓒ Ⓓ   48. Ⓐ Ⓑ Ⓒ Ⓓ
9. Ⓐ Ⓑ Ⓒ Ⓓ   29. Ⓐ Ⓑ Ⓒ Ⓓ   49. Ⓐ Ⓑ Ⓒ Ⓓ
10. Ⓐ Ⓑ Ⓒ Ⓓ   30. Ⓐ Ⓑ Ⓒ Ⓓ   50. Ⓐ Ⓑ Ⓒ Ⓓ
11. Ⓐ Ⓑ Ⓒ Ⓓ   31. Ⓐ Ⓑ Ⓒ Ⓓ   51. Ⓐ Ⓑ Ⓒ Ⓓ
12. Ⓐ Ⓑ Ⓒ Ⓓ   32. Ⓐ Ⓑ Ⓒ Ⓓ   52. Ⓐ Ⓑ Ⓒ Ⓓ
13. Ⓐ Ⓑ Ⓒ Ⓓ   33. Ⓐ Ⓑ Ⓒ Ⓓ   53. Ⓐ Ⓑ Ⓒ Ⓓ
14. Ⓐ Ⓑ Ⓒ Ⓓ   34. Ⓐ Ⓑ Ⓒ Ⓓ   54. Ⓐ Ⓑ Ⓒ Ⓓ
15. Ⓐ Ⓑ Ⓒ Ⓓ   35. Ⓐ Ⓑ Ⓒ Ⓓ   55. Ⓐ Ⓑ Ⓒ Ⓓ
16. Ⓐ Ⓑ Ⓒ Ⓓ   36. Ⓐ Ⓑ Ⓒ Ⓓ
17. Ⓐ Ⓑ Ⓒ Ⓓ   37. Ⓐ Ⓑ Ⓒ Ⓓ
18. Ⓐ Ⓑ Ⓒ Ⓓ   38. Ⓐ Ⓑ Ⓒ Ⓓ
19. Ⓐ Ⓑ Ⓒ Ⓓ   39. Ⓐ Ⓑ Ⓒ Ⓓ
20. Ⓐ Ⓑ Ⓒ Ⓓ   40. Ⓐ Ⓑ Ⓒ Ⓓ

For Section I, Part B and Section II
Formulate your responses to the short-response, data-based, and long essay questions on separate sheets of paper.

SECTION I

Part A: Multiple-Choice Questions

Time: 55 Minutes for 55 Questions
Percent of exam score—40

> **DIRECTIONS:** Each of the questions below is followed by four suggested answers. Select the one that is best in each case and then fill in the corresponding circle on the answer sheet.

Questions 1 to 3 refer to the passages below.

Whoever, not being a member of a Scheduled Caste or a Scheduled Tribe,

(i) forces a member of a Scheduled Caste or a Scheduled Tribe to drink or eat any inedible or obnoxious substance;

(ii) acts with intent to cause injury, insult or annoyance to any member of a Scheduled Caste, or a Scheduled Tribe by dumping excreta, waste matter, carcasses or any other obnoxious substance in his premises or neighbourhood;

(iii) forcibly removes clothes from the person of a member of a Scheduled Caste or a Scheduled Tribe or parades him naked or with painted face or body or commits any similar act which is derogatory to human dignity . . .

(ix) gives any false or frivolous information to any public servant and thereby causes such public servant to use his lawful power to the injury or annoyance of a member of a Scheduled Caste or a Scheduled Tribe;

(x) intentionally insults or intimidates with intent to humiliate a member of a Scheduled Caste or a Scheduled Tribe in any place within public view . . .

. . . shall be punishable with imprisonment for a term which shall not be less than six months but which may extend to five years and with fine.

> from "The Scheduled Castes and the Scheduled Tribes
> (Prevention of Atrocities) Act of 1989 (India)"

The higher-caste men greeted Mr. Sardar with a punch to the face. Then they broke his arm. Then they pinned him down. Mr. Sardar shrieked for help. Nobody came.

One higher-caste man stuffed a rag in his mouth. Another gleefully pulled out a razor. He grabbed Mr. Sardar's scalp and began to lift and cut, lift and cut, carving off nearly every inch of skin.

"Take that!" Mr. Sardar remembers them saying. "Tell everyone we scalped you!"

Mr. Sardar is a Dalit, a class of Indians who are not just considered lower caste but technically outcaste—what used to be called untouchable. Bound at the bottom of India's Hindu society for centuries, the Dalit population, now estimated at more than 300 million, has been abused for as long as anyone can remember.

And now, according to crime statistics, the violence against them is rising.

> from "How Caste Still Rules in India,"
> *New York Times* (November 17, 2018)

1. The disparity between the above text is best explained by which of the following?

    (A) The unwillingness of large segments of the Indian population to embrace modernity

    (B) The weakness of the rule of law in India after independence from Great Britain

    (C) The limited effectiveness of official legislation when it comes to eliminating prejudicial attitudes

    (D) The persistence of racial hierarchies imposed on India during the British colonial period

2. What trend in contemporary India would be most likely to encourage the sort of episode described in the second passage?

    (A) Sikh separatism in the northern provinces

    (B) The resurgence of Hindu nationalism in recent years

    (C) Heightened tensions between India and Pakistan over frontier regions such as Kashmir

    (D) Socioeconomic inequality caused by the rapid rise of high-tech industry in certain parts of India.

3. The policy outlined in the first passage most closely resembles which of the following in terms of intent and context?

    (A) The U.S. Civil Rights Acts of the 1960s

    (B) The widespread expansion of women's suffrage during and after World War I.

    (C) Repeal of the White Australia Policy during the 1970s

    (D) The dismantling of residential schools for First Nations children in postwar Canada

Questions 4 to 6 refer to the chart below.

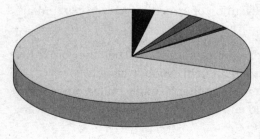

2016 HIV-positive population by region (in millions)

- North America (1.3 m)
- Latin America & the Caribbean (2 m)
- Western Europe (.75 m)
- Eastern Europe & Central Asia (1.5 m)
- Middle East & North America (.23 m)
- Asia & Oceania (5.2 m)
- Sub-Saharan Africa (25.5 m)

4. Which of the following conclusions does the chart above most safely support?

    (A) Sub-Saharan Africa has a larger population than Asia and Oceania combined.

    (B) Developed regions with sophisticated public health systems seem best able to combat the spread of diseases such as HIV/AIDS.

    (C) Rates of sexual promiscuity are higher in Asia and Africa than in most parts of Europe.

    (D) Western Europe has a smaller population than North America.

5. Which of the following most distinguishes HIV/AIDS from other pandemics of the 1900s and 2000s, such as Ebola, the Zika virus, and the Spanish flu?

(A) Spread principally via transmission of blood and sexual fluids, HIV/AIDS is more easily countered by educational efforts.

(B) HIV/AIDS has proved to be far less deadly than most other pandemic outbreaks.

(C) Efforts to prevent and treat HIV/AIDS have consistently enjoyed more enthusiastic support and higher levels of funding.

(D) HIV/AIDS strikes impoverished populations more readily and thoroughly than most other pandemic diseases.

6. What additional information would do most to increase this chart's usefulness in measuring the impact of HIV/AIDS on a given region?

(A) The number of medical-care professionals in each region

(B) Sex-education policies and budgets for each region

(C) The amount of money each region spends annually on HIV/AIDS prevention

(D) Each region's total population

Questions 7 to 10 refer to the map below.

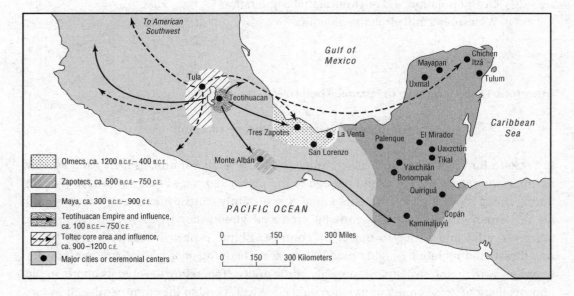

7. Which of the following conclusions about pre-Columbian Mesoamerica is best supported by the information contained in this map?

(A) The region was governed by a centralized state.

(B) Cultures there did not trade extensively.

(C) Much of Mesoamerica was heavily urbanized.

(D) Mesoamerican societies remained isolated from each other.

8. Which of the following was the clearest sign of mutual cultural influence among the societies depicted on the map?

    (A) The prevalence of human sacrifice and pyramid building
    (B) Development of a common calendar and system of writing
    (C) A single language shared throughout the region
    (D) Universal adoption of the concept of zero

9. What goods were most likely to have been traded among the cities shown on the map?

    (A) Corn and beans
    (B) Rice and sugar
    (C) Millet and coffee
    (D) Sorghum and wheat

10. Which of the following is <u>not</u> among the factors thought by most historians to have played a role in disrupting relations among the Mayan cities included on the map?

    (A) The arrival of European colonizers
    (B) Warfare among major urban centers
    (C) Overpopulation and environmental degradation
    (D) Widespread and virulent epidemics

Questions 11 to 13 refer to the passage below.

Gunpowder Weaponry: Europe vs. China

In Western Europe during the 1200s through the 1400s, early cannon, as heavy and as slow to fire as they were, proved useful enough in the protracted sieges that dominated warfare during this period that governments found it sufficiently worthwhile to pay for them and for the experimentation that eventually produced gunpowder weapons that were both more powerful and easier to move. By contrast, China, especially after the mid-1300s, was threatened mainly by highly mobile steppe nomads, against whom early gunpowder weapons, with their unwieldiness, proved of little utility. It therefore devoted its efforts to the improvement of horse archer units who could effectively combat the country's deadliest foe.

11. The argument in this passage most closely relates to which of the following large-scale questions about global history?

    (A) How societies shared strategically important technologies with each other
    (B) Why European states went on to attain military superiority over non-Western powers in the modern era
    (C) Why Silk Road commerce dwindled across the breadth of Eurasia after 1500 C.E.
    (D) How the medieval climatic optimum affected the process of cultural diffusion

12. According to this passage, why did the Chinese, despite inventing gunpowder, fail to lead in the innovation of gunpowder weaponry?

    (A) They were discouraged by Confucian traditionalism from doing so.
    (B) They put too much faith in the numerical strength of their existing armed forces.
    (C) They logically decided to develop weapons better suited to their immediate military needs.
    (D) They could not afford the initial expense of converting to a new military technology.

13. What traditional view of world history does this passage seem to challenge?

    (A) That China has always been less technologically adept than most Afro-Eurasian societies
    (B) That China's rigid form of dictatorial rule suppressed any spirit of military or technological innovation
    (C) That China was hindered by religious fundamentalism when it came to modernizing efforts
    (D) That China was surpassed by Europe in global power because it turned a blind eye to the obvious benefits of technological change

Questions 14 to 16 refer to the verses below.

O ye who believe! Strong drink and games of chance and idols . . . are only an infamy of Satan's handiwork. Leave it aside in order that ye may succeed.

the Qur'an, Sura 5:89

When once you hear the roses are in bloom,
Then is the time, my love, to pour the wine.

the *Rubáiyát* of Omar Khayyám

14. Both verses relate most closely to

    (A) key economic processes within Islamic society.
    (B) production of food and drink in Islamic society.
    (C) religious regulation of personal behavior in Islamic society.
    (D) changing gender relations in Islamic society.

15. The tone of the <u>first</u> verse best reflects which of the following modes of religious discourse?

    (A) A puritanical injunction to adhere to a strict code of conduct
    (B) An ecumenical call for religious tolerance
    (C) A sermon about respecting political authority
    (D) A spirited attempt to convert nonbelievers

16. A comparison of both verses would best support which of the following conclusions?

(A) Many Muslims inclined toward atheism in the premodern era.

(B) Religious restrictions were not universally observed by all Muslims.

(C) Christian missionaries were steadily winning converts among Muslim populations.

(D) Muslim intellectuals were generally hostile to traditional religious practice.

Questions 17 to 19 refer to the chart below.

Troop Strength of the Army of the British East India Company, 1793–1815

	1793	1798	1805	1815
European troops	18,768	22,116	24,891	31,611
Native troops	69,661	91,147	167,674	195,572
TOTAL	88,429	113,313	192,565	227,183

17. The information presented in the chart above is best interpreted in light of which of the following contexts?

(A) Colonial efforts to transfer technological skills to native populations

(B) Colonial attempts to mobilize military strength overseas

(C) Colonial desires to inculcate Western values among native troops

(D) Colonial intentions to segregate white colonizers from native inhabitants

18. Which of the following most likely motivated the policy whose operation the above chart depicts?

(A) The provision of training for British troops in a colonial setting

(B) The instillation of patriotic pride among Indians by allowing them to serve as soldiers

(C) The minimizing of the cost of maintaining imperial authority abroad

(D) The separation of white soldiers from native troops

19. The policy depicted in the chart above left British colonial authority particularly vulnerable during which of the following events?

(A) The Salt March of 1930

(B) The Second and Third Maratha Wars of 1803–1818

(C) The Amritsar Massacre of 1919

(D) The Indian Revolt of 1857

Questions 20 to 22 refer to the image below.

20. The image above is best understood as an example of which of the following trends?

    (A) Religious fundamentalism
    (B) Transnational migration
    (C) Nonviolent decolonization
    (D) Economic globalization

21. Which of the following can be seen as the most reasonable explanation for the development shown in the image above?

    (A) U.S. military domination over the Middle East
    (B) Foreign takeover of U.S. corporations
    (C) Cultural autonomy in the non-Western world
    (D) The global influence of U.S. mass culture

22. An intellectual or artist local to the region in question would most likely make which of the following complaints about the presence of the company depicted in the photograph?

    (A) The presence of the company disrupts agriculture by encouraging too much migration from farms to cities.
    (B) The presence of the company threatens to overshadow brands and cultural symbols indigenous to the region.
    (C) The presence of the company puts local people out of work.
    (D) The presence of the company violates key precepts of the region's majority religion.

Leonard Parkinson, Maroon resistance fighter, Jamaica, ca. 1796

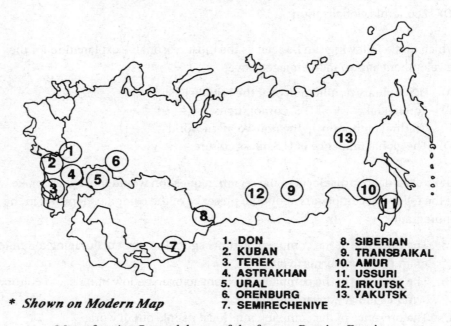

1. DON	8. SIBERIAN
2. KUBAN	9. TRANSBAIKAL
3. TEREK	10. AMUR
4. ASTRAKHAN	11. USSURI
5. URAL	12. IRKUTSK
6. ORENBURG	13. YAKUTSK
7. SEMIRECHENIYE	

* Shown on Modern Map

Map of major Cossack hosts of the former Russian Empire

23. When taken together, both images above are best understood in which of the following contexts?

   (A) Societies consisting of refugees from slave status
   (B) Societies practicing a schismatic religion
   (C) Societies governed by warrior elites
   (D) Societies existing on the periphery of large states

24. Which historical development contributed most to the formation of the society associated with the first image?

   (A) The Atlantic slave trade
   (B) The flow of refugees caused by the Seven Years' War
   (C) The segregation of races imposed by British colonial authorities
   (D) The migratory patterns encouraged by the arrival of smallpox from Europe

25. Which of the following statements is most solidly supported by the information contained in the map shown in the second image?

   (A) Cossack communities devoutly adhered to a conservative strain of Russian Orthodox Christianity.
   (B) Cossack hosts frequently rebelled against the centralizing authority of the Russian Empire.
   (C) Cossack military units consisted of highly skilled horseback warriors.
   (D) Cossack ethnic identity was shaped by intermarriage with non-Russian peoples on the empire's frontiers.

26. The ultimate fate of the societies depicted in both images was

   (A) to win their full independence.
   (B) to be hunted down and eradicated.
   (C) to be absorbed by the states neighboring them.
   (D) to migrate to distant territories elsewhere.

Questions 27 to 30 refer to the passages below.

In fact, the peculiar aggravation of the Cawnpore massacres was this, that the deed was done by a subject race—by black men who dared to shed the blood of their masters, and that of poor helpless ladies and children. Here we had not only a servile war, but we had a war of religion, a war of race, and a war of revenge, of hope, of national promptings to shake off the yoke of a stranger, and to re-establish the full power of native chiefs, and the full sway of native religions. Whatever the causes of the mutiny and the revolt, it is clear enough that one of the modes by which the leaders, as if by common instinct, determined to effect their end was, the destruction of every white man, woman or child who fell into their hands.

British journalist William Howard Russell, *My Indian Mutlny Diary*, 1860

Violence, it must be emphasized, was an essential component of the British presence in India. A dominant power is always uneasy with violence directed against it. The right to violence is, therefore, everywhere a privilege that authority enjoys and refuses to share with those under it: power always insists on violence as its exclusive monopoly. British rule in India, as an autocracy, had meticulously constructed a monopoly of violence. The revolt of 1857 shattered that monopoly by matching an official, alien violence by an indigenous violence of the colonized. The bodies of the British had acquired certain dignities in India that were predestined by birth and by the colour of their skin. This was the condition of their domination, of their superiority: rulers and ruled were arranged hierarchically as superior and inferior races, as civilized and uncivilized. And this superiority manifested itself by denying to the Indians a "humanness"; by treating them and conceiving of them as animals.

Rudrangshu Mukherjee, "The Kanpur [Cawnpore]
Massacres in India in the Revolt of 1857," 1990

27. The passages above can best be connected with which of the following forms of violence?

(A) Banditry due to socioeconomic breakdown
(B) Killing of civilians during wartime
(C) Collateral damage caused by weapons of mass destruction
(D) State-sponsored campaigns of genocide

28. From the perspective of the first passage, the death of British citizens at Cawnpore

(A) seems to mark a betrayal of a "higher" race by a "lesser" race.
(B) should be seen as a regrettable but avoidable mistake.
(C) can be said to have been brought on by the British themselves.
(D) was seen by those who killed them as a religious duty.

29. According to the second passage, the Cawnpore Massacre

(A) was justifiable according to local military custom, even if it violated Western military norms.
(B) can be viewed as a reaction to the systemic brute force with which the British governed India.
(C) should be praised as a brave patriotic blow against British colonial oppression.
(D) seems to have been the product of a well-organized and long-premeditated conspiracy.

30. In the short term, the events discussed in both passages led to which of the following outcomes?

(A) The expulsion of the British East India Company and partial home rule for India

(B) British victory over Indian rebels and the strengthening of the British East India Company

(C) Indian military success and the attainment of full independence from British authority

(D) The defeat of Indian rebels and the imposition of direct rule by the British government

Questions 31 to 34 refer to the chart below.

WORLD GDP, 1600–1870 (in millions of dollars, calculated to 1990 value)

	1600	Share of World Total	1700	Share of World Total	1870	Share of World Total
Great Britain	6,007	1.8%	10,709	2.88%	100,179	9.1%
Western Europe (excluding Britain)	65,955	20%	83,395	22.5%	370,223	33.61%
China	96,000	29%	82,800	22.3%	189,740	17.23%
India	74,250	23%	90,750	24.4%	134,882	12.25%
WORLD TOTAL	329,417		371,369		1,101,369	

Source: Angus Maddison, *Contours of the World Economy*, 2007

31. Which of the following best describes economic trends in China during the time span covered in the chart above?

(A) China's economy steadily shrank in absolute terms and as a percentage of world GDP.

(B) China's economy gained ground relative to Western Europe's in absolute terms but not proportionally to world GDP.

(C) China's economy grew in absolute terms but shrank as a percentage of world GDP.

(D) China's economy lost ground to India's in absolute terms and proportionally to world GDP.

32. Which of the following had an important direct effect on the economic developments depicted in the chart above?

(A) The abolition of the Atlantic slave trade in the 1800s

(B) The rise of Chinese naval power in the 1700s

(C) The industrialization of European economies in the 1700s and 1800s

(D) The revival of Silk Road trade in the 1600s and 1700s

33. Which of the following factors would have had the most significant impact on economic developments in India during the time span covered in the chart above?

(A) The global silver glut caused by Spanish mining in the Americas
(B) The growing demand in South Asia for Chinese tea and silk
(C) The expanding commercial influence of the British East India Company
(D) The adoption of the gold standard by European and North American states

34. British economic interactions with India during the time span covered in the chart above would have been chiefly concerned with which of the following commodities?

(A) Cotton
(B) Spices
(C) Ivory
(D) Opium

Questions 35 to 38 refer to the passages below.

An Act to place certain restrictions on Immigration and to provide for the removal from the Commonwealth of Prohibited Immigrants.

...

3. The immigration into the Commonwealth of the persons described in any of the following paragraphs in this section (hereinafter called "prohibited immigrants") is prohibited, namely

(a) Any person who when asked to do so by an officer fails to write out at dictation and sign in the presence of the officer a passage of fifty words in length in a European language directed by the officer;

(b) Any person in the opinion of the Minister or of an officer to become a charge upon the public or upon any public or charitable organisation;

...

(g) Any persons under a contract or agreement to perform manual labour within the Commonwealth: Provided that this paragraph shall not apply to workmen exempted by the Minister for special skill required by Australia . . .

Immigration Restriction Act of 1901 (Australia)

Whereas in the opinion of the Government of the United States the coming of Chinese laborers to this country endangers the good order of certain localities within the territory thereof;

Therefore,

Be it enacted by the Senate and House of Representatives of the United States of America in Congress assembled, That from and after the expiration of ninety days next after the passage of this act, the coming of Chinese laborers to the United States be suspended; and during such suspension it shall not be lawful for any Chinese laborer to come, or having so come after the expiration of said ninety days to remain within the United States.

SEC. 2. That the master of every vessel who shall knowingly bring within the United States on such vessel, and land or permit to be landed, any Chinese laborer, from any foreign port or place, shall be deemed guilty of a misdemeanor, and on conviction thereof shall be punished by a fine of not more than five hundred dollars for each and every such Chinese laborer so brought, and may be also imprisoned for a term not exceeding one year. . . .

Chinese Exclusion Act of 1882 (United States)

35. The first passage can be regarded as the cornerstone of which of the following official initiatives?

(A) The White Australia Policy
(B) The Commonwealth Literacy Crusade
(C) The Australian Economic Diversification Program
(D) The Australian Migrant Exclusion Campaign

36. The emphasis on language in the first passage is most safely interpreted as

(A) a concern for high educational standards in a rapidly growing society.
(B) a tactic allowing the exclusion of non-Europeans without referring directly to race.
(C) a measure to ensure that all immigrants possessed useful expertise.
(D) an attempt to bar all immigrants regardless of origin.

37. Which of the following economic activities did the most to drive the rising levels of immigration that led to the enactment of the law described in the second passage?

(A) Railroad construction
(B) Fertilizer harvesting
(C) Sugarcane production
(D) Gold mining

38. What broad trend from the 1800s formed the background for the enactment of the laws described in both passages?

(A) The growing appeal of Christianity among Indian and Chinese populations
(B) European and American colonial domination of India and China
(C) The Pacific-wide migration of Indian and Chinese indentured laborers
(D) Gradual industrialization of the Indian and Chinese economies

Questions 39 to 41 refer to the passage below.

No task is more urgent than that of preserving peace. Without peace our independence means little. The rehabilitation and upbuilding of our countries will have little meaning. Our revolutions will not be allowed to run their course. What can we do? We can do much! We can inject the voice of reason into world affairs. We can mobilize all the spiritual, all the moral, all the political strength of Asia and Africa on the side of peace. Yes, we! We, the peoples of Asia and Africa, 1.4 billion strong.

>   Indonesian leader Sukarno, keynote address to the Bandung Conference, 1955

39. The passage above is most associated with which of the following developments?

    (A) The formation of the nonaligned movement
    (B) Global disarmament and nuclear nonproliferation
    (C) The Green Revolution in agriculture
    (D) Mobilization of pan-Asian ideology

40. The "revolutions" spoken of by Sukarno in the passage above most likely relate to which of the following causes?

    (A) Gender equality
    (B) Communism
    (C) Decolonization
    (D) Environmental conservation

41. Like numerous other leaders in Africa, Asia, and the Middle East, Sukarno attempted to maintain but did not completely succeed in maintaining a neutral stance during

    (A) the Arab-Israeli conflict.
    (B) the Korean War.
    (C) the Cold War.
    (D) the Vietnam conflicts.

PRACTICE TEST 1

Questions 42 to 44 refer to the passage below.

Now if divorce is your wish, I cannot blame you. For the waiting has been long. And I do not know whether the Creator will grant relief immediately so that I can come home, or whether matters will take time, for I cannot come home with nothing. Now the matter is in your hand. If you wish to end our marriage, accept this bill of repudiation, and you are free. May God inspire you with the right decision.

                                        Letter from a Jewish trader in India to his wife in Cairo, ca. 1200

42. The passage above is best seen in light of which of the following historical developments?

   (A) The formation of far-flung diaspora communities as a result of interregional commerce
   (B) The continued use of organized religion to justify patriarchy
   (C) The permanent division of families due to armed conflict along established trade routes
   (D) The evolution of family structure among polytheistic populations

43. Which of the following is the most probable cause of the marital strain evident in the passage above?

   (A) The strain placed on merchant families by long periods of separation
   (B) Religious disagreements arising from the merchant's exposure to Hinduism
   (C) A decision on the part of the merchant to remain permanently in India
   (D) Bankruptcy stranding the merchant far from home

44. Based on the document's historical context, which of the following inferences seems most probable?

   (A) The marital code in question appears to have operated to a high degree on assumptions of gender equality.
   (B) If the trader in question was wealthy enough to support more than one wife, he may have been legally married to a woman in India as well.
   (C) The wife would likely have found it difficult or impossible to end this marriage had her husband been opposed to a divorce.
   (D) Dissolutions of marriage for reasons similar to this were common among merchants who traded along the Mediterranean coast and the Indian Ocean basin.

African hunters harvesting elephant ivory, Belgian Congo, ca. 1880s

45. The image above most likely depicts which of the following?

(A) African hunters pursuing their traditional livelihood
(B) African hunters exploiting resources under orders from colonial masters
(C) African hunters engaged in trade with Westerners on equal terms
(D) African hunters taking charge of ivory harvesting to keep whites from depleting supplies

46. Which of the following resources would have been pursued even more intensely in the colony depicted in the above image?

(A) Gold
(B) Cinnamon
(C) Rubber
(D) Diamonds

47. In which of the following ways can the above image most reasonably be faulted for providing an incomplete view of how the colony in question was administered?

(A) It fails to show the notorious mutilations inflicted by Belgian overseers on workers who fell short of quotas.
(B) It omits the lived experience of village women under Belgian colonial rule.
(C) It gives little indication of the complex social stratification that prevailed during the Belgian colonial era.
(D) It shows nothing of the way Belgian authorities deliberately encouraged racial tensions between neighboring tribal groups.

New York! I say New York, let black blood flow into your blood.
Let it wash the rust from your steel joints, like an oil of life
Let it give your bridges the curve of hips and supple vines …
See your rivers stirring with musk alligators
And sea cows with mirage eyes …
Just open your eyes to the April rainbow
And your eyes, especially your ears, to God
Who in one burst of saxophone laughter
Created heaven and earth in six days,
And on the seventh slept a deep Negro sleep.

Senegalese poet Léopold Sédar Senghor, "To New York," 1956

48. The verse above is best seen as belonging to which of the following modern cultural developments?

(A) The triumph of avant-garde literary styles over traditional realism
(B) The adaptation of Western literary forms by non-Western authors
(C) The political use of art and literature for propagandistic purposes
(D) The response of interwar literary figures to the horrors of World War I

49. Which of the following is likeliest to have inspired the imagery in the verse above?

(A) Nostalgia for the romantic imagery of the previous century
(B) The rise of mass media
(C) Homesickness for Africa
(D) The Jazz Age

50. Which of the following best explains the phenomenon of an African poet writing so lyrically about New York?

(A) Outmigration from Africa due to political violence
(B) Stronger transatlantic influences linking art in Afro-Eurasia with that in the Americas
(C) Preference on the part of African intellectuals for Western cultural advancements
(D) Lack of a rich indigenous artistic tradition in Africa

51. This verse is best categorized as belonging to which of the following cultural/intellectual trends?

(A) Antiwar Dadaism
(B) The impact of abstraction on literature
(C) Socialist realism
(D) The negritude movement

Questions 52 to 55 refer to the chart below.

LITERACY RATES AMONG THE RUSSIAN-SPEAKING POPULATION OF LATE IMPERIAL RUSSIA AND THE SOVIET UNION, 1897–1955

	Literacy Rate
1897	24%
1917	45%
1926	56%
1937	75%
1939	81.1%
1955	99.9%

Source: Census data and Soviet Ministry of Education

52. The information presented in the above chart is best understood in which of the following historical contexts?

(A) Educational reform in the modern era
(B) Centralized and state-directed campaigns of modernization
(C) Experimentation with syndicalist forms of socioeconomic organization
(D) Second-stage industrialization in the non-Western world

53. Which of the following segments of the Russian/Soviet population would probably have benefited most from the rising literacy rates depicted in the chart above?

(A) The rural peasantry
(B) Members of the Russian Orthodox clergy
(C) The urban middle class
(D) Officers in the armed forces

54. Dictatorial societies such as the Soviet Union typically prioritized the use of educational systems for what additional purpose besides the transmission of skills and knowledge?

(A) Creating a pool of skilled military personnel
(B) Encouraging critical thinking skills among the general public
(C) Fostering loyalty to the regime by means of political indoctrination
(D) Enabling upward mobility for economically backward citizens

55. A historian sympathetic to Soviet communism would most likely use the above chart as evidence to support which of the following propositions?

(A) The ideals of the Russian Revolution were betrayed by the Leninist and Stalinist regimes.
(B) Lenin and Stalin vastly improved Russian military preparedness.
(C) Communism has been made to work more efficiently in Russia than in China.
(D) Despite abuses on the part of Lenin and Stalin, the Soviet regime managed significant achievements.

SECTION I

Part B: Short-Answer Questions

Time: 40 Minutes for 3 Questions
Percent of exam score—20

> **DIRECTIONS:** Complete THREE of the following four questions. You must answer questions 1 AND 2. After that, choose question 3 OR question 4.

1. Use the passage below to answer all parts of the question that follows.

For all the apparent gulf between the market-dominated economies of the West and the centrally planned economies of the communist world, when it comes to attitudes to the natural world their outlook turns out to be remarkably similar.

Clive Ponting, *The Green History of the World*, 1991

    A.   Identify and explain ONE historically specific example of human interaction with the environment during the twentieth century that would support the author's argument.

    B.   Identify and explain ONE historically specific example of human interaction with the environment during the twentieth century that would challenge the author's argument.

    C.   Identify and explain ONE twentieth-century development that likely explains historians' interest in the subject of the passage.

2. Use the image below to answer all parts of the question that follows.

Propaganda poster from Nazi Germany proclaiming "Death to Lies"
and depicting a stalwart Nazi crushing a serpent bearing the labels
"Marxism" and "High Finance."

A. Describe ONE change in twentieth-century European economic life that gave rise to the political extremism that produced the image accompanying this question.

B. Identify ONE way that the image accompanying this question reflects a continuity in European economic life during the twentieth century.

C. Explain ONE way in which German economic life changed as a result of the rise of Nazism there.

3. Answer all parts of the question that follows.

A. Identify ONE similarity in the way bubonic plague affected Eurasia in the 1300s C.E. and the way smallpox affected the Americas in the 1400s and 1500s C.E.

B. Identify ONE difference in the way bubonic plague affected Eurasia in the 1300s C.E. and the way smallpox affected the Americas in the 1400s and 1500s C.E.

C. Explain ONE reason for the difference between the impact of bubonic plague on Eurasia and the impact of smallpox on the Americas.

4. Answer all parts of the question that follows.

A. Describe ONE change in agricultural production in Asia during the period between 1900 and the present.

B. Describe ANOTHER change in agricultural production in Asia during the period between 1900 and the present.

C. Describe ONE continuity in agricultural production in Asia during the period between 1900 and the present.

SECTION II: FREE-RESPONSE QUESTIONS

Part A: Document-Based Question

(Suggested planning and writing time—45 minutes, plus 15-minute reading period)
Percent of exam score—25

> **DIRECTIONS:** The following question is based on the accompanying documents. The documents have been edited for the purpose of this exercise.

1. Using the documents and your knowledge of world history, compare and contrast European and non-European encounters with unfamiliar religious traditions between roughly 1300 and 1600 C.E.

DOCUMENT 1

Source: Thomas Coryate, English traveler in Turkey, on witnessing Sufi dervishes (1613).

There is a College of Turkish Monks in Galata, that are called [Dervishes], . . . who every Tuesday and Friday do perform the strangest exercise of Devotion that ever I saw or heard of. . . .

A little after I came into the room, the Dervishes repaired into the middle void space, sitting Cross-legged, bending their Bodies low toward the floor for Religion['s] sake, even almost flat upon their Faces . . . the whole company of them were about two and fifty. . . .

[A] certain Singing-man sitting apart in an upper room began to sing certain Hymns, but with the most unpleasant and harsh notes that ever I heard, exceedingly differing from our Christian Church singing, for the yelling and disorderly squeaking did even grate mine ears. . . . [T]hree Pipers sitting in the room with the Singer began to play upon certain long Pipes not unlike Tabors, which yielded a very ridiculous and foolish Music . . . whereupon some five and twenty of the two and fifty Dervishes suddenly rose up bare-legged and bare-footed, and casting aside their upper Garments, some of them having their breasts all uncovered, they began by little and little to turn about the Interpreter of the Law. Afterward they redoubled their force and turned with such incredible swiftness, that I could not choose but admire it.

DOCUMENT 2

Source: Council of the Aztec city of Huejotzingo, letter to the king of Spain (1560).

Catholic Royal Majesty!

When your servants the Spaniards reached us and your captain general Don Hernando Cortés arrived, not a single town surpassed us here in New Spain, in that first and earliest we threw ourselves toward you.

. . . we also say and declare before you that [when] your padres, the sons of St. Francis, entered the city of Huejotzingo, of our own free will we honored them and showed them esteem. When they [told us to] abandon the wicked belief in many gods, we did it. Very willingly we destroyed, demolished, and burned the temples. . . .

But now we are taken aback and very afraid, and we ask, have we done something wrong, have we somehow behaved badly, or have we committed some sin against almighty God?

DOCUMENT 3

Source: Jean Bodin, French philosopher (1530–1596), on Ottoman religious policy.

The King of the Turks, who rules over a great part of Europe, safeguards the rites of religion as well as any prince in this world. He constrains no one, but on the contrary permits everyone to live as his conscience dictates. What is more, even in his seraglio at Pera he permits the practice of four diverse religions, that of the Jews, the Christian according to the Roman rite, and according to the Greek rite, and that of Islam.

DOCUMENT 4

Source: Photograph of the Shrine of the Twenty-Six Martyrs, Nagasaki, Japan. Dedicated to twenty-six Japanese converts and Catholic priests crucified in 1597 at the orders of Japanese ruler Toyotomi Hideyoshi.

DOCUMENT 5

Source: Dante Alighieri, Florentine poet, *The Inferno*, Canto XXVIII, 28–36 (ca. 1307).

I stood and stared at him from the stone shelf;
   he noticed me and opening his own breast
   with both hands cried: "See how I rip myself!

See how Mahomet's mangled and split open!
   Ahead of me walks Ali in his tears
   his head cleft from the top-knot to the chin.

All the other souls that bleed and mourn
   along this ditch were sowers of scandal and schism:
   as they tore others apart, so are they torn."

DOCUMENT 6

Source: Baha ad-Din, Kurdish historian, *The Life of Saladin* (ca. 1190) [trans. Francesco Gabrieli, *Arab Historians of the Crusades* (1969)]

While I was standing thus, Saladin turned to me and said: "I think that when God grants me victory over the rest of Palestine, I shall divide my territories, make a will stating my wishes, then set sail on this sea for their far-off lands and pursue the Franks there, so as to free the earth of anyone who does not believe in God, or die in the attempt.

DOCUMENT 7

Source: Alvise da Cadamosto, Italian explorer sailing for Portugal, upon meeting the West African chieftain Budomel (1455)

I was permitted to enter the mosque there they pray: arriving toward evening, [Budomel] entered with some of his chief lords into a certain place. There they prayed in this fashion: standing upright and frequently looking up at the sky, they took two paces forward, and recited some words in a low voice: then bowed down very often and kissed the earth. When he had finished, he asked me what I thought of it. I told him that his faith was false, and that those who had instructed him in such things were ignorant of the truth. On many grounds I got the better of his learned men in argument, and [Budomel] laughed at this, saying that our faith appeared to him to be good . . . I am certain it would have been easy to have converted him to the Christian faith, if he had not feared to lose his power.

Part B: Long Essay Question

(Suggested planning and writing time—40 minutes)
Percent of exam score—15

DIRECTIONS: Choose ONE from questions 2, 3, and 4.

2. In the period 1200 to 1450, the rise of interregional trade led to the formation of diaspora communities in several parts of the world.

   Develop an argument that evaluates the ways in which the rise of interregional trade in the Indian Ocean basin contributed to the formation of diaspora communities in Africa and South Asia.

3. In the period 1750 to 1900, economic globalization widened the scope of migration in many parts of the world.

    Develop an argument that evaluates the ways in which economic globalization widened the scope of Chinese and Indian migration throughout the Pacific during this period.

4. In the period after 1900, warfare caused the mass displacement of civilian populations in many parts of Afro-Eurasia.

    Develop an argument that evaluates the ways in which warfare caused mass displacement of civilian populations in one or more parts of Afro-Eurasia during this period.

ANSWER KEY
Practice Test 1

SECTION I

Part A

1. **C**	21. **D**	41. **C**
2. **B**	22. **B**	42. **A**
3. **A**	23. **D**	43. **A**
4. **B**	24. **A**	44. **C**
5. **A**	25. **D**	45. **B**
6. **D**	26. **C**	46. **C**
7. **C**	27. **B**	47. **A**
8. **A**	28. **A**	48. **B**
9. **A**	29. **B**	49. **D**
10. **A**	30. **D**	50. **B**
11. **B**	31. **C**	51. **D**
12. **C**	32. **C**	52. **B**
13. **D**	33. **C**	53. **A**
14. **C**	34. **A**	54. **C**
15. **A**	35. **A**	55. **D**
16. **B**	36. **B**	
17. **B**	37. **A**	
18. **C**	38. **C**	
19. **D**	39. **A**	
20. **D**	40. **C**	

ANSWER EXPLANATIONS

Section I

PART A: MULTIPLE-CHOICE

1. **(C)** The passage of laws to protect minority rights does not automatically do away with the popular biases that cause minorities to be treated unequally in the first place, a sad reality described by the correct answer, which is C. India has become steadily more modern since independence, and as the world's largest democracy, it has an effective constitution as the basis of its legal system, making A and B incorrect. While some colonial powers indeed encouraged racial or class divisions in parts of Africa and Asia, the British authorities in India had in fact discouraged caste-based discrimination, making D wrong as well.

2. **(B)** All four answers describe real sources of stress in present-day India. However, only B is associated with the sort of extremism that would use traditional interpretations of religion to justify blatant defiance of laws meant to protect minority populations.

3. **(A)** Each answer describes ending or repairing the effects of an unfair policy. In the case of India's "selected" castes, the wrong has to do with depriving a wide range of rights from a subgroup that has long existed within a particular society. Anti-immigrant sentiment does not quite fit the analogy, making C less relevant, and while women suffered many forms of inequality, the right to vote is more narrowly focused, excluding B. The position of First Nations people in Canada (and Native Americans in the United States) bears a stronger resemblance to that of the "selected" populations that the Indian Constitution attempts to protect, but the specific issue of residential schools is not wide enough to match the many issues listed in the first passage. Answer A redressed many wrongs for a population that was long looked down upon. Also, considering that not all racial tensions have been eliminated in the contemporary United States, the same limitations apply when it comes to the power of an official law to eradicate popular prejudice.

4. **(B)** The chart says nothing about human behavior, and stereotypes about behavior based on region are risky at best, so C must be discarded. The only thing concretely measured by the chart is the number of people ill with HIV/AIDS in a given region, but it does not necessarily follow that a region with more HIV-positive patients is more populous than one with fewer patients—Asia, after all, is the world's most populous continent—making A and D bad bets. Answer B is best by process of elimination, and it is also a reasonable inference even if the chart does not speak to the fact directly.

5. **(A)** Although HIV/AIDS is no longer fatal as long as a patient has access to the proper medication (and can afford it), it killed almost all of its victims for many years. Even today, many of those who contract HIV/AIDS cannot obtain treatment and die. Answer B is therefore false. Especially in the 1980s and 1990s, especially when its most visible victims were gay, HIV/AIDS was heavily stigmatized by large portions of the public in many places, and even now, some assign higher priority to treating and preventing other diseases, making C false. While HIV/AIDS spreads more easily in poorer areas that lack robust public health systems, it also strikes affluent societies as well, casting doubt on D. The fact that HIV/AIDS is not airborne or easily waterborne or insect-borne keeps it from spreading as easily as other pandemic diseases, making A the correct answer.

6. **(D)** It is always a useful skill to be able to identify the limitations of a source or data set. Arguably, the percentage of people affected by HIV/AIDS would be the best measure of the disease's impact on a given region. (The number of fatalities would be useful as well, but not quite as much.) For that, the total population for each region—as in D—is needed. The information described by the other answers would be interesting but not as directly relevant.

7. **(C)** This question requires use of evidence. Be careful in these cases not to pick answers that may be true according to general knowledge but not proved or indicated by the map (or whatever stimulus material is provided). The map contains no evidence for A, and the directional arrows make B or D unlikely. The proliferation of cities in such a relatively small space makes C the best choice.

8. **(A)** This question requires outside information related to the stimulus material but not referred to directly by it. Knowledge of Mesoamerican societies, most of whose cultures were built on the legacy of the Olmecs, leads most readily to A. Answers B, C, and D are true of some Mesoamerican cultures at certain times but are not universal enough to satisfy the terms of the question.

9. **(A)** As with the prior question, this requires outside information related to the stimulus material but not referred to directly by it. The goods listed in B, C, and D are associated more strongly with other parts of the world and in some cases were not available prior to the Columbian Exchange.

10. **(A)** While the peoples themselves remained (especially the Maya), the cultures depicted on the map had gone into *political* decline before the arrival of Spanish conquistadors. The Mesoamerican civilization that confronted Europeans most directly—the Aztecs (or Mexica)—are not shown on the map, further indicating that A is not relevant to the disruption referred to in this question. The downfall of the Maya, Toltecs, and others remains a matter of debate, with B, C, and D among the chief theories proposed for it.

11. **(B)** Answer D can be readily dismissed as irrelevant to the text, and C, while somewhat related to the exchange of goods and ideas, is tangential. The technology transfer described in A is not unrelated to the question, but aside from the fact that China did not "share" gunpowder directly or on purpose with Europe, the text is clearly more concerned with the broader historical question addressed by B.

12. **(C)** This question is centered on historical argumentation and historical interpretation as well as causation. The passage's clear purpose is to show that Chinese lack of interest in early gunpowder weaponry was rational and not culturally or economically short-sighted, as Western historians have traditionally supposed.

13. **(D)** This question, related to the one preceding it, involves historical argumentation even more directly. Answer D relates directly to the earlier view described above.

14. **(C)** While both texts refer to drink, the production of it (as in B) is not relevant, and gender (as in D) is alluded to only in the second text. Personal behavior, as described in C, is of far more central importance than the economic issues referred to in A.

15. **(A)** By forbidding strong drink and gambling, this passage from the Qur'an is clearly trying to regulate how individuals conduct themselves.

16. **(B)** This question calls for contextualization, historical argumentation, and historical interpretation. The passage from the Qur'an presents a cultural norm that religious doctrine sought to enforce—in this case Islam's famous restriction on the consumption of alcohol—while the second indicates that the restriction was not always observed in real life.

17. **(B)** This question focuses on techniques used by colonizing states to maintain imperial presence abroad. Answers A, C, and D address concerns acted upon by colonial administrators, but they are unconnected to the military matters connected with the recruitment and training of sepoys, or native Indian troops, to supplement the British troops that could be sent over by the British East India Company.

18. **(C)** This question requires use of evidence and historical interpretation, and it also involves causation. If A were true, the number of British troops in India might be expected to rise over time, and there is no evidence in the chart to indicate that B or D was a priority (even though mixing between Europeans and natives was discouraged). Answer C touches on a money-saving strategy used widely by most colonial powers.

19. **(D)** This question requires knowledge related to the stimulus material but beyond what is presented in it. In this case, understanding of the aftermath is crucial. Answers A and C are *very* long-term consequences associated with the Indian independence movement of the 1900s and have nothing to do with sepoys. Sepoys helped the British to win the wars mentioned in B. It was during the revolt described in D that the sepoys' expertise in Western ways of war (and their large numbers) threatened to topple British colonial authority.

20. **(D)** This McDonald's sign is instantly recognizable, despite the words' having been translated into Arabic. The global prominence of a company that originated in the United States is a classic hallmark of the trend described in D. (The formation of transnational corporations—another topic of interest in the AP World History: Modern course—would also have been an acceptable answer had it been an option.)

21. **(D)** This question relies on use of evidence and historical interpretation. Answer A refers to "hard" power (enforced by military and geopolitical might) rather than the "soft" power associated with cultural and economic influence. While answer B refers to a trend that has unfolded in many parts of the Third World, it generally involves the nationalization and transformation of Western corporations. Answer C would imply no role at all in the Western world for a corporation like McDonald's, so D is left as the correct answer.

22. **(B)** The arrival of multinational corporations has triggered complaints similar to those listed in all of the questions, especially A, B, and D. Answer C is relevant to a degree as well, although often the impact is less to put people out of work than it is to undermine traditional forms of work, causing locals to accept employment with the new multinational—sometimes for lower pay and under worse working conditions. Intellectuals and artists would most probably be concerned with the erasing of local cultural identity by popular outside media or commercial forces—as in B—a phenomenon that some have condemned as "coca-colonization."

23. **(D)** While A applies to the first image and while C could be interpreted as applying to the second, neither applies to both. There is nothing to indicate any connection to religious faith in either image. The key historical trend at play here is the formation of societies on the frontiers or edges of larger nations.

24. **(A)** This question requires knowledge related to the stimulus material but not explicitly depicted in it. Here, background is pertinent. Maroon societies in Latin America, the Caribbean, and the Gulf of Mexico formed around communities of escaped slaves brought over from Africa.

25. **(D)** This question requires you to avoid drawing conclusions that cannot be supported by information from the stimulus material. Answers A, B, and C are all factually correct, but nothing in the second image would allow you to draw those conclusions. The location of Cossack communities on non-Russian frontiers makes D a reasonable answer.

26. **(C)** This question likewise requires knowledge related to the stimulus material but not explicitly depicted in it, but it is focused instead on aftermath and consequences. The broad historical context here involves the gradual incorporation of peripheral societies into more centralized states.

27. **(B)** Answers C and D belong to a later time period than that covered by the texts, and both texts speak of a more systematic type of violence than banditry. Wars in the modern era have seen a steady upswing in the rate of civilian casualties.

28. **(A)** This question requires contextualization and the interpretation of a particular point of view. The author, a British reporter who lived at the time in question, would have been likely to sympathize with his compatriots and also to share the prejudices common to his time and place, including a sense of racial superiority over darker-skinned peoples. Nothing in the passage speaks to answers B, C, or D.

29. **(B)** This question also requires interpretation of a point of view and also touches on historiographical issues. The author here is an academic historian and also from India. He does not excuse the Cawnpore Massacre, but his purpose is to place it in a larger context of mutual violence and disrespect. In his view, the British did not "deserve" to suffer violence, but neither were they blameless for the mass outbreak of brutality.

30. **(D)** This question requires contextualization and knowledge related to the stimulus material but not referred to directly by it. The direct aftermath of the Indian Revolt was the suppression of the sepoy rebels and the assumption of colonial authority by the British crown, as opposed to the British East India Company.

31. **(C)** This question relies on interpretation of data. Answer A is false, because China's GDP was higher in 1870 than in 1600 (even though it experienced a dip in 1700), and B is false because its GDP was lower than Western Europe's *both* in absolute terms and as a percentage of global GDP. Answer D can be easily proved incorrect as well.

32. **(C)** This question calls for contextualization by calling on knowledge related to the stimulus material but not directly referred to by it. Answers B and D refer to trends that did not in fact occur, while A—as economically important as the abolition of slavery was—would not have affected patterns of GDP growth as profoundly as industrialization.

33. **(C)** This question also calls for knowledge related to the stimulus material but not referred to directly by it. In the 1600s, the British East India Company had only a few footholds in India; its imprint on India had grown significantly by 1700, and by 1870, all of India had been directly colonized by Great Britain. Answer B did not occur, while A and D would have had a minor impact at best on Indian economic growth.

34. **(A)** Likewise, this question calls for knowledge related to the stimulus material. Understanding the importance of Indian cotton as a trade commodity is key to contextualizing this question.

35. **(A)** This question involves contextualization and requires knowledge related to the stimulus material without being explicitly referred to by it. Answer A is the infamous policy line inaugurated by the law excerpted in the first passage.

36. **(B)** For the most part, the White Australia Policy sought to exclude Asians without saying so overtly. The emphasis on language allowed the authorities to enact a fundamentally racist policy while claiming only to be concerned with skills and education.

37. **(A)** Again, this question requires understanding of context and knowledge related to the stimulus material but not specifically mentioned by it. Chinese immigrants to the Americas worked in a number of economic sectors, including those alluded to in B, C, and D, but in the United States (and Canada), large numbers worked on railroads.

38. **(C)** This question focuses on contextualization. The AP topic most directly connected to the documents at hand is that described in C.

39. **(A)** This question tests contextualization and historical knowledge. Sukarno is not speaking of agriculture or nuclear weapons, so B and C are not likely choices. While he was interested in advancing Asian interests, his appeal at the Bandung Conference was aimed more widely than D would suggest. The Bandung Conference was a hallmark moment in the creation of the Third World nonaligned movement, making A the best answer.

40. **(C)** The broad historical context related to this question is the postwar success of national-liberation efforts in the so-called Third World. Between the 1940s and the 1970s, colonial possessions in Africa, Asia, and elsewhere freed themselves in a massive wave of decolonization, making C the best answer.

41. **(C)** To leaders like Sukarno, Kwame Nkrumah of Ghana, Gamal Nasser of Egypt, and Jawaharlal Nehru of India, "nonalignment" meant neutrality during the Cold War. Suspicious of the Western powers that had colonized so much of the world and also distrustful of the USSR, Third World nations often tried to remain at arms' length from both. However, most ended up trading with or even forming military alliances with one or the other, especially if they wanted assistance with modernization efforts or in local wars against neighboring countries.

42. **(A)** Judaism is a monotheistic religion, making D incorrect, and while Judaism can be considered patriarchal, nothing in the letter speaks to this, making B unlikely. Family separation is clearly at stake, but there is no talk of war in the letter, making A (which speaks to a key AP topic) a better choice than C.

43. **(A)** This question calls for interpretation and close reading of evidence. Nothing in the letter gives any support to B, C, or D. Diaspora communities frequently experienced the strains of long-term separation from loved ones.

44. **(C)** It is Islam, not Judaism, that sanctions polygamy, so B is factually wrong. Nothing in the source material speaks to the frequency of such divorces, so while D may be true, the passage gives no proof of it. The tone of the merchant seems quite reasonable, and he himself may have indeed been so, but A is a risky choice, both because one should not generalize from a single case and because few places prior to the modern era afforded women any kind of true equality in matters of marriage. Women in most societies and most eras had much less control over how and whether a divorce took place. This case would not likely have been an exception, and C speaks best to that reality.

45. **(B)** This question requires knowledge of broad trends and the ability to contextualize them. Answer C is unlikely in an era when Africa was so thoroughly colonized, and neither the pursuit of traditional hunting (as in A) nor the attempt to harvest ivory against white interests (as in D) would likely be captured by Western photography. Forcing natives to exploit local resources was an all-too-common practice in colonial regimes, making B the best answer.

46. **(C)** This question requires knowledge related to the stimulus material but not referred to directly by it. The commodity most prized by colonial officials in the Belgian Congo was rubber. Gold and diamonds were more important elsewhere in Africa, especially in the south.

47. **(A)** This question requires historiographical thinking and also outside knowledge related to the stimulus material. The brutality of colonial administration in the Belgian Congo was notorious, even by the standard of the day, and while the photograph gives no hint of it, workers—especially on rubber plantations—suffered terrible beatings and amputations for failure to fulfill work quotas.

48. **(B)** Politics and war appear to be absent from this poem, making C and D unlikely choices. While the style can be viewed as modernist, making answer A possible, the fact that an African poet is writing in a form very much associated with Western literature makes B an even better response.

49. **(D)** This question calls for the contextualization of the stimulus material. Romanticism does not suit the tone of the poem, and while the poet is African, the poem itself deals with Africa only in the most indirect sense. Modern music could be seen to have some connection to mass media, but the references to "blackness"—Senghor is a key figure in the negritude movement—and saxophones are best associated with the Harlem Renaissance and the Jazz Age.

50. **(B)** Nothing in the verse gives evidence for A (and neither does basic knowledge of the negritude poets), and D is based on a factual falsity. While non-Western intellectuals became interested in using Western artistic forms, it did not necessarily mean they *preferred* them, making B a better answer than C.

51. **(D)** This question calls for context and outside knowledge. Dadaism put a premium on absurdity and satire, and abstraction tended to complicate meaning and interpretation more than Senghor's verse does, making A and B unlikely. Socialist realism was associated with propagandistic heroization, especially in Stalin's USSR, and its obvious, heavy-handed symbolism is absent in this poem. Senghor is known as a major proponent of the negritude cultural movement.

52. **(B)** This question calls for contextualization. Answer C has to do with fascist economics, and the industrialization spoken of in D has little to do with the chart's subject. Answer A is obviously related to the subject and may seem correct. However, modernization, as in B, is a larger and more profound historical trend and is directly related to the history of the USSR, a highly centralized state.

53. **(A)** The social groups described in B, C, and D would all tend to have relatively high rates of literacy. Regardless of nationality, rural populations are generally the slowest to benefit from the spread of education and the creation of school systems.

54. **(C)** Governments use educational systems to pursue many goals, including the ones listed in A, B, and D. However, schools are extremely effective tools for the inculcation of political values—even in democratic systems—and dictatorial regimes rarely if ever pass up the chance to use them for the purposes of propaganda and indoctrination.

55. **(D)** This question is related to historiography and argumentation. Soviet and Russian historians have made arguments similar to those in B and C and have even—in some cases—agreed with A. However, the pro-Soviet argument that best relates to the improvement of literacy rates is described in D.

PART B: SHORT-ANSWER QUESTIONS

1. During the 1900s, both capitalist and communist economies focused on large-scale industrial production and mammoth projects involving construction and resource extraction. Examples to satisfy Part A might include massive mining and metallurgical efforts (Pittsburgh in the United States, Magnitogorsk and other sites built during the First Five-Year Plan); the use of nuclear power plants in Western and Eastern Europe alike; or the construction of huge hydroelectric dams. All of these affected the natural world significantly.

    Part B looks for differences between capitalist and communist economies with respect to their impact on nature. One very clear distinction involves the degree to which governments in Europe and North America tended to impose strict regulations on businesses to limit their effects on the environment. Few if any such rules operated in twentieth-century communist regimes, and the extent of damage there was much greater, a fact evident even now. As for Part C, a major historical trend of the twentieth century (and the twenty-first) has been the escalating impact of industrial activity and fossil-fuel consumption on the environment, most visibly in the form of pollution and global warming, with dramatically noticeable and potentially harmful consequences for ecosystems and plant and animal species.

2. The easiest way to answer Part A is to link the rise of Nazism in Germany with the economic stress—particularly mass unemployment—caused by the Great Depression. Because Nazism also based its appeal on a vigorous rejection of communism (note the poster's reference to "Marxism"), you could also mention the increased influence of communism as a causal factor. Alternatively, you might tie this fact to Part B, arguing that opposition between right-wing extremism (fascism) and left-wing extremism (communism) led to a recurring struggle in twentieth-century Europe. You could also talk about the periodic resurgence of right-wing economic resentments as a force in European political life in the 1900s.

As with most forms of fascism, Nazism ushered in a form of state capitalism that could be described by way of answering Part C of this question.

3. The most obvious similarity that applies to Part A involves the astounding number of deaths that each disease caused, both in absolute terms and by percentage. Wherever it struck in fourteenth-century Eurasia, the bubonic plague killed roughly a third of the existing population. Smallpox, upon reaching the Americas, slew an unknown proportion of the indigenous population, but reputable estimates range from 40 to 90 percent. Both diseases also spread as a result of interaction between different cultures.

   One difference that could be used to answer Part B is the fact that while the bubonic plague traumatized Eurasian societies deeply, it did not tend to cause their downfall. By contrast, the devastation inflicted on Native Americans by smallpox and other diseases carried across the Atlantic proved so terrible that it left even the most powerful states and cultures open to European conquest. The principal reason asked for in Part C to explain the difference between Eurasia's and the Americas' experiences is that having been in perpetual contact and interaction for many centuries, the various peoples of Eurasia were less vulnerable in a large-group sense to each other's diseases, while the peoples of the Americas had existed in complete isolation from those in Afro-Eurasia for thousands of years. This left them with virtually no resistance to new European diseases.

4. General changes in Asian agricultural production during the 1900s and 2000s include increased output and greater mechanization. Episodes and trends specific to this era include the Green Revolution, which reached South Asia from Latin America during the post–World War II decades and boosted agricultural yields by encouraging the use of new technology and scientific methods. This made mass hunger—such as the devastating Bengal famine of the 1940s—less common but also increased water consumption and the use of pesticides. Another change involved the rapid modernization of agricultural production under Mao Tse-tung, principally by means of Soviet-style collectivization. (One tragic result in the short term was a famine that killed uncounted millions and ranks as one of the worst in history.)

   One continuity linking this era with earlier time periods would be the persistence of rice, soybeans, and millet as staple crops throughout China, Japan, India, and other parts of East, South, and Southeast Asia. Also, in certain areas with more poverty and less technology, methods of agricultural production have remained less industrialized and more labor-intensive.

Section II: Free-Response Questions

PART A: DOCUMENT-BASED QUESTION

1. Remember that your **thesis** must address both the designated skill (comparison, accounting for similarities *and* differences) and the topic indicated by the documents (European and non-European reactions to unfamiliar religions). A useful thesis for this question might suggest that while both Europeans and non-Europeans reacted with a mix of hostility and toleration to unfamiliar religions during the years in question, the reaction of non-Europeans seems more often to have been conditioned by European efforts to bring Christianity to them, including by force.

Grouping is less important for the DBQ than it used to be. Still, in this case, one could discuss Document 1 and Document 3 as examples of European reactions to Islam that are mixed (in the case of Document 1) or even positive, as Document 3 is. Document 5 and Document 7 can be considered negative depictions of Islam by Europeans, although be careful to note that while the former is highly hostile, the latter is more mild in its opposition to Islam—clearly convinced that Christianity is "true," whereas Islam is "false," but not so ferocious in tone. Finally, Document 2, Document 4, and Document 6 could be examined in tandem as non-European reactions to Christianity—the latter two explicitly antagonistic, the first more complex. Other groupings, of course, are possible, although any grouping scheme should support the thesis.

You are required to discuss **point of view** (or purpose, audience, historical situation, or context) for several documents at a minimum and as many as possible for maximum credit. Document 1 comes from the Elizabethan traveler Thomas Coryate, famed for his travels through Europe and Asia. Even if you have not heard of him, you can conclude that he is reasonably educated and intellectually and culturally curious, writing for an educated public back home. He seems open-minded and receptive, especially in an era—the 1600s—when religious conflict was common. Much the same can be said of Document 3, authored by the French legal philosopher Jean Bodin. Writing during the 1500s, when France was torn apart by religious warfare between Protestants and Catholics, Bodin was one of several thinkers—including Michel de Montaigne—who advocated religious tolerance and who used the Ottoman sultans, with their policy of allowing religious minorities to keep their faiths, as an example for Europeans to imitate. (It did not hurt that at this time, France happened to have allied with the Ottoman Turks in their wars against the Habsburg Holy Roman Empire.) Document 2 curiously blends perspectives: it is written by Aztecs who have adopted Catholicism in the wake of the Spanish conquest—but feel doubts about having done so. The fact that they have become Christian by means of forced conversion should certainly be taken into account. Document 4 commemorates Catholic martyrs in Japan, killed during one of the leadership's campaigns of anti-Christian persecution. Consider why Japanese converted to Christianity to begin with and why leaders such as Hideyoshi would have reacted so violently against this. Finally, the renowned poet Dante, in his poetic cycle *The Divine Comedy*, outlines what it means to be a medieval Catholic—and while it may be unfortunate from a modern-day perspective, it is not surprising that a devout Catholic of the 1200s would consign Mohammed to hell. Document 7 provides the perspective of a Catholic traveler insisting upon the superiority of Christianity to Islam and quick to debate the point but not necessarily violent in this encounter. It would be interesting to speculate whether he is reading the African chieftain's reaction correctly—is Budomel really as receptive to Christianity as Cadamosto thinks? Or is he simply being polite? Document 6 involves the perspective of a famous Muslim ruler and warrior, the great general Saladin, whose hostility toward Christianity can be attributed both to religious difference and his resentment of European political and military encroachments during the Crusades.

The DBQ rubric asks you to demonstrate knowledge of the **broader historical context** surrounding the question. In this case, most of the documents deal with the age of exploration and colonization (Document 5 is an exception), a process that forced many of these encounters. Europe's broader engagement with systems of international trade also provides context. Also recall that you must discuss at least one **additional piece of evidence** that could shed light on the topic that the available documents do not. What about the perspective of a non-Christian visitor to Europe observing Catholic or Protestant worship for the first time? Or the point of view of Christians or Africans who encounter Islam as a result of Muslim trade or military expansion? Other examples could work as well.

Finally, the rubric calls for the repeated and meaningful use of **evidence**. Marshal as many facts and details as you can about the topic at hand. As much as possible, make every piece of evidence appear distinct and separate; the more of these you can convince the reader you are providing, the better—although quality matters as much as, if not more than, quantity.

PART B: LONG ESSAYS

2. This question tests causation as its historical **reasoning skill**. (Note that all long essay questions in a given exam will be based on the same reasoning skill.) You should discuss both causes *and* effects. The topic involves the prevalence of diaspora communities throughout the Indian Ocean trade network.

   In advancing your **thesis**, you could focus on navigational techniques as a cause to go along with the general appetite throughout this region for foreign goods; the development of dhows and other vessels using lateen sails—which took particular advantage of monsoon winds—allowing the large-scale movement of goods and people throughout the large Indian Ocean basin. On the other hand, travelers were still limited by the vast distances involved, meaning that merchants—often with their families—had to spend long periods of time living far from their home or even had to relocate permanently. As for the effects brought about by this formation of diaspora communities, these include religious and cultural diffusion, technology transfer, and in some cases the mixing of racial and ethnic populations.

   As you move on to **context**, **evidence**, and **analysis**, you might mention the fusion of African, Arab, and Southeast Asian cultures along the East African coast, the many Islamic enclaves found throughout East and South Asia (as far away as China's Pacific shores), the spread of important foodstuffs like sugar and various fruits from South Asia to the rest of Afro-Eurasia, and so on.

3. As with all the long essay choices in this exam, causation is the historical **reasoning skill** being tested. Be sure to consider causes *and* effects. The topic involves the migration of Chinese and Indian laborers throughout the Pacific in the 1800s.

   In advancing your **thesis**, you could focus on causes such as overpopulation, changing economic circumstances (including diminishing employment opportunities thanks to Western enterprises crowding out local crafts and cottage industries in Asia), and disruptive political and military episodes like the Taiping Rebellion and the Indian Mutiny. Also, make note of what seemed to be legitimate offers of employment abroad but often turned out to be forms of coerced labor. Chinese and Indian workers would sign contracts promising good jobs, only to be shipped to harsh work environments such as railroads, mines, guano islands, and factories.

The major effects include immigrant communities in places such as Australia, Hawaii, and the western coasts of North and South America. Discussion of **context**, **evidence**, and **analysis** would make mention of cultural mixing but also anti-immigrant sentiment and the struggle for legal equality in all the above-mentioned places.

4. As with all the long essay choices in this exam, causation is the historical **reasoning skill** being tested. Be sure to consider causes *and* effects. The subject is population displacement in Afro-Eurasia from 1945 to the present.

   Examples abound, but the most obvious cause of population movement in this part of the world is war. The most obvious effects involve the formation of émigré communities, the creation of refugee populations, and—very often—anti-immigrant resentment.

   Regarding **context**, **evidence**, and **analysis**, you could discuss the displacement of peoples caused by World War II and the Cold War division of Europe, the mass movement of refugees brought about by the Arab-Israeli conflict or the ongoing Syrian civil war (or other Middle Eastern crises), or the mass migration to Europe of those fleeing various wars throughout Africa.

   The search for employment and better economic conditions could provide an alternative cause-and-effect relationship to write about. Consider the Turkish guest worker population in Germany, for example, or similar cases.

ANSWER SHEET
Practice Test 2

SECTION I

Part A

1. Ⓐ Ⓑ Ⓒ Ⓓ   21. Ⓐ Ⓑ Ⓒ Ⓓ   41. Ⓐ Ⓑ Ⓒ Ⓓ

2. Ⓐ Ⓑ Ⓒ Ⓓ   22. Ⓐ Ⓑ Ⓒ Ⓓ   42. Ⓐ Ⓑ Ⓒ Ⓓ

3. Ⓐ Ⓑ Ⓒ Ⓓ   23. Ⓐ Ⓑ Ⓒ Ⓓ   43. Ⓐ Ⓑ Ⓒ Ⓓ

4. Ⓐ Ⓑ Ⓒ Ⓓ   24. Ⓐ Ⓑ Ⓒ Ⓓ   44. Ⓐ Ⓑ Ⓒ Ⓓ

5. Ⓐ Ⓑ Ⓒ Ⓓ   25. Ⓐ Ⓑ Ⓒ Ⓓ   45. Ⓐ Ⓑ Ⓒ Ⓓ

6. Ⓐ Ⓑ Ⓒ Ⓓ   26. Ⓐ Ⓑ Ⓒ Ⓓ   46. Ⓐ Ⓑ Ⓒ Ⓓ

7. Ⓐ Ⓑ Ⓒ Ⓓ   27. Ⓐ Ⓑ Ⓒ Ⓓ   47. Ⓐ Ⓑ Ⓒ Ⓓ

8. Ⓐ Ⓑ Ⓒ Ⓓ   28. Ⓐ Ⓑ Ⓒ Ⓓ   48. Ⓐ Ⓑ Ⓒ Ⓓ

9. Ⓐ Ⓑ Ⓒ Ⓓ   29. Ⓐ Ⓑ Ⓒ Ⓓ   49. Ⓐ Ⓑ Ⓒ Ⓓ

10. Ⓐ Ⓑ Ⓒ Ⓓ   30. Ⓐ Ⓑ Ⓒ Ⓓ   50. Ⓐ Ⓑ Ⓒ Ⓓ

11. Ⓐ Ⓑ Ⓒ Ⓓ   31. Ⓐ Ⓑ Ⓒ Ⓓ   51. Ⓐ Ⓑ Ⓒ Ⓓ

12. Ⓐ Ⓑ Ⓒ Ⓓ   32. Ⓐ Ⓑ Ⓒ Ⓓ   52. Ⓐ Ⓑ Ⓒ Ⓓ

13. Ⓐ Ⓑ Ⓒ Ⓓ   33. Ⓐ Ⓑ Ⓒ Ⓓ   53. Ⓐ Ⓑ Ⓒ Ⓓ

14. Ⓐ Ⓑ Ⓒ Ⓓ   34. Ⓐ Ⓑ Ⓒ Ⓓ   54. Ⓐ Ⓑ Ⓒ Ⓓ

15. Ⓐ Ⓑ Ⓒ Ⓓ   35. Ⓐ Ⓑ Ⓒ Ⓓ   55. Ⓐ Ⓑ Ⓒ Ⓓ

16. Ⓐ Ⓑ Ⓒ Ⓓ   36. Ⓐ Ⓑ Ⓒ Ⓓ

17. Ⓐ Ⓑ Ⓒ Ⓓ   37. Ⓐ Ⓑ Ⓒ Ⓓ

18. Ⓐ Ⓑ Ⓒ Ⓓ   38. Ⓐ Ⓑ Ⓒ Ⓓ

19. Ⓐ Ⓑ Ⓒ Ⓓ   39. Ⓐ Ⓑ Ⓒ Ⓓ

20. Ⓐ Ⓑ Ⓒ Ⓓ   40. Ⓐ Ⓑ Ⓒ Ⓓ

For Section I, Part B and Section II
Formulate your responses to the short-response, data-based,
and long essay questions on separate sheets of paper.

SECTION I

Part A: Multiple-Choice Questions

Time: 55 Minutes for 55 Questions

Percent of exam score—40

> **DIRECTIONS:** Each of the questions below is followed by four suggested answers. Select the one that is best in each case and then fill in the corresponding oval on the answer sheet.

Questions 1 to 4 refer to the passages below.

Whether the question be to continue or to discontinue the practice of sati, the decision is equally surrounded by an awful responsibility. To consent to the consignment year after year of hundreds of innocent victims to a cruel and untimely end, when the power exists of preventing it, is a predicament which no conscience can contemplate without horror. But, on the other hand, to put to hazard by a contrary course the very safety of the British Empire in India is an alternative which itself may be considered a still greater evil. When we had powerful neighbours and greater reason to doubt our own security, expediency might recommend a more cautious proceeding, but now that we are supreme my opinion is decidedly in favour of an open and general prohibition.

> William Bentinck, Governor-General of India, "On the Suppression of Sati," 1829

I have made it my study to examine the nature and character of the Indians [who trade with us], and however repugnant it may be to our feelings, I am convinced they must be ruled with a rod of iron, to bring and keep them in a proper state of subordination, and the most certain way to effect this is by letting them feel their dependence on [the foodstuffs and manufactured goods we sell them].

> George Simpson, Head of Northern Department, Hudson's Bay Company, 1826

1. The tone of the first passage best supports which of the following suppositions about British motivations for eradicating the sati ritual?

    (A) The British intended principally to Christianize India's Hindu population.
    (B) The British sought to end what they considered an inhumane practice without endangering their own authority.
    (C) They acted out of a progressive concern for women's equality.
    (D) They were impelled by a racially prejudiced disdain for all Indian customs.

2. Which of the following resources would the author of the second passage have been most likely interested in obtaining from local natives?

(A) Ivory
(B) Tobacco
(C) Silver
(D) Furs

3. The first passage can be said to undermine which commonly held assumption about Western imperialism?

(A) That European colonizers sometimes interfered with native religious practices
(B) That European colonizers concerned themselves deeply with turning profits
(C) That European colonizers were uniformly eager to force their cultural norms on native populations
(D) That European colonizers often resorted to armed force to impose their will on imperial subjects

4. The authors of both passages served institutions associated with which of the following colonial techniques commonly used by Western imperial powers?

(A) Direct rule by the crown
(B) Complete privatization of colonial authority
(C) Martial law enforced by sizable armies
(D) The chartering of companies to assume costs and share profits

Questions 5 to 7 refer to the image below.

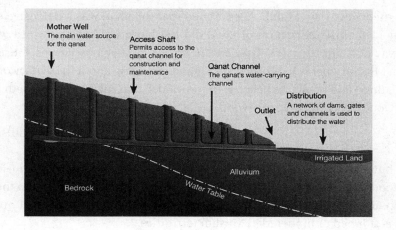

5. The innovation depicted in the image above is best regarded as

    (A) an advanced system of water management.
    (B) an example of monumental architecture.
    (C) a method for fortifying cities.
    (D) an agricultural technique associated with the Green Revolution.

6. What practice was this innovation meant to support?

    (A) Urban expansion
    (B) The creation of infrastructure for trade routes
    (C) Intensification of agriculture
    (D) The centralization of political authority

7. Which of the following can most reasonably be concluded about the kind of society that would build the structure depicted in the image above?

    (A) It was located near a plentiful supply of water.
    (B) It lacked political centralization.
    (C) It was highly militaristic.
    (D) It possessed an impressive capacity to build infrastructure.

Questions 8 to 10 refer to the passages below.

While some theorists in the Middle Ages argued that the jihad was a defensive war… most authorities held that the obligation of jihad did not lapse until all the world was brought under the sway of Islam. The *Bahr* [*al-Fava'id*, or "Sea of Precious Virtues"] insists that the first duty of a Muslim ruler is to prosecute the jihad and bring about the victory of Islam, and if he does not do so and he makes peace with the infidel, that ruler would be better dead than alive, for he would be corrupting the world.

Robert Irwin, "Islam and the Crusades," 1995

It is strange how the Christians round Mount Lebanon, when they see any Muslim hermits, bring them food and treat them kindly, saying that these men are dedicated to the Great and Glorious God and that they should therefore share with them. Likewise, not one Christian merchant was stopped or hindered in Muslim territories.

Ibn Jubayr, Muslim scholar, traveling to Mecca and Jerusalem, ca. 1200

8. These two passages are best understood in the context of which of the following?

   (A) The influence of religion on interaction between cultures
   (B) The use of religion to justify armed violence
   (C) The syncretic fusion of different religious traditions
   (D) The attempt of a religious group to proselytize to those following another faith

9. The first passage tends to support which of the following traditional historical assumptions?

   (A) That the majority of Muslims were more peaceful than Christians during the crusading era
   (B) That most Muslims were interested only in protecting their own territory during the crusading era
   (C) That many Muslims during the crusading era were driven by Islamic faith to be inherently violent
   (D) That the ideology of holy war was taken seriously by Muslim elites during the crusading era

10. The second passage undermines traditional historical assumptions by

   (A) showing that state-level antagonisms in the Middle East during the crusading era were not always reflected in personal or economic life.
   (B) showing how Middle Eastern Muslims during the crusading era did not take religious obligations as seriously as Christians did.
   (C) showing how Muslims were on the whole kinder than Christians in the Middle East during the crusading era.
   (D) showing how, in the Middle East during the crusading era, economic factors trumped all other considerations.

Questions 11 to 14 refer to the passages below.

Every two months His Majesty sends from Lima 60,000 pesos to pay for the mita of the Indians. Up on the Huanacavelica range there are 3,000 or 4,000 Indians working in the mercury mine, with picks and hammers, breaking up the ore. And when they have filled up their little sacks, the poor fellows, loaded down, climb up those ladders and rigging, so distressing that a man can hardly get up them. That is the way they work in this mine, with many lights and the loud noise of the pounding and great confusion. Nor is that the greatest evil; that is due to thievish and undisciplined superintendents. According to His Majesty's warrant, the mine owners at Potosí have a right to the mita of 13,300 Indians. These mita Indians earn each day 4 reals. Besides these there are others not under obligation, who hire themselves out voluntarily: these each get from 12 to 16 reals, and some up to 24, according to how well they wield their picks or their reputation for knowing how to get the ore out.

> Antonio Vasquez de Espinosa, report on mining in Huanacavelica and Potosí, 1620s

The third principal reason the local Yakut and Tungus natives are ruined is that from the time they first came under Russian control, they have been forced to pay *yasak* tribute. Some have paid in sables, others in red foxes, still others in cash. At first there were plenty of fur-bearing animals there, but now there are no sables and not many foxes in those lands, from the shores of the Arctic Ocean all the way south to the great Lena River. Moreover, almost half the natives cannot hunt because they no longer have horses, many of which have been pawned to the *yasak* collectors.

> Heinrich von Füch, "On the Treatment of Natives in Northeast Siberia," 1744

11. Both passages are best seen in the context of which of the following broad developments?

    (A) Emerging systems of coerced labor
    (B) The expansion of chattel slavery
    (C) Increased reliance on prison-camp workforces
    (D) Colonization of overseas territories by joint-stock companies

12. The system of labor described in the first passage came into being in which of the following ways?

    (A) Spanish colonists enslaved Native American populations outright.
    (B) Spain refused to purchase slaves from Africa, relying instead on Native American labor.
    (C) Spanish authorities adapted local forms of labor mobilization for their own purposes.
    (D) Spanish landowners came to depend heavily on plantation monoculture.

13. According to the second passage, which of the following contributed most to the burden faced by native Siberians attempting to fulfill their tribute obligations?

    (A) Interference by Russian Orthodox missionaries
    (B) Native inexperience in hunting deep into the subarctic tundra
    (C) Competition from Russian hunters and trappers
    (D) Overhunting and depletion of fur-bearing animals

14. Which of the following factors, not mentioned in the second passage, would have been most likely to create added difficulties for native Siberians attempting to fulfill their tribute obligations?

    (A) The arrival of rival hunters from China and Japan
    (B) The impact of epidemic diseases brought by Russian settlers
    (C) The general warming of the climate during this time period
    (D) The reduced demand for furs among European and Asian elites

Questions 15 to 18 refer to the chart below.

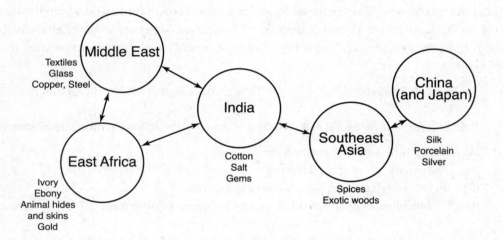

Flow of major goods and commodities, Indian Ocean trade networks, ca. 1200 to 1450

15. Which of the statements below is most solidly supported by the information contained in the chart above?

    (A) China produced the highest volume of trade goods in this system of exchange.
    (B) India served as the geographical hub of this system of exchange.
    (C) East Africa experienced an accelerated rate of urbanization as a result of this system of exchange.
    (D) The Middle East produced the highest-quality goods in this system of exchange.

16. Which of the following technological innovations played the largest role in enabling this system of exchange?

    (A) The outrigger canoe
    (B) Lateen sails
    (C) The lodestone compass
    (D) Stern rudders

17. This system of exchange would have encouraged which of the following social and cultural developments most directly?

    (A) The diffusion of Buddhism throughout Asia
    (B) The weakening of traditional social hierarchies
    (C) The formation of merchant diaspora communities
    (D) The rise of Islamic patriarchalism in East Africa

18. The economic relationships associated with this system of exchange was most disrupted by which of the following?

    (A) The sudden decline in the value of silver along the Silk Road
    (B) The conquest of East Africa by Omani Arabs
    (C) The shifting of oceanic currents due to the Little Ice Age
    (D) The arrival of European merchants and explorers

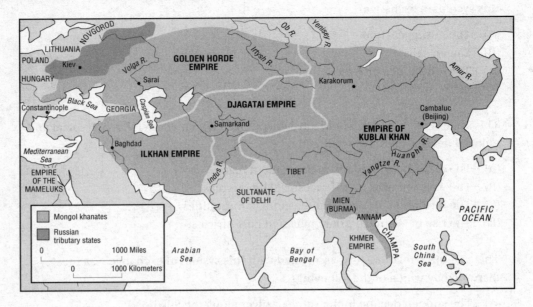

19. The map above depicts which of the following historical processes?

    (A) The consolidation of a continent-wide state
    (B) The formation of an alliance system against a common enemy
    (C) The disintegration of an empire into smaller entities
    (D) The emergence of religious divisions within a large nation

20. The economic impact of the process depicted by the map would have been felt <u>most strongly</u>

    (A) in the Indian Ocean.
    (B) along the Silk Road.
    (C) in the Mediterranean Sea.
    (D) in the Pacific Ocean.

21. Which of the following religions became more firmly established as a result of the process depicted by the map?

    (A) Confucianism and Islam
    (B) Buddhism and Christianity
    (C) Islam and Buddhism
    (D) Christianity and Islam

22. In China, the developments depicted by the map resulted in which of the following political outcomes?

    (A) The Mongolization of Chinese culture and enslavement of much of the population
    (B) A high degree of political autonomy under a Mongol leadership that interfered only infrequently
    (C) Rebellion and quick victory against a short-lived Mongol rulership
    (D) Rule by a Mongol regime that recentralized the country and adapted in many ways to Chinese custom

Questions 23 to 26 refer to the passages below.

Woman, wake up; the bell of reason is being heard throughout the whole universe; discover your rights. Enslaved man has multiplied his strength, [but] having become free, he has become unjust to his companion. Oh, women, women! When will you cease to be blind? What advantage have you received from the Revolution? A more pronounced scorn, a more marked disdain. If our leaders persist, courageously oppose the force of reason to their empty pretentions of superiority. Regardless of what barriers confront you, it is in your power to free yourselves!

   Olympe de Gouges, "Declaration of the Rights of Woman and the Female Citizen," 1791

The independence? Nothing of what I hoped for was achieved. I had expected that my children would be able to have an education, but they did not get it. We were poor peasants then, we are poor peasants now. Nothing has changed. Everything is the same. The only thing is that we are free, the war is over, we work without fear—but apart from that, nothing has changed.

   Halima Ghomri, interviewed in the 1970s, after Algeria's war of independence

23. Which of the following observations about revolutions and gender is best supported by the first passage?

    (A) Revolutionary progressivism does not always concern itself with gender equality.
    (B) Women typically assume leadership roles during times of revolution.
    (C) Women rarely support revolutions and therefore receive little benefit from them.
    (D) Revolutionary movements are generally uninterested in women's rights.

24. Publication of the first passage was followed by which of the political outcomes described below?

    (A) French women, like Jews, Protestants, and freed blacks, attained political equality after only a short delay.
    (B) French women quickly gained the right to vote but not to hold political office.
    (C) French women found their status even lower than it had been before the French Revolution.
    (D) French women remained without full political rights until well into the following century.

25. Which of the following factors is likeliest to have prevented the sort of progress hoped for by the speaker in the second passage?

(A) Failure to eradicate Islamic traditionalism
(B) Lack of industrial assets or infrastructure
(C) Hostility to women's rights on the part of new elites
(D) Prioritization of national liberation over social reform

26. Based on both passages, which of the following conclusions can be most reasonably made about revolutions?

(A) The new liberties gained by revolution are rarely worth the bloodshed.
(B) The new liberties gained by revolution typically fail to benefit women or ethnic minorities.
(C) The new liberties gained by revolution are sometimes distributed unequally or inconsistently.
(D) The new liberties gained by revolution do not always bring about economic improvement.

Questions 27 to 30 refer to the passage below.

By what principle of reason then, should these foreigners send in return a poisonous drug? Without meaning to say that the foreigners harbor such destructive intentions in their hearts, we yet positively assert that from their inordinate thirst after gain, they are perfectly careless about the injuries they inflict upon us! And such being the case, we should like to ask what has become of that conscience which heaven has implanted in the breasts of all men? We have heard that in your own country opium is prohibited with the utmost strictness and severity. This is a strong proof that you know full well how hurtful it is to mankind. Since you do not permit it to injure your own country, you ought not to have this injurious drug transferred to another country, and above all others, how much less to the Inner Land! Of the products which China exports to your foreign countries, there is not one which is not beneficial to mankind in some shape or other.

Lin Zexu, Chinese trade commissioner, letter to Queen Victoria, 1839

27. The passage above is most closely related with which of the following broad developments?

(A) Europe's enslavement of Chinese citizens
(B) Europe's expansion of missionary activity in China
(C) Europe's economic domination of China
(D) Europe's colonization of Chinese territory

28. On which of the following arguments does the author of the passage above principally base his appeal?

   (A) It is hypocritical to sell one country a substance banned as harmful in one's own.
   (B) Confucian teachings forbid the use of all narcotics as inherently immoral.
   (C) Addiction is causing China to suffer an unfavorable balance of trade.
   (D) Britain is unwise to risk the wrath of a militarily more powerful state.

29. Which of the following background facts persuaded Europeans to engage in the actions described in the above passage?

   (A) China had recently placed an embargo on exports of silk.
   (B) The price of Chinese tea had risen higher than European buyers found acceptable.
   (C) China refused to allow a meaningful volume of European goods to be sold there.
   (D) China's emperor had repeatedly insulted the British ambassador.

30. Which of the outcomes listed below followed the delivery of Lin Zexu's letter?

   (A) Chinese naval defeat and new trade terms more favorable to the West
   (B) A successful ban of the opium trade in all Chinese territories
   (C) Violent uprisings on the part of China's pro-British Muslim minority
   (D) The expulsion of all foreigners from Chinese territory

Questions 31 to 33 are based on the chart below.

World Human Population Growth: 1 C.E.–1999	
Year	***Population***
1 C.E.	200 million
1650	500 million
1850	1 billion
1930	2 billion
1975	4 billion
1999	6 billion

31. Which of the following would most historians consider the best explanation for the rapid changes depicted in the chart shown above?

    (A) The global movement of peoples, enabled by industrial-era transportation
    (B) The eradication of major famines by improvements in agricultural science
    (C) The decreased impact that modern wars have had on civilian populations
    (D) The effect of modern medical innovations and increased access to vaccines

32. Based on the information presented in the chart, the highest rate of growth was experienced during which of the following periods?

    (A) 1650–1850
    (B) 1850–1930
    (C) 1930–1975
    (D) 1957–1999

33. Which of the following statements about recent and future population growth is best supported by the data contained in the chart above?

    (A) Population growth has declined in recent years and shows little sign of rebounding.
    (B) Population growth continues at roughly the same pace as over the past half century and shows no signs of slowing.
    (C) Population growth has evened out in recent years and seems likely to continue on that track.
    (D) Population growth continues but at a noticeably slower pace than over the past few decades.

Questions 34 to 37 are based on the images below.

Woodcut of Japanese musket troops, ca. late 1500s

Senegalese troops in French service, ca. late 1800s–early 1900s

34. When taken together, both images are most closely connected with which of the following historical developments?

   (A) Western imperial domination of non-Western powers
   (B) The impact of technology transfer on military affairs
   (C) Agrarian revolutions against abusive centralizing powers
   (D) The worldwide industrialization of weapons production

35. Deployment of the weapons depicted in the first image

   (A) threatened the elite warrior status traditionally afforded to Japanese samurai.
   (B) rendered horseback warfare completely obsolete in Japan.
   (C) brought about the full democratization of Japanese society.
   (D) caused the rapid destruction of castles built during Japan's feudal era.

36. Which of the following can be most safely concluded about the African troops pictured in the second image?

   (A) The French Empire equipped them with Western gear mainly for the purposes of show.
   (B) They were issued Western weapons due to the French Empire's desire to defuse racial tensions.
   (C) They French Empire gave them Western uniforms to indicate commitment to racial equality.
   (D) They were trained in Western style to maximize the French Empire's military manpower.

37. When viewed from a comparative perspective, the Senegalese troops depicted in the second image most resemble

   (A) Ottoman janissaries.
   (B) Roman legionaries.
   (C) Indian sepoys.
   (D) Spartan hoplites.

Questions 38 to 40 are based on the chart below.

World's Major Consumers of Primary Energy (1998) Measured in quadrillions of British thermal units (Btu)	
United States	94.57 quadrillion Btu
China	33.93 quadrillion Btu
Russia	25.99 quadrillion Btu
Japan	21.21 quadrillion Btu
Germany	13.83 quadrillion Btu
India	12.51 quadrillion Btu
Canada	11.85 quadrillion Btu
France	10.00 quadrillion Btu
United Kingdom	9.75 quadrillion Btu
Brazil	8.08 quadrillion Btu

38. The data contained in the chart above <u>most clearly</u> reflects which of the following environmental developments?

(A) Expansion of the global total of land under agricultural cultivation
(B) Fossil-fuel extraction
(C) Industrialization in the less developed world
(D) Large-scale resource consumption

39. What present-day environmental issue can be associated most directly with the energy consumption measured in the chart above?

(A) Desertification
(B) Global warming
(C) Soil erosion
(D) Growing stockpiles of nuclear waste

40. Based on the data presented in the chart above, which of the following conclusions can one safely make?

(A) The top energy-consuming nations are to be found mainly in the developed world.
(B) Brazil has a smaller population than China does.
(C) Russia is a more efficient consumer of energy than China is.
(D) Japan has a larger population than India does.

Questions 41 to 43 are based on the passage below.

I don't know whether this world has meaning that transcends it. But I know that I do not know that meaning and that it is impossible just now for me to know it. What can a meaning outside my condition mean to me? I can understand only in human terms.

Albert Camus, "The Myth of Sisyphus," 1955

41. The passage above is best seen as exemplifying which of the following intellectual trends?

    (A) A postwar reassertion of traditional religious values
    (B) An expression of patriotic pride thanks to victory in World War II
    (C) A modernist tendency to question the validity of faith-based moralities
    (D) An increased willingness to embrace radical Marxism

42. The author of the above passage was most associated with which of the following movements?

    (A) Existentialism
    (B) Religious fundamentalism
    (C) New age syncretism
    (D) Liberation theology

43. In broad context, the perspective expressed in the passage can be seen to have grown out of which trend from the century before?

    (A) The rising influence of socialist ideologies
    (B) Antiwar sentiment
    (C) Popular anxiety about industrialization
    (D) The Western crisis of faith

Questions 44 to 46 refer to the image below.

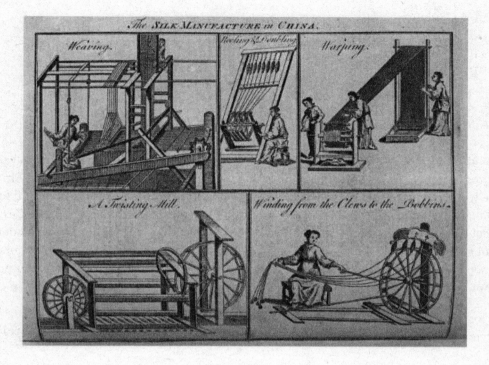

Thomas Astley and John Greene, "The Silk Manufacture in China," ca. 1750

44. The image above relates most directly to which economic trend or practice?

   (A) Inclusion of women in the workplace
   (B) Protoindustrialization
   (C) Standardization of weights and measures
   (D) The rise of coerced labor in traditional modes of production

45. The scenes depicted in the image above appear to contradict what commonly held assumption about China during the 1700s?

   (A) Gender discrimination, justified by Confucian ideology, kept women from working outside the home.
   (B) Complacency discouraged eighteenth-century China from modernizing economic production.
   (C) China's rulers focused most of their economic policy making on building a more efficient army and navy.
   (D) Technological innovation occurred in China only rarely and without major impact.

46. If the silk whose production is depicted above was sold to European merchants, it would most likely have been traded for which of the following commodities?

(A) Opium
(B) Metalware
(C) Tea
(D) Silver

Questions 47 to 49 refer to the passage below.

Is it not unity alone that can weld us into an effective force, capable of creating our own progress and making our valuable contribution to world peace? Which independent African state will claim that its financial structure and banking institutions are fully harnessed to its national development? Which will claim that its material resources and human energies are available for its own national aspirations? We are fast learning that political independence is not enough to rid us of the consequences of colonial rule. We have been too busy nursing our separate states to understand fully the basic need for union, rooted in common purpose, common planning and common endeavour.

Ghana's president, Kwame Nkrumah, addressing
the Organization of African Unity, 1963

47. The speaker in the passage above is espousing which of the following causes?

(A) Nationalism
(B) Socialism
(C) Pan-Africanism
(D) Neocolonialism

48. Which of the following diplomatic postures toward the Cold War would Nkrumah most likely have wished African nations to take?

(A) Alliance with the United States and NATO nations
(B) Nonalignment with respect to the superpowers
(C) Cautious cooperation with the Soviet Union
(D) Armed defiance against former colonizing powers such as Britain and France

49. Which of the following factors was most important in preventing the fulfillment of the political dreams described in the passage above?

(A) A lack of common ethnicity, language, or religion
(B) The spread of communism throughout the continent
(C) Armed intervention on the part of the Cold War superpowers
(D) Africa's shortage of natural resources

Questions 50 to 52 refer to the map below.

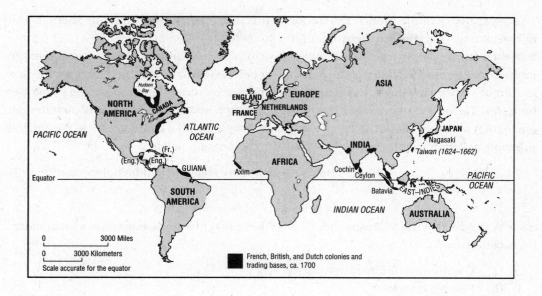

50. The map above most clearly indicates that which of the following is true about European colonization of the non-Western world in the 1600s and 1700s?

    (A) The English were particularly interested in controlling North Atlantic whaling grounds.
    (B) French, Dutch, and English colonial authority extended primarily to places easily reached by sea.
    (C) Dutch colonial expansion came in many cases at the expense of the Portuguese.
    (D) The English, Dutch, and French were less interested than Spain in overseas colonization.

51. Which of the following scientific or technological innovations most directly enabled the colonial expansion depicted by the map above?

    (A) The shipboard chronometer
    (B) The lateen sail
    (C) The sailing gunship
    (D) The sternpost rudder

52. Colonial interest in the Caribbean during this era was motivated primarily by which of the following?

    (A) The fur trade
    (B) Rich fishing stocks
    (C) Silver mining
    (D) Sugar production

Questions 53 to 55 refer to the passage below.

This great purity of the French Revolution is precisely what causes both our strength and our weakness. Our strength, because it gives to us rights of the public interest over private interests; our weakness, because it rallies all vicious men against us. We must smother the internal and external enemies of the Republic or perish with it; now in this situation, the first maxim of your policy ought to be to lead the people by reason and the people's enemies by terror. Terror is nothing other than justice, prompt, severe, inflexible; it is therefore an emanation of virtue; it is not so much a special principle as it is a consequence of the general principle of democracy applied to our country's most urgent needs.

French revolutionary leader Maximilien Robespierre, 1794

53. With which of the following threats does the speaker in the passage above seem most concerned?

(A) Counterrevolutionary opponents
(B) Foreign invaders
(C) Communist agitators
(D) Transnational corporations

54. The passage above appears to articulate which of the following political principles?

(A) From each according to his abilities, to each according to his needs
(B) Might makes right
(C) The end justifies the means
(D) The government is best that governs least

55. The passage above can be said to call into question what common understanding of the French Revolution?

(A) That it achieved economic equality for all social classes
(B) That it enshrined widespread respect for individual liberties and the right to due process
(C) That it significantly improved the plight of ordinary working people
(D) That it greatly advanced the cause of gender equality

SECTION I

Part B: Short-Answer Questions

Time: 40 Minutes for 3 Questions

Percent of exam score—20

> **DIRECTIONS:** Complete THREE of the following four questions. You must answer questions 1 AND 2. After that, choose question 3 OR question 4.

1. **Use the passage below to answer all parts of the question that follows.**

   Most people believe that technology is a staunch friend. It makes life easier, cleaner, and longer. But it is the kind of friend that asks for trust and obedience. There is a dark side to this friend. Its gifts are not without a heavy cost. The accusation can be made that the uncontrolled growth of technology destroys the vital sources of our humanity. It creates a culture without a moral foundation. It undermines certain mental processes and social relations that make human life worth living. Technology, in sum, is both friend and enemy.

   Neil Postman, Technopoly: The Surrender of Culture to Technology, 1993

   A. Identify and explain ONE historically specific example of technological impact on human society during the period ca. 1800 to the present that would support the author's argument.

   B. Identify and explain ONE historically specific example of technological impact on human society during the period ca. 1800 to the present that would challenge the author's argument.

   C. Identify and explain ONE nineteenth- or twentieth-century development that likely explains historians' interest in the subject of the passage.

2. **Use the map below to answer all parts of the question that follows.**

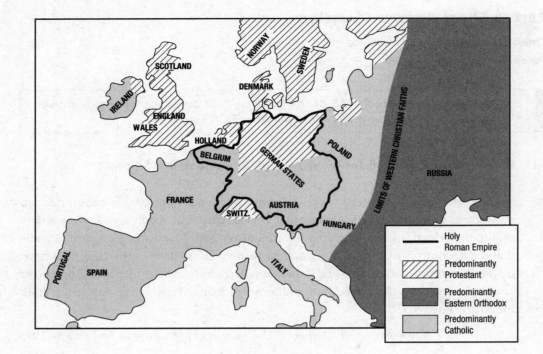

A. Describe ONE <u>change</u> in European religious practice during the fifteenth and sixteenth centuries that triggered the development depicted in the map accompanying this question.

B. Identify ONE way that the map accompanying this question reflects a <u>continuity</u> in European religious practice during the fifteenth and sixteenth centuries.

C. Explain ONE way in which European religious practice changed as a result of the development depicted in the map accompanying this question.

3. **Answer all parts of the question that follows.**

A. Identify ONE <u>similarity</u> in how women's roles were defined in the Middle East and in East Asia between 1200 and 1450.

B. Identify ONE <u>difference</u> in how women's roles were defined in the Middle East and in East Asia between 1200 and 1450.

C. Explain ONE reason for the difference between the Middle East's and East Asia's definition of women's roles between 1200 and 1450.

4. **Answer all parts of the question that follows.**

   A. Identify ONE similarity in the impact that nongovernmental organizations have had on global politics from 1945 to the present with the impact that transnational corporations have had.

   B. Identify ONE difference in the impact that nongovernmental organizations have had on global politics from 1945 to the present with the impact that transnational corporations have had.

   C. Explain ONE reason for the difference between the impact of nongovernmental organizations and that of transnational corporations.

SECTION II: FREE-RESPONSE QUESTIONS

Part A: Document-Based Question
(Suggested planning and writing time—45 minutes, plus 15-minute reading period)
Percent of exam score—25

> **DIRECTIONS:** The following question is based on the accompanying documents. The documents have been edited for the purpose of this exercise.

1. Using the documents and your knowledge of world history, identify and explain continuities and changes in the way the USSR controlled its national economy between the Russian revolution of 1917 and the death of Joseph Stalin in 1953.

DOCUMENT 1

Source: Vladimir Lenin, Soviet leader, "Advice to Workers and Peasants," in the official newspaper *Pravda*, February 6, 1918.

You must organize and consolidate Soviet power in the villages. There you will encounter kulaks [rich, landowning peasants] who will hinder your work at every step. Make it clear to ordinary peasants that the kulaks must be expropriated in order to achieve a fair and equitable distribution of goods. The bourgeoisie are hiding in their coffers the riches they have plundered. We must catch the plunderers and compel them to return the spoils, otherwise we shall perish.

DOCUMENT 2

Source: Poster entitled "What the October Revolution Has Given Female Workers and Peasants," 1920. Captions on the buildings in the background read: "House for Mothers and Children" [daycare facility], "Council of Female Workers and Peasant Deputies," "Adult Education," "Kindergarten," "Library," "Dining Hall," and "Workers' Club."

DOCUMENT 3

Source: Dmitrii Debabov, "Construction at Magnitogorsk," 1930.

DOCUMENT 4

Source: Letter from a Soviet construction worker to his uncle in Leningrad, 1931.

Hello, Uncle Fedya. Greetings from Magnitogorsk. They did a poor job of meeting us here. The first night we slept on the bare ground; so began our camp life. They don't give us work since nobody knows when the machine installation will begin. For days we did nothing, or sat in tents, or walked around looking for the bosses. A large number of us leave to go back to where they came from every day. It's very hard to get out of here, but no matter what I'm coming back since life here is impossible: the chow is awful, we're living in tents, and the weather is cold and rainy all the time. When we were being sent off, we heard pretty, sweet words. The project can't proceed without you, they said. But in fact there is such a mess here that you wouldn't be able to make heads or tails of it. Our big shots here are nothing but bureaucrats. There's complete confusion, you can't find anything.

DOCUMENT 5

Source: Miron Dolot, Ukrainian farmer and famine survivor, from his memoir *Execution by Hunger*, 1987.

To safeguard the 1932 crop against the starving farmers, the Party and government passed several strict laws. One of the cruelest laws was enacted on August 7, 1932. This law declared that all collective farm and cooperative property such as the crops in the fields, livestock, and so forth were to be considered as state-owned. The penalties for theft were execution by firing squad, and confiscation of all property of the guilty one. There could be no amnesty for these so-called felons.

DOCUMENT 6

Source: Operational order of July 30, 1937, issued by Nikolai Yezhov, USSR People's Commissar of Internal Affairs (head of Stalin's secret police).

II. On Means of Punishment of Those to Be Repressed, and the Number of Those Subject to Repression

1. All repressed kulak [rich, landowning peasant], criminal, and other anti-Soviet elements are to be divided into two categories:

a) The first category are the most hostile of the enumerated elements. They are subject to immediate arrest, and after their cases have been considered by a three-person tribunal they are TO BE SHOT.

b) In the second category are the other less active though also hostile element. They are subject to arrest and imprisonment in a camp for 8 to 10 years, and the most evil and socially dangerous of these to incarceration for the same period in prison, as determined by the three-person tribunal.

In accordance with data determined by the people's commissars of the republic-level NKVD [People's Commissariats of Internal Affairs] the following numbers of individuals are subject to repression.

	First Category	Second Category	Total
1. Azerbaijan Soviet Socialist Republic	1,500	3,750	5,250
2. Armenian Soviet Socialist Republic	500	1,000	1,500
3. Belorussian Soviet Socialist Republic	2,000	10,000	12,000
[...]			
39. Leningrad region	4,000	10,000	14,000
40. Moscow region	5,000	30,000	35,000
[...]			
[...]			
Total	72,950	177,500	250,450

III. The operation is to begin on August 5, 1937, and to be completed in four months.

DOCUMENT 7

Source: "International Communist Women's Day," celebratory article in the official newspaper *Pravda*, March 9, 1939.

Yesterday, on March 8, a celebration of International Communist Women's Day took place in the Bolshoi Theater. Comrade K. I. Nikolayeva talked about the heroic and energetic path taken by the women of our country, and about the concern for women shown by the Soviet government and by the party of Lenin and Stalin. Her speech showed how the Soviet woman has secured an honored place in the political and public life of our country. Deputies to the Supreme Soviet include 189 women. What a clear example of the political maturity of the Soviet woman! Comrade Nikolayeva spoke about the heroism of Soviet women and the unforgettable [record-breaking polar] flight taken by pilots Valentina Grizodubova, Polina Osipenko, and Maria Raskova. The heroines were located right there, and the hall greeted them with warm applause. Comrade Nikolayeva cited the example of Zinaida Troitskaya, who successfully mastered the complex craft of driving a locomotive engine, became an engineer, and now is the director of the Moscow regional railway. Her success was recognized with warm applause.

Part B: Long Essay Question

(Suggested planning and writing time—40 minutes)
Percent of exam score—15

> **DIRECTIONS:** Choose ONE from questions 2, 3, and 4.

2. In the period 1200 to 1500, major states employed political techniques to centralize and consolidate their authority.

   Develop an argument that evaluates the techniques employed by states in East Asia in comparison with those used by South Asian states during this period.

3. In the period from 1400 to 1800, states and societies in non-Western parts of the world were forced to respond to European colonization efforts.

   Develop an argument that evaluates the responses of African states and societies to European colonization in response to the responses of American states and societies during this period.

4. In the period 1750 to 1900, revolutionary processes unfolded in many parts of the Atlantic world.

   Develop an argument that evaluates the unfolding of revolutionary processes in Haiti during this period in comparison to those that unfolded in Latin American during the same period.

ANSWER KEY
Practice Test 2

SECTION I

Part A

1. **B**	21. **C**	41. **C**
2. **D**	22. **D**	42. **A**
3. **C**	23. **A**	43. **D**
4. **D**	24. **D**	44. **B**
5. **A**	25. **D**	45. **B**
6. **C**	26. **C**	46. **D**
7. **D**	27. **C**	47. **C**
8. **A**	28. **A**	48. **B**
9. **D**	29. **C**	49. **D**
10. **A**	30. **A**	50. **B**
11. **A**	31. **D**	51. **C**
12. **C**	32. **B**	52. **D**
13. **D**	33. **B**	53. **A**
14. **B**	34. **B**	54. **C**
15. **B**	35. **A**	55. **B**
16. **B**	36. **D**	
17. **C**	37. **C**	
18. **D**	38. **D**	
19. **C**	39. **B**	
20. **B**	40. **A**	

ANSWER EXPLANATIONS

Section I

PART A: MULTIPLE-CHOICE

1. **(B)** This question involves use of evidence and historical interpretation. As the leading official in a joint-stock company operating under a government charter, Bentinck was concerned above all with profits and the maintenance of British power, as in B. He was only moved to act on his moral and religious convictions once his main priorities were met. The BEIC actively discouraged—but did not prevent—Christian missionary activity, and it often ignored local customs it found objectionable, precisely because it understood how native discontent might destabilize its position. So A and D are incorrect. Bentinck, although seemingly sincere in disliking the deaths of women caused by sati, gives no indication that he favored women's equality.

2. **(D)** This question requires contextualization and knowledge related to the stimulus material, even if not directly referred to by it. The Hudson's Bay Company had many economic interests in Canada, but the fur trade was paramount during the time period in question.

3. **(C)** This question requires use of evidence and an understanding of historical argumentation. Bentinck's reluctance to interfere with a long-standing Indian custom directly rebuts C, an accusation commonly launched by some historians against colonizing powers.

4. **(D)** Both Bentinck and Simpson were administrators of companies that enjoyed government-chartered monopolies to economically exploit colonial territory. Techniques of colonial administration are a topic of key interest on the AP exam.

5. **(A)** This question relies on interpretive skill. Impressive as it may be, the qanat depicted here is clearly not a fortification or a piece of monumental architecture, making B and C incorrect. The Green Revolution, mentioned in D, involved agricultural techniques, but it was a twentieth-century trend and far too late in time to be relevant to this image.

6. **(C)** Sources of water are crucial to the growth of cities—and also the maintenance of trade routes—so A and B are not unreasonable guesses. However, no city is actually depicted in this diagram, while irrigated fields are shown in the lower right, indicating that agriculture was the main purpose, as in C. Some degree of centralization may have been needed to mobilize the labor needed to build this qanat, but that would not have been its purpose.

7. **(D)** This question also depends on interpretation and logical reasoning. Nothing about the qanat speaks to willingness or unwillingness to fight wars, and it is unlikely that a decentralized society could mobilize the labor to build such a structure, so B and C are not good choices. A ready supply of water would make the qanat less necessary, making A unlikely. Irrigation systems, especially this elaborate, would qualify as works of infrastructure.

8. **(A)** This question calls for contextualization and interpretation. The broad historical trend at work here is religious interchange between cultures. All the answers connect with that trend to one extent or another, but proselytization and syncretism, as in D and C, are not spoken of in the texts, and only the first text refers to linkages between religion and war, as in B. The widest possible take on the trend, expressed in A, is correct.

9. **(D)** This question calls for contextualization, historical argumentation, and historical interpretation. Answers A and B are contradicted by the text, and C overstates the text's basic message. Answer D is the best encapsulation of the text's core thesis.

10. **(A)** This question also calls for contextualization, historical argumentation, and historical interpretation. The passage discussing conceptions of jihad is more relevant to rulers and political elites, whereas the second deals with the lived experience of people at the lower levels of society, where Crusade-related hostility would not have been as likely to be so heartfelt.

11. **(A)** This question calls for contextualization and knowledge of broad trends emphasized by the AP exam. Neither case describes workers who are actually owned by other people, and prison-camp labor is not referred to, so B and C are incorrect. Both texts involve colonization, but Siberia was not an overseas territory for Russia, and joint-stock companies were not involved with Spanish colonization of the Americas.

12. **(C)** This document refers to the mit'a system of corvée labor that had been used by several Andean societies, including the Incan Empire, prior to the arrival of the Europeans. After attempting to enslave Native Americans by means of the encomienda system, Spanish colonizers mobilized labor by both relying on slaves from Africa *and* forcing Native Americans to work according to the dictates of the preexisting mit'a system. This was not technically slavery but counts as a form of coerced labor.

13. **(D)** This question calls for interpretation and careful reading. Answer B makes little sense, given how well native populations generally adapted to their home territories. Answers A and C refer to troubles that frequently plagued native Siberians, but the passage refers specifically to the growing shortage of the fur-bearing animals whose pelts formed the tribute payments that natives owed their Russian colonizers.

14. **(B)** This question requires contextualization and knowledge of broad trends associated with the stimulus material but not necessarily mentioned by it. Quite commonly, native populations suffered terribly from epidemic diseases brought to their communities by colonizers from far away. Native Siberians who encountered Russian settlers and trappers were no exception.

15. **(B)** This question calls for interpretation. The chart provides a sense of the directional flow of goods but no data beyond that. Answer A cannot be supported by the information given, and the same is true of D, which is also subjective. Answer C is actually true but likewise cannot be supported by the chart.

16. **(B)** This question calls for knowledge related to the stimulus material but not referred to it directly. Answer A applies more to the Pacific, and while C and D were important, the development of lateen sails, which used wind more efficiently than older sailing systems, was key to the open-water navigation necessary for the creation of the Indian Ocean trade network.

17. **(C)** This question also calls for knowledge related to the stimulus material and tests causation as well. Answer A applies more to the Silk Road, and B and D are even less relevant to the chart. The Indian Ocean trade network is famous for having created far-flung merchant communities from East Africa to China.

18. **(D)** Likewise, this question tests causation and contextualization and requires knowledge related to the stimulus material. The development described in B actually took place but *after* the cause of the true disruption, which is given in D. Answers A and C are decoys.

19. **(C)** This question requires interpretation and contextualization. The map depicts the separation of a once-united Mongol Empire into smaller states.

20. **(B)** This question tests causation and requires knowledge related to the stimulus material but not directly alluded to by it. While all the locations listed were connected by trade, the network which overlapped the most with Mongol territory—and was most affected by political trends in the Mongol Empire—was the overland Silk Road.

21. **(C)** This question likewise tests causation and requires knowledge related to the stimulus material but not explicitly mentioned by it. While Mongol conquerors were highly adaptable when it came to religion (and adopted all the faiths listed in the possible answers), the two faiths that they turned to in the largest numbers were Buddhism (both in Central Asia and East Asia) and Islam (mainly in Central Asia).

22. **(D)** This question tests knowledge beyond but related to the source material. China, already divided before the Mongol expansion, fell in the 1200s. Full conquest was achieved by Kublai Khan, who established the Yuan dynasty, known for adopting Chinese ways quite thoroughly—as in answer D.

23. **(A)** This question requires close reading and interpretation. While in both texts, women are expressing dissatisfaction with the outcomes of revolutions they have taken part in, their complaints do not support B or D and certainly not C. Answer A best captures the general trend—the *tendency* of many revolutions to neglect women's concerns—without overstating the case.

24. **(D)** This question calls for understanding of consequences and knowledge related to the stimulus material without being mentioned directly by it. Political freedoms for all French eventually increased as a result of the revolution, making C incorrect, but the revolution did not give full rights to women or even the right to vote, making A and B wrong as well. Not until the liberation of France from Nazi rule during World War II did French women receive the right to vote.

25. **(D)** This question requires interpretation, contextualization, and like the one above, knowledge related to the stimulus material. Both close reading of Ghomri's words and general understanding of the Algerian war of independence should be enough to exclude A and B. The war, after all, did not fail to win freedom or modernization; it was the leadership that failed to follow through on socioeconomic concerns—more out of neglect than actual hostility—making D a better answer than C.

26. **(C)** This question relies on interpretation and contextualization. Neither speaker is denying the revolutions' accomplishments, making A wrong. The second speaker is not addressing the issues spoken of in B, and the first is not concerned with D. The failure common to both revolutions is best described by C.

27. **(C)** This question requires contextualization and the knowledge of key trends emphasized by the AP exam. China was not enslaved or colonized outright, making A and D incorrect. While Western missionaries became quite active in Asia, their Christianizing efforts increased after the mid-1800s and are not mentioned by the author of this letter. The moment in question—the origins of the First Opium War—is tied to the economic domination referred to in C.

28. **(A)** This question involves use of evidence, historical interpretation, and historical argumentation. However true B might be, Commissioner Lin makes no reference to it, nor does he base this part of his letter on threats, making D incorrect as well. Answer C touches on a point of concern for the Chinese, but Lin leaves this unspoken, hoping (in vain) to shame the British by showing that they are acting in violation of their own value system.

29. **(C)** This question tests the same skills as the one related to it above but also requires contextualization. Answers A and B are not true, and while British delegates had been treated high-handedly before the Opium Wars, this was not nearly as decisive as European frustration at their inability to sell goods in China, while China happily sold European nations tea, silk, and other products.

30. **(A)** This question tests causation and contextualization and also requires knowledge related to the stimulus material. Lin Zexu's actions, including the confiscation of British-owned opium, led to the First Opium War and the first of the many "unequal" treaties that Britain and Europe imposed on China during the second half of the 1800s, forcing onerous trade terms on the Chinese as the century progressed.

31. **(D)** This question tests use of evidence and historical interpretation as well as causation. Answer A has little to do with population growth, while the steadily increasing impact of war on civilian populations makes C false. Answers B and D are commonly given as reasons for population growth, but most historians favor medical improvements as a prime cause.

32. **(B)** This question tests interpretation and understanding of numerical data. *Rate* of growth does not necessarily involve the difference between raw numbers but what percentage of difference there is between the earlier figure and the later one. By that standard, period B clearly experienced the largest change.

33. **(B)** This question requires knowledge of current trends as well as of information related to but not directly mentioned by the stimulus material. Population growth continues at a steady pace, and the potential for overpopulation is a key concern of the present day.

34. **(B)** This question tests interpretation and the ability to contextualize broad historical trends. These images depict the diffusion of gunpowder technology from Western armies to non-Western ones, as in B. Nothing about the images proves that the weapons are being industrially produced by the non-Western peoples in question, making D wrong. While the viewer can infer an imperial relationship from the second image, there is no evidence of one in the first, so A is unlikely. No evidence for C exists in either image.

35. **(A)** This question tests causation. It also requires knowledge connected with the stimulus material but not referred to directly by it. Early gunpowder weapons did not render castles or cavalry obsolete, either in Europe or Japan, so B and D do not apply. Japan did not democratize until well after the trend depicted in the image. As they did with knights in Europe, gunpowder weapons threatened Japan's samurai elite, whose status depended on their skill with pregunpowder arms and armor.

36. **(D)** This question tests interpretation and contextualization of broad trends, and it requires knowledge connected with the stimulus material but not directly referred to by it. Answers B and C are unlikely due to the prevailing ideologies of imperialism and racial superiority among many Europeans in the 1800s. While A is not impossible, D refers to a standard technique used by imperial regimes.

37. **(C)** This question tests comparison, and it requires knowledge connected with the stimulus material but not directly referred to by it. Other imperial nations trained native troops in Western styles of fighting in order to reduce the costs of defending colonial territories. The troop type that fits this category is the Indian sepoy, as in C. No other choice applies.

38. **(D)** This question tests interpretation. Most of the answers provided are at least somewhat related to what the chart measures. However, the phrase "most clearly" indicates that you should look for what can be safely concluded from information contained only in the chart. While farming consumes energy, land under cultivation is a topic far removed from this chart, making A irrelevant. The energy consumed is undoubtedly based in large part on fossil fuels, but the chart does not specify energy type, making B a risky option. The nations are a mix of developed and less developed, so C is a weak choice. Resource *consumption*, a key environmental trend, is the main subject of the chart.

39. **(B)** The world currently faces all of these environmental issues, and all of them can be tied to one degree or another to energy consumption. Answer D relates only to one specific form of energy, and A and C are less directly connected to energy consumption. Scientific consensus agrees that consuming all but the most renewable forms of energy contributes to climate change and global warming, as in B.

40. **(A)** This question requires use of evidence. Since it does not provide population data, this chart does not allow safe conclusions to be reached about efficiency or per capita consumption, making B, C, and D poor choices—even though B is in fact true.

41. **(C)** This question requires interpretation and contextualization. The opening statement, which communicates doubt about whether anything that cannot be seen or physically experienced has meaning, points away from the abstract ideals referred to in A, B, and D. Skepticism about traditional or religious sources of ethics is a hallmark of much modernist thinking and especially of the existentialist school to which Camus belonged.

42. **(A)** This question tests historical interpretation. All of the worldviews listed belong to the quotation's time frame. But even without knowing the identity or prominence of Camus, it can be inferred from the speaker's embrace of uncertainty—and his acceptance of the idea that he must find meaning on his own terms, without the comfort of knowing that life has an external meaning—that this is an existentialist essay.

43. **(D)** While all the answers allude to attitudes that grew stronger in nineteenth-century Europe and while Camus himself sympathized with the political left (as in A), the doubts expressed in the quotation about life's meaning grow directly out of the crisis of faith that took hold in the Western world during the 1800s. Scientific and philosophical insights from thinkers such as Darwin, Nietzsche, and Freud contributed to a mounting lack of confidence in traditional forms of religion to provide spiritual comfort or explain the workings of the universe.

44. **(B)** The image shows the use of machines in Chinese silk production, similar to many of the devices that were simultaneously being incorporated into Europe's textile industries, pointing clearly to B. The image gives no indication of the conditions under which silk workers labored, and since one should not make assumptions based on other cultures' clothing and hairstyles, even the gender of the workers remains unclear, so A and D are not safe answers. However important standardization is to a modern economy, it is not relevant to this image, excluding C.

45. **(B)** While gender discrimination was prevalent in eighteenth-century China, it has little relevance to this question, making A wrong. Answer D is simply untrue, considering that China was the source of some of the world's most important inventions, such as gunpowder and the magnetic compass. China's leaders failed to address, never mind accomplish, the military improvements mentioned in C. What is valid as a general trend—even though the mechanization depicted in the image undercuts and qualifies it somewhat—is the overconfidence of China's Qing rulership in the 1700s, which caused China to lag behind the nations of the West in terms of economic and technological advancement.

46. **(D)** This question requires an understanding of the broader context related to the stimulus material. China produced metalware of equal or superior quality to anything available elsewhere, and it was a major exporter of tea, so B and C are poor choices. In the 1700s and early 1800s, the balance of trade between China and European merchants greatly favored the former; China sold luxury goods, including silk, in exchange for massive quantities of silver currency but allowed few foreign goods into the country. This makes D the best answer. While the Chinese indeed purchased opium, as in A, this was part of an illegal trade encouraged by Western merchants angered at the uneven balance of trade.

47. **(C)** This question involves use of evidence, historical interpretation, and contextualization. The ideologies named in A and D are diametrically opposed to Nkrumah's worldview, and although he had some sympathy for socialism, it is not the subject of this speech. Nkrumah's great political goal was to persuade the newly liberated countries of Africa to put aside their national differences and join together in a strong pan-Africanist union.

48. **(B)** Knowledge of context would be enough to recall that Nkrumah, like Nasser in Egypt and Sukarno in Indonesia, was a major figure in the nonaligned movement, as in B. Beyond that, his focus on African self-reliance and unity—and the lack in his speech of any aggressive language or declared preference for either superpower—also allows the reader to reason toward B to the exclusion of the other possible answers.

49. **(A)** This question, related to the previous one, touches on the same skills but also focuses on causation. Even more so than Nasser's pan-Arab aspirations, Nkrumah's pan-Africanism proved limited in potential. The factors described in answers B and C had some bearing on this, but D most certainly did not—Africa is incredibly rich in natural resources, which include gold, diamonds, oil, and uranium. Unfortunately for Nkrumah, Africa is so diverse in terms of ethnicity, language, and culture that pan-Africanists had few if any unifying factors on which to base their movement.

50. **(B)** This question requires use of evidence and some contextualization. As always with this sort of question, be careful not to choose answers that are correct in fact but not supported by the image, map, or chart provided. While the map shows that the territorial extent of French, Dutch, and English colonies was smaller than that of Spain's empire, it says nothing about those countries' lack of interest in colonies, making D wrong. Lack of information about intentions similarly excludes A, nor does the map provide information to support C—even though C describes what actually happened. The map does show that at least for now, these three nations maintained a colonial presence only where sea power could readily support it.

51. **(C)** This question requires information related to the stimulus material but not directly referred to by it. In this case, the issue has to do with background and causation. Answer B is more appropriate to the Indian Ocean trade network, and the influence of D was felt earlier than the time period depicted in the map. Answer A refers to a later innovation (which allowed for the relatively easy calculation of longitude). The sailing gunship referred to in C allowed the European projection of force and also permitted the French, English, and Dutch to compete with rivals like the Spanish and Portuguese for control over colonies and sea routes.

52. **(D)** This question tests knowledge beyond the stimulus material. European exploration and colonization in the Americas was driven by a desire for all the goods listed, but fur hunting and fishing, as in A and B, dominated in the northern latitudes, while the principal sources of silver, as in C, were in South America. For years, the Caribbean was the world's center for sugarcane production—a development that, unfortunately, encouraged the Atlantic slave trade.

53. **(A)** This question requires the ability to contextualize the stimulus material as well as the interpretation of evidence. Answers C and D do not fit the time period. The speaker refers to "internal and external enemies," and the French revolutionary government indeed faced both types of foes, making A and B both viable. Terror, however, as opposed to military force, would be easier to apply to the former.

54. **(C)** This question tests use of evidence and historical interpretation. Answer A is a famous Marxist formula, and B is a cynical expression of power politics in the vein of Machiavelli. Robespierre has little to say about the idea contained in D but argues that when protecting a noble ideal, terrible times require terrible solutions. The same logic has been applied by many extremist politicians throughout history.

55. **(B)** This question deals with both context and cause and effect. While in the long run, revolutions like the one in France encouraged a general trend toward greater liberties for all, the French Revolution fell short on the gender question and was slow at times to redress the economic inequalities suffered by the lower rather than middle classes. Answers A, C, and D seem less likely. More important, they are not really touched on in Robespierre's address, which talks more of how a dire emergency situation requires France to set aside the principle of due process for certain enemies. It is this violation of the revolution's own ideals that makes B the best answer.

PART B: SHORT-ANSWER QUESTIONS

1. Unhappy and unintended consequences of new technology—the subject of Part A—could include the unemployment of workers due to the mechanization or automation of industrial processes (examples range from the Luddite revolts to the impact of computers and robots today). Or the loss of privacy due to improved surveillance technology. Or the fraying of face-to-face human interactions because of social media.

   To answer Part B, use examples of how technology has more unambiguously improved human life—advancements in health care would do, as would the greater availability of knowledge, art, and culture due to the Internet or technology that promotes clean energy consumption (such as solar panels or modern wind turbines). As for Part C, a good response would be the Industrial Revolution, along with the sustained improvement and refinement of technology and engineering it sparked.

2. The collapse of Catholic religious hegemony over most of Europe, culminating in the Protestant Reformation, is the best answer for Part A.

   One continuity that would satisfy Part B is the fact that Christianity remained the dominant religion in Europe, even if new Christian denominations appeared in the 1500s. To reply to Part C, you might speak of how Protestant denominations allowed priests to marry or encouraged worshippers to read the Bible or jettisoned many of the ritual practices favored by Catholics.

3. Women occupied a distinctly secondary status in both of these regions during the time in question, allowing an easy way to answer Part A. (Another possible answer: both had to regulate their appearance and conduct in strict ways, either by veiling themselves in the Middle East or binding their feet in places like China.)

   Most women in the Middle East were subject to Islamic law and custom and therefore had to veil themselves in a way that was less common in East Asia. They also appeared in public less often and under more stringent conditions. Both facts can be used to answer Part B (as could the fact that women in East Asia had more opportunities to assume roles of religious leadership, even if these were much more limited than men's roles). A key difference that can be identified to fulfill part C is the role of Islam in shaping women's lives in the Middle East.

4. In discussing Part A, you could mention that NGOs and transnational corporations have each managed to exert significant influence on governmental policy in a wide variety of countries, all at the same time. NGOs such as Greenpeace or Amnesty International, for instance, have shaped environmental and human-rights laws and policies in many places, just as transnational corporations such as Ford and McDonald's have done.

Part B can be answered by noting the contrast between the goals and tactics of most NGOs, which is to use public pressure and idea-based advocacy (convincing a government of the rightness of its cause) to bring about change, and corporations, which generally seek economic advantage (including tax breaks or the elimination of various rules and regulations) by persuading governments that they will bring new jobs and increase overall wealth if they choose to operate in a certain country. Therefore, the impact of NGOs is mainly to change laws and policies regarding a particular cause, while the impact of corporations on policy is mainly to alter policy in a way to maximize their own profits. The reason for this—as related to Part C—is that the purpose of a corporation is to make money, whereas the purpose of an NGO is typically more abstract and less self-interested.

Section II: Free-Response Questions

A: DOCUMENT-BASED QUESTION

1. Bear in mind that your **thesis** must address both the designated skill (continuity and change over time, accounting for *both* elements) and the topic indicated by the documents (political economy in the USSR under Lenin and Stalin). A useful thesis for this question might propose that throughout the Lenin and Stalin periods, Soviet economic policy consistently aimed for the creation of a modern industrial economy whose benefits were to be equally shared by all (continuity) but that the level of force and coercion employed by the state in the attempt to accomplish this goal varied considerably over time (change).

    Grouping is less important for the DBQ than it used to be. Here, there are several possibilities. One is to link Documents 2, 3, and 7 together as examples of the benefits that the Soviet regime strove for and claimed to be providing its people. Document 4 shows some of the disillusionment that resulted when Soviet reality fell short of the state's declared aspirations. Documents 1, 5, and 6 demonstrate how the regime was willing to use violence to further its economic goals. Another scheme might involve discussing Documents 1, 5, and 6 together as related to agriculture and the regime's treatment of peasants, then looking at Documents 3 and 4 in tandem to talk about industrialization, and finally clustering Documents 2 and 7 to see how the regime treated women (or at least claimed to). Other groupings, of course, are possible, although remember that any grouping scheme ought to support the thesis.

    You are required to discuss **point of view** (or purpose, audience, historical situation, or context) for several documents at a minimum and as many as possible for maximum credit. The points of view here range from official, even famous, to anonymous. Lenin himself is the author of Document 1, and the head of the secret police is outlining policy goals in Document 6. The media—controlled by the state, of course—speaks in Document 7 (the official newspaper *Pravda*) and Documents 2 and 3 (visual imagery). Miron Dolot (in Document 5) is a famous survivor of the human-made famine in Ukraine, Kazakhstan, and southern Russia by Stalin's agricultural policies, and an ordinary worker confesses his negative feelings in Document 4.

    The DBQ rubric asks you to demonstrate knowledge of the **broader historical context** surrounding the question. This subject has to do with state-sponsored centralization as an economic strategy in the modern era, especially the twentieth century. Soviet policies such as the collectivization of agriculture and Stalin's First

Five-Year Plan fit squarely into this topic, as does the entire Soviet modernization project as a whole. Related issues would include the Russian civil war, Lenin's New Economic Policy, the Stalinist famine of 1932–1933, and the great purges of the later 1930s. Also, do not forget to discuss at least one **additional piece of evidence** that could shed light on the topic in a way that the available documents do not. In this instance, the testimony of actual women living under Leninist or Stalinist rule would be useful as a comparison to the idealized messages conveyed by Documents 2 and 7 (much as Document 4 provides something of a reality check in contrast to Document 3). It would also be good to have statistics and figures measuring actual economic growth. Other examples could serve this purpose as well.

Finally, the rubric calls for the repeated and meaningful use of **evidence**. Marshal as many facts and details as you can about the topic at hand. As much as possible, make every piece of evidence appear distinct and separate; the more of these you can convince the reader you are providing, the better—although quality matters as much as, if not more than, quantity.

PART B: LONG ESSAYS

2. This question tests comparison as its historical **reasoning skill**. (Note that all long-essay questions in a given exam will center on the same reasoning skill.) You need to include both similarities *and* differences. Your topic is state-building techniques used by states in East Asia and South Asia between 1200 and 1500.

    Your key example from East Asia should be China—ruled by the Yuan and Ming dynasties during this period—and you might include Japan, although its collapse into feudalism during these years might complicate your answer. India, dominated by the Delhi Sultanate, should represent South Asia.

    Your **thesis** might highlight how, while major states in both regions strove for greater centralization, Chinese dynasties emphasized cultural continuity and had the advantage of greater religious uniformity, while outside conquest and religious differences were the norm in India and elsewhere in the region.

    Looking more closely into **contextualization**, the use of **evidence**, and **analysis** (which should emphasize comparison, as per the prompt), you could mention how both the Yuan and Ming dynasties used Confucian ideology and concepts like the mandate of heaven to create links with the past and justify their rule. (Even though the Mongols were foreign conquerors, they Sinicized, or adopted Chinese ways, and the Ming, of course, were native to China.) Centralization proved quite successful under both. (If you decide to mention feudal Japan, you'll have to note how it qualifies or complicates your thesis.) In the case of India, not only did the Delhi Sultanate invade from outside, it also imposed a new faith—Islam—on much of the territory it took over. While it successfully centralized much of India, religious and ethnic differences ran deeper and made it more difficult to maintain long-term authority. Hindu states like the Vijayanagara Empire resisted and threw off Delhi's rule over time. You could also bring up examples from elsewhere in South (and Southeast) Asia where Islam, Hinduism, several forms of Buddhism, and other faiths coexisted, illustrating the struggles that states like the Khmer and Majapahit Empires had when it came to politically uniting lands with such diverse populations. These are just some of the issues you could dwell on to answer this question.

3. As with all the long essay choices in this exam, comparison is the historical **reasoning skill** being tested. Make sure to consider similarities *and* differences. The topic asks how societies in Africa and the Americas responded to European colonial pressures between the 1400s and the 1600s C.E.

    The obvious likeness that your **thesis** could focus on is the fact that both regions experienced many military defeats and terrible economic exploitation at the hands of European colonial powers. On the other hand, a key difference lies in the fact that much of Africa remained unconquered, in contrast to the Americas, where European powers dominated more thoroughly.

    Regarding **context**, **evidence**, and **analysis**, use concrete examples such as the Aztecs, the Inca, the societies of West Africa (whose degree of success or failure in repelling Europeans varied), and the temporary domination of the Portuguese along parts of the East African coast. The impact of European diseases on the Americas is an important factor and a good point of contrast with Africa. What about religious conversion in each region? Discuss the way Africans coped with the slave trade (either being victimized by it or cooperating with Europeans in enslaving their neighbors) as opposed to peoples of the Americas dealing with labor regimes like the encomienda system? There is certainly much to compare and contrast here.

4. As with all the long essay choices in this exam, comparison is the historical **reasoning skill** you will use here. Be sure to consider similarities *and* differences. The subject is revolution during the 1700s and early 1800s—both in Haiti and in Latin America.

    In developing a **thesis**, it is easy to find likenesses—both revolutions were sparked by events in Europe related to the French Revolution (although Haiti's came first and was more directly connected, while the Latin American revolts were triggered by Napoleon's toppling of the Spanish government in the years following the French Revolution). They were both animated by the natural-rights philosophy of the Enlightenment and inspired by the ideals of the American and French Revolutions. The most obvious difference is that the Haitian rebellion began as a more straightforward slave uprising, whereas the Latin American wars of independence were more complex and driven largely by political elites.

    Your inclusion of **context**, **evidence**, and **analysis** should lead you to discuss Toussaint L'Ouverture, the religious influence of vodun on the Haitian rebellion (and the importance of the Virgin of Guadalupe as a rallying symbol in Mexico), the role of the creole elite in the Latin American wars, and figures such as Hidalgo in Mexico and, farther to the south, Bolívar and San Martín.

Appendix: Map of Selected World Regions

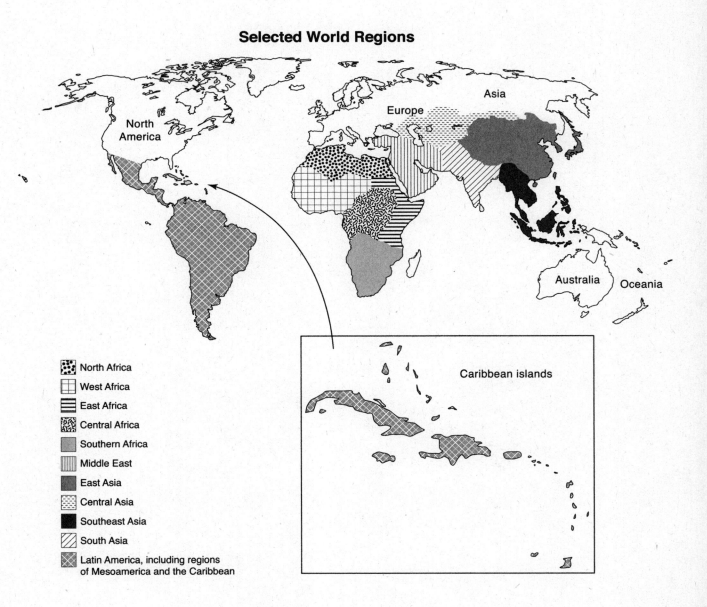

Selected World Regions

North America

Europe

Asia

North Africa

West Africa

East Africa

Central Africa

Southern Africa

Middle East

East Asia

Central Asia

Southeast Asia

South Asia

Latin America, including regions of Mesoamerica and the Caribbean

Australia

Oceania

Caribbean islands

Index

J

Janissary troops, 90
Japan
    Ashikaga regime, 94
    class diversification, 273
    Fujiwara clan, 94
    Heian period, 94
    Kamakura regime, 94
    nationalism in, 316
    Tokugawa, 165, 242, 273
Jefferson, Thomas, 225
Jesus of Nazareth, 56–57
Jewish diaspora, 53
Jim Crow laws, 371–372
Jizya, 96
Joan of Arc, 86, 128
Judaism, 52–53
Junk, 116, 120

K

Kahlo, Frida, 351
Kamakura regime, 94
Kant, Immanuel, 251
Karma, 54, 55
Kashgar, 118
Katipunan, 251
Kemal, Mustafa, 314
Kepler, Johannes, 183
Keynes, John Maynard, 362, 364
Khan, Genghis, 94–95
Khmer Empire, 50, 97
Knights, 85
Kongo, 91, 163, 235
Korean War, 328
Kublai Khan, 92, 94, 95, 97, 104
Kyoto Protocol, 381

L

Labor, specialization of, 61, 62, 124
Land ownership, 61
Languages, transnational, 104
Laozi, 56
Lateen sail, 116, 120, 180
Latin America
    authoritarianism in, 316–318
    class diversification, 272–273
    racial inequality, 247–249
    slavery in, 274–275
    wars of independence, 228–229
Law of Manu (Hindu text), 54
League of Nations, 309–310, 311, 319
Legalism, 56
Liberal Democratic Party (LDP), 339
Lines of demarcation, 155
Lingua franca, 52
Literary traditions, 52
Little Ice Age, 134, 164, 202
Liturgical languages, 52
Llama, 100, 115
Locke, John, 175, 225, 251, 255
Long-count calendar, 99
Louisiana Purchase, 228, 246
L'Ouverture, François Toussaint, 228
Lusitania, 308
Luther, Martin, 171

M

Machu Picchu, 102, 112
Madrasas, 90, 107
Magellan, Ferdinand, 155
Magna Carta, 86
Magnetic compass, 92, 115, 116, 180
Mahayana Buddhism, 55
Maimonides, 107
Maize (corn), 99, 100
Majapahit Empire, 97
Maji Maji revolt, 258
Malaria, 64, 92
Mali, 91, 108–109, 120
Mamluks, 90–91, 126
Mandate of Heaven, 55, 165
Mandela, Nelson, 338–339
Mansa Musa, 91
Manzikert, Battle of, 90
Mao Tse-tung, 316, 328, 340
Maps, precise, 180
Maratha Empire, 166, 243
Marco Polo, 104–105, 118
Marine chronometer, 180
Maritime technology, 116
Marketplaces, 59
Marshall Plan, 328, 333, 365
Marx, Karl, 256
Marxism, 316, 342, 351
Mass media, 352
Mauryan Empire, 50
Mayan culture, 51, 99
Measles, 64, 133, 156
Mecca, 58
Medicine, 114, 359–360
Medieval climatic optimum, 134
Medieval Europe, 84–87
Medieval period, 105–107
Mediterranean Sea, 118–119
Mediterranean trade network, 60
Meiji Restoration, 242–243, 270, 273, 279
Melaka, 97, 159
Mercantilism, 188
Mercantilist policy, 225
Mesa Verde, 98
Mesoamerica
    in 1200–1450, 98–100
    slavery in, 125–126
Mexican-American War, 246
Mexican Revolution, 247, 318
Mexico
    in 1200–1450, 98–100
    in 1900–1939, 317–319
    in 1945–1991, 343–344
Mexican War of Independence, 229
    women's rights in, 318
Middle East
    in 1200–1450, 58–59, 68–78, 88–90,
        107–108
    in 1450–1750, 161–162
    in 1750–1900, 233–235
    in 1900–1939, 313–314
    in 1900–present, 289, 292, 295, 297,
        299
    in 1945–1991, 335–337
    class diversification, 273

cross-cultural exchange, 114–115
    Islam, 58–59, 107–108
Migration, 49, 63, 275–276
Militarism, 257–258
Militaristic nationalism, 313, 316
Mill, John Stuart, 255, 267
Ming Dynasty, 93, 192
Mining, 63
Minority populations, 62
Missionary activity, 52, 351
Mississippian civilization, 51, 98
Mit'a system, 100, 156, 195
Moche, 100
Modes of economic production, 59
Mohammed, 58
Monarchy, 49
Money, metal coinage, 59
Mongols, 92, 94–96
Monotheism, 52–53
Monroe Doctrine, 246
Monsoon winds, 116, 120
Montesquieu, Charles de, 252
Monumental architecture, 52
Moses, 53
Movable-type printing, 92, 115
Mughal Empire, 243
Muhammad Ali Jinnah, 288, 317, 341,
    349, 352–354
Multiculturalism, 288, 349, 352–354
Munich Agreement, 320
Mussolini, Benito, 313

N

Nanak, Guru, 173
Napoleonic Code, 227
Nationalism, 224, 232, 257
National Organization for Women
    (NOW), 374
Nation-states, 151–153
Native Americans, 103, 155
Natural rights, 255
Navigational technologies, 153–154,
    179–180
Nazis, 313–314, 324
Nazi-Soviet Pact, 320
Neo-Confucianism, 56, 92, 103–104, 109
Neo-Confucian principles, 103–104, 109
New Deal, 364
New Economic Policy (NEP), 312
New Spain, 155–156
Newton, Isaac, 183
Nicaragua, 330, 344
Nicaraguan Revolution, 344
Nirvana, 55
Nkrumah, Kwame, 332, 337
Nomadic peoples, 49, 61
Non-Aligned Movement (NAM), 332
Norman Conquest, 86
North America, 97–100, 277–278
North American Free Trade Agreement
    (NAFTA), 366
North Atlantic Treaty Organization
    (NATO), 328
Northeast Passage, 157
Northern wave exploration, 157–159

Northwest Passage, 154
Nortre Dame, Cathedral of, 106
Nuclear arms race, 329–330
Nuclear Non-Proliferation Treaty, 330
Nuremberg Laws, 314
Nuremberg Trials, 324

O
Oases, 120
Oceania
    in 1200–1450, 68–77, 109–111
    in 1750–1900, 243–246
    in 1900–present, 290, 292, 295, 298,
       300
    cultural developments in 1200–1450,
       109–111
October Revolution, 312
Oligarchy, 49
Olmecs, 51, 98
Omani Arbs, 164
Omani-European rivalry, 167, 188
Open Door Policy, 241
Open-water navigation, 116
Operation Barbarossa, 320
Operation Desert Storm, 337
Opium Wars, 288
Oral traditions, 52
Organization of American States (OAS),
    343
Organization of Petroleum Exporting
    Countries (OPEC), 335, 365
Oslo Accords, 336
Ottoman-European conflict, 167
Ottomanism, 258
Ottoman-Safavid rivalry, 167
Ottoman Turks, 90–91, 161–162
"Out of Africa" thesis, 63
Overland transport, 59, 115

P
Pack animals, 115
Pakistan, 317, 341
Palestinian Liberation Organization
    (PLO), 336
Panama Canal, 249, 282, 317
Pandemics, 63–64
Paper money, 59, 92, 115
Paris Agreement, 381
Paris Peace Conference, 309
Parliamentarism, 159–160
Passover, 53
Pastoralism, 59, 61
Pathogens, 63
Patriarchalism, 58, 62
Paul, Apostle, 57
Pax Mongolica, 94
Pearl Harbor, 322
Peasant uprisings, 92, 126–127, 134
Penicillin, 359
People of the book, 58
People's Republic of China, 328, 340
Persia, 50, 104
Peter, Apostle, 57
Peter the Great, 160
Philippine-American War, 245

Philippines, 231, 245, 341
Philosophy, 52, 106, 225
Pinochet, Augusto, 343
Piracy, 187
Pizarro, Francisco, 155
Plantation agriculture, 203
Pocahontas, 199
Polio vaccine, 359
Political, 255
Political centralization, 194
Pollution, 203, 380–381
Polo, Marco, 92, 153
Polygamy, 129, 198
Polynesian migrations, 63, 97, 132–133
Polytheistic systems, 52
Portugal, Iberian wave, 154–157
Potatoes, 100
Powered flight, 358
Prague Spring, 329, 333
Pre-Columbian era, 97–102
Prince Henry the Navigator, 154
Printing, 92, 115
Printing press, 170
Prison labor, 62
Privateering, 187
Private property, 61
Proletariat, 272
Propaganda, 312–314, 352
Protestant Reformation, 170–172
Proto-industrialization, 188
Ptolemy, 114
Putin, Vladimir, 345
Pyramids, 52, 98, 100, 112

Q
Qin Dynasty, 50
Qing Dynasty, 164
Quantum theory, 262, 357
Quipu, 100

R
Rabban bar Sawma, 105
Race relations, in 1900–present, 372–374
Racially segregated policies, 273
Rajput kingdoms, 96
Rape of Nanjing, 316, 320
Realism, 252
Reconquista, 87
Red Turban Revolts, 92–93, 127
Reign of Terror, 227
Reincarnation, 54, 55
Religions, 52
    in 1450–1750, 170–173
    in 1900–present, 354–355
    atheism, 261
    deism, 252
    human sacrifice, 98–100, 112
    Islamic theology, 58–59, 89, 107–108
    missionary activity, 172–173
Renaissance, 86, 105–107, 175
Resources, extraction of, 63, 203
Rice, Champa, 63
Rig Veda, 54
Roman Catholicism, 57–58, 105
Romanticism, 252

Rome, 50
Rousseau, Jean-Jacques, 252
Rumi, 108
Russia, 159
Russo-Japanese War, 233, 243

S
Sailing ships, 116, 180
Saladin, 88
Salt, 120
Samurai, 94, 165, 242
Sati, ritual of, 96
Schlieffen Plan, 306
Scholasticism, 106
Science and technology, 52
    in 1450–1750, 169–170, 179–183
    in 1900–present, 357–360
Scientific method, 113–114, 183
Scientific Revolution, 181–183
Scramble for Africa, 236–238
Sealed bulkheads, 116
Second Battle of the Marne, 308
Second Industrial Revolution, 263–265
Secularism, 251, 261–262
Sedentary societies, 49, 61
Separation of church and state, 255, 261
September 11, 2001, 326, 348
Serfdom, 125, 160, 189, 192, 194, 195,
    232, 274
Seven Years' War, 158, 166, 167
Shakespeare, William, 175
Shamanism, 52
Sharia law, 58, 89, 166
Sheep farmers, 245
Shiva, 54
Shogunate, 94, 165
Sikhism, 173
Silk industry, 92
Silk Road, 61, 92, 94, 118
Silver, 164
Silver currency, 93
Singapore, 245, 322
Sino-Japanese War, 241
Sino-Soviet split, 330
Sinosphere, 94
    1683 siege of Vienna, 162, 167
Slavery, 62, 120
    in 1200–1450, 126–127
    in 1450–1750, 194–196
    in America, 248
    Arab trade in, 91
    in Asia, 274
    Atlantic slave trade, 157, 159, 162,
      195–196
    chattel, 194
    encomienda system, 156
    indentured servitude, 274–275
    serfdom, 125, 160, 189, 192, 194, 232,
      274
Sleeping sickness, 92
Smallpox, 64, 133, 156, 159
Smith, Adam, 255–256, 266
Smoot-Hawley Tariff Act, 364
Social classes, 61
Social contract, 255